MEMORY UNION & EMPIRE

Memory Union & Empire

George Bagby

Tall Men Books

Contents

5
Historiography   **613**

Charles Francis Adams, Jr.

Foreword

A Magnanimous Brahmin

The famous Puritans, ever critical of their own heritage, built a distinctive civilization that passed along the critical snobbery and talent for analysis while the religious belief and demographic gradually died off or converted to other faiths. This left Utah our best contemporary example of religious Puritans in the world today, and Vermont, arguably, the best example of Puritans living in their native habitat without the influence of the urban immigrants. Both states remain testaments to the character of the breed. The division of the demographic from the attitude is, of its nature, confusing and difficult, and so obscures the story of these heritage Americans and their view of the Union: especially as they fell into decline after their greatest success: "the conquest of America by Massachusetts" in 1865.

These noble elites of Boston and Plymouth, true innovators and compelling leaders, have few devotees in a cynical age so well known for patricidal fashions. We may well identify the Puritans themselves with this Western trait of discomfort with one's own inheritance, or oikophobia, as Sir Scruton had it. The English settlers of Massachusetts Bay had brought their families to a rocky and cold land in repudiation of their heritage to the degree they had deemed it religiously impure. They dared to reinvent England in New England, experimenting with a new system of weights and measures, deeming the adornment of food and clothing "needless," and actually naming their children such things as "Humiliation," "Hate-Evil," "Kill-Sin," and "Flee-Fornication." The oddities of this separated people who self-consciously tinkered with their folkways was always in contrast with the Southern colonies, who had consciously attempted to "transplant" a beloved heritage in a new environment, as in Virginia, or who had taken their heritage more-or-less for granted, as with the Scotch-Irish. Thus, the Puritans and other radical Protestants in the North planted a durable conviction in America that the tradition was impure and always subject to reform and radical excision.

The origin of the various little states of New England was born partly in religious differences and partly in a democratic and participatory politics that mirrored the congregational church government Fent of the Puritans. The founding of Connecticut by Thomas Hooker in 1636 was born partly from schism with his Puritan brethren in Boston, and he succeeded in winning a charter for his slightly smaller colony after removing himself and his followers to Hartford. Like his Puritan and Pilgrim forebears, Hooker had contended and disagreed with authorities secular and sacred in his native England, his adopted Holland, and his newly settled Boston. Roger Williams of Rhode Island fame also left the Boston after preaching and publishing the errors of all Massachusetts authorities for some years and being "permitted to escape" to what became Rhode Island, also in 1636. Even New Hampshire was carved out of Massachusetts territory because of political and religious disagreements with the Boston elites. The scruples and particularism of the radical reformation had transplanted a rationalist tradition that would be incapable of conserving but fruitful in intellectual and even mystical innovations.

The children of the Revolution were already witnessing the falling away from orthodox theology in the religious movement of John Adams into Unitarianism. Massachusetts and her diaspora into upstate New York, Ohio, Michigan, Wisconsin, and Illinois were known in the generations after the Revolution for their religious innovation, enthusiasm, and uncertainty. The Presbyterians and Episcopalians of the South had not supposed their English heritage was itself poisoned by Catholic error, and had continued to brandish the cross, use heritage liturgies, sing with musical notation, and enjoy flavorful foods. The Puritan skepticism ran too deep for these, and the attitude did not find rest in the New World, but like a gnawing hunger, ate up the orthodox Puritan civilization from within. Eventually, as Richard Weaver put it, "the right to criticize and even reject the dogmas of Christianity came at length to overshadow the will to believe them." Always inspired by new prophets that gave exposition of past errors and innovative a-priori analysis of theology and society, the Puritans were susceptible to the vegetarian utopianism of Graham, the "primitive" Unitarianism of Buckminster and Channing, the communists of Brook Farm, the eunuchs of Shakerism, and the restorationism of Joseph Smith. Always theoretical, the Puritans carried more obvious seeds of self-destruction than most, yet in their decline they were fruitful. Emerson, Melville, Hawthorne, and Thoroeau were Puritans – not to mention the politically creative, the martial heroes, and other incarnations of manly conviction and inspiration. This "type of American individualism" in the words of Weaver, was born of "an egotistical and self-willed people [who] made assent a matter of intellectual conviction."

The leadership of New England in the early republic were initially jealous of their own home states, with the early histories of Rhode Island, Vermont, and Maine all full of local concerns, insistence on state sovereignty, and even separatist traits that may have been transmitted through the colonial origins of several of these small states in church factionalism. Vermont's "Republican period," amid territorial disputes with New Hampshire and New York, was part of this heritage, as was Rhode Island's defiant and disruptive heritage of vetoes in the Continental Congress and initial rejection of the Philadelphia Constitution. Maine, under the thumb of the

Massachusetts Puritans without being deeply settled by them, achieved statehood and separation from Massachusetts in 1820 partly on a campaign for local authority and local responsibility: Massachusetts having neglected to defend the region in the War of 1812.

The War of 1812 saw the famous abstention of New England from supplying her militias for the common defense and the remarkable Hartford Convention, which discussed the secession of New England in defiance of the deeply unpopular purchase of Louisiana and the embargo. The subsequent embarrassments of Jackson's victory at New Orleans and the favorable Treaty of Ghent sent the Federalist Party, now the advocates of New England sectional interests at the Hartford Convention, reeling and discredited: both bits of news arriving while the Convention was still in session. Routed by a swell of Unionist feeling in the "Era of Good Feelings," the wiser and less preferential leadership of James Monroe awarded massive contracts for coastal fortifications and shipbuilding for the U.S. Navy to New England concerns. With trade routes re-opened, Napoleon defeated, and the embargo a fading memory, the Federalist faction utterly collapsed and the advocates of secession at Hartford were ousted from office, and President Monroe re-elected without opposition in 1820.

The incredible extinction of the Federalists, the party of Washington and Hamilton, both the creators and the ambitious secessionists from the Union, was an opportunity for renewal and nationalism for New England. The skepticism of orthodoxy- damaging to the traditions of Calvin as it ultimately was even to the traditions of Channing, wore away the embarrassing political memories as surely as it wore away the creeds of the Church Fathers. By 1830, an impressive and impassive Senator Daniel Webster declared that "New England... looks upon the states as united. [...] In our contemplation, Carolina and Ohio are parts of the same country." When Senator Hayne of South Carolina attempted to use the heritage of the Federalists at Hartford as evidence of a shared "states-rights" heritage, Webster rejected the argument as the "South Carolina Doctrine," and declared the authority of the general government to be founded on the people in the aggregate: "the people brought it into existence, established it, and have hitherto supported it, for the very purpose, amongst others, of imposing certain salutary restraints on state sovereignties." Driven by the abstract theory and by intellect, Webster proved a political Puritan equal to the dismissal of even very recent experiences. As the Federalists had seen themselves the erstwhile heirs of the offices of the Union and frustrated by their exclusion, Webster and the new generation of New England nationalists, calling "liberty and Union, now and forever, one and inseparable," and starting on a clean slate, purified of experience and its unpleasant memories of limits and tragedy. The Federalists were frustrated Yankee elites, unable to influence the power centers in the midst of the flowering of the Virginia dynasty. Webster's abstract nationalism, fed by a new era of New England innovations and optimism, rode a boom of immigration and industrialism into political power and dominance.

Ralph Waldo Emerson, a guide and voice for the new elite consciousness in the northeast, spoke prophetically of American ambition and independence from older forms. Echoing Thomas Paine, his brother in repudiating what had come before and forging his own path, Emerson wrote, "What is man born for but to be a reformer and re-maker of the world?" – a sentiment repeated today by leaders as seemingly antagonistic to one another as Ronald Reagan and Hillary Clinton. Emerson joined in sentiment the ambitions of John Winthrop, the original leader of the Massachusetts Bay Colony, with his goal of building the "shining city on a hill," the example of reform that would be a model for the whole world. Emerson's confidence and optimism overwhelmed Winthrop's modesty. Emerson was sure enough of his reforming plans that he was willing to push the issue and not willing to serve as a mere model. The optimistic and universalist humanitarianism became the standard of the region, which was the wellspring of the single greatest reform of American history: the victory of the North in the Civil War. This "re-founding" of the Union accomplished the "reconstruction" of the relation between the states and the general government along nationalist lines while accomplishing the secondary goal that is the only justification of such a sacrifice in the minds of most today: the unplanned emancipation and sudden enfranchisement of the slaves. The religious instinct, invested in the optimistic, pseudo-religious "universalism" described by Yarvin as better related to the Quaker tradition of the "inner light," has adapted itself from a regional peculiarity to the establishment opinion of polite society in the West. However removed it certainly is from the orthodox Puritans who settled New England, the tradition largely originates there, and their victory in American institutions was staged from that forgotten homeland of radical innovators.

The political aristocracy of New England was remarkably manifest in the Adams family, which produced a veritable dynasty of leaders and statesmen for at least four generations. John Adams, John Quincy Adams, Charles Francis Adams Sr., and the illustrious sons of the latter all contributed in executive leadership, diplomacy, the writing of history, and as executives in business: a recent example of successive generations of parents who managed to pass their rare traits to their children. A father and a son took turns as Massachusetts' only Presidents until JFK. Charles Francis Adams, Sr. served in the vital role as ambassador to the Court of St. James as Her Majesty's government openly talked of recognizing the Confederate States and sold them thousands of weapons and some powerful warships. Charles Francis Adams, Sr. sent his three sons, Henry, Brooks, and Charles Jr., to Harvard and intended them for careers in public service. Not one could oblige him in this family tradition, but all three proved to be remarkable intellects with careers as a triumvirate of blue-blooded historians. Most remarkable was the genius of the lot: Henry, who produced both tomes of history and novels. Brooks' passion was historiography, and became, with Spengler and Toynbee, a "prophet of decline" and a proponent of cyclical history. It was for Charles, Jr., hereafter simply Charles, to examine the themes of the Union, of the narrative of history for Americans, of the controversial imperial policies of 1898, and to pass judgement on the optimistic "universalism" of New England.

Charles Adams was raised in wealth and privilege. Although already a member of one of the most illustrious families in Boston, Charles Sr. had managed to marry Abigail Brooks: the heiress of a gigantic shipping fortune, but the new family preserved a healthy drive and maintained high standards for their remarkable sons. Newly graduated from Harvard and a new member of the Massachusetts Bar, the grandson of a President and the son of the ambassador to England was not a man expected to serve in the War. The cost of a substitution was trifling for such a wealthy family. His younger brother, Henry, went to London to serve as his father's secretary. Brooks, the youngest, went to Harvard. Charles opted to take a commission as lieutenant in the First Massachusetts Volunteer Cavalry and saw service near Charleston, Sharpsburg, Gettysburg, and Petersburg. He ended the war as a colonel, and was made brevet brigadier general in 1866 by the recommendation of President Johnson. He was in every way the equal of Thomas Garland Jefferson of VMI and John Augustine Washington, relatives of the Virginians, who did not shrink behind their illustrious names, but dared death and met it on the field of honor.

The manly Charles Adams, returned from war and awarded generous and often increasing pensions, did not relax. Driven by a noble inheritance of character, he resolved to learn what he could about the new business of railroads: the new giant corporations established by Lincoln and the first federally chartered businesses in America since Washington's Bank of the United States. After serving on a state board of railroad regulation, he was impressed with the actions of lobbyists and tycoons in the business combinations and authored his first major work of history with his brother, Henry: *Chapters of Erie* (1871). He became identified with the mugwumps: a group of reformers who deprecated the corruption in high places that characterized the Republican domination of the Reconstruction period, in which the Federal Government and the South were run as a one-party state. Charles associated with the "Liberal Republicans" who proposed replacing the scandal-ridden U. S. Grant with the New York editor Horace Greeley, but failed dramatically in their effort. Later, Charles joined his father in favoring the election of the Democrat Samuel Tilden over the Republican Rutherford B. Hayes and 1876. Meanwhile, he worked his way onto the board of the Union Pacific, and finally served as the executive officer. His career was difficult and he wrote of exhaustion and depression with the job, but worked in railroad administration until his resignation in 1890.

Adams' reputation rests on his contribution as an historian and his perspective as a latter-day member of the Massachusetts elite in the midst of a new Union and at the dawn of a new imperial age. His opinions in this pivotal epoch make him a figure of enduring interest. In some respects, he embraced the progressive optimism about the direction of the country, but in several respects he remains outstanding for his conservatism, his magnanimity to his former opponents in battle, his skepticism of empire, and his repudiation of the egalitarian dogmas of his section.

Historiography, according to Adams' biographer Edward Kirkland, was not a strong suit. Adams' major effort in the field was a speech, "The Sifted Grain and the Grain Sifters," delivered to the Wisconsin Historical Society in 1900, but it reveals much about the progressive historiography as well as the conservative reservations of Adams. First, he claims that Darwin's works, which he calls a new "dispensation", revolutionized history into a scientific discipline in which each stage of history is now scientifically understood as part of a larger whole: the story of progress. Adams often speaks of the developments of history as an inevitability. Simply put, Adams is revealed as a Whig historian, which was a typical and fashionable opinion then as it is now. Just as liberalism eroded the authorities of religion first in Europe and later in Massachusetts, Adams says that nationality in America was the progressive development destined to triumph over the interests of states and sections. He pays tribute to the nationalism of his own grandfather, John Quincy, as prophetic of the destiny of the Union. Notably, he inserts a qualification about the War, that "it was not a question of slavery; it was one of nationality." In other contexts, Adams mentions the Hartford Convention, but classifies them as disloyal reactionaries, "on the wrong side of history," as it were. He claims Massachusetts as the progressive bastion: the home of the prophets of the new school.

At the end of his 1900 address, Adams reveals a trait of reservation and, by our standards, reaction. Speaking to the sparsely settled and agricultural Wisconsin, he says that "the ideas of the founders will more especially rest in the hands of those agricultural communities of the Northwest, where great aggregations of the civic populace are few." Adams had grown convinced by the scandals and demagoguery of urban Massachusetts that the quality of leadership had substantially declined, and suspected that the corruption of government and even political rhetoric increased with the urbanization of America. In his early journalism on the "Butler Canvass" and the war pension program we see this side of Adams substantiated. Remarkably, in his 1908 lecture in Richmond entitled, "On the 'Solid South' and the Afro-American Race Problem," Adams admits he is "an individualist – in that respect a disciple of Jefferson… a strict constructionist, especially since the Civil War… a disbeliever in costly armaments. A believer in minding one's own business, I have seen my country masquerading, as I consider it, in the absurd character of an imperialistic World Power." This was a remarkable self-description of a man of his station and experience: a conservative man in age with no conservative faction, and a pessimistic wisdom in an age of optimistic hubris.

In spite of the special effort and investment in the mammoth "Sifted Grain" statement of philosophy, which Adams poured himself into, according to Kirkland, we find evidence in many works that he grew more restrained and pessimistic in his perspective in later years. In a superior essay of historiography, "An Undeveloped Function" (1902), Adams attempts elucidation of the insights to be harvested from the scientific approach to history. He is especially interested, as the Philippine-American War wound to a close, in the progressive approach to empire. Adams early opposed the Spanish War with his "Imperialism" speech, but later made a qualified withdrawal from the Anti-Imperialist League he helped to found when he deemed his colleagues unconstructive and even irresponsible. Adams grew interested in the inequalities of the races for two reasons: the legacy of inequality of black Americans since the War and the "new-caught sullen peoples" in the Caribbean and in the Pacific.

Adams contends that history furnishes no examples of "race-elevation" through "tutelage." Although he elsewhere commends the antebellum Southerners for their paternalism, calling them humanitarian in their instincts towards their slaves and the close relations it fostered in their households, he denies that "paternalism" can do anything but emasculate in an imperial relationship, and instead advises increased autonomy while the capable population administrates. He cites Britain's dominion in Egypt and India as positive examples of success.

On the subject of the Union, Adams fulfills many expectations of his heritage. He counts the Civil War as the true "War of Independence:" the independence of the Federal Government from the claims of the states. He acknowledges the basis of the claims of the states, but argues that the progressive movement of history towards consolidation had made the legacy of the state jealousies reactionary and destined to fail.

On the subject of race in the Union he reveals a more interesting point of view, differentiating between a successful union of European races, which he terms "cognate races" in his "Undeveloped Function," which may live in a state of temporary dependency or inferiority but "we absorb, or assimilate" them. In Adams' "Doctrine of Equality," written as the introduction in an historical series in 1913, he further develops the theme. Rejecting the thought that the United States is the home of an Anglo-Saxon nation, he returns to thought that "political equality" is based upon a principle of "race absorption," and those races that established American peoples will intermarry with can assimilate into American institutions. He does not dwell on this most mysterious process, but he insists that the depth of error in the "universalist" humanitarians is "thoroughly wrong." The reformers in the saddle, promising equality to the emancipated black believed that, in spite of appearances, white and black were "essentially the same" and the black man "had never had a chance." "Scientific observation" is recruited by our writer as a modern support for what any number of earlier Western observers had long seen in books such as Helper's *Negroes in Negroland: A Compilation* (1865). Experience itself counted as evidence that the African was distinct from the European in many respects and the two did not easily mix.

Adams' perspective on empire and race was strongly influenced by his 1906 journey through Egypt to the British-ruled Sudan, which he wrote a most interesting article about in *The Century*, entitled "Reflex Light From Africa." He speaks of the "scales falling from his eyes" on the differences in races. Dismissing the "appalling amount of error and cant" from "the philanthropists and theorists of New England" who imagine all races to be interchangeable, he suggests that "those who indulge in such theories go to the Soudan and pass a week at Omdurman. That place marks in commerce, in letters and in art, in science and architecture, the highest point of development yet reached by any African race." From this point in his career, Adams takes a decidedly pessimist and critical perspective on the humanitarian progressives he had earlier treated gently.

While Adams advocated an imitation of the British Raj for America's new holdings in the Philippines and Cuba, he was explicitly against paternalist administration for American minorities, for it would make the enduring inequalities excuses for increasing government interventions. To Adams, it was irrational and dangerous to make administrators responsible for rectifying natural differences among men, and he expressed a similar concern about socialism. He ironically commented in his Richmond speech that, although he and Confederate Georgian Robert Toombs recognized Uncle Tom as a totally imaginative character, he found himself in agreement with Toombs that any institution that could take an "African savage" and acculturate him into an Uncle Tom is an institution that has justified itself. This ambiguous statement invites examination, for slavery indisputably communicated many things to the African, including English, Christianity, a Western diet, and many folkways. Adams' own meaning and thoughts on this kind of assimilation remain obscure and provocative. He concluded his thoughts on the administration of minorities by saying that imperial administration of racially distinct populations seems necessary and humanitarian, while paternalist efforts to improve the communities is undesirable. The anti-imperialist was nuanced. The experience of administrative separation in Liberia, he said, was a disaster for everyone involved. Indeed, the modern example of Liberia, which includes the near-complete genocide of the unfortunate Americo-Liberians, only puts an exclamation mark on Adams' point.

Adams' career was particularly fruitful in a constructive perspective concerning the War. A conservative nationalist, an anachronistic Jeffersonian who preferred the participatory and property-owning America to the brave new world of megalopolis, Adams took many speaking engagements to propose constructive and positive views of the common heritage of the North and South. Adams is properly credited for helping to make Robert E. Lee a national hero for an era. He published several speeches and papers on the subject of Lee's legacy and gave an especially compelling argument in his piece, "Shall Cromwell Have a Statue?" which he delivered to the Phi Beta Kappa Society in Chicago in 1902. Here, his Whig historiography gave him a wise insight that has yet proven untrue as concerns the Civil War.

Adams argued that, as time passes, passions fade, and thus our perspective of history grows more rational. This is not peculiar to the Whig theory, but lends some credibility to the Whig view of history as a progression towards an inevitable improvement and enlightenment. Just as a Millennial does not expect an impartial and dispassionate account of Vietnam or the administration of JFK from a Boomer, so Adams assumed that the passage of time would better reveal the virtues of the defeated Confederates as it would the excesses of the Union – especially in Reconstruction, which he often deplored. If anything, the passions concerning the War have risen in recent history, and the sesquicentennial of the War had scarcely passed before the massive riots of 2020 saw the widespread desecration and removal of the Confederate monuments that Adams had celebrated and supported. The reasoning for the discontent in 2020 was the perceived failure of American institutions to elevate African-Americans since the Civil War, or at least the Civil Rights Movement. The rhetoric of MLK in his famous "I Have A Dream" speech makes this clear: that the Declaration of Independence and the Gettysburg Address were analogous to a check drawn on the bank, and that the racial minorities –overwhelmingly black- had come to the Federal Government to cash-in on the "deferred promise" of equality. The white liberals of the time rationalized through the rhetoric of the "equality of opportunity" that would result from the dismantling of legal segregation, removing all impediments or quality controls at the poll, and inaugurating a variety of Federal programs meant to raise living standards and relieve the widespread dysfunction in black families. The result of these reforms in 2024 has not satisfied anyone but the bureaucrats whose existence relies upon these agencies and programs. America is, arguably, more divided along racial lines today than in 1963, when MLK delivered his famous speech, but this is far afield. What is most notable in this context is the assumption of Adams and his audiences that the national union that was accomplished or "saved" by Lincoln's victory in 1865 was a union of strains from Europe who had amalgamated into an English-speaking, still overwhelmingly Protestant nation. The African-Americans had been admitted in a time of war because of the idealism and optimism of some factions, and, according to Adams, the experiment of black-run administrations in the South during Reconstruction was an unmitigated disaster that proved a point. "The reconstruction policy," he said, "[that] we forced on the helpless States of the Confederacy was worse than a crime; it was a political blunder, as ungenerous as it was gross."

Adams believed what he did about the South and Reconstruction because he believed the ethnic component of the American Union was still essential even after the Civil War. The amalgamation of European stocks in the American environment was a reasonable expectation verified by experience since, but the immigration of Catholic strains has also disrupted the heritage of New England in an astounding way. One hardly knows how to understand contemporary New England given the influx of several groups of Catholics and the decline of the WASP, but nowhere does Adams mention it. His vision of the Union, however, absolutely included the valuable contributions and characters of the South, which he recognized as more stable, obviously more agrarian, and thus more Jeffersonian than his own section. He put great stock in these traits to preserve communities "where the ideas of [the] founders remain dominant… preserving the ark of our covenant," as he put it in his "Sifted Grain."

The conservative nationalism of Adams was a vague ideal, and he frequently reflected on the transition to this newer notion of the constitution New England had played such a role in promoting. He regarded the change as part of the inevitable progress of which he spoke, and said the primary American loyalty became "to Nation rather than to State," as he put it in "Shall Cromwell Have a Statue." A modern Whig would condemn the resisting reactionaries as blind and pitiful at best and as enemies of enlightenment and goodness as worst. Adams does neither, but surprises us with the magnanimity of a confident and content man. He is most generous to his foes. In his "Lee at Appomattox," Adams praises Lee for accepting the political responsibility of surrender when meaningful struggle was no longer possible. In his "Confederacy and the Transvaal: A People's Obligation to Robert E. Lee," Adams reflects on the ongoing guerilla conflict in the Boer War and notes that Lee's bold acceptance of political responsibility, even if only symbolically, at Appomattox, saved America from such a fate.

Lee was the heir of an older American republicanism who thought of himself primarily as a Virginian, which Adams describes, appreciates, and praises. Although Adams still acknowledges the Hartford "disloyalty" with approbation, he admits more to the Confederate legal position as regards the Constitution than Webster does in the 1830 debate. Adams does not argue, as Jefferson Davis did, about the delegated authorities of the states to the Federal government, the republican right to dissolve "political bands" should the government prove tyrannical, or any of the finer points of "independency" as known to John Adams. Instead, he simply notes that times have changed, and the conflict about sovereignty is secured to the general government "of the people, by the people, and for the people," without the regional and state preferences and loyalties. Adams nevertheless saw the valor of the Confederate South, contending that "all the loyalty, all the patriotic devotion and self-sacrifice were not then, any more than all the courage, on the victor's side. True! the moral right, the spirit of nationality, the sacred cause of humanity even, were on our side; but among those opposed, and who in the end went down, were men not less sincere, not less devoted, not less truly patriotic according to their lights than he who among us was first in all those qualities. Men of whom it was and is a cause of pride and confidence to say –'They too were countrymen!'"

One of Adams' most brilliant displays of quality is in his brief discourse on the tactic of total war, which he entirely disavows as immoral. He contrasts Sherman's ruthlessness to the chivalric restraint of his Southern brethren and finds yet another point in the South's favor.

These generous sympathies and noble understanding in victory is enough, in a cynical age, to make Adams an outstanding specimen of aristocracy and high-mindedness. This example of his writings gives us a glimpse of a neglected position in the development of the American Empire. An unkindly critic might claim that Adams was a self-satisfied bourgeois with comfortable opinions that fit well among his peers and did not risk his social status. This is not a fair position. Adams was a man who pursued excellence. Born entitled to the greatest fortune in Boston, he did not at any time in his life seek comfort and security alone, but put himself first into rigorous military service and then went into the most dynamic and corrupt industry of his age. Inside the railroad business, he wrote accounts of corruption and the need for regulation, which must have made his position most uncomfortable and risky. A Union man and a Republican, he opposed the Republican leadership of his own state and in the Federal government during Reconstruction on the grounds of their demagoguery, corruption, scandals, and pillage of the postwar South. He bolted the Republican Party to campaign for Cleveland, which was hardly popular in his own circles. In 1898, he joined an intellectual minority that vocally opposed the Spanish War and the acquisition of imperial provinces abroad, but also broke with them when they refused to recognize the *fait accompli* and the according responsibilities of the government. The man's principled character shines through his biography as it does in his historical opinions. His Whig progressivism is a marker of mainstream acceptability, yet it also promises intensely enjoyable and yet unknown correspondence on the subject with his radical brother, Brooks. Adams was certainly aware of other historiography, but never suffered the social uproar his younger brother endured.

The old breed of Boston gave way to the new immigrant elites of the Kennedy dynasty: an incredible qualitative decline that marked the passing of the demographic Adams seemed confident could amalgamate and communicate its qualities to the new immigrants. Although Adams spoke in terms of progress and improvement, he simultaneously voiced misgivings and foreboding. In his "Sifted Grain," a major work of his intellect, he makes several asides about the decline in the quality of American statesmen and particularly the decline of their rhetoric and vocabulary. In this, he is united with both Henry and Brooks Adams, who wrote more forcefully concerning it and its larger meaning. In a larger context, Adams was a Whig who observed decline but kept his theory. The durable and intellectual conviction in a theory in the face of experience is certainly a regional characteristic. Although the "Blue Nose" Boston Brahmins managed to communicate their accent, their "universalist" optimism, and their snobbery to the Italians and Irish that displaced them, they did not communicate an organic connection to the place and people. The modern O'Brian or Lombardi in Beacon Hill or the North End has no connection to the Old North Church, the graves on Copp's Hill, or the blood spilt on the slopes of Breed's Hill across the River Charles. The Puritan radicals, who breathed fire concerning all things Catholic, are distant from these Ellis Islanders. Those connections could be made through marriage and the mystery of common ancestry, but Adams saw partial possibilities in this respect. The Puritan critical attitude that broke down the Christian orthodoxy of his fathers fragments and dissolves every people that adopts the attitude. The Catholic heirs of New England were only likely to marry into the older demographic once they had embraced nominalism and rejected heritage identities in place, people, and faith on principle.

Oscar Handlin, in his *Boston's Immigrants*, notes the separatism practiced by the Catholic immigrants in Massachusetts and the traditional practice of intermarriage only with other Catholics: frequently of the same ethnic group. It was under those cultural norms that Catholicism became the dominant faith of New England, Boston only claiming a 30% Protestant population in 1900. The critical and atheist heirs of the Pilgrim Fathers and Puritans, still identifiable as a legacy population in the Gilded Age, faded away because of a final inability to communicate identity to their own heirs: a function organically connected to religion. A Bostonian of Irish heritage who patriotically identifies with the colonial stock is as charming and curious as a Southerner who does so.

Adams recognized the victory of the Northern elites in the 19th century, and he knew he was one. He often speaks of his identity and heritage, saying "I and mine were and are at least as much identified with Massachusetts as was Lee and his with Virginia; - traditionally, historically, by blood and memory and name." This organic connection was not based in identification with the state of Massachusetts, according to Adams, but more broadly with the region united in interests by the Federalists. "I have heard of a New Englander, of a Green Mountain boy, of a Rhode Islander, of a "Nutmeg," of a "Blue-nose" even, but never of a Massachusettensian. The word somehow does not lend itself to the mouth, any more than the thought to the mind." The regional identity was, perhaps, displaced or forgotten in the 1840's and 1850's as the Bostonians found themselves at the fore of every celebrated movement and political cause. Adams, having seen the baseness of Reconstruction, is more level headed about his nationalism, but the tidy and intellectual New Englander of 1870 may well have thought himself the rightful heirs of the whole country and its proper leadership class. Adams is certainly aware of this perspective, but was wise enough to avoid the hubris. Instead, he endeavored to build a "national pantheon," as he put it, that included all the excellent traits of the South.

The national position of that era seemed singularly unconcerned with the antebellum Constitution and its conflicts. Adams recognizes the good will, logic, and sincerity of the "States' Rights" school defeated in '65, but he treats the arguments and experience as irrelevant in the face of the progressive theory, which reveals how things must inevitably be for the American nation. For him, this nation is much more defined and racially exclusive, and his audience requires no qualifications because these are broad and unspoken agreements. And yet, tragically, he admits to his Richmond friends of his "strict-constructionist" convictions and decries the tyranny of Reconstruction. This position is better articulated by Adams' friend and comrade in the Anti-Imperialist League, the dynamic and prolific Carl Schurz.

Adams' nationalism is in stark contrast to the constitutional conservatism of his unreconstructed Southern brethren such as the former Confederate President Jefferson Davis, who wrote carefully the historical and constitutional arguments for the Southern position in his 1881 tome, *The Rise and Fall of the Confederate Government.* The two elites, Northern and Southern, could not be living in more different worlds or have more different, yet American, imaginations in that year of 1881. Davis was thinking as he had thought his whole career: of the antebellum experience and the place of states and individual loyalties as regards the limits of the Federal government. He was also defeated and unrepentant, caring for the broken bodies of Confederate wounded at his estate in Biloxi: literally a man without a country and without citizenship. Adams was the CEO of the Union Pacific, often invited to give papers at the Massachusetts Historical Society and influential in politics and policy. The fact that Adams not only could but made a sustained effort to commemorate Lee and his comrades in arms while also believing the constitutional arguments of Davis an irrelevant anachronism is grand. When Adams begins his tributes to Lee he seems to appreciate the superlative generosity in his status, dwelling frequently on his own regional identity. Adams' gesture at the end of his own family's prestige in national life is one of the best monuments to the greatness of his heritage that any aristocratic lineage could desire.

Adams produced important works on education while a trustee at Harvard. He was influential in reforming the old classical curriculum with a more modern and, fittingly enough, progressive approach. Adams produced a corpus of work on railroads, scandals related to railroad corporations, and railroad regulation. He is also an important writer in the history of Massachusetts itself, publishing a famous work of local history on his own hometown of Quincy and a trilogy of essays formerly published together of episodes in the colonial history of Massachusetts. This volume reproduces none of this work. Mrs. Wendell Garrett and L. H. Butterfield published, in *The Proceedings of the Massachusetts Historical Society* an "Annotated Checklist" or bibliography of all known works by Adams.

The impetus for this volume has been the oft repeated desire for a collection of Adams' opinions and productions on the War and of his thoughts on Lee. Adams had proposed a diplomatic history of the War, which was based partly on his own father's key role in diplomacy in London. This work received some attention but was never finished. His several speeches and essays concerning Lee were partly collected with other works in *Lee at Appomattox and Other Works*, which was released by Houghton Mifflin in 1902, but have never since been collected. Adams' historiography and his conservative nationalism are of an antiquarian interest for those who itemize lost perspectives. At the dawn of an empire made possible by Lincoln's conquest and prophesied by Lee to Lord Acton, Adams called for a halt. This was remarkable, and so here are included his important remarks and pieces on modern war, American empire, imperial policy, and related questions of race at home and abroad.

Outside of the major themes of railroads, education, and the local or colonial history of Massachusetts, this volume is an attempt to collect the shorter works of

Charles Francis Adams, Jr. on the themes described and to do the man justice by extended memory among the living.

George Bagby,
Rockland, Maine
Summer of 2024

1

War

1

Lincoln's Offer to Garibaldi

From the *Proceedings* of the Massachusetts Historical Society, March, 1908

At a recent meeting of an Historical Congress held at Perugia, Italy, in September, Mr. H. Nelson Gay, an American now resident in Rome, submitted an interesting paper, being a part of a work upon which he is engaged, entitled " Le relazioni fra l'Italia e gli Stati Uniti." This paper was based upon original material which Mr. Gay had unearthed in the archives of the American legation at Brussels, and related to an offer of a high command in the Army of the United States made to Garibaldi during the summer of 1861, shortly after the disgraceful rout known as the first Battle of Bull Run. Henry Shelton Sanford, of Connecticut, was then the United States Minister at Brussels, and the material in question was part of Mr. Sanford's official correspondence.

Subsequently Mr. Gay put this material into the form of a paper entitled "Lincoln's Offer of a Command to Garibaldi light on a disputed point of history," which appeared in the last November (1907) issue of "The Century Magazine." He there gives the history of this offer which,

now forgotten, at the time caused some discussion ; but the details connected with it are now for the first time revealed. It will be remembered
that Garibaldi, in 1861, was living in retirement. The present kingdom of Italy, under the rule of Victor Emmanuel, had been brought
into existence as the result of the operations in which Garibaldi had
taken so famous and prominent a part in the summer of 1860, but did
not yet include the Papal temporality. The seat of government of the
newly united Italy had been established at Florence ; but Garibaldi was
looking forward to the occupation of Rome as the capital of the kingdom. His fame was, of course, world-wide. Mr. Gay now makes public
a correspondence which passed at the time, and in which Mr. Sanford
took a prominent part. As is well known, nothing resulted from the
most ill-considered move to which it relates ; but none the less it has an
historical interest, and moreover it conveys a lesson. The correspondence took place during the earlier months of my father's seven years
of diplomatic service in England, he having reached London during
the previous May. He knew nothing of it until it was over ; but I find
in his diary the following long entry, under date of Friday, September
20, 1861, which has a certain significance in connection with Mr. Gay's
article in the November " Century." I reproduce it in full:

Had visits also from Mr. Sanford and Mr. Motley, both of whom
came to dine with me. The former seemed very anxious to explain
to both of us his agency in the invitation extended to Garibaldi to
go to America. This matter has given occasion to a good deal of
unpleasant remark in Europe, as indicating that we did not feel
competent to manage our business, with our own officers. I had
been consulted about it by Mr. Lucas, who wished authority to
contradict it, which I could not give him excepting in so far as
the story affirmed that the supreme command had been offered
to [Garibaldi], I gave him on Tuesday my version of the matter,
which was this. That probably some irresponsible individual had
first sounded [Garibaldi] as to his disposition to go. Then that

the government on receiving information of this had authorized an offer of a command: — That Garibaldi had demanded a general power, which could not be admitted, and the negotiation had gone off on this issue. My conjecture proved in the main correct, though there were material additions in the narrative of Mr. Sanford. It seems that one James W. Quiggle, officiating as consul at Antwerp, some time since whilst travelling in Italy made acquaintance enough with Garibaldi to induce him to volunteer a letter of enquiry as to his feeling on the American question. The reply was of such a kind as to induce Mr. Quiggle to send a copy to the Department of State. This had brought a letter of instructions to Mr. Sanford to go and make Garibaldi an offer of a position of Major General, being *the highest army rank* in the gift of the President. At the same time it eulogized Mr. Quiggle, and directed Mr. Sanford to offer him any place under the General that he might prefer. Sanford, professing to be well aware of the responsibility resting on him, and desirous of keeping the control of the matter in his hands, yet posts off first of all to Mr. Quiggle and reads him the instruction as well as the compliment to himself. Quiggle insists upon seeing and reading it, is cunning enough to take a copy, and then on the strength of it anticipated poor Sanford by writing at once to Garibaldi to appraise him that the government had forwarded him a formal invitation to *take the supreme command* in America, of which he would receive due notice presently. Finding this misconception fastened on the mind of Garibaldi by this folly of his own, his next task was to remedy the evil in the best way he could. Accordingly he goes to Turin, where he finds a friend of Garibaldi who has come from him to notify the King of Sardinia that he is ready to go to America if his services are not wanted in Italy. In other words, he threatens to withdraw the aid of his popularity to the King if he refuses to advance forthwith upon Rome. The King is too wary to be drawn into the trap ; so, with great professions of good will, reluctantly grants his consent to the chief's departure. It follows that Garibaldi mortified at the failure of his scheme has no resource but to execute his threat. But here again Mr. Sanford is compelled to intervene to protect the American Government from the effects of Garibaldi's misconception. To that end he pays him a visit and discloses to him the fact that he can have a command, but not the supreme control. This of course changes his views again. He cannot think of going to America without having the power of a Dictator, and the contingent right to proclaim emancipation to the slaves. On this point the negotiation went off. A strange medley of blunders. Garibaldi however felt so awkwardly placed by his failure to carry the King off his feet, that he still clung to the idea of paying a visit to America as a private citizen. Mr. Sanford offered him every facility to go out as a guest, but he declined it all, and finished by saying that if he decided to go it should be in his own way. This seems to me a lucky escape; for our officers have too much sense of honor not to feel that the introduction of a foreigner to do their work is a lasting discredit to themselves. At best it is little more than a clap-trap. Mr. Seward is unquestionably a statesman of large and comprehensive views, but in his management of his office he betrays two defects. One a want of systematic and dignified operation in the opinion of the world — the other, an admixture of that earthly taint which comes from early training in the school of New York State politics. The first shows itself in a somewhat brusque and ungracious manner towards the representatives of foreign nations. The second, in a rather indiscriminate appliance of means to ends. Mr. Sanford evidently felt that he had not gained much in this melee, but I made no remark beyond expressing a fear of the effect upon Generals Scott and McClellan.

This distinctly humiliating foot-note, for it amounts to that, in the early history of our War of Secession, is curiously suggestive of a very similar episode which had occurred some eighty years before, during the progress of our War of Independence. My attention has been recently drawn to the similarity of the experiences while reading Sir George Otto Trevelyan's last volume of his work entitled " The American Revolution."

Sir George, in there recounting the operations of the third year (1778) of the war, refers to the strange antics of Silas Deane, then established at Paris in the anomalous position described as "business agent of the Revolutionary government." "Silas Deane, with ineffable folly," Sir George proceeds to remind us, "was at this time [1778] scheming to get the Commander-in-Chief of the American army superseded, and his functions transferred to the Comte de Broglie, — a restless, and not very successful, diplomatist, and a fifth-rate general."[1] "Mr. Deane's mad contract with Monsieur du Coudray and his hundred officers" is also referred to,[2] and the fact that a wretched French adventurer, as ignorant of both American conditions and character as of the English language, was actually contracted with on terms which would have led to his superseding General Knox in command of Washington's artillery. Naturally, such an appointment led to a tender of

resignation on the part of Greene, Knox and Sullivan, who all found themselves outranked and felt humiliated. And so in 1861 history repeated itself, the earlier page of 1778 being quite forgotten ; though it is only fair to bear in mind the fact, in a degree redeeming, that Garibaldi was not a Comte de Broglie, nor Sanford a Silas Deane. Even this much, however, cannot be said of the personage designated as "one James W. Quiggle, officiating [in 1861] as consul at Antwerp." But, no matter how charitably viewed, the more recent episode of the two, seen through the perspective of nearly half a century, is, it must be conceded, far from being in strict accordance with a proper sense of national self-respect.

The two incidents, separated by more than three-fourths of a century, are, indeed, suggestive of a certain element of provincialism and lack of self-confidence, so to speak, paradoxical as it sounds, in the American people. We seem never to have quite got over the colonial, or rather the provincial, feeling that, somehow or in some way, the old countries of Europe contain material of which we ourselves are more or less barren. For instance, in "The Boston Herald" for Tuesday of this very week, February 11, there is an editorial entitled "A Prophet and his Prophecy." In this article a "distinguished French journalist" now visiting this country — whose name, however, does not appear — is quoted as saying that, in case of a war between Japan and this country, as the result of earlier successes on the part of the Asiatic nation, "American money will be inducing soldiers of fortune from all lands to join the forces of the United States. Then the United States will win." The quotation is suggestive of that most illuminating paper of the late James Russell Lowell, written in 1869, shortly after the close of our War of Secession, entitled "On a Certain Condescension in Foreigners." That condescension we seem actually through both the eighteenth and nineteenth centuries to have gone out to seek. We invited it; and at no time in our history do we seem to have been more prone to this tacit self-confession of foreign superiority than during the years which immediately preceded the War of Secession. As Mr. Lowell, writing in 1869,[3] says:

> Before our war we were to Europe but a huge mob of adventurers and shop-keepers. Leigh Hunt expressed it well enough when he said that he could never think of America without seeing a gigantic counter stretched all along the seaboard.

Mr. Lowell then goes on:

> Democracy had been hitherto only a ludicrous effort to reverse the laws of nature by thrusting Cleon into the place of Pericles. But a democracy that could fight for an abstraction, whose members held life and goods cheap compared with that larger life which we call country, was not merely unheard-of, but portentous.

None the less, Mr. Gay's paper in "The Century Magazine" reminds us how in the early stages of that struggle we advertised to the world through our highest officials — the President and Secretary of State — our lack of self-confidence, and went forth to invite a manifestation of " condescension in foreigners." But it is curious now to consider what might have occurred had the offer to Garibaldi been accepted. At best, from a military point of view, a daring partisan leader, the probabilities are great that the liberator of the two Sicilies would have sustained a lamentable loss of prestige.

He, it is true, was exceptional; but in the "Reminiscences" of Carl Schurz, recently published, there is a most suggestive passage bearing upon these foreign military adventurers taken as a whole, — "soldiers of fortune," as they were called, — who came under Mr. Schurz's own observation. He says that, after his return (1862) from his mission to Spain, and when he had himself been offered a brigadier-generalship in our army by President Lincoln:

> While I was waiting in Washington for my confirmation and assignment, I had again to undergo the tribulations of persons who are supposed to be men of "influence." The news had gone abroad that in America there was a great demand for officers of military training and experience. This demand could not fail to attract from all parts of the globe adventurous characters who had, or pretended to have, seen military service in one country or another, and who believed that there was a chance for prompt employment and rapid promotion, Washington at that period fairly swarmed with them. Some were very respectable persons, who came here well recommended, and subsequently made a praiseworthy record. Others belonged to the class of adventurers who traded on their good looks or on the fine stories they had concocted of their own virtues and achievements [ii. 338].

Mr. Schurz then goes on to specify instances:

A young man, calling himself Count von Schweinitz, presented himself to me neatly attired in the uniform of an Austrian officer of Uhlans. He was very glib of tongue, and exhibited papers which had an authentic look, and seemed to sustain his pretensions. But there were occasional smartnesses in his conversation which made me suspicious. He may have noticed that I hesitated to trust him, for suddenly he ceased to press me with his suit. I learned afterwards that he had succeeded in obtaining some appointment, and also in borrowing considerable sums of money from two foreign Ministers. Finally it turned out that his mother was a washerwoman, that he had served an Austrian officer of Uhlans as a valet, and that as such he had possessed himself of his uniform and his master's papers [ii. 339].

Recalling these somewhat unsavory reminiscences, it is not without interest to ask ourselves whether this state of affairs will ever wholly cease to be : whether the time will at last indeed come when we Americans will look upon the older European nations as otherwise than in some way superior ; or, on the other hand, whether those nations will ever approach us without a certain sense of that condescension of the foreigner upon which Mr. Lowell animadverted half a century ago. At present it seems to have assumed a most unsavory phase, but one which is perhaps the natural result of the rapid accumulation of vast wealth in the hands of the self-made individual, — the purchase of titles, always encumbered by a man, by American young women, or for American young women by their families, who wish in this way to identify themselves with an aristocracy. It is, in fact, difficult to-day to take up a newspaper without coming across a reference to such cases, usually in the divorce courts, — an Italian prince, an English duke or earl, or a French count, more or less, as the evidence shows, a degenerate, married to a rich Americaness. It is the same old weakness; but, whether studied in the pages of Trevelyan, in Mr. Gay's paper, or in the scandal-mongering columns of to-day's society journals, it is not inspiring ; and

I confess to a certain sense of satisfaction in thus putting on record the evidence that, with sturdy Americanism, Mr. Adams, when he heard of the Seward-Garibaldi incident of 1861, saw the thing in its true light, and most properly, as well as correctly, characterized it.

Notes:

1. G. 0. Trevelyan, *The American Revolution*, Part III. (New York, 1907), 42.

2. *Ibid.* 40.

3. J. R. Lowell, *My Study Windows* (Boston, 1885), 76, 77.

2

The Crisis of Foreign Intervention in the War of Secession, 1862

This paper was published in the *Proceedings* of the Massachusetts Historical Society in April of 1914.

At the November meeting, 1911 — thirty months since — it may
by some be remembered I submitted a paper — "The Trent Affair;
An Historical Retrospect" — which now appears in its proper place
in our *Proceedings.* The episode then discussed was one of indisputable
historical interest, and I was able to speak of it to a certain extent from
personal recollection. What I now submit amounts to a sequel. I then
had occasion to refer in some detail to the Confederate Commissioners
arrested in transit by Capt. Wilkes — James M. Mason of Virginia, and
John Slidell of Louisiana. I described their seizure, their subsequent
detention at Fort Warren, their release, and, finally, their arrival at
their original destinations in the two European capitals — London and
Paris — there to represent the Confederacy.

The present narrative has in it not a few of the elements which enter into works of fiction; and, on behalf of the Confederacy, it was John Slidell who at that juncture arranged the diplomatic program about to be described. Such being the case, it is historically interesting, in view of what subsequently occurred, to recall the impression once made on his contemporaries by Mr. Slidell; for, so highly developed was his faculty of political management supposed to be, he was popularly regarded as little short of a magician. This impression was shared also by those exceptionally competent to form opinions on that head. For instance, in his publication, *My Diary, North and South,* W. H. Russell thus describes a social call at New Orleans, May 24, 1861, immediately after the fall of Fort Sumter. He says:

In the evening I visited Mr. Slidell, whom I found at home with his family. ... I rarely met a man whose features have a greater finesse and firmness of purpose than Mr. Slidell's; his keen grey eye is full of life, his thin, firmly-set lips indicate resolution and passion. Mr. Slidell, though born in a Northern state, is perhaps one of the most determined disunionists in the Southern Confederacy; he is not a speaker of note, nor a ready stump orator, nor an able writer; but he is an excellent judge of mankind, adroit, persevering, and subtle, full of device, and fond of intrigue; one of those men, who, unknown almost to the outer world, organizes and sustains a faction, and exalts it into the position of a party — what is called here a "wire-puller." Mr. Slidell is to the South something greater than Mr. Thurlow Weed has been to his party in the North. . . . Mr. Slidell and the members of his family possess naivete, good sense, and agreeable manners; and the regrets I heard expressed in Washington society, at their absence, had every justification.

This was written in May. Six months later Mr. Slidell emerged into world-wide notoriety, and Russell, then still sending his "Special Correspondent" letters to the Times, thus referred to him immediately after the Trent affair, the letter, written in Washington, appearing in the Times issue for December loth:

Mr. Slidell, whom I had the pleasure of meeting in New Orleans, is a man of more tact and he is not inferior to his colleague, Mr. Mason, in other respects. He far excels him in subtlety and depth, and is one of the most consummate masters of political manoeuvre in the States. He is what is here called a "wire-puller," — a man who unseen moves the puppets on the public stage as he lists — a man of iron will and strong passions, who loves the excitement of combinations, . . . and who in his dungeon [at Fort Warren], or whatever else it may be, would conspire with the mice against the cat sooner than not conspire at all. . . . Originally a northern man, he has thrown himself into the southern cause and staked his great fortune on the issue without hesitation, and with all the force of his intellect and character.

Commenting on the above, I thus expressed myself in the paper on the Trent affair:

Slidell, on the other hand, was considered one of the most astute and dangerous of all Confederate public characters. An intriguer by nature, unscrupulous in his political methods, he . . . was generally looked upon as the most dangerous person to the Union the Confederacy could select for diplomatic work in Europe. The first object of the envoys was to secure the recognition of the Confederacy.[1]

In the present study my purpose is to describe, in the light of material to which access has since been obtained, the work done by this master of political management, this diplomatic magician, during the eight months immediately succeeding his arrival in Europe. The narrative, an extraordinary one, involves, as I shall show, the crisis of our Civil War. Well designed, the scheme — plot, it cannot properly be termed — at one time seemed almost certain to prove a triumph of diplomatic art. In the event it failed, and failed utterly; but its failure was due to a combination of circumstances highly improbable of occurrence, and quite beyond the control of Mr. Slidell. Not long surviving the cause he had furthered, Mr. Slidell died in exile. No biography of him has since been published, and his papers, like those of his colleague in the Senate and Chief in the Confederate State Department during the Civil War, Judah P. Benjamin, have been destroyed. In his share in what then occurred, however, so far as the record survives, I find nothing provocative of censure, nothing which an opponent would be justified in stigmatizing as otherwise than in accordance with the accepted rules of the game. On this point my judgment is also worth something; as, first so to do, I have been privileged to read the confidential correspondence between him and Mr. Mason.

July, 1863, witnessed the Gettysburg struggle and the fall of Vicksburg. That month, consequently, is by general historical consent looked upon as marking the climax and turning-point of the War of Secession. Perhaps it did; but it may none the less fairly be questioned whether for sympathisers in the cause of the Union, the previous September did not furnish occasion for a deeper solicitude. In it the crisis became acute; and, until the ensuing July, it continued to be so.

To summarize briefly the course of events, it will be remembered that in August, 1862, the great Union advance inaugurated, East and West, in the preceding February, had spent its force; and, in Virginia, ceasing to be aggressive, it was thrown back to such an extent that Washington, and not Richmond, stood in danger of hostile occupation. At the same time, the European situation was far from satisfactory. Not only was the Confederate cotton campaign in progress, but every indication favored for it an early and successful issue; and that issue involved nothing less than the outcome of the struggle. Was Cotton not indeed King? This had, in the summer of 1862, become a world question; and the machinery and life incident to and dependent upon the cotton production and the cotton textile industries, whether in Great Britain, on the continent, or in Asia, were disorganized. The social unrest and economical suffering, necessarily incident to a commercial confusion literally world-wide, were at their height. This condition of affairs was, moreover, by common consent, attributed to the American War. The blockade of the Southern cotton-shipping ports by the National Government of the United States was accepted as the obvious cause of ills and disturbances in Hindustan and China no less than in Lancashire.

The question of foreign action in some form, bearing on this situation — whether an offer of mediation, or through the formal recognition of the Confederacy as a member of the family of nations, or through a refusal farther to recognize the blockade — now presented itself. It had been in the air since the commencement of the struggle. Indeed, weeks before the attack on Fort Sumter, M. Mercier, the French Minister in Washington, had become so convinced that a permanent separation, South from North, was impending and inevitable, that he had even gone so far as to suggest to Lord Lyons that it was desirable that he, the British Minister at Washington, acting in connection with the representative of France, should be clothed with discretionary power to recognize the Confederacy. This was in March.[2] The conviction further on assumed in Mercier 's mind the shape almost of an obsession;[3] and, naturally, it colored his official dispatches, operating immediately on the minds of the Emperor and his advisers in potent furtherance of the program which had early outlined itself in Mr. Slidell's busily scheming brain. Indeed, that program may be said to have originated with the French representative; for, in April, 1862, Mercier obtained a permit to visit the Confederate capital. Judah P. Benjamin was then acting as the Confederate Secretary of State, and with him, Creole Senator from Louisiana up to the previous February, the French Minister had, during their common residence in Washington, held social relations of a peculiarly friendly character. Lord Newton, in his *Life of Lord Lyons*, says of Mercier in this connection, "after the manner of French diplomatists of the period, he could not resist the temptation of trying to effect a striking coup."[4] Whether such was or was not his moving impulse, Mercier had concealed from Lord Lyons his project until it was too late to endeavor to dissuade him from it. Indeed, he was bent upon it. More cautious in his disposition than his colleague, Lord Lyons apprehended that in going to the Confederate capital at that time he was "as likely to get himself into a scrape as to do anything else." And it so turned out. It was an officious act, characteristic of the man and of the imperial diplomatic service.

Mercier got back on the 24th of April.[5] He returned more than ever persuaded that a restoration of the Union was impossible;[6] that unless the Powers of Europe intervened the war would last for years; that in the end the independence of the South would have to be recognized;

that the evils incident to a cotton shortage would meanwhile be intensified; and that, in view of these conditions, the Governments of Europe should be on the watch for any favorable opportunity of exerting themselves in such a way as to end the war. His dispatches would in this connection be of great historic value; and, at some future time, will probably be accessible. At present, however, they are buried in the archives of the French Foreign Office; but the Minister of course freely communicated his views whether to the Emperor personally or to his official superior in the department of the French Foreign Affairs. Those views also, it so chanced, chimed in most opportunely with the plans of the Emperor in connection with the Mexican enterprise on which he was at the time fully embarked. Napoleon III, therefore, was under every inducement to exert himself actively and openly to bring the proposed intervention about.[7] A little later, the French Minister of Foreign Affairs, M. Thouvenel, was in England, and the Emperor then sent him a telegram desiring him unofficially to ascertain whether the British Government did not think the time had come for recognizing the South. This was in July. Thouvenel replied that from conversations which had already taken place between him and Lord Palmerston, and from the language which the Premier had just used in Parliament, it did not seem to him expedient to press the matter further at that time.[8]

The course of ensuing events must next be noted in close connection with military operations then going on both in the United States and in Mexico. The reverses to the Union arms which marked the months of July, August and early September, 1862, were already foreshadowed. On the i8th of July, it was reported in London and Liverpool that McClellan 's army either had surrendered or was on the point of capitulation.[9] Under pressure of disaster, a military reorganization in face of a victorious opponent had become a necessity. So General Halleck, called from the West to Washington, superseded at the seat of government McClellan, his senior in commission. General Pope had already been put at the head of a newly organized force, intended to act in cooperation with the Army of the Potomac, but wholly independent of it. The succession of military disasters was thus provoked, which, a few weeks later, resulted in the Union forces being driven or withdrawn from Virginia soil. On the 29th of July, moreover, to the unconcealed satisfaction of Parliament as well as a large preponderance of the English press, the Alabama, eluding the customs officials, got to sea. It was in position to begin its work, the character of which was well and generally understood. A British-built, British-armed and British-manned Confederate commerce-destroyer had been let loose on the American merchant marine.

The second French expeditionary force to Mexico was in course of active preparation. The Emperor had been advised by the commander of the first force, sent out a year before, that in point of discipline, organization and morale, the French were so superior to the Mexicans that he (Gen. Lorencez) felt able to "assure the Emperor that at the head of six thousand men [he] would undertake to become complete master of Mexico." Thus officially informed, Louis Napoleon, constitutionally a dreamer, was imbued with a belief that it was his mission to establish in West Indian waters a firm government, which "shall give to that Latin race beyond the ocean its ancient strength and power. "[10]

From Gibraltar to Kronstadt, all Europe was intently following the above course of events. Thus, through a wholly fortuitous concurrence of circumstances, Mr. Slidell found himself in that situation for which Nature had especially designed him. The atmosphere was one of intrigue, and every condition of the environment, whether in France, in England, in Mexico, or in the Confederacy, invited manipulation. He was also in fairly close personal touch with the Emperor, at that time looked upon as the European Sphinx, and himself the busiest schemer of the day. About the middle of April the Confederate Commissioner had with him a personal interview, of which Slidell sent to Mason the following account:

My interview lasted seventy minutes (one hour, ten minutes); he was particularly gracious, I may even say cordial. I had expected him to be reserved, taking little part in conversation, making or suggesting questions and replying briefly. Far from this he talked freely, frankly, and unreservedly, spoke in the most decided terms of his sympathy and his regret that England had not shared his views. He said that he had made a great mistake in respecting a blockade which had for six months at least not been effective, that we ought to have been recognized last summer while our ports were still in our own possession. He spoke freely of the Mexican question and the probability of its soon bringing him into collision with the United States, that the treaty with Mexico if ratified by the Senate, would place them inevitably in a hostile position towards him. He asked if he offered mediation how the question of boundaries could be settled? What we would insist on? I said that we would insist on all the States where a majority of the people had already determined by their votes to join our Confederacy, leaving the people of Kentucky, Missouri and Maryland to decide further — such as whether they could or would associate their fortunes with ours. He expressed his regret that he had not been able sooner to see me and on parting said that he hoped for the future I should have less difficulty in seeing him.

On the whole he left on my mind the impression that if England long persists in her inaction he would be disposed to act without her, although of course he did not commit himself to do so. He said that he had reason not to be wholly satisfied with England, she had not appreciated as she should have done his support in the Trent affair. There is an important part of our conversation that I will give you through Mr. Mann. On the whole my interview was highly satisfactory.[11]

At this time a sharp personal stimulus was administered to Mr. Slidell's activities. The surrender of New Orleans to the Union fleet under command of Admiral Farragut took place April 26. Immediately on receipt of the news of this event in Paris, Slidell wrote to Mason that in an interview with M. Thouvenel, the Foreign Secretary, he had frankly admitted that this occurrence "would be most disastrous, as it would give the enemy the control of the Mississippi and its tributaries, that it would not in any way modify the fixed purpose of our people to carry on the war even to an extermination. He [Thouvenel] said that was the opinion of everyone here."[12] Referring to the effect of the capture on his personal circumstances, Slidell added in the same letter: " The taking of New Orleans cuts me off from all resources while the war lasts, and that will probably be very many months. Under other circumstances, I should not care about receiving anything from Richmond. This, is now to me a matter of consequence."[13]

Slidell's line of diplomatic activity was now clearly defined. Aware that concurrent action with Great Britain was fundamental in the policy of the Second Empire, Slidell's purpose was to make the most effective use possible of France to influence Great Britain in favor of a joint European recognition of the Confederacy, and, if possible, of intervention in the blockade. This failing, he further hoped so to commit Napoleon through his Mexican enterprise that, in case of a failure to bring about concurrent action, the independent recognition of the Confederacy by France would become for the Emperor a logical necessity, implying the presence of a formidable fleet in the waters of the Gulf, strong enough to keep [that coast] clear of every Federal cruiser." Such a naval armament had in fact already been provided as a necessary adjunct to the Mexican outfit. As Slidell now expressed it to Mason, "I shall be very much surprised and disappointed if the Emperor do not take the matter in hand on his own hook." This was written August 3. Three days later, on the 6th, Slidell further wrote to the same effect. Referring to a discussion which occurred in the House of Lords two days previous, in the course of which Earl Russell, being questioned, had made certain statements, Slidell thus expressed himself:

> I think that it may now be assumed that England will not move, and I can only account for the inaction of the English Ministry on the hypothesis that they desire to see the North entirely exhausted

and broken down, that they are willing in order to attain this object to suffer their own people to starve, and [themselves to] play the poltroon in the face of Europe. [Russell's] answer must have been given without any consultation with this Government. If I am right in this opinion, the Emperor has been treated with a rudeness approaching to indignity, which will make him the better disposed to pursue his own policy without consulting England. If he do, Russell's prompt reply ought not to be regretted. France will for us be a safer ally than England.

With this program rapidly assuming shape in his mind, on July 17 Slidell had submitted to the Emperor a direct and definite proposition, which was also a little later communicated in writing to Thouvenel, the Minister for Foreign Affairs. This proposition was based on formal instructions drawn up by Benjamin, the Confederate Secretary of State, at the time of Mercier's visit to Richmond. Benjamin's instructions ran in part as follows:

It is well understood that there exists at present a temporary embarrassment in the finances of France, which might have the effect of deterring that government from initiating a policy likely to superinduce the necessity for naval expeditions. If, under these circumstances, you should after cautious inquiry be able to satisfy yourself that the grant of a subsidy for defraying the expenses of such expeditions would suffice for removing any obstacle to an arrangement or understanding with the Emperor, you are at liberty to enter into engagements to that effect.[14]

Slidell, accordingly, construing his instructions broadly, now proposed to Louis Napoleon that, in return for Confederate recognition, France was to receive in bales of cotton what amounted to the equivalent in cash of a hundred million francs, together with most favorable tariff arrangements; and, so far as Mexico was concerned, an immediate alliance offensive and defensive was to be arranged.[15] This was in every way an opportune as well as tempting inducement; and the Emperor encouraged the Confederate representative by assuring him that he, the Emperor, had moved in the matter, and was exerting himself to bring about combined action by European powers. A diplomatic intimation meanwhile shortly after reached Mr. Slidell to the effect that it was undesirable the special inducements held forth should come to the knowledge of the English Government;[16] and, accordingly, when Slidell confidentially communicated with his London colleague on this topic, he did not fail to intimate to him that the existence of an understanding so markedly advantageous to the French Government had best not reach those the Emperor proposed to have associated with him in the contemplated movement. It was presumably at this stage of proceedings that the telegraphic message from the Emperor personally to Thouvenel, already referred to, was sent.

Thus Slidell was putting in most effective diplomatic work, and the tide not only seemed to be setting, but, from all directions, actually was setting in favor of the Confederacy, and that strongly. On the 7th of August Parliament was prorogued, and the Government, relieved of its presence for some months to come, felt comparatively free. The situation in Lancashire was, however, most disturbing. It even threatened to get beyond all available means of relief, and not impossibly of control. The market was in a condition of unprecedented excitement, for American cotton was quoted at thirty pence per pound, while great uneasiness was felt because of a belief that the next steamer from America might not improbably bring news of the Confederates being in Washington. In such case, as the result of some European offer of mediation, a speedy recognition of the Confederacy was anticipated, and Liverpool might find itself flooded with cotton arrivals. The most prudent and the most daring were equally at a loss. The suffering in the Lancashire districts was at the same time rapidly intensifying. The number of those either actually paupers or dependent upon others for relief was mounting up at the rate of approximately a thousand each day; and it was reported that as compared with the previous year there had been an increase of over 113,000 persons in receipt of parochial relief, or some 263 per cent. In five manufacturing centres, 32,718 operatives were reported as working short time, while 33,651 were wholly unemployed; 14,530 only were working full time. The weekly loss of wages in those five unions alone amounted to £27,430.[17]

In view of these facts and the situation thus set forth, the minds of both Lord Palmerston and Earl Russell naturally a little later on turned to the question of policy as respects the American conflict. Was not the time actually come, or at least probably at hand, when a new attitude should be assumed? If so, what form should it take? Should the cooperation of other European powers be invited? And, so far as France was concerned, the intimations, direct and indirect, semi-official and un-official, received first through Mr. Lindsay and later through M. Thouvenel, bore fruit.[18] As Palmerston expressed it, "France, we know, is quite ready, and only waiting for our concurrence."[19] So far as the cause of Confederacy was concerned, all the indications were favorable.

Lord Palmerston accordingly now broached the subject in characteristic fashion to Earl Russell; and the two, as the result of an interchange of views, agreed on both the expediency and nature of ministerial action looking, as respects the American conflict, to a radical change of policy. This subject, however, elsewhere discussed, is familiar history, and I

Notes:

1. *Proceedings*, xiv. 40.

2. Newton, *Life of Lord Lyons*, I. 3

3. Ib., 90.

4. Newton, *Life of Lord Lyons*, I. 82; *Lyons to Russell*, April 14, 1862.

5. *Lyons to Russell*, April 25, 1862.

6. See Butler, *Judah P. Benjamin*, 288.

7. Rhodes, IV. 94.

8. Walpole, *Twenty-five Years*, II. 55.

9. Adams, Ms. Diary; *Mason to Slidell*, July 18, 1862.

10. Martin, *Maximilian in Mexico*, 107, 108.

11. *Slidell to Mason*, April 20, 1862.

12. *Slidell to Mason*, May 19, 1862.

13. *Slidell to Mason*, May 14, 1862.

14. April 12, 1862. Richardson, *Messages and Papers of the Confederacy*, 11. 229.

15. *Slidell to Benjamin*, July 25, 1862.

16. *Slidell to Mason*, July 30, 1862.

17. *Index*, I. 354.

18. *Slidell to Mason*, August 6, 1862; Butler's *Benjamin,* 299.

19. Walpole's *Russell,* 11. 362.

20. *Life of C. F. Adams* (Am. Statesmen Series), chap, xv; *Studies, Military and Diplomatic,* 400-412; *Trans- Atlantic Historical Solidarity,* 97-106. See, also, Rhodes, iv, and, generally, the researches of Callahan, Latané and others.

3

The Trent Affair

This speech was given to the Massachusetts Historical Society
in November of 1911.

As, doubtless, all of us have had frequent occasion to observe, there
are few occurrences which in their relative connection with other occurrences or with things at large do not assume with the lapse of time
aspects strangely different. The passage of fifty years is a great dissol-
vent and clarifier. The international incident, still memorable, known
as the affair of the Trent and the seizure by Captain Charles Wilkes,
then commanding the *San Jacinto*, of Messrs. Mason and Slidell, the two
Confederate envoys, occurred on the 8th of November, and the fiftieth
recurrence of that date accordingly came about yesterday.

One living in those times who had then attained even a degree of
maturity, that is, any man or woman now over sixty-five years of age,
cannot but retain, if American, a distinct recollection of the incident,
and a general memory at least of the excitement caused by it, and the
intense interest with which every stage of its development was awaited.

For such, however, it is necessary also to bear in mind that the present great majority, those of the younger generations, do not have this vivid personal recollection of the events of that memorable period, and there are many whose ideas concerning the affair of the Trent are vague and, to say the least, unsettled. For instance, as an illustration in point let me relate an incident told me by my friend Mr. Moorfield Storey. Among the guests on one occasion at Mr. Storey's house was an intelligent young fellow, either a recent Harvard graduate or, possibly, in one of the older classes. He was also in a general way not ill informed, as men of that age go. Incidentally a reference was made to the as sault of Preston Brooks on Charles Sumner in the United States Senate chamber, — very fresh and vivid in Mr. Storey's recollections. To his utter surprise this young man listened with interest, and then asked for further details, observing that he knew nothing about it, never having heard of the occurrence before! To us who lived in those times, such a lack of information upon really momentous historical events seems incomprehensible, almost astounding. Yet from personal experience I have reason to believe the case was in no wise exceptional.

With us of the Civil War generation the events of that period are, on the contrary, in the language of Milton, "writ large." They stand forth in memory, belittling where they do not altogether obscure the historical episodes of very considerable importance which have since occupied attention. It is, there fore, always peculiarly interesting to us — now lingerers from that bygone generation — to look back on those events through the perspective of fifty years, and, recalling our feelings at the time, note the different aspects those events now wear. Few are more well worth consideration from this point of view than the episode I have referred to, — the taking of the Confederate envoys, Messrs. Mason and Slidell, from the steamer Trent on November 8, 1861.

In pursuance of my present purpose, I do not propose to enter into any detailed narrative of what then occurred. So far as the facts are concerned, the incident has taken its place, and presumably its proper place, in recorded history. The field too has been thoroughly gleaned; and, though nearly twenty years have passed since the publication of

Mr. Thomas L. Harris's very thorough monograph entitled *The Trent Affair*, little light of value has in the intervening time been cast on the subject. The conclusions therein reached have been revised in no essential respect. In his *Life of William H. Seward*, Mr. Frederic Bancroft devotes to this incident his thirty-third chapter, and in that gives a thoroughly un prejudiced -and critical account of what occurred. Reading it afresh, Mr. Bancroft's narrative strikes me as judicial; and, moreover, so far as Seward is concerned, while he in it nothing extenuates, he sets down naught in malice.

Before entering in the casual way now proposed on my retrospect, I must first submit certain broad conclusions in regard to the affair, and the influences and conditions under which it occurred.

Speaking generally, I think I do not remember in the whole course of the half-century's retrospect — equal to the period which elapsed between the surrender at Yorktown and the presidency of Andrew Jackson — any occurrence in which the American people were so completely swept off their feet, for the moment losing possession of their senses, as during the weeks which immediately followed the seizure of Mason and Slidell. Everything combined to this result. In the first place, when the incident occurred the community was in a wholly over wrought nervous condition. On the 8th of November, 1861 , seven months had elapsed since the firing on Fort Sumter, and nearly four months since the mortifying Bull Run experience. It was exactly a year from the election to the presidency of Abraham Lincoln. That election, it will be remembered, had been immediately followed by the initial movement of South Carolina in the direction of secession. Then followed the trying winter of 1860 and 1861, during which State after State seceded, the war cloud in the South ever gathering, and assuming day by day a more threatening aspect. The five months which elapsed between the election of 1860 and the firing on Fort Sumter were probably the most trying period, psychologically, this country has ever passed through. The inevitable was constantly assuming a more portentous shape. At last in April war broke out. Thus in November, 1861, the country had been on tenter-hooks, so to speak, for twelve entire months, and during the last six of those months one mortification and failure had followed sharp on another. The community, in a state of the highest possible tension, was constantly hoping for a successful coup somewhere and by someone executed in its behalf. It longed for a man who would do, taking the responsibility of the doing. While it was in this state of mind, the telegraph one day announced that the United States sloop of war *San Jacinto,* under the command of Captain Wilkes, had arrived at Fortress Monroe, having on board the two Confederate envoys, Mason and. Slidell, taken on the high seas from the British mail steamer *Trent.* At last the hour seemed come, and with it a man. By one now seeking an explanation of what then occurred, all this must be borne in mind.

Thus worked up to the highest pitch of excitement, the feeling of the country had also been slowly fermenting to one of acute hostility towards Great Britain; and this for two rea sons. In the first place, it had seemed as if, in view of its antislavery preachings during the last thirty years, and its some what Pharisaic, better-than-thou attitude to-wards America as respects the negro and his condition, Great Britain had failed to evince that sympathy towards us which was expected be cause of the Slaveholders' rebellion, and had, to say the least, done nothing to forward the cause of the Union in a crisis brought on by the aggressive action of the South. On the contrary, the attitude of Eng-land in general had been sneering as well as adversely critical; and the tone of the London *Times,* in particular, — for the *Times,* still known as "The Thunderer," was recognized as the first and most influential newspaper in the world, — had been distinctly unsympathetic, not to say antagonistic and otherwise acutely irritating. William H. Russell, the famous Crimean War correspondent, was also at that time in this country, and his letters regularly appearing in the Times as "from our special correspondent" were republished and read in America to an extent which can hardly now be understood. Anxiously waited for, and printed in extenso in all the leading journals, extracts from them were to be found in every paper in the land. Russell had been to a certain extent present at Bull Run, and a witness of our dis grace. While his account of what he saw on that occasion was photographic and strictly correct, we none the less had become morbidly conscious that there was "a chiel amang [us] taking notes," and the "notes" he took when seen in "prent" caused a degree of irritation at this day difficult to describe or overstate. Thus morbidly excited and intensely sensitive, the country was in a thoroughly unreasoning and altogether unreasonable condition, very necessary now to emphasize; for it needed only the occurrence of some accident to lead to a pronounced explosion of what can only be described as Anglo phobia. Discouraged, we had in fact only begun to settle down to the conviction that a long and uncertain struggle was before us. With all conditions, therefore, explosive, so to speak, in character, the incident of the *Trent* came like a bolt from a clouded and lowering sky; but it was a shell exploding in a powder magazine rather than a spark falling in a mass of combustible matter.

The course of events, briefly stated, was as follows : — Immediately after the firing upon Fort Sumter, Jefferson Davis, President of the then newly organized Confederate States, had sent out to Europe agents to forward the interests of the pro posed nationality. These agents had there spent some seven months, accomplishing little. Disappointed at their failure, Davis determined upon a second and more formal mission . The new representatives were designated as "Special Commissioners of the Confederate States of America, near the Government" whether of Great Britain or of France, as the case might be. James Murray Mason of Virginia and John Slidell of Louisiana were selected, the first named for London, the second for Paris. Both, it will be remembered, had recently been Senators of the United States, Slidell having withdrawn from the Senate February 4, 1861, immediately after the passage of the Ordinance of Secession by the State of Louisiana; while Mason, having absented himself about March 20, during the session of the Senate for executive business, did not again take his seat. Virginia seceded April 17, and Mason, together with several other Southern Senators, was in his absence expelled by formal vote (July 11) at the special session of the Thirty-Seventh Congress, which met under the call of President Lincoln, July 4, 1861. Probably no two men in the entire South were more thoroughly obnoxious to those of the Union side than Mason and Slidell. The first was, in many and by no means the best ways, a typical Virginian. Very provincial and in tensely arrogant, his dislike of New England, and especially of Massachusetts, was pronounced, and exceeded only by his contempt.[1] It was said of him at the time that when trouble was brewing and he was invited to make a speech in Boston, he. had replied that he would not again visit Massachusetts until he went there as an ambassador. Slidell, on the other hand, was considered one of the most astute and dangerous of all Confederate public characters. An intriguer by nature, unscrupulous in his political methods, he was credited with having fraudulently defeated, by secret manipulations, the Clay ticket in Louisiana in the 1844 presidential election, and was generally looked upon as the most dangerous person to the Union the Confederacy could select for diplomatic work in Europe.[2] The first object of the envoys was to secure the recognition of the Confederacy. The ports of the Confederate States were then blockaded; but the blockade had not yet become really effective. The new envoys selected Charleston as their port of embarkation, and October 12 as its date. The night of the 12th was dark and rainy, but with little or no wind, conditions altogether favorable for their purpose. They left Charleston on the little Confederate steamer *Theodora*, evaded the blockading squadron, and reached New Providence, Nassau, two days later, the 14th. It had been the intention of the envoys to take passage for Europe at Nassau on an English steamer; but, failing to find one which did not stop at New York, the Theodora continued her voyage to Cardenas in Cuba, whence the envoys and those accompanying them proceeded overland to Havana. Arriving at Havana about the 22d of October, Messrs. Mason and Slidell remained there until the 7th of November. They then embarked on the British steamer *Trent*, the captain of the *Trent* having full knowledge of their diplomatic capacity as envoys r of an insurgent community, and giving consent to their embarkation. The *Trent* was a British mail packet, making regular trips between Vera Cruz, in the Republic of Mexico, and the Danish Island of St. Thomas. She was in no respect a blockade runner; was not engaged in commerce with any American port; and was then on a regular voyage from a port in Mexico, by way of Havana, to her advertised destination, St. Thomas, all neutral ports. At St. Thomas direct connection could be made with a line of British steamers running to Southampton. The envoys, therefore, when they left Havana, were on a neutral mail steamer, sailing under the British flag, on a schedule voyage between neutral points.

At just that time the United States war steamer, *San Jacinto*, a first-class screw sloop mounting fifteen guns, was returning from a cruise on the western coast of Africa, where for twenty months she had been part of the African squadron engaged in suppressing the slave trade. She was commanded by Captain Wilkes, who had recently joined her. Returning by way of the Cape Verde Islands, Captain Wilkes there learned from the newspapers about the last of September of the course of public events in the United States, and rumors reached him of Confederate privateers, as they were then called, destroying American vessels in West India waters. He determined to make an effort at the capture of some of these "privateers." On October loth the *San Jacinto* reached the port of St. Thomas, and subsequently touched at Cienfuegos on the south coast of Cuba. There Captain Wilkes learned, also from the newspapers, that the Confederate envoys were at that very time at Havana, and about to take passage for Southampton. Reaching Havana on the 28th of October, the commander of the *San Jacinto* further learned that the commissioners were to embark on the steamer *Trent,* scheduled to leave Havana on the 7th of November. Captain Wilkes then conceived the design of intercepting the *Trent,* exercising the right of search, and making prisoners of the envoys. No question as to his right to stop, board, and search the *Trent* seems to have entered the mind of Captain Wilkes. He did, however, take into his confidence his executive officer, Lieutenant Fairfax, disclosing to him his project. Lieutenant Fairfax entered, it is said, a vigorous protest against the proposed action, and strongly urged on Captain Wilkes the necessity of proceeding with great caution unless he wished to provoke international difficulties, and not impossibly a war with Great Britain. He then suggested that his commanding officer consult an American Judge at Key West, an authority on maritime law; which, however, Captain Wilkes declined to do. Leaving Key West on the morning of November 5th, Captain Wilkes directed the course of the *San Jacinto* to what is known as the Bahama Channel, through which the *Trent* would necessarily pass on its way to St. Thomas, and there stationed himself. About noon on the 8th of November, the *Trent* hove in sight, and when she had approached sufficiently near the *San Jacinto*, a round shot was fired athwart her course; the United States flag was run up at the mast head at the same time. The approaching vessel showed the English colors, but did not check her speed or indicate a disposition to heave to. Accordingly, a few instants later, a shell from the *San Jacinto* was exploded across her bows. This had the desired effect. The Trent immediately stopped, and a boat from the *San Jacinto* proceeded to board her. It is unnecessary to go into the details of what then occurred. For present purposes it is sufficient to say that the two envoys, together with their secretaries, were identified and forcibly removed, being taken on board the *San Jacinto;* which, with out interfering with the mails or otherwise subjecting the *Trent* to search, then laid its course for Fortress Monroe. Arriving there on the 15th, news of the capture was immediately flashed over the country. The *Trent,* on the other hand, proceeded to St. Thomas, where her passengers were transferred to another steamer, and completed the voyage to Southampton. They arrived and the report of the transaction was made public in Great Britain November 27th, twelve days after the arrival of the *San Jacinto* at Fortress Monroe, and the publication of the news of the arrest in the United States.

Such were the essential facts in the case, and, while a storm of enthusiastic approval was sweeping over the northern part of the United

States in the twelve days between November 15th and November 27th, a storm of indignation of quite equal intensity swept over Great Britain between November 27th and the close of the year.[3] Most fortunately there was no ocean cable in those days, and the movement of the Atlantic steamers was comparatively slow. Accordingly the first intimations of the commotion caused in Great Britain by the action of Captain Wilkes did not reach America until the arrival of the Hansa at New York, December 12. Strange as it now seems, there fore, almost an entire month had elapsed between the arrival of the *San Jacinto* at Fortress Monroe (November 15) and the receipt in America (December 12) of any information as to the effect of the seizure of the envoys on the British temper. A most important fact to be now borne in mind.

In reading the accounts of what occurred in America between November 15 and December 26, and seeing the recorded utterances of persons whose names carried authority, it is now most curious to observe the confusion of idea which seemed to exist as to the principles of international law involved, and the apparent utter inability of all concerned to exercise their reason to the extent of preserving consistency of thought or action. The affair was looked at from diverse and several points of view ; and the point of view implied a great deal. The situation re minds one, in fact, of Browning's poem of "The Ring and the Book," where, it will be remembered, the poet approaches the mystery from the point of view of each participant in it,— whether the woman who was murdered, the husband who murdered her, the counsel of the one and of the other, the gossip of one half of Rome and the other half of Rome, and finally from the standpoint of the Pope. So, to understand what was then said and done, the status and capture of the Confederate envoys has to be looked at from the Confederate point of view, from the Union point of view, from the English point of view, and, primarily, from the Captain Charles Wilkes point of view. Seen through the perspective of fifty years, it may now with reasonable assurance be asserted that, in the controversy which ensued, the United States did not have, and never had, in reality, a justifying leg to stand upon, and least of all was there any possible justification for the course pursued by Captain Wilkes. In the first place, Wilkes, commanding a United States ship of war, had not been in communication with his government for months. He had received no instructions; he was not even officially advised of the existence of a blockade; and only through the newspapers and current gossip did he know of the attitude his own government had assumed towards the so-called Confederacy. According to his own statement subsequently made, he did have some treatises on international law in the cabin of the *San Jacinto*, and he consulted them.[4] From these he satisfied himself that accredited envoys were "contraband"; but he ignored the fact that the Confederacy had not been recognized by the United States Government, or by any foreign government, and that the so-called "envoys" were merely "private gentlemen of distinction," citizens of certain States then in insurgency, trying to effect a transit to foreign countries. They were unquestionably embarked under a neutral flag, upon a mail steamer making its regular passage from one neutral port to another. Nevertheless, *pro hac vice.* Captain Wilkes invested the envoys in question with an official character which his government distinctly refused to allow them, and then proceeded on the assumption that ambassadors were "embodied des patches," to exercise on the high seas a right of search of a most questionable character; and, in so doing, he further constituted himself, in the person of his subordinate, a Prize Court, adjudicating on the deck of a neutral ship forcibly halted in its passage as to what personages should be seized, what persons and property should be exempted from seizure, as to how far the process of search should be carried, and generally what course under the conditions given should be pursued. Accordingly, while forcible possession was taken of the persons of the two envoys, no inquiry whatever was made as to their despatch bags, which, when the purpose of the procedure was suspected, had been handed over by the Commissioners to the British mail agent, and been by him deposited in his mail-room. They were subsequently in due course delivered to the agents of the Confederacy in England.

Incidentally it may here be observed that this proceeding on the part of Commander Williams, the mail agent in question, was in plain violation both of recognized British principles and precedents regulating the obligations of neutrals as also of the Queen's proclamation of the previous May; for that ordinance specifically warned all British subjects against "carrying officers, soldiers, despatches ... for the use or service of either of the said contending parties." An English publicist of recognized authority was, moreover, at that very time pronouncing the conveyance of despatches a "service" of the "most noxious and hostile character." Clearly, then, Commander Williams by the acceptance of these despatches, knowing them to be such, from a recognized envoy of one of the belligerents, gravely compromised the steamer *Trent* as well as himself. On this point there was no room for doubt; but, on the other hand, every Cunard steamer which crossed the Atlantic — and no others crossed it then — carried despatches from the other belligerent, officially received and delivered as such, and this not between neutral ports, but between New York or Boston and Liverpool. Indeed, if the carrying of despatches and envoys had been disallowed, in strict accordance with the letter of the proclamation of May, it would have been necessary at that time for the United States Government to have installed an armed ocean mail and passenger service of its own. It cannot be denied that, as the British authorities laid the law down, and Captain Wilkes put it in practical operation, the ocean situation was mixed. Or, as an American publicist writing at the time, but without the slightest sense of suppressed humor, observed, "it must be admitted that the subject is an embarrassing one."[5] In point of fact it was a farrago of absurdities, contradictions and incongruities, over which learned men pondered and young girls prattled,[6] with results about equally satisfactory.[7]

Recurring from this digression to what occurred November 8th in the Bahama Channel, the officer deputed for the work by Captain Wilkes, acting under his instruction, thus, it appeared, arrested and seized only the "embodied despatches"; the despatches themselves were, it would seem, not made matter even of inquiry. As to this theory of "embodied despatches" in the persons of "private gentlemen of distinction," known by general fame to be the agents of certain States in insurrection and an admitted "belligerent" but not as yet a recognized nationality, that was a figment of international law for which no precedent could be found in the treatises, devised *pro hac vice* by Captain Charles Wilkes, U. S. N.

Dismissing for the moment the extraordinary international law propositions involved, and recurring to the Wilkes point of view, it is obvious that today any' such action as that then taken by him would on the part of a naval officer be simply inconceivable. A similar hypothetical case needs only to be suggested in connection with the hostilities now going on in the Mediterranean between the Kingdom of Italy and the Ottoman Empire. Such a thing as a United States mail steamer running between New York, Gibraltar and Alexandria may not now exist, but it is supposable; and in such case the flag would certainly be found to signify something as respects personages as well as mail-bags. The celebrated Koszta case of more than half a century ago, though not a precedent strictly in point, would be revived in memory, and the spirit therein displayed again invoked. The conduct of a commander of a United States armed ship of superior force who, chancing to be in those waters, at once intervened, and forcibly "rescued" both mail-bags and persons from those who had thus exercised an alleged right of search and seizure, would be promptly approved and sustained. But, under the conditions I have referred to as prevailing in this country in the autumn and early winter of 1861, Captain Wilkes' conduct was officially approved by certain of those in authority, especially by the Secretary of the Navy and by the United States House of Representatives. It was even contended by high authorities that his acts were in substantial accordance with well-established principles of international law, to which, of course, when our turn came, we would yield a cheerful and graceful acquiescence. In other words, just fifty years later, the contentions and war of 1812 were on our part all a mistake; the British attitude at that time was correct; and the right of search, arrest and impressment were at last by us fully conceded!

Such was the logical aspect of the matter from the Wilkes point of view. Next perhaps to be considered in this cool semi-centennial perspective light are the popular, the official and the juristic points of view then assumed. So doing really now makes one who then lived and actively participated feel a little foolish; there is, however, a discipline, and even lesson perhaps, in a remorseless retrospect.

Personally, I have a vivid recollection of the day when the news of the seizure was flashed to Boston, and hurriedly placarded on the newspaper bulletin boards.[8] A youthful legal practitioner, I was then a man of twenty-six. I had studied, or made an at least honest pretence of so doing, in the office of Richard H. Dana, Jr. Mr. Dana was deemed as high an authority on maritime law as there was at the American bar. Reading the announcement on the bulletin board, I hurried up to his office, and communicated the startling news. Well do I remember his reception of it. His face lighted up, and, clapping his hands with satisfaction over the tidings, he expressed his emphatic approval of the act, adding that he would risk his " professional reputation" on its legality.. And this was the view universally expressed and generally accepted.

The *San Jacinto*, having put into Fortress Monroe on the 1 5th of November, was, for various reasons, ordered to proceed at once to New York, and thence to Boston; there to deliver its prisoners for safe keeping. Captain Wilkes anchored his ship in Boston harbor on the 24th of November, and two days later a dinner was given him and his officers at the Revere House, the Hon. J. Wiley Edmands presiding. Mr. Edmands, prominent among the solid business men of Boston of that period, lived at Newton and was treasurer of the Pacific Mills; a Webster Whig in politics, he had been a member of the Thirty-third Congress. The speakers on this occasion seemed to vie with each other in establishing a record from which there after it would be impossible to escape. For instance, John A. Andrew, then Governor of Massachusetts, a man really great but of somewhat impulsive disposition, had been present in the office of the Secretary of the Navy when the news of the seizure came in. Literally swept off his feet, he had then sprung upon a chair and been prominent. in the tumult of cheering which followed the announcement. He now at this public dinner[8] declared that Captain Wilkes had shown "not only wise judgment, but [his act was marked by] manly and heroic success." He referred to it as "one of the most illustrious services that had made the war memorable"; and then most unnecessarily capped the climax of indiscretion by informing a delighted audience "that there might be nothing left [in the episode to] crown the exultation of the American heart, Commodore Wilkes fired his shot across the bows of the ship that bore the British Lion at its head." On the same occasion George T. Bigelow, then Chief Justice of Massachusetts, committed himself to an almost though not quite similar extent. First he voiced the very prevalent feeling already referred to, saying: — "In common with all loyal men of the North, I have been sighing, for the last six months, for some one who would be willing to say to himself, 'I will take the responsibility'; and who would not only say this, but when the opportunity offered would take the responsibility." The Chief Justice of our Supreme Court then went on to declare that "Commodore Wilkes acted more from the noble instincts of his patriotic heart, than from any sentence he read from a law book"; adding .that, under such circumstances, "a man does not want to ask counsel, or j to consult judges upon his duty; his heart, this instinct, tells him what he ought to do." Well might the London *Times* in commenting on the affair observe shortly after — "These are wild words from lawyers." Captain Wilkes then, in language indicative of singular confusion of thought, said that before he had decided on his course, he had examined the authorities, and satisfied himself that these so-called envoys had none of the rights attaching to such functionaries when properly appointed; and, concluding that it was within his function to capture written despatches, assumed consequently that he had a right to take from under a neutral flag personages of distinction as the embodiment of despatches.

At Washington the Secretary of the Navy next addressed a congratulatory letter to Captain Wilkes on the "great public service" he had rendered, giving to his proceeding the "emphatic approval of this department." He, however, took pains to insist that the forbearance of the commander of the *San Jacinto* in this instance in not seizing the *Trent* and sending it into port for adjudication by a Prize Court "must by no means be permitted to constitute a precedent hereafter for the treatment of any case of similar infraction of neutral obligations." In his annual official report a few days later, Secretary Welles further stated that the "prompt and decisive action of Captain Wilkes on this occasion merited and received emphatic approval." On Monday, December 2, Congress assembled, and before the close of the first day's session Mr. Lovejoy, of Illinois, offered a joint resolution thanking Captain Wilkes, "for his brave, adroit and patriotic conduct in the arrest and detention of the traitors, James M. Mason and John Slidell." This resolution was passed by a unanimous vote; and, furthermore, the President was requested to present to Captain Wilkes "a gold medal with suitable emblems and devices, in testimony of the high sense entertained by Congress of his good conduct," etc.[10] As to the irresponsible outpourings and journalistic utterances of those delirious three weeks, it is no exaggeration to say that, read to-day, they are more suggestive of the incoherences of the inmates of an insane asylum than of any well-considered expression of the organs of a sober and policed community, — a community which half a century only before had gone to war in defence of the great principles of immunity from ocean search, and seamen's rights.

But, most noticeable and, perhaps, most suggestive of all the phases of that madness, were the utterances of the publicists, the supposed authorities on international law, and those who should have shown themselves the calmly poised leaders of public opinion. Here are some of them: — Theophilus Parsons was Dane professor of law at Harvard. Professor Parsons hurried into print with the following dictum: — "I am just as certain that Wilkes had a legal right to take Mason and Slidell from the *Trent*, as I am that our Government has a legal right to block-ade the port of Charleston." Caleb Gushing, in the administration of Franklin Pierce Attorney General of the United States, was a publicist, and a reputed legal authority. Mr. Gushing now wrote: — "To conclude then: In my judgment, the act of Captain Wilkes was one which any and every self-respecting nation must and would have done by its own sovereign right and power, regardless of consequences. It was an act which it cannot be denied Great Britain would have done under the same circumstances. At the same time, it was an act amply justified by the principles and doctrines of international jurisprudence."

I have already referred to R. H. Dana, and his exclamation on first hearing of Captain Wilkes' performance. Mr. Dana now wrote in an unsigned communication to the Boston *Advertiser.* — "In the present case, the mission [of the two envoys] is in its very nature necessarily and solely a mission hostile to the United States. It is treason within our municipal law, and an act in the highest degree hostile within the law of nations. If a neutral vessel intervenes to carry such persons on such a mission she commits an act hostile in the same degree. . . . We rather look to see Mr. Seward or Mr. Adams call the immediate attention of Her Majesty's Government to this violation of neutrality than to see Lord Lyons or Earl Russell addressing our Government on the subject."

Finally, Edward Everett, formerly the representative of the country at the Court of St. James and an ex-Secretary of State, than whom no one stood higher in general estimation as an authority on topics of this character, thus publicly ex pressed himself: — "You see that there is not the slightest ground for apprehension that there is any illegality in this detention of the mail packet; that the detention was perfectly lawful, the capture was perfectly lawful, their confinement in Fort Warren will be perfectly lawful, and as they will no doubt be kept there in safety until the restoration of peace — which we all so much desire — we may, I am sure, cordially wish them a safe and speedy deliverance."[11]

But the time at our disposal would not nearly admit of going through all the kaleidoscopic phases of this singular but most interesting and instructive international episode. The point of view now changes. We must imagine ourselves in London, and Englishmen.

On Tuesday, November 12, four days after the actual seizure of Messrs. Mason and Slidell, but fifteen days before an intimation of it reached England, Mr. Adams, then representing the country at the Court of St. James, made this diary entry — "Received a familiar note from Lord Palmerston, asking me to call and see him between one and two o'clock." The note, of the briefest possible character, read as follows : —

92 PICCADILLY, 12 Nov., 1861.

MY DEAR SIR:

I should be very glad to have a few minutes conversation with you; could you without inconvenience call upon me here today at any time between one and two.

Yrs faithfully

PALMERSTON.

The Honbl. Mr. Adams.

Though Mr. Adams had at this time been nearly six months in London, his official relations had been exclusively with Earl Russell; and, though he had met Lord Palmerston several times, and more than once been a guest at Cambridge House, their intercourse had been social only. A few days before Mr. Adams had been present at the Lord Mayor's dinner, and had been one of the speakers on that occasion. In his diary entry is the following: "The only marking speech being one from Lord Palmerston which had his customary shrewdness. He touched gently on our difficulties and at the same time gave it clearly to be understood that there is to be no interference for the sake of cotton." Shortly after, but before the news of the *Trent* affair arrived, Mr. Adams made the following further diary entry: — "In the evening Mrs. Adams and I went by invitation to Lady Palmerston's. A few persons only, after one of her dinners. We had been invited to dine our selves, last Saturday, and are again invited for next Saturday evening. This civility is so significant that it must by no means be declined. ... I touched Lord Palmerston a little on the event of the day, [the burning of the *Harvey Birch* by the Confederate cruiser *Nashville*], and reminded him of the connection which the *Nashville* had with our former conversation. He seemed good-natured and rather desirous to get information as to grounds on which to act." The relations between the two men had accordingly thus far been of an altogether friendly character. The diary entry of November 12 goes on as follows: —

This (Lord Palmerston's note) took me by surprise, and I speculated on the cause for some time without any satisfaction. At one o'clock I drove from my house over to his, Cambridge House in Piccadilly. In a few minutes he saw me. His reception was very cordial and frank. He said he had been made anxious by a notice that a United States armed vessel[12] had lately put in to Southampton to get coal and supplies. It had been intimated 'to him that that object was to intercept the two men, Messrs. Mason and Slidell, who were understood to be aboard the British West India steamer expected to arrive tomorrow or next day. He had been informed that the Captain, having got gloriously drunk on brandy on Sunday had dropped down to the mouth of the river yesterday as if on the watch. He did not pretend to judge absolutely of the question whether we had a right to stop a foreign vessel for such a purpose as was indicated. Even admitting that we might claim it, it was yet very doubtful whether the exercise of it in this way could lead to any good. The effect of it here would be unfavorable, as it would seem as if the vessel had come in here to be filled with coal and sup plies, and the Captain had enjoyed the hospitality of the country in filling his stomach with brandy, only to rush out of the harbor and commit violence upon their flag. Neither did the object to be gained seem commensurate with the risk. For it was surely of no consequence whether one or two more men were added to the two or three who had already been so long here. They would scarcely make a difference in the action of the government after once having made up its mind.

The remainder of this diary entry is long, and not germane to the present occasion. I, therefore, omit it. But the ex treme significance of the intimation thus unofficially and pleas antly conveyed was not apparent at the time; indeed it was not fully disclosed until half a century later. Mr. Adams never knew the motive cause of the interview he was describing, and consequently never appreciated the really kind purpose behind this most friendly action of the man at the head of the government to which he was accredited. It was an effort to forestall and prevent an international complication even more objectless than it was dangerous, a senseless wrangle over two men who were of no consequence anyway.

To appreciate the true significance of the interview described in his diary by Mr. Adams it is necessary to bear in mind that it took place on the 1 2th of November, the Confederate envoys having been taken on the 8th from the Trent. On the day preceding his talk with Mr. Adams, Lord Palmerston, it now appears, had addressed the following letter to J. T. Delane, the editor of the *Times*:

94, PICCADILLY, November 11, 1861.

MY DEAR DELANE:

It may be useful to you to know that the Chancellor, Dr. Lushington, the three Law Officers, Sir G. Grey, the Duke of Somerset, and myself, met at the Treasury today to consider what we could properly do about the American cruiser come, no doubt, to search the West Indian packet supposed to be bringing hither the two South ern envoys; and, much to my regret, it appeared that, according to the principles of international law laid down in our courts by Lord Stowell, and practised and en- forced by us, a belligerent has a right to stop and search any neutral not being a ship of war, and being found on the high seas and being suspected of carrying enemy's despatches; and that consequently this American cruiser might, by our own principles of international law, stop the West Indian packet, search her, and if the Southern men and their despatches and credentials were found on board, either take them out, or seize the packet and carry her back to New York for trial. Such being the opinion of our men learned in the law, we have determined to do no more than to order the *Phaeton* frigate to drop down to Yarmouth Roads and watch the proceedings of the American within our three-mile limit of territorial jurisdiction, and to prevent her from exercising within that limit those rights which we cannot dispute as belonging to her beyond that limit.

In the meanwhile the American captain, having got very drunk this morning at Southampton with some excellent brandy, and finding it blow heavily at sea, has come to an anchor for the night within Calshot Castle, at the entrance of the Southampton river.

I mention these things for your private information. Yours sincerely,

PALMERSTON.

And, the following day, immediately after his talk with Mr. Adams, he further wrote : —

MY DEAR DELANE:

I have seen Adams today, and he assures me that the American paddle-wheel was sent to intercept the *Nashville* if found in these seas, but not to meddle with any ship under a foreign flag. He said he had seen the commander, and had advised him to go straight home; and he believed the steamer to be now on her way back to the United States. This is a very satisfactory explanation.

Yours sincerely,

PALMERSTON.

While the opinion of the officers of the Crown referred to was no mystery at the time, and is mentioned, though in much more general language, by Spencer Walpole in his *Life of Lord Russell* (n. 354-356), yet the statement here made of that opinion by Lord Palmerston is well calculated to excite surprise. It will be noticed that the officers referred to — the Lord Chancellor, Westbury, and Dr. Lushington being among them — are said to have laid it down as law that the belligerent had a right to stop and search any neutral, not being a ship of war, on the high seas, suspected of carrying enemy's despatches. Consequently, then, in this case, the Southern insurgents having been granted belligerent rights, the *San Jacinto* might, on English principles of international law, stop the *Trent,* search her, and if the Southern men were on board, either do exactly what Captain Wilkes had already just done, — take them out, and then allow the packet to proceed on its voyage, — or seize the packet and carry her to some American port for trial and adjudication as prize.

Here is indeed another turn of the *Trent* kaleidoscope, — a British turn! That just half a century ago such an opinion as this should have been advanced as accepted international law seems incredible. It indicates clearly how confused, as well as archaic, the principles of that law were at the time in question in the minds of those supposed to be learned in it. No war involving maritime rights to any considerable extent had occurred since Waterloo. The precedents established in the English Prize Courts in the days of Napoleon's "Continental System" and the British "Orders in Council," and the principles then laid down, utterly regardless as they notoriously had been of the rights of neutrals, were held to be still law. Those precedents and rulings were of the most miscellaneous description and arbitrary character. Meanwhile, the world had progressed. It is, therefore, simply astounding to us in 1911 that the law officers of the Crown should in 1861 have advised her Majesty's government that an American ship-of-war might lie in the straits of Dover, and, having reason to suppose that an emissary of the Confederacy, carrying despatches, was on a certain steamer, — the Calais packet, for instance, — could stop the steamer in question, subject it to search, and either take out the envoy referred to, and his despatches, leaving the steamer then to complete its course, or could pronounce her a prize of war for violation of neutrality, and send her into port for adjudication! Or, to put the case in a different way, difficulties of a revolutionary character have recently occurred in Mexico, and are now, as is well known, agitating Portugal. Is it supposable that a Mexican or Portuguese man-of-war commissioned by the recognized government, rights of belligerency having for reasons of commerce or humanity been conceded, — is it, I say, even remotely sup posable that, under such circumstances, a Mexican or Portuguese battleship could now lie in wait off Long Island on the course of the trans-Atlantic steamers, and, having sufficient reason to believe that either despatches were being carried in those steamers, or that a Mexican or Portuguese envoy was among its passengers, could proceed to stop and search the ocean-liner, forcibly arrest the persons in question, and with them steam away, or, then and there, compel the ship — the *Lusitania* or the *Oceanic,* let us say — to abandon its voyage, and send it into a Mexican or Portuguese port for adjudication![13] The thing is too absurd for a moment's consideration. Yet then it seems to have been laid down as the accepted law of Great Britain; and according to Lord Chancellor Westbury and Dr. Lushington, Mr. George Sumner, the brother of the Senator of the same name, was not wrong when at this time (November 22) he wrote to the New York *Tribune* that, "The act of Commodore Wilkes was in strict accordance with the principles of international law recognized in England, and in strict conformity with English practice." One American at least seems here to have then spoken correctly and by the book. He said "English principles" and "English practice"! If it was law and practice in Great Britain then, it was law and practice nowhere else; least of all in the United States.

But was the position thus taken sound as a proposition of even British law? This is open to grave question; nor did it pass unchallenged at the time. The point was well put by the Duke of Argyll, himself a member of the British ministry, in a letter to Mr. Adams written on the 25th of the following January.[14] Referring to the objection subsequently made to the act of Captain Wilkes that the *Trent* was not taken into port for adjudication, he characterized it as one made on "a narrow and technical ground." He then proceeded as follows: "This is a very minor objection, tho' so far as it goes, a sound one. But the real objection I hold to be a much stronger one, *viz.* that a neutral vessel, with a bona fide, *neutral destination,* cannot contain contraband of war at all, and that civilians, especially, bound for a neutral country cannot, under any circumstances, be held to be subject to seizure as Contraband. I venture to affirm that no decision of any of our Judges, nor any act of our Government can be cited as inconsistent with this doctrine."

This, even if advanced by a layman, was certainly good sense, and probably sound law. Admitting, however, that as a mere proposition of existing law, wise or not wise as a question of policy, the British precedents and practice were as laid down by the law-advisers of the Crown, if such a contingency as that of the Trent arose there was but one course to be pursued by any self-respecting nation. If such was once the law, the world had outgrown it; it was law no longer. In any event, it could not possibly be observed as such by any nation powerful enough to set it at naught. The case did not admit of argument.

The course, therefore, to be pursued by the British Government under the circumstances which then confronted it, was simple, and exactly the course that was pursued. The matter was referred back to the law officers of the Crown, with instructions to reconsider the subject. The subject was reconsidered, and different conclusions arrived at. Nevertheless, those conclusions commend themselves little more to present judgment than the previous opinion. It was now held that what had been done in the Trent case was illegal because in assuming authority under the accepted law of nations, as laid down in the reports and treatises, Captain Wilkes had under taken to pass upon the issue of a violation of neutrality on the spot, instead of sending the Trent as a prize into port for judicial adjudication. There is about the position thus assumed in 1 86 1 something which seems in 1911 little short of the grotesque. Nevertheless, so the case stood at that time; and, as mere technical law, the point probably was, as the Duke of Argyll said in his letter to Mr. Adams, well taken. At any rate it met in a way the requirements of that particular occasion, and was gravely advanced and argued over pro and con by able and adroit men holding high official positions. It was, however, recognized all through as a solemn farce. As a question of practical statesmanship, the world manifestly had burst asunder those particular swaddling clothes. It is contentions of this character which bring law into contempt.

One more turn of the kaleidoscope, and I am through for this occasion. Leaving London and the legal advisers of Her Majesty's Government, we travel back to Boston. The *San Jacinto*, with the two Confederate envoys on board, — more guests of the Captain than prisoners of state,[15] — steamed into Boston harbor on the 24th of November. Fort Warren had been designated as, *pro hac vice,* the American Tower, or Bastile. Fort Warren is situated on George's Island, commanding the main ship-channel, so called, at the entrance of Boston harbor. Small in area, the island is almost entirely covered by the fort; and, as is well known, the sea-shore of Massachusetts Bay is, as a winter resort, inclement. Though, as already mentioned, both Mr. Mason and Mr. Slidell were peculiarly obnoxious to the loyal North and especially to New Englanders, there were a number of residents of Boston who had in one way or another been personally associated with them in former times, and even under obligations to them. Among these was Mr. Robert C. Winthrop, long a member of Congress from Massachusetts, speaker of the national House of Representatives, and, for a time, the occupant of a seat in the United States Senate. Those were the days of the comparatively "simple life" in Washington, and while in the Senate together Mr. Mason and Mr. Winthrop had belonged to the same "mess," as the boarding-house arrangements of those days were termed. As Mr. Winthrop now wrote in a familiar letter to Mr. John P. Kennedy, another of his Congressional associates, referring to the dedication in 1857 of the statue of Joseph Warren in Bunker Hill monument, when he had introduced both Mr. Mason and Mr. Kennedy, — "His tone was insolent enough on that occasion,[16] yet I will not triumph over him now. ... I sent down some sherry a fortnight ago, and offered to go myself, but the officer said I could speak to none of them. ... I also helped to get some great coats to prevent the North Carolina soldiers from freezing." There certainly was biblical authority for such action under these circumstances on the part of Mr. Winthrop. At the same juncture, it so chanced that Colonel H. Raymond Lee and Major

Paul J. Revere, of the 2oth Massachusetts Volunteers, were with other Massachusetts officers prisoners of war at Richmond. It cannot be denied that as such they were treated with great severity, almost indeed as if they had been common criminals. If, however, at that time any prominent citizen of Richmond, who had previously received attentions at their hands in Boston, had endeavored to alleviate the hardships of prison life, we can feel assured he would have been denounced by the Southern press as supplying luxuries to those who could only be compared with the minions of Attila or some other great barbarian destroyer. In those days somewhat exaggerated metaphors and comparisons were in over-common use, and, as will immediately be seen, history quite failed to supply either of the two sides with precedents or examples equal to the occasion's requirements. Until then the lowest depths of depravity had not been sounded; "history did not record, "etc., etc.! And yet even at that juncture such Samaritan action as that suggested on the part of some Richmond resident towards Lee and Revere would hardly have been regarded in Boston as conduct suitable for bitter denunciation only. Thus viewed, *in alterant partem,* it is curious now to read the bitter words in which the very simple courtesy of Mr. Winthrop and others was denounced by the New England press. The Boston *Transcript,* for instance, in its issue of Thursday evening, December 12, 1861, gave vent to the following growl: "We beg to suggest to those whom it may concern to leave the care of men, one of whom is the personification of arrogance, and the other of craft, to the proper authorities. We beg them not again to outrage public opinion by sending their champagne and other luxuries to the avowed enemies of the United States." And yet this merely echoed an utterance from Governor Andrew, conveyed in a private but published letter dated at the State House, December nth. Referring to what he termed "the numerous manifestations of misplaced sympathy by some citizens of Boston with the rebel prisoners confined at Fort Warren," Governor Andrew then said: "I fully appreciate your feelings in this matter, and share with the writer of the *Post* in his condemnation of that sympathy with traitors, which makes men in comparison with whom Benedict Arnold was a saint, comfortable in their confinement, while our own brave defenders of liberty and Union and the rights of man, are cut off from all such sympathy by the rigorous despotism of the Southern oligarchy, — but I do not know of anything that I can do to prevent it." When such utterances emanate from a man of the high character and natural kindliness of Governor Andrew, it is possible for those who did not, as well as for those who did live in those times, to imagine the grim murkiness, so to speak, of the language elsewhere heard. For example, here is an illustrative extract from the newspapers of the time: "Mr. Wendell Phillips, in a lecture delivered at the New Music Hall on the evening of Wednesday, November 27, 1861, observed: 'If at the outbreak' of the present troubles Breckinridge, Mason, Slidell, Toombs, Hunter, Wise, and others had been hung, and a frigate or two had been sent to Charleston, Savannah and New Orleans, and shelled those cities, there never would have been any rebellion." Mr. Phillips was never conspicuous for tolerance or for moderation of speech, nor could any marked degree of sanity of judgment be fairly attributed to him; it is, however, at this distance of time curious to learn that even he should in 1861 have so utterly misjudged the courage as well as the earnestness of the South. But in 1911 it has an even more curious and exaggerated sound to hear John A. Andrew referring to the two Confederates in question as men in comparison with whom " Benedict Arnold was a saint." Whatever may be said against either Mr. Mason or Mr. Slidell, — and much certainly can in both justice and truth be said, — it can never be asserted that they were guilty of treachery or of secret treasons. They proclaimed their opinions loudly enough, and thereon, early and late, "made good." Nevertheless, Mr. Winthrop's attitude towards them on this occasion excited so much feeling that he wrote to his friend Kennedy as follows: "A miserable clamor has been raised by a few of our bitter spirits because some per sons have sent down a few creature comforts to alleviate the condition of old friends. One of our malignant presses calls us sympathizers in Rebellion and threatens to send our names to the Secretary of State! I hope you will give Seward to under stand that a malicious spirit of misrepresentation prevails in this quarter, which vents itself upon everybody who is not ready to embark in an Abolition Crusade. For myself, I have done so little for the prisoners, that I feel a compunction at having seemed wanting in kindness. It is wretched policy not to treat them with humanity and consideration." This episode constitutes a mere insignificant footnote in the record of that period; but it brings forcibly to mind the morbid and unreasoning state of public opinion.

One point further, and a point curiously illustrative of the thoroughness with which this particular piece of historical ground has been gone over, and the difficulty of now reaching any novel conclusions in regard to those who played their parts in connection with it. As a final result of recent investigations I had reached the conclusion that, among those occupying positions of prominence and political responsibility in American public life at the time, two only preserved their poise throughout the Mason and Slidell episode, and, taking in all the aspects of the situation, both acted with discretion and counselled wisely. These two were Montgomery Blair, the Postmaster General in Lincoln's Cabinet, and, somewhat strange to say, Charles Sumner. They alone, using the vernacular, did not "slop over," prematurely and inconsiderately committing either themselves or the country, whether in private speech or public utterance. Though not quoted at the time, Mr. Blair's attitude was the more pronounced. According to Secretary Welles, he "from the first denounced Wilkes's act as unauthorized, irregular and illegal"; and even went so far as to advise that Wilkes be ordered to take the San Jacinto and go with Mason and Slidell to England, and deliver them to the British Government.[17] In view of the excitement and unreasoning condition of the public mind such a disposition of the question was, perhaps, practically impossible; though even this admits of question. Nevertheless, seen through the vista of half a century, this would clearly have been the wisest as well as the most dignified course to pursue, far more so than that ultimately adopted; for, as Secretary Welles, a dozen years later, wrote, " the prompt and voluntary disavowal of the act of Wilkes, and delivering over the prisoners, would have evinced our confidence in our own power, and been a manifestation of our in difference and contempt for the emissaries, and a rebuke to the alleged intrigues between the rebels and the English cabinet."[18] Mr. Welles might have further remarked that such a disposition of the matter, besides being in strict consistency with a long-proclaimed international policy, would have afforded for the navy a most salutary disciplinary example.

As I have said, the attitude and bearing of Mr. Sumner throughout those trying days was above criticism. With a proper sense of the responsibility due to his official position, that of Chairman of the Senate Committee on Foreign Relations, he was silent, biding his time; and, when that time came, he used his influence in such a way as to produce results not wholly unworthy of a great nation passing through a trying ordeal. This conclusion I had reached, and was prepared to set forth as one that might have a certain degree of novelty as well as weight, the matured judgment of half a century subsequent to the event. Fortunately for myself, before so doing, I glanced once more over the pages of our associate, Mr. James Ford Rhodes. In the chapter of his *History* (in. 523-524) in which he deals with the affair of the *Trent,* I then found the following: — "Of all the men in responsible positions, Sumner and Blair saw the clearest. They were in favor of at once surrendering to England the Confederate Commissioners."

My "novel" judgment, slowly reached at the close of half a century, had been, it would thus appear, anticipated by my associate here by about sixteen years!

But there is another aspect of the Trent affair and its out come, which, from the historical point of view, is, I believe, novel; and that in closing I propose to bring to view, emphasizing it as forcibly as I can. But in order to appreciate this aspect of the affair it is necessary clearly to bear in mind the sequence of events, the intervals of time which elapsed and the exact date of each occurrence. The arrest of the *Trent* and the seizure of the two envoys took place in the Bahama Channel, November 8; the interview between Lord Palmerston and Mr. Adams at Cambridge House, at which Lord Palmerston suggested that the presence of the two envoys in Europe was "of no consequence" and "would scarcely make a difference in the action of the government" was on the i2th, and the despatch of Mr. Adams conveying this most significant intimation to Secretary Seward was received by the latter before November 30. This was fourteen days after the news of the seizure had been made known in the United States (November 16) and the public excitement had already begun to sub side. Tidings of the affair had reached England three days only before, on the 27th, and the despatch of Earl Russell to Lord Lyons demanding the immediate surrender of the two envoys, dated November 30, reached Washington December 1 8, or a little over a full month after the news of the seizure of the envoys had made wild the American public.

At the time great emphasis was laid on the general preparations for war entered upon by the British government in case of a refusal to yield to the ultimatum presented. It was here pronounced unnecessary, irregular, minatory, and insulting; and subsequent American historical investigators and publicists have continued to so pronounce it. There is no question that Great Britain was in dead earnest in its demand for immediate reparation, and acted accordingly. The arsenals were busy; all available forces were mobilized; troops embarked for Canada.

> And why such daily cast of brazen cannon,
> And foreign mart for implements of war;
> Why such impress of shipwrighters, whose sore task
> Does not divide the Sunday from the week.
> What might be toward . . .

The answer was ready; as was then alleged, and has since been reiterated, it was on the part of Great Britain a case of uncalled for, unnecessarily offensive braggadocio and bullying; and it was resented as such. Yet something was, and is, fairly to be said on the other side. The critics were not careful as to their facts, the sequence of events and the natural operation of cause and effect. Again it is necessary to bear dates clearly in mind. Commenting on this phase of the "affair," R. H. Dana, for instance, with singular carelessness says in his elaborate note in his edition of Wheaton — "The news of the capture of Messrs. Mason and Slidell reached Washington about the same time it reached London."[19] This is erroneous, and the error vitiates Mr. Dana's whole criticism on the minatory course pursued by Great Britain. The news of the seizure, not " capture," reached Washington November 16; the same news did not reach London until the 29th, or eleven days later. Those eleven days of difference were pregnant with consequences; for during them the United States went crazy, and it was then that the news both of the seizure and of the storm of American approval thereof reached London " about the same time." The announcement a few days later of the Governor of Massachusetts at the Wilkes dinner in Boston (November 26) that "a shot fired across the bows of the ship that bore the English lion's head" had filled to the brim the cups of America's satisfaction over the event, followed hard by the "emphatic approval" of the act of the Secretary of the Navy and its unanimous endorsement by Congress — these surely were not utterances or incidents calculated either to allay British excitement or to lead to a countermand of warlike preparation. Even on the very eve of the surrender, it was publicly alleged and on excellent authority that the President had emphatically announced: — "I would sooner die than give them up." This probably was not true; it was, however, believed both in Washington and in London. In London also it was suspected, especially in inner ministerial circles,[20] — and on good grounds it has since appeared, — that Mr. Seward had, only a few months previously, desired to provoke trouble with Great Britain with ulterior purposes in view. The opportunity for so doing had now presented itself; nor was there any reason to suppose that the views of the Secretary had recently undergone change. Under such circumstances, however, it was perhaps in no way so remarkable, nor did it afford just ground for animadversion, that the din of preparation for war in the one country was con current with the din of approval of the seizure in the other.

Meanwhile the news of the excitement occasioned throughout Great Britain by Wilkes' act had reached America on the 12th, six days before the arrival of Russell's ultimatum. The dates necessary to bear in mind are therefore the 16th of November, when the news of the seizure reached America; the 29th, when the same news reached Europe; the 12th of December, when the extreme seriousness of the situation first dawned on the American mind through tidings of the British excitement and consequent demands; and, finally, the 18th of December, when it became apparent that a decision as to the course to be by it pursued had to be reached within one week by the American Government. Thus, between the date of the arrival of the *San Jacinto* at Hampton Roads (November 15), and the announcement from Washington that the envoys would be surrendered (December 26) forty days elapsed. This was a most important factor; for, as the result showed, during that period the popular effervescence had time in which to subside, while by the forty-first day the sober second thought might to a degree be invoked with some assurance of a response. An Anglo-Saxon community rarely goes daft permanently.

It was so in this case; and, though both in public and private, some, like Hale of New Hampshire and Lovejoy of Illinois in Congress, and two of the sons of Mr. Adams in private correspondence, foamed at the mouth, swearing inextinguishable hatred of Great Britain and asseverating an unalterable determination to bide their time for revenge on that arrogant and overbearing nationality,[21] so far as the great body of public opinion was concerned the insanity passed away almost as suddenly as it had asserted itself. Reason resumed its sway.

And yet, while this greatly to the credit of the American people proved in the outcome to be the case, at the time such grave doubt was felt as to the popular reception of the decision to surrender the envoys that they were actually smuggled out of Boston harbor, Province town being selected as the point of delivery to a British frigate. This was suggested by Mr. Seward to Lord Lyons as the better course, the Secretary being "apprehensive that some outrage would be offered by the populace to the prisoners and the British flag." No sufficient grounds in reality existed for any such apprehension, but at the same time a reliable correspondent wrote from Boston to Charles Sumner that "the whole population were terribly excited, ready to plan any kind of an expedition to sink the vessel that should be sent to convey the Rebels from Fort Warren."[22] So general was this belief that Russell, the *Times* correspondent, then at Washington and in very direct daily communication with the best informed authorities, "resolved to go to Boston being satisfied that a great popular excitement and uprising will, in all probability, take place."[23] The delivery did not, however, in fact, occasion a ripple of lawlessness.

Such being the facts of the "affair" and the dates of the occurrences in its development, it is of interest now, and certainly not without its value as matter of experience, to consider the courses then possible to have been pursued by the United States and to contrast them, coolly and reflectively, with that which was actually pursued. And in so doing the thought which first suggests itself is one not conducive in us to an increased sense of national pride. What an opportunity was then lost! How completely our public men, and through them our community, failed to rise to the height of the occasion! For, viewed in the perspective of history, it is curious, and for an American of that period almost exasperating, to reflect upon what a magnificent move in the critical game then conducted would have been made had the advice of Montgomery Blair been followed to the letter and in spirit. To carry out the simile, by such a playing of the pieces on the board as he suggested, how effectually a checkmate would have been administered to the game of both the Confederates and their European sympathizers! In the first place, the act of Wilkes, as was subsequently and on better reflection universally con ceded, was ill-considered, improper, and in violation of all correct naval usage. It should have been rebuked accord ingly, and officers should have been taught by example and at the commencement that they were neither diplomatic representatives nor judicial tribunals administering admiralty law. It was for them to receive instructions and implicitly to obey them. A reprimand of much the same nature was at almost this very time administered to General John C. Fremont, when in Missouri he undertook by virtue of martial law to proclaim the freedom of the slave throughout the military department under his command. His ill-considered order was revoked; and he was officially instructed that he was to confine himself to his military functions, and that the administration reserved to itself all action of a political character. So much for Captain Wilkes, and the reprimand he should have received because of his indiscreet and unauthorized proceeding.

Next, such a line of conduct would have been on the part of the Government in severe and manly adherence to the past contentions of the United States. It would have recognized in the action taken by Wilkes an attempt to carry the right of search and power of impressment far beyond any precedent ever established by the British Government, even in the days of its greatest maritime ascendency, and consequent arrogance. In the strong and contemptuous language of Mr. Adams, America, in sustaining Wilkes, was consenting "to take up and to wear [Britain's] cast-off rags." If, instead of so bedizening itself, the United States had boldly, defiantly, and at once now adhered to its former contentions, its attitude would have been simply magnificent; and, as such, it would have com manded respect and admiration.

Nor was this aspect of the situation wholly unseen by some at the time; for, writing from his post in London to J. L. Motley in Vienna on the 4th of December, 1861, the date at which the tension between the United States and Great Britain was at the breaking point, Mr. Adams thus expressed himself: "It ought to be remembered that the uniform tendency of our own policy has been to set up very high the doctrine of neutral rights, and to limit in every possible manner the odious doctrine of search. To have the two countries virtually changing their ground under this momentary temptation would not, as it seems to me, tend to benefit the position of the United States.[24] Whereas, a contrary policy might be made the means of securing a great concession of principle from Great Britain. Whether the government at home will remain cool enough to see its opportunity, I have no means of judging.'7 And a few days later — December 7, 1861 — John Bright, writing to Charles Sumner, expressed himself to the same effect: "You may dis appoint your enemies by the moderation and reasonableness of your conduct, and every honest and good man in England will applaud your wisdom. Put all the fire-eaters in the wrong, and Europe will admire the sagacity of your Government." "Sagacity of your Government!" That phrase expressed ex actly what the situation called for, and got only in a very mod ified degree.

Taken immediately and openly in the presence of the whole world, the position advised by Blair would have indicated the supreme confidence we felt in our national power, and the pronounced contempt in which we held both those whom we called "rebels" and those whom they termed their "envoys." If reached and publicly announced after mature deliberation during the week which followed the announcement of the seizure from Fortress Monroe (November 23), as trans-Atlantic communication was conducted in those days the news would scarcely have reached England before the 3d of December, just three days after the peremptory and somewhat offensive despatch of Earl Russell demanding the immediate surrender of the arrested envoys was beyond recall or modification, well on its way to America. A situation would have resulted almost ludicrous so far as Great Britain was concerned, but, for the United States, most consistent, dignified and im posing. Excited, angry, arrogant, bent on reparation or war, Great Britain would have* been let down suddenly, and very hard and flat. Its posture would, to say the least, have been the reverse of impressive. But for us it would have established our prestige in the eyes of foreign nations, and once for all silenced the numerous emissaries who were sedulously working in every part of Europe to bring about our undoing through foreign interference. In particular, the immediate delivery of the envoys, in advance of any demand therefor and on the very ship which had undertaken to exer cise the right of search and seizure under the command of the officer who had thus exceeded his authority and functions, would, so to speak, have put the Government of Great Britain thenceforth under bonds, so far as the United States was concerned. Thereafter any effort, either of the "envoys" thus contemptuously surrendered or of other Confederate emissaries, would, so far as this country was concerned, have been futile. Reciprocity would from that moment have been in order, and all question of foreign recognition would have ceased. The whole course of international events in the imme diate future would probably have been far different from what it was; for with what measure we had used, it would neces sarily have been measured to us again.

Such a line of conduct immediately decided on and boldly declared would have been an inspiration worthy of a Cavour or a Bismarck; but, though actually urged in the Cabinet meetings by Montgomery Blair, its adoption called for a grasp of the situation and a quickness of decision which, very pos sibly, could not reasonably be expected under conditions then existing. It also may even yet be urged that, if then taken and announced, such a policy would have failed to command the assent of an excited public opinion. That it would have failed to do so is, however, open to question; for it is more than possible, it is even probable, that American intelligence would even then have risen at once to the international possibilities presented, and in that crisis of stress and anxiety would have measured the extent to which the "affair" could be improved to the public advantage. The national vanity would unquestionably have been flattered by an adherence so consistent and sacrificing to the contentions and policies of the past. The memories of 1812 would have revived. However, admit ting that a policy of this character, now obviously that which should have been pursued', was under practical and popular conditions then prevailing at least inadvisable, it remains to consider yet another alternative.

Assuming that the course pursued remained unchanged an entire month after the seizure, and up to the i2th of December, when the news arrived in America of the excitement occasioned by the seizure in Great Britain and the extreme seriousness of the situation resulting therefrom, — assuming this, it is now obvious that the proper policy then and under such con ditions to have been adopted, although it could not have produced the results which would have been produced by the policy just considered if adopted and announced ten days earlier, would still have been consistent and dignified, and, as such, would have commanded general respect. It was very clearly outlined by Mr. Adams in a letter written to Cassius M. Clay, then the representative of the country at St. Petersburg, in the following month. He expressed himself as follows: — "Whatever opinion I may have of the consistency of Great Britain, or of the temper in which she has prosecuted her latest convictions, that does not in my judgment weigh a feather in the balance against the settled policy of the United States which has uniformly condemned every and any act like that of Captain Wilkes when authorized by other nations. The extension of the rights of neutrals on the ocean and the protection of them against the arbitrary exercise of mere power have been cardinal principles in the system of American statesmen ever since the foundation of the Government. It is not for us to abandon them under the transient impulse given by the capture of a couple of unworthy traitors. What are they that a country like ours should swerve one hair from the line of its ancient policy, merely for the satisfaction of punishing them?"

If the advisers of Mr. Lincoln had viewed the situation in this light, when his Secretary of State sat down to prepare his answer to the English demand he would at once with a bold sweep of the hand have dismissed as rubbish the English precedents and authorities, reverting to the attitude and contentions uniformly and consistently held by the Government for which he spoke, during the earlier years of the century. The proceeding of Captain Wilkes would then have been pro nounced inconsistent with the traditions and established policy of the United States, and the line of action by it to be pursued in the case immediately presented would have been dictated thereby. The course to be pursued on the issue raised was clear, and the surrender of the envoys must be ordered accordingly; — and this in no degree because of their small importance, as suggested by Lord Palmers ton in his talk with Mr. Adams — though unquestionably the fact would have secretly exercised no little influence on the mind of the Secretary — and still less was it ordered because of any failure of Captain Wilkes to seize the Trent as prize on the ground of alleged breach of neutrality: but exclusively for the reason that the seizure in question was unauthorized, in direct disregard of the established policy of the United States and its contentions in regard to the rights of neutrals, clearly and repeatedly set forth in many previous controversies with the Government represented by Earl Russell. From that policy, to quote the language of Mr. Adams, "this country was not disposed to swerve by a single hair's breadth." In accordance with it, delivery of the so-called "envoys" was ordered.

Again, an opportunity was lost! Such an attitude would have been dignified, consistent and statesmanlike. It would have had in it no element of adroitness and no appearance of special pleading. It could hardly have failed immediately to commend itself to the good judgment as well as pride of the American people, and it would certainly have commanded the respect of foreign nations.

Of the elaborate, and in many respects memorable, despatch addressed by Secretary Seward to Lord Lyons, in answer to the categorical demand for the immediate release of the two envoys,[25] it is not necessary here to speak in detail. It is historical, and my paper has already extended far beyond the limits originally proposed. Of this state paper I will therefore merely say that, reading it now, "clever," not "great," is the term which suggests itself as best descriptive. Much commended at the time, it has not stood the test.[26] In composing it, the writer plainly had his eye on the audience ; while his ear, so to speak, was in manifest proximity with the ground. Indeed, his vision was directed to so many different quarters, and his ear was intent on such a confusion of rumblings that it is fair matter for surprise that he acquitted himself even as success fully as he did. In the first place, it was necessary for him to persuade a President who had " put his foot down," and whose wishes inclined to a quite different disposition of the matter. In the next place, the reluctant members of a divided Cabinet were to be conciliated and unified. After this, Captain Wilkes, the naval idol of the day, must be justified and supported. Then Congress, with its recent commitments as respects ap proval, thanks, gold medals, etc., had to be not only pacified, but reconciled to the inevitable; and, finally, an aroused and patriotic public opinion was to be soothed and gently led into a lamb-like acquiescence. The situation in the aspect it then bore, was, it cannot be denied, both complicated and delicate. Accordingly, one is conscious, in reading the Secretary's communication to Lord Lyons of December 26, 1861, of a distinct absence therein of both grasp and elevation. That "bold sweep of the hand" before suggested, is conspicuous for its absence. The English and British precedents were by no means dis missed as antiquated "rubbish "; while, on the contrary, our own earlier and better contentions were silently ignored. In their stead, British principles were adopted as sound and of established authority; and thus the final action of the United States in delivering the, so called, envoys was rested on what the Duke of Argyll presently, and most properly, character ized in his letter to Mr. Adams as "a narrow and technical ground." Captain Wilkes, it was argued, while acting in strict accordance with law and precedent, had failed to seize the *Trent* as lawful prize, and as such, send her into an American port for adjudication. It was a complete abandonment of the traditional American contentions in favor of the arrogant and high-handed policies formerly pursued by Great Britain, but now by her silently dismissed as antiquated and inconvenient — "her cast-off rags "!

It can, therefore, now hardly be denied that there was more than an element of truth in the criticisms passed upon the Secretary's momentous reply to Lord Russell's demand by Hamilton Fish, in a letter to Charles Sumner, written at the time. Mr. Fish, then in retirement, not impossibly entertained feelings of a nature not altogether friendly towards Mr. Seward, whose colleague he had been in the Senate, and whom later he was to succeed in charge of the Department of State. They were both from New York, and had been contemporaneously active in New York politics. Those also whose attention has been called to the grounds of comparison will, perhaps, hardly be disposed to deny that for natural grasp of the spirit and underlying principles of international law, Hamilton Fish was better endowed than either Seward or Sumner. Fish now wrote: - "In style [the letter] is verbose and egotistical; in argument, flimsy; and in its conception and general scope it is an abandonment of the high position we have occupied as a nation upon a great principle. We are humbled and disgraced, not by the act of the surrender of four of our own citizens, but by the manner in which it has been done, and the absence of a sound principle upon which to rest and justify it. ... We might and should have turned the affair vastly to our credit and advantage; it has been made the means of our humiliation."

The ultimate historical verdict must apparently be in accordance with the criticism here contemporaneously expressed. The Seward letter was inadequate to the occasion. A possible move of unsurpassed brilliancy on the international chessboard had, almost unseen, been permitted to escape us.

Notes:

1. The course of subsequent events in no way mollified these antipathies. Writing from London to a daughter in Virginia thirteen months (April 5, 1866) after the delivery of Lincoln's second inaugural, he thus expressed himself: — "In my varied intercourse with the world, I have met with some whom I held in disesteem, with others in contempt, as unworthy, and some few who were essentially bad; but, in looking back, I do not recognize that my feelings toward any such amounted to acrimony, or insuperable hate. Now it is otherwise. I confess, that toward every man or thing North, there has arisen within me a feeling of detestation that I cannot express or qualify, if I would. In the war they waged against us, they were demons — in victory, they proved themselves fiends. There are, of course, individual exceptions I doubt not, but I have yet to learn of one prominent man there who has, since the rupture, expressed a sentiment, or evinced a feeling, that would not be held a disgrace to manhood elsewhere." *The Public Life and Diplomatic Correspondence of James M. Mason*, 581.

2. W. H. Russell thus wrote of Mr. Slidell in a letter to the Times, which appeared in its issue of December 10, 1861 : — "Mr. Slidell, whom I had the pleasure of meeting in New Orleans, is a man of more tact and he is not inferior to his colleague Mr. Mason in other respects. He far excels him in subtlety and depth, and is one of the most

consummate masters of political manoeuvre in the States. He is what is here called a ' wire-puller ' — a man who unseen moves the puppets on the public stage as he lists — a man of iron will and strong passions, who loves the excitement of combinations, . . . and who in his dungeon [at Fort Warren], or whatever else it may be, would conspire with the mice against the cat sooner than not conspire at all. . . . Originally a northern man, he has thrown himself into the southern cause and staked his great fortune on the issue without hesitation, and with all the force of his intellect and character. And even he believed that England must break the blockade for cotton."

3. Two exceptionally well-informed Americans, long resident in Great Britain, then wrote, the one from London to Mr. Seward, and the other from Edinburgh to his uncle, a citizen of New York: — "There never was within memory such a burst of feeling as has been created by the news of the boarding of the [*Trent*]. The people are frantic with rage, and were the country polled, I fear that 999 men out of a thousand would declare for immediate war. Lord Palmerston cannot resist the impulse if he would; " the other, under the same date, November 29: — "The excitement consequent upon the insult to the British flag by the U. S. Frigate, *San Jacinto*, has entirely monopolized the public mind. I have never seen so intense a feeling of indignation exhibited in my life. It pervades all classes, and may make itself heard above the wiser theories of the Cabinet officers."

— *War Records, Series* II. n. 1107, 1131.

4. "When I heard at Cienfuegos on the south side of Cuba of these commissioners having landed on the Island of Cuba and that they were at the Havana and would depart in the English steamer on the 9th of November, I determined to intercept them and carefully examined all the authorities on international law to which I had access, viz., Kent, Wheaton and Vattel, besides various decisions of Sir William Scott and other judges of the admiralty court of Great Britain which bore upon the rights of neutrals and their responsibilities." Official report

of Captain Wilkes to the Secretary of the Navy. *War Records,* Series II. n. 1098.

5. Dana, *Wheaton,* 659 n.

6. Rhodes, *History,* III. 522 n.

7. The quite unintelligible and somewhat ludicrous state of what is termed Law, of the International variety, so far as the topic here in question is concerned, is presented in a concrete shape in Moore's *Digest,* vn. 768-779. The authorities are there cited, and the discussions of the Trent precedent referred to. The difficulty seems to arise from the attempt seriously made to apply the principles laid down by Vattel, etc., and the precedents established by Lord Stowell to present conditions. The existence of modern lines of common-carrier transportation of passengers, merchandise and mails under neutral flags between points not actually blockaded — lines like the Peninsula and Oriental, the Cunard and the White Star — seems not to have occurred to the publicists; while in fact the applying to the ships of such lines the rules under which Captain Wilkes thought he proceeded, and the application of which Mr. Seward afterwards gravely dis cussed, is hardly less opposed to reason and common sense than would be the attitude and efforts of a tailor who endeavored to adjust the dress of a seven-year old boy to the body and limbs of the same boy when grown to be a man of un precedented size. In each case the attempt is, or would be, unfortunate, and lead inevitably to results unexpected if not impossible. This apparently is the one real lesson the world derived from the *Trent* affair. It seems to be questionable, however, whether either the statesmen at the time took in the fact or the publicists since have realized it, and the consequent utter futility of what they attempted. Let the investigator substitute *Lusitania* for *Trent,* and consider what would necessarily result. To-day, the procedure of Captain Wilkes would, if of possible occurrence, be justly looked upon as showing prima facie evidence of insanity in the case of a naval officer responsible for it. Its single possible justification by his government would be found in Juvenal :

Hoc volo, sic jubeo, sit pro ratione voluntas.

[Editor's note: "Let my will stand for the reason."]

8. Saturday, November 16. On the afternoon of that day the following despatch was sent from Washington: "The intelligence of the capture of Slidell and Mason has diffused the greatest possible joy among all the citizens, including the Government officials from the President down to the humblest messenger."

9. An account of the affair will be found in the *Boston Evening Transcript,* November 27, 1861.

10. *War Records,* Series II. n. 1113.

11. In an address on the State of the Country, delivered before the Middlesex Mechanics' Association, at Lowell, on Tuesday evening, December 24, 1861.

There has been a diversity of statement as respects Lewis Cass and his attitude and utterances in this connection. By some it has been asserted that he also was positive that the action of Captain Wilkes was justifiable, both on principle and by precedent. Such, however, was in no degree the case. On the contrary, the only recorded expression of opinion by Mr. Cass is refreshing from its correctness; its practical view of the matter also strongly coincided with what Lord Palmerston, as will next be seen, had said to Mr. Adams shortly before. The conclusions of General Cass are found in a letter addressed to Secretary Seward from Detroit, on the 19th of December, 1861. In his retirement from active political life, General Cass then wrote: — "Though I think it was justifiable upon the grounds laid down and acted upon by England, yet I considered it a most useless and unfortunate affair — an affair which from its evident importance should never have been undertaken by Captain Wilkes with out express orders from his Government, and his interference is the more inexcusable as he states in his report that in his search into the authorities upon the law of nations he could find no such case decided and was brought to consider the rebel commissioners as the ' embodiment of despatches ' — I think is his phrase — in order to justify the arrest; a strange reason to be officially given for such a procedure. And what has amazed me more than anything else in this whole affair are the laudations bestowed upon Captain Wilkes for his courage in taking three or four unarmed men out of an unarmed vessel." *War Records,* Series II. n. 1132. This position evinced consistency also, as Cass, when Secretary of State, had clearly and fully laid down the American principles of neutral rights in a despatch, June 27, 1859, addressed to John Y. Mason, then Minister to France, and a brother of James M. Mason.

12. The *James Adger,* commanded by Captain J. B. Marchant. In regard to this incident, see Charles Francis Adams (Am. Statesmen Series), 222-224; *Records of Union and Confederate Navies,* I. 128, 224;. Adams, *Studies:* Military *and Diplomatic,* 394.

13. These very instances were at the time cited as possibilities by Earl Russell in his despatch to Lord Lyons, closing the discussion on the side of the British government. In addition thereto the following — "So also a Confederate vessel-of-war [e.g. the *Alabama*] might capture a Cunard steamer on its way from Halifax to Liverpool, on the ground of its carrying despatches from Mr. Seward to Mr. Adams." It is difficult now of belief that in 1861 an experienced American naval officer should have undertaken to establish a precedent logically implying such obvious consequences, and this on his own initiative; that the most learned legal authorities in America should have unequivocally sustained him in such an act, insisting on its unquestionable legality, fairly surpasses belief. Yet the evidence is conclusive that at the time American public opinion was well-nigh unanimous in support of the proposition, and had persuaded itself, or was persuaded, that Great Britain should be held to a future strict responsibility and account for failing to give immediate and willing assent to it.

14. See *Mass. Hist. Soc. Proceedings,* Vol. 45, p. 137.

15. Mason, *Public Life,* 224, 225.

16. But on this point see Mason, *Public Life,* 123-125.

17. This course was, it is said, also at the moment advocated by General McClellan, then organizing the Army of the Potomac, and

practically commander-in-chief in succession to General Scott. Russell, *My Diary*, II. 405

18. *Lincoln and Seward* (1874), 186-187. This was an opinion formed later and on more mature reflection. At the time of the occurrence of the "affair" the attitude of Secretary Welles was pronounced, and his utterances were peculiarly indiscreet as well as precipitate. See *Diary*, I. 299, 466, 490.

19. *Wheaton*, 654, n.

20.The Duke of Newcastle, who had accompanied the Prince of Wales in his visit to America in the summer and autumn of 1860, was at this time Colonial Secretary in the Palmerston-Russell government. On June 5, 1861, five months before the occurrence of the Trent affair, he thus wrote in an official letter to Sir Edmund Head, Governor-General of Canada: — "I entirely concur in what you say in your letter of the 18th May about Mr. Seward's speculations and unfriendly views towards Canada, but I think you hardly make sufficient allowance for his hyper-American use of the policy of bully and bluster. When I saw him at Albany last October he fairly told me he should make use of insults to England to secure his own position in the States, and that I must not suppose he meant war. On the contrary, he did not wish war with England, and he was confident we should never go to war with the States — we dared not and could not afford it."

On December 5th following, in the heat of the excitement of the *Trent* affair, Newcastle wrote to Lord Monck, then in command of the forces in Canada: — "Soon after your last letter was written [November 16] you must have learnt of the affair of the *Trent*, and the serious complications which it must produce. I am bound to warn you that war is too likely to be the result. Such an insult to our flag can only be atoned by the restoration of the men who were seized when under its protection, and with Mr. Seward at the helm of the United States, and the mob and the Press manning the vessel, it is too probable that this atonement may be refused."

To the same effect, William H. Russell wrote as follows to the Times: — "In the present temper of the American people, no concessions can avert serious complications very long, or the surrender of all the boasted privileges of the Civis Romanus. . . .

"There is a popular passion and vengeance to be gratified by the capturing and punishment of Mr. Mason and Mr. Slidell, and I believe the Government will retain them at all risks because it dare not give them up, not being strong enough to do what is right, in the face of popular sentiment. ... I was much struck with the deep spirit of animosity displayed by some friends of mine, for whom I entertain a great respect, in speaking of the probable act of Great Britain: — ' If we are forced now in our hour of weakness to give up Mason and Slidell, I trust to God that every man in America will make a solemn resolve to let England feel the force of our resentment and an undying revenge when next she is involved in any difficulty.'" Letter of November 12, printed in the issue of the *Times* for December 3, 1861.

"As I write there is a rumour that Messrs. Mason and Slidell are to be sur rendered. If it be true this Government is broken up. There is so much violence of spirit among the lower orders of the people, and they are so ignorant of every thing except their own politics and passions, so saturated with pride and vanity that any honorable concession even in this hour of extremity would prove fatal to its authors." From letter dated November 25, in the issue of the *Times* of December 10, 1861.

The general understanding and accepted popular conviction in Great Britain was thus set forth in an editorial in the *Illustrated London News* of December 14, 1861: "While it is broadly stated on all hands on this side of the water that a restoration of the old Union is assuming the aspect of an impossibility, it has been whispered that such an opinion has secretly taken root in the minds of the Cabinet at Washington, and that a contest with England is adopted as a policy out of which may spring a pretext for the ultimate acknowledgment of the independence of the South. If this is really the case, why, all ground for argument is cut away, and it must be readily admitted that no course more calculated to attain that end could have been selected than that of bringing on a quarrel with this country."

21. The absurdities and excesses of speech into which the prevailing epidemic of excitement led people at this juncture seem now simply incredible. For in stance, one gentleman rushed into print proposing as a remedy for existing conditions that Mason and Slidell should at once be tried, convicted of treason, sentenced, and hanged, — this before Great Britain could formulate demands for their surrender. The whole difficulty, he claimed, would thus be disposed of.

The favorite formula, however, seems to have been of a Hamilcarian character, — that is, the swearing of one's offspring to eternal hatred. Of this there were many cases; for example, Mr. Lovejoy, a member of Congress, of Illinois, thus expressed himself on the floor of the House of Representatives on the afternoon of January 7, when the correspondence between Secretary Seward and the British Government, relative to the Trent case, were laid before the House: "I am made to renew the horrible grief which I suffered when the news of the surrender of Mason and Slidell came. I acknowledge it, I literally wept tears of vexation. I hate it; and I hate the British government. I have never shared in the traditional hostility of many of my countrymen against England. But I now here publicly avow and record my inextinguishable hatred of that government. I mean to cherish it while I live, and to bequeath it as a legacy to my children when I die. And if I am alive when war with England comes, as sooner or later it must, for we shall never forget this humiliation, and if I can carry a musket in that war I will carry it. I have three sons, and I mean to charge them, and do now publicly and solemnly charge them, that if they shall have at that time reached the years of manhood and strength, they shall enter into that war."

To the same effect Captain Dahlgren, of the navy, vowed to Mr. Russell that if England should avail herself "of the temporary weakness of the United States to get back the rebel commissioners by threats or force, every American should make his son swear eternal hostility to Great Britain."

Finally, one of Mr. Adams' sons, writing to his father, expressed himself in the same vein, as follows: — "I at least would care to impress but one thing on a son of mine, and that should be inveterate, undying, immortal hatred of Great Britain. In this I do not feel that I am at all exaggerating the general feeling here." He wrote December 30, 1861.

A curious collection might be made of utterances of the same import at that juncture.

22. *Works,* VIII. 102.

23. Russell, *My Diary,* n. 428-429.

24. The timidity and hesitation with which Americans then advanced, for it cannot be said they really advocated, the traditional American policy, are fairly matter of surprise. For instance, in a letter to the London *Times,* printed in its issue of December 14, — a letter which Mr. Adams criticised at the time as being "a little too smooth and deprecating," — Mr. Thurlow Weed thus cautiously referred to the law as laid down by Lord Stowell: "Were I at all qualified to enter into the legal argument I should be inclined to accept your view of the question, to wit, that time and circumstances have so far changed the practice, reformed the principles of international maritime law as to render the earlier precedents and authorities largely inapplicable to existing cases." *Memoir of Thurlow Weed,* n. 354.

25. In his official despatch conceding the surrender of the envoys, Mr. Seward observed that the British claim for reparation was not made "in a discourteous manner." A later writer, however, has referred to the "indecent haste and manifest unfairness of the whole proceeding, as well as the bombast and implied threats" contained in Lord Russell's letters to Lord Lyons. Without going into details on this subject, it may however be observed that, so far as the United States is concerned, the despatch in question, as respects either language or peremptoriness of tone, would compare not unfavorably with the subsequent attitude and utterances of our spokesmen in the case of the difficulty of this country with Chili, as set forth in President Harrison's message of January 12, 1892, anent the assault on American sailors in Valparaiso; or with

those of President Cleveland as embodied in the memorable Venezuela message directed at Great Britain, December 17, 1895; or with those of President McKinley in his message of April n, 1898, communicating his ultimatum preceding the war with Spain; or with the course adopted by President Roosevelt in February, 1904, towards the United States of Colombia, as respects the independent Republic of Panama, proclaimed as per arrangement the day previous by a band of trembling conspirators. To the record in all these cases it is unnecessary in this connection more particularly to refer.

26. A far harsher criticism must, however, be passed on the memorandum of Secretary Chase, read at the Cabinet meeting of December 26, 1861, and printed in Warden, *Private Life and Public Letters of Salmon P. Chase,* 393, 394. It was distinctly childish; for Mr. Chase then said of Captain Wilkes' act: — "How ever excused or even justified by motives, the act of removing [Messrs. Mason and Slidell] as prisoners from the *Trent,* without resort to any judicial cognizance, was in itself indefensible. We could not deny this without denying our history. Were the circumstances reversed, our government would, Mr. Chase thought, accept the explanation, and let England keep her rebels; and he could not divest himself of the belief that, were the case fairly understood, the British government would do likewise. ... It is gall and wormwood to me. Rather than consent to the liberation of these men, I would sacrifice everything I possess." It is hardly necessary to observe that it has not been the practice of either Great Britain or the United States to yield up political refugees, or "rebels" asking right of asylum, on the demand of any Government claiming their allegiance, to "keep her rebels." The Koszta case is here distinctly in point. Secretary Chase appears when writing this memorandum to have been somewhat oblivious of that precedent.

4

Some Phases of the Civil War: An Appreciation and Criticism of of Mr. James Ford Rhodes's Fifth Volume

Published in the *Proceedings* of the Massachusetts Historical
Society, Vol. 19, 1905.

This volume covers the twenty-one momentous and ever memorable months between December, 1864, and August, 1866. Not a few of those who read the narrative themselves bore a part, subordinate, perhaps, but still a part, in the vast military and naval operations therein described; and, when the war drums ceased to beat and the battle-flags were furled, they were deeply interested in the subsequent political agitation. Passing their own recollections in review, they have thus lived to hearken to the verdict of the historian.

Based on the careful study of a vast mass of material, patiently gathered and judicially considered, Mr. Rhodes's book is literary in tone and calm in spirit, — a thoroughly good piece of up-to-date historical work. The significance of the period dealt with will, moreover, only increase with the lapse of time, and to its history this volume is a contribution of lasting value. If for no other reason, it will so prove from the fact that it is not to such a degree removed from the time of which it treats as to cease to be contemporaneous. He who writes has in this case shared in the intensity of that of which he writes ; with his own eyes he has seen many of the actors in the events of which he tells, and his ears have drunk in their own descriptive words. How great an advantage this may prove to one competent to avail himself of it has been shown more recently by Clarendon and Thiers, as in the classic times by Tacitus and Thucydides. What is more, the judgments now rendered by Mr. Rhodes, as to both men and events, based on an exhaustive study of material, are not only cautiously reached but they are expressed in measured terms, quite devoid of either zeal or preconception. Neither a partisan nor a theorist, Mr. Rhodes is nothing unless critical. It is, therefore, not unsafe even now to predict that his conclusions will prove in essentials in harmony with the ultimate verdict. Nor is this something to be lightly said; for the events and men of the period of Gettysburg and Emancipation will be studied and weighed not less closely by the historians and historical investigators of the twenty-third century than were those of the Naseby and Commonwealth period by Masson, by Carlyle, by Macaulay and by Gardiner in the century we recently closed.

But, in writing history, especially the narrative of events still to a large extent contemporaneous, much necessarily depends on the point of view. The direction of approach involves, indeed, nothing less than the question of perspective, — the relative proportion of parts. On these, in turn, depend to some extent the conclusions reached.

Mr. Rhodes approaches his subject in a general way. Neither a politician nor a soldier, he is as unskilled in practical diplomacy as he is innocent of any study of international law ; nor can he be classed as a publicist. Once, indeed, a man of affairs, he is now a judicially minded general investigator, bringing much hard common-sense to bear, always modestly, on the complex problems of a troubled and eventful period. Now it so chances that as a participant in the earlier time, and, more recently, through the study of historical material as yet unpublished, I have looked upon the same problems from other points of view. In what I now have to say, therefore, I propose to discuss, in a spirit of criticism wholly friendly, what from those points of view seem to me deficiencies and shortcomings in Mr. Rhodes's treatment. They will prove not inconsiderable. Indeed, they go, in my judgment, to the heart of the mystery.

At the close of his summary of the war, in that chapter devoted to a consideration of the internal affairs of the Confederacy during the struggle, Mr. Rhodes suggests a query which many others have often put to themselves, and over which, first and last, they have pondered much. Tersely stated, it is this: How was it that we succeeded in overcoming the seceded States? A task truly Titanic! — and, looking back now through a vista of more than forty years, one still instinctively asks — How did we ever accomplish it?

Seeking an answer to this far from self-explanatory query, Mr. Rhodes says: "A certain class of facts, if considered alone, can make us wonder how it was possible to subjugate the Confederates. It could not have been accomplished without great political capacity at the head of the Northern government, and a sturdy support of Lincoln by the Northern people." 1 This, I submit, is an inadequate answer to a per-
. plexing question, — a question which goes to the heart of any correct historical treatment of our Great Rebellion, to adopt Clarendon's title. Surely it goes without saying that to overcome a combination of numbers, resources and territory such as that composing the Southern Confederacy implied great political capacity in the overcoming power, and the sturdy popular support of him upon whom the task devolved. As Shakespeare causes Horatio to observe in another connection, " There needs no ghost come from the grave to tell us this." But the question suggested by Mr. Rhodes cannot, I submit, being one of a

very perplexing character, satisfactorily be disposed of by generalities. To formulate an answer at once definite and satisfactory, we must, descending to particulars, be more specific.

The usual and altogether conventional explanation given is the immense preponderance of strength and resources — men and material — enjoyed by one of the two contending parties. The census and the statistics of the War Department are then appealed to, and figures are arrayed setting forth the relative population and wealth, — the resources, manufactures and fighting strength of the two sides. As the result of such a showing, a certain amount of astonishment is finally expressed that the Confederacy ever challenged a conflict; and the conclusion reached is that, under all the circumstances, the only real cause for wonder is that such an unequal contest was so long sustained. But this answer to the question will hardly bear examination. After the event it looks well, — has a plausible aspect; but in 1861 a census had just been taken, and every fact and figure now open to study was then patent. The South knew them, Europe knew them; and yet in the spring of 1861, and from Bull Run in July of that year to Gettysburg and Vicksburg in 1863, no unprejudiced observer anywhere believed

that the subjugation of the Confederacy and the restoration of the old Union were reasonably probable, or, indeed, humanly speaking, a possibility. Mr. Gladstone, a man wise in his generation, and as a contemporaneous observer not unfriendly to the Union side, only expressed the commonly received and apparently justified opinion of all unprejudiced on-lookers, when at Newcastle, in October, 1862, he made his famous declaration in public speech that " Jefferson Davis and other leaders of the South . . . have made a nation. . . . We may anticipate with certainty the success of the Southern States so far as regards their separation from the North. I cannot but believe that that event is as certain as any event yet future and contingent can be." No community, it was argued, numbering eight millions, as homogeneous, organized and combative as the South, inhabiting a region of the character of the Confederacy, ever yet had been overcome in a civil war; and there was no sufficient reason for supposing that the present case would prove an exception to a hitherto universal rule. All this, moreover, was so. Wherefore, then, the exception? How was it that, in the result of our civil war, human experience went for nothing?

Was, then, the unexpected really due to preponderance in force? Confederate authorities have, of late, evinced a strong disposition to insist upon this as the correct and sufficient explanation. Their contention has been discussed here very recently by our associate Colonel Livermore. 1 In order to make out even a prima facie showing, the Confederate authorities have assumed, or endeavored to show, that the South never, from Sumter to Appomattox, had over 600,000 men in the aggregate in arms; and these, first and last, were opposed by, as they assert, some 2,800,000 on the part of the Union. Admitting these figures to be correct of both sides, — a large admission, and one which the analysis of Colonel Livermore has effectually disposed of, — it is none the less obvious that a force six hundred thousand strong, made up of fighting material of the most approved character, wholly homogeneous, acting on the defensive, mustered for the protection of the hearthstone, is something not easily overcome. It constitutes in itself a very large army; and one more especially formidable when the minds of those composing it are to the last degree

embittered against an opponent whose courage, as well as capacity, they held in almost unmeasured contempt. Such a force would, under the conditions existing in 1861 and 1862, unquestionably have considered itself, and been pronounced by others, quite adequate for every purpose of Southern defence.

But this estimate of Confederate field force obviously invites criticism of another character. It calls for explanation. The Confederate historians and investigators responsible for it do not seem to realize that, in the very act of advancing it, they cast opprobrium on the community they belong to and profess to honor. If this estimate is sustained, the verdict of the historian of the future cannot be escaped. He will say that if 600,000 men were all the Confederacy, first and last, could get into the field, it is clear that the South went into the struggle in a half-hearted way, and, being in it, showed but a craven soul. No effort of the government, no inducement of pride or patriotism, sufficed to get even a moiety of its arms-bearing men into the fighting line.

Such a showing on the part of the Confederacy, if established, will certainly not compare favorably with the forty years' later record of the Boers in the very similar South African struggle. Accepting the Confederate figures as correct, how do the two cases stand? Territorially the Confederacy covered some 712,000 square miles, — a region considerably (30,000 square miles) larger than the combined European areas of Austro-Hungary, Germany, France and Italy, with Belgium, Holland and Denmark thrown in. This vast space was inhabited by five million people of European descent, with three millions of Africans who could be depended upon to produce food for those of European blood in active service. In the course of the conflict, and before admitting themselves beaten, every white male in the Confederacy between the ages of seventeen and fifty capable of bearing arms was called out. Wherever necessary to preclude evasion of military duty the writ of habeas corpus was suspended, and the labor, property and lives of all in the Confederacy were by legislation of the most drastic character put at the disposal of an energetic executive. The struggle lasted four full years; and during that period the eighth part of a generation grew up, yielding its quota of arms-bearing men. Consequently, under any recognized method of computation, the Confederacy, first and last, contained within itself some 1,850,000 men capable of doing military duty. This result, also, is in accordance with the figures of the census of 1860.[1] During the war the Confederate army was reinforced by over 125,000 sympathizers[2] from the sister slave States not included in the Confederacy. The upshot of the contention thus is, out of a population of 5,600,000 whites, only 475,000 put in an appearance in response to a many-tongued and often reiterated call to arms, — a trifle in excess of one man to each twelve inhabitants. There were, moreover, more than 500,000 able-bodied negroes well adapted in every respect for all the numerous semi-military services, — such as teamsters, servants, hospital attendants and laborers on fortifications, the call for which always depletes the number present for duty of every army.3 Yet it is now maintained by Confederate authorities that all the efforts of the Richmond government, backed by every feeling of pride, patriotism, protection of the domestic roof-tree and hate of the enemy, could only induce or compel a comparatively Spartan band to turn out and strike for independence.

How was it, under very similar circumstances, with the South Africans? On Confederate showing they are a braver, a more patriotic and self-sacrificing race. Two communities, the Transvaal and the Orange Free State, were engaged in a defensive struggle against Great Britain. They included within their bounds an area of 160,000 square miles, — less than a fourth of that included in the Confederacy. Their entire white population was but about 325,000, and, when the war commenced, it was estimated they could muster a force not in excess of 48,000. In countries equally defensible, the Confederates had seven whites to a square mile of territory, the Boers had two. Yet in their two years of resistance the Boers, it is computed, had 90,000 men, first and last, in actual service, or more than one in four of their population, as against the one out of twelve in the case of the Confederacy.[4] The preponderance of force opposed to the Boers was as five to one ; the preponderance of force in the case of the Confederates, according to this latest estimate of their historians, was at most but four and a half to one.[5]

Such an estimate is, however, as far from the mark as, were it based on actual facts, it would be discreditable to Confederate manhood. It is simply unbelievable that, measured by the proportion of fighting men to the total populations, the Boer spirit was to the spirit of the Confederacy as three is to one. The statement carries its own refutation ; and the Southerners of that period were no such race of miching, mean-spirited, stay-at-home skulkers as their self-constituted and most ill-advised annalists would apparently make them out. On the contrary, as matter of historical fact, they did both turn out in force and they fought to a finish. Undoubtedly there was, towards the close of the contest, a large desertion from the Confederate ranks. The army melted imperceptibly away. The men would not stay by the colors. When, in

April, 1865, Jefferson Davis, after his flight from Richmond, met, at Greensboro', North Carolina, Joseph E. Johnston, then in command of the army confronting Sherman, a species of council was held at which the course to be pursued, in the then obviously desperate condition of affairs, was discussed. Johnston, knowing well the condition of things, and the consequent feeling among his men, when appealed to for his opinion bluntly said that the South felt it was whipped, and was tired of the war. Davis, on the other hand, was eager to continue the struggle. He insisted that in spite of the "terrible" disasters recently sustained, he would in three or four weeks have a large army in the field; and, further, expressed his confident belief that the Confederates could still win, and achieve their independence, if, as he expressed it, "our people will turn out."[7]

That Davis even then honestly so thought is very probable; and, looking only to the number of fighting men on each side available for service under proper conditions, he was right. And yet under existing conditions he was altogether wrong. As respects mere numbers, it is capable of demonstration that, at the close of the struggle, the preponderance was on the side of the Confederacy, and distinctly so. The Union at that time had, it is said, a million men on its muster rolls. Possibly that number were consuming rations and drawing pay. If such was the case, acting on the offensive and deep in a vast hostile country, the Union might possibly have been able to put 500,000 men in the fighting line. On the other side, notwithstanding the heavy drain of four years of war, the fighting strength of the Confederacy at the close cannot have been less than two-thirds of its normal strength. The South should have been able to muster, on paper, 900,000 men.. Such a force, or even the half of it, acting on the defensive in a region inadequately supplied with railroad facilities, — and these, such as they were, very open to attack, — should have been ample for every purpose. Texas alone had in 1860 a white population larger by nearly 100,000 than the white population of the Transvaal and Orange Free State combined in 1899.[8] Texas covered an area of 265,780 square miles, as against the 161,296 of the combined African republics; and this vast region was rendered accessible in 1861 by some 300 miles of railroad, or about one mile of railroad of most inferior construction to each 900 square miles of territory.[9] The character of the soil made heavy movement, slow and difficult always, at times impossible. In such a region and under such conditions, how could an invading force have been fed or transported, or kept open its lines of communication? Thus, on the face of the facts, Davis was right, and the South, if it chose to defend itself, was invincible.

And here we find ourselves face to face with one of the greatest of the many delusions in the popular, conception of practical warfare. In his remark at the Greensboro' conference about the South "turning out," Jefferson Davis seems to have fallen into it. The South, at that stage of the conflict, simply could not "turn out." So doing was a physical impossibility. It was Napoleon who said that an army was like a serpent, it moves on its belly. In dealing with practical conditions in warfare, it has always to be borne in mind that an army is a most complex organization; and its strength is measured and limited not by the census number of men available, but the means at hand of arming, equipping, clothing, feeding and transporting those men. Mere numbers in excess of those means constitute not strength, but an encumbrance. The supernumeraries are in the way ; they not only tumble over each other, but they aggravate the shortages. It was so with the Confederate army in the last stages of the Civil War. The men were there; nor did the leaders want more just so long as they were unable to arm, clothe, feed and transport those they already had. Both Lee's army and Johnston's army melted away as the alternative to starvation. Under such circumstances, if all the men in the South had flocked to the colors it would only have made matters worse; the rations and ammunition would have given out so much the sooner. The artillery and commissariat trains could not be hauled when the horses were dead of inanition. In other words, after January, 1865, the possibility of organized resistance on the part of the Confederacy no longer existed. The choice lay between surrender and disbandment; or, as General Johnston subsequently wrote: — "We, without the means of purchasing supplies of any kind, or procuring or repairing arms, could continue this war only as robbers or guerillas."[10]

The next question is, — How had this result been brought about? How did it happen that five millions of people in a country of practically unlimited extent, and one almost invulnerable to attack, were physically incapable of further organized resistance? How did they come to be so devoid of arms, food, clothing and means of transport? In other words, what is the correct answer to the query suggested by Mr. Rhodes? He certainly does not give it; but, perplexing as the question is, a plausible answer can surely at this late day at least be approximated.

Lord Bacon long ago, in some passage I well remember but have not been able now to find, compares the judgment passed on current events by foreign nations with that of posterity. We may there, as he points out, find the necessary detachment and sense of proportion; also that absence of prejudice and passion which, to some extent, makes good deficiencies of knowledge. Turning over the pages of an English periodical lately, I came, in its issue for July, 1866, across a somewhat elaborate paper entitled "The Principles and Issues of the American Struggle."[11] Philosophizing over the outcome of the struggle rather more than a year after it had been brought to a close, the writer of the article thus answered Mr. Rhodes's query some thirty-eight years in advance of the time when Mr. Rhodes put it : —

"By dint of obstinate endurance — by dint of illimitable paper money and credit — by dint of foreign soldiers from Ireland and Germany who swarmed into the country, allured by bounties on enlistment varying from £100 to £200 sterling per head — by dint of sacrificing general after general, however brave and able, who could not gain a victory — by dint of a blockade of the sea-board, producing in due time a famine, or something very like it, through the most fertile portions of the South ; and last, but by no means least, by dint of the cowardice or incapacity of the British government, that refused to unite with that of France in acknowledging the independence of the South — the Northern people conquered their Southern brethren."

Here, then, is a foreign contemporaneous explanation, and one, in some respects, close to the mark. Yet it is not wholly satisfactory. It again is too general ; for, though the writer is specific enough, he generalizes in his specification, omitting nothing that suggests itself, and emphasizing everything about equally. Further elimination and a more severe analysis are necessary.

Six contributing causes are specified. Let us, through the perspective of forty years, see which still stand as material. The initial two, "obstinate endurance" and "illimitable paper dollars and credit," we may pass over. The first goes without saying; and the last would not in itself have sufficed to accomplish the end sought in 1865 any more than it had sufficed to accomplish the end then sought, when an advantage in the hands of Great Britain in the struggle that ended in 1783. The third count also cuts no considerable figure in a revised summary. The backbone of the Union army at the close of the struggle, as at its beginning, was made up of Americans. The number of foreigners, Irish or German, drawn to the country by the temptation of bounties may have been considerable; but, as an advantage on the side of the Union, it was far more than counterbalanced by the drastic conscription enforced throughout the Confederacy. Three factors now only remain for consideration. One of these, the sacrificing of those leaders who failed to win victories, is a feature of all warfare, and in no way peculiar to our civil strife. As a factor in results it was not peculiarly in evidence there. The allusion is apparently to McClellan; but, in his case, history, and the coming to light, of historical material, have more than justified the course finally pursued by Lincoln and Stanton. Of the two remaining factors of success, — the blockade and absence of foreign intervention, — the last may be left out of consideration, "it is useless to discuss historical problems from the point of view of what would have happened if something had occurred which in point of fact never did occur. On this foreign and contemporaneous judgment of conditions we are thus through elimination brought down to one factor, the blockade, as the controlling condition of Union success. In other words, that success was made possible by the undisputed naval and maritime supremacy of the North. Cut off from the outer world and all exterior sources of supply, reduced to a state of inanition by the blockade, the Confederacy was pounded to death.

Or, to put the proposition in yet another form, in the game of warfare, maritime supremacy on the part of the North — what Captain Mahan has since developed historically as the Influence of the Sea Power — even more than compensated for the military advantage of the defensive, and its interior strategic lines, enjoyed by the South. Such being the case, the greater command by one party to the conflict of men, supplies, munitions and transportation worked its natural result.

Unquestionably much could be said in support of this contention. More than plausible, it fairly explains an outcome otherwise inexplicable now, as contrary to all foreign expectation then. Without, however, going into any elaborate discussion of the arguments for and against it as a satisfactory historical postulate, but for present purposes accepting it as such, a distinct grasp and full recognition of the advantage in the struggle pertaining to the mastery of the sea is to my mind the most marked deficiency in Mr. Rhodes's treatment of the outcome of the conflict. In this respect his narrative is lacking in a proper sense of proportion. As compared with the space devoted to the movements on land, he fails to give to the sea operations the emphasis properly belonging to them. Towards the close of that portion of his fifth volume devoted to a summary of the preceding narrative, Mr. Rhodes, it is true, does incidentally say that the " work of the United States navy was an affair of long patience unrelieved by the prospect of brilliant exploits; lacking the incitement of battle, it required discipline and character only the more. But the reward was great; for the blockade was one of the effective agencies in deciding the issue of the war."[12] This is a somewhat faint recognition of services really decisive; but, such as it is, it may pass. As one reads Mr. Rhodes's narrative, however, it would hardly be supposed that a blockade existed at all, much less that it entered into the struggle as the essential pivot on which turned many of the most important of those land movements so fully described. For instance, an undisputed maritime supremacy made possible Sherman's march to the sea.

To this general criticism, an exception must be made in the case of the action between the Monitor and the Merrimac. To that a sufficiency of space (five pages) is given; for, obviously, on its result depended McClellan's strategy. Besides being temptingly dramatic in itself, it had to be dealt with in connection with land operations. But the capture of Hatteras Inlet (August 26, 1861) and of Port Royal (November 7, 1861) are incidentally mentioned in part of a twenty-three line paragraph, though strategically they were, and subsequently proved, of the utmost consequence, distinctly foreshadowing that process of devitalization as a result of which the Confederacy ultimately collapsed. Again, the taking of New Orleans, from every point of view one of the most important events of the war as well as one of its most striking episodes, — a knife-thrust in the very vitals of the Confederacy is disposed of in two pages; the sinking of the Alabama by the Kearsarge is truly enough referred to "as of no moment towards terminating the war"; but its moral effect in Europe at a critical period was very memorable. Finally, to assert that the achievements of Admiral Farragut contributed not less than those of General Sherman to the downfall of the Confederacy may or may not be an exaggeration; but, on the part of the navy, it may safely be claimed that the running of the forts at the mouth of the Mississippi, and the consequent fall of New Orleans, was as brilliant an operation, and one as triumphantly conducted, as the march through Georgia. It struck equal dismay into the hearts of the Southern leaders. Yet the name of Farragut appears but once in the index of Mr. Rhodes's fifth volume, in which he summarizes the war; and that once is in connection with Andrew Johnson's famous "swinging-round-the-circle" performance. Twelve lines of text are devoted to the battle of Mobile Bay, while two lines only are made to suffice for the capture of Wilmington, which closed the last inlet of the Confederacy, hermetically sealing it. Here, then, from Hatteras Inlet to Fort Fisher, — between August, 1861, and January, 1865, — is a consecutive series of operations, prime factors in the final result, and they are disposed of in ninety lines of a narrative covering 1,350 pages. About a sixth of one per cent of the entire space is given to them. With Hilton Head, Hatteras Inlet, New Orleans, Hampton Roads, Mobile Bay, Wilmington and Cherbourg blazing imperishably on the record, Mr. Rhodes incidentally remarks that the work of the navy was "unrelieved by the prospect of brilliant exploits"! Nor do the names of those identified with our naval triumphs thunder in the general index. Judged by that test, six lines suffice for the allusions to Farragut, and five for those to Porter; while four solid columns are judged scarcely adequate for Grant, and two for Sherman. This, I submit, is disproportionate. In some future edition an entire chapter for each year would not be too much to devote to an account of the operations of that arm of the Union service which on the sea counterbalanced that advantage of interior lines on the land the Confederates so confidently counted upon, and of which all the military strategists or critics, whether domestic or foreign, so everlastingly wrote. Throttling the Confederacy throughout, the navy was also a spear-thrust in its back.

Passing to another topic of scarcely less importance, the sense of correct proportion is again at fault. The Confederacy did not go into the conflict unadvisedly. On the contrary, its leaders gave what at the time they considered full consideration to all the factors on either side essential to success.[13] As was apparent in the outcome, they reckoned without their host; but, none the less, they did reckon. Unfortunately for it, the Southern community in the years prior to 1861 was phenomenally provincial. Judged by its , literature and the published utterances of its men and women, particularly its women, it seemed — intellectually, socially, economically and physically — to be conscious only of itself. This characteristic, among many other phases of development, was in- * ordinately and most offensively apparent in an undervaluation of its prospective opponent both for character and courage, and in an overvaluation of the importance of the South as a commercial world-power. As respects the undervaluation of # the prospective opponent, the mental condition of the South in 1861 has since been very tersely stated by General Bradley T. Johnson himself a Confederate, though born in Maryland, — at once jurist and veteran : — u The Southern people for several generations had trained themselves into a vainglorious mood toward the Northern men. They believed that they were inconquerable by the North, and that the men of the North were not their physical nor mental equals."[14] And, reviewing the conflict and outcome through the vista of thirty years, this typical Southron reached a conclusion, bearing directly on the query suggested by Mr. Rhodes: — "The Confederate States were not crushed by overwhelming resources nor overpowering numbers. They were out-thought by the Northern men."[15] As respects the other great factor of self-deception, the overvaluation of itself by the South as a commercial worldpower, the mere mention of that delusion recalls to memory the once familiar, now quite forgotten, postulate, — "Cotton is King!" To the South its infatuation on this point was the fruitful mother of calamity; for the commercial supremacy of cotton, accepted as a fundamental truth, was made the basis of political action. The unquestioning faith in which that patriarchal community cherished this belief has now passed out of memory, and the statement of it savors of exaggeration. As a matter of fact it does not admit of exaggeration. For instance, what modern historical presentation could be so framed as to exceed in strength, broadness and color the following from a speech delivered in the United States Senate, March 4, 1858 ? James H. Hammond, representing South Carolina, then said : —

"But if there were do other reason why we should never have war, would any sane nation make war on cotton? Without firing a gun, without drawing a sword, should they make war on us we could bring the whole world to our feet. The South is perfectly competent to go on one, two, or three years without planting a seed of cotton. . . . What would happen if no cotton was furnished for three years? I will not stop to depict what every one can imagine, but this is certain : England would topple headlong and carry the whole civilized world with her, save the South. No, you dare not make war on cotton. No power on earth dares to make war upon it. Cotton is King. Until lately the Bank of England was king, but she tried to put her screws as usual, the fall before the last, upon the cotton crop, and was utterly vanquished. The last power has been conquered. Who can doubt, that has looked at recent events, that cotton is supreme?"[16]

It would not be difficult to multiply almost indefinitely utterances like the above ; but for the purpose in hand this one will suffice. Intensely provincial, the idea was vulgar; in the jargon of the Stock Exchange the South thought she had a corner on Cotton, and, if she so willed it, the World must walk up to her counter, and settle on any terms she saw fit to prescribe! As Russell, of the London Times, observed, — "These tall, thin, fine-faced Carolinians are great materialists. Slavery perhaps has aggravated the tendency to look at all the world through parapets of cotton-bales and rice-bags, and though more stately and less vulgar, the worshippers here are not less prostrate before the ' almighty dollar ' than the Northerners."[17]

Thus, in complete provincialism and childlike faith a community was willing to venture, and actually did venture, life, fortune and sacred honor on its contempt for those composing the largest part of the community of which they were themselves but a minority, and on the soundness of a commercial theory. In regard to the extent and implicit character of the faith held on both these points no better witness could testify than Dr. William H. Russell, the once famous *Times* Crimean correspondent just referred to. Russell certainly had no prejudice against the South, or Southern men. On the contrary, he liked both; while he did not take kindly to the North as a whole, or to its people. He was, however, a foreign observer with a remarkable faculty for vivid description, and here to take notes and to portray things as they appeared. He was in South Carolina immediately after the bombardment of Sumter, and there mixed freely with the exponents of public sentiment. In his Diary he thus describes what he heard on the subject of Southern superiority and cotton supremacy, — he is recording what occurred at the Charleston Club on the evening of April 16, 1861, ex-governors of the State, senators, congressmen, and other prominent South Carolinians being of the company: —

"We talked long, and at last angrily, as might be between friends, of political affairs.

"I own it was a little irritating to me to hear men indulge in extravagant broad menace and rodomontade, such as came from their lips. 'They would welcome the world in arms with hospitable hands to bloody graves.' 'They never could be conquered.' 'Creation could not do it,' and so on. I was obliged to handle the question quietly at first — to ask them ' if they admitted the French were a brave and warlike people I ' ' Yes, certainly.' l Do you think you could better defend yourselves against invasion than the people of France ? ' 'Well, no; but we 'd make it pretty hard business for the Yankees.' 'Suppose the Yankees, as you call them, come with such preponderance of men and *materiel*, that they are three to your one, will you not be forced to submit?' 'Never.' 'Then either you are braver, better disciplined, more warlike than the people and soldiers of France, or you alone, of all the nations in the world, possess the means of resisting physical laws which prevail in war, as in other affairs of life.' 'No. The Yankees are cowardly rascals. We have proved it by kicking and cuffing them till we are tired of it; besides, we know John Bull very well. He will make a great fuss about non-interference at first, but when he begins to want cotton he 11 come off his perch.' I found this was the fixed idea everywhere. The doctrine of 'cotton is king' — to us who have not much considered the question a grievous delusion or an unmeaning babble — to them is a lively all-powerful faith without distracting heresies or schisms."[18]

The following day, Dr. Russell was one of a party on an excursion down Charleston harbor, visiting Forts Sumter and Moultrie. In the course of the trip he met, among others, L. T. Wigfall, the notorious Texan who had recently resigned a seat in the Senate of the United States to throw in his fortunes with the Confederacy. Dr. Russell says in his Diary, April 17 : —

"For me there was only one circumstance which marred the pleasure of that agreeable reunion. Colonel and Senator Wigfall, who had not sobered himself by drinking deeply, in the plenitude of his exultation alluded to the assault on Senator Sumner as a type of the manner in which the Southerners would deal with the Northerners generally, and cited it as a good exemplification of the fashion in which they would bear their 'whipping.'"[19]

A day or two later, Mr. Bunch, the British consul at Charleston, who not long afterwards achieved a most unhappy diplomatic notoriety, entertained Dr. Russell at dinner. It was a " small and very agreeable party," but of the talk at that table the guest recorded : —

"It was scarcely very agreeable to my host or myself to find that no considerations were believed to be of consequence in reference to England except her material interests, and that these worthy gentlemen regarded her as a sort of appanage of their cotton king- dom. 'Why, sir, we have only to shut off your supply of cotton for a few weeks, and we can create a revolution in Great Britain. There are four millions of your people depending on us for their bread, not to speak of the many millions of dollars. No, sir, we know that England must recognize us,' &c.

"Liverpool and Manchester have obscured all Great Britain to the Southern eye. I confess the tone of my friends irritated me."

He next visited the leading merchants, bankers, and brokers : —

"In one office I saw an announcement of a company for a direct communication by steamers between a southern port and Europe. 'When do you expect that line to be opened?' I asked. 'The United States cruisers will surely interfere with it.' 'Why, I expect, sir,' replied the merchant, ' that if those miserable Yankees try to blockade us, and keep you from our cotton, you'll just send their ships to the bottom and acknowledge us. That will be before autumn, I think.' It was in vain I assured him he would be disappointed. 'Look out there,' he said, pointing to the wharf, on which were piled some cotton bales; 'there 's the key will open all our ports, and put us into John Bull's strong box as well.' "

A guest shortly after on the island plantation of Mr. Trescot, he there met Edmund Rhett, a member of a family prominent in South Carolina public life. The Rhett dwelling house and plantation were on Port Royal Island, a few miles only from the smaller island on which Mr. Trescot dwelt. They thus were neighbors. The stranger and guest describes the South Carolinian as " a very intelligent and agreeable gentleman," but from his lips also came the same old story. "Look,' he said, 'at the fellows who are sent out by Lincoln to insult foreign courts by their presence.' I said that I understood Mr. Adams and Mr. Dayton were very respectable gentlemen, but I did not receive any sympathy ; in fact, a neutral who attempts to moderate the violence of either side, is very like an ice between two hot plates. Mr. Rhett is also persuaded that the Lord Chancellor sits on a cotton bale. 'You must recognize us, sir, before the end of October.'"[20]

As respects the outcome of what may well enough be called the South's cotton campaign, Mr. Rhodes's narrative seems to me deficient. That campaign was in fact the most far-reaching and, in world effect, the most important inaugurated and carried out by the Confederacy; and in its result they sustained complete and disastrous defeat, — a defeat which entailed on them in the midst of the contest and in presence of the enemy, an entire change of front, economical, financial and diplomatic. This nowhere appears in Mr. Rhodes's narrative; and yet on this phase of the struggle both Confederate finance and Confederate diplomacy hinged. And here again the blockade comes to the front.

Had the theory as respects the potency of cotton on which the South went into the war been sound, the blockade would have proved the Confederacy's most potent ally ; for the blockade shut off from Europe its supply of cotton as it could have been shut off by no other possible agency. In so far the government of the Union played the game of the Confederacy, and played it effectively. In the early days of the struggle, they talked at Richmond of an export duty on their one great staple, and of inhibiting its outgo altogether; the blockade made any action of this nature quite unnecessary. Through the blockade the cotton-screw, so to speak, was applied to the fullest possible extent. Nor was the overthrow of the potentate brought about easily. He was well entrenched, and dethroning him entailed on the commercial, world one of the most severe trials it has ever been called upon to pass through. In this phase of the struggle Lancashire was the field of central battle; and there, as the result of a struggle extending through eighteen months, the Confederate ikon was tumbled down. The catastrophe was complete; and the whole Southern programme, economical, fiscal, and, at last, strategic, where it did not utterly collapse, underwent great change. The summer of 1862 marked the crisis; before that, as Mr. Rhodes truly states,1 the Confederate policy was to keep cotton at home, and by withholding it to compel foreign recognition; after that, the one effort was to get it to market with a view to its conversion into ships, munitions of war and necessaries of life. But Mr. Rhodes, in my judgment, disposes of this crucial Confederate defeat altogether too lightly. Mr. Rhodes says: " As we have seen, [England and France] when they could not get cotton from America, got it elsewhere." I do not know on what authority this statement is made; but it is not in accordance with the facts. In the early months of 1861 the estimated weekly consumption of cotton in Great Britain was 50,000 bales; at the close of 1862 it had fallen to 20,000 bales, inferior in weight as well as quality. Indeed so bad was the quality that its manufacture was destructive to machinery. Of this greatly reduced quantity, moreover, a considerable portion — some twenty per cent — was the American product, run through the blockade. So great was the dearth that in September, 1862, the staple, which two years before had sold in Liverpool for fourpence a pound, had gone up until it touched the unheard-of price of half a crown. Cotton simply was not forthcoming from any quarter, and the commercial world was everywhere in search of substitutes for it.

To this subject, from my point of view, Mr. Rhodes might well have devoted a chapter. As it stands, it is a case of anticlimax; introduced with a loud blast of trumpets, the potentate simply vanishes, — so to speak, he evaporates. How, and what became of him, nowhere appears. Judging by Mr. Rhodes's narrative, one would infer that it was a case of insensible dissolution; but, as an historical fact, it was very far otherwise. Not all that Mr. Hammond and others predicted, or that the Confederate leaders confidently looked to see happen, actually did happen ; but, none the less, the process involved a commercial and industrial disturbance of the first magnitude, and the most complete and disastrous defeat sustained by the Confederacy in the whole course of the war. The episode, too, carried with it a most instructive historical lesson as to the danger even nations incur from indulging with undue confidence in a theory, — in other words, the old South furnished in 1860-61 a very striking illustration of the homely truth that the evils incident to what is humanly known as a condition of mental "cocksureness" are not confined to individuals. In 1860 that whole Southern community was socially and economically daft. But no people and no period are exempt from such states of delusion. Within the memory of those now living this country has been subject to a dozen such ; in the eyes of not a few it is to-day suffering under more than one. Fortunately, so far as deep water and destruction are concerned, the experience of the South was exceptional. It was a dream ; but a dream from which the awakening must have been terribly bitter. The first indication I have found of a recurrence to common-sense was in a speech made by William L. Yancey at an impromptu reception given him in the rotunda of the St. Charles Hotel at New Orleans, on his return in March, 1862, from that wholly abortive mission to Europe on which he had been sent by Jefferson Davis a year before. He had learned something in the course of his travels, and he then significantly said: " It is an error to say that 'Cotton is King.' It is not. It is a great and influential power in commerce, but not its dictator." A little foreign travel had educated that particular Southern prophet out of some bf his provincialism. Almost immediately his words found an echo in Richmond, a Louisiana Senator there sadly declaring in debate, " We have tested the powers of King Cotton and have found him to be wanting."[21] While three months later, in June, 1862, Alexander H. Stephens enunciated too late the correct principle. They had been possessed with the idea, he told them, that "cotton was a political power. There was the mistake, — it is only a commercial power."[22]

Passing to the other topics in the treatment of which the narrative of Mr. Rhodes, though sufficiently full, seems from my point of view open to criticism, I next refer to his account of Sherman's famous march to the sea in November, 1863, and Grant's advance on Richmond in May, 1864. Mr. Rhodes quotes General Sherman as saying in his Memoirs : " Were I to express my measure of the relative importance of the March to the Sea and of that from Savannah northward, I would place the former at one and the latter at ten, or the maximum." We are then told, in a foot-note to the same page,[23] that General Schofield was of a different opinion. "Considered," he said in his *Forty-six Years* (p. 348), "as to its military results, Sherman's march cannot be regarded as more than I have stated — a grand raid. The defeat and practical destruction of Hood's army in Tennessee was what paved the way to the speedy termination of the war, which the capture of Lee by Grant fully accomplished; and the result ought to have been essentially the same as to time if Sherman's march had never been made."

On this point Mr. Rhodes expresses no opinion. He wisely leaves it for the military critics to fight it out among themselves. I can, however, say that at the time, and in Europe, this view of the relative importance of operations did not obtain. Far from it. Schofield, of course, refers to Sherman's march north from Savannah, through the Carolinas ; but I gravely doubt whether his estimate of the strategic importance of that march, or Sherman's estimate of its relative importance as compared with that through Georgia, are either of them correct. While, so far as the fall of the Confederacy was concerned, both exercised great influence on the outcome, from my point of view I incline to the belief that the march through Georgia was the more potent in influence of the two. It was so for an obvious reason. In war, as in most other affairs in which mankind gets itself involved, moral effects count for a good deal; and especially is this so with somewhat volatile and excitable communities, such as that inhabiting the South unquestionably was. But, so far as Europe was concerned, it is safe to assert that no other operation of the entire war was productive of a moral effect in any way comparable with that caused by the march to the sea. Indeed, coming as it did and when it did, it is not too much to say it was an epochal event in that it marked the turning of the tide of European and especially of English opinion as respects the United States and things American. James Russell Lowell wrote a well-remembered essay " Upon a Certain Condescension in Foreigners"; and, during the earlier stages of the Civil War, this well-understood "condescension" resolved itself quite naturally into a studied tone of scorn, in no way veiled. The change which has since become so marked in this respect began with Sherman's march. That march in a way smote the foreign imagination ; and the whole course of subsequent events, down to the treaty negotiated last summer at Portsmouth, has served to promote what has now developed into a revolution in tone and estimate. As every one realizes,

Lowell's "foreigner" has undergone a total change; his "condescension " is of the past. The beginning of that change I had occasion to trace through the utterances of the European press. Up to the autumn of 1864, and the re-election of Lincoln, the general tone of the European and especially of the English periodicals and papers was one of exaggerated admiration for Confederate valor and leadership; while, on the other hand, the leadership and courage of the Union side were referred to with studied contumely. Sometimes, however, the contempt was equally distributed over both parties to the fray. The famous remark attributed at least to Von Moltke is still remembered, that he "did not have time to devote to the study of the combats of two armed mobs." But a much more curious and illustrative utterance was one of Charles Lever, the Irish military novelist, who, most unfortunately for himself, chose as the time and place in which to deliver himself the January Blackwood's of 1865. The paper was, of course, prepared some time before. By mere ill luck, however, it appeared in London just as Sherman put in his appearance at Savannah. In this paper Mr. Lever undertook to compare the American combatants to two inmates of a lunatic asylum playing chess. They went through moves similar to those of chess, but without the slightest comprehension of the game. He then goes on, — "Now, does not this immensely resemble what we are witnessing this moment in America? There are the two madmen engaged in a struggle, not one single rule nor maxim of which they comprehend. Moving cavalry like infantry, artillery like a wagon train, violating every principle of the game, till at length one cries Check-mate, and the other, accepting the defeat that is claimed against him, deplores his mishap, and sets to work for another contest. . . . Just however, as I feel assured, nobody who ever played chess would have dignified with that name the strange performance of the madmen, so am I convinced that none would call this struggle a war. It is a fight — a very big fight, if you will, and a very hard fight too, but not war."[24] There is much more to the same effect, the intensely ludicrous side of which at just that juncture the genial Irishman himself subsequently appreciated most keenly. What I have quoted will, however, suffice for the purpose of present illustration. At the very time Mr. Lever was thus rashly committing himself in cold print, General Sherman was entering on his famous march ; and, while that march was in progress, the daily tone of the London newspapers was pitched in much the same key as that of Mr. Lever's lucubration in the forthcoming number of Blackwood. The outcome of the move of the "Yankee" General was looked for with a contemptuous interest; it clearly was not war; a hare-brained effort, dictated probably by desperation, it could end only in disaster; most probably it was an ill-considered attempt at getting out of an impossible military situation. But one day the tidings came that the heads of Sherman's columns had emerged on the sea-coast, that they had made short work of the forces there found to oppose them, and that Savannah had fallen. The army and the navy had struck hands! The announcement seemed absolutely to take away the breath of the foreign critics, military and journalistic. A brilliant strategic blow had been struck; an operation, the character of which could neither be ignored nor mistaken, had been triumphantly carried through to a momentous issue; the thrust — and such a thrust! — had penetrated the vitals of the Confederacy; — what next? From that moment the end was plainly foreshadowed. Europe recognized that a new power of un-known strength, but undeniable military capacity, was thenceforth to be reckoned with.

To one feature, and one feature only, in Mr. Rhodes's account of this memorable war episode, do I care to call attention. The historian, I fear, passes somewhat gently over the pronounced vandalism which characterized Sherman's operations from Atlanta to Savannah, and yet more from Savannah to Raleigh. It is referred to, indeed, both gener-ally, and, more especially, in connection with what occurred in South Carolina, reaching a climax at Columbia; but the treatment is, notwith-standing, distinctly perfunctory.[25] The other, and I very much fear, the truer and more realistic, side is portrayed in sufficient detail, and with reference to chapter and verse, in General Bradley T. Johnson's Life of Joseph E. Johnston.[26] It there appears what Sherman meant by his famous aphorism — " War is Hell." The truth is that in 1864-65 the conflict had lasted too long for the patience of the combatants, and the defence of the South had been very stubborn. The rules and limitations of civilized warfare, so far as non-combatants were concerned, were no longer observed, and Sherman's advancing army was enveloped and followed by a cloud of irresponsible stragglers, known throughout the country as " bummers," who were simply for the time being desperadoes bent on pillage and destruction, — subject to no discipline, amenable to no law. They were looked upon then by the North, weary of the war, with a half-humorous leniency ; but, in reality, a band of Goths, their existence was a disgrace to the cause they professed to serve. For a Northerner it is not a pleasant admission, but the historic, if ungrateful, truth is that, as respects what are euphemistically termed the " severities " of warfare, the record made by our armies during the latter stages of the conflict will not bear comparison with that of the Army of Northern Virginia while in Pennsylvania during the Gettysburg campaign. Lee's memorable general order (No. 73) dated at Chambersburg, Pennsylvania, June 27, 1863, is well known, and need not be quoted; but there was truth in the reference to those opposed to him when in it he said, " No greater disgrace could befall the army, and through it our whole people, than the perpetration of barbarous outrages upon the unarmed and defenceless, and the wanton destruction of private property, that have marked the course of the enemy in our own country. It will be remembered that we make war only upon armed men." It was my fortune to be a participant in the Gettysburg campaign,[27] and, forty years later, I was glad when occasion offered to bear my evidence to the scope and spirit in which Lee's order was at the time observed by his followers. "I doubt if a hostile force ever advanced into an enemy's country, or fell back from it in retreat, leaving behind it less cause of hate and bitterness than did the Army of Northern Virginia in that memorable campaign."[28] Our own methods during the final stages of the conflict were sufficiently described by General Sheridan, when, during the Franco-Prussian War, as the guest of Bismarck, he declared against humanity in warfare, contending that the correct policy was to treat a hostile population with the utmost rigor, leaving them, as he expressed it, " nothing but their eyes to weep with over the war."[29]

In other words, a veteran of our civil strife, General Sheridan, advocated in an enemy's country the sixteenth-century practices of Tilly, described by Schiller, and the later devastation of the Palatinate policy of Louis XIV., commemorated by Goethe. In the twenty-first century, perhaps, partisan feeling as regards the Civil War performances having by that time ceased to exist, American investigators, no longer regardful of a victor's self-complacency, may treat the episodes of our struggle with the same even-handed and outspoken impartiality with which Englishmen now treat the revenges of the Restoration, or Frenchmen the dragonnades of the Grand Monarque. But when that time comes, the page relating to what occurred in 1864 in the valley of the Shenandoah, in Georgia, and in the Carolinas, — a page which Mr. Rhodes somewhat lightly passes over, — will probably be rewritten in characters of far more decided import.[30]

One final topic ; dealt with by Mr. Rhodes in his fourth volume rather than in the fifth, it still occupies a prominent place in his narrative, and its treatment necessarily involves a man who, first and last, for good or evil, will assuredly stand forth in history as one of Massachusetts' most conspicuous contributions to our Great Rebellion period. The topic is that Virginia campaign which made sadly memorable the spring and summer of 1864: the individual, General B. F. Butler. To my mind Mr. Rhodes has neither done justice, nor fully meted out justice, to the episode or to the man.

And, primarily, in the matter of Grant's strategy in that famous campaign. It seems to me to have been much better considered, and more creditable to him, than would be inferred from Mr. Rhodes's narrative. Mr. Rhodes then, secondarily, as I see it, fails to place where it belongs the grave responsibility for the failure of Grant's plan of campaign, with the awful loss of life that failure involved. My understanding has always been that Grant's plan assumed the active and harmonious co-operation of three distinct armies, — that of the Potomac, under General Meade ; that of the James, under General Butler ; and, finally, the Ninth Corps, 15,000 strong, under the command of General Burnside. Meade, with the Army of the Potomac, was to advance and engage Lee, holding the Confederate army of Northern Virginia fully occupied ; Burnside, meanwhile, was to be in reserve, immediately in Meade's rear; and, while Lee was thus engaged, Butler, with the Army of the James, composed of two corps, the Tenth and Eighteenth, and in all some 35,000 to 40,000 strong, was to push forward vigorously, threatening Richmond, and jeopardizing Lee's communications. Thus an important, if not vital, part in the plan of operations depended on Butler and the Army of the James, Opposed to him, with his completely equipped and numerically formidable command, was a wholly inadequate and widely scattered force under General Beauregard, recently (April 15) assigned to that department, and not yet on the ground.[31] If by an offensive movement, intelligently conceived and skilfully as well as vigorously handled, the Confederate line could be broken and thrown back into Richmond, Lee's rear would be exposed, his lines of communication threatened, and he must, abandoning Richmond, have fallen back towards Lynchburg or the Carolinas. Grant then proposed to follow- him up, hanging doggedly on his .rear, and catch Lee between an upper and a nether mill-stone, — the Army of the James holding him in check until the Army of the Potomac, hurrying up, could force a decisive battle.

As a strategic plan this was open to criticism. Two distinct armies were to operate conjointly in wholly separate fields, with an active enemy between them, enjoying, of course, the advantage of shorter interior lines. By a rapid concentration of forces it was obvious that Lee might crush Butler, and then swiftly turn to confront Meade either from within the 'defences of Richmond or in the open. Not impossibly the Army of the Potomac might then be doomed to undergo, on the same ground, a repetition of its experiences of two years before. General Beauregard, it has since appeared, did indeed almost at once take in the situation from this point of view, and devised a plan of campaign accordingly.[32] Nevertheless, though involving some risk in the presence of two such commanders as Lee and Beauregard, both at once alert and vigorous, Grant's scheme of campaign was well considered and practical. He enjoyed a large numerical preponderance, and each of the three independent armies, if skilfully as well as energetically handled, was amply sufficient to take care of itself.

Had, accordingly, Grant's plan been carried out in all its parts, — south of the James as well as north of Richmond, — the terrible fighting of May and June in the Wilderness, and on the road to the James and Petersburg, would have been avoided. Richmond assuredly must have fallen; while the fate of Lee and his army would have been at least problematical. Though it is not probable that Appomattox could have been anticipated by a year, the Confederacy would have lost its capital, and Lee, with one of his two lines of communication with the Carolinas cut off, would have been confronted by the three Union armies, undepleted and combined under Grant.

If such was Grant's plan, as I at the time and since have always understood, Mr. Rhodes gives no hint of it. He treats the campaign as if it had developed on the lines originally intended. If so, and I am right in my understanding, this does Grant great strategic injustice. His campaign failed, — failed in the beginning, and failed through the gross military incompetency of the General commanding the Army of the James.

An army could not well enter on an active campaign more auspiciously than did the Army of the Potomac in April, 1864. With full ranks, well disciplined, admirably equipped, inured to service, with confidence in itself and its commanders, it felt equal to any emergency of warfare. It was in fact a most formidable fighting machine; but, formidable as it was, the test to which it was subjected exceeded endurance. Plunging into the Wilderness, it found itself confronted by Lee at the head of the even more veteran Army of Northern Virginia, fighting on the defensive in a country peculiarly susceptible of an effective defence.[33] Mr. Rhodes has described what ensued. In forty days the force in Lee's front reported 55,000 casualties. Meanwhile, what had become of the Army of the James ? Why did it not play its part, working a diversion ? Well do I remember, at the time and on the spot, when the news came that Beauregard, with a mere handful of men, — hardly more than a heavy skirmish line, — had foiled Butler. No relief was to be looked for from that quarter. It was at this juncture that Grant characteristically remarked that "Butler was as safe as wax; bottled up at Bermuda Hundred!" But the plan of campaign then went to pieces; while Lee, relieved from all anxiety because of Richmond and his rear, with his communications assured, was left free to oppose his entire force to the enemy before him. What ensued, Mr. Rhodes has sufficiently told in a previous volume.

In the volume now under consideration, however, Mr. Rhodes deals with Benjamin F. Butler judicially, — as one standing at the bar of history. The sentence he passes upon him is severe, and the more severe because carefully restrained in expression. But it is confined to questions of mere lucre,— "beyond reasonable doubt," Mr. Rhodes says, he [Butler] was making money [illicitly] out of his country's life struggle." That is bad; but, however bad it may be, it is in my judgment the rendering on a very minor count in the long indictment to which Massachusetts' senior Major-General of the Civil War should be made to answer. His departmental dishonesty may be measured in dollars and cents ; his headquarters incompetence cost blood and grief both unmeasured and immeasurable. Who was responsible for the greater part of that awful loss of life, — a loss numerically nearly equal to the entire army Napoleon had on the field at Waterloo ? Primarily, it was that commander of the Army of the James who so utterly failed in doing the work he had himself insisted should be assigned him to do;[34] and, secondarily, to the commander-in-chief who left a charlatan and an incompetent in the place to which he should have designated his trustiest lieutenant.[35] It was a parallel case to that of Grouchy, — the fatal mistake of the man at the head in the choice of a tool. Years ago, during the life of our late associate John C. Ropes, I frequently discussed with him — once (1894), I remember, on the field of Waterloo — what turn other than that history has recorded might have been given to the momentous 15th of June, 1815, had Davout, instead of being at the time Minister of War and in Paris, been, as he should have been, in command of Napoleon's right wing. It hardly admits of question that the victor of Auerstadt and Eckmiihl, instinctively taking in the strategic situation, would have kept in close touch with the Emperor, and that Bliicher would have found the road from Wavre to Waterloo effectually blocked. Napoleon's right arm would not then have been paralyzed ; he would have been free to throw his whole army on Wellington's flank and rear. Fortunately for Wellington, Grouchy, and not Davout, was that day in command of Napoleon's detached wing. Butler's command and mission in the Virginia campaign of 1864 were almost exactly similar to the command and mission of Grouchy in the Waterloo campaign of 1815 ; and now to discuss the operations of the Army of the Potomac in the Wilderness and at Spottsylvania without constant reference to what the Army of the James was on those days doing south of the James, is a treatment no less defective than it would be to try to explain what took place at Waterloo without giving any consideration to Grouchy's blundering march from Gembloux to Wavre. Butler, like Grouchy, was left by the commander-in-chief to act, under general instructions, as the conditions of time and place, and the movements of the enemy in his front, might make more expedient, the plan of campaign and general strategic situation being always clearly in mind. Both failed, and failed utterly. In each case incalculable disaster ensued. My point is that, in the narrative of Mr. Rhodes, Butler does not figure as the Grouchy of the Wilderness.

It is obvious enough now, and, when too late, was plain enough to Grant then, that a blunder of selection entailing infinite detriment was made. In planning his campaign of 1864 Grant should have taken no chances ; and it is safe to say that at no subsequent period would he have entrusted to Butler any military operations. Probably at the time he relied on General W. F. ("Baldy") Smith, assigned to the command of the Eighteenth Corps, and second in rank in the Army of the James, to supply Butler with that military guidance of which he stood in such crying need. If this was so, Grant was wrong again. Smith was then fresh from Chattanooga, where he had shown great skill immediately under Grant's eye; and perhaps no one available in the whole Union army at that time promised a more brilliant future. So high an opinion did Grant then hold of Smith that when the newly appointed Lieutenant-General came East in February, 1864, to take full charge, he brought Smith with him, with the half-formulated idea of substituting him for Meade in command of the Army of the Potomac. This idea Grant subsequently abandoned, finding a place for Smith in the Army of the James; but, unfortunately, he did not substitute him for Butler as he had proposed to do for Meade. Instead of so doing he endeavored, taking a half-way course, by indirections to work directions out. As usual, when in military operations that feat is attempted, a terrible mistake was made. Smith was, in fact, a skilful engineer; in all respects a good soldier; and, in some, a brilliant commander. But Butler, though himself a military harlequin, was a man not easy to guide; nor was "Baldy" Smith the man to guide him. On the contrary, he was almost the last of those high in rank to whom that task, at once difficult and delicate, should have been assigned.[36] A year later, General Grant would unquestionably have selected Sheridan to do the work thus hesitatingly assigned ; but, in May, 1864, Sheridan had not forged to the front as he afterwards so rapidly did. None the less, just as it is curious to consider what would have been the result in June, 1815, had Davout filled the position in Napoleon's command held by Grouchy, so we are free to philosophize to any extent we see fit over what might have happened in May and June, 1865, had Beauregard then found himself confronted by Sheridan instead of by Butler.

The recollection of events and talk of more than forty years ago was the sole basis for the statements made in the text, and the conclusions drawn therefrom. Throughout the period in question I was attached in a subordinate capacity to the headquarters of the Army of the Potomac, and was, almost of necessity, more or less familiar with operations then going on in the field, and the views generally held at and about headquarters of them, and of those who had had them in charge. But, however vivid and distinct it may be, the memory of what was asserted, or actually occurred, more than the lifetime of a generation ago is no basis for any historical statement. While revising this paper I have therefore sought to refresh my memory and verify my recollections by consulting portions of the vast mass of material put in print since 1865, especially the *War Records,* Grant's *Personal Memoirs* (1885), *Butler's Book* (1892), Roman's *Military Operations of General Beauregard* (1884), W. F. Smith's *Chattanooga to Petersburg* (1893), and, on the whole as illuminating as any, our late associate John C. Ropes's paper (1884) entitled *Grant's .Campaign in Virginia.*[37] While from these authorities I have learned much I did not before know as to details, I have come across nothing affecting the general correctness of the impressions I at the time received.

Grant's original plan of combined campaign for the spring of 1864 was exactly that described. To quote his own language in his instructions to Meade, " Lee's army will be your objective point. Wherever Lee goes, there you will go also. Gillmore will join Butler with about 10,000 men from South Carolina. Butler can reduce his [Fortress Monroe garrison] so as to take 23,000 men into the field directly to his front. The force will be commanded by Major-General W. F. Smith. With Smith and Gillmore, Butler will seize City Point, and operate against Richmond from the south side of the river. His movement will be simultaneous with yours."[38] At the same time Grant wrote to Butler as follows: — Major-General Smith "is ordered to report to you to command the troops sent into the field from your own department. . . . The fact that Richmond is to be your objective point, and that there is to be co-operation between your force and the Army of the Potomac, must be your guide." Butler was at once to seize City Point, and there, Grant wrote, "concentrate all your troops for the field as rapidly as you can. From City Point directions cannot be given at this time for your further movements." Holding a firm base on the south bank of the James, Butler was thus left free to move in any direction he saw fit; and "should the enemy be forced into his intrenchments in

Richmond, the Army of the Potomac would follow, and by means of transports the two armies would become a unit."[39] Such were Butler's instructions; meanwhile of Smith, who was "to command the troops sent into the field," Grant at the same time wrote to Halleck, General Smith "is possessed of one of the clearest military heads in the army; is very practical and industrious. No man in the service is better qualified than he for our largest commands."[40] General Smith "is really one of the most efficient officers in service, readiest in expedients;, and most skilful in the management of troops in action."[41] On the night of May 5th Butler debarked at Bermuda Hundred. The movement was a complete surprise to the Confederates. By mere chance General Hagood's South Carolina brigade was moving by rail to Richmond, when, on the 6th of May at Walthall Junction, between Petersburg and Richmond, they encountered a brigade thrown forward by Butler to seize the railroad at that point. The Confederates "jumped off the platform cars upon which they were borne, the [Union] brigade . . . was in view, some thousand yards off, across an open field, advancing in line of battle, and supported by artillery ... a brisk action ensued. The [Union brigade] made two direct attacks, and, after a second repulse, at nightfall withdrew."[42] "Thus were Petersburg and Richmond barely saved by the opportune presence and gallant conduct of Hagood's command. It was upon that occasion that General Butler's forces were baffled and beaten off in their attempt to seize the Richmond railroad above Petersburg."[43] " The authorities at Richmond were now in a state of great excitement. The enemy had been repulsed on the Richmond railroad, and, to all appearance, had abandoned his original intention of investing Petersburg; but where he would next attempt to strike was the all-absorbing question."[44] At this juncture Beauregard had not yet arrived from Weldon; nor were there 3,000 men all told south of Walthall Junction, or available for the defence of Petersburg. The key to the whole military situation was unprotected. " Meanwhile troops were hastily called for from all quarters," and on the 10th Beauregard arrived, with the first body of reinforcements. The golden opportunity was rapidly passing. On the evening of the 9th Generals Gillmore and Smith, being then at

Swift's Creek, about four miles north of Petersburg, united in a written communication to General Butler suggesting that the whole command should be directed on Petersburg instead of Richmond, as previously agreed. They claimed that " all the work of cutting the [railroad, and perhaps capturing the city, can be accomplished in one day." Refusing even to consider the suggestion, General Butler, the same evening, returned a reply beginning as follows: —

> " Generals, — While I regret an infirmity of purpose which did not permit you to state to me, when I was personally present, the suggestion which you made in your written note, but left me to go to my head-quarters under the impression that another and far different purpose was advised by you, I shall not yield to the written suggestions, which imply a change of plan made within thirty minutes after I left you. Military affairs cannot be carried on, in my judgment, with this sort of vacillation. The information I have received from the Army of the Potomac convinces me that our demonstration should be toward Richmond, and I shall in no way order a crossing of the Appomattox for the purpose suggested in your note."[45]

The date of this correspondence (May 9) is important. The battle of the Wilderness had been fought on May 5th and 6th, that of Spottsylvania was to begin on May 10th, and not until the 12th was the famous assault made on Lee's salient. The Confederate army was hard pressed. To what extent at just this juncture would sudden tidings of the capture of Petersburg, and the consequent severing of his line of southern sea-coast communication, have affected Lee's mind and the entire strategic situation? And it was just then that Butler, contemptuously and insolently ignoring the recommendations of his two subordinates, allowed Beauregard to establish himself at Petersburg, while the Army of the James made "a demonstration" toward Richmond! In his official report of the whole campaign Grant subsequently said of this "demonstration" that " the time thus consumed lost to us the benefit of the surprise and capture of Richmond and Petersburg, enabling, as it did, Beauregard to collect his loose forces in North and South Carolina, and bring them to the defence of those places."[46] The occasion was great, and Beauregard showed himself equal to it. Rapidly concentrating his scattered and scanty command, he, on the 15th, assumed the offensive. The next day (16th) he attacked Butler at Drewry's Bluff. " Butler's army was driven back, hemmed in, and reduced to comparative impotency, though not captured. The danger threatening Richmond was, for the time being, averted."[47]

At that time the Army of the Potomac was fighting at Spottsylvania fiercely and futilely, and not until June 3d, a fortnight later, did the slaughter of Cold Harbor occur. The great opportunity of May 9th, pointed out to Butler by his lieutenants, had been allowed wholly to escape; Lee's rear and communications were secure ; Butler was safely "bottled up"; the Army of the Potomac, sorely crippled, had sustained losses as heavy as they were unnecessary; Grant's whole plan of campaign had gone to pieces. Had Butler on May 9th, correctly taking in the military situation, complied with the suggestion of his two corps commanders, Petersburg must have fallen into his hands; Lee would perforce have been compelled to fall back on Richmond; the Cold Harbor assaults would not have occurred; and all subsequent operations would have been other than they were.

Prior to this, May 7th, General Butler had written a letter marked "Confidential" to Senator Wilson of Massachusetts, then on the Senate Military Committee, beginning thus: "My Dear Sir: — I must take the responsibility of asking you to bring before the Senate at once the name of General Gillmore, and have his name rejected by your body." Nominated for promotion to the rank of Major-General, the nomination of General Gillmore was then pending.[48] Under such circumstances the state of affairs in the Army of the James not unnaturally became in May so unsatisfactory that General Halleck at the request of General Grant sent (May 21st) Generals Meigs and Barnard to investigate. On the 24th they gave it as their opinion that " an officer of military experience and knowledge [should be placed] in command. . . . General Butler . . . has not experience and training to enable him to direct and control movements in battle. . . . General Butler evidently desires to retain command in the field. If his desires must be gratified, withdraw Gillmore, place Smith in command of both corps under the supreme command of Butler. . . . You will thus have a command which will be a unit, and General Butler will probably be guided by Smith, and leave to him the suggestions and practical execution of army movements ordered. Success would be more certain were Smith in command untrammelled, and General Butler remanded to the administrative duties of the departments."[49]

Difficulties naturally suggested themselves to the adoption of the course thus recommended. General Gillmore was relieved of his command early in June,[50] and the ill-feeling between Butler and Smith culminated, June 21st, in a characteristic and extremely sharp correspondence,[51] as a result of which General Smith requested to be relieved of the command of the Eighteenth Corps. Then followed one of the most extraordinary and inexplicable episodes of the war. Grant wrote (July 1) to Halleck, advising him of the situation. He said: "I regret the necessity of asking for a change of commanders here, but General Butler, not being a soldier by education or experience, is in the hands of his subordinates in the execution of all orders military." Grant, however, hesitated "to recommend his [Butler's] retirement."[52] This brought out a most suggestive reply (July 8) from Balleck. Jn it he said: "It was foreseen from the first that, you would eventually find it necessary to relieve General B. on account of his total unfitness to command in the field, and his generally quarrelsome character."[53] The Chief of Staff then went on to discuss the several dispositions which might be made of Butler, significantly pointing out the danger to be apprehended from "his talent at political intrigue, and his facilities for newspaper abuse." He finally suggested: "Why not leave General Butler in the local command of his department, including North Carolina, Norfolk, Fort Monroe, Yorktown, &c, and make a new army corps of the part of the Eighteenth under Smith?" The letter closed with a sentence indicative of the personal apprehension General Butler seemed to excite in the breasts of those put in any position antagonistic to him. The official Chief of Staff said: "As General Butler claims to rank me, I shall give him no orders wherever he may go, without the special direction of yourself or the Secretary of War." Three days later, July 6th, Grant wrote to Halleck: "Please obtain an order assigning the troops of the Department of Virginia and North Carolina serving in the field to the command of Maj. General W. F. Smith, and order Major General Butler, commanding department, to his head-quarters, Fortress Monroe." In accordance with this request, General Order No. 225 was at once issued. Curiously enough the original order, forwarded both to Butler and Smith,[54] read that "Maj. Gen. Smith is assigned by the President to the command of the corps," etc.; in the order as formally made public the words "by the President" do not appear. This order, though in conformity with the recommendation of Generals Meigs and Barnard of six weeks before (May 24), was highly objectionable to General Butler. Immediately on receipt of it at Bermuda Hundred he rode over to the head-quarters of General Grant, and asked if "this was his act and his desire." Grant replied: "But I don't want this." Colonel Mordecai afterwards wrote: "Gen'l Butler returned to camp about dusk, as I recall it, and, as he dismounted from his horse, remarked to a number of his staff officers who were near him, 'Gentlemen, the order will be revoked to-morrow.'"[55] Not only was the order revoked, but General Butler's field command was extended so as to include the Nineteenth Corps, while General Smith was "relieved from the command of the Eighteenth Army Corps, and [directed to] proceed to New York, and await further orders."[56]

As respects the details of what transpired at the interview above referred to, General James H. Wilson, whose relations at the time and subsequently were intimate with both General Grant and Smith, wrote in 1904 as follows, in that Memoir of "Baldy" Smith already referred to : —

"It must be confessed that Grant's explanations of his later attitude towards Smith, and of the reasons for relieving him and restoring Butler to command, were neither full nor always stated in the same terms. He ignores the subject entirely in his memoirs, but it so happens that Mr. Dana, then Assistant Secretary of War, was sitting with General Grant when Butler, clad in full uniform, called at headquarters, and was admitted. Dana describes Butler as entering the General's presence with a flushed face and a haughty air, holding out the order relieving him from command in the field, and asking: 'General Grant, did you issue this order? ' To which Grant in a hesitating manner replied: 'No, not in that form.' Dana, perceiving at this point that the subject under discussion was an embarrassing one, and that the interview was likely to be unpleasant, if not stormy, at once took his leave, but the impression made upon his mind by what he saw while present was that Butler had in some measure 'cowed' his commanding officer. What further took place neither General Grant nor Mr. Dana has ever said. Butler's Book, however, contains what purports to be a full account of the interview, but it is to be observed that it signally fails to recite any circumstance of an overbearing nature."[57]

The disposition of commands made in Special Order No. 62, above referred to, continued in force until the Wilmington expedition and the famous powder-boat explosion of the following December. During the months intervening much had happened. July, 1864, came about during one of the most depressing, if not the most depressing, period of the whole struggle. Grant's movement against Richmond and Lee's army had failed, after excessive loss of life; Sherman's movement against Atlanta had not yet succeeded; Washington was threatened from the valley of the Shenandoah; a presidential election was immediately impending; the country at large was in a state of extreme discouragement; the administration and the generals in the field stood in manifest fear of Butler's "talent for political intrigue and his facilities for newspaper abuse." Six months later the whole aspect of affairs had undergone a complete and, indeed, almost magical change. Grant, it is true, was still held in firm check before Petersburg: but Sherman had marched through Georgia and captured Savannah; Sheridan had won his victories in the valley; Lincoln had been re-elected; the Confederacy was believed to be in extremities. Under these circumstances that might safely be done which in July had seemed to involve a political risk. Accordingly, on January 4, 1865, Grant wrote to the Secretary of War: " I am constrained to request the removal of Maj. Gen. B. F. Butler from the command of the Department of Virginia and North Carolina. I do this with reluctance, but the good of the service requires it. In my absence General Butler necessarily commands, and there is a lack of confidence felt in his military ability, making him an unsafe commander for a large army. His administration of the affairs of his department is also objectionable."[58] Three days later (January 7) the following was issued from the War Department : —

"General Orders No. 1.

"I. By direction of the President of the United States, Maj. Gen. Benjamin F. Butler is relieved from the command of the Department of North Carolina and Virginia. . . .

"II. Major-General Butler on being relieved will repair to Lowell, Mass., and report by letter to the Adjutant- General of the Army."

Of General Butler as a field officer in active military service General W. F. Smith wrote to General Grant, after asking to be relieved from further service in the Department of Virginia and North Carolina: " I want simply ... to ask you how you can place a man in command of two army corps, who is as helpless as a child on the field of battle and as visionary as an opium-eater in council?"[59] Of the same commander, Admiral David D. Porter wrote to the Secretary of the Navy, December 29, 1864, immediately after the withdrawal of the first expedition against Wilmington, subsequently to the powder-boat fiasco of

December 24: "If this temporary failure succeeds in sending General Butler into private life, it is not to be regretted."[60]

Notes:

1. The exact number, arithmetically computed on the census returns of 1860, but of course to a certain extent inaccurate and deceptive, was 1,356,600.

2. An exact statistical statement of the number of sympathizers from Maryland, West Virginia, Kentucky, Tennessee, and Missouri, who, first and last, found their way into the ranks of the Confederate army, is, of course, impossible. It has been asserted that there were 316,424 "Southern men in the Northern army." This large contingent, so far as not imaginary, would naturally have come in greatest part from the " Border States," so called. It would be not unnatural to assume that these States furnished an equal number of recruits to the Confederacy; but such an assumption would, on the basis above given, be manifestly absurd. The War Records contain lists of all military organizations of the Confederate army referred to in that publication. Including regiments, battalions and companies belonging to all branches of the service, regular and provisional, these numbered 279 from the four States, Kentucky, Maryland, Missouri and Tennessee. Included in these were 238 full regiments. If these averaged, from first to last, only 600 each, they included an aggregate of 148,000 men. No less than 182 lesser organizations, battalions, and companies, and all individual enlistments, remain to be allowed for. Colonel Livermore, in view of these facts, writes me under date of October 24, 1906, "I think a larger estimate than 135,000 in the Confederate army from these States might safely be made."

3. "I propose to substitute slaves for all soldiers employed out of the ranks — on detached service, extra duty, as cooks, engineers, laborers, pioneers, or any kind of work. Such details for this little army amount to more than 10,000 men. Negroes would serve for such purposes, better than soldiers. . . . The plan is simple and quick. It puts soldiers and negroes each in his appropriate place; the one to fight, the other

to work. I need not go into particulars." (Gen. J. E. Johnston to Confederate Senator L. T. Wigfall, January 4, 1864. Mrs. D. G. Wright, *A Southern Girl in '61*, pp. 168, 169.)

4. To be exact, one out of each eleven and eight-tenths.

5. We hare census (1860) figures of the population of the States of the Confederacy at the breaking out of the Civil War ; but the Confederate muster-rolls, showing actual enlistments, are confessedly defective. It is not easy to reach any accurate figures as to either the population of the two South African republics, or the number of men actually put into the field by them during the war. The "total number of officers and men of all Regular and Auxiliary [British] Forces in the South African War from the beginning to the end" is officially stated as 448,435. At the beginning of the war the Intelligence Division of the British War Office estimated the total available forces of the Transvaal at 29,917, and those of the Orange Free State at 13,104, or an aggregate of 43,021 combatants. At the close of the war, however, the total number accounted for was 72,974 Transvaal and Free State combatants, with 16,400 "Rebels," "Renegades and Foreigners," or a grand total of 89,874. The British officials content themselves with saying "it is difficult to explain the excess over the Boer official returns [preceding the conflict] unless, indeed, these purposely understated the actual strength of the burghers." (Report (1903) of "His Majesty's Commissioners appointed to Inquire into the Military Preparations and Other Matters Connected with the War in South Africa," pp. 85, 158, 168.) Excluding in each case foreign sympathizers, the two South African republics apparently put into the field as combatants one man to each four and two-tenths (4.2) of their entire population ; on the claim of the Southern historians the nine States of the Confederacy put into the field one combatant to each eleven and eight-tenths (11.8) of their total white population. The relative aggregate fighting force of the Boers was to that of the British almost exactly one to five. The force of the Confederacy (600,000), as claimed by Southern authorities, to that of the Union, as stated by the same authorities (2,778,304), was about as one to four and a half.

7. Alfriend, *Life of Jefferson Davis*, pp. 622-626 ; B. T. Johnson, *Life of Joseph E. Johnston*, p. 219; Roman, *Military Operations of General Beauregard*, vol. ii. p. 665. Roman here prints a letter, dated March 30, 1868, from J. E. Johnston to Beauregard, giving his recollections of what was said and took place at the Greensboro' meeting of April 12-13, 1861.

8.According to the best authorities, the combined white population of the two South African states at the beginning of hostilities was approximately 323,113; the white population of Texas was returned in the census of 1800 at 421,204.

9.The census of 1860 returned 307 miles of railroad in operation in Texas; in 1903 it was stated that 11,256 miles were in operation. The proportion of railroad mileage to area was, in 1860, one mile to each 865 square miles of territory ; in 1903 it was one mile to each 24 square miles.

10. Johnston to Beauregard, March 80, 1868: Roman, *Beauregard,* vol. ii. p. 666.

11. Black wood's *Edinburgh Magazine,* July, 1866, vol. c. p. 31.

12. Vol. V, p. 399.

13. For instance, in the very matter of a blockade, as an incident to war, James H. Hammond, then in the Senate from South Carolina, in a speech delivered in 1858, and presently referred to, thus summarily dismissed the idea as an absurdity: "We have three thousand miles of continental sea-shore line so indented with bays and crowded with islands that when their shore lines are added, we have twelve thousand miles. . . . Can you hem in such a territory as that? You talk of putting up a wall of fire around eight hundred and fifty thousand square miles so situated! How absurd." (Selections from Letters and Speeches of James H. Hammond, pp. 311, 312.)

14. "Vulgar, fanatical, cheating Yankees — hypocritical, if as women they pretend to real virtue; and lying, if as men they pretend to be honest" (W. H. Russell, *My Diary North and South,* chap, xix.)

15. *Memoir of the Life and Public Service of Joseph E. Johnston* (1891), pp. 60,61.

16. *Selections from the Letters and Speeches of James H. Hammond* (New York, 1866), pp. 316, 317.

17. *My Diary North and South*, chap. xv.

18. *My Diary North and South*, chap. xiii. Later, April 19, the Times correspondent called on the Governor of the State, F. W. Pickens. Of him he wrote : — "The Governor writes very good proclamations, nevertheless, and his confidence in South Carolina is unbounded. If we stand alone, sir, we must win. They can't whip us." (Ibid. chap, xvi.)

19. A month later Mr. Wigfall received, through his wife, from a correspondent in Providence, Rhode Island, an ardent sympathizer with the Confederacy, a warning curiously characteristic of the period, and most suggestive of the estimate in which the Northern community was then held by those impregnated with Southern ideals : —

"I think, however, that you at the South are wrong to undervalue the courage and resources of the Northern States. They are no doubt less accustomed to the use of firearms — there are very few who know how to ride, and they are less fiery in their impulses. They are less disposed to fight, but they are not cowardly where their interests are concerned and will fight for their money. Where their property is at stake they will not hesitate to risk their lives. ... I would not advise you of the South to trust too much in the idea that the Northerners will not fight ; for I believe they will, and their numbers are overwhelming." (Mrs. D. G. Wright, *A Southern Girl in '61*, pp. 52, 53.)

20. This meeting was on April 28. A few days only more than six months later both the Rhetts and Mr. Trescot hurriedly abandoned their homes, immediately after the bombardment and capture of the forts at Hilton Head, November 7, 1861, by the expedition under command of Captain, afterwards Admiral, Dupont. All of the South Carolina sea-islands, as they were called, were thenceforth occupied by the Union forces.

21. Appleton's *Annual Cyclopaedia*, 1862, p. 261, quoted by Rhodes, vol. v. p. 411.

22. What is known as the alternative Confederate fiscal policy is referred to, and discussed, by Mr. Rhodes (vol. v. pp. 381, 382). There is in the appendix to Roman's *Life of Beauregard* (vol. ii. pp. 674-680) an elaborate letter on this subject written by Mr. Stephens to Beauregard in 1882, seventeen years after the close of the struggle. In the letter he quoted at length from a speech made by him at Crawfordville, Georgia, in the fall of 1862. He then said: "The great error of those who supposed that King Cotton would compel the English ministry to recognize our government and break the blockade, and who will look for the same result from the total abandonment of its culture, consists in mistaking the nature of the kingdom of the potentate. His power is commercial and financial, not political."

23. Vol. v. p. 107.

24. Cornelius O'Dowd upon Men and Women and other Things in General : Part XII., " The Fight over the Way." *Blackwood's Edinburgh Magazine,* vol. xcvii. pp. 57-59.

25. "It seems probable that the inhabitants of North Carolina were better treated than had been those of the sister State. Nevertheless correction of the bad habits engendered in the soldiery by the system of foraging upon the country was only gradually accomplished and the irregular work of stragglers was not circumscribed by State boundary lines. . . . The men who followed Sherman were probably more humane generally than those in almost any European army that marched and fought before our Civil War, but any invading host in the country of the enemy is a terrible scourge. On the other hand there is considerable Southern evidence of depredations committed bv Wheeler's cavalry." (Vol. V. pp. 102, 104.)

26. Chapters xi., xii., xiii. pp. 119-225.

27. *Proceedings,* 2d series, vol xiii. p. 106.

28. Speech at thirteenth annual dinner of the Confederate Veterans Camp of New York, at the Waldorf-Astoria, January 26, 1903; the annual Confederate commemoration of General Lee.

29. "Thursday, September 8, 1870. — The Chancellor gives a great dinner, the guests including the Hereditary Grand Duke of Mecklenburg-Schwerin, Herr Stephan, the Chief Director of the Post Office, and the three Americans. Amongst other matters mentioned at table were the various reports as to the affair at Bazeilles. The Minister said that peasants could not be permitted to take part in the defence of a position. Not being in uniform, they could not be recognized as combatants — they were able to throw away their arms unnoticed. The chances must be equal for both sides. Abeken considered that Bazeilles was hardly treated, and thought the war ought to be conducted in a more humane manner. Sheridan, to whom MacLean has translated these remarks, is of a different opinion. He considers that in war it is expedient, even from the political point of view, to treat the population with the utmost rigour also. He expressed himself roughly as follows: 'The proper strategy consists in the first place in inflicting as telling blows as possible upon the enemy's army, and then in causing the inhabitants so much suffering that they must long for peace, and force their Government to demand it. The people must be left nothing but their eyes to weep with over the war/ Somewhat heartless, it seems to me, but perhaps worthy of consideration." (*Bismarck: Some Secret Pages of his History,* Busch, vol. ii. p. 127.) To the same effect General Sherman subsequently declared: "I resolved to stop the game of guarding their cities, and to destroy their cities. We were determined to produce results, and now what were those results'? To make every man, woman and child in the South feel that if they dared to rebel against the flag of their country they must die or submit."

The subsequent influence on the American army of General Sherman's famous "War is Hell" aphorism, and its illustration in his campaigns in Georgia and the Carolinas, is deserving of notice.

Lieutenant-General S. B. M. Young spoke to the same effect as General Sheridan, at Prince Bismarck's table, at a public dinner given by the New York Chamber of Commerce at the Arlington Hotel, Washington, in honor of the representatives of certain foreign commercial bodies then in America, November 13, 1902. General Young then pronounced "all the army's defamers densely ignorant of what constitutes the laws of war," and added, "To carry on war, disguise it as we may, is to be cruel, it is to kill and burn, burn and kill, and again kill and burn." If the word "humane" could be applied to war, he would define it as one "fast and furious and bloody from the beginning." He added, "When war has been decided on by our nation I agree with the German Emperor's sentiments and believe that the American army should leave such an impression that future generations would know we had been there." (N. Y. Tribune, November 14, 1902.)

The utterance of the German Emperor here referred to was his famous speech at Bremenhaven, July 27, 1900, to the first contingent of his army then embarking for China. He said: "When you meet the foe you will defeat them. No quarter will be given; no prisoners will be taken. Let all who fall into your mercy be at your mercy. Just as the Huns a thousand years ago, under the leadership of Attila, gained a reputation in virtue of which they still live in historical tradition, so may the name of Germany become known in such a manner in China that no Chinaman will ever again dare to look askance at a German."

At a court-martial convened in Manila twenty-one months after this utterance, Brigadier-General Jacob H. Smith declared that in operations conducted by him as General in command he had instructed a subordinate " not to burden himself with prisoners"; that he told him "that he wanted him to kill and burn in the interior and hostile country ; and did also instruct him that 'The interior of Samar must be made a howling wilderness'; and did further instruct him that he wanted all persons killed who were capable of bearing arms and were actively engaged in hostilities against the United States ; and that he did designate the age limit of ten years."

The court in this case found General Smith guilty of "conduct to the prejudice of good order and military discipline," and sentenced him to be admonished by the reviewing authority. The court declared itself thus lenient "in view of the undisputed evidence that the accused did not mean everything that his unexplained language implied; that his subordinates did not gather such a meaning ; and that the orders were never executed in such sense." (57th Congress, 2d Session, Senate Document No. 213.)

Historically, however, it is noticeable that the instructions given by General Smith were in strict accordance with the "War is Hell" principles on which operations in a hostile country should be conducted as laid down on the occasion specified, by Lieutenant-General Sheridan, September 8, 1870, by the German Emperor, July 27, 1900, and by Lieutenant-General Young, November 13, 1902.

30. In his work entitled " Ohio in the War " (1868), Mr. Whitelaw Reid says of the burning of Columbia, " it was the most monstrous barbarity of the barbarous march. There is no reason to think that General Sherman knew anything of the purpose to burn the city, which had been freely talked about among the soldiers through the afternoon. But there is reason to think that he knew well enough who did it, that he never rebuked it, and made no effort to punish it. . . . He did not seek to ferret out and punish the offending parties. He did not make his army understand that he regarded this barbarity as a crime. He did not seek to repress their lawless course. On the contrary, they came to understand that the leader, whom they idolized, regarded their actions as a good joke, chuckled over them in secret, and winked at them in public. ... In both campaigns [that from Atlanta to Savannah, and from Savannah to Goldsboro'] great bodies of men were moved over States and groups of States with the accuracy and precision of mechanism. In neither was any effort to preserve discipline apparent, save only so far as was needful for keeping up the march.

"Here, indeed, is the single stain on the brilliant record. Before his movement began, General Sherman begged permission to turn his army loose in South Carolina and devastate it. He used this permission to the full. He protested that he did not wage war on women and children. But, under the operation of his orders, the last morsel of food was taken from hundreds of destitute families, that his soldiers might feast in needless and riotous abundance. Before his eyes rose, day after day, the mournful clouds of smoke on every side, that told of old people and their grandchildren driven, in midwinter, from the only roofs there were to shelter them, by the flames which the wantonness of his soldiers had kindled. With his full knowledge and tacit approval, too great a portion of his advance resolved itself into bands of jewelry-thieves and plate-closet burglars. Yet, if a single soldier was punished for a single outrage or theft during that entire movement, we have found no mention of it in all the voluminous records of the march. He did indeed say that he 'would not protect' them in stealing 1 women's apparel or jewelry.' But even this, with no whisper of punishment attached, he said, not in general orders, nor in approval of the findings of some righteously severe court-martial, but incidentally — in a letter to one of his officers, which never saw the light till two years after the close of the war. He rebuked no one for such outrages; the soldiers understood that they pleased him. Was not South Carolina to be properly punished?

"This was not war. It was not even the revenge of a wrathful soldiery, for it was practised, not upon the enemy, but upon the defenceless 'feeble folk ' he had left at home. There was indeed one excuse for it — an excuse which chivalric soldiers might be slow to plead. It injured the enemy — not by open fight, where a million would have been thought full match for less than a hundred thousand, but by frightening his men about the situation of their wives and children!" (*Ohio in the War*, vol. i. pp. 475-479.)

31. Beauregard was at Weldon, North Carolina, from April 22 to May 10, awaiting the development of the Union plan of campaign. He did not reach Petersburg until May 10.

32. Roman, *Beauregard*, vol. ii. pp. 201, 202.

33. In his Memoir of General William Farrar Smith, in the "Heroes of the Civil War Series," General James H. Wilson, both a very competent critic and one who on this subject spoke from intimate personal knowledge, attributed the ensuing failure of the campaign in greatest part to the very defective organization of the headquarters staff. For this, of course, Grant was wholly responsible. General Wilson says: "Without pausing here to recapitulate the arguments for and against the line and general plan of operations actually selected by General

Grant, or to consider further his choice of subordinate commanders, it may be well to call attention to the fact that the organization and arrangements made by him for the control and co-operation of the forces in Virginia are now generally regarded by military critics as having been nearly as faulty as they could have been. ... It was in the nature 'of things impossible to make either the armies or the separate army-corps work harmoniously and effectively together. The orders issued from the different headquarters were necessarily lacking in uniformity of style and expression, and failed to secure that prompt and unfailing obedience that in operations extending over so wide and difficult a field was absolutely essential, and this was entirely independent of the merits of the different generals or the peculiarities of their Chiefs of Staff and Adjutants General. The forces were too great; they were scattered too widely over the field of operations; the conditions of the roads, the width of the streams and the broken and wooded features of the battlefields were too various, and the means of transport and supply were too inadequate to permit of simultaneous and synchronous movements, even if they had been intelligently provided for, and the generals had uniformly done their best to carry them out.

"But when it is considered that Grant's own staff, although presided over by a very able man from civil life, and containing a number of zealous and experienced officers from both the regular army and the volunteers, was not organized for the arrangement of the multifarious details and combinations of the marches and battles of a great campaign, and indeed under Grant's special instructions made no efforts to arrange them, it will be apparent that properly co-ordinated movements could not be counted upon. ... In addition to the defective organization and inefficient staff arrangements which have been mentioned, neither the Union government nor the Union generals ever made provisions, or seemed to understand the necessity, for a sufficient preponderance of force, to neutralize the advantages which the Confederate armies enjoyed, when fighting on the defensive, or to render victory over them reasonably certain."

34. Yet in his farewell order to the Army of the James of January 8, 1865, Butler boasted — " The wasted blood of my men does not stain my garments." *War Records*, Serial No. 96, p. 71.

35. "Lastly, to put such an important operation as this under the charge of a civilian who had never made any military reputation was really an unwarrantable piece of folly. If, as Badeau says, Mr. Lincoln insisted upon it on political grounds, it would have done Mr. Lincoln no harm for General Grant to have reminded him, in distinct and not to be misunderstood speech, that the . Congress of the United States had placed him, Grant, in charge of the armies of the United States for the very purpose of seeing to it that this sort of thing should not occur in the future, as it had so often in the past." (J. C. Hopes, *Papers of Military Historical Society of Massachusetts*, vol. iv. p. 369.)

36. "General Smith, whilst a very able officer, is obstinate, and is likely to condemn whatever is not suggested by himself." (Grant to Hancock, May 21, 1865.)

37. This paper appears as Number XV. (pp. 363-405) in the volume entitled " The Wilderness Campaign," of the publications of the Military Historical Society of Massachusetts.

38. Grant to Meade, April 9, 1864, *Personal Memoirs*, vol. ii. p. 135.

39. Grant to Butler, April 2, 1864, *Butler's Book*, p. 630; *War Records*, Serial No. 95, p. 15.

40. Grant to Stanton, November 12, 1863, Chattanooga to Petersburg, p. 15.

41. Grant to Halleck, July 1, 1864, *ibid.* p. 29.

42. Roman, *Beauregard*, vol. ii. p. 552.

43. Roman, *Beauregard*, vol. ii. p. 108.

44. *Ibid.* p. 199.

45. *War Records*, Serial No. 68, p. 35.

46. *War Records*, Serial No. 95, p. 19.

47. Roman, *Beauregard*, vol. ii. p. 209.

48. Butler's *Book*, pp. 644, 1065.

49. *War Records*, Serial No. 69, p. 178.

50. Butler's *Book*, p. 679.

51. *War Records,* Serial No. 81, pp. 299-301; *From Chattanooga to Petersburg,* pp. 28, 155, 186-188.

52. *War Records*, Serial No. 81, p. 659.

53. *Ibid.* p. 598.

54. Butler's *Book*, p. 695; *From Chattanooga to Petersburg*, p. 33.

55. *Chattanooga to Petersburg,* p. 180.

56. Special Orders No. 62, July 19, 1864 ; Butler's *Book,* p. 1087.

57. *Life and Services of W. F. Smith,* pp. 112, 113.

58. *War Record*, Serial No. 96, p. 29.

59. *Chattanooga to Petersburg,* p. 37; *War Records,* Serial No. 81, p. 596.

60. Butler's *Book*, p. 1123.

2

Reconstruction

5

Lessons of the Butler Canvass

Published in *The Nation*, Vol. 13, October 5th, 1871.

IT is a thing sad to reflect upon, but the world will probably never know the exact frame of mind with which Mr. Wendell Phillips, on the morning subsequent to the recent Worcester Convention in Massachusetts, meditated the proceedings therein of his friend, "the grim soldier of New Orleans." He must, indeed, have thought that a more melancholy spectacle had not often offended the eyes of gods and men. But a few days before, he of "the silver tongue" had kindled thousands into enthusiasm over the proprietor of "the one great, iron right hand," who was at once "the judge and executioner of the Republican party," and who, "instead of waiting, his eye taking in the future, flings away his chances, and comes out to lead the new enterprises of the coming epoch." All this egregious nonsense had been uttered by Mr. Phillips upon the 13th of September; upon the 27th of the same month, exactly a fortnight later, the Worcester Convention was held. "Grim soldiers" do not usually lead their followers into the enemy's camp, and there surrender them at discretion; men who "over the stagnant waters of office-holding wave a new idea" (whatever the process thus referred to may be), do not, we presume, ride that idea as a hobby until they think it may fail them, and then make haste to cut loose from it; men who "fling away their chances, and come out to lead the new enterprises of the coming epoch "--who say, "I represent this, or I die in the attempt "-these men do not bawl and bluster through the length and breadth of a commonwealth in order that they may more perfectly collapse when the pinch comes, and so leave the "new enterprise" to take care of itself.

It by no means needs to be said that we are no admirers of either Mr. Wendell Phillips or the labor-reform brethren of Massachusetts. We have hardly more sympathy with the extreme prohibition leaders, and, if anything, rather less with the female suffragists. Together, they certainly constitute a motley gathering. Their present discomfiture, however, bears with it a lesson which ought not to be lost upon better men. For years they have been sedulously laboring in Massachusetts to build up distinct political organizations, through which they might give practical effect to their peculiar ideas. They have claimed to con-stitute parties by themselves. They have voted for their own candi-dates, and elected their own representatives to the Legislature of the State. however, they, as well as the Democrats, indulged in a "new departure." They all pinned their faith to a political charlatan, and through him sought, not to fight their own battles, but to take posses-sion of another and distinct party organization. In their efforts to accomplish this they stuck at nothing. They systematically invaded primary meetings into which they had no right to come; they turned caucuses into mobs; they broke down all the barriers intended to secure the true representation of popular opinion; and the occasion only, and not the will, was lacking which prevented their breaking up the State Convention in a riot. And in what did it all result? The man of whom they sought to make a tool, but who, in truth, was making them his tools, utterly failed them at the decisive moment. All through his angry, boastful, blackguard canvass, he tolled them along with the fond belief that, failing their attempt to take possession of the Republi-can party for him, he would himself break from it and split it for them- that he would be their leader, even if to lead them he was forced for a time into that minority which constitutes the politician's Gethsemane. They trusted him and they followed him. How well they trusted him and how faithfully they followed him, no one needs to be told who at all watched that disgraceful canvass. A large minority of the voters of the old Puritan commonwealth gave conclusive proof that none of the famous election precincts of New York City could teach them anything as regards ballot-stuffing, repeating, or mob rule at elections in general. And so they tagged after their chosen representative into the convention. All through the proceedings of that convention they yielded him the obedience of dogs; they cheered to the echo his harlequin tricks; they adopted as their own all his gross breaches of decency and decorum; they were prepared either to force his nomination there or to bolt with him and nominate him elsewhere. They got their reward. When the decisive moment came, the wretched charlatan was as a reed shaken by the wind. He, "the grim soldier," the man of the "great, iron right hand," who had led them trustingly out of their own camp into that of the enemy, "to represent them, or die in the attempt," there surrendered them, while he himself clumsily dropped the rôle of "judge and executioner" in order to pass, as best he might, under the Caudine Forks of party discipline. So much for expecting a quack to do the work of a hero.

The good people of Massachusetts, however, no less than the motley crowd of blatherskite reformers, may draw a very significant, though somewhat alarming, lesson from the singular canvass they have just witnessed. They have had a very great deliverance, it is true, and may well be very thankful for it; but, at the same time, they had best look at the danger carefully, even if for the time it has ceased to threaten. What was the significance of this strange conflict? Was it, after all, anything less than the bold attempt of a thoroughly bad demagogue to take possession of the whole politics of the State, through the agency of its discontented factions? Was it not the organization, prematurely and under false colors, but still the organization of such a commune as America would now supply? No reflecting man will deny that it was this, and there are few who will not allow that it came dangerously near to success. Is it not matter for reflection with Massachusetts men that their State, young, prosperous, enlightened, wealthy withal, and as yet untried by adversity, should contain so many discontented elements, ready to the hand of the disorganizer?-elements to which the idea of a personal government, a government of men and not of laws, strongly commended itself, provided only that it was their Cæsar or their Cleon who governed.

Whence came these elements? They are not far to seek. Butler's strength throughout his canvass lay almost exclusively in the large manufacturing towns. Lawrence, Lowell, Haverhill, Lynn, New Bedford, Fall River, Springfield, Fitchburg, and North Adams, all of them among the most thriving places in the State, either showed a united front in his favor or elected a majority of his supporters. The opposition to him, on the contrary, came in a very large degree from the small farming towns, sending but from one to three delegates, and lying away from the manufacturing centres. A close analysis of the list of delegates, and a very superficial review of the primary meetings, show conclusively that this was a clean-drawn struggle between the manufacturing and other operatives of the State, in combination with the Sentimentalist reformers of the Phillips school, on the one side, and the more well-to-do and observing classes, aided by the old New England yeomanry, which, up to this time, has constituted the moral backbone of Massachusetts politics, upon the other. Such a division at this time is very significant in the light of the figures of the last census. As we have had occasion more than once to notice in the Nation, the shrewd, hard-headed, stubborn New England farmer is rapidly disappearing. Amateur successors of the George B. Loring type by no means supply his place as the basis of a political structure. It is questionable whether, within the last five years, there is a single purely agricultural town in Massachusetts which has enjoyed more than a nominal increase; on the other hand, it is safe to say that of the towns in the State which, during that period, have suffered an absolute decrease, nine out of ten are either agricultural or fishing towns. The recent canvass was, therefore, a contest between two forces, the one of which is slowly but surely declining, while the other is rapidly increasing. The whole policy of the State also necessarily looks towards this transfer of power. Massachusetts, as an agricultural community, has no future; railroads are killing it; and nothing but heavy protective duties upon the products of the rich soil of the West can save it. Indeed, between the "pauper labor of Europe" on the one hand, and the bottom lands of the Mississippi Valley on the other, the soul of the Massachusetts protectionist must be sorely perplexed. Meanwhile, materially, Massachusetts has but one policy to pursue. It must, as a community, fling itself heart and soul into the complete development of its manufacturing industries. This necessarily involves the rapid increase of the manufacturing population, and the speedy and total transfer of all political power to the manufacturing centres. The political tendencies of the population gathered at these centres should, therefore, constitute a very interesting subject of study to the Massachusetts philosophers.

In so far as they have been developed in the political campaigns of General Butler, these tendencies are far from reassuring. We had fondly hoped that a deep-seated admiration of "smartness," regardless of truth, character, courage, or decency, might be confined to Essex County. The recent canvass has indicated otherwise. It seems to be a criterion of political merit common to the New England manufacturing centres. While the citizens of Massachusetts, therefore, may well take pride in the good courage and prudent conduct which at the eleventh hour saved them from a very grave peril, it yet behooves them very seriously to consider the deplorably low condition of political morality which the events of the last two months have unmistakably revealed as existing throughout what is soon to be their controlling class. Having maturely considered this subject, they had best, while there is yet time, energetically bestir themselves in regard to it. Should they fail to do so, some demagogue bolder than Butler, and as unscrupulous, will yet illustrate to them the great difference which exists between popular institutions emanating from those who follow the sea and till the soil, and the same institutions in the hands of those who crowd the tenement-houses and workshops of manufacturing cities.

6

The Civil War Pension Lack-Of-System

Published in *The World's Work* in a series of articles in 1911 and 1912.

A FOUR-THOUSAND-MILLION RECORD OF LEGISLATIVE INCOMPETENCE
TENDING TO GENERAL POLITICAL CORRUPTION

"I want to say this, here and now, though I realise the effect of my vote upon this question, that $50,000,000 a year is too big a price for the country to pay to bring me hack to Congress." — Hon. William Hughes, M. C. — Congressional Record, January 10, 1911, page 750.

Introduction

On Tuesday, December 12th last, the anticipated occurred. The so-called "Sherwood" or "Dollar-a-day" pension bill, referred to and discussed in the following papers, was acted upon as the earliest considerable measure taken up at the first regular session of the Sixty-third Congress; and that by a Democratic National House of Representatives pledged to an economical expenditure, "wise, efficient and effective." The vote stood 229 yeas, against 92 nays. The character of the debate, and of the speeches which preceded the taking of the vote, is elsewhere referred to. Sentimental to the last degree, it was neither creditable in tone nor in accordance with the ascertained facts of history.

The pension disbursements in the year 1910-11 because of the Civil War amounted approximately to $150,000,000. Since the close of that war an aggregate of four thousand million dollars has been disbursed from the National Treasury, pensions paid because of physical injuries sustained, or services rendered, or alleged to have been rendered, in that struggle. Should the Sherwood "Dollar-a-day" bill become a law, it is estimated by the Pension Bureau that a further amount of $75,000,000 a year will be added to that disbursed in 1910- 11, or an increase of fifty per cent. And this, forty-seven years after Appomattox!

Under the coming allotment the country is to be parcelled out for the next ten years into 435 congressional districts. In each of these districts in 37 States, an average sum of $400,000 will be annually disbursed under already existing legislation. Should the "Dollar-a-day" bill become a law, this annual disbursement will be further increased by $200,000. In each of the districts in the States referred to, there is now an average of 2600 recipients of pensions.

The natural political result of such conditions at once suggests itself.

The subject matter discussed in the! following paper is momentous, reaching down as it does to the very base of our American institutions — the purity of the constituencies. The fast developing pension system is nothing more nor less than the initial step in what will, and at no remote day, surely become an established policy of general bribery and corruption. At present, in dealing with the subject, members of Congress and others are either short-sighted or foolish enough to say that, though the amount expended is large, and steadily increases, it will be but for a brief time. In ten years the "Veterans" will all, or nearly all, be dead; the thing will then stop of itself.

Nothing of the sort will occur! On the contrary, it is vastly more probable that ten years hence the pension roll of this country will be three hundred million dollars a year than that it will be less than it now is. What has hitherto been done in this way, or is now being done, is merely the entering wedge. It is so safe, as well as so personally inexpensive, for members of Congress to buy votes with the public money!

The order of future events will proceed somewhat as follows: — We now have a "Veteran" pension system affecting, on an average, about 2,600 voters in every congressional district north of the Potomac and, with a few exceptions only, in all of those west of the Mississippi. The parties openly and avowedly bid against each other for that vote — Democrat against Republican. It already involves an annual disbursement of about $400,000 a year in each congressional district. Under the proposed " Dollar-a-day " largess measure, this amount will be increased to about $600,000 a year in each district. Next in order will be the Volunteer Officers, Retired List, involving an annual expenditure of about $15,000,000 a year — $50,000 on an average, in each district. Next come the widows and dependents of the "Veterans," involving an amount impossible now to estimate. If fixed at $20 a month, as proposed, it will probably be $100,000,000 a year for an indefinite future period, and affect a number of households not easy to calculate. That the "old militia men and teamsters and telegraphers and the other men who did so much for the Union cause" should now be given a pensionable status is next urged. And why not? They also have votes in congressional elections!

The system thus fairly inaugurated, the next move, already agitated, is to pension the Civil Service officials. These are some 300,000 in number, or about 700 in each congressional district, which, added to the 2,600 already referred to makes an aggregate of 3,400. Behind that comes the Old Age Pension System, and other gratuity projects, of which echoes from abroad and suggestions at home already reach us.

It is not too much to say, therefore, that, on the road we have now fairly entered, and upon which we by leaps and bounds are so rapidly advancing, within the next fifteen years the annual pension disbursements of this country will amount not improbably to five hundred millions, representing over a million of annual gratuities paid out in every congressional district, affecting no less than from five to seven thousand voters therein.

Under the system hitherto in vogue in this country of progressive pensions — that is, annual increases promised by candidates for office — it is not too much to say that at a not remote period the government will thus at each election be practically put up at auction. Each congressional candidate will travel through his district, hat in hand, promising to be more liberal in the way of pensions, etc., than his opponent. "Codlin's the friend, not Short. Short's very well as far as he goes, but the real friend is Codlin — not Short!" The result of such competitive election bidding any disinterested citizen can with no considerable difficulty work out for himself.

As one of the most sagacious and experienced members of the present Congress observed a short time since: — "Under the natural development of the system inaugurated by the Old-age Civil War Pension roll, within ten, or at the most fifteen, years, the pensioned dependents on the National Treasury, each looking eagerly for an early increase in the 'mere pittance' now 'doled out' to him, will represent six thousand votes to a district, or the controlling factor in almost every election."

In this progressive system, the move immediately impending is an increase of the Old-age Veteran pensions from an aggregate of $150,000,000 a year to one of $225,000,000 a year, or, as has already been said, the enlargement of the annual disbursement in each of 435 congressional districts from $5400,000 to $600,000. Of this large total, moreover, some six per cent, only is disbursed in ten states, once members of the so-called Confederacy. Ninety-four per cent, of it will be disbursed in congressional districts north of the Potomac and Ohio, and west of the Mississippi.

The writer has frequently been asked why, in face of the apparently inevitable, he assumed the not inconsiderable task of preparing the following papers. His reply is simple. Having himself done military duty in the Civil War for a period little short of four years, his sole object is, in so far as may be in his power, to bear witness against what he considers, and what many others consider, one of the most individually demoralizing and politically debauching acts of which record exists, and altogether the most ill-concealed and unblushing piece of political jobbery, corruption and bribery as yet to be found inscribed in American annals. Nor is any end to it yet in sight!

Charles Francis Adams,

Col. and Brevet Brig. Gen. 1865. Washington,

1 January, 19 12.

1

Spare at the Spigot and Spill at the Bung: The Modern Practical Observance of a Political Mandate Looking to a Wise, Efficient and Effective Administration of Public Affairs With a View to a Retrenchment of Expenditures: Campaign Promise and Congressional Performance: The Carcass and the Vultures.

The publication known as the Congressional Record is an awkward, as well as an enduring fact; and, with it at hand for ready reference by political opponents, habitually to reconcile utterances and votes of a wholly contradictory tenor, involves, on the part of the average member of Congress, recourse by no means infrequent to a fineness of distinction bearing close resemblance to bare-faced sophistry. So gross is this, indeed, as at times to seem indicative of scant respect for the intelligence of those, constituents or otherwise, to confuse and deceive whom it is designed. A somewhat striking illustration of this commonplace is now apparently in order for January, 1912, an illustration to be writ large and in dollars; in fact, in the scores of millions of dollars.

The special session of the 62nd Congress, convened in April last, adjourned on the 25th of August. Called in advance of the regular date of meeting to consider and act upon the proposed commercial pact with the Dominion of Canada, Congress, in so far as was practical, confined its action to the business immediately in hand, attempting no general legislation; but, at its closing session, Mr. Oscar W. Underwood of Alabama, the official and recognized leader of the dominant party in the House of Representatives, made a statement in regard to the economies in national expenditure so far effected, as a result of the incoming of the political party of which he was the mouthpiece. The amount was not considerable; in fact, as national expenditures go, it was trivial. In Mr. Underwood's own language, "the total saving in money as a result of the enforcement of Democratic policies during the present session of Congress is $308,836.67." But he then went on further to say that "a determined effort will be made to effect proportional savings in the administration of the Government in every department"; and he added — "This House is pledged to reform the administration of public affairs and to retrench public expenditures. . . . Not a dollar will be appropriated which a careful investigation does not demonstrate should be expended in a wise, efficient, and effective administration of public affairs."

The programme to which Mr. Underwood thus committed his party was excellent as well as pronounced. The effect, however, was somewhat impaired by a subsequent remark of Ex-Speaker Cannon, to the effect that he believed "the country will not approve the waste of time over the saving of cents here and there, when the great affairs touching expenditures that aggregate nearly a thousand million dollars are neglected!" and he might have said "ignored."

The saving referred to by Mr. Underwood, so far merely in the nature of an earnest, was thus, he explicitly asserted, the first step in a systematic house-cleaning policy, both sweeping and drastic. So much for the special session of the 62nd Congress, and its Record. Meanwhile, throughout that session there was, from its beginning to its end, in spite of its assurances and commitments, an undertone curiously and distinctly ominous so far as any reduction of the aggregate of public expenditures was concerned — an undertone most suggestive of the ancient adage as respects saving at the spigot and wasting at the bunghole. While a jealous and watchful eye was kept on the spigot of House expense, the pension "Bung Hole" was with difficulty kept stopped. The opening thereof, it was well understood, awaited merely a more opportune, though not remote occasion. Judging from the official report of what was said and done at the special session, that occasion cannot apparently be deferred far beyond the beginning of the new year.

For present purposes it is not necessary here to enlarge upon the existing pension system of the United States. It is sufficient to say that the world has not heretofore in its history seen, as respects volume, anything like it — anything even approaching it. In the year 1866, that immediately following the close of the Civil War, the national appropriation for the payment of pensions, though supposedly covering, under existing legislation, cases of wounds and disability therein incurred, amounted to a little in excess of $15,000,000, annually. Forty-five years later, in 1911, the exact amount reported as expended under that head was $157,325, 160.35, and for the three years 1909, 1910, and 1911 the average annual disbursement because of pensions considerably exceeded $160,000,000. The exact aggregate for those years was $487,300,304.85; a sum so large that giving it conveys no idea to the ordinary mind. In other words, fifty years after the close of the Civil War, the pension payments because of that war having increased in volume tenfold, were still on the ascending grade. And that they were still on the ascending grade was clearly indicated both in the debates and in the parliamentary action of the special session of the 62nd Congress. Moreover, that, so far as the House of Representatives was concerned, it was not then increased by an amount variously estimated at from $20,000,000 to $50,000,000 annually, was due solely to the fact that, by a recourse to ingenious parliamentary expedients on the part of those anxious to make a showing of economies, action was prevented on a measure upon the calendar — action both persistently and strenuously pressed. Into the nature of the expedients thus resorted to, it is for present purposes unnecessary to enter. So doing would involve the explanation of a complicated system of parliamentary procedure. The fact, however, was patent that, those responsible for the conduct of affairs knew perfectly well that could a way under the rules be found to compel a vote on the measure in question, it would have been passed by an overwhelming majority of an opposition house, pledged to a reduction in the volume of public expenditures. And this in spite of the fact that the measure in question necessitated an increased treasury outgo of some fifty millions a year — a bare-faced largess, in no possible way contributing to a "wise, efficient, and effective administration of public affairs."

When, in December, the 62nd Congress meets in its first regular session, recourse can apparently no longer be had to parliamentary expedients to prevent action. Like a sword of Damocles, the measure impends. It will have to be met; and it will have to be disposed of. The present purpose is to discuss the true nature of the impending measure; the reason for inferring that no adequate opposition will or can be offered to its passage; and finally, its defects, and the character of the possible measure which should be substituted for it. The modest origin and phenomenal growth of our pensions has been alluded to. Both the system and the abuses which accompanied its growth have been described in recent numbers of the *World's Work*[1] The question is no longer of the past; that speaks for itself in the figures of a disbursement in excess of four thousand million dollars. The present discussion relates to what is proposed to be done in the immediate future; the objections to it; and, finally, the substitute policy, which, better late than never, should now be adopted.

The previous favorite measure, the passage of which was narrowly prevented by recourse to a strict observance of the rules of procedure in the Senate during the final days of the closing session of the 61st Congress, was known as the Sulloway Service Pension Bill. As reported with a favorable recommendation to the Senate, after its passage by the House, this measure would have imposed upon the Treasury an additional draft estimated by the Pension Office at $50,000,000 a year. In a minority committee report then submitted, it was stated that, during the last four years, or since February 6, 1907, Congress had increased the pension disbursements by the sum of $29,000,000, per annum. The act known as that of 1907 increased them by $16,000,000, and the act of April 19, 1908, added another $13,000,000 to this amount. And now, a simple amendment to existing laws, strongly urged, granting $30 a month indiscriminately to every soldier of the war over 70 years of age, would, it was estimated, swell these aggregates by $9,000,000 more. There would thus be a total increase of $38,000,000 in the pension payments within four years. An average of, approximately, ten millions increase a year.

That preference in the order of business was not accorded this measure, and that it should, solely because of a recourse to parliamentary expedients by those opposed to it, fail of passage, was, it is needless to say, warmly resented by a large class of would have-been beneficiaries. As one of those objecting to its precipitate consideration — a public character of long and varied legislative experience — at the time ruefully expressed it, while in daily receipt of remonstrances, nearly all "denunciatory" and many "excessively abusive," the natural inference would be that a government now disbursing a hundred and fifty millions a year in pensions "had never done anything for the soldiers of the Civil War, and that this measure (to which precedence over other measures had been denied) was an effort to get some slight recognition for their services."

The 6 1 St Congress expired on the 4th of last March, and the 62nd Congress met a month later. The House of Representatives of the old Congress had been strongly Republican; that of the new was as strongly Democratic. This House had, moreover, been chosen in an outspoken spirit of protest against the extravagant and even reckless scale of public expenditure alleged to have been indulged in — a scale necessitating most onerous taxation. Thus the popular branch of the 62nd Congress was chosen under a distinct mandate — the inauguration of a system of economical reform. The cost of living, already excessive, was manifestly increasing; and a halt was accordingly called to an era of inordinate and extravagant public profusion. With an eye to this mandate, the committees of the new House were in due time appointed. Over those committees Democratic

chairmen presided; Democrats predominated in their membership. Among the committees thus appointed was that on Invalid Pensions. It met, and at once proceeded to the work assigned it — that of a reformed and economical administration involving far the largest single item of national disbursement.

As a result, it may be assumed, of full and deliberate consideration, it at last, on August 19th, reported what must be taken for its idea of an improved economical substitute for the so-called Sulloway bill — that measure which had so narrowly failed of passage by the previous Congress. Of this bill — the Sherwood bill — more presently. Meanwhile, through some parliamentary legerdemain unnecessary to consider, another measure was already before the House. This was known as the Anderson bill, and was a measure of the character usually known as a "blanket bill." That is, it provided for an indiscriminate and large increase of pensions under provisions of the most sweeping character, including not only veterans of the war but the widows of deceased soldiers and sailors; and it was estimated that, if it became a law, it would increase the draft on the Treasury by some $50,000,000 a year — in other words, raise that draft in the aggregate to the two hundred million mark. This bill, it was alleged, had been so to speak, "sneaked" into its position on the calendar; and the charge, which was apparently advanced in numerous papers, led, on the 31st of July, to a somewhat unseemly altercation on the floor of the House between two members, both from Ohio — General Sherwood, the chairman of the Committee on Invalid Pensions, and Mr. Anderson, a member of the committee, the introducer of the bill. Mr. Anderson asserted that, though he might have "sneaked" in his bill, he at least did not "sneak into the corridors and fail to vote when the bill came up for action," thus intimating that the chairman of the committee, claiming paternity of another measure, had in this way sought to evade responsibility. Passing by these amenities of debate as immaterial to the main issue, it is not necessary, for present purposes, seriously to consider the so-called Anderson bill. It would, however, be difficult to suggest anything in its favor. Crude and slovenly in form, it was in its provisions indiscriminate, grossly inequitable and wildly profuse. "Blanket" legislation of the most pronounced and vicious character, it was well calculated to promote mendicancy, destroying all sense of respect in the beneficiaries under it. But this measure has been practically superseded by the so-called Sherwood bill, formally reported, after much deliberation in committee, with one dissentient only. It thus embodies the final conclusions of sixteen members of the present House, ten of whom are Democrats, while six are Republicans. Six of the number were born subsequent to 1860, and three only saw any actual Civil War service. The measure and the accompanying report were, after presentation, referred to the Committee of the Whole House on the State of the Union. Under the rules it is thus in position to be called up for action on any specified Tuesday of the coming session. Over the head of the Democratic House, about to fulfil its Mandate of Economy, this bill now hangs.

In the report which accompanied this bill much space was, for appearance sake, allotted to an enumeration of economies to be effected thereby. The measure itself is framed on the basis of what is known as the "dollar-a-day pension bill," first introduced by the chairman of the present Committee, General Sherwood — "Old Dollar-a-day Sherwood" as he likes to have himself designated — then a newly elected member, early in December, 1907. Re-introduced in December, 1909, it was pending before the Committee on Invalid Pensions up to the end of the 6ist Congress. In the report now accompanying its appearance in a new and perfected form, much emphasis is laid upon the fact that, during the preceding year, the Government had paid out over $700,000 for medical boards and special examiners. It was now proposed that these boards, to a certain extent barriers against abuse, were to be done away with, as being no longer required. This was a measure of economy! Furthermore, it is stated that, during the previous year, $300,000 was paid out for special pension examiners, nearly all of which, it was argued, could now be saved, and the money paid direct to the soldiers. A second barrier against abuse done away with in the name of economy!

A further "economy" feature was that, under the sweeping provisions of this measure, the Pension Bureau would be in a position largely to reduce its office force. Over $1,000,000, it is claimed, now spent in salaries could thus be saved, and paid direct to the soldiers. And yet, even while advancing this argument, those who advance it know perfectly well that the measure they are advocating will increase the work of the Pension Bureau for years to come, necessitating a large addition to its clerical force if the avalanche of claims which pour in is to be disposed of within any reasonable estimate of the lifetime yet remaining to the "decrepit" and "halting" pension claimant. But it is so throughout! The utter futility and falseness of the arguments made and the considerations advanced by those advocating more "liberal" pension legislation are conceivable only by those who make a study of the Record. The audacity of assertion, plainly contradictory, exceeds belief.

Without repealing any existing pension law, or in any way modifying, restricting, or changing the laws or rules governing the payment of present pensions to the inmates of national soldiers' homes, the so-called Sherwood, or dollar-a-day bill seeks to provide that every soldier who served in the Civil War, no matter where, when, or how, for the period of ninety days should receive $15 per month for the remainder of his life; every soldier who served 6 months, $20; every one who served 9 months was to get $25; and he who served one year or more, irrespective of his present age, was to receive $30 per month. All these payments, it is to be borne in mind, were to be made to men who suffered no wound or injury during their term of service, nor incurred therein any physical disability. Such are already cared for by virtue of other legislation. The payments now provided were to be a pure gratuity, based upon the fact that the recipient, at a period nearly fifty years ago, performed some sort of military service for ninety days, or six months, or nine months, or one year or more. Upon the theory that all the money to be appropriated should go to soldiers in distress, a provision was added that no ex-soldier enjoying a net income of $1000 a year or more, should draw any additional pension under the provisions of this act. The word "additional" here should be noted. It is a word of much significance in this connection.

While this bill was being drafted and was still in committee, it was referred to the Pension Bureau for the usual estimate of the cost likely to be entailed thereby should it become a law. The Pension Bureau refused, however, to make the called-for estimate, on the ground that, owing to the section which excluded soldiers with a net private income per year of $1,000 or more, no data existed upon which an estimate could be based. Thereupon the Committee proceeded to make an estimate of its own. By virtue of this "estimate," the possible number of pension recipients was reduced from 20 to 30 per cent; that number of "veterans" it was "guessed" enjoying incomes of over $1,000 a year. Other deductions of somewhat similar character were then made; and finally an estimate — a final "guess" — was reached that the aggregate increased draft on the Treasury during the first year of the operation of the bill was not likely to exceed $20,000,000. But, as the great mass of the claims are necessarily acted upon during subsequent years (the Bureau being swamped by the number thereof), and all operate back to the time the claim was filed, it is not unsafe to estimate that for the second year the draft made on the Treasury by virtue of this measure would be in the neighborhood of at least $40,000,000.[2] The report then goes on to state that under this bill no provision was made for the soldiers of the Mexican War; while any further measure for the benefit of soldiers' widows, etc., was to be considered in a separate bill to be reported by another committee. It would thus appear that, under the measure now favorably acted on by the Committee on Invalid Pensions, the $160,000,000 paid out by the Pension Bureau, according to its report in 1910, is to be increased by the sum of from $50,000,000 to $75,000,000 in the not remote future; further provision being yet to be made for the soldiers of the Mexican War, for soldiers' widows, etc., etc., etc.

Sweeping and extravagant as this measure is, it does have one feature of improvement, and of marked improvement, over previous legislation. It recognizes to a certain degree the period of service — it is at least an effort in the direction of manifest justice. The ninety-days man, the six-months man, the nine-months man, and the three-years man are not all lumped together and dealt with as if the mere fact of service at all or of any sort alone called for consideration. Under this system, which has permeated all previous legislation, men who had never heard a hostile shot, or seen a Confederate flag outside of a museum, men who, as had notoriously been the case, had taken advantage of the expiration of a brief term of service to march home to the sound of the enemy's cannon after battle had been actually joined[3] — such were not set down as the equals in every respect of those who went in for the whole war. A distinction was recognized between the eleventh hour recruit and he who had borne the heat and burden of the entire day. The bill was at least an attempt to recognize the one great essential distinction — differences of time in the manifold enlistments. It had in this respect much to commend it as an advance upon all previous efforts at pension legislation. So much, at least, must be said in commendation of it.

Conceding this, the present "Sherwood" bill — that under immediate consideration — is, as presented, none the less in other respects a somewhat noticeable example of that absence of care and exactness characteristic of all " blanket " legislation. A slovenly piece of work, badly drawn, not grammatical and at points meaningless,[4] it was in these respects in thorough keeping with the mass of pension enactments. It, moreover, invites concealment, deception, fraud, and perjury. Take, for example, that clause upon which so much emphasis in the accompanying report is laid, intended to confine pension payments under this act to the needy. Under a previous pension measure of a different character reported in the Senate in 1909 (Senate 4183), it was provided that a beneficiary under that act should first "make affidavit that his income derived from private sources and including the income of his wife" did not exceed a specified amount; but in the Sherwood bill, it will be observed, it is merely provided that a pension under the act should not be paid to any soldier whose annual income is $1,000 or more. As already stated, it was then crudely estimated that from 20 to 30 per cent, of the possible beneficiaries would be excluded by the operations of this clause. If so, they must, it would appear, be excluded at their own option. No affidavit is required; no provision is made for examination of individual cases; there is no exception because of income derived from a wife. The possible beneficiary is left to settle the matter with his own conscience. Practically, the exception thus amounts to nothing. Moreover, what at most, or in any case, does it amount to? The accompanying report especially says that the bill does not repeal or modify any existing pension law. The exclusion, therefore, of cases in which the possible recipient has a private income of $1000 or more, would only prevent his drawing the difference between the pension provided under a previous law and a pension provided under the proposed law. The economy upon which so much emphasis in the report is laid, thus amounts to nothing at all. It is an economical blind, devised to "save the face," so to speak, of a committee uneasily conscious of a mandate to reduce the public outgo.[5]

It has already been stated that no precedent exists in the history of the human race for such indiscriminate and promiscuous giving as that already provided for under the existing pension laws of the United States, or for anything even approaching it. Of this the British Old Age Pension act is illustrative. This act — at the time of its passage deemed one of unprecedented liberality outside of our own pension system — it was estimated, would impose a draft on the Imperial Treasury of about six million sterling ($30,000,000) a year. Experience is uniform and invariable to the effect that every measure of indiscriminate public giving far exceeds, in its practical operation, any preceding estimate made of the cost thereof. It proved so in the case of the British Old Age Pension act, the provisions of which were most general. The originally estimated disbursement of six million sterling a year, will, in the third year of the operation of the act be thirteen million — the equivalent of some $65,000,000, in American money. The annual pension drain on the American Treasury, because of a war fought close upon fifty years ago, already considerably more than twice that amount, will, under the proposed legislation, should it become a law, exceed it by more than threefold. Nor is the limit reached, or the end even remotely in sight.

It is a safe and good rule for legislators, whether municipal, state, or national, to measure every proposed public expenditure by their individual and private standards — in other words, to do for and with the public as under similar conditions and circumstances they would do for themselves, with their own. When

for instance, it is a question of making a draft on the public treasury, the strictly conscientious legislator would err on the right side only, should he be actuated, *mutatis mutandis*, by the same considerations of reasonable expenditure which would actuate him were he signing a check or authorizing a draft on his own bank deposit.

The matter of provision to be made for those who for any reason are insufficiently provided for, is no new question. On the contrary, in one form or another, it has, as a problem, occupied the attention of the individual man, the legislator, and the business administrator or director almost since the beginning of time. And if, as a result of all human experience, through largesses, distributions, charitable bequests and foundations, poor-laws and work-houses, doles, out-door reliefs, asylums, and pensions — the *panem et circenses* of all times and kinds — one fact stands forth more distinct and indisputable than most others, it is that promiscuous and indiscriminate benefactions and givings are a curse to all concerned. In such case the demand always exceeds the supply; feeding on itself, the thing fed grows with an exceeding growth. Impairing self-respect, it saps the desire of self-help. It creates dependents and begets mendicants.

It remains to apply these rules of action and results of experience to the United States pension legislation. Did any one ever hear of a private individual or a large business concern which, in providing for employees and dependents, pursued the policy which has for the last thirty years been pursued by the United States Congress, as respects what are known as the "veterans" of the Civil War, or those dependent upon them? Did any one, either in a private capacity, a corporate capacity, or a public capacity, ever hear of a system under which equal amounts were distributed in the form of annuities to every one who had been in a public or private or corporate employ, at a given period of time — provided only it was in excess of ninety days — and wholly irrespective of his means, present occupation, earning capacity, or physical condition? A private individual who, dealing with his own funds, adopted such a policy, would unquestionably at an early day be in bankruptcy; provided always he was not put under guardianship by a court-of-law on petition of members of his family or those dependent on him. The directors of a business corporation, no matter how large, who pursued such a policy, would unquestionably be held personally liable for perversion of corporate funds. Yet this is exactly the course which, in the case of the Civil War pension roll, has, for the last thirty years, been pursued by a succession of Congresses.

Custom has habituated the country to the spectacle; and the extreme crudeness, and consequent waste and incidental abuses and corruption of the system are taken as matters of course. They excite neither notice nor criticism. To realize the situation it becomes necessary to get a glimpse of it objectively — to see ourselves as others must see us. Let a case be supposed. Reference has already been made to the British Old Age Pension system. By virtue of that act, ill-considered in many respects and confessedly open to grave criticism, weekly payments are made under clauses necessarily general in their phraseology, to all persons coming under their purview. These of course are numbered by tens of thousands. Now let it be assumed that, in addition to general legislative action. Parliament were to assume both administrative and judicial functions; inviting individual applications, exceptional in character, and undertaking to pass upon each separate appeal; granting special exemptions and favors, and in cases even correcting and setting aside the judgments and sentences of judicial tribunals, declaring him not a criminal who is a criminal of record ; and if this were done habitually and in thousands of cases each year (pensioning and pardoning being recognized as a parliamentary perquisite) such a system, indiscriminate, illogical, wasteful and confused, we would at once pronounce unworthy of a civilized country and impossible of continued operation. Yet that is the exact system in use in the United States. As a result of its workings, a hundred and sixty million dollars were, in 1910, drawn out of the Treasury, and under those workings it is proposed to draw out over two hundred and twenty-five millions in 191 3. Were this not a fact, the statement of it would seem incredible.

The question, therefore, naturally suggests itself, why is such a system continued? And much more, how has it come about that the extension of such a system is not only proposed but is so sure of passage, that, can it once be brought to a vote, action can be forestalled only by recourse to parliamentary expedients? To any one who makes a study, even a superficial study, of existing conditions, the answer is obvious. Much has been heard of late of the trusts and of great trade combinations which control legislation, greatly to the public detriment, while more conducive yet to private emolument — "predatory wealth," the phrase goes. It is safe, however, to say that there is to-day in Washington, or in the world, no influence which, in its power to break down opposition and to bring about the legislative results it desires, is at all comparable to the influence which has grown up and become organized under the existing United States pension system. That system disburses eight score millions a year. Wherever disbursements on any account run into the millions, the opportunity for what is known as "pickings" cannot but exist. To that rule no exception can be found. The Commissioner of Pensions, in his report for the year ending June 30, 19 10, states that more than 25,000 recognized attorneys practise before the Bureau. During the year 1909 more than $320,000 of public money was disbursed among them. He further states that there was a marked increase in the amount of attorneys' fees paid, due to claims filed and allowed under an act passed during the previous year. Every "blanket" act implies an enormous increase of attorneys' fees. A most fairfaced and plausible, but altogether deceptive clause from time to time appears in these acts to the effect that no money under the provisions thereof shall be paid to attorneys. The clause amounts to absolutely nothing. This was curiously demonstrated in the case of possible beneficiaries under the various pension laws after the Spanish War. "On the return of the army from the Philippine Islands, most of the troops were mustered out in San Francisco. In advance of their arrival at that point, the pension attorneys of Washington hurried to the spot to open offices or have their agents ready to meet the returning soldiers. According to the language of the soldiers themselves the rival agents beset them at once, importuning them to file their claims for pensions without delay. To the bewildered youth eager only to reach their homes, seventy-five attorneys seemed to be pursuing each victim, assuring him that it was his duty to file his application, whether an invalid or not. The hospitals had to be guarded against these tormentors masquerading as friends of the invalids." In the case of a single regiment composed of officers and men of exceptional physical excellence, 477 applications for pensions were filed within four months, for over twenty different diseases!

"Wheresoever the carcass is there will the eagles be gathered together." For "carcass" in the above biblical aphorism read "Pension largess" and, for "eagles," "vultures," and the situation with us as respects pension attorneys is not inadequately set forth. For them, each fresh "blanket" bill spells — "Harvest!" And it is safe to say that, if the exigencies of legislation called for it, every one of the 25,000 attorneys practising before the Pension Bureau could be depended upon for at least one telegram to some member of Congress. It is no exaggeration, therefore, to assert that, at a single indication amounting merely to a warning from the sentinel "vulture," from twenty to thirty thousand telegrams would in a single day be poured in upon Congress. The pressure also could be directed exactly at the points where pressure was most necessary or desirable. Outside of congressional circles, few have any idea of the influences which can thus be brought to bear. It is to be remembered also that, on the other side, nothing is heard. What is every one's business is proverbially no one's business; and any member of Congress, whether Senate or House, questioned on the point, would state that to one letter or message of protest against some "blanket" act involving the expenditure of tens of millions, he will receive at least a hundred urgent messages demanding its passage. If, moreover, any member of Congress raises his voice against such a measure, he becomes at once the recipient of letters of remonstrance, some indignant, others abusive and threatening. Most rarely, however, does he get a letter of commendation or sympathy. The logical result follows. Members of Congress are somewhat exceptionally human.

Looked at from another point of view, the political influence in favor of any and every additional pension measure, no matter what its character, is apparent, and even more startling than apparent. On the 30th of June last, there were upon the rolls of the Pension Office the names of over 880,000 recipients. These of course, are unequally distributed. They represent, however, on an average, considerably more than 2,000 recipients for each present congressional district of the country. In Indiana, for instance, there are 4,176 pensioners to a district; in Maine there are 3,773. The six New England states average 2,985 recipients to each district. In twelve other states — New York, Pennsylvania, New Jersey, Ohio, Indiana, Illinois, Michigan, Wisconsin, Iowa, Missouri, Oklahoma, and Kansas — the districts average a trifle more than 2,800 each. On the other hand, in the eleven states which constituted the Confederacy, represented in the aggregate by 98 members of Congress, there are but 754 recipients to a district. The two states of the Confederacy having the largest number of pensioners are Arkansas and Tennessee with a fraction more than 1,640 to a district; but Georgia with eleven representatives averages 310 pensioners only to each district; while South Carolina with seven representatives has but 275. In seven former Confederate states having an aggregate of sixty-eight representatives, the pensioners average 490 only to a district, as compared with 3,258, the average in six populous Northern states returning 89 members of the House. Furthermore, the pensioners in the Southern states referred to are, presumbly, nearly all pensioners coming down from earlier wars — the Mexican War or even that of 1812 — and the provisions of the pending Sherwood bill, with its fifty millions of increased annual outgo, affect the states named in no appreciable degree;[6] while, on the other hand, six Northern states — Ohio, Illinois, Indiana, Wisconsin, Iowa, and Kansas — have at least

120,000 would-be beneficiaries under that bill, averaging not less than 1,300 to a congressional district.

For reasons that at once suggest themselves, no considerable opposition to this indiscriminate but unequal distribution of public money has as yet been made by the representatives of the Southern states; though, in addition to their share of the heavy burden of taxation imposed generally by the national pension payments, each of these states supports a local system making provision for the disabled and necessitous yet living, among those furnished by it to the armies of the Confederacy. Incidentally, it may be observed that some of those Confederate pension measures as respects administration as well as the measure of relief furnished, might well afford material for congressional study. Carefully framed, while assisting the deserving and needy, they do not hold out temptation to fraud or actively stimulate and foster mendicancy. For instance, under the pension law of South Carolina there is a provision that property sufficient to produce $75 in the applicant's own or his wife's name, debars a possible beneficiary from receipt of a pension. Furthermore, it is credibly asserted that in the Confederacy the veteran "who possesses even a moderate competence, who has sons or daughters able to provide for him, would regard it as a humiliation to be offered a pension by the State."

2

Pension Beneficiaries as a Political Factor

and Menace: Those Once Battle-scared now

the Battle-scarred: The Travesty of Special

Enactments: The Conscription Scarecrow:
The Bounty Jumper and Deserter: President
Lincoln on "Rottenness" in the Army of
1862: More than 500,000 Cases of Recorded
Desertion.

Referring, in April last, incidentally and in the course of some remarks on another but cognate subject, to the Civil War pension system, the present Secretary of the Treasury, Mr. Franklin MacVeagh, observed that it had lost its patriotic aspects and now become a political list. In Washington this fact is understood and appreciated; for, while it is true that all pensioners are not actual voters, it is equally true that those who are not voters, largely women, when it comes to political action are probably more formidable as factors than an equal number of the opposite sex. As petitioners for relief, women are apt to be both tearfully importunate and persistently persuasive; men, when not sympathetic, are notoriously good-natured. As a class the pensioners, whether male or female, act as a unit ; and exciting the hostility of the pensioners is to a politician like challenging an organized phalanx actuated throughout by the strongest motives of self-interest. Of this fact Secretary MacVeagh afforded a good illustration as a result of his altogether truthful assertion just referred to. It excited a storm of angry protest, which was perhaps best and most typically voiced by a leading orator on the following Decoration Day, who declared that the Secretary had recently made himself ridiculous "by raising an outcry against pensions"; adding, "if I were President of the United States and had such an ingrate in my Cabinet, I would fire him as far as Chicago so quickly it would make his head swim." Let one example suffice; but generally it may not unsafely be asserted that if any member of

Congress,— or indeed citizen in private life of sufficient prominence to excite remark at all — ventures on a criticism, much more an analysis, of the pension roll, he may with tolerable certainty count on a response in no way dissimilar to that visited on Secretary MacVeagh; nor need he hope for either fairness of treatment or moderation of speech. He may, on the contrary, rest assured that the denunciation will be personal, abusive and mendacious — that usually experienced from the sturdy and persistent mendicant to whom alms are denied. To the outsider, this, in accordance with the everlasting order of things, matters little; but to him who is playing the game of politics it counts for much. It may to-day safely be asserted that any member of Congress representing a district north of the Potomac, who dares to criticize, much less to challenge a measure involving an increase in the appropriation for pension payments, practically takes his political life in his hand.

Massachusetts furnishes an example. Under the last census fourteen congressional districts were apportioned to Massachusetts. The average number of pensioners in each district of Massachusetts is just 2,700. At the election in November, 1910, in which the members of the present Congress (62d) were chosen, the vote in Massachusetts, Republican and Democratic, was almost exactly equal, 203,136 Republican, 203,624 Democratic. In five districts in which an aggregate of 182,000 votes were cast, the total of the pluralities of the successful candidates, one way or the other, amounted to only 2,806. In those six districts there were probably 18,000 pensioners. The average plurality to a district was 450. Such figures speak for themselves.

It is idle as well as false to assert in this connection that the pensioner, in point of fact, has not made himself actively felt as a political factor. The contrary is susceptible of proof. In recent debates in Congress it was asserted that, during the campaign of 19 10, United States Senators went through certain sharply contested districts, throwing their whole weight for or against the respective candidates on the pension issue alone. It was urged in advocacy of one man that he had introduced a "dollar-a-day" pension bill; while against another it was charged that his whole course had been one consistent effort to "fool the soldier."

Elsewhere districts were flooded with letters and circulars emanating directly from the organization of pension applicants, advocating or opposing candidates on this issue, and this issue alone. Statements to this effect made openly in course of debate met with no denial. Members of Congress who had been defeated for reelection attributed that result to these circulars. Thus, when Secretary MacVeagh, in the occasional speech which has been referred to, spoke of the pension list as no longer a Roll of Honor, but as a political list, he used language of moderation. He might truthfully and fairly have referred to it as an enormous instance of political jobbery of the most far-reaching character, deeply affecting, both in its direct and its indirect outcome, not merely the Treasury, but the moral health and lasting well-being of the whole body politic. In plain English, the legislation under that head is to a large extent simply a disguised method of bribery and corruption on the largest possible scale, and with money paid out of the National Treasury instead of from the pockets of candidates.

Take, for instance, the gross abuse of special pension legislation as a political factor. Since 1861 there have been granted to individuals under special acts no less than 32,401 original pensions or increases of existing pensions. In the 39th Congress, that immediately succeeding the close of the Civil War, when exceptional cases of peculiar hardship were naturally fresh in memory or sight, 138 cases only were provided for in this way. Subsequently it became an understanding in Congress that each member of either house was entitled, as a perquisite or special bit of personal pocket patronage, to two acts at a session — a sort of congressional extra. The custom thus obtained a foothold; the usual result followed. In the second session of the 61st Congress there were 6,063 individual cases provided for by special acts, at rates varying from $6 a month, of which there were three, to f 100 a month, of which there was a single instance. The great mass of beneficiaries, far exceeding in number all others combined, were those to whom was granted $24 a month of which there were 2,639, and those granted $30 a month of which there were 1,921 — in all, 4,560 cases of beneficiaries at either $24 or $30 a month. And this by special acts including perhaps 600 beneficiaries in a lump, passed with hardly a word of debate, and no criticism or remonstrance. These figures represent an average of rather more than thirteen special beneficiaries to each member of either house, in a single session thereof. A very respectable bit of patronage, which the average Senator and Representative feels little disposition to forego! The question naturally suggests itself: how would it be under conditions at all analogous were that Senator or Member acting for himself or as the director of a business corporation — much more as a trustee, which last a legislator in strictness is? A breach of trust, such action is a travesty of legislation.

Nor, in this respect, is the outlook alluring; for, during the special session of the 62d Congress, just closed, the records show what may not unfairly be described as a flood of special cases presented and referred to the proper committees, sometimes as many as thirty by a single member in one day's sitting; and it has been officially stated that 30,000 applications of this character are now on file in the office of the proper House Committee alone.

The condition of affairs existing in the room of that committee at the beginning of the last session of the 61st Congress was indeed forcibly set forth in a report presented December 15, 1910, by Mr. Fuller, one of its members, speaking on its behalf. The really curious thing, however, in connection with the report referred to, was its unconscious betrayal of the mental condition, as respects what is known as a system of constructive legislation, of the member who drew the document up, and of the committee which authorized its presentation; for it was therein stated that there was not a member of either branch of Congress who was not besieged with hundreds of applications for relief by special act, there being no "existing law to cover these distressing cases." The report then goes on to say: "The pension committees of Congress, working by night and by day, have been able

to bring relief to a few thousand soldiers, yet in comparison with the thousands who are still knocking at its doors for help, it is but a drop in the bucket. In this Congress alone, there has been referred to the two pension committees of the House of Representatives, more than 20,000 bills for private legislation."

The committee in question is thus depicted, graphically though unconsciously, as a shifting and necessarily unorganized charity bureau, indiscriminately distributing money not its own.

Under these circumstances, it might naturally be supposed that a committee composed of men of average intelligence and business experience would reach the conclusion that, when the exceptional cases under the system in use had grown to such dimensions and the system itself had fairly broken down, some other system — a system based on well-considered, constructive legislation — was altogether desirable, indeed, quite essential; for such alone would meet the exigencies of the situation. Nothing of the sort seems to have suggested itself. On the contrary, all that the committee had to propose was the passage of yet another "blanket" bill of the customary, indiscriminate kind, raising existing pensions in a lump and to an extent which would constitute an additional fifty-million draft on the Treasury. It was then innocently observed that, though this was a large sum to be added to the present pension appropriation of $160,000,000 a year, yet it was necessary to grant it if Congress was to be relieved of a vast amount of special pension legislation! That the passage of the proposed bill would only increase the scale but in no degree correct the evil referred to, seems no less apparent than that, just so long as the old system is thus continued, special cases of particular alleged individual hardship will arise, and importunately present themselves. Members of Congress will, moreover, be just as desirous of at once signalizing their fidelity to their duties and incidentally making themselves solid with their constituencies by obtaining consideration for such applications on the new scale as they were on the old. Thus, the whole experience of forty years went in this case for nothing. The general increase proposed was simply, in other words, another entering wedge.

But, in other respects, the debate on the so-called Fuller bill (January 10, 1911), which accompanied this report, and the speeches — not delivered in the course thereof, but subsequently published by permission in the Record (January 12, 1912) — are curiously, and far from pleasantly, suggestive to one who actively participated in the military operations of the Civil War. Rhetorical, and evidently intended for use in the various districts of the members thus delivering themselves, they certainly are not indicative of close acquaintance with the facts in the case, or even of desire to present those facts with any approach to either accuracy or realism.

It is, of course, to be borne in mind that nearly all those responsible for the utterances referred to, besides being politicians, were born either subsequent to the Civil War, or had not at that time attained an age of distinct memory, much less of accurate knowledge. Accordingly, those engaged in the war are uniformly referred to in somewhat stilted terms as "veterans" and "heroes"; as being "battle-scarred," and invariably as "deserving and worthy"; men who "enlisted at the call of duty with no thought of emoluments, pay, or pension. They were patriots then and they are patriots now"; — and so forth and so on! Furthermore they are uniformly described as "old and infirm, some blind, some crippled, some bed-ridden; most of them poor and many destitute." It is furthermore alleged of them as a body that those who are not dependent on others or the public for support constitute "so few exceptions as to be negligible."

To those who themselves personally took part in the struggle, none of these statements or implications commend themselves. They are simply absurd in their exaggeration. Speaking coldly, and bearing witness as one personally acquainted with the facts in the case, the army of the Union, numbering more than two million, was a very miscellaneous body, composed of material of all sorts and conditions; and this, moreover, was a necessary result of the radically vicious and wasteful system pursued in recruiting its loss and waste.

The original enlistments, those of the first eight months following April, 1861, constituted probably as fine a body of raw military material as was ever got together. It was composed of the very pick of American youth of that period. Those men did indeed enroll themselves in a storm of enthusiasm and from a sense of duty. Enlisting for three years, and at the expiration of those three years to a large extent reenlisting, they formed the nucleus of the Union Army. Too much cannot be said in their praise.

The beginning of a war is always in the nature of a picnic — a stimulating novelty; everyone is anxious to have a hand in it, in some shape or manner. Men almost shed tears if rejected as recruits. But after the glow of the first call to arms dies away, and real war reveals its grim, repulsive aspect, the response to each renewal of that call-to-arms grows less and less in volume; until, in the case of our Civil War, within the very first year of the struggle (April, 1862) volunteering practically ceased. Under such circumstances, as everyone at all informed on that subject knows perfectly well, there is but one true course to pursue — recourse should be had to a system of conscription, exacting, stern, and even cruel. Permitting the fewest possible grounds of exemption, it should accept no excuses. Our Government in the Civil War, however, never dared have a real recourse to that drastic but alone effective measure. Conscription, in the states of the Confederacy, a stern, unrelenting reality, was in the loyal states a scarecrow. Enacted under the pressure of necessity into a law, that law was used as a threat to compel local communities to band together to fill their quotas — somehow! Recourse was then naturally had to the bounty system; and this early in the second year of the war. The frightful losses incurred in McClellan's Peninsular Campaign thus had to be made good.

The communities, local and otherwise, then combined; enlisting agencies were established; and men sold themselves and were bought and delivered singly and in lots at so much a head, like cattle. It was a wretched system, cowardly, wasteful, inhuman; but, under it — and it was pursued for three years — men were quoted much as bullocks at Smithfield — a fair average valuation being, say, three to six dollars a pound — the only difference from the Smithfield basis of dealing being that quality was not considered. Anything went!

Needless to say, the material forwarded to the front under such a system — the bogus conscription system — constantly deteriorated. In the army, this was notorious — notorious not only to everyone who held a commission, but to every man in the ranks called upon to associate with those forwarded under guard to fill up the war-worn battalions. Desertion and "bounty-jumping," having become a calling, were reduced to a system. As the war went on, the "recruits," recent importations from Europe, or picked up in the slums and from the gutters of the great cities, were notoriously looked upon by the veterans of '61 with averted eyes — objects of contempt; they were treated with scant consideration. Yet these, "the cankers of a calm world and a long peace, " to a large extent, constituted what are now known as "war-worn veterans," "glorious heroes," and "worthy patriots!"

To one who personally recalls the events of that struggle — its hard, realistic and mercenary features — the present day utterances concerning it are a constant source of amused astonishment. In skimming over the columns of the *Congressional Record*, such cannot but marvel at the amount of cant and fustian — nauseating twaddle, perhaps, would not be too extreme a term — deemed useful properly to lubricate the creaking district machinery. Any detailed recurrence to the facts and evidence is, however, apt to be denominated "muckraking," and denounced as such. Perhaps, however, a brief reference in this connection might be permitted to such standard authorities as Mr. James Ford Rhodes's *History,* and Secretary Gideon F. Welles's *Diary.* Mr. Rhodes would inform the gushy members of Congress referred to that — "The Government, the states, the counties, and other political divisions were munificent in their officers of bounties, of which a salient example is seen in the advertisement of the New York Volunteer Committee: '30,000 Volunteers Wanted.' The following are the pecuniary inducements offered: 'County bounty, cash down, $300; State bounty, $75; United States bounty to new recruits, $302; additional to veteran soldiers, $100'; making totals, respectively, of $677 and $777 for service which would not exceed three years, which was likely to be less, and which turned out to be an active duty of little more than one year — besides the private soldiers' pay of $16 per month with clothing and rations. The bounty in the county of New York was more than that generally paid throughout the country, although in some districts it was even higher." As respects the "bounty-jumper," the inevitable product of such a system, Mr. Rhodes next says: — "The Provost-Marshal General stated in his final report that 'A man now in the Albany penitentiary, undergoing an imprisonment of four years, confessed to having jumped the bounty thirty-two times.' It was stated that 'out of a detachment of 625 recruits sent to reinforce a New Hampshire regiment in the Army of the Potomac, 137 deserted on the passage, 82 to the enemy's picket line, and 36 to the rear, leaving but 370 men.'" (Rhodes, Vol. IV, pp. 430-1.)

Recurring next to the recently published diary of Gideon F. Welles, President Lincoln's Secretary of the Navy, the following is from the report, written down at the time, of a species of council of magnates held at the White House, September 1, 1862, before the war was yet eighteen months old: "... In these remarks the President concurred, and said he was shocked to find that of 140,000 whom we were paying for in Pope's army only 60,000 could be found. McClellan brought away 93,000 from the Peninsula, but could not to-day count on over 45,000. As regarded demoralization, the President said, there was no doubt that some of our men permitted themselves to be captured in order that they might leave on parole, get discharged, and go home. Where there is such rottenness, is there not reason to fear for the country?" — (*Diary of Gideon Welles*, Vol.1 , p. 1 17.) Later on, as is well known, Andersonville put an effectual stop to that familiar game; but it went briskly on at first. Lincoln and his advisers called it "rottenness"; but now they differentiate it in Congress as only a form of *nostalgia!* The poor lads, fresh from their innocent homes, labored under such an un- controllable desire to get back to their mammas and the vine-covered cottage, that they instinctively sought the enemy's lines as being the most direct road thereto. They were, however, all good boys, though a bit guileless perhaps; but, all "heroes" now, every one, without discrim- ination, is to have for life a dollar a day pension money!

Historically speaking, it is a fact not to be denied that the bounty-bought material constituted a large percentage of the whole Civil War levy — how large it is impossible to say; but it certainly sounds strange to the ears of those personally cognizant of the facts, and is, to say the least, an incorrect use of language to assert that those men enlisted without "thought of emoluments, pay or pension." They did nothing of the kind; nor were they "patriots" either then or now. They sold themselves for bounty money; and they got it! Simply and avowedly mercenaries, they were constantly referred to by the older and more reliable as the "seven-dollars-a-pound fellows." As food for powder, such were paid at the time all, and more than all, they were worth. And to the truth of every word of this statement any officer who had, during the last two years of the war, charge of recruits on their way to the front — and there were many such — can bear testimony still. The great difficulty of preventing these "patriots" and "worthy soldiers" from deserting the moment they had handled their bounty money was one of the problems of the service. Then, far more battle-scared than now battle-scarred, they are indiscriminately pensioned as "disinterested heroes!"

Much the same tone of reckless exaggeration is noticeable in the references made to the present condition of those who served. It is little less than a libel to speak of them as a class as prematurely old, or decrepit, or unable to support themselves, or as dependents, or as a band of virtual paupers. As a mass they do not in any of these respects differ from the great body of other American citizens. It was asserted in the recent congressional debate referred to that there are some 800,000 or 900,000 of these men still surviving. This again was a gross exaggeration. There are in fact somewhere in the neighborhood of half a million; but, speaking of the survivors of the Civil War as a whole, wounds and disabilities apart — and such cases are liberally provided for in the pension acts — there was nothing connected with the service or life in the army which differentiated such in any noticeable respect from those who had passed through no similar experience. The drunkard, the "bounty-jumper," the deserter, the malingerer, the "dead beat," after his term of service expired, was just what he was before it began. He in time became a dependent, in many cases a pauper. He was born that way, and traveled to his destined end; but the great mass of those who obtained an honorable discharge, especially those of volunteering days, were subsequently self-respecting and self-supporting, and such as survive to-day are as well-to-do and quite as sufficiently provided for as the average American. Two years after Cromwell's Puritan army of the British Commonwealth was disbanded, following the Stuart restoration in 1660, the Royalist office holder, Samuel Pepys, wrote in his diary, "of all the old army now you cannot see a man begging about the street; but what? You shall have this captain turned a shoemaker; the lieutenant a baker; this a brewer; that a haberdasher; this common soldier a porter; and every man in his apron and frock, etc., as if they never had done anything else." And much the same might have been said of the earlier enlistments of the Civil War during the years that immediately followed its close. Then the politicians and pension-mongering vote-buyers got after them with the usual demoralizing result. Even then they were and are as other American citizens; and surely it would be a libel on the average of American citizens to assert that the greater part of them, or indeed that more than a small percentage, are unable to obtain even the necessaries of life without assistance from the public. Those who composed the bone and sinew of the army of the Union were in these respects certainly not below the American average. To assert of them, as has been asserted in Congress, that 96 per cent, of them would be paupers if they were not pensioners — a grotesque perversion of facts — is remote from the truth.

So also as respects deserters, toward whom, judging by the Record, a most lenient congressional disposition exists — "amending" or "correcting" the record, the wise call it. Bills to effect this result — in other words bills seeking by legislative action to set aside court records — are introduced by the score on every private-bill legislative day. All duly referred, they were formerly acted upon by committees so carelessly, and consequently so favorably, that the thing grew to be a scandal. The committees were finally notified that the President would feel obliged to veto such acts. Measures looking to a "correction of records" with a view to the extended drawing of pensions have, accordingly, dwindled in number. Nevertheless, our Civil War annals, as respects desertions, are not pleasant reading. As a matter of history, the subject has never been thoroughly investigated; but this, together with the bounty abuse just referred to, would constitute for youthful and rhetorical members of Congress a field of inquiry at once fruitful and instructive. If called for, or if the assertions here made are challenged, the record can be produced. That muck-heap would not require much raking to yield malodorous results.

For present purposes it can be briefly disposed of. It has been asserted that, in the whole course of the Franco-Prussian war of 1870, so far as the German army was concerned, there were recorded but seventeen cases of established desertion. The reason is obvious. The deserter from that service had nowhere to go. His apprehension was certain; the consequences thereof, not less so. In our Civil War it was otherwise; and the official records of the Adjutant-General's office at Washington report the almost incredible number of 508,494 as the grand total of desertions during the war, a number exceeding twenty-five per cent. — one quarter part — of the total enlistments'! And "at the close of the Civil War, notwithstanding the many efforts of the Government, through the promise of pardon and restoration to duty, to secure their return, there were still 117,247 deserters at large, exclusive of non-reporting drafted men." Largely congressional "heroes" and "worthy soldiers" now; and, in altogether too many cases, the recipients of "liberal pensions"!

But in gentle and kindly extenuation of this terrible but ineffaceable record it is sometimes urged that the number was largely, if not in greatest part, made up of men who, having served faithfully until hostilities ceased, then disappeared, or failed to report back for duty, because of their eagerness to return to their families and to civil life. That some such cases occurred is indisputable; but they were only rare exceptions. As any company or regimental officer who served in that war knows and will testify — General Isaac R. Sherwood of Ohio, for example — those men who, having served in the war, served it out, were not indifferent whether the word "Deserter" was then inscribed against their names on the last regimental muster-roll. Proud of what they had done, they wanted honorable discharge. Beyond this, the deserter forfeited his pay and emoluments; he forfeited transportaiton to his home. The plea in extenuation just stated shows in fact only the simple-minded ignorance — the charitable disposition perhaps — of him who advances it. Those who witnessed what was probably the most notable display of the nineteenth century — the review of the Union army at Washington after the close of hostilities — cannot but retain a distinct recollection of the occasion, and of the character and bearing of the men who figured in it. How many of those who there tramped in review before President and Commander-in-Chief is it supposed subsequently deserted, without pay and transportation, in their eagerness to get back to their families and homes? Safe to say, not one!

But, as matter of history, the deserter was, in the army of the Union, referred to with scorn and treated with contumely; and any one who commanded either a company or a regiment will now bear witness that those who deserted from it were almost invariably of the scum and dregs thereof. As a rule, their absence, unaccounted for, was better than their "Present" at roll-call. One and all, they then deserved to be shot; now, by act of Congress, they are pensioned by the score! More extraordinary still, not infrequently a suggestion has been heard on the floor of Congress to this effect — "Isn't it about time to let up on the deserters?" As respects such, the "blanket" pension bill is unquestionably convenient. Nor was it with undue strength of speech that Mr. Underwood, the leader of the majority in the present House, recently referred in debate to a measure of this description, which it was proposed to introduce out of the regular order, as "a bill to pension deserters who have had the charge of desertion removed by this House; to pension men who were never within five hundred miles of a firing line; men who did not serve over thirty days in the army." And, when his attention was called to the fact that the particular "blanket" bill then in question provided for a somewhat longer period of service, he answered with a manifest sneer: "Yes, it says ninety days instead of thirty days!"

It remains to consider the measure of remedial constructive legislation manifestly called for to meet such conditions. One of those who last winter participated in the House debate on the so-called Sulloway bill, truly observed that, if our national pension system policy were "tested by the pension policy of any civilized government in history, such a measure as that then proposed [the Sulloway bill], ignoring the cardinal factors of merit and need, could never stand. The country has already gone too far in the pension policy in confounding the deserving with the undeserving, and the stupendous expenditures for unworthy cases is sure at last to imperil the cause of the deserving. The time has come when our pension policy is tending to pauperize able-bodied men and restrict the funds available for really needy soldiers and their dependents." The facts thus stated are indisputable; but, before considering the remedy, it is necessary to have a clear understanding of the cause of the scandal and abuse.

3

The Pension Bureau an Overworked Factory of Pauperism: Mendicancy Stimulated: Self-support at a Discount: The Entering Wedge and the Flying Wedge: The Volunteer Officers' Retired List: Special Enactments by the Thousand: A Committee Worked Day and Night: A System of Publicity Necessary to a Purging of the Roll of Honor: The Great Desideratum, Constructive and Scientific Pension Legislation as a Substitute for the Blanket, Makeshift, Piecemeal Travesty of Such Now in Operation.

Forty-six years after the echoes of the last gun discharged in the Civil War had died away, it was officially estimated that rather more than 550,000 of those who served therein in any military capacity still survived, and that 96 per cent, of those surviving were the recipients of pensions. Such a statement, including, as the aggregate of survivors necessarily must, those whose term or character of service was merely nominal, those who were in advance paid for all they did, and paid most liberally, those who are otherwise amply provided for, and those who for various causes are undeserving of assistance — and when men gathered up promiscuously are numbered by the hundreds of thousands the percentage of such is of necessity invariably large — taking all these cases into consideration, the statement speaks for itself. Such a showing is not creditable. On its face it is suggestive of reckless and indiscriminate giving on the part of the public, and of fraud and false pretence on the part of the recipients. That more than one quarter of those who genuinely participated in a war half a century ago still survive is, to say the least, surprising. If substantiated, however, the fact speaks volumes for the excellent physical condition in which they came out of it. On the other hand, the implication that no less than ninety-six out of a hundred of these survivors of the stalwart American youth of 1861, are now if not virtually paupers yet dependent for a comfortable support on others or on the public, is certainly in no degree conducive to an increased national self-complacency. The simple fact is, neither of the things stated is really so. No such number of proper and worthy recipients of public assistance survive; no such proportion (96 per cent.) of average American citizens of any class stand in need of assistance from the public. If any faith at all can be put in the statistics of American life, or, throwing statistics aside, if any reliance can be put on ordinary, every-day observation, it is manifest that more than half of the enormous sum ($157,325,160.35) thus expended in 1910-11 was worse than thrown away; that is, if the rule universally deduced from human experience — that profuse and indiscriminate giving is a curse — holds good in this case also. That our pension system tends to pauperize the community by undermining that sense of self-respect always incident to self-support, hardly admits of denial; that indiscriminate giving, regardless of individual requirements, restricts the funds available for the relief of the truly deserving and really needy, is a self-evident proposition. That such a condition of things calls for reform is obvious; but before a proper measure of reform can be devised, it is necessary to have a clear understanding of the real cause of difficulty — the root of the evil.

In the case of the pension system, that root of evil is found in the legislative policy which has for nearly thirty years been steadily followed in regard to it — a piecemeal, instalment-plan policy, gradually assuming shape through an ill-considered succession of progressive "blanket bill" enactments. In other words, while perpetually legislating, no measure has ever been even suggested which professed, much less which was intended, to be comprehensive and final. Itself avowedly an entering wedge, the passage of each measure is forced through by a system of tactics which might most aptly be described as the "flying wedge." In other words, the organization having this legislation in charge — the General Pension-Staff, we will call it — first considers what can probably be obtained under conditions at the time prevaillng — the particular political party in control, the state of the Treasury, and the greater or less proximity of an election. A measure is then introduced intended for immediate action, with a distinct intimation that further and ulterior results are in view, but reserved for a more opportune occasion! The measure selected is as much as can probably be made to go now. As the result of a varied experience stretching through the lifetime of an entire generation, the General Pension-Staff is well advised as respects both pension strategy and congressional tactics. The method of procedure has been reduced to a system. In the last Congress it was time and again asserted in debate that the end ultimately in view was the securing of legislation which would give what is known as the "dollar-a-day" pension to every man who, having served 90 days during the Civil War, had received an honorable discharge, and ^20 a month to the widows of such, regardless of the date of marriage. The so-called Sulloway bill, it was claimed, would "at once put at least 75 per cent, of all soldiers on the roll at $30 per month, and the balance will receive a like amount before long." The widows, dependents, hospital nurses, teamsters, camp-followers generally, and even militia, were to follow, an endless procession — as long as the money held out !

The legislation thus immediately proposed, which would unquestionably have gone through could it have been brought to a vote, would easily have lifted the appropriation above the two-hundred-millions-a-year mark. Upon this the "flying" wedge was directed; but this again was merely an "entering" wedge. Judging by the experience of the past it can admit of no question that if the Sulloway bill had become a law, and the dollar-a-day pension basis had been established, the cry would next have been heard that the cost of living had so increased that a-dollar-and a-half a day was in purchasing power now no more than a dollar a day at the time the measure was first advocated. The pensions should in "justice" be increased accordingly. Furthermore, under no measure yet even introduced, much less made law, has any attempt been made toward reducing to a system legislation by special act covering individual cases. On the contrary, it was distinctly stated in the debate on the Sulloway bill, nor was the statement denied, that, if the most extreme of the present " blanket " measures were passed the future introduction of special acts would in no way be restricted. Rather, a new life would be infused into that vicious practice, but on a higher level.

Every bill, therefore, yet introduced has been of the "blanket" and "entering wedge" character — an instalment only.

The "flying wedge" is then brought into legislative play. All the forces behind every possible description of pension act, whether reported, contemplated, or hoped for, are concentrated in solid phalanx behind that measure which immediately holds the stage. That carried, the next is in order!

Next, thus in order, to the Sherwood Dollar-a-day bill — now actually reported and immediately impending — the measure known as the Volunteer Officers' Retired List affords in its history an apt illustration of the "entering wedge" tactics. This measure originated in 1905. On March 3, of that year. Gen. Joseph R. Hawley and Gen. P. J. Osterhaus, officers of the Volunteer Civil War service, were placed by special act on the pension roll as Major Generals "retired." A precedent was thus created; the narrow edge had been inserted. The principle was at once pronounced excellent; its further application was proposed. So the next year a bill was prepared and submitted, generalizing, but in moderation only, the exceptional case. Presented May 7, 1906, and referred to the Committee on Military Claims, this measure, strictly limited, had a most plausible sound. As such it appealed. In fact, as soon became apparent, it was only the second blow upon the wedge inserted the previous year. Under this bill (59th Congress, Document No. 489, reported June 1 3, 1906), it was proposed to create a special roll to be known as the Volunteer Retired List. A place upon this roll was limited to those 70 years and upward of age, who had, after an actual Civil War service of two and one half years, attained the rank of Major General or Brigadier General of Volunteers, or who, being field officers of volunteer regiments, had been brevetted Major General or Brigadier General. Eligibility to this roll was very properly extended to all who, without reference to the length of their service, having attained the above rank, had in the line of duty sustained injuries of a specified character. Those on the roll were to be entitled to three fourths pay on the scale received by officers of like rank in the regular army. A somewhat imperfect list was prepared, assumedly containing the names of 191 persons reported as possible beneficiaries under this act, should it become law. The passage of the act, would, it was stated, involve an annual expenditure of about $550,000; not, for the end in view and under the conditions set forth, a considerable or unreasonable addition to an annual pension appropriation exceeding $150,000,000.

At first glance the measure commended itself. The length of service rendered — thirty months — the rank achieved — that of general — the age attained before becoming eligible as a beneficiary — 70 years — serving as guarantees, all established limitations. Here was honorable recognition and reasonable reward for exceptional service, long rendered. It soon became apparent, however, that this bill, in the form proposed, stood no chance of passage; and this on obvious grounds. For, whereas, a "blanket" pension bill covering enlisted men as well as officers would affect some six or eight hundred thousand voters, a bill which affected less than two hundred voters only, no matter how individually deserving, was plainly lacking in political merit ; for, in considering proposed pension legislation, the voting strength of those affected is in the congressional mind the prime consideration. The measure now suggested went home to but half a vote on the average in each congressional district; argal, as Shakespeare's clown would have discoursed, it was undeserving of consideration. Though a strenuous effort was made toward the passage of this measure, nothing could be effected. Obviously, it was necessary to enlarge it. It would be purposeless here to follow it through its several subsequent stages. Annually brought up, and ever in a new and more attractive form pressed upon the notice of Congress, it made no progress; and so, gradually assuming new shape, it at last became thoroughly comprehensive — so to speak, broad-bottomed! The age limit disappeared; the length of service was reduced; one after another, every grade of commissioned officer was included in its scope.

A little "log rolling" was also at this stage expedient. The consideration and passage of the measure could tacitly but most advantageously be combined with the consideration and passage of another "blanket" measure in favor of the enlisted man; a measure affecting, it was said, 800,000 beneficiaries, and adding $55,000,000 to the pension payments. This was business! In thirty states of the Union the two measures would, if combined, probably affect an average of 3,000 beneficiaries in each congressional district; and, while it was true the establishing of the retired list alone would in those states probably affect on the average hardly more than one hundred voters in each district, yet they were active and influential voters!

In its final shape, and so accompanied, the original bill of 1906 had thus assumed a wholly new aspect. The measure as now framed applied to all ever having held a commission in the Civil War Volunteer Army, without regard to age, provided only that the entire term of service of the proposed beneficiary had exceeded six months. In other words, every individual who had received a commission during the Civil War and had served half a year or more, whether as enlisted man or officer, at the front or in the snug retirement of a recruiting office, was placed for the remainder of his life on the Retired Volunteer Officers' Pension Roll, with two thirds pay, quite irrespective of whether he had received injury during his period of service, which had to a degree already been provided for under other legislation, and without regard to his extraneous means of support. And yet it is safe to say that quite a large proportion of these proposed beneficiaries had, during their period of military service, been the recipients of larger salaries than had ever subsequently come their way.

The innocent looking, strictly limited measure introduced in 1906 had thus in 1910 become "blanket" legislation of the widest and most vicious character. As such, it was estimated that it would include 22,000 beneficiaries, instead of less than 200 as originally proposed, and, instead of $550,000 a year, it would add $14,600,000 to the annual pension roll of $155,000,000. Though favorably reported, this handsomely enlarged measure still failed in obtaining the necessary support. In other words, it did not even yet represent a sufficient number of votes to make its passage worth while in the average congressional estimate. Nor did the rank and file of the pension roll, so to speak, regard it with favor. In the eye of the enlisted man, the commissioned officer had already enjoyed sufficient advantages; he was in no way entitled to further favors. That the bill should again be recast, and reappear in a still more seductive form was reluctantly recognized as essential. This work was accordingly next taken in hand, and, on February 21, 1911, the measure was 'reported in the Senate in an entirely new and altogether more reasonable shape. It now included all surviving volunteer commissioned officers who had served during the Civil War for a term or terms aggregating two years. They were to receive a reasonable retiring allowance at a diminishing rate, running from $900 per annum in the case of a colonel, or grades higher than colonel, those holding the same having served two years and more, to $450 to lieutenants having served in excess of one year; *provided* that no ex-officer should be entitled to, or should receive the retired allowance until he should have arrived at the age of 70 years, nor until he should first make affidavit that his income, derived from private sources, including the income of his wife, did not exceed $1200 per annum. It was estimated that the first year's net cost of the measure thus recast and limited would be approximately $5,000,000 in excess of all pensions ($3,000,000) now paid to the proposed beneficiaries under existing pension laws. It might apply in all, it was assumed, to about 15,000 persons; and right of admission to the roll without retired pay was very properly extended to all surviving officers who had served six months or more, irrespective of age or private income; a merely honorary recognition.

Reduced to this final form, the measure may be considered as now pending, and ready for consideration by the present Congress at its first regular session; that is, practically, after the passage of a previous "blanket" measure, satisfactory to a much larger number of the rank-and-file, has been secured. That has the right of way! In the form it now bears, the Volunteer Officers' bill is plausible. Nevertheless, under the established and prescriptive system of pension legislation, this measure also if now passed, will in all human probability prove to be merely another stage of the Hawley-Osterhaus wedge. Once it becomes law, the cry will be raised — Why this discrimination between the list of the Regular Service and the Civil War Volunteer list? The limitation of age will hardly be swept away, because the number of the Civil War commissioned officers already less than 70 years old is inconsiderable. The other limitations would, however, one by one be removed, until finally all distinctions between the volunteer retired list and the regular army retired list would cease. The Hawley-Osterhaus precedent would, in the joint names of Justice and Honorable Recognition, be applied universally!

The arguments most confidently urged in its support are, if calmly considered from a detached point of view, the most curious feature in the very earnest advocacy of this measure by those interested in its passage. And apparently those who advance these arguments actually believe in them ! They never weary of asserting, until they have convinced themselves, that the measure is one of right ; that it merely carries out a solemn pledge made by Congress and confirmed by Abraham Lincoln during the first year of the Civil War (July, 1861) — a promise to the effect that those mustered into the volunteer Civil War service should be placed on the same footing as to pay and allowances as similar corps of the regular army. The proposed beneficiaries then go on somewhat strenuously to ask — "How has the Government kept this promise?" And it is pointed out that since 1866 Congress has passed various acts conferring honors and benefits on officers of the regular army, solely on account of their Civil War service; but has passed no acts of a similar character in favor of the officers of the volunteer service.

The passage of similar measures relating to the volunteer officers is next demanded as an act of simple justice — the redemption of a solemn contract volunteered by the Government when in dire need, etc., etc. The fact is conveniently ignored that no one of the several measures referred to applied to officers of the regular service who had subsequent to the war been mustered out of that service. It applied only to officers of continued and consecutive service lasting until those to whom the acts applied had been retired for age or incapacity. No one of these acts applied to those who had been mustered out, least of all those who had been mustered out more than forty years before at their own request and in order that they might enter upon other occupations which at the time had seemed to them likely to be more remunerative, or in other respects desirable. There is, consequently, no analogy whatever between the two cases, and no pledge was ever made which the Government can justly be called upon now to redeem. Regulars and volunteers are on precisely the same footing. Yet those who would be beneficiaries under the proposed act have actually argued themselves into a firm belief that, in demanding a great preference, they are merely insisting upon the fulfilment of an obligation which has up to date been unduly and unrighteously withheld!

A similar analogy is drawn between the officers of the Civil War and the officers of the, so-called. Revolutionary army, wholly oblivious again of the fact that there is no real analogy between the two cases. No benefits or pensions of any description were conferred upon the officers of the Revolutionary army until the lapse of close upon half a century after that struggle closed. During the Civil War the officers of the volunteer army were paid, as were the officers of the regular army, what belonged to the grades they held in the legal-tender money then in use — "the blood-sealed greenback," as the beloved and congressionally consecrated monetary medium of that period was designated — which possessed a recognized value. The officers of the Revolutionary army, on the contrary, were paid in a continental money, constantly depreciating and finally altogether valueless. Every officer of the Civil War who has seen fit to claim it has since been the recipient of a regular pension, the same as that of the enlisted man. No real analogy, therefore, exists between the two cases; and yet the analogy is constantly urged, as if it were perfect at every point, and as if a right conceded to the officers of the earlier struggle had been denied to those of the later. In other words, a Preference is importunately demanded in the names of Justice and Equality!

Such, as respects pensions, is the system of progressive, patchwork, instalment-plan, blanket legislation which has been pursued for the last forty years, and is still being pursued. Nor is any end in sight, or limit proposed. It simply feeds on itself — and $150,000,000 a year of public money, soon to be $200,000,000! Under such circumstances, what the occasion now calls for is obvious. It calls, and it calls imperatively, for some measure of a wholly new character — at once constructive, definite, and final. A measure which will discharge the overloaded and groaning committees of Congress from all further consideration of pension acts, general or special. The framing of such a measure should also, it would seem, be easy; nor in framing it would it be necessary to tax the knowledge or ingenuity of the congressional Committee on Invalid Pensions. On the contrary, such a measure would best be prepared under instruction and for the use of that committee in the Pension Bureau and the office of the Adjutant-General. Then, prepared by experts in the full light of a vast accumulated experience, it would be so framed as to make provision, at once suitable and liberal, for all ordinary classes, as also to provide for cases of exceptional hardship.

The business of Congress is to legislate, not sit as a tribunal, whether executive, administrative, judicial, or eleemosynary.

The first existing condition manifestly calling for attention in such a measure would be a purging of the roll. It is useless to assert, as is generally asserted, that no purging of the roll in the case is necessary; or that, so far as it is necessary, the machinery for it already exists. Neither statement is true. During the year closing June 30 last, in consequence of repeated allegations of extensive fraud, the Commissioner of Pensions has instituted what he terms a "checking of the pension roll." It amounts, however, to nothing more than the ascertainment that, in the localities selected for investigation, the person receiving the pension was actually the person entitled to draw it. Beyond that somewhat immaterial consideration there was no attempt to go. The charge is that in this, as in all similar cases, the inducement to fraud has begotten fraud. Measures of a more searching and drastic character are called for, and, in the case of a private company engaged in the business of insurance or the payment of annuities, would be in use. But even allowing that a machinery, such as it is, for the elimination of fraud already exists and is in use, the charge is made, and moreover is supported by reference to cases judicially and otherwise exposed, that the existing pension roll is largely factitious, built upon perjury, mis-representation, and evasion. Notoriously, it is a sealed book. Within the last year it has been, in private, confidently asserted by officers of the Government, than whom none have better means of reaching a correct conclusion, that if the existing roll were as thoroughly purged as a similar roll would be by a private business organization, the amount paid out thereunder would be reduced by one half.

Such cases as the following, too numerous to specify, are on record and have in course of recent debate been brought to the notice of Congress. A responsible man, himself a veteran of the war, wrote from a town in Ohio that he "could name at least twenty men in the same company to which he belonged who are receiving under special pension acts $24 a month, and who never stood in line of battle." Still another case was specified on the floor of the last House of a man "who enlisted in 1864, got a big bounty, stayed in the hospital until discharged, never fired a gun or did a day's duty at the front, came home, was examined, was pensioned at $12 per month for the last stages of consumption, and is living yet." A system under which such abuses exist, and are practically connived at, is one not improperly characterized as a "system which offers every possible inducement to mendicancy and conceals every possible inducement to fraud."

Without going into the exact truth, or possible exaggeration, of such statements, it should be sufficient that they are made, publicly made, and in congressional debate. The pension beneficiaries, in this respect resembling all other recipients of public money, should be peculiarly sensitive under such imputations. Demanding inquiry, they should challenge searching investigation. The pension roll, it is claimed, is one of honor. If it be one of honor, those who discredit it by their presence should be exposed, and their names stricken therefrom.

The first and obvious step to this end would be publicity. The fullest light should be let on. This would be brought about by the annual publication of a list of pensioners, indicating in each case the name, place of residence, and the amount of which the beneficiary is in regular receipt. It should be by state, county, and congressional district, town and ward, the appeal being to persons dwelling in the immediate vicinage of the recipient.

Against this most obvious remedial measure two arguments are advanced — arguments singularly contradictory as well as futile. In fact, in this respect as in others when pensions are in question, great mental ingenuity is displayed in the invention of objections to any measure looking to public enlightenment. 1 n the first place, the pension roll is proclaimed a roll of honor. It is then, however, immediately argued that the acceptance of public money savors of pauperism, and places the recipient thereof somewhat in the position of a mendicant. His presence on the roll is, in some respects, agreeable; but, savoring of charity, they prefer it should not be disclosed. In other words, the roll altogether ceases to be one of honor! "Veterans" are sensitive; and their sense of delicacy should not be so outraged. Next, and with increasing ingenuity, it is asserted that the publication of such a roll subjects those whose names thereon appear to receiving applications from attorneys, "green-goods" men, dealers in quack medicines, and other well-known solicitors of patronage, and in this way subjects the battle-scarred veteran to unnecessary annoyances; which, however, are shared in common by them with the ten to twelve thousand persons whose names appear in " Who's Who in America" and other similar publications.

The simple fact is that those advancing these ingenious arguments, as well as others of similar character, do so for the excellent reason that they well know the existing pension roll would not bear the glare of the limelight. Cases of fraud by the thousand would, it is alleged, at once become patent, were that light let on. Those who take a proper pride in the presence of their names upon the roll of honor should on this score alone demand that the roll be made public.

Finally, it is urged that this and the other measures proposed involve an annual expenditure of large sums, which had much better be saved and given to the veteran under the "blanket" system, without formal examination or prying inquiry into the particular case. Any private corporation distributing annually considerable amounts in the form of pensions to superannuated employees, or employees injured in the service of the company, would unquestionably consider 5 per cent, of the amount distributed well expended in the work of administering its relief. Were 5 per cent, of the United States pension appropriations so expended it would amount to no less than the absurdly unnecessary sum of $8,000,000 a year. One half of that amount would amply provide for all existing Pension Bureau expenses and also pay the cost of the most drastic investigation, including the annual publication of the roll of beneficiaries. The argument for economy through dispensing with effective administrative work is merely a cover for a public expenditure fraudulently profuse.

Publicity and the consequent purging of the roll being then first provided for, the next step would be to prepare, in the light of the experience of fifty years, a definitive and comprehensive measure understood to be of a final character, covering all possible cases and classes of cases, both ordinary and exceptional. It is useless to argue that such a measure is difficult of preparation. All the material necessary for framing it must have been accumulated, and is now in the hands of bureaus and officials amply competent to frame a measure accordingly. It only needs that they should be set to work. That the ordinary member of a Committee on Invalid Pensions is not qualified, or in any respect competent, to prepare so complex a measure, is obvious. He has not the knowledge of precedents and statistics, nor could he devote to the framing of the bill the necessary amount of time and thought. It should be prepared to his hand; taking the place of one of those slip-shod "blanket" measures so discreditable to legislators, but which committees seem always ready to accept and report.

The course now to be pursued by the honestly sympathetic but yet conscientious Congressman would thus seem tolerably plain. When the next bill providing for an indiscriminate increase of pensions is proposed, he should not oppose it as a measure of relief to the "worthy soldier" and "veteran," but, objecting to its form, he should ask that it be referred back to the committee reporting it, with instructions to prepare a bill of a definitive character, understood to be final as well as comprehensive, covering all cases which a century's experience has shown likely to arise; the same to be reported as a substitute for the last pending specimen of "blanket" legislation. After all these years and in the face of such an accumulation of experience, involving more than four thousand millions of public money already actually disbursed, no measure, not so framed and reported as final, is entitled to respectful consideration.

Finally, a comprehensive measure, understood to be definitive, and as such doing away with all necessity for future congressional action, having been prepared, it would remain to provide the administrative machinery necessary to its effective working. This should not be difficult. It was, in fact, clearly pointed out in the debate on the Sulloway bill by Mr. Payne of New York. The committee in its report had complained in terms already referred to of being hopelessly overworked; it was unable by utmost exertion — "day and night" put forth — to dispose of more than one in fifty of the cases referred to it. In reply Mr. Payne said that, if the committee was not able to reach all these "distressing cases," he wished to point out to them that, by "enacting into general law the rules which they enforce when bills are brought before that committee, giving the administration of it to the Pension Bureau, they would relieve the committee of the consideration of nearly all these cases." To enact into law "the rules adopted by the pension committees of the two houses, under which they are reporting special bills, and give the Commissioner of Pensions authority to grant pensions in accordance with those rules would be far more just than the passage of the 'blanket' bill then pending. The affidavits which are now examined hastily by the committees, from the necessities of the case, would then have to undergo the scrutiny of the Pension Bureau, and the facts could be far more easily and accurately established." Such a disposition of the matter would, however, it must be confessed, be inconsistent with the economical theories, more popular in the congressional mind, advanced in the same debate by a Representative from Ohio. This gentleman thus expressed himself: "I would, in a spirit of real economy abolish the brass ornaments and expensive machinery of the Pension Bureau, muster out the army of agents, examiners, and medical boards, and then grant without question a pension to every Civil War veteran holding an honorable discharge or being able to satisfactorily account for its absence. Thus would millions be saved annually to the Government which it now expends in useless salaries."

The administrative method here suggested has certainly the merit of simplicity. It would effectually do away with every barrier to a free access to the Treasury. The most ardent supporter of pension appropriations could hardly ask for more. On this head, however, the gentleman just quoted is hardly entitled to the consideration which properly belongs to Mr. Payne. That, however, the Committee on Invalid Pensions will, or any other congressional committee similarly situated would, take such a rational view of the subject as that suggested by him can scarcely be hoped; for, under the legislative system now in vogue, the Committee on Invalid Pensions has a larger patronage at its disposal than probably any other committee of Congress, perhaps larger than all others. Able to report favorably, or to refuse to act, on any one of some 30,000 applications for pensions on its files, with the number increased by many hundreds each legislative week, the members of that committee can exercise a political influence most considerable. That they should willingly divest ' themselves of it, is scarcely to be hoped. They can be divested of it only by action from without; but, until they are divested of it, the abuse of special pension legislation, which has now grown to unprecedented dimension, cannot be corrected. None the less, the simple measure alone necessary for its correction is obvious. Mr. Paine pointed it out, and his remarks in so doing can be found in the *Record*.[7]

Tribunals would thus be provided sufficient in number to insure reasonably prompt action on all cases which presented themselves; and to them, by standing rule, would be referred every application of exceptional character. Such tribunals would be in the nature of a Court of Claims. Instead of the committee undertaking to pass upon the individual application, the members of it thus assuming judicial or administrative functions, it would confine itself to proper legislative work. Framing and enacting general rules, it would receive each application for special relief, refer the same at once to the proper branch of the Pension Bureau, by which the application would be intelligently and locally passed upon, and the applicant either refused or given that measure of relief provided in the general act.

Could such a system as that here outlined be adopted even at this late day, it would do away with the necessity of any further pension legislation, whether blanket or individual. The Committee on Invalid Pensions would be at once relieved of its congestion — its groans would cease for lack of occasion therefor. This result attained, it would be of comparatively little importance how liberal, within reason, the provisions of the general and definitive act might be, or what addition it might make to the present drain upon the Treasury. The "entering wedge" and instalment-plan system would be brought to an end; but, until that system is brought to an end, no reduction of the pension roll disbursements can be expected. On this point no one can longer either be deceived or deceive himself. It is always and regularly admitted that the present appropriation is large and the amount already expended, running into the billions, is beyond human comprehension. Yet it is argued with wearisome iteration that the additional relief now provided is but temporary, and within the next ten years will cease through the death-rate. Nothing of the sort will occur. Under the existing system every year new acts will be reported and passed, and ever increasing recourse had to special acts. The future will, in this respect, be merely a repetition of the past. This slovenly makeshift and manifest fraud should stop; and stop now. Were it made to stop, the life of the pension system would admit of actuarial computation. The process of regular reduction and ultimate extinction would begin, and could be figured to a nicety. For instance, take the measure already referred to, introduced in the last Congress, and providing for a Volunteer Officers' Retired List. It was estimated that under the proposed bill there would be at first 21,995 possible beneficiaries. The annual reduction which would occur was then computed, with the result that, while the measure would, in 1911, call for an appropriation of $13,521,393, in 1912 the amount required under it would be reduced to $179,940. There would then remain only 243 beneficiaries.

Under any well-considered measure of constructive legislation it should be the same with the general pension list. To-day there are upon that list more than 900,000 names. Of these, it is computed, some 40,000 and upward are dropped from natural causes each year. The computation is, however, to a degree deceptive. If even such a proportion were maintained the existing roll would practically disappear during the life of the next generation. We all know nothing of the sort will take place, and that the last name will hardly have been removed from that roll when the twenty-first century is ushered in. On this head, the experience of the Revolutionary past is instructive.

Any such action as that here outlined — action at once obvious, simple, effective, and economical of the public money — is most improbable; and it is made improbable by the condition of affairs which admits of easy illustration. In the course of the debate of January last on the Sulloway bill (*Record,* Jan. 10, 1911; p. 750), one member voiced his opposition in few words, closing thus — " Yet I want to say this here and now, though 1 realize the effect of my vote upon this question, that $50,000,000 a year is too big a price for the country to pay to bring me back to Congress." The nail was here hit on the head; but the average member of the House is not afflicted with any similar excess of modesty. In his estimation no price seems to be too considerable to pay for his retention in Congress, provided always the money paid to bring that result about comes not out of his private resources, but from the National Treasury. Hence in the same debate another member proclaimed himself not only in favor of the pending measure — the dollar-a-day pension — but also of the most unquestioning private legislation in addition thereto, and the sweeping away of all limitation of the date of marriage in the case of soldiers' widows and increasing the amount in such cases to $20 per month. Obviously, a somewhat excessive premium on immorality; but it, also, meant votes! Furthermore, he advocated the extension of this beneficent system to cover all the militia of the war period, who, though "never technically mustered into the service of the United States," yet "served their country." Those men, he claimed, "should in justice and honor be granted military status and the accruing benefits." Here was indeed a bid for votes! It included not only the aged and war-worn veterans and the "spring chicken" relict, but that body of participants known in civic processions as "citizens generally." This gentleman evidently set not fifty, but a hundred and fifty millions a year as the value to the country of a retention of his presence in the national council chamber.

The case of this member will, however, sufficiently exemplify what the particular measure then under discussion — the Sulloway bill — meant as a political factor in a single district — *ex pede, Herculem!* In the absence of a detailed statement it is not possible to specify the aggregate number of pensioners, or the number of pensioners of each description, resident in the district in question. The average number in each district of the state, which the member in part represented, is almost exactly 2,300. Assuming that his particular district did not fall behind the average, it is not unfair to assume that one half at least of those receiving pensions were "veterans," and would be beneficiaries under the provisions of the measure then pending. The average amount of the pension paid under the existing law is $15.00 a month; this it was proposed to double in the case of the beneficiaries under the pending measure, making it $30.00 a. month. The net result would be that in this particular district the passage of the Sulloway bill meant the gratuitous disbursement among the voters of an additional sum of $17,000 a month, a similar sum being already disbursed, or $200,000 per annum in addition to the $200,000 provided by existing law. The plurality received by the member in question at the last election was 2,500 in a total vote of 46,000. Comment is unnecessary; the inference suggests itself.

There are at this time two senatorial scandals exciting much public attention. Of these, one involves the use made of a fund of $50,000 raised to effect the result; the other the use made of a sum of $117,000 furnished by the successful candidate for senatorial honors. The two amounts seem large; the last so excessive as to be scandalous. Here, however, is a sum of $200,000 a year — $400,000 for a single congressional term — voted by a member out of the National Treasury "to bring me back to Congress." And in his view, even this does not suffice! The alleged corruption funds so interminably discussed in the Lorimer and Stephenson cases sink into insignificance.

As already observed at the commencement of this series of papers, the party of political opposition elected under a mandate to restrict a too profuse public expenditure, is now in control of the National House of Representatives. Measures are pending looking to the increase of the present appropriation for payment of pensions merely because of the age of the recipients thereof, from $157,000,000 a year to $225,000,000 and more. "Progressive" measures are in agitation and warmly advocated which, if they become law, would increase this amount to $250,000,000. An average sum of $600,000 to be each year gratuitously disbursed in every congressional district of the entire country! The measure immediately impending involves the additional gratuitous annual disbursement of approximately $175,000 in each of the congressional districts of the more northern section of the country; the more southern section will not participate in it to any considerable extent. Each of its districts may possibly get from it $2,000 a year — crumbs from the table! At the close of the opening session of the present Congress, Mr. Underwood, the leader of the Democratic party, on the floor of the House declared, in language already quoted, that "This House is pledged to reform the administration of public affairs and to retrench public expenditures. . . . Not a dollar will be appropriated which a careful investigation does not demonstrate should be expended in a wise, efficient and effective administration of public affairs." The issue will soon be presented, and it remains to be seen whether the gratuitous expenditure of seventy-five millions a year in addition to the $157,000,000 already provided, "to bring Me back to Congress," is in the estimation of a majority of the present House of Representatives, a sum "expended in a wise, efficient and effective administration of public affairs."

Appendix

PENSIONS GRANTED BY SPECIAL ACT DURING THE THIRD SESSION OF THE SIXTY-FIRST CONGRESS

RATES SPECIFIED	NUMBER GRANTED	RATES SPECIFIED	NUMBER GRANTED
$60	1	$14	1
$55	1	$12	211
$50	44	$10	3
$40	84	$6	4
$36	132	Inoperative:	
$35	4	$50	2
$30	1,116	$36	3
$27	1	$30	20
$25	14	$24	16
$24	1,636	$20	3
$20	212	$15	1
$18	1	$12	3
$17	6		
$16	58	Total	3,586
$15	9		

PENSIONS OF THE SEVERAL WARS AND OF THE PEACE ESTABLISHMENT

The amounts that have been paid for pensions to soldiers, sailors, and marines, their widows, minor children, and dependent relatives on account of military and naval service in the several wars and in the regular service since the foundation of the Government to June 30, 1911, are as follows:

War of the Revolution (estimate)	$70,000,000.00
War of 1812 (service pension)	45,853,024.19
Indian Wars (service pension)	11,192,205.52
War with Mexico (service pension)	45,279,686.83
Civil War	3,985,719,836.93
War with Spain and insurrection in Philippine Islands	34,142,976.37
Regular establishment	21,705,852.33
Unclassified	16,488,147.99
Total disbursements for pensions	$4,230,381,730.16

DISBURSEMENTS FOR PENSIONS AND FOR MAINTENANCE OF PENSION SYSTEM, 1866 TO 1911

FISCAL YEAR	PAID AS PENSIONS	COST, MAINTENANCE AND EXPENSES	TOTAL	NUMBER OF PENSIONERS
1866	$15,450,549.88	$407,165.00	$15,857,714.88	126,722
1867	20,784,789.69	490,977.35	21,275,767.04	155,474
1868	23,101,509.36	553,020.34	23,654,529.70	169,643
1869	28,513,247.27	564,526.81	29,077,774.08	187,963
1870	29,351,488.78	600,997.86	29,952,486.64	198,686
1871	28,518,792.62	863,079.00	29,381,871.62	207,495
1872	29,752,746.81	951,253.00	30,703,999.81	232,229
1873	26,982,063.89	1,003,200.64	27,985,264.53	238,411
1874	30,206,778.99	966,794.13	31,173,573.12	236,241
1875	29,270,404.76	982,695.35	30,253,100.11	234,821
1876	27,936,209.53	1,015,078.81	28,951,288.34	232,137
1877	28,182,821.72	1,034,459.33	29,217,281.05	232,104
1878	26,786,009.44	1,032,500.09	27,818,509.53	223,998
1879	33,664,428.92	837,734.14	34,502,163.06	242,755
1880	56,689,229.08	935,027.28	57,624,256.36	250,802
1881	50,583,405.35	1,072,059.64	51,655,464.99	268,830
1882	54,313,172.05	1,466,236.01	55,779,408.06	285,697
1883	60,427,573.81	2,591,648.29	63,019,222.10	303,658
1884	57,912,387.47	2,385,181.00	60,747,568.47	322,756
1885	65,171,937.12	3,392,576.34	68,564,513.46	345,125
1886	64,091,142.90	3,245,016.61	67,336,159.51	365,783
1887	73,752,997.08	3,753,400.91	77,506,397.99	406,007
1888	78,950,501.67	3,515,057.27	82,465,558.94	452,557
1889	88,842,720.58	3,466,968.40	92,309,688.98	489,725
1890	106,093,850.39	3,526,382.13	109,620,232.52	537,944
1891	117,312,690.50	4,700,636.44	122,013,326.94	676,160
1892	139,394,147.11	4,898,665.80	144,292,812.91	876,068
1893	156,906,637.94	4,867,734.42	161,774,372.36	966,012
1894	139,986,726.17	3,963,976.31	143,950,702.48	969,544
1895	139,812,294.30	4,338,020.21	144,150,314.51	970,524
1896	138,220,704.46	3,991,375.61	142,212,080.07	970,678
1897	139,949,717.35	3,987,783.07	143,937,500.42	976,014
1898	144,651,879.80	4,114,091.46	148,765,971.26	993,714
1899	138,355,052.95	4,147,517.73	142,502,570.68	991,519
1900	138,462,130.65	3,841,706.74	142,303,887.39	993,529
1901	138,531,483.84	3,868,795.44	142,400,279.28	997,735
1902	137,504,267.99	3,831,378.96	141,335,646.95	999,446
1903	137,759,653.71	3,993,216.79	141,752,870.50	996,545
1904	141,093,571.49	3,849,366.25	144,942,937.74	994,762
1905	141,142,861.33	3,721,832.82	144,864,694.15	998,441
1906	139,000,288.25	3,523,269.51	142,523,557.76	985,971
1907	138,155,412.46	3,309,110.44	141,464,522.90	967,371
1908	153,093,086.27	2,800,963.36	155,894,049.63	951,687
1909	161,973,703.77	2,852,583.73	164,826,287.50	946,194
1910	159,974,056.08	2,657,673.86	162,631,729.94	921,083
1911	157,325,160.35	2,517,127.06	159,842,287.41	892,098
Total	4,133,936,285.93	120,879,861.74	4,254,816,147.67	

PENSIONERS ON THE ROLL JUNE 30, 1911, AND JUNE 30, 1910

	1911	1910	GAIN	LOSS
Revolutionary War:				
Daughter	....	1	....	1
War of 1812:				
Widows	279	338	....	59
Indian Wars:				
Survivors	1,387	1,560	....	173
Widows	2,629	2,822	....	193
War with Mexico:				
Survivors	1,639	2,042	....	403
Widows	5,982	6,359	....	377
Civil War:				
Act Feb. 6, 1907 —				
Survivors	356,830	362,433	....	5,603
General Law —				
Invalids	113,063	121,581	....	8,518
Widows	67,509	70,587	....	3,078
Minor Children	385	445	....	60
Mothers	1,877	2,391	....	514
Fathers	278	368	....	90
Brothers, sisters, sons, and daughters	353	300	53	....
Helpless children	508	533	....	25
Act June 27, 1890 —				
Invalids	59,991	78,601	....	18,610
Minor children	3,983	4,009	....	26
Helpless children	375	335	40	....
Act Apr. 19, 1908 —				
Widows	228,198	220,826	7,372	....
Army nurses	406	442	....	36
War with Spain:				
Invalids	23,383	22,783	600	....
Widows	1,217	1,183	34	....
Minor children	326	330	....	4
Mothers	3,032	3,072	....	40
Fathers	522	512	10	....
Brothers, sisters, sons, and daughters	9	7	2	....
Helpless children	1	2	....	1
Regular establishment:				
Invalids	13,757	13,180	577	....
Widows	2,799	2,727	72	....
Minor children	149	136	13	....
Mothers	1,066	1,011	55	....
Fathers	152	152	....	....
Brothers, sisters, sons, and daughters	8	7	1	....
Helpless children	5	8	....	3
Total	892,098	921,083	8,829	37,814
Net loss	....	....	....	28,985

The number of soldiers and sailors on the pension roll at the close of the year was 570,050, the number of dependents and widows was 321,642, and the number of army nurses was 406.

Notes:

1. See the series of five articles entitled "The Pension Carnival," by William Bayard Hale in the issues of the *World's Work* for October, November, and December, 1910, and January and February, 1911.

2. Subsequently, the Secretary of the Interior, in an official communication addressed to the Hon. P. J. McCumber, Chairman of the Senate Committee on Pensions, estimated the aggregate number of pensioners for the several periods of service prescribed in this measure at 471,336, and the total increase of pension payments per annum at $75,651,548. The average increase per annum per pensioner was fixed at $106.50. It was further estimated that the number of those entitled to a rate of $30 per month would be 357,474, implying an annual disbursement on their account alone of $128,690,640. These totals are so considerable as to carry no significance to the average mind. Meanwhile, by way of comparison, it may be observed that the total amount paid out since the foundation of the Government on account of the War of Independence up to this time is estimated at 170,000,000, or less than the mere increase provided for by one year's operation of the Sherwood "Dollar-a-day" bill.

3. As a matter of practical experience, and speaking from the strictly military point of view, the three, six, and nine months organizations of the Civil War were worse than useless. Costly in point of money, they had a demoralizing effect upon the armies in which they served. Of use as a training-school for reenlistments for longer terms, these organizations in themselves did not know how to march, and could not be depended upon to fight. In other words, the periods of their enlistments did not afford time in which to ripen and harden them for the real work of warfare. There is in the files of the State Department a curious letter, incidentally bearing on this subject, addressed by John Lolhrop Motley to Mr. Seward, the Secretary of State. Written from England a few months only after the battle of Bull Run, Mr. Motley therein gave an account of a conversation held with Earl Russell, at that time the British Foreign Secretary. Referring to the first Bull Run, Earl Russell then said he "thought that much less effect had been produced

in England by the defeat and the rout than by the circumstance of so many regiments leaving on the eve of active operations because their term of enlistment had expired." As respects these short-term organizations, this was true throughout the entire conflict. They could not be depended upon. Those composing them are, however, now clamorous applicants for "more liberal pensions" in consideration of services which, as a rule, were of less than no real military value.

4. See speech of Mr. Evans of Illinois, December 9, 191 1, *Record*, 62d Congress, Second Session, pp. 144-45.

5. Subsequently, this provision was stricken from the bill by a vote of 157 yeas to 93 nays. This action was markedly characteristic of the temper of the House throughout the debate on the Sherwood Bill in the following December. Any effort to limit the aggregate disbursement or to reduce in any way the number of benficiaries under the act was manifestly repugnant to a majority of the body elected under a direct mandate to reduce public expenditures. In the course of the debate attention was emphatically called to this by Mr. Fitzgerald of New York, who said of the Sherwood Bill: — "Its enactment sounds the death knell of the hopes of the Democratic party successfully to reduce expenditures and to lower substantially tariff taxes." *Record*. December 12, 191 1, page 221.

6. Less than 6 per cent, of the total amount paid out for pensions is disbursed in ten states which include 25 per cent, of the whole number of congressional districts. This fact accounts for the extreme eagerness of the present House of Representatives to make most liberal provision in any pension act that might be passed for the surviving "veterans" of the Mexican War. It was desired to conciliate the states of the old Confederacy, giving them what is known in Washington as their "share of the pork." On this subject Mr. Edwards of Georgia, made some exceptionally well considered and suggestive remarks in the course of the final debate on the Sherwood bill. (*Record*, December 1 2, 1 9 1 1 , pp. 23 5-6.)

7. The speech of Mr. Payne is in the Record of January 17, 1911;
pp. 10, 33 — 34. The rules referred to of the Committee on Invalid
Pensions are to be found in the *Record* of January 16, 1911; p. 958.

7

Reform in City Government

Published in *The Proportional Representation Review*, Vol. 1, in March of 1894.

Few deny that in the matter of municipal government of large centers of population there is something wrong in our body politic-something wrong, and so seriously wrong as to be indicative even of political blood poisoning,-political "plague spots" some observers have called them. Without going so far as this in his language; Prof. Bryce, in that work of his on America, which has attracted so much attention, adopting an illustration from Dante, likens the United States in the matter of city government to a sick man tossing upon a bed of pain and restlessly turning from side to side, but no where finding relief.

There is a general consensus of opinion to the effect that one marked trouble with our city governments is that the best men in our great civic committees,—those who are at the front in the ordinary transactions of life when any work of moment is to be done,-appear less frequently than they should, or even scarcely at all, in the departments of municipal affairs, especially in the legislative departments;

and so the management of those affairs, by what seems to be a natural process of gravitation, falls into inferior hands; witness New York.

The first question then is-Why this is thus? The second question will be-What can be done to remedy it? My own belief is that the disorder under which our municipalities are suffering is due to an excess of localism, The idea of territorial representation has been carried too far; and resulted, as when looked at coolly, it is seen it must result, when carried to excess, in a species of petty provincialism,—a narrowminded disregard of the best interests of a large whole, in a morbid watchfullness over the supposed immediate needs of a small part of the whole. This particular form of political disease might be well enough defined as the malady of ward politics. Ward politics lead naturally to an eruption on the surface of the body politic known best as ward politicians; so the symp- toms I have alluded to are the methods employed by ward politicians and the results to which those methods lead. I do not believe there has been any falling off in public spirit. On the contrary, as the service everywhere rendered on our un-paid commissions conclusively shows, there never was a time when the men most regarded in private life came forward more freely in response to a public call. The trouble is not that such men refuse to serve in municipal life, so to speak, perform their tour of duty; it is that the matters are so arranged and so managed that they are not called upon to perform it. If this is the case, and I think it undeniably is the case, the fault is in the machinery and not inherent. That which is needed is there; the problem is how to get at it.

Assuming this diagnosis to be correct, the next question is-How did the trouble originate? It will then remain to consider how, if at all, it may be corrected. Such observations as I have made leads me to believe that the trouble may have originated, and probably did originate, in the fact that our cities in their original organization departed in a most unnecessary degree from the fundamental lines of our municipal development. It is a thing by no means generally ap-preciated that our whole municipal organization-the New England town of which so much has been said-began in a business corporation.

Not only is this true of the Massachusetts town, it is equally true of the Commonwealth itself. Massachusetts originated in a purely business corporation, just as much a business corporation as any bank or manufacturing company, or railway company, or insurance company in the state to-day. The very names and titles preserved bear witness to this fact. The company of Massachusetts Bay was organized at about the same time of the Bank of England and the East India Company. Like the Bank of England and the East India Company it had a governor who was what we should now call the president of the corporation, and it had a General Court, which was in fact the stockholders' meeting. The stockholders assembled in that General Court to transact company business. Even to-day in London they are talking of the governor and directors of the Bank of England; and we read of the General Courts of the stockholders of the East India company. The commonwealth developed, therefore, from a business corporation. In like manner our towns were in the beginning similar corporations" plantations"— as they were termed, or land companies as we should call them. They, too, had their general courts, which subsequently became town meetings; and in those courts the stockholders assembled, choosing a board of directors, who a little later on were known as selectmen. This organization lasted, giving general satisfaction, until the body of stockholders became in some cases too large to meet in their general courts, and there transact business. Then, unfortunately, instead of pursuing the course which other business corporations—banks and railroads and manufacturing companies have pursued when they reached this stage, the people became possessed with the idea that a city government must in some manner resemble the government of a state or a nation; and so it became a body politic, instead of remaining a business corporation. Our city governments did not develop along the original and simple business lines, they followed the analogies of the more complicated political system, that of the state or of the United States, dividing themselves up into petty representative districts called wards, having two legislative chambers, and generally seeking to make the machine as complicated as possible through systems of checks and balances. The result we now see naturally followed. The bullfrog sped the ox, but for all that when he opened his mouth he emitted only a croak. So, with us, sixty years ago, the little body politic was modeled on the great body politic; but, naturally enough it evolved in time only the little "ward boss" and not the great civic statesman. It had to be so. It was only the inevitable which occurred. Yet we wonder at it! The municipal "boss" is a mere symptom of the deeper seated ward-line disease; for municipal ward-lines inevitably lead to ward politics; ward politics to ward politicians. If the diagnosis is correct the first step toward improvement is the breaking up, the utter abolishing of ward lines, and a return to that original system under which business corporations still elect their directors—that is, the system of election by general ticket, and the choice of a legislative board by the whole body of stock- holders from the whole body of stockholders. No man should represent a given section of brick and mortar, including such and such streets and alleys. Each citizen should have the right to name those who are to represent him from the whole body of citizens.

It will naturally be objected that under a system of this sort the dominant party would elect the entire city government, that the individual would be extinguished, and the power of influencing results would be taken from the smaller divisions, where it now is, and transferred to the whole. If such results really followed a return to the simple corporation plan, the idea of returning to it could not for a moment be entertained. Fortunately, it is not so, it is in no degree so. Methods have been devised and are now in operation in Belgium and Switzerland which obviate all these difficulties, and, if utilized in municipal affairs, would enable the body of those composing each community to bring the best men in it into the management of those affairs.

These devices are the various forms of proportional representation, having as their cardinal principles the two requirements that the voting shall be done from the city at large and the representatives shall be distributed among the various political bodies or groups in proportion to the votes polled by them respectively. There need be little contention regarding the particular method employed so long as it embodies these two requirements. We may adopt the Limited Vote, which allows the citizen to vote for a certain part of the whole number, fifteen out of twenty-one, and allow the voter to cumulate his fifteen votes as he pleases. Or we may have the Free List system, which is now in operation in Switzerland and Belgium. This method allows of the voting for party nominations, as is now done in this country, and then apportions the successful candidates among the several parties in proportion to the votes cast by them, and takes the required number from those standing highest on their respective party polls. Again, we might have what is known as the Gove System, which is a combination of the original Hare System and the Free List. As any one of these would work the desired reform the choice could be left to each locality that it might adopt that which most nearly accords with its present system.

By the adoption of proportional representation the greatest possible scope would be secured to intelligent individual action at the polls; but, and this is all important and deserves careful thought, the whole basis of constituency would be changed. It would rest, not as now, on the accident of residence in a given locality-the same ward-but on the community of political opinion and identical ends in view. No longer artificially segregated and restricted, the constituency would be left absolutely free to crystalize in such a way as it saw fit. Those who thought alike and desired the same results would be left to seek each other out, and act together. The ward line now keeps them apart.

Consider what an enormous influence this would give to the intelligent individual voter! How it would bother the municipal "boss!" Voters are now divided up and segregated by artificial lines; they are in this way so placed that they can be manipulated by astute political managers to the utmost possible extent. Their efforts at a better state of things can be thwarted. Under the system proposed they would be free from all restraints and put in position where the individual could make himself felt, provided he desired so to do. He could not be tied hand and foot.

Take the City of New York. We all know the character of those composing the legislative department of the city. It is notorious-it could not be worse than it is. Suppose that in- stead of the present board of aldermen and its common council the city of New York were to elect one legislative body in such a way that every proportionate part of the voters should have one representative. Suppose every vote to bear directly upon the final result, with all useless majorities and wasted minorities given their proper effect. If the council consisted of 21 members any body of citizens numbering one 21st part of the whole number of voters could and would have one representative. Would not the inevitable result be the nomination as candidates by citizen organizations of at least a certain number of men, who, if elected would give weight and character to that body! Would not the result naturally be that men of the class now composing the legislative department of New York city either would not be brought forward as candidates at all, or if brought forward before the constituency as a whole, and no longer in wards, would be left in the election at the foot of the poll? Every reform organization hoping to represent one twenty-first part of the total vote thrown would be under the highest possible inducement to put forward as its candidate the man of the strongest character, and the man most widely and favorably known. The objection to bringing forward men who were only locally known would be equally great. The object of each organization would necessarily be to nominate candidates who would draw to themselves the greatest number of votes in the constituency at large. The political prison lines, now known as ward lines, would be thrown down.

But the final and crowning advantage of such a system remains to be pointed out. Elected in this way, who could refuse to serve? Con- sider the prestige-the weight of authority and influence-with which any man could walk into a council chamber, who entered it at the head of the poll under such a system as this! No citizen, whether of New York or of Boston, so elected, could or would refuse to obey the mandate of his fellow citizens. And so it would be in the power of any considerable body of voters to lay a hand on the shoulder of any man, no matter how eminent or how busy he might be, and call upon him to perform his tour of municipal duty. Public opinion should exact obedience. Every man owes to the municipality in which he lives something more than the payment of any annual tax bill.

If then my diagnosis of the disease is correct, if the trouble is that, through minute territorial divisions, an excess of political differentiation, men are as a matter of fact continually brought to the front who would not be brought to the front under a larger and less complicated system, if, in a word, the country long has been and now is sick of "wardism," then I confidently submit that under the system proposed we might fairly hope to get down to the root of the disease and remove it. By so doing only, I also submit, the patient can be restored to health. It is useless to waste time over symptoms, and we do not need more complicated charters. We must, on the contrary, go back to first principles: and first principles are always simple. Complete freedom of action must be restored to the individual voter, and he must be so placed that he can influence results in the largest possible degree. There is nothing the "ward boss" fears so much as an intelligent ballot not restrained within local lines. The system as it has long existed and now does exist suits him exactly. It brought him into existance; he grew up under it; he understands it; he will labor to per- petuate it. We should labor to destroy it altogether. By destroying it we will destroy him. For, as the Jew of Venice said of old:-

> You take my house, when you do take the prop
> That doth sustain my house; you take my life
> When you do take the means whereby I live.

3

Memory

8

Lee at Appomattox

This speech was delivered to the American Antiquarian Society on October 30, 1901.

THE present seems a sufficiently proper occasion, and this an appropriate place, to call attention to a matter perhaps only germane to the purpose of this Society, because as yet hardly antiquarian. None the less, historical in character, it conveys a lesson of grave present import.

One of the most unhappy, and, to those concerned in it, disastrous wars since the fall of Napoleon, is, in South Africa, now working itself to a close apparently still remote, and in every way unsatisfactory. There is reason to think that the conflict was unnecessary in its inception; that by timely and judicious action it might long since have been brought to a close ; and that it now continues simply because the parties to it cannot be brought together to discuss and arrive at a sensible basis of adjustment, — a basis upon which both in reality would be not unwilling to agree. Nevertheless, as the cable despatches daily show, the contest drags wearily along, to the probable destruction of one of the combatants, to the great loss of the other, and, so far as can be seen, in utter dis regard of the best interests of both.

My immediate purpose, however, is to draw attention to the hairbreadth escape we ourselves had from a similar experience, now thirty-six years ago, and to assign to whom it belongs the credit for that escape. In one word, in the strong light of passing events, I think it now opportune to set forth the debt of gratitude this reunited country of ours — Union and Confederate, North and South — owes to Robert E. Lee, of Virginia.

Most of those here — for this is not a body of young men — remember the state of affairs which existed in the United States, especially in what was then known as the Confederate States, or the rebellious portion of the United States, in April, 1865. Such as are not yet as mature as that memory implies have read and heard thereof. It was in every respect almost the identical state of affairs which existed in South Africa at the time of the capture of Pretoria by General Roberts, in June a year ago.

On the 2d of April, 1865, the Confederate army found itself compelled to abandon the lines in front of Petersburg ; and the same day — a very famous Sabbath — Jefferson Davis, hastily called from the church services he was attending, left Richmond to find, if he might, a new seat of government, at Danville. The following morning our forces at last entered the rebel capital. This was on a Monday; and, two days later, the Confederate President issued from Danville his manifesto. In it he said to the people of the South, — " We have now entered upon a new phase of the struggle. Relieved from the necessity of guarding particular points, our army will be free to move from point to point, to strike the enemy in detail far from his base. If, by the stress of numbers, we should be compelled to a temporary withdrawal from her [Virginia's] limits, or those of any other border State, we will return until the baffled and exhausted enemy shall abandon in despair his endless and impossible task of making slaves of a people resolved to be free." The policy, and line of military action, thus indicated were precisely those laid down and pursued by the Boer leaders during the last sixteen months.

It is unnecessary for me even to refer to the series of events which followed our occupation of Richmond, and preceded the surrender of Appomattox. It is sufficient to say that on the Friday which followed the momentous Sunday, the capitulation of the Army of Northern Virginia had become inevitable. Not the less for that, the course thereafter to be pursued as concerned further resistance on the part of the Confederacy was still to be decided. As his Danville proclamation showed, Jefferson Davis, though face to face with grave disaster, had not for an instant given up the thought of continuing the struggle. To do so was certainly practicable, — far more practicable than now in South Africa, both as respects forces in the field and the area of country to be covered by the invader. Foreign opinion, for instance, was on this point settled; it was in Europe assumed as a certainty of the future that the conquest of the Confederacy was "impossible." The English journals had always maintained, and still did maintain, that the defeat of Lee in the field, or even the surrender of all the Confederate armies, would be but the close of one phase of the war and the opening of another, — the final phase being a long, fruitless effort to subdue a people, at once united and resolved, occupying a region so vast that it would be impossible to penetrate every portion of it, much less to hold it in peaceful subjection. As an historical fact, on this point the scales, on the 9th of April, 1865, hung wavering in the balance; a mere turn of the hand would decide which way they were to incline. Thus, on the morning of that momentous day, it was an absolutely open question, an even chance, whether the course which subsequently was pursued should be pursued, or whether the leaders of the Confederacy would adopt the policy which President Krüger and Generals Botha and De Wet have in South Africa more recently adopted, and are now pursuing.

The decision rested in the hands of one man, the commander of the Army of Northern Virginia. Fairly reliable and very graphic accounts of interviews with General Lee during those trying days and in the morning hours of April 9th have either appeared in print or been told in conversation, and to two of these accounts I propose to call attention. The first I find in a book, entitled *The End of an Era,* recently published by John Sargent Wise, a son of Henry A. Wise, once prominent in our national politics. Though in 1865 but a youth of nineteen, John S. Wise was a hot Confederate, and had already been wounded in battle.

At the time now in question he chanced, according to his own account, to have been

sent by Jefferson Davis, then on his way to Danville, with despatches to Lee. At length, after many hair breadth escapes from capture, he reached the Confederate headquarters late in the night following the disastrous battle of Sailor's Creek. By it the line of march of the Confederate army towards Danville had been intercepted, and it had been forced to seek a more circuitous route in the direction of Lynchburg. " It was past midnight," writes Mr. Wise, " when I found General Lee. He was in an open field north of Rice's Station and east of the High Bridge. A camp-fire of rails was burning low. Colonel Charles Marshall sat in an ambulance with a lantern and a lap-desk. He was preparing orders at the dictation of General Lee, who stood near, with one hand resting on a wheel and one foot upon the end of a log, watching intently the dying embers, as he spoke in a low tone to his amanuensis."

Explaining his mission to the Confederate leader, Mr. Wise passed the remaining hours of the night in bivouac near by ; and early in the morning, the head quarters having moved, he again set out on his quest. It was now Friday, the 7th. He had not gone far when he stumbled across his father, in bivouac with his brigade. Henry A. Wise was then nearly sixty years of age ; but the son found him wrapped in a blanket, stretched on the ground like a common soldier, and asleep among his men. Essentially a Virginian, and in many respects typically a Southerner and "fire-eater," Henry A. Wise was governor at the time of the John Brown Harper's Ferry raid, in October, 1859, his term expiring shortly after Brown's execution. A member of the Virginia Convention which, immediately after the fall of Sumter, passed the ordinance of secession, Wise, though an extreme States-rights man, had been in favor of "fighting it out in the Union," as the phrase then went; but when Virginia became plainly bent on secession, he unhesitatingly "went with his State." Commissioned as a brigadier-general almost at once, he had served in the Confederate army throughout the war, and was in the thick of the fight at Sailor's Creek. Now, on the morning after that engagement, aroused from an un easy sleep by the unexpected appearance of his son, almost the first wish he expressed was to see General Lee, and he asked impetuously of his whereabouts. The two started together to go to him. John S. Wise has described vividly the aspect of affairs as they passed along: — "The roads and fields were filled with stragglers. They moved looking behind them, as if they expected to be attacked and harried by a pursuing foe. Demoralization, panic, abandonment of all hope, appeared on every hand. Wagons were rolling along without any order or system. Caissons and limber-chests, without commanding officers, seemed to be floating aimlessly upon a tide of disorganization. Rising to his full height, casting a glance around him like that of an eagle, and sweeping the horizon with his long arm and bony forefinger, my father exclaimed: "This is the end!" It is impossible to convey an idea of the agony and the bitterness of his words and gestures." Then follows this description of the interview which ensued: —

"We found General Lee on the rear portico of the house that I have mentioned. He had washed his face in a tin basin, and stood drying his beard with a coarse towel as we approached. ' General Lee,' exclaimed my father, 'my poor, brave men are lying on yonder hill more dead than alive. For more than a week they have been fighting day and night, without food, and, by God, sir, they shall not move another step until somebody gives them something to eat!'

"Come in, general," said General Lee soothingly. "They deserve something to eat, and shall have it; and meanwhile you shall share my breakfast." He disarmed everything like defiance by his kindness.

"It was but a few moments, however, before my father launched forth in a fresh denunciation of the conduct of General Bushrod Johnson[1] in the engagement of the sixth. I am satisfied that General Lee felt as he did; but, assuming an air of mock severity, he said, "General, are you aware that you are liable to court-martial and execution for insubordination and disrespect toward your commanding officer?"

"My father looked at him with lifted eyebrows and flashing eyes, and exclaimed: 'Shot! You can't afford to shoot the men who fight for cursing those who run away. Shot! I wish you would shoot me. If you don't, some Yankee probably will within the next twenty-four hours."

"Growing more serious, General Lee inquired what he thought of the situation.

"'Situation? ' said the bold old man. 'There is no situation! Nothing remains, General Lee, but to put your poor men on your poor mules and send them home in time for spring ploughing. This army is hopelessly whipped, and is fast becoming demoralized. These men have already endured more than I believed flesh and blood could stand, and I say to you, sir, emphatically, that to prolong the struggle is murder, and the blood of every man who is killed from this time forth is on your head, General Lee.'

"This last expression seemed to cause General Lee great pain. With a gesture of remonstrance, and even of impatience, he protested: 'Oh, general, do not talk so wildly. My burdens are heavy enough. What would the country think of me, if I did what you suggest?'

"Country be d----- d! " was the quick reply.

"There is no country. There has been no country, general, for a year or more. You are the country to these men. They have fought for you. They have shivered through a long winter for you. Without pay or clothes, or care of any sort, their devotion to you and faith in you have been the only things which have held this army together. If you demand the sacrifice, there are still left thousands of us who will die for you. You know the game is desperate beyond redemption, and that, if you so announce, no man or government or people will gainsay your decision. That is why I repeat that the blood of any man killed hereafter is upon your head.'

> "General Lee stood for some time at an open window, looking out at the throng now surging by upon the roads and in the fields, and made no response."[2]

It will be remembered that John Sargent Wise was individually present at this conversation, a youth of nineteen. I have as little respect as any one well can have for the recollection of thirty years since as a basis of history. Nevertheless, it would seem quite out of the question that a youth of only nineteen could have been present at such a scene as is here described, and that the words which then passed, and the incidents which occurred, should not have been indelibly imprinted upon his memory. I am disposed, therefore, to consider this reliable historical material. Mean while, it so chances that I am able to supplement it by similar testimony from another quarter.

Some years ago I was, for a considerable period, closely associated with General E. P. Alexander, who, in its time, had been chief of artillery in Longstreet's famous corps ; and it was General Alexander who, on the morning of July 3, 1863, opened on the Union line at Gettysburg what Hancock described as "a most terrific and appalling cannonade," intended to prepare the way for the advance of Pickett's division. In April, 1865, General Alexander was, if my recollection serves me right, in command of the artillery of the Army of Northern Virginia. In many connections I had found occasion to notice the singular tenacity of his memory. He seemed to forget nothing; nor was he less accurate in matters of detail than in generalities. He delighted in reminiscence of the great war, and he recalled its incidents with the particularity of a trained officer of the general staff. He thus many times, always with the same precision, repeated to me, or in my hearing, the details of interviews with Lee during the retreat from Peters burg, and more especially of one, on the morning of April 9th. Of what he said I have since retained a vivid memory. During Friday, April 7th, the day Wise found his way to Lee's headquarters, the weary Confederate army pressed forward, vainly trying to elude the hot pursuit of the Union advance, led by Sheridan. On Saturday, the 8th, according to General Alexander, the leading Confederate officers became so demoralized that one of them, General Pendleton, was authorized by a sort of informal council to wait on Lee, and to tell him that, a surrender seeming inevitable, they were prepared to take the responsibility of advising it. Recognizing his military obligations, and not yet convinced that his command was hopelessly involved, Lee distinctly resented the advice. He told General Pendleton that there were too many men yet remaining in the ranks to think of laying down arms, and his air and manner conveyed a rebuke.

Twenty-four additional hours of fasting, marching, and fighting put a new face on the situation. Two days before, on the 7th, shortly after the Wise interview, General Alexander had met Lee at Farmville, and a consultation over the maps took place. Alexander had then pointed out Appomattox as "the danger point," the roads to Lynchburg there intersecting, and the enemy having the shortest line. Sheridan did not lose his advantage, and, on Sunday, the 9th of April, Lee found his further progress blocked. That morning General Alexander again met Lee. Both realized the situation fully. Moreover, as chief of artillery, Alexander was well aware that the limber-chests were running low; his arm of the service was in no condition to go into another engagement. Yet the idea of an abandonment of the cause had never occurred to him as among the probabilities.

All night he had lain awake, thinking as to what was next to be done. Finally he had come to the conclusion that there was but one course to pursue. The Confederate army, while nominally capitulating, must in reality disperse, and those composing it should be instructed, whether individually or as part of detachments, to get each man to his own State in the most direct way and shortest possible time, and report to the governor thereof, with a view to a further and continuous resistance. Thus, exactly what is now taking place in South Africa was to take place in the Confederacy. General Alexander told me that, as he passed his batteries on his way to headquarters, the men called out to him, in cheery tones, that there were still some rounds remaining in the caissons, and that they were ready to renew the fight. He found Lee seated on the trunk of a fallen tree before a dying camp-fire. He was dressed in uniform, and invited Alexander to take a seat beside him. He then asked his opinion of the situation, and of the course proper to be pursued. Full of the idea which dominated his mind, Alexander proceeded at once to propound his plan, for it seemed to him the only plan worthy of consideration. As he went on, General Lee, looking steadily into the fire with an abstracted air, listened patiently. Alexander said his full say. A brief pause ensued, which Lee finally broke in somewhat these words: "No! General Alexander, that will not do. You must remember we are a Christian people. We have fought this fight as long as, and as well as, we knew how. We have been defeated. For us, as a Christian people, there is now but one course to pursue. We must accept the situation; these men must go home and plant a crop, and we must proceed to build up our country on a new basis. We cannot have re course to the methods you suggest." I remember being deeply impressed with Alexander's comment, as he repeated these words of Lee. They had evidently burned themselves into his memory. He said: "I had nothing to urge in reply. I felt that the man had soared way up above me, — he dominated me completely. I rose from beside him; silently mounted my horse; rode back to my command; and waited for the order to surrender."

Then and there, Lee decided its course for the Confederacy. And I take it there is not one solitary man in the United States to-day, North or South, who does not feel that he decided right.

The Army of Northern Virginia, it will be remembered, laid down its arms on the 9th of April. But General Joseph Johnston was in command of another Confederate army then confronting Sherman, in North Carolina, and it was still an open question what course he would pursue. His force numbered over 40,000 combatants ; more than the entire muster of the Boers in their best estate. Lee's course decided Johnston's. S. R. Mallory, who was present on the occasion, has left a striking account of a species of council held at Greensboro, North Carolina, on the evening of the 10th of April, by Jefferson Davis and the members of his cabinet, with General Johnston. Davis, stubborn in temper, and bent on a policy of continuous irregular resistance, expressed the belief that the disasters recently sustained, though "terrible," should not be regarded as "fatal." "I think," he added, "we can whip the enemy yet, if our people will turn out." When he ceased speaking, a pause ensued. Davis at last said, "We should like to hear your views, General Johnston." Whereupon Johnston, without preface or introduction, and with a tone and manner almost spiteful, remarked in his terse, concise, demonstrative way, as if seeking to condense thoughts that were crowding for utterance: "My views are, sir, that our people are tired of the war, feel themselves whipped, and will not fight."[3]

We all know what followed. Lee's great military prestige and moral ascendency made it easy for some of the remaining Confederate commanders, like Johnston, to follow the precedent he set; while others of them, like Kirby Smith, found it imposed upon them. A firm direction had been given to the course of events; an intelligible policy was indicated.

I have in my possession a copy of the *Index*, the weekly journal published in London during our civil war. The official organ of the Confederate agents in Europe, it was intended for the better enlightenment of foreign opinion, more especially the English press. The surrender of Lee was commented upon editorially in the issue of that paper for April 27th. " The war is far from concluded," it declared. "A strenuous resistance and not surrender was the un alterable determination of the Confederate authorities, . . . and if the worst comes to the worst there is the trans-Mississippi department, where the remnant of [Johnston's] army can find a shelter, and a new and safe starting-point."[4] On the 11th of May following, the surrender of Johnston's army was announced on the same terms as that of Lee ; but in summing up the situation, the *Index* still found "the elements of a successful, or, at least, a protracted resistance." On the 25th of May, it had an article entitled "Southern Resistance in Texas," in which it announced that, "Such a war will be fierce, ferocious, and of long duration," - - in a word, such an expiring struggle as we are to-day witnessing in South Africa. In its issue of June 1st, the Index commented on "The capture of President Davis;" and then, and not until then, forestalling the trans-Mississippi surrender of Kirby Smith, brought to it by the following mail, it raised the wailing cry, " *Fuit Ilium.*[5] . . . The South has fallen."

Comparing the situation which then existed in the Confederacy with that now in South Africa, it must also be remembered that General Lee assumed the responsibility he did assume, and decided the policy to be pursued in the way it was decided, under no ameliorating conditions. Politically, unconditional surrender was insisted upon ; and Lee's surrender was, politically, unconditional. Even more so was Johnston's; for, in Johnston's case, the modifying terms of capitulation agreed on in the first place between him and Sherman were roughly disallowed at Washing-ton, and the truce, by an order coming thence, abruptly terminated. Then Johnston did what Lee had already done; ignoring Davis, he surrendered his army.

In the case of the Confederacy, also, an absolutely unconditional political surrender implied much. The Emancipation Proclamation of January, 1863, which confiscated the most valuable chattel property of the Confederacy, remained the irreversible law of the land. The inhabitants of the South were, moreover, as one man disfranchised. When they laid down their arms they had before them, first, a military government; and, after that, the supremacy of their former slaves. A harder fate for a proud people to accept could not well be imagined. The bitterness of feeling, the hatred, was, too, extreme. It may possibly be argued that the conditions in this country then were different from those now in South Africa, inasmuch as here it was a civil war, — a conflict between communities of the same race and speech involving the vital question of the supremacy of law. This argument, however, seems to imply that, in case of strife of this description, a general severity may fairly be resorted to in excess of that permissible between nations ; in other words, that we are justified in treating our brethren with greater harshness than we would treat aliens in blood and speech. Obviously, this is a questionable contention.

It might possibly also be claimed that the bitter ness of civil war is not so insurmountable as that of one involving a question of race dominance. Yet it is difficult to conceive bitterness of greater intensity than existed between the sections at the close of our civil war. There is striking evidence of this in the book of Mr. Wise, from which I have already quoted. Toward its close he speaks of the death of Lincoln. He then adds the following : —

"Perhaps I ought to chronicle that the announcement was received with demonstrations of sorrow. If I did, I should be lying for senti-ment's sake. Among the higher officers and the most intelligent and conservative men, the assassination caused a shudder of horror at the heinousness of the act, and at the thought of its possible consequences; but among the thoughtless, the desperate, and the ignorant, it was hailed as a sort of retributive justice. In maturer years I have been ashamed of what I felt and said when I heard of that awful calamity. However, men ought to be judged for their feelings and their speech by the circumstances of their surroundings. For four years we had been fighting. In that struggle, all we loved had been lost. Lincoln incarnated to us the idea of oppression and conquest. We had seen his face over the coffins of our brothers and relatives and friends, in the flames of Richmond, in the disaster at Appomattox. In blood and flame and torture the temples of our lives were tumbling about our heads. We were desperate and vindictive, and whosoever denies it forgets or is false. We greeted his death in a spirit of reckless hate, and hailed it as bringing agony and bitterness to those who were the cause of our own agony and bitterness. To us, Lincoln was an inhuman monster, Grant a butcher, and Sherman a fiend."

Indeed, recalling the circumstances of that time, it is fairly appalling to consider what in 1865 must have occurred, had Robert E. Lee then been of the same turn of mind as was Jefferson Davis, or as implacable and unyielding in disposition as Krüger or Botha have more recently proved. The national government had in arms a million men, inured to the hardships and accustomed to the brutalities of war; Lincoln had been freshly assassinated; the temper of the North was thoroughly aroused, while its patience was exhausted. An irregular warfare would inevitably have resulted, a warfare without quarter.[6] The Confederacy would have been reduced to a smouldering wilderness, — to what South Africa to-day is. In such a death grapple, the North, both in morale and in means, would have suffered only less than the South. From both sections that fate was averted.

It is not my purpose to enter into any criticism of the course of events in South Africa, or of the policy there on either side pursued. It will be for the future to decide whether the prolonged, irregular resistance we are witnessing is justifiable, or, if justifiable, whether it is wise. Neither of these questions do I propose to discuss. My purpose simply is to call attention, in view of what is now taking place elsewhere, to the narrow escape we ourselves, thirty-six years ago, had from a similar awful catastrophe. And I again say that, as we look to-day upon Krüger and Botha and De Wet, and the situation existing in the Transvaal and the Orange Free State, I doubt if one single man in the United States, North or South, — whether he participated in the civil war or was born since that war ended, — would fail to acknowledge an infinite debt of gratitude to the Confederate leader, who on the 9th of April, 1865, decided, as he did decide, that the United States, whether Confederate or Union, was a Christian community, and that his duty was to accept the responsibility which the fate of war had imposed upon him, — to decide in favor of a new national life, even if slowly and painfully to be built up by his own people under conditions arbitrarily and by force imposed on them.

In one of the Confederate accounts of the great war[7] is to be found the following description of Lee's return to his Richmond home immediately after he had at Appomattox sealed the fate of the Confederacy. With it I will conclude this paper. On the afternoon of the previous day, the first of those paroled from the surrendered Army of Northern Virginia had straggled back to Richmond. The writer thus goes on: "Next morning a small group of horsemen appeared on the further side of the pontoons. By some strange intuition it was known that General Lee was among them, and a crowd collected all along the route he would take, silent and bareheaded. There was no excitement, no hurrahing; but as the great chief passed, a deep, loving murmur, greater than these, rose from the very hearts of the crowd. Taking off his hat and simply bowing his head, the man great in adversity passed silently to his own door; it closed upon him, and his people had seen him for the last time in his battle harness."

AFTER preparing the foregoing paper, I wrote to General Alexander, asking him to verify my recollection of the account of what passed at his meeting with General Lee at Appomattox. His reply did not reach me in time for the meeting of the American Antiquarian Society, at which the paper was read. He wrote in part as follows: "I am greatly interested in what you wish, having often thought and spoken of the contrast between Lee's views of the duty of the leaders of a people, and those held at the time by President Davis, and now held by Kriiger and the Boer leaders; and I have written of it, too, in my own war recollections, which I am writing out for my children.

"Essentially, your recollections are entirely correct; though some of the details are not exact. Two days before, I had talked with General Lee over his map, and noted Appomattox Courthouse as the danger point.' When I came up on the 9th to where he had halted on the road, he called me to him, and began by referring to previous talk, and then he asked me, — ' What shall we do to-day ? ' For an account of our conversation I will cut out of a scrap-book two pages which contain a clipping from the Philadelphia Press of a letter I wrote twenty years ago."

In the course of his letter, General Alexander further said, — "The gist of my argument to General Lee was that the governors of the Southern States might make some sort of Terms, which would bar trials for treason, etc.; and it was based on the assumption that Grant would demand 'unconditional surrender.' And I certainly think, too, that Grant deserves equal praise and gratitude for his high-mindedness in his liberal treatment of his foe — more absolutely at his mercy than was Buckner at Fort Donelson, or Pemberton at Vicksburg." . . .

"I particularly remember, too, his (Lee's) dwelling on the fact that the men were already, as it were, demoralized by four years of war, and would but too easily become mere bushwhackers."

The clipping referred to was from an issue of the *Press* of July, 1881. The narrative contained in it, now not easily accessible, is of such interest and obvious historical value, as throwing light on what was passing in Lee's mind at one of the most critical moments in the national history, that I here reproduce it in full: —

"The morning of the 9th of April, 1865, found the Confederate army in a position in which its inevitable fate was apparent to every man in it. The skirmishing which had begun in its front as its advance guard reached Appomattox Courthouse the night before had developed into a sharp fight, in which the continuous firing of the artillery and the steady increase of the musketry told to all that a heavy force had been thrown across our line of march, and that reinforcements to it were steadily arriving. The long trains of wagons and artillery were at first halted in the road and then parked in the adjoining fields, allowing the rear of the column to close up and additional troops to pass to the front to reinforce the advanced guard and to form a reserve line of battle in their rear, under cover of which they might retire when necessary. While these dispositions were taking place, General Lee, who had dismounted and was standing near a fire on a hill about two miles from the Court house, called the writer to him, and, inviting him to a seat on a log near by, referred to the situation and asked: ' What shall we do this morning? 'Although this opportunity of expressing my views was unexpected, the situation itself was not, for two days before, while near Farmville, in a consultation with General Lee over his map, the fact of the enemy's having the shortest road to the Appomattox Court house had been noted and the probability of serious difficulty there anticipated, and in the mean time there had been ample opportunity for reflection on all of the emergencies that might arise. Without replying directly to the question, however, I answered first that it was due to my command (of artillery) that I should tell him that they were in as good spirits, though short of ammunition and with poor teams, as they had ever been, and had begged, if it came to a surrender, to be allowed to expend first every round of ammunition on the enemy, and surrender only the empty ammunition chests. To this General Lee re plied that there were remaining only two divisions of infantry sufficiently well organized and strong to be fully relied upon (Field's and Mahone's), and that they did not number eight thousand muskets together; and that that force was not sufficient to warrant him in undertaking a pitched battle. 'Then,' I answered, 'general, there are but two alternatives, to surrender or to order the army to abandon its trains and disperse in the woods and bushes, every man for himself, and each to make his best way, with his arms, either to the army of General Johnston, in North Carolina, or home to the governor of his State. We have all foreseen the probability of such an alternative for two days, and I am sure I speak the sentiments of many others besides my own in urging that rather than sur render the army you should allow us to disperse in the woods and go, every man for himself.'

'"What would you hope to accomplish by this?"' I answered: 'If there is any hope at all for the Confederacy or for the separate States to make terms with the United States or for any foreign assistance, this course stands the chances, whatever they may be; while if this army surrenders this morning, the Con federacy is dead from that moment. Grant will turn 150,000 fresh men against Johnston, and with the moral effect of our surrender he will go, and Dick Taylor and Kirby Smith will have to follow like a row of bricks, while if we all take to dispersing in the woods, we inaugurate a new phase of the war, which may be indefinitely prolonged, and it will at least have great moral effect in showing that in our pledges to fight it out to the last we meant what we said. And even, general, if there is no hope at all in this course or in any other, and if the fate of the Confederacy is sealed whatever we do, there is one other consideration which your soldiers have a right to urge on you, and that is your own military reputation, in which every man in this army, officer or private, feels the utmost personal pride and has a personal property that his children will prize after him. The Yankees brought Grant here from the West, after the failure of all their other generals, as one who had whipped everybody he had ever fought against, and they call him "Unconditional Surrender " Grant, and have been bragging in advance that you would have to sur render too. Now, general, I think you ought to spare us all the mortification of having you to ask Grant for terms, and have him answer that he had no terms to offer you.'

"I still remember most vividly the emotion with which I made this appeal, increasing as I went on, until my whole heart was in it ; and it seemed to me at the moment one which no soldier could resist and against which no consideration whatever could be urged ; and when I closed, after urging my suggestions at greater length than it is necessary to repeat, looking him in the face and speaking with more bold ness than I usually found in his presence, I had not a doubt that he must adopt some such course as I had urged.

"He heard me entirely through, however, very calmly, and then asked: ' How many men do you estimate would escape if I were to order the army to disperse? '

"I replied: 'I suppose two thirds of us could get away, for the enemy could not disperse to follow us through the woods.'

"He said: ' We have here only about sixteen thousand men with arms, and not all of those who could get away would join General Johnston, but most of them would try and make their way to their homes and families, and their numbers would be too small to be of any material service either to General Johnston or to the governors of the States. I recognize fully that the surrender of this army is the end of the Confederacy, but no course we can take can prevent or even delay that result. I have never believed that we would receive foreign assistance, or get our liberty otherwise than by our own arms. The end is now upon us, and it only remains to decide how we shall close the struggle. But in deciding this question we are to approach it not only as soldiers but as Christian men, deciding on matters which involve a great deal else besides their own feelings. If I should order this army to disperse, the men with their arms, but without organization or control, and without provisions or money, would soon be wandering through every State in the Confederacy, some seeking to get to their homes, and some with no homes to go to. Many would be compelled to rob and plunder as they went to save themselves from starvation, and the enemy's cavalry would pursue in small detachments, particularly in efforts to catch the general officers, and raid and burn over large districts which they will other wise never reach, and the result would be the inauguration of lawlessness and terror and of organized bands of robbers all over the South. Now, as Chris tian men, we have not the right to bring this state of affair upon the country, whatever the sacrifice of personal pride involved. And as for myself, you young men might go to bush-whacking, but I am too old; and even if it were right for me to disperse the army, I should surrender myself to General Grant as the only proper course for one of my years and position. But I am glad to be able to tell you one thing for your comfort: General Grant will not demand an unconditional surrender, but offers us most liberal terms — the paroling of the whole army not to fight until exchanged.' He then went on to speak of the probable details of the terms of surrender, and to say that about 10 A.M. he was to meet General Grant in the rear of the army, and would then accept the terms offered.

"Sanguine as I had been when he commenced that he must acquiesce in my views,' I had not one word to reply when he had finished. He spoke slowly and deliberately, and with some feeling; and the complete ness of the considerations he advanced, and which he dwelt upon with more detail than I can now fully recall, speaking particularly of the women and children, as the greatest sufferers in the state of anarchy which a dispersion of the army would bring about, and his reference to what would be his personal course if he did order such dispersion, all indicated that the question was not then presented to his mind for the first time.

"A short time after this conversation General Lee rode to the rear of the army to meet General Grant and arrange the details of the surrender. He had started about a half hour when General Fitz Lee sent word to General Longstreet that he had broken through a portion of the enemy's line, and that the whole army might make its way through. General Longstreet, on learning this, directed Colonel Haskell of the artillery,[8] who was very finely mounted, to ride after General Lee at utmost speed, killing his horse, if necessary, and re call him before he could reach General Grant. Colonel Haskell rode as directed, and a short distance in rear of the army found General Lee and some of his staff dismounted by the roadside. As he with difficulty cheeked his horse, General Lee came up quickly, asking what was the matter ; but, without waiting for a reply, said: 'Oh! I'm afraid you have killed your beautiful mare. What did you ride her so hard for?' On hearing General Longstreet's message, he asked some questions about the situation, and sent word to General Longstreet to use his own discretion in making any movements; but he did not himself return, and in a short while another message was received that the success of the cavalry under General Fitz Lee was but temporary, and that there was no such gap in the enemy's line as had been supposed. Soon afterward a message was brought from the enemy's picket that General Grant had passed around to the front and would meet General Lee at Appomattox Courthouse, and General Lee accordingly returned.

"Meanwhile, as the Confederate line under General Gordon was slowly falling back from Appomattox Courthouse after as gallant a fight against overwhelming odds as it had ever made, capturing and bringing safely off with it an entire battery of the enemy's, General Custer, commanding a division of Federal cavalry, rode forward with a flag of truce, and, the firing having ceased on both sides, was conducted to General Longstreet as commanding temporarily in General Lee's absence. Custer demanded the surrender of the army to himself and General Sheridan, to which General Longstreet replied that General Lee was in communication with General Grant upon that subject, and that the issue would be determined between them. Custer replied that he and Sheridan were independent of Grant, and unless the surrender was made to them they would 'pitch in' at once. Longstreet's answer was a peremptory order [to Custer] at once [to return] to his own lines, and try it if he liked.' Custer was accordingly escorted back; but fire was not reopened, and both lines remained halted, the Confederate about a half mile east of the Courthouse.

"General Lee, returning from the rear shortly after ward, halted in a small field adjoining Sweeney's house, a little in rear of his skirmish line, and, seated on some rails under an apple-tree, awaited a message from General Grant. This apple-tree was not only entirely cut up for mementos within two days afterward, but its very roots were dug up and carried away under the false impression that the surrender took place under it.[9]

"About noon a Federal staff officer rode up and announced that General Grant was at the Courthouse, and General Lee with one of his staff accompanied him back. As he left the apple-tree General Longstreet's last words were: Unless he offers you liberal terms, general, let us fight it out.'

"It would be a difficult task to convey to one who was not present an idea of the feeling of the Confederate army during the few hours which so suddenly, and so unexpectedly to it, terminated its existence, and with it all hopes of the Confederacy. Having been sharply engaged that very morning, and its movements arrested by the flag of truce, while one portion of it was actually fighting and nearly all the rest, infantry and artillery, had just been formed in line of battle in sight and range of the enemy, and with guns unlimbered, it was impossible to realize fully that the war, with all its hopes, its ambitions, and its hardships, was thus ended. There was comparatively very little conversation, and men stood in groups looking over the scene ; but the groups were unusually silent. It was not at first generally known that a surrender was in evitable, but there was a remarkable pre-acquiescence in whatever General Lee should determine, and the warmest expressions of confidence in his judgment. Hanks and discipline were maintained as usual, and there is little doubt that, had General Lee decided to fight that afternoon, the troops would not have disappointed him. About 4 P.M. he returned from the Courthouse, and, after informing the principal officers of the terms of the surrender, started to ride back to his camp.

"The universal desire to express to him the unabated love and confidence of the army had led to the formation of the gunners of a few battalions of artillery along the roadside, with orders to take off their hats in silence as he rode by. When he approached, however, the men could not be restrained, but burst into the wildest cheering, which the adjacent infantry lines took up; and, breaking ranks, they all crowded around him, cheering at the tops of their voices. General Lee stopped his horse, and, after gaining silence, made the only speech to his men that he ever made. He was very brief, and gave no excuses or apologies for his surrender, but said he had done all in his power for his men, and urged them to go as quickly and quietly to their homes as possible, to resume peaceful avocations, and to be as good citizens as they had been soldiers ; and this advice marked the course which he himself pursued so faithfully to the end."

BOSTON, November 6, 1901.

Notes:

1. Elsewhere in his book (pp. 358, 359), and in another connection, J. S. Wise is equally severe in his characterization of Bushrod Johnson.

2. *The End of an Era,* pp. 433-435.

3. Alfriend: *Life of Jefferson Davis,* pp. 622-626.

4. Captain Raphael Semmes, of *Alabama* fame, wrote as follows, in a private letter to an English friend, published in the *London Morning Herald,* during March, 1865: "The State of Texas alone has within her limits all the materials, and is fast getting the appliances, for equipping and maintaining armies, and when you reflect that she has three times as much territory as France, and that countless herds of horses and beef cattle wander over her boundless prairies, you can well imagine with what contempt this warlike people regard the insane threat

of subjugation. If our armies were driven to-morrow across the Mississippi River, we could still fight the enemy for a century to come in Texas alone. So dismiss all your fears, my friend, our independence is an accomplished fact, let the war continue as long as the Yankee pleases, and with what varying results it may." In its issue of March 15, 1865, the *London Times* editorially said: "These territories are too vast to be occupied, and the elements of rebellion they contain are too rife to be left to themselves. They may be penetrated in every direction, but we do not see how they are to be held or subdued."

5. Editor's Note: *Fuit Ilium:* "Troy has been. (Is no more.)" This is a quote from Virgil's *Aeneid*.

6. Commenting on the " Suddenness of the Collapse," the *Index* said, editorially, in its issue of June 8, 1805: "The loss of the armies left no alternative but private war, which never yet redeemed a country without foreign help, and which is as much directed against society as against a public foe. Such a course was inconsistent with the genius of the Southern people, which is eminently law-abiding and orderly. Brave men know how to accept defeat, and the Southerners have accepted theirs, bitter though it is, as only brave men can."

7. De Leon: *Four Years in Rebel Capitals,* p. 367.

8. Colonel J. C. Haskell, of South Carolina; "a born and a resourceful artilleryman, [who] knew no such thing as fear." General Longstreet evidently used General Alexander's paper in the Philadelphia Press in preparing the account, contained in his Manassas to Appomattox, of what occurred on the day of Lee's surrender. A further reference to Colonel Haskell may be found in Wise: *The End of an Era* (p. 360). Long-street says that, at Appomattox, " there were ' surrendered or paroled ' 28,356 officers and men." A week previous to the capitulation, Lee's and Johnston's combined forces numbered considerably over 100,000 combatants. [C. F. A.]

9. The surrender took place in the house of a Mr. McLean, a gentleman who, by a strange coincidence, owned a farm on Bull Run at the beginning of the war. General Beauregard's headquarters were at

McLean's house, just in the rear of Blackburn's ford, during the first battle fought by the army, July 18, 1861. McLean moved from Bull Run to get himself out of the theatre of war. The last battle took place on his new farm, and the surrender in his new residence.

End Note: While the foregoing- was passing through the press, there appeared in the *Century* magazine for April, 1902 (volume IXIII pp. 921-944), a series of papers relating to the surrender of Appomattox. One of these papers, entitled "Personal Recollections of the Break-up of the Confederacy," was by General Alexander. Another was by Colonel Charles Marshall, the military secretary to General Lee, referred to by Mr. John Sargent Wise. (Supra, page 5.) In the Century paper General Alexander recounts the circumstances of his interview with General Lee more in detail, and with greater exactness, than in his contribution to the Philadelphia Press of twenty years before; but the two narratives differ in no material respect.

9

The Constitutional Ethics
of Secession

Speech to the New England Society of Charleston
"ΑΝΑΓΚΗ"[1]
December 22, 1902

Mr. President, and Ladies and Gentlemen of the New England Society of Charleston : —

Though this is a Yule-tide festival, being, by descent at least, a Puritan, I shall, after the fashion of the Puritans, open with a text, thence proceeding to "improve the occasion." If you will turn to the twelfth chapter of Exodus, you will there find it written : —

"And this day shall be unto you for a memorial; and ye shall keep it a feast to the Lord throughout your generations ; ye shall keep it a feast by an ordinance forever.

"And it shall come to pass, when your children shall say unto you, What mean ye by this service?

"That ye shall say. It is the sacrifice of the Lord's passover, who passed over the houses of the children of Israel in Egypt, when he smote the Egyptians.

"Now the sojourning of the children of Israel, who dwelt in Egypt, was four hundred and thirty years.

"And it came to pass at the end of the four hundred and thirty years, even the self-same day it came to pass, that all the hosts of the Lord went out from the land of Egypt."

As it was of old with the children of Israel, even so is it now with us of New England ; and, when our children say unto us, what mean you by this service, we say unto them, it is the feast of the passover, when our fathers, having passed over the ocean, set foot in the promised land. A day of retrospection, it is a day also of reckoning, — a day meet for reflection. I propose so to utilize it this evening. Discussing grave topics gravely, I crave patience.

Two hundred and sixty-four years ago a schism, since become historic, occurred in the infant colony of Massachusetts Bay. It was rent in twain; and so, as the Father of Massachusetts has recorded, "finding, upon consultation that two so opposite parties could not continue in the same body without apparent hazard to the ruin of the whole, [those in the majority] agreed to send away some of the principal." And again, " by the example of Lot in Abraham's family, and after Hagar and Ishmael, he [Gov. John Winthrop] saw they must be sent away." Those thus proscribed went accordingly into banishment; and so, by another passover, Rhode Island came into existence. This was in 1638; and, in 1640, the chief of those thus thrust into exile having occasion to write to the magistrate who had enforced the order of banishment, said, with a pathos reached only by words of simplicity, "what myself and wife and family did endure in that removal, I wish neither you nor yours may ever be put unto"; but again, and at almost the same time, writing from his new home in Newport, Gov. William Coddington expressed to Gov. John Winthrop the approval he felt "of a speech of one of note amongst you, that we were in a heate and chafed, and were all of us to blame; in our strife we had forgotten that we were brethren."

The expression is apt; the admission appropriate. More, much more than two years ago, — longer ago than the lifetime of a generation,— Massachusetts and South Carolina got in "a heate and chafed" one with the other, and fell into bitter strife. Forgetting that we were brethren, were we also "all of us to blame"?

Not long since, circumstances led me into a dispassionate re-examination of the great issues over which the country divided in the mid-years of the last century. As a result thereof, I said in a certain Phi Beta Kappa Society address delivered in June, at Chicago, copies of which some of you may have seen, — "legally and technically, — not morally, again let me say, and wholly irrespective of humanitarian con-siderations, — to which side did the weight of argument incline during the great debate which culminated in our Civil War? If we accept the judgment of some of the more modern students and investigators of history, — either wholly unprejudiced or with a distinct Union bias, — it would seem as if the weight of argument falls into what I will term the Confederate scale." And I then referred to some recent utterances of Prof. Goldwin Smith and Mr. Henry Cabot Lodge. Incited by those utterances to yet further inquiry of my own, the result thereof was, to me at least, curious; — suggestive of moralizing, and moralizing, too, of a sort highly appropriate for the Passover period.

The question is now one purely historic; but on that question of the weight of authority and argument as respects the right of secession, I found a divergence of opinion existing to-day so great as hardly to admit of reconciliation. On the one side it was — I am told still is — taught as an article of political faith that not only was the right of peace-able secession at will plain, manifest, and expressly reserved, but that, until a comparatively recent period, it had never been even disputed. In the words of one writer of authority — "through a period of many years, the right of secession was not seriously questioned in any quarter except under the exigencies of party politics." On the other hand, in the section of the country where my lot has been cast, this alleged heresy is sternly denounced, and those propounding it are challenged to their proofs. With equal positiveness it is claimed that, from the time of the adoption of the Constitution down to a comparatively recent day, "there was not a man in the country who thought or claimed that the new system was anything but a perpetual Union."

Which contention, I asked, is right? And separating myself from my present environment, I tried to go back to the past, and to see things, not as they now are, but as they were; as they appeared to those of three generations gone, — to the fathers, in short, of our grandfathers. It was a groping after forgotten facts and conditions in places dark and unfamiliar. The results reached, also, were, I confess, very open to question. But, while more or less curious, as well as unexpected, they were such as a Massachusetts man, forty years ago at this time in arms for the Union, need not hesitate to set forth in South Carolina, where the right of secession, no longer proclaimed as a theory, was first resorted to as a fact.

It was Alexander Pope, hard on two centuries ago (1733), who wrote: —

> "Manners with fortunes, humors turn with climes,
> Tenets with books, and principles with times."

And, again, Tennyson in our day has said : —

> "The drift of the Maker is dark, an Isis hid by the veil.
> Who knows the ways of the world, how God will bring them about?
> Our planet is one, the suns are many, the world is wide.
> We are puppets, Man in his pride, and Beauty fair in her flower;
> Do we move ourselves, or are moved by an unseen hand at a game
> That pushes us off from the board, and others ever succeed?"

As I delved into the record, I concluded that humors turned quite as much with climes in the nineteenth century as they did in the eighteenth; and that, in the later as in the earlier period, principles, so called, bore a very close relation to times. We, too, had also been "puppets" moved by "an unseen hand at a game." As, in short, I pursued my inquiries, the individual became more and more minimized; chance and predestination cut larger figures; and, at last, it all assumed the form of a great fatalistic process, from which the unexpected alone was sure to result.

But to come to the record. For more than a century, lawyers, jurists and publicists, — journalists, politicians and statesmen, — have been arguing over the Federal Constitution. Sovereignty carries with it allegiance. Wherein rested sovereignty? Was it in the State or in the Nation? Was the United States a unit, — "an indissoluble Union of imperishable States," — or was it a mere confederacy of nations, held together solely by a compact upon possible infringements of which each one, so far as it was concerned, was a final judge? Each postulate has been maintained from the beginning; for that matter, is maintained still. Each has been argued out with great legal acumen and much meta-physical skill to results wholly satisfactory to those that way inclined; and yet absolutely illogical and absurd to the faithful of the other side. It was the old case of the shield of the silver and golden sides. That the two sides were irreconcilable made no difference. Be it silver or gold, the thing to him who had eyes to see was in his sight silver or gold, as the case might be. And yet, as I pursued my inquiries, I gradually felt assured, not that the thing was in this case either silver or gold, but that it was both silver and gold. Everybody, in short, was right; no one wrong. Conditions changed, and with them not only appearances but principles, and even facts. The inevitable and unexpected had occurred.

This I propose for my thesis.

In dealing with these questions the lawyers, I find, start always with the assumption that, at a given time in the past, to wit, at or about 1788, there was in the thirteen States, then soon to become the present United States, a definite consensus of public opinion, which found expression in a written compact, since known as the Federal Constitution. But was this really the case? Public opinion, so called, is a very elusive and uncertain something, signifying things different at different times and in different places. Especially was this the case in the States of the old Federation. So far as I can ascertain, every State of the Federation became a member of the Union with mental reservations, often unexpressed, growing out of local traditions and interests, in the full and correct understanding of which the action of each must be studied. Dissatisfied with the past and doubtful of the future, jealous of liberties, to the last degree provincial and suspicious of all external rule, intensely common-sensed, but illogical and alive with local prejudice, the one thing our ancestry united in most apprehending was a centralized government. From New Hampshire to Georgia such a government was associated with the idea of a foreign regime. The people clung to the local autonomy, — the Sovereignty of the State. With this fundamental fact the framers of the Constitution had to deal. And they did so, in my opinion, with consummate skill. Accepting things as they were, they went as far as they could, leaving the outcome to time and the process of natural growth. The immediate result was a nation founded on a metaphysical abstraction, — a condition of unstable equilibrium. It could not endure. But the great mass of people composing a community — Lincoln's "plain people" — are not metaphysicians, and do not philosophize. Loving to argue, in argument they are not logical. Even in Virginia they were not then all abstractionists; and, while, in a vague way, the Virginians wanted to become part of one people, they never proposed to cease to be Virginians, or to permit Virginia to become other than a Sovereign State. It was so with the others.

Confronted with this fact, what did the framers of the Constitution propose? Taking refuge in metaphysics, they proposed a contradiction in terms — a divided sovereignty. Sovereignty, it was argued, was in the People. But who are the People? The People of the United States, it was replied, are the aggregate of those inhabiting the particular States. Then they began to apportion sovereignty, oblivious of the fact that sovereignty does not admit of apportionment. Pursuing some vague analogy of the solar system, and conceiving of States as planets in their orbits, the People of the particular States assigned to the Nation a modicum of sovereignty, conferred another modicum on the State governments, and reserved whatever remained to themselves. Now it is written, " No man can serve two masters : for either he will hate the one and love the other ; or else he will hold to the one, and despise the other." The everlasting truth of this precept in the fulness of time held good in our case. From the moment the fathers sought to divide the indivisible, the result was written on the wall. It was a mere question of years and of might. Sovereignty had to be somewhere, and accepted as being there.

Thus, intentionally by some of the most far-seeing, unintentionally by others anxious to effect only a more perfect union, a pious fraud was in 1788 perpetrated on the average American, and his feet were directed into a path which inevitably led him to the goal he least designed for his journey's end.[2]

> " Through the Valley of Love I went,
> In the lovingest spot to abide,
> And just on the verge where I pitched my tent,
> I found Hate dwelling beside."

The bond was deceptive; for, on this vital point of ultimate sovereignty, — To whom was allegiance due in cases of direct issue and last resort? — on this crucial point of points the Constitution was not self-explanatory, — explicit. Nor was it meant to be. The framers — that is, the more astute, practical and far-seeing — went as far as they dared. The difficulty — the contradiction involved— was explicitly, and again and again, pointed out. It is impossible to believe that a man so intellectually acute as Hamilton failed to see the inherent weakness of the plan proposed. He did see it; but, under existing conditions, it was, from his point of view, the best attainable. Madison, though a man of distinctly constructive mind, was also an abstractionist. He seems really to have had faith in the principle of an unstable political equilibrium. At a later day, that faith was put to a rude test; and, in 1814, while the Hartford Convention was in session, the scales fell from his eyes. He had all he wanted of a divided sovereignty in practical operation. Lawyers, meanwhile, have since argued on this point; philosophers and publicists have refined over it; historians have analyzed the so-called original materials of history ; and men with arms in their hands have fought the thing to a final result. Nevertheless, the real facts in the case seem quite clear, and altogether otherwise than they are usually assumed to have been.

When the Federal Constitution was framed and adopted, — "an indestructible Union of imperishable States," — what was the law of treason, — to what or to whom, in case of final issue, did the average citizen owe allegiance? Was it to the Union, or to his State? As a practical question, seeing things as they then were,- sweeping aside all incontrovertible legal arguments and metaphysical disquisitions, -I do not think the answer admits of doubt. If put in 1788, or indeed at any time anterior to 1825, the immediate reply of nine men out of ten in the Northern States, and of ninety-nine out of a hundred in the Southern States, would have been that, as between the Union and the State, ultimate allegiance was due to the State.

A recurrence to the elementary principles of human nature tells us that this would have been so, and could have been no otherwise. We have all heard of a famous, much-quoted remark of Mr. Gladstone to the effect that the Constitution of the United States was the most wonderful piece of constructive work ever wrought by man at a single effort. This may or may not be so. I do not propose to controvert it here and now; but, however wonderful, it would have been more than wonderful, it would have been distinctly miraculous, had it on the instant so wrought on men as at once to transfer the allegiance and affection of those composing thirteen distinct communities from their old traditional governments to one newly improvised. The thing hardly admits of discussion. The change was political and far-reaching; but it produced no immediate effect on the feelings of the people. As well say that the union of the crowns of Scotland and England immediately broke up Scotch clanship. It did break it up; but the process was continuous through one hundred and fifty years. The union was a fact; but its consequences no Campbell nor Cameron foresaw. So with us in 1788. allegiance to State had only a few years before proved stronger than allegiance to the Crown or to the Confederation, and no one then was "foolish enough to suppose that" the executive of the Union "would dare enforce a law against the wishes of a sovereign and independent State"; the very idea was deemed "preposterous." "That this new government, this upstart of yesterday, had the power to impose its edicts on unwilling States was a political solecism to which they could in no wise assent."[3]

I am sure that all this was so in 1788. I am very confident it remained so until 1815. I fully believe it was so, though in less degree, until at least 1830. A generation of men born in the Union had then grown up, supplanting the generations born and brought up in the States. Steam and electricity had not yet begun to exert their cementing influence ; but time, sentiment, tradition, — more, and most of all, the intense feeling excited North and South by our naval successes under the national flag in the war of 1812, — had in 1815 in large part done their work. The sense of ultimate allegiance was surely, though slowly as insensibly, shifting from the particular and gravitating to the general, — from the State to the Union. It was not a question of law, or of the intent of the fathers, or the true construction of a written instrument ; for, on that vital point, the Constitution was silent, — wisely, and, as I hold it, intentionally silent. In studying the history of that period, we are again confronted by a condition and not a theory; but, as I read the record and understand the real facts of that now-forgotten social and political existence, in case of direct and insoluble issue between sovereign State and sovereign Nation between 1788 to 1861, every man was not only, free to decide, but had to decide for himself; and, whichever way he decided, he was right. The Constitution gave him two masters. Both he could not serve; and the average man decided which to serve in the light of sentiment, tradition and environment. Of this I feel as historically confident as I can feel of any fact not matter of absolute record or susceptible of demonstration.

I have already referred to the academic address I some months ago had occasion to deliver. In response to it I received quite a number of letters, one of which, bearing on this point, seemed very notable. It was from the president of an historic Virginia college, who himself bears an historic Virginia name. In the address alluded to I had said that, " however it may have been in 1788, in i860 a nation had grown into existence." This I take to be indisputable. In no way denying the fact, my correspondent, quoting the words I have given, thus wrote: " But is it not true that this nationality was after all a Northern nationality? Did the South share in it to any extent? On the contrary, the Confederate character of the Union was more strongly impressed upon the South in 1861 than in 1788. So that it may be more truly said that the Secessionists' recourse in 1861 was to peaceable separation, and not to the sword. If the North was really the only national part of the Union, and its national character reached out after the South, must not the responsibility for the use of the sword be visited upon the North, and not on the South? Both North and South started out from the same constitutional standpoint of secession; but, while the South adhered to the same idea, the North fused into a nation, which, in 1861, determined to conquer the other and conservative part. That the South had ever suffered nationalization in spirit or in fact, previous to 1861, I think your address clearly disproves."

Again, Tennyson's "unseen hand at a game"! — a game in which we are "puppets." But, after all, what is that "unseen hand"? And how did it manifest itself in our national life during the three-fourths of a century, between 1788 and 1861? That "unseen hand," theologically known as an "inscrutable providence," I take to be nothing more nor less than those material social, industrial and political conditions, domestic and public, which, making up our environment, mould our destiny with no very great regard for our plans, our hopes, our traditions or our aspirations. All of which is merely our nineteenth century agnostical way of putting the fifteenth century aphorism that "Man proposes, but

God disposes." With a political instinct which now seems marvellous, Madison, in the course of debate in the constitutional convention of 1788, casting a prophetic glance into futurity, said: "The great danger to our general government is, that the Southern and Northern interests of the continent are opposed to each other, not from their difference of size, but from climate, and principally from the effects of their having or not having slaves. Defensive power ought to be given, not between the large and small states, but between the Northern and Southern." And again, " The greatest danger is disunion of the States " ; and, " It seems now well understood that the real difference of interests lies, not between the large and small, but between the Northern and Southern States." Based on this line of broad difference, the contest was " between the fear of the centripetal and the fear of the centrifugal force in the system." On the other side of the Atlantic, a shrewd observer and pioneer economist, profoundly opposed to the British policy during our War of Independence, had thus, shortly before, cast a horoscope of the American people, "The mutual antipathies and clashing interests of the Americans, their difference of governments, habitudes and manners, indicate that they will have no centre of union and no common interest. They never can be united into one common empire under any species of government whatever; a disunited people to the end of time, suspicious and distrustful of each other, they will be divided and subdivided into little commonwealths or principalities, according to the natural boundaries, by great bays of the seas and by vast rivers, lakes, and ridges of mountains."[4]

Into the details of the conflict over sovereignty which dragged along for seventy years, it is needless for me here to enter. A twice-told tale, I certainly have no new light to cast upon it; but in reviewing it recently, that aspect of it which has impressed me was its resemblance to the classic. Throughout Fate, the inevitable, "the unseen hand," are everywhere now apparent, — destiny had to be fulfilled. In connection with the history of those momentous years, we read much of men; and, indeed, it is a galaxy of great names, — Washington, Hamilton, Jefferson, Marshall, Madison, Webster, Calhoun: — but, as I went back to the deeper underlying influences, — the profound currents of thought and action which in the end worked results, — one and all those bearing even these names became Tennyson's "puppets" moved by the "unseen hand at the game." In this respect our story is suggestive of some cosmic theory, — the process by which suns and planets and satellites are evolved; — and gradually it seems as if the individual man were able to affect the course of events and final results as respects the outcome of the one as much as he does of the other. The elaborate legal arguments, the metaphysical theories and historical disquisitions, — even the rights and wrongs of the case, — became quite immaterial, and altogether insignificant. In obedience to underlying influences, and in conformity with natural laws, a system is crystallizing. Discordant elements blend; assimilation, willing or reluctant, goes on.

See how the sides change — how rapidly "humors turn with climes"; while, as to the principles involved, the mutation is only less complete than sincere. Nationality, as we see it to-day, had its birth in Virginia; and the Sovereignty of the Union assumed shape through the agency of Washington and was slowly perfected by Marshall, both more or less consciously responding to a natural movement, and working in harmony with it. Next, Virginia, and her offspring Kentucky, are passing the resolutions of 1798, and arraying themselves under the standard of decentralization. The government then passes into the hands of the protestants; and, almost at once, again in response to an underlying, unseen influence too strong to resist, the process of a more complete crystallization enters on a new phase; and, as it does so, catholic suddenly becomes protestant, and while Federalist New England formally pronounces the Union at an end, Jeffersonian Virginia supplies fresh aliment to nationality.

Meanwhile, the "unseen hand" is again at work, and the "puppets" duly respond. They thought, and we once thought, they were free agents. Not at all. In the light of development it is clear to us now that they merely went through their motions in obedience to influences of the mere existence of which they were at most but vaguely conscious. The drama was drawing insensibly to a crisis; the forces were arraying themselves in opposing ranks on the lines forecast by Madison in 1788. With much confidence I assert, in its fundamentals there was no right or wrong about it; it was an inevitable, irrepressible conflict, — the question of sovereignty was to be decided, and either side could offer good ground, historical and legal, for any attitude taken in regard to it. That shield did actually have a silver as well as a golden side.

Historically speaking, from the close of our second War of Independence, — commonly known as that of 1812, — the ebb and flow of the great currents of influence had set in new and definite channels. Gradually they assumed irresistible force therein. Side by side two civilizations — a Chang and Eng[5] — were developing. North of the Potomac and the Ohio a community was taking shape the whole tendency of which was national. Very fluid in its elements, commercial and manufacturing in its diversified industries, it was largely composed of Europeans or their descendants, who, knowing little of States, cared nothing for State Sovereignty, which, indeed, like the unknown God to the Greeks, was to them foolishness. This vast discordant migration the railroad, the common school and the newspaper were rapidly merging, coalescing and fusing into a harmonious whole. Naturally it found a mouthpiece ; and that mouthpiece preached Union. It was not exactly a consistent utterance; for, less than a score of years before, the same voice had been loud and emphatic in behalf of State Sovereignty. But manners change with fortunes, and principles with times.

So much for Chang, north of the Potomac and the Ohio; but with Eng, south of those streams, it was altogether otherwise. Under the influence of climate, soil, and a system of forced African labor the Southern States irresistibly reverted to the patriarchal conditions, becoming more and more agricultural; and, as is always the case with agricultural races and patriarchal communities, they clung ever more closely to their traditions and local institutions. Then it was that Calhoun, the most rigid of logicians, in obedience to an irresistible influence of the presence and power of which he was unconscious, — Calhoun, the unionist of the War of 1812 and protectionist of 1816, turned to the Constitution; he began that "more diligent and careful scrutiny into its provisions in order to ascertain fully the nature and character of our political system." Needless to say, he there found what he was in search of. But a similar scrutiny was at the same time going on in New England. As a result of the two scrutinies, Chang and Eng both changed sides. Before, Chang's side of the shield was gold, while that of Eng was silver; now, Chang saw quite clearly that it was silver after all, while Eng recognized it as burnished gold of the purest stamp. Both were honest, and both fully convinced. Both also were right; the simple truth being that no man can serve two masters, and two masters the fundamental law prescribed. The inevitable ensued.

But what was the inevitable? That again, as I read the story of our development, was purely a matter of circumstance and time. Fate, — the Greek necessity, — intervened in those lists and decided the issue of battle. To my mind, the record is from its commencement absolutely clear on one point. After the 25th of July, 1788, when the last of the nine States necessary to the adoption of the Federal Constitution acted favorably thereon, a withdrawal from the Union, all theories to the contrary notwithstanding, became practically an issue of might. Into the abstract question of right I will not enter, — least of all here and now. But, conceding everything that may be asked on the point of abstract right, — looking only on imperfect and illogical man as he is, and as he acts in this world's occasions and exigencies, — I adhere on this point to my own belief. In 1790 Rhode Island was spared from being "coerced" into the Union only by a voluntary, though very reluctant, acceptance of it; and from that day to 1861 any attempted withdrawal from the Union would, after long argument over the question of right, have ultimately resolved itself into an issue of might.

Here again the elements of the Greek drama once more confront us — the Fates, necessity. What at different epochs would have been the probable outcome of any attempt at withdrawal? That ever, at any period of our history since 1790, a single State, — no matter how sovereign, even Virginia, — could alone have made good, peaceably or otherwise, a withdrawal in face of her unitedly disapproving sister States, I do not believe. Naturally, or as a result of force applied, the attempt would have resulted in ignominious failure. But how would it have been at any given time with a combination of States, acting in sympathy — a combination proportionately as considerable when measured with the whole as was the Confederacy in 1861? I hold that, here again, it was merely a question of time, and that such a withdrawal as then took place would never have failed of success at any anterior period in our national history. It was steam and electricity which then settled the issue of sovereignty; not argument, not military skill, not wealth, courage, or endurance; not even men in arms. Before 1861 steam and electricity, neither on land nor water, had been rendered so subservient to man as to make him equal to the prodigious, the unprecedented, task then undertaken and finally accomplished. In that case, might in the end made right; but the end was in no degree a foregone conclusion.

In my own family records I find a curious bit of contemporary evidence of this, and of the line of thought and reasoning then resulting therefrom. Following the foresight of Madison, J. Q. Adams, noting the set of the currents in 1820, became instinctively persuaded that the North and the South would be swept into collision by the forces of inherent development. Again and again did he put this belief of his on record. Contemplating such an eventuality, he, in 1839, thus expressed himself in a public utterance, in words which I have of late more than once seen quoted in support of the abstract constitutional right of secession. Speaking in New York on what was called the jubilee of the Constitution, or the fiftieth anniversary of its adoption, he said: "If the day should ever come (may Heaven avert it!) when the affections of the people of these States shall be alienated from each other, when the fraternal spirit shall give way to cold indifference, or collisions of interest shall fester into hatred, the bands of political association will not long hold together parties no longer attracted by the magnetism of conciliated interests and kindly sympathies; and far better will it be for the people of the disunited States to part in friendship from each other than to be held together by constraint. Then will be the time for reverting to the precedents which occurred at the formation and adoption of the Constitution, to form again a more perfect union by dissolving that which could no longer bind, and to leave the separated parts to be reunited by the law of political gravitation to the centre."[7]

In other words, forecasting strife, and measuring the coercive force available at a time when steam on land and water was in its stages of earlier development, J. Q. Adams regarded the attempt at an assertion of national sovereignty as so futile that, though he most potently and powerfully believed in that sovereignty, he looked upon its exercise as quixotic, and, consequently, not to be justified. A dissolution of the Union, at least temporarily, he believed to be inevitable. So strongly was he convinced of the power of the disintegrating influence as contrasted with the cohesive force, that the late Robert C. Winthrop, then a young man of twenty-seven, writing in 1836, described him as saying, in the course of dinner-table talk, that "he despaired of the Union, believing we are destined soon to overrun not merely Texas, but Mexico, and that the inevitable result will be a break-up into two, three, four, or more confederacies." "Inevitable"! The unexpected alone is inevitable. These two utterances were, the one in 1836, the other in 1839. In 1839 there were not five hundred miles of constructed railroad in the United States; steam had not been applied to naval construction; electricity was a toy. So far as he could look into the future, Mr. Adams was right; only — the unexpected was to occur! It did occur; and it settled the question. In 1788 the preponderance of popular feeling and affection was wholly in the scale of State Sovereignty as opposed to Nationality; in 1800 the Union was, in all probability, saved by being taken from the hands of its friends, and, so to speak, put out to nurse with its enemies, who from that time were converted to unity; in 1815 the final war of independence gave a great impetus to Nationality, and the scales hung even; in 1831 the irrepressible conflict began to assert itself, and now they inclined slightly but distinctly to Nationality, the younger of the two sovereigns asserting a supremacy; between 1831 and 1861 science threw steam and electricity into his scale, and, in 1865 they made the other kick the beam. But, when all is said, merely a fresh illustration had been furnished of the truth of that scriptural adage in regard to a divided service.

Such are the conclusions reached from a renewed and somewhat careful review of a record frequently scanned by others. They found in it the outcome of great orations, labored arguments, and the teaching of individuals. I cannot so see it. It is, as I read it, one long majestic Greek tragedy.

" Like to the Pontic sea.
Whose icy current and compulsive course
Ne'er feels retiring ebb, but keeps due on
To the Propontic and the Hellespont," —

so that great drama swept on to its inevitable catastrophe; — Fate and Necessity ever the refrain of its chorus, — until, at the end, the resounding clash of arms.

For better, for worse, a new era then opened. In what I have this evening said I have dealt with a past in which, as I see it, the forces of nature — "the unseen hand at the game" — decided the issues involved. But there are times also when men have their turn, both asserting and establishing their superiority over fate, — shaping destiny to their desires, — triumphing amid the slings and arrows of outrageous fortune. In closing, were I to look for such a spectacle, I fancy it would not be in vain, nor would my search be far or long. I should find it here in the South, and not least in Charleston, in a manly adaption to unsought-for conditions, in the resiliency of a vigorous race casting calamity lightly aside, — "a dew-drop from the lion's mane." To what extent the issues of the past are bygone, my being here this night, and discussing them in this presence, bear conclusive evidence. And indeed, coming from Massachusetts to South Carolina, it glads my heart here to see, if I may in closing use the great language of Milton, "a noble and puissant nation rousing herself like a strong man after sleep, and shaking her invincible locks; an eagle mewing her mighty youth, and kindling her undazzled eyes at the full mid-day beam."

Notes:

1. Editor's Note: ΑΝΑΓΚΗ or Ananke is the mother of the mythical fates and sister to Chronos: Father Time. She has authority over final destiny.

2. " The convention framed a constitution by the adoption of which thirteen peoples imagining themselves still independent and sovereign, really acknowledged themselves to be but parts of a single political whole. But they made this acknowledgment unconsciously. They continued to think of themselves as sovereigns who indeed permitted an agent to exercise some of their functions for them, but who had not abdicated their thrones. If the constitution had contained a definite statement of the actual fact; if it had said that to adopt it was to acknowledge the sovereignty of the one American people, no part of which could sever its connections from the rest without the consent of the whole, it would probably have been rejected by every State in the Union." J. P. Gordy, *Political Parties in the United States* (Edition 1900), vol. i, p. 79.

3. Gordy, *Political Parties in the United States,* vol. i, pp. 203, 341.

4. Josiah Tucker, Dean of Gloucester, quoted by Bancroft, *History of the Formation of the Constitution,* i, 65.

5. Editor's Note: Cheng and Eng Bunker, 1811-1874, were the original "Siamese twins" and circus performers who married Anglo sisters in North Carolina, became planters, sired nearly two dozen children, and died within an hour of one another near Mount Airy, NC.

6. J. Q. Adams, *Jubilee of the Constitution* (April 30, 1839), p. 69.

10

'Tis Sixty Years Hence

*Founder's Day Address to the University of South Carolina
January 16, 1913*

In the single hour self-allotted for my part in this occasion there is much ground to cover,--the time is short, and I have far to go. Did I now, therefore, submit all I had proposed to say when I accepted your invitation, there would remain no space for preliminaries. Yet something of that character is in place. I will try to make it brief.

As the legend or text of what I have in mind to submit, I have given the words "'Tis Sixty Years Since." As some here doubtless recall, this is the second or subordinate title of Walter Scott's first novel, "Waverley," which brought him fame. Given to the world in 1814,--hard on a century ago,--"Waverley" told of the last Stuart effort to recover the crown of Great Britain,--that of "The '45." It so chances that Scott's period of retrospect is also just now most appropriate in my case, inasmuch as I entered Harvard as a student in the year 1853--"sixty years since!" It may fairly be asserted that school life ends, and what may in contradistinction thereto be termed thinking and acting life begins, the day the young man passes the threshold of the institution of more advanced education. For him, life's responsibilities then begin. Prior to that confused, thenceforth things with him become consecutive,--a sequence. Insensibly he puts away childish things.

Owing to its length, this "Address" was compressed in delivery, occupying one hour only. It is here printed in the form in which it was prepared,--the parts omitted in delivery being included.

In those days, as I presume now, the college youth harkened to inspired voices. Sir Walter Scott belonged to a previous generation. Having held the close attention of a delighted world as the most successful story-teller of his own or any preceding period, he had passed off the stage; but only a short twenty years before. Other voices no less inspired had followed; and, living, spoke to us. Perhaps my scheme to-day is best expressed by one of these.

When just beginning to attract the attention of the English-speaking world, Alfred Tennyson gave forth his poem of "Locksley Hall,"--very familiar to those of my younger days. Written years before, at the time of publication he was thirty-three. In 1886, a man of seventy-five, he composed a sequel to his earlier effort,--the utterance entitled "Locksley Hall Sixty Years After." He then, you will remember, reviewed his young man's dreams,--dreams of the period when he

> " ... dip't into the future, far as human eye could see,
> Saw the Vision of the world, and all the wonder that would be,"

--threescore years later contrasting in sombre verse an old man's stern realities with the bright anticipations of youth. Such is my purpose to-day. "Wandering back to living boyhood," to the time when I first simultaneously passed the Harvard threshold and the threshold of responsible life, I propose to compare the ideals and actualities of the present with the ideals, anticipations and dreams of a past now somewhat remote.

To say that in life and in the order of life's events it is the unexpected which is apt to occur, is a commonplace. That it has been so in my own case, I shall presently show. Meanwhile, not least among the unexpected things is my presence here to-day. If, when I entered Harvard in 1853, it had been suggested that in 1913, I,--born of the New England Sanhedrim, a Brahmin Yankee by blood, tradition and environment--had it been suggested that I, being such, would sixty years later stand by invitation here in Columbia before the faculty and students of the University of South Carolina, I should under circumstances then existing have pronounced the suggestion as beyond reasonable credence. Here, however, I am; and here, from this as my rostrum, I propose to-day to deliver a message,--such as it is.

And yet, though such a future outcome, if then foretold, would have seemed scarcely possible of occurrence, there, after all, were certain conditions which would have rendered the contingency even at that time not only possible, but in accordance with the everlasting fitness of things. For, curiously enough, personal relations of a certain character held with this institution would have given me, even in 1853, a sense of acquaintance with it such as individually I had with no other institution of similar character throughout the entire land. It in this wise came about. At that period, preceding as it did the deluge about to ensue, it was the hereditary custom of certain families more especially of South Carolina and of Louisiana,--but of South Carolina in particular--to send their youth to Harvard, there to receive a college education. It thus chanced that among my associates at Harvard were not a few who bore names long familiarly and honorably known to Carolinian records,--Barnwell and Preston, Rhett and Alston, Parkman and Eliot; and among these were some I knew well, and even intimately. Gone now with the generation and even the civilization to which they belonged, I doubt if any of them survive. Indeed only recently I chanced on a grimly suggestive mention of one who had left on me the memory of a character and personality singularly pure, high-toned and manly,-- permeated with a sense of moral and personal obligation. I have always understood he died five years later at Sharpsburg, as you call it, or Antietam, as it was named by us, in face-to-face conflict with a Massachusetts regiment largely officered by Harvard men of his time and even class,--his own familiar friends. This is the record, the reference being to a marriage service held at St. Paul's church in Richmond, in the late autumn of 1862: "An indefinable feeling of gloom was thrown over a most auspicious event when the bride's youngest sister glided through a side door just before the processional. Tottering to a chancel pew, she threw herself upon the cushions, her slight frame racked with sobs. Scarcely a year before, the wedding march had been played for her, and a joyous throng saw her wedded to gallant Breck Parkman. Before another twelvemonth rolled around the groom was killed at the front."[1] Samuel Breck Parkman was in the Harvard class following that to which I belonged. Graduating in 1857, fifty-five years later I next saw his name in the connection just given. It recorded an incident of not infrequent occurrence in those dark and cruel days.

It was, however, in Breck Parkman and his like that I first became conscious of certain phases of the South Carolina character which subsequently I learned to bear in high respect.

So far as this University of South Carolina was concerned, it also so chanced that, by the merest accident, I, a very young man, was thrown into close personal relations with one of the most eminent of your professors,--Francis Lieber. Few here, I suppose, now personally remember Francis Lieber. To most it gives indeed a certain sense of remoteness to meet one who, as in my case, once held close and even intimate relations with a German emigrant, distinguished as a publicist, who as a youth had lain, wounded and helpless, a Prussian recruit, on the field above Namur. Occurring in June, 1815, two days after Waterloo, the affair at Namur will soon be a century gone. Of those engaged in it, the last obeyed the fell sergeant's summons a half score years ago. It seems remote; but at the time of which I speak Waterloo was appreciably nearer those in active life than are Shiloh and Gettysburg now. The Waterloo campaign was then but thirty-eight years removed, whereas those last are fifty now; and, while Lieber was at Waterloo, I was myself at Gettysburg.

Subsequently, later in life, it was again my privilege to hold close relations with another Columbian,--an alumnus of this University as it then was--in whom I had opportunity to study some of the strongest and most respect-commanding traits of the Southern character. I refer to one here freshly remembered,--Alexander Cheves Haskell,--soldier, jurist, banker and scholar, one of a septet of brothers sent into the field by a South Carolina mother calm and tender of heart, but in silent suffering unsurpassed by any recorded in the annals whether of Judea or of Rome. It was the fourth of the seven Haskells I knew, one typical throughout, in my belief, of what was best in your Carolinian development. With him, as I have said, I was closely and even intimately associated through years, and in him I had occasion to note that almost austere type represented in its highest development in the person and attributes of Calhoun. Of strongly marked descent, Haskell was, as I have always supposed, of a family and race in which could be observed those virile Scotch-Irish and Presbyterian qualities which found their representative types in the two Jacksons,--Andrew, and him known in history as "Stonewall." To Alec Haskell I shall in this discourse again have occasion to refer.

Thus, though in 1853, and for long years subsequent thereto, it would not have entered my mind as among the probabilities that I should ever stand here, reviewing the past after the manner of Tennyson in his "Locksley Hall Sixty Years After," yet if there was any place in the South, or, I may say, in the entire country, where, as a matter of association, I might naturally have looked so to stand, it would have been where now I find myself.

But I must hasten on; for, as I have said, if I am to accomplish even a part of my purpose, I have no time wherein to linger.

Not long ago I chanced, in a country ramble, to be conversing with an eminent foreigner, known, and favorably known, to all Americans. In the course of leisurely exchange of ideas between us, he suddenly asked if I could suggest any explanation of the fact that not only were the publicists who had the greatest vogue in our college days now to a large extent discredited, but that almost every view and theory advanced by them, and which we had accepted as fixed and settled, was, where not actually challenged, silently ignored. Nor did the assertion admit of denial; for, looking back through the vista of threescore years, of the principles of what may be called "public polity" then advanced as indisputable, few to-day meet with general acceptance. To review the record from this point of view is curious.

When in 1853 I entered Harvard, so far as this country and its polity were concerned certain things were matters of contention, while others were accepted as axiomatic,--the basic truths of our system. Among the former--the subjects of active contention--were the question of Slavery, then grimly assuming shape, and that of Nationality intertwined therewith. Subordinate to this was the issue of Free Trade and Protection, with the school of so-called American political economy arrayed against that of Adam Smith. Beyond these as political ideals were the tenets and theories of Jeffersonian Democracy. That the world had heretofore been governed too much was loudly acclaimed, and the largest possible individualism was preached, not only as a privilege but as a right. The area of government action was to be confined within the narrowest practical limits, and ample scope was to be allowed to each to develop in the way most natural to himself, provided only he did not infringe upon the rights of others. Materially, we were then reaching out to subdue a continent,--a doctrine of Manifest Destiny was in vogue. Beyond this, however, and most important now to be borne in mind, compared with the present the control of man over natural agencies and latent forces was scarcely begun. Not yet had the railroad crossed the Missouri; electricity, just bridled, was still unharnessed.

I have now passed in rapid review what may perhaps without exaggeration be referred to as an array of conditions and theories, ideals and policies. It remains to refer to the actual results which have come about during these sixty years as respects them, or because of them; and, finally, to reach if possible conclusions as to the causes which have affected what may not inaptly be termed a process of general evolution. Having thus, so to speak, diagnosed the situation, the changes the situation exacts are to be measured, and a forecast ventured. An ambitious programme, I am well enough aware that the not very considerable reputation I have established for myself hardly warrants me in attempting it. This, I premise.

Let us, in the first place, recur in somewhat greater detail to the various policies and ideals I have referred to as in vogue in the year 1853.

First and foremost, overshadowing all else, was the political issue raised by African slavery, then ominously assuming shape. The clouds foreboding the coming tempest were gathering thick and heavy; and, moreover, they were even then illumined by electric flashes, accompanied by a mutter of distant thunder. Though we of the North certainly did not appreciate its gravity, the situation was portentous in the extreme.

Involved in this problem of African slavery was the incidental issue of Free Trade and Protection,--apparently only economical and industrial in character, but in reality fundamentally crucial. And behind this lay the constitutional question, involving as it did not only the conflicting theories of a strict or liberal construction of the fundamental law, but nationality also,--the right of a Sovereign State to withdraw from the Union created in 1787, and developed through two generations.

These may be termed concrete political issues, as opposed to basic truths generally accepted and theories individually entertained. The theories were constitutional, social, economical. Constitutionally, they turned upon the obligations of citizenship. There was no such thing then as a citizen of the United States of and by itself. The citizen of the United States was such simply because of his citizenship of a Sovereign State,--whether Massachusetts or Virginia or South Carolina; and, of course, an instrument based upon a divided sovereignty admitted of almost infinitely diverse interpretation. It is a scriptural aphorism that no man can serve two masters; for either he will hate the one and love the other, or else he will hold to the one and despise the other. And in the fulness of time it literally with us so came about. The accepted economical theories of the period were to a large extent corollaries of the fundamental proposition, and differing material and social conditions. Beyond all this, and coming still under the head of individual theories, was the doctrine enunciated by Thomas Jefferson in the Declaration of Independence,--the doctrine that all men were created equal,--meaning, of course, equal before the law. But the theorist and humanitarian of the North, accepting the fundamental principle laid down in the Declaration, gave to it a far wider application than had been intended by its authors,--a breadth of application it would not bear. Such science as he had being of scriptural origin, he interpreted the word "equal" as signifying equal in the possibilities of their attributes,--physical, moral, intellectual; and in so doing, he of course ignored the first principles of ethnology. It was, I now realize, a somewhat wild-eyed school of philosophy, that of which I myself was a youthful disciple.

But, on the other hand, beside these, between 1850 and 1860 a class of trained and more cautious thinkers, observers, scientists and theologians was coming to the front. Their investigations, though we did not then foresee it, were a generation later destined gently to subvert the accepted fundamentals of religious and economical thought, literary performance, and material existence. The work they had in hand to do was for the next fifteen years to be subordinate, so far as this country was concerned, to the solution of the terrible political problems which were first insistent on settlement; yet, as is now apparent, an initial movement was on foot which foreboded a revolution world-wide in its nature, and one in comparison with which the issues of slavery and American constitutionality became practically insignificant,--in a word, local and passing incidents.

Finally, it remains to consider specifically the political theories then in vogue in their relation to the individual. In this country, it was the period of the equality of man and individuality in the development of the type. It was generally believed that the world had hitherto been governed too much,--that the day of caste, and even class, was over and gone; and finally, that America was a species of vast modern melting-pot of humanity, in which, within a comparatively short period of time, the characteristics of all branches of Indo-Aryan origin would resolve themselves. A new type would emerge,--the American. These theories were also in their consequences far-reaching. Practically, 1853 ante-dates all our present industrial organizations so loudly in evidence,-- the multifarious trades-unions which now divide the population of the

United States into what are known as the "masses" and the "classes." As recently as a century ago, it used to be said of the French army under the Empire, that every soldier carried the baton of the Field-Marshal in his knapsack. And this ideal of equality and individuality was fixed in the American mind.

Not that I for a moment mean to imply that in my belief the middle of the last century, or the twenty years anterior to the Civil War, was a species of golden age in our American annals. On the contrary, it was, as I remember it, a phase of development very open to criticism; and that in many respects. It was crude, self-conscious and self-assertive; provincial and formative, rather than formed. Socially and materially we were, compared with the present era of motors and parlor-cars, in the "one-hoss shay" and stove-heated railroad-coach stage. Nevertheless, what is now referred to as "predatory wealth" had not yet begun to accumulate in few hands; much greater equality of condition prevailed; nor was the "wage-earner" referred to as constituting a class distinct from the holders of property. Thus the individual was then encouraged,--whether in literature, in commerce, or in politics. In other words, there being a free field, one man was held to be in all respects the equal of the rest. Especially was what I have said true of the Northern, or so-called Free States, as contrasted with the States of the South, where the presence of African slavery distinctly affected individual theories, no matter where or to what extent entertained.

Such, briefly and comprehensively stated, having been the situation in 1853, it remains to consider the practical outcome thereof during the sixty years it has been my fortune to take part, either as an actor or as an observer, in the great process of evolution. It is curious to note the extent to which the unexpected has come about. In the first place, consider the all-absorbing mid-century political issue, that involving the race question, to which I first referred,--the issue which divided the South from the North, and which, eight years only after I had entered college, carried me from the walks of civil life into the calling of arms.

And here I enter on a field of discussion both difficult and dangerous; and, for reasons too obvious to require statement, what I am about to say will be listened to with no inconsiderable apprehension as to what next may be forthcoming. Nevertheless, this is a necessary part of my theme; and I propose to say what I have in mind to say, setting forth with all possible frankness the more mature conclusions reached with the passage of years. Let it be received in the spirit in which it is offered.

So far, then, as the institution of slavery is concerned, in its relations to ownership and property in those of the human species,--I have seen no reason whatever to revise or in any way to alter the theories and principles I entertained in 1853, and in the maintenance of which I subsequently bore arms between 1861 and 1865. Economically, socially, and from the point of view of abstract political justice, I hold that the institution of slavery, as it existed in this country prior to the year 1865, was in no respect either desirable or justifiable. That it had its good and even its elevating side, so far at least as the African is concerned, I am not here to deny. On the contrary, I see and recognize those features of the institution far more clearly now than I should have said would have been possible in 1853. That the institution in itself, under conditions then existing, tended to the elevation of the less advanced race, I frankly admit I did not then think. On the other hand, that it exercised a most pernicious influence upon those of the more advanced race, and especially upon that large majority of the more advanced race who were not themselves owners of slaves,--of that I have become with time ever more and more satisfied. The noticeable feature, how-ever, so far as I individually am concerned, has been the entire change of view as respects certain of the fundamental propositions at the base of our whole American political and social edifice brought about by a more careful and intelligent ethnological study. I refer to the political equality of man, and to that race absorption to which I have alluded,--that belief that any foreign element introduced into the American social system and body politic would speedily be absorbed therein, and in a brief space thoroughly assimilated. In this all-important respect I do not hesitate to say we theorists and abstractionists of the North, through-out that long anti-slavery discussion which ended with the 1861 clash of arms, were thoroughly wrong. In utter disregard of fundamental, scientific facts, we theoretically believed that all men--no matter what might be the color of their skin, or the texture of their hair--were, if placed under exactly similar conditions, in essentials the same. In other words, we indulged in the curious and, as is now admitted, utterly erroneous theory that the African was, so to speak, an Anglo-Saxon, or, if you will, a Yankee "who had never had a chance,"--a fellow-man who was guilty, as we chose to express it, of a skin not colored like our own. In other words, though carved in ebony, he also was in the image of God.

Following out this theory, under the lead of men to whom scientific analysis and observation were anathema if opposed to accepted cardinal political theories as enunciated in the Declaration as read by them, the African was not only emancipated, but so far as the letter of the law, as expressed in an amended Constitution, would establish the fact, the quondam slave was in all respects placed on an equality, political, legal and moral, with those of the more advanced race.

I do not hesitate here,--as one who largely entertained the theoretical views I have expressed,--I do not hesitate here to say, as the result of sixty years of more careful study and scientific observation, the theories then entertained by us were not only fundamentally wrong, but they further involved a problem in the presence of which I confess to-day I stand appalled.

It is said,--whether truthfully or not,--that when some years ago John Morley, the English writer and thinker, was in this country, on returning to England he remarked that the African race question, as now existing in the United States, presented a problem as nearly, to his mind, insoluble as any human problem well could be. I do not care whether Lord Morley made this statement or did not make it. I am prepared, however, to say that, individually, so far as my present judgment goes, it is a correct presentation. To us in the North, the African is a comparatively negligible factor. So far as Massachusetts, for instance, or the city of Boston more especially, are concerned, as a problem it is solving itself. Proportionately, the African infusion is becoming less--

never large, it is incomparably less now than it was in the days of my own youth. Thus manifestly a negligible factor, it is also one tending to extinction. Indeed, it would be fairly open to question whether a single Afro-American of unmixed Ethiopian descent could now be found in Boston. That the problem presents itself with a wholly different aspect here in Carolina is manifest. The difference too is radical; it goes to the heart of the mystery.

As I have already said, the universal "melting-pot" theory in vogue in my youth was that but seven, or at the most fourteen, years were required to convert the alien immigrant--no matter from what region or of what descent--into an American citizen. The educational influences and social environment were assumed to be not only subtle, but all-pervasive and powerful. That this theory was to a large and even dangerous extent erroneous the observation of the last fifty years has proved, and our Massachusetts experience is sadly demonstrating to-day. It was Oliver Wendell Holmes, who, years ago, when asked by an anxious mother at what age the education of a child ought to begin, re-marked in reply that it should begin about one hundred and fifty years before the child is born. It has so proved with us; and the fact is to-day in evidence that this statement of Dr. Holmes should be accepted as an undeniable political aphorism. So far from seven or fourteen years making an American citizen, fully and thoroughly impregnated with American ideals to the exclusion of all others, our experience is that it requires at least three generations to eliminate what may be termed the "hyphen" in citizenship. Not in the first, nor in the second, and hardly in the third, generation, does the immigrant cease to be an Irish-American, or a French-American, or a German-American, or a Slavonic-American, or yet a Dago. Nevertheless, in process of tune, those of the Caucasian race do and will become Americans. Ultimately their descendants will be free from the traditions and ideals, so to speak, ground in through centuries passed under other conditions. Not so the Ethiopian. In his case, we find ourselves confronted with a situation never contemplated in that era of political dreams and scriptural science in which our institutions received shape. Stated tersely and in plain language, so far as the African is concerned--the cause and, so to speak, the motive of the great struggle of 1861 to 1865--we recognize the presence in the body politic of a vast alien mass which does not assimilate and which cannot be absorbed. In other words, the melting-pot theory came in sharp contact with an ethnological fact, and the unexpected occurred. The problem of African servitude was solved after a fashion; but in place of it a race issue of most uncompromising character evolved itself.

A survivor of the generation which read "Uncle Tom's Cabin" as it week by week appeared,--fresh to-day from Massachusetts with its Lawrence race issues of a different character, I feel a sense of satis-faction in discussing here in South Carolina this question and issue in a spirit the reverse of dogmatic, a spirit purely scientific, observant and sympathetic. And in this connection let me say I well remember re-peatedly discussing it with your fellow-citizen and my friend, Colonel Alexander Haskell, to whom I have already made reference. Rarely have I been more impressed by a conclusion reached and fixed in the mind of one who to the study of a problem had obviously given much and kindly thought. As those who knew him do not need to be told, Alexander Cheves Haskell was a man of character, pure and just and thoughtful. He felt towards the African as only a Southerner who had himself never been the owner of slaves can feel. He regarded him as of a less advanced race than his own, but one who was entitled not only to just and kindly treatment but to sympathetic consideration. When, however, the question of the future of the Afro-American was raised, as matter for abstract discussion, it was suggestive as well as curious to observe the fixed, hard expression which immediately came over Haskell's face, as with stern lips, from which all suggestion of a smile had faded away, he pronounced the words:--"Sir, it is a dying race!" To express the thought more fully, Colonel Haskell maintained, as I doubt not many who now listen to me will maintain, that the nominal Afro-American increase, as shown in the figures of the national census, is deceptive,--that in point of fact, the Ethiop in America is incurring the doom which has ever befallen those of an inferior and less advanced race when brought in direct and immediate contact, necessarily and inevitably competitive, with the more advanced, the more masterful, and intellectually the more gifted. In other words, those of the less advanced race have a fatal aptitude for contracting the vices, both moral and physical, of the superior race, in the end leading to destruction; while the capacity for assimilating the elevating qualities and attributes which constitute a saving grace is denied them. Elimination, therefore, became in Haskell's belief a question of time only,--the law of the survival of the fittest would assert itself. The time required may be long,--numbered by centuries; but, however remotely, it nevertheless would come. God's mill grinds slowly, but it grinds uncommon small; and, I will add, its grinding is apt to be merciless.

The solution thus most pronouncedly laid down by Colonel Haskell may or may not prove in this case correct and final. It certainly is not for me, coming from the North, to undertake dogmatically to pass upon it. I recur to it here as a plausible suggestion only, in connection with my theme. As such, it unquestionably merits consideration. I am by no means prepared to go the length of an English authority in recently saying that "emancipation on two continents sacrificed the real welfare of the slave and his intrinsic worth as a person, to the impatient vanity of an immediate and theatrical triumph."[2] This length I say, I cannot go; but so far as the present occasion is concerned, with such means of observation as are within my reach, I find the conclusion difficult to resist that the success of the abolitionists in effecting the emancipation of the Afro-American, as unexpected and sweeping as it was sudden, has led to phases of the race problem quite unanticipated at least. For instance, as respects segregation. Instead of assimilating, with a tendency to ultimate absorption, the movement in the opposite direction since 1865 is pronounced. It has, moreover, received the final stamp of scientific approval. This implies much; for in the old days of the "peculiar institution" there is no question the relations between the two races were far more intimate, kindly, and even absorptive than they now are.

That African slavery, as it existed in the United States anterior to the year 1862, presented a mild form of servitude, as servitude then existed and immemorially had almost everywhere existed, was, moreover, incontrovertibly proven in the course of the Civil War. Before 1862, it was confidently believed that any severe social agitation within, or disturbance from without, would inevitably lead to a Southern servile insurrection. In Europe this result was assumed as of course; and, immediately after it was issued, the Emancipation Proclamation of President Lincoln was denounced in unmeasured terms by the entire London press. Not a voice was raised in its defence. It was regarded as a measure unwarranted in civilized warfare, and a sure and intentional incitement to the horrors which had attended the servile insurrections of Haiti and San Domingo; and, more recently, the unspeakable Sepoy incidents of the Indian mutiny. What actually occurred is now historic. The confident anticipations of our English brethren were, not for the first time, negatived; nor is there any page in our American record more creditable to those concerned than the attitude held by the African during the fierce internecine struggle which prevailed between April, 1861, and April, 1865. In it there is scarcely a trace, if indeed there is any trace at all, of such a condition of affairs as had developed in the Antilles and in Hindustan. The attitude of the African towards his Confederate owner was submissive and kindly. Although the armed and masterful domestic protector was at the front and engaged in deadly, all-absorbing conflict, yet the women and children of the Southern plantation slept with unbarred doors,--free from apprehension, much more from molestation.

Moreover, as you here well know, during the old days of slavery there was hardly a child born, of either sex, who grew up in a Southern household of substantial wealth without holding immediate and most affectionate relations with those of the other race. Every typical Southern man had what he called his "daddy" and his "mammy," his "uncle" and his "aunty," by him familiarly addressed as such, and who were to him even closer than are blood relations to most. They had cared for him in his cradle; he followed them to their graves. Is it needful for me to ask to what extent such relations still exist? Of those born thirty years after emancipation, and therefore belonging distinctly to a later generation, how many thus have their kindly, if humble, kin of the African blood? I fancy I would be safe in saying not one in twenty.

Here, then, as the outcome of the first great issue I have suggested as occupying the thought and exciting the passions of that earlier period, is a problem wholly unanticipated,--a problem which, merely stating, I dismiss.

Passing rapidly on, I come to the next political issue which presented itself in my youth,--the constitutional issue,--that of State Sovereignty, as opposed to the ideal, Nationality. And, whether for better or worse, this issue, I very confidently submit, has been settled. We now, also, looking at it in more observant mood, in a spirit at once philosophical and historical, see that it involved a process of natural evolution which, under the conditions prevailing, could hardly result in any other settlement than that which came about. We now have come to a recognition of the fact that Anglo-Saxon nationality on this continent was a problem of crystallization, the working out of which occupied a little over two centuries. It was in New England the process first set in, when, in 1643, the scattered English-speaking settlements under the hegemony of the colony of Massachusetts Bay united in a confederation. It was the initial step. I have no time in which to enumerate successive steps, each representing a stage in advance of what went before. The War of Independence,--mistakenly denominated the Revolutionary War, but a struggle distinctly conservative in character, and in no way revolutionary,--the War of Independence gave great impetus to the process, resulting in what was known as Federation. Then came the Constitution of 1787 and the formation of the, so called, United States as a distinct nationality. The United States next passed through two definite processes of further crystallization,--one in 1812-1814, when the second war with Great Britain, and more especially our naval victories, kindled, especially in the North, the fire of patriotism and the conception of nationality; the other, half a century later, presented the stern issue in a concrete form, and at last the complete unification of a community--whether for better or for worse is no matter--was hammered by iron and cemented in blood. It is there now; an established fact. Secession is a lost cause; and, whether for good or for ill, the United States exists, and will continue to exist, a unified World Power. Sovereignty now rests at Washington, and neither in Columbia for South Carolina nor in Boston for Massachusetts. The State exists only as an integral portion of the United States. That issue has been fought out. The result stands beyond controversy; brought about by a generation now passed on, but to which I belonged.

Meanwhile, the ancient adage, the rose is not without its thorn, receives new illustration; for even this great result has not been wrought without giving rise to considerations suggestive of thought. Speaking tersely and concentrating what is in my mind into the fewest possible words, I may say that in our national growth up to the year 1830 the play of the centrifugal forces predominated,--that is, the necessity for greater cohesion made itself continually felt. A period of quiescence then followed, lasting until, we will say, 1865. Since 1865, it is not unsafe to say, the centripetal, or gravitating, force has predominated to an extent ever more suggestive of increasing political uneasiness. It is now, as is notorious, more in evidence than ever before. The tendency to concentrate at Washington, the demand that the central government, assuming one function after another, shall become imperial, the cry for the national enactment of laws, whether relating to marital divorce or to industrial combinations,--all impinge on the fundamental principle of local self-government, which assumed its highest and most pronounced form in the claim of State Sovereignty. I am now merely stating problems. I am not discussing the political ills or social benefits which possibly may result from action. Nevertheless, all, I think, must admit that the tendency to gravitation and attraction is to-day as pronounced and as dangerous, especially in the industrial communities of the North, as was the tendency to separation and segregation pronounced and dangerous seventy years ago in the South.

To this I shall later return. I now merely point out what I apprehend to be a tendency to extremes--an excess in the swinging of our political pendulum.

We next come to that industrial factor which I have referred to as the issue between the Free Trade of Adam Smith and Protection, as inculcated by the so-called American school of political economists. The phases which this issue has assumed are, I submit, well calculated to excite the attention of the observant and thoughtful. I merely allude to them now; but, in so far as it is in my power to make it so, my allusion will be specific. I frankly acknowledge myself a Free-Trader. A Free-Trader in theory, were it in my power I would be a Free-Trader in national practice. There has been, so far as I know, but one example of absolute free trade on the largest scale in world history. That one example, moreover, has been a success as unqualified as undeniable. I refer to this American Union of ours. We have here a country consisting of fifty local communities, stretching from the Atlantic to the Pacific, from tropical Porto Rico to glacial Alaska, representing every conceivable phase of soil, climate and material conditions, with diverse industrial systems. With a Union established on the principle of absolutely unrestricted commercial intercourse, you here in South Carolina, and more especially in Columbia, are to-day making it, so to speak, uncomfortable for the cotton manufacturer in New England; and I am glad of it! A sharp competition is a healthy incentive to effort and ingenuity, and the brutal injunction, "Root hog or die!" is one from which I in no way ask to have New England exempt. When Massachusetts is no longer able to hold its own industrially in a free field, the time will, in my judgment, have come for Massachusetts to go down. With communities as with children, paternalism reads arrested development. One of the great products of Massachusetts has been what is generically known as "footwear." Yet I am told that under the operation of absolute Free Trade, St. Louis possesses the largest boot and shoe factory in its output in the entire world. That is, the law of industrial development, as natural conditions warrant and demand, has worked out its results; and those results are satisfactory. I am aware that the farmer of Massachusetts has become practically extinct; he cannot face the competition of the great West: but the Massachusetts consumer is greatly advantaged thereby. So far as agricultural products are concerned, Massachusetts is to-day reduced to what is known as dairy products and garden truck; and it is well! Summer vegetables manufactured under glass in winter prove profitable. So, turning his industrial efforts to that which he can do best, even the Massachusetts agriculturalist has prospered. On the other hand, wherever in this country protection has been most completely applied, I insist that if its results are analyzed in an unprejudiced spirit, it will be pronounced to have worked unmitigated evil,--an unhealthy, because artificially stimulated and too rapid, growth. Let Lawrence, in Massachusetts, serve as an example. Look at the industrial system there introduced in the name of Protection against the Pauper Labor of Europe! No growth is so dangerous as a too rapid growth; and I confidently submit that politically, socially, economically and industrially, America to-day, on the issues agitating us, presents an almost appalling example of the results of hot-house stimulation.

Nor is this all, nor the worst. There is another article, and far more damaging, in the indictment. Through Protection, and because of it, Paternalism has crept in; and, like a huge cancerous growth, is eating steadily into the vitals of the political system. Instead of supporting a government economically administered by money contributed by the People, a majority of the People to-day are looking to the government for support, either directly through pension payments or indirectly through some form of industrial paternalism. Incidentally, a profuse public expenditure is condoned where not actually encouraged. Jeffersonian simplicity is preached; extravagance is practised. As the New York showman long since shrewdly observed: "The American people love to be fooled!"

But I must pass on; I still have far to go. As respects legislation, I have said that sixty years ago, when my memories begin, the American ideal was the individual, and individuality. This, implied adherence to the Jeffersonian theory that heretofore the world had been governed too much. The great secret of true national prosperity, happiness and success was, we were taught, to allow to each individual the fullest possible play, provided only he did not infringe on the rights of others. How is it to-day? America is the most governed and legislated country in the world! With one national law-making machine perpetually at work grinding out edicts, we have some fifty provincial mills engaged in the same interesting and, to my mind, pernicious work. No one who has given the slightest consideration to the subject will dispute the proposition that, taking America as a whole, we now have twenty acts of legislation annually promulgated, and with which we are at our peril supposed to be familiar, where one would more than suffice. Then we wonder that respect for the law shows a sensible decrease! The better occasion for wonder is that it survives at all. We are both legislated and litigated out of all reason.

Passing to the other proposition of individuality, there has been, as all men know and no one will dispute, a most perceptible tendency of late years towards what is known as the array of one portion of the community--the preponderating, voting portion--against another--the more ostentatious property-holding portion. It is the natural result, I may say the necessary as well as logical outcome, of a period of too rapid growth,--production apportioned by no rule or system other or higher than greed and individual aptitude for acquisition. I will put the resulting case in the most brutal, and consequently the clearest, shape of which I am capable. Working on the combined theories of individualism controlled and regulated by competition, it has been one grand game of grab,--a process in which the whole tendency of our legislation, national or state, has during the last twenty years been, first, to create monopolies of capital and, later, to bring into existence a counter, but no less privileged, class, known as the "wage-earner."

Of the first class it is needless to speak, for, as a class, it is sufficiently pilloried by the press and from the hustings. Much in evidence, those prominent in it are known as the possessors of "predatory wealth"; "unjailed malefactors," they are subjects of continuous "grilling" in the congressional and legislative committee rooms. The effort to make them "disgorge" is as continual as it is noisy, and, as a rule, futile. It constitutes a curious and in some respects instructive exhibition of mis-directed popular feeling and legislative incompetence. None the less, the existence of a monopolist class calls for no proof at the bar of public opinion. Not so the other and even more privileged class,--the so-called "wage-earner"; for, disguise it as the trades-unionist will, angrily deny it as he does, the fact remains that to-day under the operation of our jury system and of our laws, the Wage-earner and the member of the Trades-Union has become, as respects the rest of the community, him-self a monopolist and, moreover, privileged as such. Practically, crimes urged and even perpetrated in behalf of so-called "labor" receive at the hands of juries, and also not infrequently of courts, an altogether exces-sive degree of merciful consideration. At the same time, both here and in Europe, Organized Labor is instant in its demand that immunity, denied to ordinary citizens, and those whom it terms "the classes," shall by special exemption be conferred upon the Labor Union and upon the Wage-earner. The tendency on both sides and at each extreme to inequality in the legislature and before the law is thus manifest.

Viewing conditions face to face and as they now are, no thoughtful observer can, in my judgment, avoid the conviction that, whether for good or ill, for better or for worse, this country as a community has, within the last thirty years--that is, we will say, since our centennial year, 1876--cast loose from its original moorings. It has drifted, and is drifting, into unknown seas. Nor is this true of English-speaking America alone. I have already quoted Lord Morley in another con-nection. Lord Morley, however, only the other day delivered, as Chancellor of Manchester University, a most interesting and highly suggestive address, in which, referring to conservative Great Britain, he thus pictured a phase of current belief: "Political power is described as lying in the hands of a vast and mobile electorate, with scanty regard for tradition or history. Democracy, they say, is going to write its own programme. The structure of executive organs and machinery is undergoing half-hidden but serious alterations. Men discover a change of attitude towards law as law; a decline in reverence for institutions as institutions."

While, however, the influences at work are thus general and the manifestations whether on the other side of the Atlantic or here bear a strong resemblance, yet difference of conditions and detail--constitutional peculiarities, so to speak--must not be disregarded. One form of treatment may not be prescribed for all. In our case, therefore, it remains to consider how best to adapt this country and ourselves to the unforeseeable,--the navigation of uncharted waters; and this adaptation cannot be considered hi any correct and helpful, because scientific, spirit, unless the cause of change is located. Surface manifestations are, in and of themselves, merely deceptive. A physician, diagnosing the chances of a patient, must first correctly ascertain, or at least ascertain with approximate correctness, the seat of the trouble under which the patient is suffering. So, we.

And here I must frankly confess to small respect for the politician,--the man whose voice is continually heard, whether from the Senate Chamber or the Hustings. There is in those of his class a continual and most noticeable tendency to what may best be described as the *post ergo propter* dispensation. With them, the eye is fixed on the immediate manifestation. Because one event preceded another, the first event is obviously and indisputably the cause of the later event. For instance, in the present case, the cause or seat of our existing and very manifest social, political and financial disturbances is attributed as of course to some peculiarity of legislation, either a subtreasury bill passed in the administration of General Jackson, or a tariff bill passed in the administration of Mr. Taft, or the demonetization of silver in the Hayes period,--that "Crime of the Century," the Crucifixion of Labor on the Cross of Gold! Once for all, let me say, I contemplate this school of politicians and so-called "thinkers" with sentiments the reverse of respectful. In plain language, I class them with those known in professional parlance as quacks and charlatans. Not always, not even in the majority of cases, does that which preceded bear to that which follows the relation of cause and effect. A marked example of this false attribution is afforded in more recent political history by the everlasting recurrence of the statement that American prosperity is the result of an American protective system. Yet in the Protectionist dispensation, this has become an article of faith. To my mind, it is undeserving of even respectful consideration.

If I were asked the cause of that change, little short of revolutionary, if indeed in any respect short of it, which has occurred in the material condition of the American people, and consequently in all its theories and ideals, within the last thirty years, I should attribute it to a wholly different cause. Mr. Lecky some years ago, in his book entitled "Liberty and Democracy," made the following statement, in no way original, but, as he put it, sufficiently striking: "The produce of the American mines [incident to the discoveries made by Columbus] created, in the most extreme form ever known in Europe, the change which beyond all others affects most deeply and universally the material well-being of men: it revolutionized the value of the precious metals, and, in consequence, the price of all articles, the effects of all contracts, the burden of all debts."

In other words, referring to the first half of the sixteenth century,-- the sixty years, we will say, following the land-fall of Columbus,--the historian attributed the great change which then occurred and which stands forth so markedly in history, to the increased New-World production of the precious metals, combined with the impetus given to trade and industry as a consequence of that discovery, and of the mastery of man over additional globe areas. Now, dismissing from consideration the so-called American protective system, likewise our currency issues and, generally, the patchwork, so to speak, of crazy-quilt legislation to which so much is attributed during the last thirty years, I confidently submit that in the production of the results under discussion, they are quantities and factors hardly worthy of consideration. The cause of the change which has taken place lies far deeper and must be sought in influences of a wholly different nature, influences developed into an increased and still ever increasing activity, over which legislation has absolutely no control. I refer, of course, to man's mastery over the latent forces of Nature. Of these Steam and Electricity are the great examples, which, because always apparent, at once strike the imagination. These, as tools, it is to be remembered, date practically from within one hundred years back. It may, indeed, safely be asserted that up to 1815, the end of the Wars of Napoleon and the time of your Professor Lieber, steam even had not as yet practically affected the operations of man, while electricity, when not a terror, was as yet but a toy. Commerce was still exclusively carried on by the sailing ship and canal-boat. The years from the fall of Napoleon to our own War of Secession--from Waterloo to Gettysburg--were practically those of early and partial development. Not until well after Appomattox, that is, since the year 1870,--a period covering but little more than the life of a generation,--did what is known to you here as the Applied Sciences cover a range difficult to specialize. As factors in development, it is safe to say that those three tremendous agencies--Steam, Electricity, Chemistry--have, so to speak, worked all their noticeable results within the lifetime of the generation born since we celebrated the Centennial of Independence. The manifestations now resulting and apparent to all are the natural outcome of the use of these modern appliances, become in our case everyday working tools in the hands of the most resourceful, adaptive, ingenious and energetic of communities, developing a virgin continent of undreamed-of wealth. Naturally, under such conditions, the advance has been not only general and continuous, but one of ever increasing celerity. So Protection and the Currency become flies on the fast revolving wheel!

But what has otherwise resulted?--An unrest, social, economical, political. Not contentment, but a lamentation and an ancient tale of wrong! We hear it in the continual cry over what is known as the increased cost of living, and feel its pressure in the higher standard of living. What was considered wealth by our ancestors is to-day hardly competence. What sufficed for luxury in our childhood barely now supplies what are known as the comforts of life. Take, for instance, the motor,--the automobile. I speak within bounds, I think, when I say there are many fold more motors to-day racing over the streets, the highways and the byways of America than there were one-horse wagons thirty-five years ago. Six hundred, I am told, are to be found within the immediate neighborhood of Columbia; and, since I have been here I have seen in your streets just one man on horse-back! These figures and that statement tell the tale. A few years only back, every Carolinian rode to town, and the motor was unknown. A single illustrative example, this could be duplicated in innumerable ways everywhere and in all walks of life.

The result is obvious, and was inevitable. Entered on a new phase of existence, the world is not as it was in the days of Columbus, when a single new continent was discovered containing in it what we would now regard as a limited accumulation of the precious metals. It is, on the contrary, as if, in the language of Dr. Johnson, "the potentiality of wealth" had been revealed "beyond the dreams of avarice"; together with not one or two, but a dozen continents, the existence and secrets of which are suddenly laid bare. The Applied Sciences have been the magicians,--not Protection or the Currency.

And still scientists are continually dinning in our ears the question whether this state of affairs is going to continue,--whether the era of disturbance has reached its limit! I hold such a question to be little short of childish. That era has not reached its limits, nor has it even approximated those limits. On the contrary, we have just entered on the uncharted sea. We know what the last thirty years have brought about as the result of the agencies at work; but as yet we can only dimly dream of what the next sixty years are destined to see brought about. Imagination staggers at the suggestion.

What, then, has been of this the inevitable consequence,--the consequence which even the blindest should have foreseen? It has resulted in all those far-reaching changes suggested in the earlier part of what I have said to-day, as respects our ideals, our political theories, our social conditions. In other words, the old era is ended; what is implied when we say a new era is entered upon?

To attempt a partial answer to the query implies no claim to a prophetic faculty. Whether we like to face the fact or not, far-reaching changes in our economical theories and social conditions are imminent, involving corresponding readjustments in our constitutional arrangements and political machinery. Tennyson foreshadowed it all in his "Locksley Hall" seventy years ago:--"The individual withers, and the world is more and more." The day of individualism as it existed in the American ideal of sixty years since is over; that of collectivism and possibly socialism has opened. The day of social equality is relegated to what may be considered a somewhat patriarchal past,--that patriarchal past having come to a close during the memory of those still in active life.

And yet, though all this can now be studied in the political discussion endlessly dragging on, strangely and sadly enough that discussion carries in it hardly a note of encouragement. It is, in a word, unspeakably shallow. And here, having sufficiently for my present purpose though in hurried manner, diagnosed the situation,--located the seat of disturbance,--we come to the question of treatment. Involving, as it necessarily does, problems of the fundamental law, and a rearrangement and different allocation of the functions of government, this challenges the closest thought of the publicist. That the problem is here crying aloud for solution is apparent. The publications which cumber the counters of our book-stores, those for which the greatest popular call to-day exists--treatises relating to trade interests, to collectivism, to socialism, even to anarchism--tell the tale in part; in part it is elsewhere and otherwise told. Only recently, in once Puritan Massachusetts, processions paraded the streets carrying banners marked with this device, more suggestive than strange:--"No master and no God!"

What are the remedies popularly proposed? In that important branch of polity known as Political Ethics, or, as he termed them, Hermeneutics, which your Professor Lieber sixty years ago endeavored to treat of, what advance has since his time been effected?--Nay! what advance has been effected since the time, over two thousand years, of his great predecessor, Aristotle? I confidently submit that what progress is now being made in this most erudite of sciences is in the nature of that of the crab--backwards! In the discussions of Aristotle, the problem in view was, how to bring about government by the wisest,--that is, the most observant and expert. In other words, government, the object of politics, was by Aristotle treated in a scientific spirit. And this is as it should be. Take, for example, any problem,--I do not care whether it is legal or medical or one of engineering: How successfully dispose of it? Uniformly, in one way. Those problems are successfully solved, if at all, only when their solution is placed in the hands of the most proficient. Judged by the discussions of to-day, what advance has in politics been effected? Do the *Outlook* and the *Commoner* imply progress since the Stagirite? Not to any noticeable extent. We are, on the contrary, fumbling and wallowing about where the Greek pondered and philosophized.

Democracy, as it is called, is to-day the great panacea,--the political nostrum; as such it is confidently advocated by statesmen and professors and even by the presidents of our institutions of the advanced education. "Trust the People" is the shibboleth! "Let the People rule!" "The cure for too much Liberty is more Liberty!" To Democracy plain and simple--Composite Wisdom--I frankly confess I feel no call,--no call greater than, for instance, towards Autocracy or Aristocracy or Plutocracy. Taken simply, and applied as hitherto applied, all and each lead to but one result,--failure! And that result, let me here predict, will, in the future, be the same in the case of pure Democracy that, in the past, it was in the case of the pure Autocracy of the Caesars, or the case of the pure Aristocracy of Rome or of the so-called Republics of the Middle Ages. A political edifice on shifting sands.

Yet, to-day what do we see and hear in America? Tell it not in Gath; publish it not in the streets of Askalon I Two thousand years after the time of Aristotle, we see a prevailing school working directly back to the condition of affairs which existed in the Athenian agora under the disapproving eyes of the father of political philosophy. Panaceas, universal cure-alls, and quack remedies--the Initiative, the Referendum, and the Recall are paraded as if these--nostrums of the mountebanks of the county fair--would surely remedy the perplexing ills of new and hitherto unheard-of social, economical, and political conditions.

Democracy! What is Democracy? Democracy, as it is generally understood, I submit, is nothing but the reaching of political conclusions through the frequent counting of noses; or, as Macaulay two generations ago better phrased it, "the majority of citizens told by the head";--the only question at just this juncture being whether, in order to the arriving at more acceptable results, both sexes shall be "told," instead of one sex only. Moreover, I with equal confidence make bold to suggest that while conceded, and while men have even persuaded themselves that they have faith in it, and really do believe in this "telling" of noses as the best and fairest attainable means of reaching correct results, yet in so doing and so professing they simply, as men are prone to do, deceive themselves. In other words, victims of their own cant, they preach a panacea in which they really do not believe. Nor of this is proof far to seek. *Vox populi, vox Dei!* If you extend the application of this principle by a single step, its loudest advocates draw back in alarm from the inevitable. They seek refuge in the assertion--"Oh! That is different!" For instance, take a concrete case; so best can we illustrate.

One of the greatest scientific triumphs reached in modern times--perhaps I might fairly say the greatest--is the discovery of the cause of yellow fever, and its consequent control. As a result of the studies, the patient experimentation and self-sacrifice of the wisest,--that is, the most observant and expert,--the amazing conclusion was reached that not only the yellow fever but the innumerable ills of the flesh known under the caption of "malarial," were due to causes hitherto unsuspected, though obvious when revealed,--to the existence in the atmosphere of a venomous insect, in comparison with the work of which the ravages on mankind of the entire carnivorous and reptile creation were of comparatively small account. The mosquito flew disclosed, the atmospheric viper,--a viper most venomous and deadly. How was the disclosure brought about? What was the remedy applied? Was the discovery effected through universal suffrage? Was the remedy sought for and decided upon by the Initiative, or through a Referendum at an election held on the Tuesday succeeding the first Monday of a certain month and year? Had recourse in this case been had to the panacea now in greatest political vogue, we all know perfectly well what would have followed. History tells us. The quarantine, as it is called, would have been decreed, and a day of fasting, humiliation and prayer appointed. The mosquito, quite ignored, would then have gone on in his deadly work. We all equally well know that the man, even the politician or the statesman, who had suggested a solution of that problem by a count of noses would have been effaced with ridicule. Even the most simple minded would have rejected that method of reaching a result. Yet the ilia of the body politic, too, are complicated. Indeed, far more intricate in their processes and more deceitful in their aspects, they more deeply affect the general well-being and happiness than any ill or epidemic which torments the physical being, even the mosquito malaria. Yet the ills of the body politic, the complications which surround us on every side,--for these the unfailing panacea is said to lie in universal suffrage, that remedy which is immediately and of course laughed out of court if suggested in case of the simpler ills of the flesh.

This, I submit, is demonstration. The true remedy is not to be sought in that direction in the one case any more than the other.

There is a considerable element of truth, though possibly a not inconsiderable one of exaggeration, in this statement from a paper I recently chanced upon in the issue of the sober and classical *Edinburgh Review* for October last,--a paper entitled "Democracy and Liberalism":--"History testifies unmistakably and unanimously to the passion of democracies for incompetence. There is nothing democracy dislikes and suspects so heartily as technical efficiency, particularly when it is independent of the popular vote." But to-day, what is politically proposed by our senatorial charlatans and the mountebanks of the market-place? The Referendum, the constant and easy Recall, the everlasting Initiative are dinned into our ears as the cure-alls of every ill of the body politic. On the contrary, I submit that, while in the absence of any better method as yet devised and accepted, the process of reaching results by a count of the "majority told by the head" of the citizens then present and voting has certain political advantages, yet, for all this, as a final, scientific, political process, it is unworthy of consideration. A passing expedient, it in no degree reflects credit on twentieth-century intelligence.

And now I come to the crux of my discussion. Thus rejecting results reached by the ballot as now in practical use, a query is already in the minds of those who listen. At once suggesting itself and flung in my face, it is asked as a political poser, and not without a sneer,--What else or better have I to propose? Would I advise a return to old and discarded methods,--Heredity, Caste, Autocracy, Plutocracy? I respectfully submit this is a question no one has a right to put, and one I am not called upon to answer. Again, let me take a concrete case. Once more I appeal to the yellow fever precedent. The first step towards a solution of a medical, as of a political, problem is a correct diagnosis. Then necessarily follows a long period devoted to observation, to investigation and experiment. If, in the case of the yellow fever, a score of years only ago an observer had pointed out the nature of the disease and the manifest inadequacy of current theories and prevailing methods of prevention and treatment, do you think others would have had a right to turn upon him and demand that he instantly prescribe a remedy which should be not only complete, but at once recognized as such and so accepted? In the present case, as I have already observed, from the days of Aristotle down through two and twenty centuries, men had been experimenting in all, to them, conceivable ways, on the government of the body politic, exactly as they experimented on the disorders of the physical body. But only yesterday was the source of the yellow fever, for instance, diagnosed and located, and the proper means of prevention applied. The cancer and tuberculosis are to-day unsolved problems. By analogy, they are inviting subjects for an Initiative and a Referendum! Yet would any person who to-day, standing where I stand, expressed a disbelief, at once total and contemptuous, of such a procedure as respects them, be met by a demand for some other panacea of immediate and guaranteed efficiency? And so with the body politic. I here to-day am merely attempting a diagnosis, pointing out the disorders, and exposing as best I can the utter crudeness and insufficiency of the market-place remedies proposed. Have you a right, then, to turn on me, and call for some other prescription, warranted to cure, in place of the nostrums so loudly advertised by the sciolists and the dabblers of the day, and by me so contemptuously set aside? I confess I am unable to respond, or even to attempt a response to any such demand. I am not altogether a quack, nor is this a county fair.

"Paracelsus," so denominated, was one of Robert Browning's earlier poems. In it he causes the fifteenth-century alchemist and forerunner of all modern pharmaceutical chemistry, to declare that as the result of long travel and much research

> "I possess
> Two sorts of knowledge: one,--vast, shadowy,
> Hints of the unbounded aim....
> The other consists of many secrets, caught
> While bent on nobler prize,--perhaps a few
> Prime principles which may conduct to much:
> These last I offer."

So, *longo intervallo*, I have a few suggestions,--the result of an observation extending, as I said at the beginning, over the lives of two generations and a connection with many great events in which I have borne a part,--a part not prominent indeed, and more generally, I acknowledge, mistaken than correct. My errors, however, have at least made me cautious and doubtful of my own conclusions. I submit them for what they are worth. Not much, I fear.

What, then, would I do, were it in my power to prescribe alterations and curatives for the ills of our American body politic, of which I have spoken; or, more correctly, the far-reaching disturbances manifestly due to the agencies at work, to which I have made reference? Let us come at once to the point, taking the existing Constitution of the United States as a concrete example, and recognizing the necessity for its revision and readjustment to meet radically changed conditions,--conditions social, material, geographical, changed and still changing.

It was Mr. Gladstone who, years ago, made the often-quoted assertion that the Constitution of the United States was "the most wonderful work ever struck off at a given time by the brain and purpose of man." I do not think he was far wrong; though we, of course, realize that the Federal Constitution was a growth and in no degree an inspiration. That Constitution has through a century and a quarter stood the test of time and stress of war, during a period of almost unlimited growth of the community for which it was devised. It has outlasted many nationalities and most of the dynasties in existence at the time of its adoption; and that, too, under conditions sufficiently trying. I, therefore, regard it with profound respect; and, so regarding it, I would treat it with a cautious and tender hand. Not lightly pronouncing it antiquated, what changes would I make in it if to-morrow it were given me to prescribe alterations adapting it to the altered conditions which confront us? I do not hesitate to say, and I am glad to say, the changes I would suggest would be limited; yet, I fancy, far-reaching.

And, in the first place, let us have a clear conception of the end in view. That end is, I submit, exactly the same to-day which Aristotle had in view more than twenty centuries ago. It is, not to solve all political problems, but to put political problems as they arise in the hands of those whom he termed the "best,"--but whom we know as the most intelligent, observant and expert,--to be, through their agency, in the way of ultimate solution. If, adopting every ill-considered and half-fledged measure of so-called reform which might be the fancy of the day, we incorporated them in our fundamental law, but one thing could result therefrom,--ultimate confusion. The Constitution is neither a legislative crazy-quilt nor a receptacle of fads. To make it such is in every respect the reverse of scientific. The work immediately in hand, therefore, is to devise such changes in the fundamental law as will tend most effectually to bring about the solution of issues as they may arise, by the most expert, observant and reliable. This accomplished, if its accomplishment were only practicable, all possible would have been done; and the necessary and inevitable readjustment of things would, in politics as in medicine and in science, be left to solve itself as occasion arose. Provision cannot be made against every contingency.

This premised, the Constitution of the United States is an instrument through which powers are delegated by several local communities to a central government. The instrument, it was originally held, should be strictly construed and the powers delegated limited; and in this respect, with certain alterations made obviously necessary to meet changed conditions, I would return to the fundamental idea of the framers.

In saying this I feel confidence also that here in South Carolina at least I shall meet with an earnest response. The time is not yet remote when local self-government worked salvation for South Carolina, as for her sister States of the Confederacy. You here will never forget what immediately followed the close of our Civil War. As an historic fact, the Constitution was then suspended. It was suspended by act of an irresponsible Congress, exercising revolutionary but unlimited powers over a large section of the common country. You then had an illustration, not soon to be forgotten, of concentration of legislative power. An episode at once painful and discreditable, it is not necessary here to refer to it in detail. Appeal, however, was made to the principle of local self-government,--it was, so to speak, a recurrence to the theory of State Sovereignty. The appeal struck a responsive, because traditional, chord; and it was through a recurrence to State Sovereignty as the agency of local self-government that loyalty and contentment were restored, and, I may add, that I am here to-day. Ceasing to be a Military Department, South Carolina once more became a State. Not improbably the demand will in a not remote future be heard that State lines and local autonomy be practically obliterated. In that event, I feel a confident assurance that, recurring in memory to the evil days which followed 1865, the spirit of enlightened conservatism will assert itself here and in the sister States of what was once the Confederacy; and again it will prevail. In the future, as in the past, you in South Carolina at least will cling to what in 1876 proved the ark of your social and political salvation.

Taking another step in the discussion of changes, the Constitution is founded on that well-known distribution and allocation of powers first theoretically suggested by Montesquieu. There is a division, accompanied by a mutual limitation of authority, through the Judiciary, the Executive, and the Legislative. As respects this allocation, how would I modify that instrument? I freely say that the tendency of my thought, based on observation, is to conservatism. I have never yet in a single instance found that when the people of this or any other country accustomed to parliamentary government desired a thing, they failed to obtain it within a reasonable limit of time. Hasty changes are wisely deprecated; but I think I speak within limitation when I say that neither in the history of Great Britain,--the mother of Parliaments--nor in the history of the United States, has any modification which the people, on sober second thought, have considered to be for the best, long been deferred. Action, revolutionary in character, has not, as a rule, been needful, or, when taken, proved salutary. This is a record and result that no careful student of our history will, I take it, deny.

Such being the case, so far as our Judiciary is concerned, I do not hesitate to say I would adhere to older, and, as I think, better principles, or revert to them where they have been experimentally abandoned. It took the Anglo-Saxon race two centuries of incessant conflict to wrest from a despotic executive, practically an autocracy, judicial independence. That was effected through what is known as a tenure during good behavior, as opposed to a tenure at the will of the monarch. This, then, for two centuries, was accepted as a fundamental principle of constitutional government. Of late, a new theory has been propounded, and by those chafing at all restraint--constitutionally lawless in disposition--it is said the Recall should also be applied to the Judiciary. Having, therefore, wrested the independence of the Judiciary from the hand of the Autocrat, we now propose to place it, in all trustfulness, in the hands of the Democrat. To me the proposition does not commend itself. It is founded on no correct principle, for the irresponsible democratic majority is even more liable to ill-considered and vacillating action than is the responsible autocrat. In that matter

I would not trust myself; why, then, should I trust the composite Democrat? In the case of the Judiciary, therefore, I would so far as the fundamental law is concerned abide by the older and better considered principles of the framers.

Next, the Executive. Again, we hear the demand of Democracy,--the Recall! Once more I revert to the record. This Republic has now been in working operation, and, taken altogether, most successful operation, for a century and a quarter. During that century and a quarter we have had, we will say, some five and twenty different chief magistrates. There is an ancient and somewhat vulgar adage to the effect that the proof of a certain dietary article is in its eating. Apply that homely adage to the matter under consideration. What is the lesson taught? It is simply this,--during a whole century and a quarter of existence there has not been one single chief executive of the United States to whom the arbitrary Recall could have been applied with what would now be agreed upon as a fortunate result. In the Andrew Johnson impeachment case was it not better that things were as they were? On the other hand, every one of the seven independent, self-respecting Senators who then by a display of high moral courage saved the country from serious prejudice would have been recalled out-of-hand had the Recall now demanded been in existence. Its working would have received prompt exemplification; as it was, the recall was effected in time, and after due deliberation. The delay occasioned no public detriment. In this life, experience is undeniably worth something; and the experience here referred to is fairly entitled to consideration. No political system possible to devise is wholly above criticism,--not open to exceptional contingencies or to dangers possible to conjure up. Such have from time to time arisen in the past; in the future such will inevitably arise. This consideration must, however, be balanced against a general average of successful working; and I confidently submit that, weighing thus the proved advantage of the system we have against the possibilities of danger which hereafter may occur, but which never yet have occurred, the scale on which are the considerations in favor of change kicks the beam.

In view, however, of the growth of the country, the vastly increased complexity of interests involved, the intricacy and the cost of the election processes to which recourse is necessarily had, I would substitute for the present brief tenure of the presidential office--a tenure well enough perhaps in the comparatively simple days which preceded our Civil War--a tenure sufficiently long to enable the occupant of the presidential chair to have a policy and to accomplish at least something towards its adoption. As the case stands to-day, a President for the first time elected has during his term of four years, one year, and one year only, in which really to apply himself to the accomplishment of results. The first year of his term is necessarily devoted to the work of acquiring a familiarity with the machinery of the government, and the shaping of a policy. The second year may be devoted to a more or less strenuous effort at the adoption of the policy thus formulated. As experience shows, the action of the third and fourth years is gravely affected--if not altogether perverted from the work in hand--by what are known as the political exigencies incident to a succession. Manifestly, this calls for correction. The remedy, however, to my mind, is obvious and suggests itself. As the presidency is the one office under our Constitution national in character, and in no way locally representative, I would extend the term to seven years, and render the occupant of the office thereafter ineligible for reëlection. Seven years is, I am aware, under our political system, an unusual term; and here my ears will, I know, be assailed by the great "mandate" cackle. The count of noses being complete, the mind of the composite Democrat is held to be made up. It only remains to formulate the consequent decree; and, with least possible delay, put it in way of practical enforcement. Again, I, as a publicist, demur. It is the old issue, that between instant action and action on second thought, presented once more. Briefly, the experience of sixty years strongly inclines me to a preference of matured and considerate action over that immediate action which notoriously is in nine cases out of ten as ill-advised as it is precipitate. Only in the field of politics is the expediency of the latter assumed as of course; yet, as in science and literature and art so in politics, final, because satisfactory, results are at best but slowly thrashed out. As respects wisdom, the modern statute book does not loom, monumental. Its contemplation would indeed perhaps even lead to a surmise that reasonable delay in formulating his "mandate" might, in the case of the composite Democrat as in that of the individual Autocrat, prove a not altogether unmixed, and so in the end an intolerable, evil.

Thus while a change of the Executive and Legislative branches of the government might not be always simultaneously effected, by selecting seven years as the presidential term the election would be brought about, as frequently as might be, by itself, uncomplicated by local issues connected with the fortunes or political fate of individual candidates for office, whether State, Congressional, or Senatorial; and during the seven years of tenure, four, at least, it might reasonably be anticipated, would be devoted to the promotion of a definite policy, in place of one year in a term of four, as now. If also ineligible for reelection, there is at least a fair presumption that the occupant of the position might from start to finish apply himself to its duties and obligations, without being distracted therefrom by ulterior personal ends as constantly as humanly held in view.

Having thus disposed of the Judiciary and the Executive, we come to the Legislative. And here I submit is the weak point in our American system,--manifestly the weak point, and to those who, like myself, have had occasion to know, undeniably so. I am here as a publicist; not as a writer of memoirs: so, on this head, I do not now propose to dilate or bear witness. I will only briefly say that having at one period, and for more than the lifetime of a generation, been in charge of large corporate and financial interests, I have had much occasion to deal with legislative bodies, National, State and Municipal. That page of my experiences is the one I care least to recall, and would most gladly forget. I am not going to specify, or give names of either localities or persons; but, knowing what I know, it is useless to approach me on this topic with the usual good-natured and optimistic, if somewhat unctuous and conventional, commonplaces on general uprightness and the tendency to improved conditions and a higher standard. I know better! I have seen legislators bought like bullocks--they selling themselves. I have watched them cover their tracks with a cunning more than vulpine. I have myself been black-mailed and sandbagged, while whole legislative bodies watched the process, fully cognizant at every step of what was going on. This, I am glad to say, was years ago. The legislative conditions were then bad, scandalously bad; nor have I any reason to believe in a regeneration since. The stream will never rise higher than its source; but it generally indicates the level thereof. In this case, I can only hope that in my experience it failed so to do. Running at a low level, the waters of that stream were deplorably dirty.

That the legislative branch of our government has fallen so markedly in public estimation is not, I think, open to denial. To my mind, under the conditions I have referred to, such could not fail to be the case. It has, consequently, lost public confidence. Hence this popular demand for immediate legislation by the People,--this twentieth-century appeal to the Agora and Forum methods which antedate the era of Christ. It is true the world outgrew them two thousand years ago, and they were discarded; but, living in a progressive and not a reactionary period, all that, we are assured, is changed! The heart is no longer on the right-hand side of the body. To secure desired results it is only necessary to start quite fresh, as a mere preliminary discarding all lessons of experience.

Such reasoning does not commend itself to my judgment. On the contrary, the failure of the American legislative to command an increasing public confidence, while both natural and obvious, is, if my observation guides me to conclusions in any degree correct, traceable to two reasons. So far as government is concerned, the law-making branch is assumed to be made up of the wisest and the most expert. Meanwhile, it is as a matter of fact chosen by the process I have not over-respectfully referred to as the counting of noses; and, moreover, by an unwritten law more binding than any in the Statute Book, that counting of noses is with us localized. In other words, when it comes to the choice of our law-makers, reducing provincialism to a system we make the local numerical majority supreme, and any one is considered competent to legislate. He can do that, even if by common knowledge he is incompetent or untrustworthy in every other capacity. Localization thus becomes the stronghold of mediocrity, the sure avenue to office of the second-and third-rate man,--he who wishes always to enjoy his share of a little brief authority, to have, he also, a taste of public life. In this respect our American system is, I submit, manifestly and incomparably inferior to the system of parliamentary election existing in Great Britain, itself open to grave criticism. In Great Britain the public man seeks the constituency wherever he can find it; or the constituency seeks its representative wherever it recognizes him. The present Prime Minister of Great Britain, for instance, represents a small Scotch constituency in which he never resided, but by which he was elected more than twenty years ago, and through which he has since consecutively remained in public life. On the other hand, look at the waste and extravagance of the system now and traditionally in use with us. To get into public life a man must not only be in sympathy with the majority of the citizens of the locality in which he lives, but he must continue to be in sympathy with that majority; or, at any election, like Mr. Cannon in the election just held, where for any passing cause a majority of his neighbors in the locality in which he lives may fail to support him, he must go into retirement. I cannot here enlarge on this topic, vital as I see it; I have neither space nor time, and must, therefore, needs content myself with the "hints" of Paracelsus. I will merely say that as an outcome this localized majority system practically disfranchises the more intelligent and the more disinterested, the more individual and independent of every constituency. It reduces their influence, and negatives their action. It operates in like fashion everywhere. My field of observation has been at home, here in America; but it has been the same in France. For instance, while preparing this address I came across the following in that most respectable sheet, the London *Athenaum*. A very competent Frenchman was there criticising a recent book entitled "Idealism in France." Reference was by him made to what, in France, is known as the "*scrutin d'arrondissement,*" or, in other words, the district representative system. The critic declares that this system has there "created a party machine which has brought the country under the sway of a sort of Radical-Socialist Tammany, and bound together the voter and the deputy by a tie of mutual corruption, the candidate promising Government favors to the elector in return for his vote, and the elector supporting the candidate who promises most. Hence a policy in which ideas and ideals are forgotten for personal and local interests, as each candidate strives to outbid his rivals in the bribes that he offers to his constituents. Hence, finally, a general lowering in the tone of French home politics, every question being made subservient by the deputies to that of their reëlection."

I would respectfully inquire if the above does not apply word for word to the condition of affairs with which we are familiar in America.

But let me here again cite a concrete case, still fresh in memory; nothing in abstract discussion tells so much. Take the late Carl Schurz. If there was one man in our public life since 1865 who showed a genius for the parliamentary career, and who in six short years in the United States Senate--a single term--displayed there constructive legislating qualities of the highest order, it was Carl Schurz. Yet at the end of that single senatorial term, for local and temporary reasons he failed to obtain the support of a majority, or the support of anything approaching a majority, of those composing the constituency upon which he depended. Consequently he was retired from that parliamentary position necessary for the accomplishment, through him, of best public results. Yet at that very time there was no man in the United States who commanded so large and so personal a constituency as Carl Schurz; for he represented the entire Germanic element in the United States. Distributed as that element was, however, with its vote localized under our law, unwritten as well as statutory, there was no possibility of any constituency so concentrating itself that Carl Schurz could be kept in the position where he could continue to render services of the greatest possible value to the country. I, therefore, confidently here submit a doubt whether human ingenuity could devise any system calculated to lead to a greater waste of parliamentary ability, or more effectually keep from the front and position of influence that legislative superiority which was the arm of Aristotle to secure. "Cant-patriotism," as your Francis Lieber termed it; and, on this score, he waxed eloquent. "Do we not live in a world of cant," he wrote from Columbia here to a friend at the North seventy-five years ago, "that cant-patriotism which plumes itself in selecting men from within the State confines only. The truer a nation is, the more essentially it is elevated, the more it disregards petty considerations, and takes the true and the good from whatever quarter it may come. Look at history and you find the proof. Look around you, where you are, and you find it now." And, were Lieber living to-day, he would find a striking exemplification of the consequences of a total and systematic disregard of this elementary proposition in studying the United States Senate from and through its reporters' gallery. The decline in the standards of that body, whether of aspect, intelligence, education or character, under the operation of the local primary has been not less pronounced than startling. The outcome and ripe result of "cant-patriotism," it affords to the curious observer an impressive object-lesson,--provincialism reduced to a political system; what a witty and incisive French writer has recently termed the "Cult of Incompetence." Speaking of conditions prevailing not here but in France, this observer says:--"Democracy in its modern form chooses its' delegates in its own image.... What ought the character of the legislator to be? The very opposite, it seems to me, of the democratic legislator, for he ought to be well-informed and entirely devoid of prejudice." Taken as a whole, and a few striking individual exceptions apart, are those composing the Senate of the United States conspicuous in these respects? They certainly do not so impress the casual observer. That, as a body, they increasingly fail to command confidence and attention is matter of common remark. Nor is the reason far to seek. It would be the same as respects literature, science and art, were their representatives chosen and results reached through a count of noses localized, with selection severely confined to home talent.

I am well aware of the criticism which will at once be passed on what I now advance. Local representation through choice by numerical majorities within given confines, geographically and mathematically fixed, is a system so rooted and intrenched in the convictions and traditions of the American community that even to question its wisdom evinces a lack of political common-sense. It in fact resembles nothing so much as the attempt to whistle down a strongly prevailing October wind from the West. The attempt so to do is not practical politics! In reply, however, I would suggest that such a criticism is wholly irrelevant. The publicist has nothing to do with practical politics. It is as if it were objected to a physician who prescribed sanitation against epidemics that the community in question was by custom and tradition wedded to filth and surface-drainage, and could not possibly be induced to abandon them in favor of any new-fangled theories of soap-and-water cleanliness. So why waste time in prescribing such? Better be common-sensed and practical, taking things as they are. In the case suggested, and confronted with such criticism, the medical adviser simply shrugs his shoulders, and is silent; the alternative he knows is inescapable. After a sufficiency of sound scourgings the objecting community will probably know better, and may listen to reason; in a way, conforming thereto. So, also, the body politic. If Ephraim is indeed thus joined to idols, the publicist simply shrugs his shoulders, and passes on; possibly, after Ephraim has been sufficiently scourged, he may in that indefinite future popularly known as "one of these days" be more clear sighted and wiser.

None the less, so far as our national parliamentary system is concerned, could I have my way in a revision of the Constitution, I would increase the senatorial term to ten years, and I would, were such a thing within the range of possibility, break down the system of the necessary senatorial selection by a State of an inhabitant of the State. If I could, I would introduce the British system. For example, though I never voted for Mr. Bryan and have not been in general sympathy with Mr. Roosevelt, yet few things would give me greater political satisfaction than to see Mr. Bryan, we will say, elected a Senator from Arizona or Oregon, Mr. Roosevelt elected from Illinois or Pennsylvania, President Taft from Utah or Vermont. They apparently best represent existing feelings and the ideals prevailing in those communities; why, then, should they not voice those feelings and ideals in our highest parliamentary chamber?

As respects our House of Representatives, it would in principle be the same. I do not care to go into the rationale of what is known as proportional representation, nor have I time so to do; but, were it in my power, I would prescribe to-morrow that hereafter the national House of Representatives should be constituted on the proportional basis,--the choice of representatives to be by States, but, as respects the nomination of candidates, irrespective of district lines. Like many others, I am very weary of provincial nobodies, "good men" locally known to be such!

As I have already said, in parliamentary government all depends in the end on the truly representative character of the legislative body. If that is as it should be, the rest surely follows. The objective of Aristotle is attained.

Exceeding the limits assigned to it, my discussion has, however, extended too far. I must close. One word before so doing. Why am I here? I am here,--a man considerably exceeding in age the allotted threescore and ten--to deliver a message, be the value of the same greater or less. I greatly fear it is less. I would, however, impart the lessons of an experience stretching over sixty years,--the results of such observation as my intelligence has enabled me to exercise. I do so, addressing myself to a local institution of the advanced education. Why? Because, looking over the country, diagnosing its conditions as well as my capacity enables me, observing the evolution of the past and forecasting, in as far as I may, the outcome, I am persuaded that the future of the country rests more largely in the hands of such institutions as this than in those of any other agency or activity. Do not say I flatter; for, while I can hope for no advancement, I think I have not overstated the case; I certainly have not overstated my conviction. There has been no man who has influenced the course of modern thought more deeply and profoundly than Adam Smith, a Professor in a Scotch University of the second class. So here in Columbia seventy years ago, Francis Lieber prepared and published his "Manual of Political Ethics." Adam Smith and Francis

Lieber were but prototypes--examples of what I have in mind. The days were when the Senate of the United States afforded a rostrum from which thinkers and teachers first formulated, and then advanced, great policies. Those days, and I say it regretfully, are past. Unless I am greatly mistaken, however, a new political force is now asserting itself. I have recently, at a meeting of historical and scientific associations in Boston, had my attention forcibly called to this aspect of the situation now shaping itself. I there met young men, many, and not the least noticeable of whom, came from this section. They inspired me with a renewed confidence in our political future. Essentially teachers,--I might add, they were publicists as well as professors. Observers and students, they actively followed the course of developing thought in Europe as in this country. Exact in their processes, philosophical and scientific in their methods, unselfish in their devotion, they were broad of view. It is for them to realize in a future not remote the University ideal pictured, and correctly pictured, from this stage by one who here preceded me a short six months ago. They, constituting the University, are the "hope of the State in the direction of its practical affairs; in teaching the lawyer the better standards of his profession, his duty to place character above money making; in teaching the legislator the philosophy of legislation, and that the constructive forces of legislation carefully considered should precede every effort to change an existing status; in teaching those in official life, executive and judicial, that dem- agogy, and theories of life uncontrolled by true principles, do not make for success, when final success is considered, but that, if they did lead to success, they should be avoided for their inherent imperfection.... The province of the University is to educate citizenship in the abstract."

It is the presence of this class, to those composing which I bow as distinctly of a period superior to mine, that you owe my presence to-day,--whatever that presence may be worth. I regard their existence and their coming forward in such institutions as this University of South Carolina, as the arc of the bow of promise spanning the political horizon of our future.

Through you, to them my message is addressed.

Notes:

1. DeLeon, "Belles, Beaux and Brains of the Sixties," p. 158.

2. Bussell's (Dr. F.W.) "Christian Theology and Social Progress." Bampton Lectures, 1905.

11

Lee's Centennial

Delivered at Lexington, Virginia,
Saturday, January 19, 1907
On the Invitation of the President and Faculty of Washington
& Lee University

Having occasion once to refer in discussion to certain of the founders of our Massachusetts Commonwealth, I made the assertion that their force "lay in character;" and I added that in saying this I paid, and meant to pay, the highest tribute which in my judgment could be paid to a community or to its typical men. Quite a number of years have passed since I so expressed myself, and in those years I have grown older — materially older; but I now repeat even more confidently than I then uttered them, these other words — "The older I have grown and the more I have studied and seen, the greater in my esteem, as an element of strength in a people, has Character become, and the less in the conduct of human affairs have I thought of mere capacity or even genius. With Character a race will become great, even though as stupid and unassimilating as the Romans; without Character, any race will in the long run prove a failure, though it may number in it individuals having all the brilliancy of the Jews, crowned with the genius of Napoleon." We are here to-day to commemorate the birth of Robert Edward Lee, — essentially a Man of Character. That he was such all I think recognize; for, having so impressed himself throughout life on his cotemporaries, he stands forth distinctly as a man of character on the page of the historian. Yet it is not easy to put in words exactly what is meant when we agree in attributing character to this man or to that, or withholding it from another; — conceding it, for instance, to Epaminondas, Cato and Wellington, but withholding it from Themistocles, Caesar or Napoleon. Though we can illustrate what we mean by examples which all will accept, we cannot define. Emerson in his later years (1866) wrote a paper on "Character;" but in it he makes no effort at a definition. "Character," he said, "denotes habitual self-possession, habitual regard to interior and constitutional motives, a balance not to be overset or easily disturbed by outward events and opinion, and by implication points to the source of right motive. We sometimes employ the word to express the strong and consistent will of men of mixed motive; but, when used with emphasis, it points to what no events can change, that is a will built of the reason of things." The more matter-of-fact lexicographer defines Character as "the sum of the inherited and acquired ethical traits which give to a person his moral individuality." To pursue further the definition of what is generally understood would be wearisome, so I will content myself with quoting this simile from a disciple of Emerson — "The virtues of a superior man are like the wind; the virtues of a common man are like the grass ; the grass, when the wind passes over it, bends."

That America has been rich in these men of superior virtues before whom the virtues of the common man have bent, is matter of history. It has also been our making as a community. Such in New England was John Winthrop, whose lofty example still influences the community whose infancy he fathered. Such in New York was John Jay. Such, further south, was John Caldwell Calhoun, essentially a man of exalted character and representative of his community, quite irrespective of his teachings and their outcome. Such unquestionably in Virginia were

George Washington and John Marshall; and, more recently, Robert Edward Lee. A stock, of which those three were the consummate flower, by its fruits is known.

Here to commemorate the centennial of the birth of Lee, I do not propose to enter into any eulogium of the man, to recount the well-known events of his career, or to estimate the final place to be assigned him among great military characters. All this has been sufficiently done by others far better qualified for the task. Eschewing superlatives also, I shall institute no comparisons. One of a community which then looked upon Lee as a renegade from the flag he had sworn to serve, and a traitor to the Nation which had nurtured him, in my subordinate place I directly confronted Lee throughout the larger portion of the War of Secession. During all those years there was not a day in which my heart would not have been gladdened had I heard that his also had been the fate which at Chancellorsville befell his great lieutenant; and yet more glad had it been the fortune of the command in which I served to visit that fate upon him. Forty more years have since gone. Their close finds me here to-day — certainly a much older, and, in my own belief at least, a wiser man. Nay, more! A distinguished representative of Massachusetts, speaking in the Senate of the United States shortly after Lee's death upon the question of a return to Lee's family of the ancestral estate of Arlington, used these words: "Eloquent Senators have already characterized the proposition and the traitor it seeks to commemorate. I am not disposed to speak of General Lee. It is enough to say he stands high in the catalogue of those who have imbrued their hands in their country's blood. I hand him over to the avenging pen of History." It so chances that not only am I also from the State of Massachusetts, but, for more than a dozen years, I have been the chosen head of its typical historical society, — the society chartered under the name and seal of the Commonwealth considerably more than a century ago, — the parent of all similar societies. By no means would I on that account seem to ascribe to myself any representative character as respects the employment of History's pen, whether avenging or otherwise;[1] nor do I appear here as representative of the Massachusetts Historical Society:

but, a whole generation having passed away since Charles Sumner uttered the words I have quoted, I do, on your invitation, chance to stand here to-day, as I have said, both a Massachusetts man and the head of the Massachusetts Historical Society, to pass judgment upon General Lee. The situation is thus to a degree dramatic.

Though, in what I am about to say I shall confine myself to a few points only, to them I have given no little study, and on them have much reflected. Let me, however, once for all, and with emphasis, in advance say I am not here to instruct Virginians either in the history of their State or the principles of Constitutional Law ; nor do I make any pretence to profundity whether of thought or insight. On the contrary I shall attempt nothing more than the elaboration of what has already been said by others as well as by me, such value or novelty as may belong to my share in the occasion being attributable solely to the point of view of the speaker. In that respect, I submit, the situation is not without novelty; for, so far as I am aware, never until now has one born and nurtured in Massachusetts — a typical bred-in-the-bone Yankee, if you please — addressed at its invitation a Virginian audience, on topics relating to the War of Secession and its foremost Confederate military character.

Coming directly to my subject, my own observation tells me that the charge still most commonly made against Lee in that section of the common country to which I belong and with which I sympathize is that, in plain language, he was false to his flag, — educated at the national academy, an officer of the United States Army, he abjured his allegiance and bore arms against the government he had sworn to uphold. In other words he was a military traitor. I state the charge in the tersest language possible; and the facts are as stated. Having done so, and admitting the facts, I add as the result of much patient study and most mature reflection, that under similar conditions I would myself have done exactly what Lee did. In fact, I do not see how I, placed as he was placed, could have done otherwise.

And now fairly entered on the first phase of my theme, I must hurry on; for I have much ground to traverse, and scant time in which to cover it. I must be concise, but must not fail to be explicit. And first as to the right or wrong of secession, this theoretically; then practically, as to what secession in the year of grace 1861 necessarily involved.

If ever a subject had been thoroughly thrashed out, — so thrashed out in fact as to offer no possible gleaning of novelty, — it might be inferred that this was that subject. Yet I venture the opinion that such is not altogether the case. I do so moreover not without weighing words. The difficulty with the discussion has to my mind been that throughout it has in essence been too abstract, legal and technical, and not sufficiently historical, sociological and human. It has turned on the wording of instruments, in themselves not explicit, and has paid far too little regard to traditions and local ties. As matter of fact, however, actual men as they live, move and have their being in this world, caring little for parchments or theory, are the creatures of heredity and local attachments. Coming directly to the point, I maintain that every man in the eleven States seceding from the Union had in 1861, whether he would or no, to decide for himself whether to adhere to his State or to the Nation; and I finally assert that, whichever way he decided, if only he decided honestly, putting self-interest behind him, he decided right.

Paradoxical as it sounds, I contend, moreover, that this was indisputably so. It was a question of Sovereignty — State or National; and from a decision of that question there was in a seceded State escape for no man. Yet when the national Constitution was framed and adopted that question was confessedly left undecided; and intentionally so left. More than this, even: the Federal Constitution was theoretically and avowedly based on the idea of a divided sovereignty, in utter disregard of the fact that, when a I final issue is presented, sovereignty does not 1 admit of division.

Yet even this last proposition, basic as it is. I have heard denied. I have frequently had it replied that, as matter of fact, sovereignty is frequently divided, — divided in domestic life, — divided in the apportionment of the functions of government. Those thus arguing, however, do so confusedly. They confound sovereignty with an agreed, but artificial, *modus vivendi.* The original constitution of the United States was, in fact, in this important respect just that, — a *modus vivendi:* — under the circumstances a most happy and ingenious expedient for overcoming an obstacle in the way of nationality, otherwise insurmountable. To accomplish the end they had in view, the framers had recourse to a metaphysical abstraction, under which it was left to time and the individual to decide, when the final issue should arise, if it ever did arise — as they all devoutly hoped it never would arise — where sovereignty lay. There is nothing in connection I with the history of our development more interesting from the historical point of view I than the growth, the gradual development of I the spirit of nationality, carrying with it sovereignty. It has usually been treated as a purely legal question to be settled on the verbal construction of the instruments, — "We, the People," etc. Webster so treated it. In all confidence I maintain that it is not a legal question; it is purely an historical question. As such, furthermore, it has been decided, and correctly decided, both ways at different times in different sections, and at different times in opposite ways in the same section.

And this was necessarily and naturally so; for, as development progressed along various lines and in different localities, the sense of allegiance shifted. Two whole generations passed away between the adoption of the Federal Constitution and the War of Secession. When that war broke out in 1861 the last of the framers had been a score of years in his grave; but evidence is conclusive that until the decennium between 1830 and 1840 the belief was nearly universal that in case of a final, unavoidable issue, sovereignty resided in the State, and to it allegiance was due. The law was so laid down in the Kentucky resolves of 1798; and to the law as thus laid down Webster assented. Chancellor Rawle so propounded the law; and such was the understanding of so unprejudiced and acute a foreign observer as De Tocqueville.[2]

The technical argument — the logic of the proposition — seems plain and, to my thought, unanswerable. The original sovereignty was indisputably in the State; in order to establish a nationality certain attributes of sovereignty were ceded by the States to a common central organization; all attributes not thus specifically conceded were reserved to the States, and no attributes of moment were to be construed as conceded by implication. There is no attribute of sovereignty so important as allegiance, — citizenship. So far all is elementary. Now we come to the crux of the proposition. Not only was allegiance — the right to define and establish citizenship — not among the attributes specifically conceded by the several States to the central nationality, but, on the contrary, it was explicitly reserved, the instrument declaring that "the citizens of each State" should be entitled to "all Privileges and Immunities of Citizens in the several States." Ultimate allegiance was, therefore, due to the State which defined and created citizenship, and not to the central organization which accepted as citizens whomever the States pronounced to be such.[3] Thus far I have never been able to see where room was left for doubt. Citizenship was an attribute recognized by the Constitution as originating with, and of course belonging to, the several States. But, speaking historically and in a philosophical rather than in a legal spirit, it is little more than a commonplace to assert that one great safeguard of the Anglo-Saxon race — what might almost be termed its political palladium — has ever been that hard, if at times illogical, common sense which, recognizing established custom as a binding rule of action, found its embodiment in what we are wont with pride to term the Common Law. Now, just as there can, I think, be no question as to the source of citizenship and, consequently, as to sovereignty, when the Constitution was originally adopted, there can be equally little question that during the lives of the two succeeding generations a custom of nationality grew up which became the accepted Common Law of the land, and practically binding as such. This was true in the South as well as the North, though the custom was more hardened into accepted law in the latter than in the former; but the growth and acceptance as law of the custom of nationality even in the South was incontrovertibly shown in the very act of secession, — the seceding States at once crystallizing into a Confederacy. Nationality was assumed as a thing of course.

But the metaphysical abstraction of a divided sovereignty, none the less, bridged the chasm. As a *modus vivendi* it did its work. I have called it a metaphysical abstraction; but it was also a practical arrangement resulting in great advantages. It might be illogical, and fraught with possible disputes and consequent dangers; but it was an institution. And so it naturally came to pass that in many of the States a generation grew up, dating from the War of 1812, who, gravitating steadily and more and more strongly to nationality, took a wholly different view of allegiance. For them Story laid down the law; Webster was their mouthpiece; at one time it looked as if Jackson was to be their armed exponent. They were, moreover, wholly within their right. The sovereignty was confessedly divided; and it was for them to elect. The movements of both science and civilization were behind the nationalists. The railroad obliterated State lines, while it unified the nation. What did the foreign immigrants, now swarming across the ocean, care for States? They knew only the Nation. Brought up in Europe, the talk of State sovereignty was to them foolishness. Its alphabet was incomprehensible. In a word, it too "was caviare to the general." Then the inevitable issue arose; and it arose over African slavery; and slavery was sectional. The States south of a given line were arrayed against the States north of that line. Owing largely to slavery, and the practical exclusion of immigrants because thereof, the States of the South had never undergone nationalization at all to the extent those of the North had undergone it. The growing influence and power of the national government, the sentiment inspired by the wars in which we had been engaged, the rapidly improving means of communication and intercourse, had produced their effects in the South; but in degree far less than in the North. Thus the curious result was brought about that, when, at last, the long deferred issue confronted the country, and the modus Vivendi of two generations was brought to a close, those who believed in national sovereignty constituted the conservative majority, striving for the preservation of what then was, — the existing nineteenth-century Nation, — while those who passionately adhered to State sovereignty, treading in the footsteps of the fathers, had become eighteenth century reactionists. Legally, each had right on his side. The theory of a divided Sovereignty had worked itself out to its logical consequence. "Under which King, Bezonian?" — and every man had to "speak or die."

In the North the situation was simple. State and Nation stood together. The question of allegiance did not present itself, for the two sovereignties merged. It was otherwise in the South; and there the question became, not legal or constitutional, but practical. The life of the Nation had endured so long, the ties and ligaments had become so numerous and interwoven that, all theories to the contrary notwithstanding, a peaceable secession from the Union — a virtual exercise of State sovereignty — had become impossible. If those composing the several dissatisfied communities would only keep their tempers under restraint, and exercise an almost unlimited patience, a theoretical divided sovereignty, maintained through the agency and intervention of the Supreme Court, — in other words the perpetuation of the *modus vivendi*, — was altogether practicable; and probably this was what the framers had in mind under such a contingency as had now arisen. But that, after seventy years of Union and nationalization, a peaceable and friendly taking to pieces was possible, is now, as then it was, scarcely thinkable. Certainly, with a most vivid recollection of the state of sectional feeling which then existed, I do not believe there was a man in the United States — I am confident there was not a woman in the South — who fostered self-delusion to the extent of believing that the change was to come about without a recourse to force. In other words practical Secession was revolution theoretically legal. Why waste time and breath in discussion! — The situation becomes manifestly impossible of continuance where the issue between heated men, with weapons handy, is over a metaphysical distinction involving vast material and moral consequences. Lee, with intuitive common sense, struck the nail squarely on the head when amidst the Babel of discordant tongues he wrote to his son — "It is idle to talk of secession;" the national government as it then was can only be dissolved by revolution." That struggle of dissolution might be longer and fiercer, — as it was, — or shorter, and more wordy than blood-letting, — as the seceding States confidently believed would prove to be the case, — but a struggle there would be.

Historically, such were the conditions to which natural processes of development had brought the common country at the mid-decennium of the century. People had to elect; the *modus vivendi* was at an end. — Was the State sovereign; or was the Nation sovereign? And, with a shock of genuine surprise that any doubt should exist on that head, eleven States arrayed themselves on the side of the Sovereignty of the State and claimed the unquestioning allegiance of their citizens; and I think it not unsafe to assert that nowhere did the original spirit of State Sovereignty and allegiance to the State then survive in greater intensity and more unquestioning form than in Virginia, — the "Old Dominion," — the mother of States and of Presidents. And here I approach a sociological factor in the problem more subtle and also more potent than any legal consideration. It has no standing in Court: but the historian may not ignore it; while, with the biographer of Lee, it is crucial. Upon it judgment hinges. I have not time to consider how or why such a result came about, but of the fact there can, I hold, be no question, — State pride, a sense of individuality, has immemorially entered more largely and more intensely into Virginia and Virginians than into any other section or community of the country. Only in South Carolina and among Carolinians, on this continent, was a somewhat similar pride of locality and descent to be found. There was in it a flavor of the Hidalgo, — or of the pride which the Macgregors and Campbells took in their clan and country. In other words, the Virginian and the Carolinian had in the middle of the last century not undergone nationalization to any appreciable extent.

But this, it will be replied, though true of the ordinary man and citizen, should not have been true of the graduate of the military academy, the officer of the Army of the United States. Winfield Scott and George H. Thomas did not so construe their allegiance; when the issue was presented, they remained true to their flag and to their oaths. Robert E. Lee, false to his oath and flag, was a renegade! The answer is brief and to the point : — the conditions in the several cases were not the same, — neither Scott nor Thomas was Lee. It was our Boston Dr. Holmes who long ago declared that the child's education begins about two hundred and fifty years before it is born; and it is quite impossible to separate any man — least of all, perhaps, a fullblooded Virginian — from his prenatal traditions and living environment. From them he drew his being; in them he exists. Robert E. Lee was the embodiment of those conditions, the creature of that environment, — a Virginian of Virginians. His father was "Light Horse Harry" Lee, a devoted follower of Washington; but in January, 1792, "Light Horse Harry" wrote to Mr. Madison: "No consideration on earth could induce me to act a part, however gratifying to me, which could be construed into disregard of, or faithlessness to, this Commonwealth;" and later, when in 1798 the Virginia and Kentucky resolutions were under discussion, "Light Horse Harry" exclaimed in debate, "Virginia is my country; her will I obey, however lamentable the fate to which it may subject me." Born in this environment, nurtured in these traditions, to ask Lee to raise his hand against Virginia was like asking Montrose or the MacCallum More to head a force designed for the subjection of the Highlands and the destruction of the clans. Where such a stern election is forced upon a man as then confronted Lee, the single thing the fair minded investigator has to take into account is I the loyalty, the single-mindedness of the election. Was it devoid of selfishness, — was it free from any baser and more sordid worldly motive, — ambition, pride, jealousy, revenge or self-interest. To this question there can, in the case of Lee, be but one answer. When, after long and trying mental wrestling, he threw in his fate with Virginia, he knowingly sacrificed everything which man prizes most, — his dearly beloved home, his means of support, his professional standing, his associates, a brilliant future assured to him. Born a slaveholder in a race of slaveholders, he was himself no defender, much less an advocate of slavery; on the contrary, he did not hesitate to pronounce it in his place "a moral and political evil." Later, he manumitted his slaves. He did not believe in secession; as a right reserved under the Constitution he pronounced it "idle talk:" but, as a Virginian, he also added, "if the Government is disrupted, I shall return to my native State and share the miseries of my people, and save in defence will draw my sword on none." Next to his high sense of allegiance to Virginia was Lee's pride in his profession. He was a soldier; as such rank, and the possibility of high command and great achievement, were very dear to him. His choice put rank and command behind him. He quietly and silently made the greatest sacrifice a soldier can be asked to make. With war plainly impending, the foremost place in the army of which he was an officer was now tendered him; his answer was to lay down the commission he already held. Virginia had been drawn into the struggle; and, though he recognized no necessity for the state of affairs, "in my own person," he wrote, "I had to meet the question whether I should take part against my native State; I have not been able to make up my mind to raise my hand against my relatives, my children, my home." It may have been treason to take this position; the man who took it, uttering these words and sacrificing as he sacrificed, may have been technically a renegade to his flag, — if you please, false to his allegiance; but he stands awaiting sentence at the bar of history in very respectable company. Associated with him are, for instance, William of Orange, known as The Silent, John Hampden, the original *Pater Patriae*, Oliver Cromwell, the Protector of the English Commonwealth, Sir Harry Vane, once a governor of Massachusetts, and George Washington, a Virginian of note. In the throng of other offenders I am also gratified to observe certain of those from whom I not unproudly claim descent. They were, one and all, in the sense referred to, false to their oaths — forsworn. As to Robert E. Lee, individually, I can only repeat what I have already said, — if in all respects similarly circumstanced, I hope I should have been filial and unselfish enough to have done as Lee did.[4] Such an utterance on my part may be "traitorous;" but I here render that homage.

In Massachusetts, however, I could not even in 1861 have been so placed; for, be it because of better or worse, Massachusetts was not Virginia; — no more Virginia than England once was Scotland, or the Lowlands the Highlands. The environment, the ideals, were in no respect the same. In Virginia, Lee was Macgregor; and, where Macgregor sat, there was the head of the table.

Into Lee's subsequent military career, there is no call here to enter; nor shall I undertake to compare him with other great military characters whether contemporaneous or of all time. As I said when I began, the topic has been thoroughly discussed by others; and, moreover, the time limitation here again confronts me. I must press on. Suffice it for me, as one of those then opposed in arms to Lee, however subordinate the capacity, to admit at once that, as a leader, he conducted operations on the highest plane. Whether acting on the defensive upon the soil of his native State, or leading his army into the enemy's country, he was humane, self-restrained and strictly observant of the most advanced rules of civilized warfare. He respected the non-combatant; nor did he ever permit the wanton destruction of private property. His famous Chambersburg order was a model which any invading general would do well to make his own ; and I repeat now what I have heretofore had occasion to say, "I doubt if a hostile force of an equal size ever advanced into an enemy's country, or fell back from it in retreat, leaving behind less cause of hate and bitterness than did the Army of Northern Virginia in that memorable campaign which culminated at Gettysburg."

And yet that Gettysburg campaign is an episode in Lee's military career which I am loth wholly to pass over; for the views I entertain of it are not in all respects those generally held. Studied in the light of results, that campaign has been criticised; the crucial attack of Gettysburg's third day has been pronounced a murderous persistence in a misconception; and, among Confederate writers especially, the effort has been to relieve Lee of responsibility for final miscarriage, transferring it to his lieutenants. As a result reached from participation in those events and subsequent study of them, briefly let me say I concur in none of these conclusions. Taking the necessary chances incident to all warfare on a large scale into consideration, the Gettysburg campaign was in my opinion timely, admirably designed, energetically executed, and brought to a close with consummate military skill. A well considered offensive thrust of the most deadly character, intelligently aimed at the opponent's heart, its failure was of the narrowest; and the disaster to the Confederate side which that failure might readily have involved was no less skilfully than successfully averted.

I cannot here and now enter into details. But I hold that credit, and the consequent measure of applause, in the outcome of that campaign belong to Lee's opponent, and not to him. All the chances were in Lee's favor, and he should have won a great victory; and Meade should have sustained a decisive defeat. As it was, Meade triumphantly held his ground; Lee suffered a terrible repulse, his deadly thrust was foiled, and his campaign was a failure.

So far as Lee's general plan of campaign, and the movements which culminated in the battle of Gettysburg, were concerned, in war, be it always and ever remembered, a leader must take some chances, and mistakes will occur; but the mistakes are rarely, if ever, all on one side. They tend to counterbalance each other; and, commanders and commanded being at all equal, not unseldom it is the balance of misconceptions, shortcomings, miscarriages, and the generally unforeseen and indeed unforeseeable, which tips the scale to victory or defeat. I have said that I proposed to avoid comparisons; at best such are invidious, and, under present circumstances, might from me be considered as doubtful in matter of taste. I think, however, some things too obvious to admit of denial; or, consequently, to suggest comparison. About every crisp military aphorism is as matter of course attributed to Napoleon; and so Napoleon is alleged first to have remarked that — "In war, men are nothing; a man is everything." And, as formerly a soldier of the Army of the Potomac, I now stand appalled at the risk I unconsciously ran anterior to July, 1863, when confronting the Army of Northern Virginia, commanded as it then was and as we were. The situation was in fact as bad with us in the Army of the Potomac as it was with the Confederates in the Southwest. The unfortunate Pemberton there was simply not in the same class as Grant and Sherman, to whom he found himself opposed. Results there followed accordingly. So, in Virginia, Lee and Jackson made an extraordinary, a most exceptional combination. They outclassed McClellan and Burnside, Pope and Hooker;

outclassed them sometimes terribly, sometimes ludicrously, always hopelessly: and results in that case also followed accordingly. That we were not utterly destroyed constitutes a flat and final refutal of the truth of Napoleon's aphorism. If we did not realize the facts of the situation in this respect, our opponents did. Let me quote the words of one of them: "There was, however, one point of great interest in [the rapid succession of the Federal commanders], and that was our amazement that an army could maintain even so much as its organization under the depressing strain of those successive appointments and removals of its commanding generals. And to-day (1903) I, for one, regard the fact that it did preserve its cohesion and its fighting power under, and in spite of such experiences, as furnishing impressive demonstration of the high character and intense loyalty of our historic foe, the Federal Army of the Potomac."[5]

Notwithstanding the fact that until the death of Jackson and the Gettysburg campaign we were thus glaringly outclassed, and at a corresponding disadvantage in every respect save mere men and equipment, the one noticeable feature of the succession of Virginia campaigns from that of 1862 to that of 1864, was their obstinacy and indecisive character. The advantage would be sometimes on one side, sometimes on the other: but neither side could secure an indisputable supremacy. This was markedly the case at Gettysburg; and yet, judging by the Confederate accounts of that campaign which have met my eye, the inference would be that the Union forces labored under no serious disadvantage, while Lee's plans and tactics were continually compromised by untoward accident, or the precipitation or remissness of his subordinates. My study of what then took place leads me to a wholly opposite conclusion. Well conceived and vigorously carried out as that campaign was on the part of the Confederate leader, the preponderance of the accidental — the blunders, the unforeseeable, the misconceptions and the miscarriages — was distinctly in Lee's favor. On any fair weighing of chances, he should have won a decisive victory; as a matter of actual outcome, he and his army ought to have been destroyed. As usual, on that theatre of war at the time, neither result came about.

First as to the chapter of accidents, — the misconceptions, miscarriages and shortcomings. If, as has been alleged, an essential portion of Lee's force was at one time out of reach and touch, and if, at the critical moment, a lieutenant was not promptly in place at a given hour, on the Union side an unforeseen change of supreme command went into effect when battle was already joined, and the newly appointed commander had no organized staff; his army was not concentrated; his strongest corps was over thirty miles from the point of conflict; and the two corps immediately engaged should have been destroyed in detail before reinforcements could have reached them. In addition to all this — superadded thereto — the most skilful general and perhaps the fiercest fighter on the Union side was killed at the outset, and his line of battle was almost fatally disordered by the misconception of a corps commander.

The chapter of accidents thus reads all in Lee's favor. But, while Lee on any fair weighing of chances stands in my judgment more than justified both in his conception of the campaign and in every material strategic move made in it, he none the less fundamentally misconceived the situation, with consequences which should have been fatal both to him and to his command. Frederick did the same at Kunersdorf; Napoleon, at Waterloo. In the first place, Lee had at that time supreme confidence in his command; and he had grounds for it. As he himself then wrote — "There never were such men in an army before. They will go anywhere and do anything, if properly led." And, for myself, I do not think the estimate thus expressed was exaggerated; speaking deliberately, having faced some portions of the Army of Northern Virginia at the time and having since reflected much on the occurrences of that momentous period, I do not believe that any more formidable or better organized and animated force was ever set in motion than that which Lee led across the Potomac in the early summer of 1863. I It was essentially an army of fighters, — men who, individually or in the mass, could be depended on for any feat of arms in the power of mere mortals to accomplish. They would blanch at no danger. This Lee from experience knew. He had tested them; they had full confidence in him. He also thought he knew his opponent; and here too his recent experience justified him.

The disasters which had befallen the Confederates in the Southwest in the spring and early summer of 1863 had to find compensation in the East. The exigencies of warfare necessitated it. Some risk must be incurred. So Lee determined to strike at his opponent's heart. He had what he believed to be the better weapon; and he had reason for considering himself incomparably the superior swordsman. He was; of that he had at Chancellorsville satisfied himself and the world. Then came the rapid, aggressive move; and the long, desperately contested struggle at Gettysburg, culminating in that historic charge of Pickett's Virginia division. Paradoxical as it may sound, in view of the result, that charge — what those men did — justified Lee. True, those who made the charge did not accomplish the impossible; but towards it they did all that mortal men could do. But it is urged that Lee should have recognized the impossible when face to face confronted by it, and not have directed brave men to lay down their lives in the vain effort to do it. That is true; and, as Lee is said to have once remarked in another connection, "Even as poor a soldier as I am can generally discover mistakes after it is all over." After Gettysburg was over, like Frederick at Kunersdorf and Napoleon at Waterloo, Lee doubtless discovered his mistake. It was a very simple one: he undervalued his opponent. The temper of his own weapon he knew; he made no mistake there. His mistake lay in his estimate of his antagonist: but that estimate again was based on his own recent experience, though in other fields.

On the other hand, from the day I rode over the field of Gettysburg immediately following the fight, to that which now is, I have fully and most potently believed that only some disorganized fragments of Lee's army should after that battle have found their way back to Virginia. The war should have collapsed within sixty days thereafter. For eighteen hours after the repulse of Pickett's division, I have always felt and now feel, the fate of the Army of Virginia was as much in General Meade's hands as was the fate of the army led by Napoleon in the hands of Blücher on the night of Waterloo. As an aggressive force, the Confederate army was fought out. It might yet put forth a fierce defensive effort; it was sure to die game: but it was impotent for attack. Meade had one entire corps — perhaps his best, — his Sixth, commanded by Sedgwick — intact and in reserve. It lay there cold, idle, formidable. The true counter movement for the fourth day of continuous fighting would on Meade's part have been an exact reversal of Lee's own plan of battle for the third day. That plan, as described by Fitzhugh Lee, was simple. "His [Lee's] purpose was to turn the enemy's left flank with his First Corps, and, after the work began there, to demonstrate against his lines with the others in order to prevent the threatened flank from being reinforced, these demonstrations to be converted into a real attack as the flanking wave of battle rolled over the troops in their front." What Lee thus proposed for Meade's army on the third day, Meade should unquestionably have returned on Lee's army upon the fourth day. Sedgwick's corps should then have assailed Lee's right and rear. I once asked a leading Confederate general, who had been in the very thick of it at Gettysburg, what would have been the outcome had Meade, within two hours of the repulse of Pickett, ordered Sedgwick to move off to the left, and, occupying Lee's line of retreat, proceeded to envelop the Confederate right, while, early the following morning, Meade had commanded a general advance. The answer I received was immediate: "Without question we would have been destroyed. We all that night fully expected it; and could not understand next day why we were unmolested. My ammunition " — for he was an officer of artillery — *'was exhausted."

But in all this, as in every speculation of the sort, — and the history of warfare is replete with them, — the "if" is much in evidence; as much in evidence, indeed, as it is in a certain familiar Shakesperian disquisition. I here introduce what I have said on this topic simply to illustrate what may be described as the balance of miscarriages inseparable from warfare. On the other hand, the manner in which Lee met disaster at Gettysburg, and the combination of serene courage, and consequent skill, with which he extricated his army from a most critical situation commands admiration. I would here say nothing depreciatory of General Meade. He was an accomplished officer as well as a brave soldier. Placed suddenly in a most trying position, — assigned to chief command when battle was already joined, — untried in his new sphere of action, and caught unprepared, — he fought at Gettysburg a stubborn, gallant fight. With chances at the beginning heavily against him, he saved the day. Personally, I was later under deep obligation to General Meade. He too had character. None the less, as I have already pointed out, I fully believe that on the fourth day at Gettysburg Meade had but firmly to close his hand, and the Army of Northern Virginia was crushed. Perhaps under all the circumstances it was too much to have expected of him; certainly it was not done. Then Lee in turn did avail himself of his opportunity. Skilfully, proudly though sullenly, preserving an unbroken front, he withdrew to Virginia. That withdrawal was masterly.

Narrowly escaping destruction at Gettysburg, my next contention is that Lee and the Army of Northern Virginia never sustained defeat. Finally, it is true, succumbing to exhaustion, to the end they were not overthrown in fight. And here I approach a large topic, but one closely interwoven with Lee's military career; in fact, as I see it, the explanation of what finally occurred. What then was it that brought about the collapse of the Army of Northern Virginia, and the consequent downfall of the Confederacy? The literature of the War of Secession now constitutes a library in itself. Especially is this true of it in its military aspects. The shelves are crowded with memoirs and biographies of its generals, the stories of its campaigns, the records and achievements of its armies, its army corps and its regiments. Yet I make bold to say that no well and philosophically considered narrative of the struggle has yet appeared; nor has any satisfactory or comprehensive explanation been given of its extraordinary and unanticipated outcome. Let me briefly set it forth as I see it; only by so doing can I explain what I mean.

Tersely put, dealing only with outlines, the southern community in 1861 precipitated a conflict on the slavery issue, in implicit reliance on its own warlike capacity and resources, the extent and very defensible character of its territory, and, above all, on its complete control of cotton as the great staple textile fabric of modern civilization. That the seceding States fully believed in the justice of their cause, and confidently appealed to it, I do not question, much less deny. For present purposes let this be conceded in full. But, historically, it is equally clear that to vindicate the right, next to their own manhood and determination, they relied in all possible confidence on their apparently absolute control of one commercial staple. When, therefore, in 1858, with the shadow of the impending conflict darkening the horizon, a thoughtful senator from South Carolina, one on whom the mantle of Calhoun had fallen, declared that "Cotton is King," that "no power on earth dares to make war on it," that "without firing a gun, without drawing a sword," the cotton-producing South could, if war was declared upon it, bring "the whole world" to its feet, he only gave utterance to what was in the South accepted as a fundamental article of political and economical faith. Suggesting the contingency that no cotton was forthcoming from the South for a period of three years, the same senator declared, "this is certain: England would topple headlong and carry the whole civilized world with her, save the South. Who," he then exclaimed, "that has looked on recent events, can doubt that cotton is supreme." In case of conflict, cotton, if it went forth, was to supply the South with the sinews of warfare; if it did not go forth the lack of it would bring about European civil commotion, and compel foreign intervention. In either case the South was secure. As to a maritime blockade of the South, shutting it up to die of inanition, the idea was chimerical. No such feat of maritime force ever had been accomplished, it was claimed; nor was it possible of accomplishment. To "talk of putting up a wall of fire around eight hundred and fifty thousand square miles" situated as the Confederacy was, with its twelve thousand miles of seacoast, was pronounced too "absurd" for serious discussion. And, certainly, that no such thing had ever yet been done was undeniable. But, even supposing it were possible of accomplishment, the doing it would but the more effectively play the Confederate game. It would compel intervention. As well shut off bread from the manufacturing centres of Europe as stop their supply of cotton. In any or either event, and in any contingency which might arise, the victory of the Confederacy was assured. And this theory of the situation and its outcome was accepted by the southern community as indisputable.

What occurred.? In each case that which had been pronounced impossible of occurrence. On land the Confederacy had an ample force of men, they swarmed to the standards; and no better or more reliable material was ever gathered together. Well and skilfully marshalled, the Confederate soldier did on the march and in battle all that needed to be done. Nor were the two sides unequally matched so far as the land arrays were concerned. As Lee with his instinctive military sense put it even in the closing stages of the struggle — "The proportion of experienced troops is larger in our army than in that of the enemy, while his numbers exceed our own." And in warfare experience, combined with an advantageous defensive, counts for a great deal. This was so throughout the conflict; and yet the Confederate cause sank in failure. It did so to the complete surprise of a bewildered world; for, in Europe, the ultimate success of the South was accepted as a foregone conclusion. To such an extent was this the case that the wisest and most far-seeing of English public men did not hesitate to stake their reputation for foresight upon it as a result. How was the wholly unexpected actual outcome brought about .'^ The simple answer is, — The Confederacy collapsed from inanition. Suffering such occasional reverses and defeats as are incidental to all warfare, it I was never crushed in battle or on the field, until its strength was sapped away by want of food. It died of exhaustion, — starved and: gasping!

Take a living organism, whatever it may be, place it in a vessel hermetically sealed, and attach to that vessel an air pump. You know what follows. It is needless to describe it. No matter how strong or fierce or self-confident it may be, the victim dies; growing weaker by degrees, it finally collapses. That was the exact condition and fate of the Confederacy. What had been confidently pronounced impossible was done. The Confederacy was sealed up within itself by the blockade; and the complete exclusion of cotton from the manufacturing centres of Europe did not cause revolution there, nor compel intervention here. Man's foresight once more came to grief. As usual, it was the unexpected which occurred.

Thus the two decisive defeats of the Confederacy, — those which really brought about its downfall and compelled Lee to lay down his arms, — were inflicted not before Vicksburg nor yet in Virginia, — not in the field at all; they were sustained, the one, almost by default, on the ocean; the other, most fatal of all, after sharpest struggle in Lancashire. The story of that Lancashire Cotton Famine of 1861 to 1864 has never been adequately told in connection with our Civil War. Simply ignored by the standard historians, it was yet the Confederacy's fiercest fight, and its most decisive as well as most far-reaching defeat. A momentous conflict, the supremacy of the Union on the ocean hung on its issue; and upon that supremacy depended every considerable land operation: — the retention by the Confederacy of New Orleans, and the consequent control of the Mississippi; Sherman's march to the sea; the movement through the Carolinas; the operations before Petersburg; generally, the maintenance of the Confederate armies in the field. It is in fact no exaggeration to assert that both the conception and the carrying out of every large Union operation of the war without a single exception hinged and depended on complete national maritime supremacy. It is equally indisputable that the struggle in Lancashire was decisive of that supremacy. As Lee himself admitted in the death agony of the Confederacy, he had never believed it could in the long run make good its independence "unless Foreign Powers should, directly or indirectly, assist" it in so doing. Thus, strange as it sounds, it follows as a logical consequence that Lee and his Army of Northern Virginia were first reduced to inanition, and finally compelled to succumb, as the result of events on the other side of the Atlantic, largely stimulated by a moral impulse over which they could exert no control. The great and loudly trumpeted cotton campaign of the Confederacy was its most signal failure; and that failure was decisive of the war.

It is very curious, at times almost comical, to trace historical parallels. Plutarch is, of course, the standard exemplar of that sort of treatment. Among other great careers, Plutarch, as every college boy knows, tells the story of King Pyrrhus, the Epirot. A great captain, Pyrrhus devised a military formation which his opponents could not successfully face, and his career was consequently one of victory. But at last he met his fate. Assaulting the town of Argos, he became entangled in its streets; and, fighting his way out, he was struck down, and killed, by a tile thrown from a house-top by an Argive woman. The Confederacy, and, through the Confederacy, Lee underwent a not dissimilar fate; for, as an historical fact, it was a missile from a woman's hand which was decisive of that Lancashire conflict, and so doomed the Confederacy. A startling proposition; but proof quite irrefutable of it exists in a publication to which as an authority no Southern writer at least will take exception, the organ established in London by the agents of the Confederacy in 1862. Sustained as long as the conflict continued from Confederate funds, with a view to influencing European public opinion, the Index, as it was called, collapsed with the Confederacy in July, 1865. Naturally those in charge of it watched with feverish interest the progress of the cotton famine. Not only was the British pocket nerve touched at its most sensitive point, but in Lancashire starvation emphasized financial distress. The pressure thus brought to bear on public opinion in Great Britain, and, through that public opinion, on the policy of Europe, was confidently counted on for results decisive of the American struggle. Ten years before Harriet Beecher Stowe had launched through the press her *Uncle Tom's Cabin.* Translated into every civilized tongue, it had soon become world literature. In Great Britain, and especially in Lancashire, it "carried the new gospel to every cabin in the land." Whoever in those days read anything, read Uncle Tom's Cabin. That it was a correct portrayal of conditions actually existing in the region wherein the incidents[6] narrated were supposed to have occurred, is not now to be considered. That Uncle Tom himself was a type of his race, or indeed even a possibility in it, few would now be disposed to contend. Ethically, he was a Christian martyr of the most advanced description and, on the large class who accepted the work as a correct portrayal, the pathetic story and cruel fate of the colored saint, moralist and philosopher made an indelible impression. Indeed, that female and sentimentalist portrayal lent a force which has not yet spent itself to the contention that the only difference between the Ethiopian and the Caucasian is epidermal; the negro being in fact merely a white man — a Yankee, if you please — who, having a black skin, has never been given a chance! Nay, more! if Uncle Tom and Legree were to be accepted as types, the black man was superior naturally to the white; for Uncle Tom was a fully developed moralist, while Legree was a demon incarnate. And this presentation of life and manners, and this portrayal of typical racial characters were in Lancashire implicitly accepted as gospel truth! Such indisputably was the fact; and, when the final issue was joined, the fact told heavily against the Confederacy. In contemplation of it, — realizing the handicap thus imposed, the burden of which at the moment the historian has since ignored, and few consequently now appreciate, — the writers for the Index fairly cried aloud in agony. Their wail, long repeated, has in it as now read an element of the comic. The patience of the victims of the cotton famine, they declared, was the extraordinary feature of the foreign situation; and the agents of the Confederacy noted with unconcealed dismay the absence of political demonstrations calculated to urge on a not unwilling Palmerston ministry "its duty to its suffering subjects." There was but one way of accounting for it. Uncle Tom and Legree were respectively doing their work. So it was that the Index despairingly at last declared — "The emancipation of the negro from the slavery of Mrs. Beecher Stowe's heroes is the one idea of the millions of British who know no better, and do not care to know." Like the Cherubim with the flaming sword this sentiment stood between Lancashire and cotton; and the inviolate blockade made possible the subjugation of the Confederacy. With Pyrrhus, it was the tile thrown by a woman from the house-top; with Lee, it was a book by a woman issued from the printing press! The missiles were equally fatal. It was only a difference of time, and its changed conditions.

Foreign intervention being thus withheld, and the control of the sea by the Union made absolute, the blockade was gradually perfected. The fateful process then went steadily on. Armies might be resisted in the field; the working of the air pump could not be stopped : and, day and night, season after season, the air pump worked. So the atmosphere of the Confederacy became more and more attenuated, respiration sensibly harder. Air-hole on air-hole was closed. First New Orleans fell; then Vicksburg, and the Mississippi flowed free; next Sherman, securely counting on the control of the sea as a base of new operations on land, penetrated the vitals of the Confederacy; then, relying still on maritime cooperation, he pursued his almost unopposed way through the Carolinas; while Grant, with his base secure upon the James and Fortress Monroe, beleaguered Richmond. Lee with his Army of Northern Virginia calmly, but watchfully and resolutely, confronted him. The Confederate lines were long and thin, guarded by poorly clad and half -fed men. But, veterans, they held their assailants firmly at bay. As Lee, however, fully realized, it was only a question of time. The working of the air pump was beyond his sphere either of influence or operations. Nothing could stop it. As early as the close of 1863 Lee wrote of his men, "Thousands are bare-footed, a greater number partially shod, and nearly all without overcoats, blankets, or warm clothing;" and later, in the dead of winter, referring to the elementary necessities of any successful warfare, he said, — "The supply, by running the blockade, has become so precarious that I think we should turn our attention to our own resources ... as a further dependence upon those from abroad can result in nothing but increase of suffering and want." The conclusion here drawn, while necessary, was extremely suggestive. "Our own resources!" — the Confederacy had always prided itself on being a purely agricultural community. With institutions patriarchal in character, it had looked upon the people of the North as its agents and factors, and those of Europe as its skilled workmen and artisans; and now that community shut up within its own limits, under conditions of warfare active and severe, had only itself to rely upon for a supply of everything its defenders needed, from munitions to shoes, from blankets to medicines and even soap. Viewed in a half century's perspective, the situation was simply and manifestly impossible of continuance. To it there could be but one outcome; and when at last on the 16th of January, 1865, the telegraph announced the fall of Fort Fisher, the Confederacy felt itself hermetically sealed. Wilmington, its last breathing hole, was closed. Still, not the less for that, the air pump kept on in its deadly silent work.

Three months later the long-delayed inevitable occurred. The collapse came. That under such conditions it should have been so long in coming is now the only legitimate cause of surprise. That adversity is the test of man is a commonplace; that Lee and his Army of Northern Virginia were during the long, dragging winter of 1864-5 most direfully subjected to that test need not here be said; any more than it is needful to say that they bore the test manfully. But the handwriting was on the wall; the men were taxed beyond the limits of human endurance. And Lee knew it. "Yesterday, the most inclement day of the winter," he reported on February 8, 1865, the right wing of his army "had to be retained in line of battle, having been in the same condition the two previous days and nights. . . . Under these circumstances, heightened by assaults and fire of the enemy, some of the men had been without meat for three days, and all were suffering from reduced rations and scant clothing, exposed to battle, cold, hail and sleet. . . . The physical strength of the men, if their courage survives, must fail under this treatment." If it was so with the men, with the animals it was even worse. "Our cavalry," he added, "has to be dispersed for want of forage." Even thus Lee's army faced an opponent vastly superior in numbers, whose ranks were being constantly replenished; a force armed, clothed, equipped, fed and sheltered as no similar force in the world's history had ever been before. I state only indisputable facts. Lee proved equal to even this occasion. Bearing a bold, confident front, he was serene and outwardly calm ; alert, resourceful, formidable to the last, individually he showed no sign of weakness, not even occasional petulance. Inspired by his example, the whole South seemed to lean up against him in implicit, loving reliance. It was a superlative tribute to Character. Finally, when in April the summons to conflict came, the Army of Northern Virginia, the single remaining considerable organized force of the Confederacy, seemed to stagger to its feet, and, gaunt and grim, shivering with cold and emaciated with hunger, worn down by hard, unceasing attrition, it faced its enemy, formidable still. As I have since studied that situation, listened to the accounts of Confederate officers active in the closing movements, and read the letters written me by those of the rank and file, it has seemed as if Lee's command then cohered and moved by mere force of habit. Those composing it failed to realize the utter hopelessness of the situation — the disparity of the conflict. I am sure Jefferson Davis failed to realize it; so, I think, in less degree, did Lee. They talked, for instance, of recruits and of a levy in mass; Lee counselled the arming of the slaves; and when, after Lee had surrendered, Davis on the 10th of April, 1865, held his last war conference at Greensboro, he was still confident he would in a few weeks have another army in the field, and did not hesitate to express his faith that "we can whip the enemy yet, if our people will turn out." I have often pondered over what Davis had in mind when he ventured this opinion; or what led Lee to advocate the enlistment of negroes. Both were soldiers; and, besides being great in his profession, Lee was more familiar than any other man alive with actual conditions then existing in the Confederate camps. Both Davis and Lee, therefore, must have known that, in those final stages of the conflict, if the stamp of a foot upon the ground would have brought a million men into the field, the cause of the Confederacy would thereby have been in no wise strengthened ; on the contrary, what was already bad would have been made much worse. For, to be effective in warfare, men must be fed and clothed and armed. Organized in commands, they must have rations as well as ammunition, commissary and quartermaster trains, artillery horses and forage. In the closing months of the Civil War, both Lee and Davis knew perfectly well that they could not arm, nor feed, nor clothe, nor transport the forces already in the field ; they were themselves without money, and the soldiers most inadequately supplied with arms, clothing, quartermaster or medical supplies, commissariat or ammuni-tion. Notoriously, those then on the muster-rolls were going home, or deserting to the enemy, as the one alternative to death from privation — hunger and cold. If then, a million, or even only a poor hundred thousand fresh recruits had in answer to the summons swarmed to the lines around Richmond, how would it have bettered the situation? An organized army is a mighty consumer of food and material; and food and material have to be served out to it every day. It must be fed as regularly as the sun rises and sets. And the organized resources of the Confederacy were exhausted; its granaries — Georgia and the valley of the Shenandoah — were notoriously devastated and desolate; its lines of communication and supply were cut, or in the hands of the invader.

Realizing this, when the time was ripe, Lee rose to the full height of the great occasion. The value of Character made itself felt. The service Lee now rendered to the common country, the obligation under which he placed us whether of the North or South, has not, I think, been always appreciated; and to overstate it would be difficult. Again to put on record my estimate of it brings me here to-day.

That the situation was to the last degree critical is matter of history. Further organized resistance on the part of the Confederacy was impossible. The means for it did not exist; could not be had. Cut off completely from the outer world, the South was consuming itself, — feeding on its own vitals. The single alternative to surrender was disbandment and irregular warfare. As General Johnston afterwards wrote, "without the means of purchasing supplies of any kind, or procuring or repairing arms, we could continue the war only as robbers or guerrillas." But that it should be so continued was wholly possible; nay more, it was in the line of precedent, — it had been done before, and, more than once, it has since been done, notably in South Africa. It was, moreover, the course advocated by many southern participants in the struggle as that proper to be pursued; and that it would be pursued was accepted as of course by all foreign observers, and by the organ of the Confederacy in London. "A strenuous resistance and not surrender," it was there declared, "was the unalterable determination of the Confederate authorities." Lee's own son, then in the Army of Northern Virginia, but by chance not included in the surrender, has since described how surprised and incredulous he was when news of it first reached him; and, "not believing for an instant that our struggle was over," he made his way at once to Jefferson Davis, at Greensboro. At the time of his capture Davis himself, wholly unsubdued in spirit, was moving in the direction of the Mississippi intent on organizing resistance in Texas, — a resistance which the writers of the Index confidently predicted would "be fierce, ferocious and of long duration," — "a successful or at least a protracted resistance."

Indeed, had the veil over the immediate /future then been lifted, and the outrages, and I humiliations worse than outrage, of the period of so-called reconstruction, but actual servile I domination, now to ensue revealed itself, no room for doubt exists that the dread alternative would have been adopted. Even as it was, the scales hung trembling. Anything or everything was possible; even that mad pistol shot of the theatrical fool which five days later so irretrievably complicated a delicate and dangerous situation. None the less, what Lee and Grant had done at Appomattox on April 9 could not be wholly undone even by the deed in Ford's theatre of April 14; much had been secured. Of Appomattox, and what there occurred, I do not care here to speak. I feel I could not speak adequately, or in words sufficiently simple; for, in my judgment, there is not in our whole history as a people any incident so creditable to our manhood, — so indicative of our racial possession of Character. Marked throughout by a straightforward dignity of personal bearing and propriety in action, it was marred by no touch of the theatrical, no effort at posturing. I know not to which of the two leaders, there face to face, preference should be given. They were thoroughly typical, the one of Illinois and the New West, the other of Virginia and the Old Dominion. Grant was considerate and magnanimous, — restrained in victory; Lee, dignified in defeat, carried himself with that sense of absolute fitness which compelled respect. Verily ! — "he that ruleth his spirit is better than I he that taketh a city"!

The lead that day given by Lee proved decisive of the course to be pursued by his fellows with arms in their hands. At first, and for a brief space, there was in the Confederate councils much diversity of opinion as to what should or could be done. Calm and dignified in presence of overwhelming disaster, the voice of Jefferson Davis was that of

Milton's "scepter'd king:"— "My sentence is for open war!" Lee was not there; none the less, Lee, absent, prevailed over Davis. The sober second thought satisfied all but the most extreme that what he had done they best might do. Thus the die was cast. And now, forty years and more after the event, it is appalling to reflect what in all human probability would have resulted had the choice then been other than it was, — had Lee's personality and character not intervened.

The struggle had lasted four full years; the assassination of Lincoln was as oil on the Union fire. With a million men, inured to war, on the national muster rolls, men impatient of further resistance, accustomed to license and now educated up to a belief that war was Hell, and that the best way to bring it to a close was to intensify Hell, — with such a force as this to reckon with, made more reckless in brutality by the assassin's senseless shot, the Confederacy need have looked for no consideration, no mercy. Visited by the besom of destruction, it would have been harried out of existence. Fire and sword sweeping over it, what the sword spared the fire would have consumed. Whether such an outcome of a prolonged conflict — what was recently witnessed in South Africa — would in its result have been more morally injurious to the North than it would have been physically destructive to the South, is not now to be considered. It would, however, assuredly have come about.

From that crown of sorrows Lee saved the common country. He was the one man in the Confederacy who could exercise decisive influence. It was the night of the 8th of April, I lacking ten days only of exactly four full years, — years very full for us who lived through them — since that not dissimilar night when Lee had paced the floor at Arlington, communing with himself over the fateful issue, a decision on which was then forced upon him. A decision of even greater import was now to be reached, and reached by him. A commander of the usual cast would under such circumstances have sought advice — perhaps support; at least, a divided responsibility. Even though himself by nature and habit a masterful man and one accustomed to direct, he would have called a council, and harkened to those composing it. This

Lee did not do. A singularly self-poised man, he sought no external aid. Sitting before his bivouac fire at Appomattox he reviewed the situation. Doing so, as before at Arlington, he reached his own conclusion. That conclusion he himself at the time expressed in words, brief, indeed, but vibrating with moral triumph: — "The question is, is it right to surrender this army? If it is right, then I will take all the responsibility." The conclusion reached at Arlington in the April night of 1861 to some seems to have been wrong — inexcusable even; all concur in that reached before the Appomattox camp-fire in the April vigils of 1865. He then a second time decided; and he decided right.

His work was done; but from failure he plucked triumph. Thenceforth Lee wore defeat as it were a laurel crown. A few days later a small group of horsemen appeared in the morning hours on the further side of the Richmond pontoons across the James. By some strange intuition it became known that General Lee was of the party; and, silent and uncovered, a crowd — Virginians all — gathered along the route the horsemen would take. "There was no excitement, no hurrahing; but as the great chief passed, a deep, loving murmur, greater than these, rose from the very hearts of the crowd. Taking off his hat, and simply bowing his head, the man great in adversity passed silently to his own door; it closed upon him; and his people had seen him for the last time in his battle harness."

From the day that he affixed his signature to the terms of surrender submitted to him by Grant at Appomattox to the day when he drew a dying breath at Lexington, Lee's subsequent course was consistent. In his case there was no vacillation, no regretful glances backward thrown. When, four months after the last hostile shot was fired, he was invited to assume the presidency of this college, though then under indictment, in flagrant disregard of the immunity assured him when he gave his parole, he briefly set forth his views. "I think it," he wrote, "the duty of every citizen, in the present condition of the country, to do all in his power to aid in the restoration of peace and harmony, and in no way to oppose the policy of the State or General Governments directed to that object." And, four days later, writing to the Confederate Governor of

Virginia, he said — "The duty of [Virginian] citizens appears to me too plain to admit of doubt. All should unite in honest efforts to obliterate the effects of war, and to restore the blessings of peace. They should remain if possible in the country; promote harmony and good feeling; qualify themselves to vote, and elect to the State and general legislatures wise and patriotic men, who will devote their abilities to the healing of all dissensions. I have," he added, "invariably recommended this course since the cessation of hostilities, and have endeavored to practice it myself." Here was a complete exposition of duty, combined with abnegation of self; the purest patriotism, it was also the concentrated essence of statesmanship. He counselled with a wisdom not less profound because unconscious ; and what he said evinced that underlying common sense which in politics avails more than genius.

Five years of life and active usefulness yet remained to General Lee — years in my judgment most creditable to himself, the most useful to his country of his whole life; for, during them, he set to Virginia and his own people a high example, — an example of lofty character and simple bearing. Uttering no complaints, entering into no controversies, he was as one, in suffering all, that suffers nothing. His blood and judgment were well commingled; and so it fell out that he accepted fortune's buffets and rewards with equal thanks. His record and appearance during those final years are pleasant to dwell upon, for they reflect honor on our American manhood. Turning his face courageously to the future, he uttered no word of repining over the past. Yet, like the noble Moor, his occupation also was gone —

> " The royal banner, and all quality,
> Pride, pomp and circumstance of glorious war! "

But with Lee this did not imply

> " Farewell the tranquil mind! farewell content! "

Far from it; for as the gates closed on the old occupation, they opened on a new. And it was an occupation through which he gave to his country. North and South, a priceless gift.

Speaking advisedly and on full reflection, I say that of all the great characters of the Civil War, and it was productive of many whose names and deeds posterity will long bear in recollection, there was not one who passed away in the serene atmosphere and with the gracious bearing of Lee. From beginning to end those parting years of his will bear closest scrutiny. There was about them nothing venal, nothing querulous, nothing in any way sordid or disappointing. In his case there was no anti-climax; for those closing years were dignified, patient, useful ; sweet in domesticity, they in all things commanded respect. It is pleasant to catch glimpses of the erstwhile commander in that quiet Virginia life. There is in the picture something altogether human — intensely sympathetic. "Traveller," he would write, "is my only companion; I may also say my pleasure. He and I, whenever practicable, wander out in the mountains and enjoy sweet confidence." Or again we see him, always with Traveller, the famous old charger this time "stepping very proudly," as his rider showed those two little sun-bonneted daughters of a professor, astride of a plodding old horse, over a pleasant road, quite unknown to them. Once more in imagination we may ride, his companions, through those mountain roads of his dearly loved Virginia, or seek shelter with him and his daughter from a thunder-shower in the log cabin, the inmates of which are stunned when too late they realize that the courtly, gracious intruder was no other than the idolized General Lee. I Indifferent to wealth, he was scrupulous as respects those money dealings a carelessness I in regard to which has embittered the lives of so many of our public men, as not infrequently it has tarnished their fame. Lee's career will be scrutinized in vain for a suggestion even of the sordid, or of an obligation I he failed to meet. He was nothing if not self-respecting. He once wrote to a member of his family "vile dross' has never been a drug with me," yet his generosity as a giver from his narrow means was limited only by his resources. Restricting his own wants to necessities, he contributed, to an extent which excites surprise, to both public calls and private needs. But the most priceless of those contributions were contained in the precepts he inculcated and in the unconscious example he set during those closing years.

Lee was at the head of Washington College from October, 1865, to October, 1870; a very insufficient time in which to accomplish any considerable work. A man of fast advancing years, he also then had sufficient cause to feel a sense of lassitude. He showed no signs of it. On the contrary, closely studied, those years, and Lee's bearing in them, were in certain respects the most remarkable as well as the most creditable of his life; they impressed unmistakably upon it the stamp of true greatness. Unable to pass them wholly over, I shall deal very briefly with them. His own means of subsistence having been swept away by war, — the property of his wife as well as his own having been sequestered and confiscated in utter disregard not only of law, but — I add it regretfully — of decency, — a mere pittance, designated in courtesy "salary," under his prudent management was made to suffice for the needs of an establishment the quiet dignity of which even exceeded its severe simplicity. Within five months of the downfall of the Confederacy, he addressed himself to his new vocation. Coming to it from crushing defeat, about him there was nothing suggestive of disappointment; and thereafter through public trials and private misfortunes — for it pleased Heaven to try him with afflictions — he bore himself with serene patience, and a mingled firmness and sweetness of temper to which mere words fail to do justice. More than that, becoming interested in his new work, he evinced, it would seem, as the head of a college a grasp of educational problems not less clear and intelligent than he had previously shown of strategic conditions. It was indeed extraordinary that a man educated in a military school, first an engineer, then an officer of cavalry, and finally a general in charge of large field operations, should, when approaching his sixtieth year, have given proof of such mental activity and freshness. Fully realizing the needs and requirements of the present age, the former commandant of West Point was the ardent advocate of complete classical and literary culture. Utterly out of sympathy with the modern advocates of materialistic education, he yet recognized the fact that material well-being is, for a people, the condition of all high civilization; and, accordingly, sought to provide, in the institution of which he was the head, all means for the development of science, and its practical application. With a large and correct conception he planned, therefore, to connect all the departments of literary, scientific, and professional education, and to consolidate them under a common organization. He thus outlined a true university. So, at an early day he called into existence, as adjuncts of the college he found prostrate and well-nigh moribund, schools of Applied Mathematics, of Engineering and of Law; while later he submitted to its Board of Trustees a matured scheme for the complete development of the scientific and professional departments. His death, just before he had yet reached the grand climacteric, prevented the full development of his great conception. None the less, he had shown himself fully equal to the new demand upon him.

The most marked feature of his educational career was, however, the moral influence he exerted on the student body, — what has most fitly been described by one associated with him as *'the mighty influence of his personal character." Here, as in the Army of Northern Virginia, this was all-powerful. It was sorely needed, too; for the young men of the South were wild, and resented efforts at restraint. Grown up in an environment of warfare and consequent violence, they were somewhat disposed to take matters into their own hands, — to be, in a word, a law unto themselves; but, under Lee's presidency, the elevation of tone in this respect, and the consequent improvement in student conduct were, we are on good evidence assured, marked and rapid. Acts of disorder became infrequent; and in the latter years of Lee's brief administration it is said that "hardly a single case of serious discipline occurred." A Boston student of Washington College in those years — sent there because of the feelings of profound respect for Lee entertained by his Northern father — has since borne witness to me of the personal interest taken by Washington's president in the individual students. In close sympathy with the modern university spirit, the youth in question was, I have reason to suppose, far more addicted to athletics than to his text-books.

"This lack of proficiency in my studies," he has recently written me, "was, of course, a matter for which I was frequently called into the presence of General Lee; and I fully appreciate now, though I did not then, the difficulties under which he labored; for, if he had expelled me, as under similar circumstances he undoubtedly would have expelled any Southern student, it would have been considered a factional matter. He would plead most earnestly with me always that I should attend more to my studies and less to athletics, and never a harsh word during the entire period."

It remains to assign due weight and value to these precepts and this great example at just that juncture and from just that man. And here, bearing in mind the common country, — the community to which I belong as well as that I now address, — I feel I tread on dangerous ground. What I must necessarily say will be very susceptible of misconstruction. Speaking, however, in the true historical spirit, as throughout I have sought to do, I must deal with this topic also as best I can.

Because no blood flowed on the scaffold, and no confiscations of houses or lands marked the close of our war of Secession, it has always been assumed by us of the victorious party that extreme, indeed unprecedented, clemency was shown to the vanquished, and that subsequently they had no good ground of complaint or sufficient cause for restiveness. That history will accord assent to this somewhat self-complacent conviction is open to question. On the contrary, it may not unfairly be doubted whether a people prostrate after civil strife has often received severer measure than was inflicted on the so-called reconstructed Confederate States during the years immediately succeeding the close of strife. Adam Smith somewhere defined Rebels and Heretics as "those unlucky persons who, when things have come to a certain degree of violence, have the misfortune to be of the weaker party." Spoliation and physical suffering have immemorially been their lot. The Confederate, it is true, when he ceased to resist, escaped this visitation in its usual and time-approved form. Nevertheless, he was by no means exempt from it. In the matter of confiscation, it has been computed that the freeing of the slaves by act of war swept out of existence property valued at some two thousand millions; while, over and above this, a system of simultaneous reconstruction subjected the disfranchised master to the rule of the enfranchised bondsman. For a community conspicuously masterful, and notoriously quick to resent affront, to be thus placed by alien force under the civil rule of those of a different and distinctly inferior race, only lately their property, is not physical torment, it is true, but that it is mild or considerate treatment can hardly be contended. Yet this — slave confiscation, and reconstruction under African rule — was the war penalty imposed on the States of the Confederacy. That the policy inspired at the time a feeling of bitter resentment in the South was no cause for wonder. Upon it time has already recorded a verdict. Following the high precedent set; at Appomattox it was distinctly unworthy. Conceived in passion, it ignored both science and the philosophy of statesmanship; worse yet, it was ungenerous. Lee, for instance, again setting the example, applied formally for amnesty and a restoration of civil rights within two months of his surrender. His application was silently ignored; while he died "a prisoner on parole," the suffrage denied him was conferred on his manumitted slaves. Verily, it was not alone the base Indian of the olden time who "threw a pearl away richer than all his tribe"!

But on such a rejection and choice of material as this was the so-called reconstruction edifice based; nor is it matter for wonder that it speedily crumbled away. It was under these conditions that Lee's bearing and example were of special national importance. The one political result the States of the Confederacy should ever have kept steadily in view after strife closed was the restoration of local self-government; and that, under the traditions and political instincts of the American community, was sure to come. It was only a question of time; and patience and self-restraint were the two qualities most sure to hasten the steps of time. "We shall have to be patient," Lee in March, 1866, wrote to old companions in arms, "and suffer for a while at least ; . . . I hope, in time, peace will be restored to the country, and that the South may enjoy some measure of prosperity. I fear, however, much suffering is still in store for her, and that her people must be prepared to exercise fortitude and forbearance." To those to whom it was addressed, no wiser or more tactful counsel could at that juncture (March, 1866) have been imparted; for, while Lee himself possessed those virtues to a well-nigh unexampled degree, patience and self-restraint have not been generally accepted as most conspicuous among the many manly and ennobling qualities of the race to which Lee belonged.

In the passage with which I began, it was observed by Emerson that "Character denotes habitual self-possession, habitual regard to interior and constitutional motives, a balance not to be overset or easily disturbed by outward events and opinion.'* To my knowledge I never saw General Lee ; I certainly never stood in his presence, nor exchanged a word with him. On the few occasions when I was a guest in his house, he chanced to be absent. Even that was long ago; while he and his family still lived at Arlington. Thus I know him only by report, and through his letters. But, if the report of those who did know him well, and the evidence of what he wrote, may be relied on, I "habitual self-possession, habitual regard to] interior and constitutional motives, a balance \ not to be overset or easily disturbed by out/ ward events and opinion," were his to an eminent degree, — a degree which his harshest and most prejudiced critic could not ignore. That, himself a devout man and by conviction sincerely religious, he was neither ashamed nor afraid so publicly to profess himself, may be read in his repeated army orders; or, to such as prefer there to look for it, in his family letters. What more expressive of a profound religious faith could be imagined than these words written in the very shadow of Gettysburg's disaster to the dying wife of his wounded and captured son? — "In his own good time He will relieve us, and make all things work together for our good, if we give Him our love and place in Him our trust." That his immediate family circle regarded him with the affectionate devotion founded on respect which is the surest indication of those sterling and fundamental qualities which alone can cause a man to seem a hero to those near to him, — the confidants of his privacy, — appears from those family letters and recollections which have been so freely published. That he impressed himself on those about him in his professional and public life to an uncommon extent, — that the soldiers of the Army of Northern Virginia as well as those of his staff and in high command felt not only implicit and unquestioning confidence in him but to him a strong personal affection, is established by their concurrent testimony. He, too, might well have said with Brutus: —

" My heart doth joy that yet in all my life I found no man but he was true to me. I shall have glory by this losing day."

Finally, one who knew him well has written of him — "He had the quiet bearing of a powerful yet harmonious nature. An unruffled calm upon his countenance betokened the concentration and control of the whole being within. He was a kingly man whom all men who came into his presence expected to obey." That he was gifted in a prominent degree with the *mens aequa in arduis*[7] of the Roman poet, none deny.

And now, Virginians, a word with you in closing: "Show me the man you honor; I know by that symptom, better than by any other, what kind of man you yourself are. For you show me then what your ideal of I manhood is; what kind of man you long possibly to be, and would thank the Gods, with your whole soul, for being if you could. Whom shall we consecrate and set apart as one of our sacred men. Sacred; that all men may see him, be reminded of him, and, by new example added to old perpetual precept, be taught what is real worth in man. Whom do you wish to resemble? Him you set on a high column, that all men looking at it, may be continually apprised of the duty you expect from them."

"The virtues of a superior man are like the wind; the virtues of a common man are like the grass; the grass, when the wind passes over it, bends."

Appendix

In regard to the early utterances of Mr. Webster, the following is from a speech by him in the National House of Representatives, December 9, 1814, It should be borne in mind that this speech was delivered in the midst of the gloomiest period of the War of 181215, four months after the battle of Bladensburg and the capture of Washington, and one month before the British were defeated below New Orleans. The speech was first published (1902) by C. H. Van Tyne, in his edition of the *Letters of Daniel Webster* (p. 67).

"In my opinion [the law under consideration for compulsory army and military service] ought not to be carried into effect. The operation of measures thus unconstitutional and illegal ought to be prevented, by a resort to other measures which are both constitutional and legal. It will be the solemn duty of the State Governments to protect their own authority over their own Militia, and to interpose between their citizens and arbitrary power. These are among the objects for which the State Governments exist; and their highest obligations bind them to the preservation of their own rights and the liberties of their people. I express these sentiments here. Sir, because I shall express them to my constituents. Both they and myself live under a Constitution which teaches us, that 'the doctrine of non-resistance against arbitrary power and oppression is absurd, slavish, and destructive of the good and happiness of mankind.' With the same earnestness with which I now exhort you to forbear from these measures, I shall exhort them to exercise their unquestionable right of providing for the security of their own liberties."

William Rawle was in his day an eminent Philadelphia lawyer, and Chancellor of the Law Association of Philadelphia. The principal author of the revised code of Pennsylvania, he stood in the foremost rank of American legal luminaries in the first third of the nineteenth century. His instincts, sympathies, and connections were all national. His View of the Constitution, published in Philadelphia in 1825, was the standard text-book on the subject until the publication of Story's Commentaries, in 1833. It has been asserted that Rawle's View was used as a text-book for the instruction of the students at West Point until after the year 1840. (See prefatory matter to republication of paper entitled Sectional Misunderstandings, by Robert Bingham, in North American Review of September, 1904.)

"If a faction should attempt to subvert the government of a State for the purpose of destroying its republican form, the paternal power of the Union could thus be called forth to subdue it. Yet it is not to be understood that its interposition would be justifiable if the people of a State should determine to retire from the Union, whether they adopted another or retained the same form of government. (Page 289.) . . .

"The States, then, may wholly withdraw from the Union; but while they continue they must retain the character of representative republics." (Page 290.)

"The secession of a State from the Union depends on the will of the people of such State. The people alone, as we have already seen, hold the power to alter their constitution. The Constitution of the United States is, to a certain extent, incorporated into the constitutions of the several States by the act of the people. The State legislatures have only to perform certain organical operations in respect to it. To withdraw from the Union comes not within the general scope of their delegated authority. There must be an express provision to that effect inserted in the State constitutions. This is not at present the case with any of them, and it would perhaps be impolitic to confide it to them. A matter so momentous ought not to be entrusted to those who would have it in their power to exercise it lightly and precipitately upon sudden dissatisfaction, or causeless jealousy, perhaps against the interests and the wishes of a majority of their constituents.

"But in any manner by which a secession is to take place, nothing is more certain than that the act should be deliberate, clear, and unequivocal. The perspicuity and solemnity of the original obligation require correspondent qualities in its dissolution. The powers of the general government cannot be defeated or impaired by an ambiguous or implied secession on the part of the State, although a secession may perhaps be conditional. The people of the State may have some reasons to complain in respect to acts of the general government; they may in such cases invest some of their own officers with the power of negotiation, and may declare an absolute secession in case of their failure. Still, however, the secession must in such case be distinctly and peremptorily declared to take place on that event; and in such case, as in the case of an unconditional secession, the previous ligament with the Union would be legitimately and fairly destroyed. But in either case the people is the only moving power." (Pages 295, 296.)

De Tocqueville cannot, of course, be cited as an authority on American Constitutional Law. Nevertheless, an acute observer, his evidence carries great weight on the question of the views generally current on all constitutional questions at the time he collected the materials for his great work (1831-32). The following extracts bearing upon the topic under discussion are found in the translation of *Democracy in America* by Henry Reeve (London, 1889).

"In America, each State has fewer opportunities of resistance and fewer temptations to non-compliance; nor can such a design be put in execution (if indeed it be entertained) without an open violation of the laws of the Union, a direct interruption of the ordinary course of justice, and a bold declaration of revolt; in a word, without taking a decisive step which men hesitate to adopt." . . . "Here the term Federal government is clearly no longer applicable to a state of things which must be styled an incomplete national government : a form of government has been found out which is neither exactly national nor federal; but no further progress has been made, and the new word which will one day designate this novel invention does not yet exist." (Vol. i, pp. 156, 157.)

"The Union is a vast body which presents no definite object to patriotic feeling. The forms and limits of the State are distinct and circumscribed; since it represents a certain number of objects which are familiar to the citizens and beloved by all. It is identified with the very soil, with the right of property and the domestic affections, with the recollections of the past, the labours of the present, and the hopes of the future. Patriotism, then, which is frequently a mere extension of individual egotism, is still directed to the State, and is not excited by the Union." (Vol. i, p. 394.)

"The Federal Government is, therefore, notwithstanding the precautions of those who founded it, naturally so weak that it more peculiarly requires the free consent of the governed to enable it to subsist.

"If the Union were to undertake to enforce the allegiance of the Confederate States by military means, it would be in a position very analogous to that of England at the time of the War of Independence." (Vol. i, p. 395.)

"The Union was formed by the voluntary agreement of the States; and, in uniting together, they have not forfeited their nationality, nor have they been reduced to the condition of one and the same people. If one of the States chose to withdraw its name from the contract, it would be diflBcult to disprove its right of doing so; and the Federal Government would have no means of maintaining its claims directly, either by force or by right." (Vol. i, p. 396.)

"It appears to me unquestionable that if any portion of the Union seriously desired to separate itself from the other States, they would not be able, nor indeed would they attempt, to prevent it; and that the present Union will only last as long as the States which compose it choose to continue members of the confederation." (Vol. i, p. 397.)

"The dangers which threaten the American Union do not originate in the diversity of interests or of opinions, but in the various characters and passions of the Americans. The men who inhabit the vast territory of the United States are almost all the issue of a common stock; but the effects of the climate, and more especially of slavery, have gradually introduced very striking differences between the British settler of the Southern States and the British settler of the North." (Vol. i, p. 402.)

"I think that I have demonstrated that the existence of the present confederation depends entirely on the continued assent of all the confederates; and, starting from this principle, I have inquired into the causes which may induce the several States to separate from the others. The Union may, however, perish in two different ways : one of the confederate States may choose to retire from the compact, and so forcibly to sever the Federal tie; and it is to this supposition that most of the remarks that I have made apply: or the authority of the Federal Government may be progressively entrenched on by the simultaneous tendency of the united republics to resume their independence." (Vol. i, p. 412.)

"The Constitution had not destroyed the distinct sovereignty of the States; and all communities, of whatever nature they may be, are impelled by a secret propensity to assert their independence." (Vol. i, p. 415.)

Notes:

1. Possibly, and more properly, this attribute might be considered as pertaining rather to James Ford Rhodes, also a member of the Society referred to, and at present a Vice-President of it. Mr. Rhodes' characterization of General Lee, and consequent verdict on the course pursued by him at the time under discussion, can be found on reference to his *History of the United States* (vol. iii, p. 413).

2. Sec Appendix A.

3. See W. H. Fleming, *Slavery and the Race Problem at the South,* pp. 19, 20. An authoritative definition of United States citizenship, as distinct from the citizenship of a State, was first given in the fourteenth amendment to the Federal Constitution, ratified in 1868. See J. S. Wise, A Treatise on American Citizenship, pp. 6, 13, 31.

4. See *Lee at Appomattox and Other Papers* (second edition), pp. 414-416.

5. Stiles, *Four Years under Marse Robert,* p. 21.

6. J. C. Read, *The Brothers' War,* pp. 194-198. There is in Mr. Read's book, published fifty years after the appearance of Mrs. Stowe's historic tale and forty years after the Proclamation of Emancipation, a chapter (ix) entitled, " Uncle Tom's Cabin," in which are to be found the views of an observant and reflecting Georgian on the statement in the text.

7. Editor's Note: *Mens aequa in arduis:* stable mind in adversity. This line is from Horace.

12

Shall Cromwell Have a Statue?

Oration

Given to the Phi Beta Kappa Society

at the University of Chicago,

June 17, 1902

" Whom doth the king delight to honour? that is the question of questions concerning the king's own honour. Show me the man you honour; I know by that symptom, better than by any other, what kind of man you yourself are. For you show me there what your ideal of manhood is; what kind of man you long inexpressibly to be, and would thank the gods, with your whole soul, for being if you could." " Who is to have a Statue? means, Whom shall we consecrate and set apart as one of our sacred men? Sacred; that all men may see him, be reminded of him, and, by new example added to old perpetual precept, be taught what is real worth in man. Whom do you wish us to resemble? Him you set on a high column, that all men, looking on it, may be continually apprised of the duty you expect from them."

— Thomas Carlyle, " Latter-Day Pamphlets." (1850.)

At about-3 o'clock of the afternoon of September 3rd. 1658, the day of Worcester and of Dunbar, and as a great tempest was wearing itself to rest, Oliver Cromwell died. He died in London, in the palace of Whitehall; that palace of the great banqueting hall, through whose central window Charles I. had walked forth to the scaffold a little less than ten years before. A few weeks later, "with a more than regal solemnity," the body of the great Lord Protector was carried to Westminster Abbey, and there buried "amongst Kings." Two years then elapsed: and, on the twelfth anniversary of King Charles's execution, the remains of the usurper, having been disinterred by a unanimous vote of the Convention Parliament, were hung at Tyburn. The trunk was then buried under the gallows, while Cromwell's head was set on a pole over the roof of Westminster Hall. Nearly two centuries of execration ensued, until, in the sixth generation, the earlier verdict was challenged, and the question at last asked: — "Shall Cromwell have a statue?" Cromwell, the traitor, the usurper, the execrable murderer of the martyred Charles! At first, and for long, the suggestion was looked upon almost as an impiety, and, as such, scornfully repelled. Not only did the old loyal King-worship of England recoil from the thought, but. indignantly appealing to the church, it declared that no such distinction could be granted so long as there remained in the prayer-book a form of supplication for "King Charles, the Martyr," and of "praise and thanks giving for the wonderful deliverance of these kingdoms from the great rebellion, and all the other miseries and oppressions consequent thereon, under which they had so long groaned." None the less, the demand was insistent ; and at last, but only after two full centuries had elapsed and a third was well advanced, was the verdict of 1661 reversed. Today the bronze effigy of Oliver Cromwell, — massive in size, rugged in feature, characteristic in attitude, — stands defiantly in the yard of that Westminster Hall, from a pole on the top of which, twelve score years ago, the flesh crumbled from his skull.

In this dramatic reversal of an accepted verdict, — this complete revision of opinions once deemed settled and immutable, — there is, I submit, a lesson, — an academic lesson. The present occasion is essentially educational. The Phi Beta Kappa oration, as it is called, is the last, the crowning utterance of the college year, and very properly is expected to deal with some fitting theme in a kindred spirit. I propose to do so today; but in a fashion somewhat exceptional. The phases of moral and intellectual growth through which the English race has passed on the subject of Cromwell's statue afford, I submit, to the reflecting man an educational study of exceptional interest. In the first place, it was a growth of two centuries; in the second place it marks the passage of a nation from an existence under the traditions of feudalism to one under the principles of self-government; finally it illustrates the gradual development of that broad spirit of tolerance which, coming with time and study, measures the men and events of the past independently of the prejudices and passions which obscure and distort the immediate vision.

We, too, as well as the English, have had our "Great Rebellion." It came to a dramatic close thirty-seven years since; as theirs came to a close not less dramatic some seven times thirty-seven years since. We, also, as they in their time, formed our contemporaneous judgments and recorded our verdicts, assumed to be irreversible, of the men, the issues and the events of the great conflict; and those verdicts and judgments, in our case as in theirs, will unquestionably be revised, modified, and in not a few cases wholly reversed. Better knowledge, calmer reflection, and a more judicial frame of mind come with the passage of the years; in time passions subside, prejudices disappear, truth asserts itself. In England this process has been going on for over two centuries and a half, with what result Cromwell's statue stands as proof. We live in another age and a different environment; and, as fifty years of Europe out-measure in their growth a cycle of Cathay, so I hold one year of twentieth century America works more progress in thought than thirty-seven years of Britain during the interval between its Great Rebellion and ours. We who took active part in the Civil

War have not yet wholly vanished from the stage: the rear guard of the Grand Army, we linger. To-day is separated from the death of Lincoln by the same number of years only which separated "the Glorious Revolution of 1688" from the execution of Charles Stuart; yet to us is already given to look back on the events of which we were a part with the same perspective effects with which the Victorian Englishman looks back on the men and events of the Commonwealth.

I propose on this occasion to do so; and reverting to my text,— "Shall Cromwell have a Statue"- — and reading that text in the gloss of Carlyle's *Latter-Day Pamphlet* utterance, I quote you Horace's familiar precept,

Mutato nomine, de te Fabula narratur,[1]

and ask abruptly, "Shall Robert E. Lee have a Statue?" I propose also to offer to your consideration some reasons why he should, and, assuredly, will have one, if not now. then presently.

Shortly after Lee's death, in October, 1870, leave was asked in the United States Senate, by Mr. McCreery, of Kentucky, to introduce a Joint Resolution providing for the return of the estate and mansion of Arlington to the family of the deceased Confederate Commander-in chief. In view of the use which had then already been made of Arlington as a military cemetery, this proposal, involving, as it necessarily did, a removal of the dead, naturally led to warm debate. The proposition was one not to he considered. If a defect in the title of the government existed, it must in some way be cured, as, subsequently, it was cured. But I call attention to the debate because Charles Sumner, then a Senator from Massachusetts, participated in it, using the following language: — "Eloquent Senators have already characterized the proposition and the traitor it seeks to commemorate. I am not disposed to speak of General Lee. It is enough to say he stands high in the catalogue of those who have imbrued their hands in their country's blood. I hand him over to the avenging pen of History."

This was when Lee had been just two months dead; but, three-quarters of a century after the Protector's skull had been removed from over the roof of Westminster Hall, Pope wrote in similar spirit:

"See Cromwell, damn'd to everlasting fame;"[2]

and, sixteen years later, — four-fifths of a century after Cromwell's disentombment at Westminster, and reburial at Tyburn, —a period from the death of Lee equal to that which will have elapsed in 1950, Cray wrote of the Stoke Pogis churchyard —

" Some mute inglorious Milton here may rest,
Some Cromwell guiltless of his country's blood."[3]

And now, a century and a half later, Cromwell's statue looms defiantly up in front of the Parliament House. When, therefore, an appeal is in such cases made to the "avenging pen of History," it is well to bear this in stance in mind, while recalling perchance that other line of a greater than Pope, or Gray, or Sumner, —

" Thus the whirligig of time brings in his revenges."

Was then Robert E. Lee a "traitor" —was he also guilty of his "country's blood?" These questions I propose now to discuss. 1 am one of those who, in other days, was arrayed in the ranks which confronted Lee; one of those whom Lee baffled and beat, but who, finally, baffled and beat Lee. As one thus formerly lined up against him, these questions I propose to discuss in the calmer and cooler, and altogether more reasonable light which comes to most men, when a whole generation of the human race lies buried between them and the issues and actors upon which we undertake to pass.

Was Robert E. Lee a traitor? Technically, I think he was indisputably a traitor to the United States; for a traitor, as I understand it technically, is one guilty of the crime of treason; or, as the Century Dictionary puts it, violating his allegiance to the chief authority of the State; while treason against the United States is specifically defined in the Constitution as "levying war" against it, or "giving their enemies aid and comfort." That Robert E. Lee did levy war against the United States can. I suppose, no more be denied than that he gave "aid and comfort" to its enemies. This technically; but, in history, there is treason and treason, as there are traitors and traitors. And, furthermore, if Robert E. Lee was a traitor, so also, and indisputably were George Washington, Oliver Cromwell, John Hampden, and William of Orange. The list might be extended indefinitely; but these will suffice. There can be no question that every one of those named violated his allegiance, and gave aid and comfort to the enemies of his sovereign. Washington furnishes a precedent at every point. A Virginian like Lee, he was also a British subject; he had fought under the British flag, as Lee had fought under that of the United States; when, in 1776, Virginia seceded from the British Empire, he "went with his State," just as Lee went with it eighty-five years later; subsequently Washington commanded armies in the field designated by those opposed to them as "rebels," and whose descendants now glorify them as "the rebels of '76," much as Lee later commanded, and at last surrendered, much larger armies, also designated "rebels " by those they confronted. Except in their outcome, the cases were, therefore, precisely alike; and logic is logic. It consequently appears to follow, that, if Lee was a traitor, Washington was also. It is unnecessary to institute similar comparisons with Cromwell, Hampden and William of Orange. No defence can in their cases be made. traitors. Technically, one and all, they undeniably were traitors.

But there are, as I have said, traitors and traitors, — Catalines, Arnolds and Gorgeis, as well as Cromwells, Hampdens and Washingtons. To reach any satisfactory conclusion concerning a candidate for "everlasting fame," —whether to praise him or to damn him, — enroll him as saviour, as martyr, or as criminal, — it is, therefore, necessary still further to discriminate. The cause, the motive, the conduct must be passed in review. Did turpitude anywhere attach to the original taking of sides, or to subsequent act? Was the man a self-seeker? Did low or sordid motives impel him? Did he seek to aggrandize himself at his country's cost? Did he strike with a parricidal hand?

These are grave questions ; and, in the case of Lee, their consideration brings us at the threshold face to face with issues which have perplexed and divided the country since the day the United States became a country. They perplex and divide historians now. Legally, technically, —the moral and humanitarian aspects of the issue wholly apart, — which side had the best of the argument as to the rights and the wrongs of the ease in the great de bate which led up to the Civil War? Before entering, however, on this well-worn, — I might say, this threadbare — theme, as I find myself compelled in briefest way to do, there is one preliminary very essential to be gone through with. A species of moral purgation. Bearing in mind Dr. Johnson's advice to Boswell, on a certain memorable occasion, we should at least try to clear our minds of cant. Many years ago, but only shortly before his death, Richard Cobden said in one of his truth-telling deliverances to his Rochdale constituents, — "I really believe I might be Prime Minster. If I would get up and say 'you are the greatest, the wisest, the best, the happiest people in the world, and keep on repeating that, I don't doubt but what I might be Prime Minister. I have seen Prime Ministers made in my experience precisely by that process.'" The same great apostle of homely sense, on another occasion bluntly remarked in a similar spirit to the House of Commons, — "We generally sympathise with everybody's rebels but our own." In both these respects I submit we Americans are true descendants from the Anglo-Saxon stock; and nowhere is this more unpleasantly apparent than in any discussion which may arise of the motives which actuated those of our countrymen who did not at the time see the issues involved in our Civil War as we saw them. Like those whom Cobden addressed, we like to glorify our ancestors and ourselves and we do not particularly care to give ear to what we are pleased to term unpatriotic, and, at times, even treasonable, talk. In other words, and in plain, unpalatable, English, our minds are saturated with cant. Only in the case of others do we see things as they really are. Then, ceasing to be antagonistic, we are nothing unless critical. So, when it conies to rebellions, we, like Cobden's Englishmen, are wont almost invariably to sympathize with everybody's rebels but our own. Our souls go forth at once to Celt, Pole, Hungarian, Boer and Hindoo: but, when we are concerned, language quite fails us in which adequately to depict the moral turpitude which must actuate Confederate or Filipino who rises in resistance against what we are pleased really to consider, as well as call, the best and most beneficent government the world has yet been permitted to see, —Our Government. This, I submit, is cant,— pure cant; and at the threshold of discussion we had best free our minds of it, wholly, if we can; if not wholly, then in so far as we can. Philip the Second of Spain, when he directed his crusade in the name of God, Church and Government, against William of Orange, indulged in it in quite as good faith as we: and as for Charles "the Martyr" and the "sainted" Laud, for two centuries after Cromwell's head was stuck on a pole, all England every Sunday lamented in sackcloth and ashes the wrongs inflicted by sacrilegious hands on those most assuredly well-meaning rulers and men. All depends on the point of view; and, during our own Civil War, while we unceasingly denounced the wilful wickedness of those who bore parricidal arms against the one immaculate authority yet given the eye of man to look upon, the leading news paper of the world was referring to us in perfect good faith "as an insensate and degenerate people." An English member of Parliament, speaking at the same time in equally good faith, declared that, throughout the length and breadth of Great Britain, public sentiment was almost unanimously on the side of " the Southerners," — as ours was on the side of the Boers, — be cause our "rebels " were "fighting against one of the most grinding, one of the most galling, one of the most irritating attempts to establish tyrannical government that ever disgraced the history of the world."

Upon the correctness or otherwise of these judgments I do not care to pass. They certainly cannot be reconciled. The single point I make is that they were, when made, the expression of views honestly and sincerely entertained. We sympathize with Great Britain's rebels; Great Britain sympathized with our rebels. Our rebels in 1862. as theirs in 1900. sincerely believed they were resisting an iniquitous attempt to deprive them of their rights, and to establish over them a "grinding," a "galling" and an "irritating " "tyrannical government." We in 1861, as Great Britain in 1898, and Charles "the Martyr" and Philip of Spain some centuries earlier, fully believed that we were engaged in God's work while we trod under foot the "rebel" and the "traitor." Presently, as distance lends a more correct perspective, and things are seen in their true proportions, we will get perhaps to realize that our case furnishes no exception to the general ride; and that we, too, like the English " generally sympathize with everybody's rebels but our own." Justice may then be done.

Having entered this necessary, if somewhat hopeless caveat, let us address ourselves to the question — legally, technically, — again let me say not morally and not to the rights and the wrongs of the case in the great debate which led up to the Civil War? The answer necessarily turns on the abstract right of what we term a Sovereign State to secede from the Union at such time and for such cause as may seem to that State proper and sufficient. The issue is settled now: irrevocably and for all time decided; it was not settled forty years ago, and the settlement since made has been the result not of reason, based on historical evidence, but of events and of force. To pass a fair judgment on the line of conduct pursued by Lee in 1861, it is necessary to go back in thought and imagination, and see things, not as they are, but as they were. If we do so, and accept the judgment of some of the more modern students and investigators of history, — either wholly unprejudiced or with a distinct Union bias, — it would seem as if the weight of argument falls into what I will term the Confederate scale. For instance. Professor Goldwin Smith, — an Englishman, a life-long student of history, a friend and advocate of the Union during the Civil

War, the author of one of the most compact and readable narratives of our national life, — Prof. Smith has recently said —"Few who have looked into the history can doubt that the Union originally was, and was generally taken by the parties to it to be, a compact, dissoluble perhaps most of them would have said, at pleasure, dissoluble certainly on breach of the articles of Union."[5] To a like effect, but in terms even stronger, Mr. Henry Cabot Lodge, now a Senator from Massachusetts, has said, not in a political utterance but in a work of historical character, — "When the Constitution was adopted by the votes of States at Philadelphia, and accepted by the votes of States in popular conventions, it is safe to say that there was not a man in the country from Washington and Hamilton on the one side, to George Clinton and George Mason on the other, who regarded the new system as anything but an experiment entered upon by the States and from which each and every State had the right peaceably to withdraw, a right which was very likely to be exercised."[6]

Here are two explicit statements of the legal and technical side of the argument made by authority to which no exception can be taken, at least by those of the Union side. On them, and on them alone, the case for the abstract right of secession might be rested, and we could go on to the next stage of the discussion.

I am unwilling, however, so to do. The issue involved is still one of interest, and I am not disposed to leave it on the mere dictum of two authorities, however eminent. In the first place I do not altogether concur in their statement; in the next place, this discussion is a mere threshing of straw unless we get at the true inwardness of the situation. When it comes to subjects — political or moral — in which human beings are involved, meta physics are scarcely less to be avoided than cant; alleged historical facts are apt to prove deceptive; and I confess to grave suspicions of logic. Old time theology, for instance, with its pitiless reasoning, led the world into very strange places and much bad company. In reaching a conclusion, therefore, in which a verdict is entered on the motives and actions of men, acting either individually or in masses, the moral and sentimental must be quite as much taken into account as the legal, the logical and the material. This, in the present case, I propose presently to do; but, as I have said, on the facts even I am un able wholly to concur with Professor Smith and Mr. Lodge.

Mr. Lodge, for instance, cites Washington. But it so chances Washington put himself on record upon the point at issue, and his testimony is directly at variance with the views attributed to him by Mr. Webster's biographer. What are known in history as the Kentucky resolutions, drawn up by Thomas Jefferson, then Vice President, were passed by the Legislature of the State whose name they bear in November, 1798. In those resolutions the view of the framers of the Constitution as to the original scope of that instrument accepted by Prof. Smith and Mr. Lodge was first set forth. The principles acted upon by South Carolina on the 20th of December, 1860, were enunciated by Kentucky, November 10, 1798. The dragon's teeth were then sown. Washington was at that time living in retirement at Mt. Vernon. When, a few weeks later, the character of those resolutions became known to him, he was deeply concerned, and wrote to Lafayette, — "The Constitution, according to their interpretation of it, would be a mere cipher; " and again, a few days later, he expressed himself still more strongly in a letter to Patrick Henry,—"Measures are systematically and pertinaciously pursued which must eventually dissolve the Union. or produce coercion."[7] Coercion Washington thus looked to as the remedy to which recourse could properly be had in case of any overt attempt at secession. But, so far as the framers of the Constitution as a whole were concerned, it seems to me clear that, acting as wise men of conflicting views naturally would act, they did not care to incur the danger of a shipwreck of their entire scheme by undertaking to settle, distinctly and in advance, abstract questions, the discussion of which was fraught with danger. In so far as they could, they, with great practical shrewdness, left those questions to be settled, should they ever present themselves in concrete form, under the conditions which might then exist. The truth seems to be that the mass of those composing the Convention of 1787, working under the guidance of a few very able and exceedingly practical men, of constructive mind, builded a great deal better than they knew. The delegates met to harmonize trade differences; they ended by perfecting a scheme of political union that had broad consequences of which they little dreamed. If they had dreamed of them, the fabric would never have been completed. That Madison, Marshall and Jay were equally blind to consequences does not follow. They probably designed a nation. If they did, however, they were too wise to take the public into their confidence: and, today, no impartial student of our constitutional history can doubt for a moment that each State ratified the form of government submitted in the firm belief that at any time it could withdraw therefrom. Probably, however, the more far-seeing, — and, in the long' run, they alone count, — shared with Washington in the belief that this withdrawal would not be unaccompanied by practical difficulty.[8] And, after all is said and done, the legality of secession is somewhat of a metaphysical abstraction so long as the right of revolution is inalienable. As matter of fact it was to might and revolution the South appealed in 1861; and it was to coercion the government of the Union had recourse. So with his supreme good sense and that political insight at once instinctive and unerring, in respect to which lie stands almost alone, Washington foresaw this alternative in 1798. He looked upon the doctrine of secession as a heresy; but, none the less, it was a heresy then preached, and to which many, not in Virginia only but in New England also, pinned their political faith. Even the Devil is proverbially entitled to his due.

So far, however, as the abstract question is of consequence, as the utterances of Prof. Smith and Mr. Lodge conclusively show, the Secessionists of 1861 stand in history's court by no means without a case. In that case, moreover, they implicitly believed. From generation to generation they had grown up indoctrinated with the gospel, or heresy, of State Sovereignty, and it was as much part of their moral and intellectual being as was clanship of the Scotch highlanders. In so far they were right, as Governor John A. Andrew said of John Brown. Meanwhile, practically, as a common-sensed man, leading an every day existence in a world of actualities, John Brown was not right; he was, on the contrary, altogether wrong, and richly merited the fate meted out to him. It was the same with the Secessionists. That, in 1861, they could really have had faith in the practicability, — the real working efficiency, — of that peaceable secession which they pro fessed to ask for, and of which they never wearied of talking, I cannot believe. I find in the record no real evidence thereof.

Of the high-type Southron, as we sometimes designate him, I would speak in terms of sincere respect. I know him chiefly by hear-say, having come in personal contact only with individual represen-tatives of the class; but such means of observation as I have had confirm what I recently heard said by a friend of mine, once Governor of South Carolina; and so far as I know, the only man who ever gave the impossible plan of reconstruction at tempted after our Civil War a firm, fair and intelligent trial. He at least put forth an able and honest effort to make effective a policy which never should have been de-vised. Speaking from "much and varied experience," I recently heard Daniel Chamberlain say of the "typical southern Gentleman" that he considered him "a distinct and really noble growth of our American soil. For, if fortitude under good and under evil fortune, if endurance without complaint of what comes in the tide of human affairs, if a grim clinging to ideals once charming, if vigor and resiliency of character and spirit under defeat and poverty and distress, if a steady love of learning and letters when libraries were lost in flames and the wreckage of war, if self-restraint when the long delayed relief at last came, — if, I say, all these qualities are parts of real heroism, if these qualities can vivify and ennoble a man or a people, then our own South may lay claim to an honored place among the differing types of our great common race." Such is the matured judgment of the Massa-chusetts Governor of South Carolina during the Congressional re-construction period; and, listening to it, I asked myself if it was descriptive of a Southern fellow-countryman, or a Jacobite Scotch chieftian anterior to "the '45."

The Southern statesmen of the old slavery days, —the antediluvian period which preceded our mid-century cataclysm,—were the outcome and representatives of what has thus been described. As such they presented a curious admixture of qualities. Masterful in temper, clear of purpose, with a firm grasp on principle, a high sense of honor and a moral perception developed on its peculiar lines, as in the case of Calhoun, to a quality of distinct hardness, they were yet essentially abstractionists. Political metaphysicians, they were not practical men. They did not see things as they really were. They thus, while discussing their "forty-bale theories" and the "patriarchal institution" in connection with States rights and nullification, failed to realize that on the two essential features of their policy,— slavery and secession,— they were contending with the stars in their courses. The whole world was moving irresistibly in the direction of nationality and an ever increased recognition of the rights of man: while they, on both of these vital issues, were proclaiming a crusade of reaction.

Moreover, what availed the views or intentions of the framers of the Constitution? What mattered it in 1860 whether they, in 1787, contemplated a Nation or only a more compact federation of Sovereign States? Realities have an unpleasant way of asserting their existence. How ever it may have been in 1788, in 1860 a Nation had grown into existence. Its peaceful dismemberment was impossible. The complex system of tissues and ligaments, the growth of seventy years, could not be gently taken apart, without wound or hurt; the separation, if separation there was to be, involved a tearing asunder, supplementing a liberal use of the knife. Their professions to the contrary notwithstanding, this the Southern leaders failed not to realize. In point of fact, therefore, believing fully in the abstract legality of secession, and the justice and sufficiency of the grounds on which they acted, their appeal was to the inalienable right of revolution; and to that might by which alone the right could be upheld. Let us put casuistry, metaphysics and sentiment aside, and come to actualities. The secessionist recourse in 1861 was to the sword; and to the sword it was meant to have recourse.

I have thus far spoken only of the South as a whole. Much has been said and written on the subject of an alleged conspiracy in those days of Southern men and leaders against the Union; of the designs and ultimate objects of the alleged conspirators; of acts of treachery on their part, and the part of their accomplices, towards the government, of which they were the sworn officials. Into this phase of the subject I do not propose to enter. That the leaders in Secession were men with large views, and that they had matured a comprehensive policy as the ultimate outcome of their movement, I entertain no doubt. They looked unquestionably to an easy military success, and the complete establishment of their Confederacy ; more remotely, there can be no question they contemplated a policy of extension, and the establishment along the shores of the Gulf of Mexico and in the Antilles of a great semi-tropical, slave-labor republic; finally, all my investigations have tended to satisfy me that they confidently anticipated an early disintegration of the Union, and the accession of the bulk of the Northern States to the Confederacy, New England only being sternly excluded therefrom— "sloughed off," as they expressed it. The capital of the new Confederacy was to be Washington; African servitude, under reasonable limitations, was to be recognized through out its limits; agriculture was to be its ruling interest, with a tariff and foreign policy in strict accord therewith." Secession is not intended to break up the present government, but to perpetuate it. We go out of the Union, not to destroy it, but for the purpose of getting further guarantees and security," — this was said in January, 1861: and this in 1900 — "And so we believe that, with the success of the South, the 'Union of the Fathers,' which the South was the principal factor in forming, and to which she was far more attached than the North, would have been restored and re-established: that in this Union, the South would have been again the dominant people, the controlling power." Conceding the necessary premises of fact and law, —a somewhat considerable concession, but, perhaps, conceivable, — conceding these, I see in this position, then or now, nothing illogical, nothing provocative of severe criticism, certainly nothing treasonable. Acting on sufficient grounds, of which those thus acting were the sole judge, proceeding in a way indisputably legal and regular, it was proposed to reconstruct the Union in the light of experience, and on a new, and, as they considered, an improved basis, without New England. This cannot properly be termed a conspiracy; it was a legitimate policy based on certain assumed data legal, moral and economical. But it was in reality never for a moment believed that this programme could be peaceably and quietly carried into effect; and the assent of New England to the arrangement was neither asked for, assumed nor expected. New England was distinctly relegated to an outer void, —at once cold, dark, inhospitable.

As to participation of those who sympathized in these views and this policy in the councils of the government, so furthering schemes for its overthrow while sworn to its support, I hold it unnecessary to speak. Such were traitors. As such, had they met their deserts, they should at the proper time and on due process of law, have been arrested, tried, convicted, sentenced and hanged. That in certain well-remembered instances this course was not pursued, is,' to my mind, even yet much to be deplored. In such cases clemency is only another form of cant.

Having now discussed what have seemed to me the necessary preliminaries, I come to the particular cases of Virginia and Robert E. Lee. The two are closely interwoven, for Virginia was always Virginia, and the Lees were, first, over and above all, Virginians. It was the Duke of Wellington who, on a certain memorable occasion, indignantly remarked in his delightful French-English — "Mais avant tout je suis gentilhomme Anglais."[9] So might have said the Lees of Virginia of themselves.

As respects Virginia, moreover, I am fain to say there was in the attitude of the State towards the Confederacy, and, indeed, in its bearing throughout the Civil War, something which appealed strongly, — something unselfish and chivalric, — worthy of Virginia's highest record. History will, I think, do justice to it. Virginia, it must be remembered, while a Slave State was not a Cotton State. This was a distinction implying a difference. In Virginia the institution of slavery existed, and because of it she was in close sympathy with her sister Slave States; but, while in the Cotton States slavery had gradually assumed a purely material form, in Virginia it still retained much of its patriarchal character. The slave there was not a mere transferable chattel; practically, and to a large extent, he was attached to the house and the soil. This fact had a direct bearing on the moral issue; for slavery was one thing in Virginia, quite another in Louisiana. The Virginian pride was moreover proverbial. Indeed, I doubt if local feeling and patriotism and devotion to the State ever anywhere attained a higher development than in the community which dwelt in the region watered by the Potomac and the James, of which Richmond was the political centre. We of the North, especially we of New England, were Yankees; but a Virginian was that, and nothing else. I have heard of a New Englander, of a Green Mountain boy, of a Rhode Islander, of a "Nutmeg," of a "Blue-nose" even, but never of a Massachusettensian. The word somehow does not lend itself to the mouth, any more than the thought to the mind.

But Virginia was strongly attached by sentiment as well as interest to the Union. The birth-place of Washington, the mother of States, as well as of Presidents, "The Old Dominion," as she was called, and fondly loved to call herself, had never been affected by the nullification heresies of South Carolina ; and the long line of her eminent public men, though, in 1860, showing marked signs of a deteriorating standard, still retained a prominence in the national councils. If John B. Floyd was Secretary of the Interior, Winfield Scott was at the head of the Army. Torn by conflicting feelings, Virginia still held to the Nation, unwilling to sever her connection with it because of the lawful election of an anti-slavery President, even by a distinctly sectional vote. For a time she even stayed the fast flooding tide of secession, bringing about a brief but important reaction. Those of us old enough to remember the drear and anxious winter which followed the election and preceded the inauguration of Lincoln, recall vividly the ray of bright hope which, in the midst of its deepest gloom, then came from Virginia. It was in early February. Up to that time the record was unbroken. Beginning with South Carolina on the 20th of December, State after State, meeting in convention, had with significant unanimity passed ordinances of secession. Each successive ordinance was felt to be the equivalent to a renewed declaration of war. The outlook was. dark indeed ; and, amid the fast gathering gloom, all eyes, all thoughts, turned to Virginia. She represented what were known as the Border States, her action it was felt would largely influence, and might control, theirs. John Letcher was then Governor of Virginia,— a States Rights Democrat, of course ; but a Union man. By him the legislature of the State was in December called together in special session, and that legislature passed what was known as a convention bill. Practically Virginia was to vote on the question at issue. Events moved rapidly. South Carolina had seceded on the 20th of December; Mississippi on the 8th of January; Alabama and Florida only three days later on the 11th; Georgia followed on the 19th; Louisiana on the 26th, with Texas on the 1st of February. The procession seemed unending ; the record unbroken. Not without cause might the now thoroughly frightened friends of the Union have exclaimed with Macbeth —

"What! will the line stretch out to the crack of doom? Another yet? A seventh?"

If at that juncture the Old Dominion by a decisive vote had followed in the steps of the Cotton States it implied consequences which no man could fathom. It involved the possession of the national capitol, and the continuance of the Government. Maryland would inevitably follow the Virginian lead; the recently elected President had not yet been inaugurated; taken wholly by surprise, the North was divided in sentiment: the loyal spirit of the country was not aroused. It was thus an even question whether, on the 4th of March, the whole machinery of the *de facto* government would not be in the hands of the revolutionists. All depended on Virginia. This is now forgotten; none the less, it is history.

The Virginia election was held on the 4th of February, the news of the secession of Texas — seventh in the line —having been received on the 2nd. Evidently, the action of Texas was carefully timed for effect. Though over forty years ago, I well remember that day,— gray, over cast, wintry, — which succeeded the Virginia election. Then living in Boston, a young man of twenty-five, I shared, — as who did not? — in the common deep depression and intense anxiety. It was as if a verdict was to be that day announced in a case involving fortune, honor, life even. Too harassed for work, I remember leaving my office in the afternoon to seek relief in physical activity, for the ponds in the vicinity of Boston were ice-covered and daily thronged with skaters. I was soon among the number, gloomily seeking unfrequented spots. Suddenly I became aware of an unusual movement in the throng nearest the shore, where those fresh from the city arrived. The skaters seemed crowding to a common point ; and a moment later they scattered again, with cheers and gestures of relief. An arrival fresh from Boston had brought the first bulletin of yesterday's election. Virginia, speaking against secession, had emitted no uncertain sound. It was as if a weight had been taken off the mind of everyone. The tide seemed turned at last. For myself, I remember my feelings were too deep to find expression in words or sound. Something stuck in my throat. I wanted to be by myself.

Nor did we over-estimate the importance of the event. If it did not in the end mean reaction, it did mean time gained ; and time then, as the result showed, was vital. As William H. Seward, representing the President-elect in Washington, wrote during those days: — "The people of the District are looking anxiously for the result of the Virginia election. They fear if Virginia resolves on secession, Maryland will follow: and then Washington will be seized. *** The election tomorrow probably determines whether all the Slave States will take the attitude of disunion. Everybody around me thinks that that will make the separation irretrievable, and involve us in flagrant civil war.

Practically everybody will despair." A day or two later the news came "like a gleam of sun shine in a storm." The disunion movement was checked, perhaps would be checkmated. Well might Seward, with a sigh of profound relief, write to his wife: — "At least, the danger of conflict, here or elsewhere, before the 4th of March, has been averted. Time has been gained."[10] Time was gained: and the few weeks of precious time thus gained through the expiring effort of union sentiment in Virginia involved the vital fact of the peaceful delivery four weeks later, of the helm of state into the hands of Lincoln.

Thus, be it always remembered, Virginia did not take its place in the secession movement because of the election of an anti-slavery president. It did not raise its hand against the national government from mere love of any peculiar institution, or a wish to protect and to perpetuate it. It refused to he precipitated into a civil convulsion; and its refusal was of vital moment. The ground of Virginia's final action was of wholly another nature, and of a nature far more creditable. Virginia, as I have said, made State Sovereignty an article. — a cardinal article, — of its political creed. So, logically and consistently, it took the position that, though it might be unwise for a State to secede, a State which did secede could not, and should not be coerced.

To us now this position seems worse than illogical ; it is impossible. So events proved it. Yet, after all, it is based on the great fundamental principle of the consent of the governed ; and, in the days immediately preceding the war, something very like it was accepted as an article of correct political faith by men afterwards as strenuous in support of a Union re-established by force, as Charles Sumner, Abraham Lincoln, William H. Seward, Salmon P. Chase and Horace Greeley. The difference was that, con fronted by the overwhelming tide of events, Virginia adhered to it ; they, in presence of that tide, tacitly abandoned it. In my judgment, they were right. But Virginia, though mistaken more consistent, judged otherwise. As I have said, in shaping a practical outcome of human affairs logic is often as irreconcilable with the dictates of worldly wisdom as are metaphysics with common sense. So, now, the issue shifted. It became a question, not of slavery or of the wisdom, or even the expediency, of secession, but of the right of the National Government to coerce a Sovereign State. This at the time was well understood. The extremists of the South, counting upon it, counted with absolute confidence; and openly proclaimed their reliance in debate. Florida, as the representatives of that State confessed on the floor of Congress, might in itself be of small ac count; but Florida, panoplied with sovereignty, was hemmed in and buttressed against assault by protecting sister States.

So, in his history, James F. Rhodes asserts that — "The four men who in the last resort made the decision that began the war were ex-Senator Chestnut, Lieutenant-Col. Chisholm, Captain Lee, all three South Carolinians, and Roger A. Pryor, a Virginia secessionist, who two days before in a speech at the Charleston Hotel had said, "I will tell your Governor what will put Virginia in the Southern Confederacy in less than an hour by Shrewsbury clock. Strike a blow!"[11] The blow was to be in reply to what was accepted as the first overt effort at the national coercion of a Sovereign State, — the attempted relief of Sumter. That attempt, — unavoidable even if long deferred, the necessary and logical outcome of a situation which had become impossible, — that attempt, construed into an effort at coercion, swept Virginia from her Union moorings.

Thus, when the long-deferred hour of fateful decision came, the position of Virginia, be it in historical justice said, however impetuous, mistaken or ill-advised, was taken on no low or sordid or selfish grounds. On the contrary, the logical assertion of a cardinal article of accepted political faith, it was made generously, chivalrously, in a spirit almost altruistic; for, from the outset, it was manifest Virginia had nothing to gain in that conflict of which she must perforce be the battle-ground. True! her leading men doubtless believed that the struggle would soon be brought to a triumphant close, — that Southern chivalry and fighting qualities would win a quick and easy victory over a more materially minded, even if not craven, Northern mob of fanatics and cobblers and pedlars, officered by preachers ; but, however thus deceived and misled at the outset, Virginia entered on the struggle others had initiated, for their protection and in their behalf. She thrust herself between them and the tempest they had invoked. Technically it may have been treasonable ; but her attitude was consistent, was bold, was chivalrous:

"An honourable murderer if you will; For naught did he in hate but all in honour."

So much for Virginia : and now as to Robert E. Lee. More than once already, on occasions not unlike this, have I quoted Oliver Wendell Holmes's remark in answer to the query of an anxious mother as to when a child's education ought to begin, — "About 250 years before it is born;" and it is a fact, — somewhat necessitarian, doubtless, but still a fact, — that every man's life is largely moulded for him far back in the ages. We philosophize freely over fate and free will, and one of the excellent commonplaces of our educational system is to instill into the minds of the children in our common-schools the idea that every man is the architect of his own life. An admirable theory to teach: but, happily for the race, true only to a very limited extent. Heredity is a tremendous limiting fact. Native force of character, —individuality,— doubtless has something to do with results; but circumstances, ancestry, environment have much more. One man possibly in a hundred has in him the inherent force to make his conditions largely for himself; but even he moves influenced at every step from cradle to grave by ante-natal and birth conditions. Take any man you please, —yourself, for instance; now and again the changes of life give opportunity, and the individual is equal to the occasion, — the roads forking, consciously or instinctively he makes his choice. Under such circumstances, he usually supposes that he does so as a free agent. The world so assumes, holding him responsible. He is nothing of the sort; or at best such only in a very limited degree. The other day one of our humorists took occasion to philosophize on this topic, delivering what might not inaptly be termed an occasional discourse appropriate to the 22nd of February. It was not only worth reading, but in humor and sentiment it was somewhat suggestive of the melancholy Jacques. "We are made, brick by brick, of influences, patiently built up around the frame work of our born dispositions. It is the sole process of construction; there is no other. Every man, woman and child is an influence. Washington's disposition was born in him, he did not create it. It was the architect of his character; his character was the architect of his achievements. It had a native affinity for all in fluences fine and great, and gave them hospitable welcome and permanent shelter. It had a native aversion for all influences mean and gross, and passed them on. It chose its ideals for him; and out of its patiently gathered materials, it built and shaped his golden character.

"And we give him the credit."

Three names of Virginians are impressed on the military records of our civil war — indelibly impressed, — Winfield Scott, George Henry Thomas and Robert Edward Lee: The last most deeply. Of the three, the first two stood by the flag; the third went with his State. Each, when the time came, acted conscientiously, impelled by the purest sense of loyalty, honor and obligation, taking that course which, under the circumstances and according to his lights, seemed to him right; and each doubtless thought he acted as a free agent. To a degree each was a free agent: to a much greater degree each was the child of anterior conditions, hereditary sequence, existing circumstances, — in a word of human environment, moral, material, intellectual. Scott or Thomas or Lee, being as he was, and things being as things were, could not decide otherwise than as he did decide. Consider them in order; Scott first:

A Virginian by birth, early association and marriage, Scott, at the breaking-out of the Civil War, had not lived in his native State for forty years. Not a planter, he held no broad acres and owned no slaves. Essentially a soldier, he was a citizen of the United States; and, for twenty years, had been the General in command of its army. When, in April, 1861, Virginia passed its ordinance of secession, he was well advanced in his seventy-fifth year, — an old man, he was no longer equal to active service. The course he would pursue was thus largely marked out for him in advance; a violent effort on his part could alone have forced him out of his trod den path. When subjected to the test, what he did was infinitely creditable to him, and the obligation the cause of the Union lay under to him during the critical period between December, 1860, and June, 1861, can scarcely be overstated; but, none the less, in doing as he did, it cannot be denied he followed what was for him the line of least resistance.

Of George Henry Thomas, no American, North or South, — above all, no American who served in the Civil War, — whether wearer of the blue or the gray, — can speak, save with infinite respect, — always with admiration, often with love. Than his, no record is clearer from stain. Thomas also was a Virginian. At the time of the breaking-out of the Civil War, he held the rank of Major in that regiment of cavalry of which Lee, nine years his senior in age, was Colonel. He never hesitated in his course. True to the nag from start to finish. William T. Sherman, then General of the Army, in the order announcing the death of his friend and class-mate at the Academy, most properly said of him: " The very impersonation of honesty, integrity and honor, he will stand to posterity as the beau ideal of the soldier and gentleman." personified. More tersely, Thomas stands for character Washington himself not more so. And now having said this, let us come again to the choice of Hercules, — the parting of those terrible ways of 1861.

Like Scott and Lee, Thomas was a Virginian; but, again, there are Virginians and Virginians. Thomas was not a Lee. When, in 1855, the second United States cavalry was organized, Jefferson Davis being Secretary of War, Captain Thomas, as he then was and in his thirty ninth year, was appointed its junior Major. Between that time and April, 1861, fifty-one officers are said to have borne commissions in that, regiment, thirty-one of whom were from the South; and of those thirty-one, no less than twenty-four entered the Confederate service, twelve of whom, among them Robert E. Lee, Albert Sidney Johnston and John B. Hood, became General officers. The name of the Virginian, George H. Thomas, stands first of the faithful seven; but, Union or Confederate, it is a record of great names, and fortunate is the people, great of necessity their destiny, which in the hour of exigency, on the one side or the other, naturally develops from the roster of a single regiment men of the ability, the disinterestedness, the capacity and the character of Lee, Thomas, Johnson and Hood. It is a record which in spires confidence as well as pride.

And now of the two men—Thomas and Lee. Though born in Virginia, Gen. Thomas was not of a peculiarly Virginian descent. By ancestry, he was, on the father's side, Welsh; French on that of the mother. He was not of the old Virginia stock. Born in the southeastern portion of the State, near the North Carolina line, we are told that his family, dwelling on a "goodly home property," was "well to do" and eminently respectable"; but, it is added, there "were no cavaliers in the Thomas family, and not the remotest trace of the Pocahontas blood." When the war broke out, in 1861, Thomas had been twenty-one years a commissioned officer; and during those years he seems to have lived almost everywhere, except in Virginia. It had been a life at military stations; his wife was from New York; his home was on the Hudson rather than on the Nottoway. In his native State he owned no property, land or chattels. Essentially a soldier, when the hour for choice came, the soldier dominated the Virginian. He stood by the flag.

Not so Lee; for to Lee I now come. Of him it might, and in justice must, be said, that he was more than of the essence, he was of the very quintessence of Virginia. In his case, the roots and fibres struck down and spread wide in the soil, making him of it a part. A son of the revolutionary "Light Horse Harry," he had married a Custis. His children represented all there was of descent, blood and tradition of the Old Dominion, made up as the Old Dominion was of tradition, blood and descent. The holder of broad patrimonial acres, by birth and marriage he was a slave-owner, and a slave-owner of the patriarchal type, holding "slavery as an institution, a moral and political evil."

Every sentiment, every memory, every tie conceivable bound him to Virginia; and, when the choice was forced upon him, — had to be made,—sacrificing rank, career, the flag, he threw in his lot with Virginia. He did so, with open eyes and weighing the consequences. He at least indulged in no self-deception — wandered away from the path in no cloud of political metaphysics,—nourished no delusion as to an early and easy triumph. "Secession," as he wrote to his son, "is nothing but revolution. The framers of our Constitution never exhausted so much labor, wisdom and forbearance in its formation, and surrounded it with so many guards and securities, if it was intended to be broken by every member of the confederacy at will. It is idle to talk of secession." But he also believed that his permanent allegiance was due to Virginia; that her secession, though revolution- ary, bound all Virginians and ended their connection with and duties to the national government. Thereafter, to remain in the United States army would be treason to Virginia. So, two days after Virginia passed its ordinance, he, being then at Arlington, resigned his commission, at the same time writing to his sister, the wife of a Union officer, —-- We are now in a state of war which will yield to nothing. The whole South is in a state of revolution, into which Virginia, after a long struggle, has been drawn; and, though I recognize no necessity for this state of things, and would have foreborne and pleaded to the end for redress of grievances, real or supposed, yet in my own person I had to meet the question whether I should take part against my native State. With all my devotion to the Union, and the feeling of loyalty and duty of an American citizen, 1 have not been able to make up my mind to raise my hand against my relatives, my children, my home. I have, therefore, resigned my commission in the army; and, save in defense of my native State, I hope I may never be called on to draw my sword." Two days before he had been unreservedly tendered, on behalf of President Lincoln, the command of the Union army then immediately to be put in the field in front of Washington, — the command shortly afterwards held by General McDowell.

So thought and spoke and wrote and acted Robert E. Lee in April, 1861. He has, for the decision thus reached, been termed by some a traitor, a deserter, almost: in apostate, and consigned to the "avenging pen of History." I cannot so see it; I am confident posterity will not so see it. The name and conditions being changed, those who uttered the words of censure, invoking "the avenging pen," did not so see it —have not seen it so. Let us appeal to the record. What otherwise did George Washington do under circumstances not dissimilar? What would he have done under circumstances wholly similar? Like Lee, Washington was a soldier; like Lee, he was a Virginian before he was a soldier. He had served under King George's flag; he had sworn allegiance to King George; his ambition had been to hold the royal commission. Presently Virginia seceded from the British empire, — renounced its allegiance. What did Washington do? He threw in his lot with his native province. Do you hold him then to have been a traitor,—to have been false to his colors? Such is not your verdict; such has not been the verdict of history. He acted conscientiously, loyally, as a son of Virginia, and according to his lights. Will you say that Lee did otherwise?

But men love to differentiate: and of drawing of distinctions there is no end. The cases were different, it will be argued; at the time Virginia renounced its allegiance Washington did not hold the King's commission, indeed he never held it. As a soldier he was a provincial always. —he bore a Virginian commission, True! Let the distinction be conceded; then assume that the darling wish of his younger heart had been granted to him, and that he had received the King's commission, and held it in 1775: — what course would he then have pursued? What course would you wish him to have pursued? Do you not wish. —do you not know,—that, circumstanced as then he would have been, he would have done exactly as Robert E. Lee did eighty-six years later. He would first have resigned his commission; and then arrayed himself on the side of Virginia. Would you have had him do otherwise? And so it goes in this world. In such cases the usual form of speech is: "Oh! that is different! Another case altogether!" Yes, it is different; it is another case. For it makes all the difference in the world with a man who argues thus, whether it is his ox that is gored or that of the other man!

And here in preparing this address 1 must fairly acknowledge having encountered an obstacle in my path also. When considering the course of another, it is always well to ask one's self the question — What would you yourself have done if similarly placed? Warmed by my argument, and the great precedents of Lee and of Washington, I did so here. I and mine were and are at least as much identified with Massachusetts as was Lee and his with Virginia; — traditionally, historically, by blood and memory and name, we with the Puritan Common wealth as they with the Old Dominion. What, I asked my-self, would I have done had Massachusetts at any time arrayed itself against the common country, though with out my sympathy and assent, even as Virginia arrayed it self against the Union without the sympathy and assent of Lee in 1861? The question gave me pause. And then I must confess to a sense of the humor of the situation coming over me, as I found it answered to my hand. The case had already arisen; the answer had been given; nor had it been given in any un-certain tone. The dark and disloyal days of the earlier years of the century just ended rose in memory, —the days of the Embargo, the Leopard and the Chesapeake, and of the Hartford Convention. The course then taken by those in political control in Massachusetts is recorded in history. It verged dangerously close on that pursued by Virginia and the South fifty years later : and the quarrel then was foreign; it was no domestic broil. One of my name, from whom I claim descent, was then prominent in public life. He accordingly was called upon to make the choice of Hercules, as later was Lee. He made his choice; and it was for the common country as against his section. The result is matter of history. Because he was a Union man and held country higher than State or party, John Quincy Adams was in 1808 driven from office, a successor to him in the United States Senate was elected long before the expiration of his term, and he himself was forced into what at the time was regarded :us an honorable exile. Nor was the line of conduct then by him pursued,—that of unswerving loyalty to the Union, —ever forgotten or wholly forgiven. He had put country above party; and party leaders have long memories. Even so broad-minded and clear-thinking a man as Theodore Parker, when delivering a eulogy upon J. Q. Adams, forty years later, thus expressed himself of this act of supreme self-sacrifice and loyalty to Nation rather than to State: — "To my mind, that is the worst act of his public life; I cannot justify it. I wish I could find some reasonable excuse for it. *** However, it must be confessed that this, though not the only instance of injustice, is the only case of servile compliance with the Executive to be found in the whole life of the man. It was a grievous fault but grievously did he answer it ; and if a long life of unfaltering resistance to every attempt at the assumption of power is fit atonement, then the expiation was abundantly made."[12]

What more, or worse, on the other side, could be said of Lee?

Perhaps I should enter some plea in excuse of this diversion; but, for me, it may explain itself, or go un explained. Confronted with the question what would I have done in 1861 had positions been reversed and Massachusetts taken the course then taken by Virginia, I found the answer already recorded I would have gone with the Union, and against Massachusetts. None the less, I hold Massachusetts estopped in the case of Lee. "Let the galled jade wince, our withers are unwrung"; but, I submit, however it might be with me or mine, it does not lie in the mouths of the descendants of the New England Federalists of the first two decennials of the nineteenth century to invoke "the avenging pen of history" to record an adverse verdict in the case of any son of Virginia who threw in his lot with his State in 1861.

Thus much for the choice of Hercules. Pass on to what followed. Of Robert E. Lee as the commander of the Army of Northern Virginia, —at once the buckler and the sword of the Confederacy, — I shall say few words. I was in the ranks of those opposed to him. For years I was face to face with some fragment of the Army of Northern Virginia, and intent to do it harm; and during those years there was not a day when I would not have drawn a deep breath of relief and satisfaction at hearing of the death of Lee, even as I did draw it at hearing of the death of Jackson. But now, looking back through a perspective of nearly forty years, I glory in it, and in them as foes, —they were worthy of the best of steel. I am proud now to say that I was their countryman. Whatever differences of opinion may exist as to the course of Lee when his choice was made, of Lee as a foe and the commander of an army, but one opinion can be entertained. Every inch a soldier, he was as an opponent not less generous and humane than formidable, a type of highest martial character; — cautious, magnanimous and bold, a very thunderbolt in war, he was self-contained in victory, but greatest in defeat. To that escutcheon attaches no stain.

I now come to what I have always regarded, — shall ever regard, — as the most creditable episode in all American history, — an episode without a blemish, — imposing, dignified, simple, heroic. I refer to Appomattox. Two men met that day, representative of American civilization, the whole world looking on. The two were Grant and Lee, —types each. Both rose, and rose unconsciously, to the full height of the occasion, — and than that occasion there has been none greater. About it, and them, there was no theatrical display, no self-consciousness, no effort at effect. A great crisis was to be met; and they met that crisis as great countrymen should. Consider the possibilities; think for a moment of what that day might have been; —you will then see cause to thank God for much.

That month of April saw the close of exactly four years of persistent strife, — a strife which the whole civilized world had been watching intently. Democracy, —the capacity of man in his present stage of development for self-government, — was believed to be on trial. The wish the father to the thought, the prophets of evil had been liberal in prediction. It so chances that my attention has been specially drawn to the European utterances of that time; and, read in the clear light of subsequent history, I use words of moderation when I say that they are now both inconceivable and ludicrous. Staid journals, grave public men, seemed to take what was little less than pleasure in pronouncing that impossible of occurrence which was destined soon to occur, and in committing themselves to readings of the book of fate in exact op position to what the muse of history was wetting the pen to record. Volumes of unmerited abuse and false vatication, —and volumes hardly less amusing now than instructive, —- could be garnered from the columns of the *London Times* — volumes in which the spirit of contemptuous and patronizing dislike sought expression in the profoundest ignorance of facts, set down in bitterest words. Not only were republican institutions and man's capacity for self-government on trial, but the severest of sentences was imposed in advance of the adverse verdict, assumed to be inevitable. Then, suddenly, came the dramatic climax at Appomattox, —dramatic, I say, not theatrical, — severe in its simple, sober, matter-of-fact majesty. The world, I again assert, has seen nothing like it; and the world, instinctively, was conscious of the fact. I like to dwell on the familiar circumstances of the day; on its momentous outcome; on its far-reaching results. It affords one of the greatest educational object-lessons to be found in history; and the actors were worthy of the theatre, the auditory and the play.

A mighty tragedy was drawing to a close. The breathless world was the audience. It was a bright balmy April Sunday in a quiet Virginia landscape, with two veteran armies confronting each other; one, game to the death, completely in the grasp of the other. The future was at stake. What might ensue? What might not ensue? Would the strife end then and there? Would it die in a death grapple, only to reappear in that chronic form of a vanquished but indomitable people writhing and struggling in the grasp of an insatiate but only nominal victor? Such a struggle as all European authorities united in confidently predicting?

The answer depended on two men, —the captains of the contending forces. Grant that day had Lee at his mercy. He had but to close his hand, and his opponent was crushed. Think what then might have resulted had those two men been other than they were, —had the one been stern and aggressive, the other, sullen and unyielding. Most fortunately for us, they were what and who they were — Grant and Lee. More, I need not, could not say —this only let me add, — a people has good right to be proud of the past and self-confident of its future when on so great an occasion it naturally develops at the front men who meet each other as those two met each other then. Of the two, I know not to which to award the palm. Instinctively, unconsciously, they vied not unsuccessfully each with the other, in dignity, magnanimity, simplicity.

" Si fractus illabatur orbi?
Impavidum ferient ruinæ."[13]

With a home no longer his, Lee then sheathed his sword. With the silent dignity of his subsequent life, after he thus accepted defeat, all are familiar. He left behind him no querulous memoirs, no exculpatory vindication, no controversial utterances. For him, history might explain itself, — posterity formulate its own verdict. Surviving Appomattox but a little more than five years, those years were not unmarked by incidents very gratifying to American recollection; for we Americans do, I think, above all things love magnanimity, and appreciate action at once fearless and generous. We all remember how by the grim mockery of fate,—as if to test to the uttermost American capacity for self-government, — Abraham Lincoln was snatched away at the moment of crisis from the helm of state, and Andrew Johnson substituted for him. I think it no doubtful anticipation of historical judgment to say that a more unfortunate selection could not well have been made. In no single respect, it is safe to say, was Andrew Johnson adapted for the peculiar duties which Booth's pistol imposed upon him. One of Johnson's most unhappy, most ill-considered convictions was that our Civil War was a conventional old-time rebellion; — that rebellion was treason; — that treason was a crime; and that a crime was something for which punishment should in due course of law be meted out. He, therefore, wanted, or thought he wanted, to have the scenes of England's Convention Parliament and the Restoration of 1660 re-enacted here, as a fitting sequel of our great conflict. Most fortunately, the American people then gave evidence to Europe of a capacity for self-restraint and self-government not traceable to English parentage, or precedents. No Cromwell's head grinned from our Westminster Hall; no convicted traitor swung in chains; no shambles dripped in blood. None the less Andrew Johnson called for "indictments," and one day demanded that of Lee. Then outspoke Grant,— General of the Army. Lee, he declared, was his prisoner. He had surrendered to him, and in reliance on his word. He had received assurance that so long as he quietly remained at his home, and did not offend against the law, he should not be molested. He had done so, and, so long as Grant held his commission, molested he should not be. Needless, as pleasant, to say what Grant then grimly intimated did not take place. Lee was not molested; nor did the General of the Army indignantly fling his com mission at an accidental President's feet. That, if necessary, he would have done so, I take to be quite indubitable.

Of Lee's subsequent life, as head of Washington College, I have but one anecdote to offer. I believe it to be typical. A few months ago I received a letter from a retired army officer of high character from which I extract the following:—

Lee was essentially a Virginian. His sword was Virginia's, and I fancy the State had higher claims upon him than had the Confederacy, just as he supposed it had than the United States. But, after the surrender, he stood firmly and unreservedly in favor of loyalty to the Nation. A gentleman told me this anecdote. As a boy he ran away from his Kentucky home, and served the last two years in the rebel ranks. After the war he resumed his studies under Lee's presidency; and on one occasion, delivered as a college exercise an oration with eulogistic reference to the "Lost Cause," and what it meant. Later, General, then President Lee sent for the student, and, after praising his composition and delivery, seriously warned him against holding or advancing such views, impressing strongly upon him the unity of the Nation, and urging him to devote himself loyally to maintain the integrity and the honor of the United States. The kindly paternal advice thus given was,

I imagine, typical of his whole port bellum Let this one anecdote suffice. Here was magnanimity, philosophy, true patriotism: the pure American Accepting the situation loyally and in a manly, Here was magna spirit. silent way, — without self-consciousness or mental reservation, he sought by precept and yet more by a great ex ample, to build up the shattered community of which he was the most observed representative in accordance with the new conditions imposed by fate, and through constitutional action. Talk of traitors and of treason! The man who pursued that course and instilled that spirit had not. could not have had, in his whole being one drop of traitor's blood or conceived a treacherous thought. His lights may have been wrong, —according to our ideas then and now they were wrong, — but they were his lights, and in acting in full accordance with them he was right.

But, to those thus speaking, it is since sometimes replied, — "Even tolerance may be carried too far, and is apt then to verge dangerously on what may be better described as moral indifference. It then, humanly speaking, assumes that there is no real right or real wrong in collective human action. But put yourself in his place, and to those of this way of thinking Philip II. and William of Orange, — Charles I. and Cromwell, — are much the same; —the one is as good as the other, provided only he acted according to his lights. This will not do. Some moral test must be applied, — some standard of right and wrong." It is by the recognition and acceptance of these that men prominent in history must be measured, and approved or condemned. To call it our Civil War is but a mere euphemistic way of referring to what was in fact a slave-holders' rebellion, conceived and put in action for no end but to perpetuate and extend a system of human servitude, a system the relic of barbarism, an insult to advancing humanity. To the furtherance of this rebellion Lee lent himself. Right is right, and treason is treason, —and, as that which is morally wrong cannot be right, so treason cannot be other than a crime. Why then be cause of sentiment or sympathy or moral indifference seek to confound the two? Charles Stuart and Cromwell could not both have been right. If Thomas was right, Lee was wrong."

To this I would reply, that we, who take another view, neither confound, nor seek to confound, right with wrong, or treason with loyalty. We accept the verdict of time ; but, in so doing, we insist that the verdict shall be in accordance with the facts, and that each individual shall be judged on his own merits, and not stand acquitted or condemned in block. In this respect time works' wonders, leaving few conclusions wholly unchallenged. Take, for instance, one of the final contentions of Charles Sumner, that, following old world precedents, founded, as he claimed in reason and patriotism, the names of battles of the war of the rebellion should be removed from the regimental colors of the national army, and from the army register. He put it on the ground that, from the re publics of antiquity down to our days, no civilized nation ever thought it wise or patriotic to preserve in conspicuous and durable form the mementoes of victories won over fellow citizens in civil war. As the sympathizing orator said at the time of Sumner's death — " Should the son of South Carolina, when at some future day defending the Republic against some foreign foe, be reminded by an inscription on the colors floating over him, that under this flag the gun was fired that killed his father at Gettysburg?" This assuredly has a plausible sound." His father; "yes, perhaps. Though even in the immediately succeeding generation something might well be said on the other side. Presumably, in such case, the father was a brave, an honest and a loyal man, — contending for what he believed to be right; — for it, laying down his life. Gettysburg is a name and a memory of which none there need ever feel ashamed. As in most battles, there was a victor and a vanquished; but on that day the vanquished, as well as the victor, fought a stout fight. If, in all recorded warfare there is a deed of arms the name and memory of which the descendants of those who participated therein should not wish to see obliterated from any record, be it historian's page or battle-flag, it was the advance of Pickett's Virginian division across that wide valley of death in front of Cemetery Ridge. I know in all recorded warfare of no finer, no more sustained and deadly feat of arms. I have stood on either battle field, and. in scope and detail, carefully compared the two; and, challenging denial, I affirm that the much vaunted charge of Napoleon's guard at Waterloo, in fortitude, discipline and deadly energy will not bear comparison with that other. It was boy's work be side it. There, brave men did all that the bravest men could do. Why then should the son of one of those who fell coming up the long ascent, or over our works and in among our guns, feel a sense of wrong because "Gettysburg " is inscribed on the flag of the battery a gun of which he now may serve? On the contrary, I should suppose he would there see that name only.

But, supposing it otherwise in the case of the son, — the wound being in such case yet fresh and green, — how would it be when a sufficient time has elapsed to afford the needed perspective ? Let us suppose a grand son six generations removed. What Englishman, be he Cavalier or Roundhead by descent, — did his ancestor charge with Rupert or Cromwell, — did he fall while riding with levelled point in the grim wall of advancing Ironsides, or go hopelessly down in death beneath their thundering hoofs, — what descendant of any English-man who there met his end, but with pride would read the name of Nasby on his regimental flag? What Frenchman would consent to the erasure of Ivry or Moncontour? Thus in all these matters, Time is the great magician. It both mellows and transforms. The Englishman of to day does not apply to Cromwell the standard of loyalty or treason, of right and wrong, applied after the Restoration; nor again does the twentieth century confirm the nineteenth's verdicts. Even slavery we may come to regard as a phase, pardonable as passing, in the evolution of a race.

I hold it will certainly be so with our Civil War. The year 1965 will look upon its causes, its incidents and its men with different eyes from those with which we see them now, —eyes wholly different from those with which we saw forty years ago. They, — for we by that time will have rejoined the generation to which we be longed, — will recog-nize the somewhat essential fact, in dubitably true, that all the honest conviction, all the loyalty, all the patriotic devotion and self-sacrifice were not then, any more than all the courage, on the victor's side. True! the moral right, the spirit of nationality, the sacred cause of humanity even, were on our side; but, among those opposed, and who in the end went down, were men not less sincere, not less devoted, not less truly patriotic according to their lights than he who among us was first in all those qualities. Men of whom it was and is a cause of pride and confidence to say— "They too were countrymen!"

Typical of those men, — most typical, — was Lee. He represented, individualized, all that was highest and best in the Southern mind and the Confederate cause, — the loyalty to State, the keen sense of honor and personal obligation, the slightly archaic, the almost patriarchal, love of dependent, family and home. As I have more than once said, he was a Virginian of the Virginians. He represents a type which is gone, — hardly less extinct than that of the great English nobleman of the feudal times, or the ideal head of the Scotch clan of a later period : but just so long as men admire courage, devotion, patriot ism, the high sense of duty and personal honor, — all in a word which go to make up what we know as Character, — just so long will that type of man be held in affectionate, reverential memory. They have in them all the elements of the heroic. As Carlyle wrote more than half a century ago, so now— "Whom do you wish to resemble ? Him you set on a high column. Who is to have a statue? means, Whom shall we consecrate and set apart as one of our sacred men? Sacred: that all men may see him, be reminded of him, and. by new example added to old perpetual precept, be taught what is real worth in man. Show me the man you honor; I know by that symptom, better than by any other, what kind of man you yourself are. For you show me there what your ideal of manhood is; what kind of man you long inexpressibly to be, and would thank the gods, with your whole soul, for being if you could."

It is all a question of time; and the time is, probably, not quite yet. The wounds of the great War are not altogether healed, its personal memories are still fresh, its passions not wholly allayed. It would, indeed, be a wonder if they were. But, I am as convinced as an unillumined man can be of anything future, that when such time does come, a justice not done now, will be done to those descendants of Washington, of Jefferson, of Rutledge, and of Lee who stood opposed to us in a succeeding generation. That the national spirit is now supreme and the nation cemented. I hold to be unquestionable. That property in man has vanished from the civilized world, is due to our Civil War. The two are worth the great price then paid for them. But wrong as he may have been, and as he was proved by events in these respects, the Confederate had many great and generous qualities; he also was brave, chivalrous, self-sacrificing, sincere and patriotic. So I look forward with confidence to the time when they too will be represented in our national pantheon. Then the query will be answered here, as the query in regard to Cromwell's statue put sixty years ago has recently been answered in England. The bronze effigy of Robert E. Lee, mounted on his charger and with the insignia of his Confederate rank, will from its pedestal in the nation's capitol look across the Potomac at his old home at Arlington, even as that of Cromwell dominates the yard of Westminster upon which his skull once looked down. When that time comes, Lee's monument will be educational, — it will typify the historical appreciation of all that goes to make up the loftiest type of character, military and civic, exemplified in an opponent, once dreaded but ever respected : and, above all, it will symbolize and commemorate that loyal acceptance of the consequences of defeat, and the patient upbuilding of a people under new conditions by constitutional means, which I hold to be the greatest educational lesson America has yet taught to a once skeptical but now silenced world.

Notes:
1. "With a changed name, a story is told about you."
2. *Essay on Man*
3. *Elegy Written in a Country Church Yard*

4. *Twelfth Night*

5. *Atlantic Monthly Magazine* (March, 1902) vol. 89 p. 305.

6. *Webster*, American Statesmen Series, p. 172.

7. *Washington's Works*, vol. xi, pp. 378, 389.

8. Donn Platt, *George H. Thomas*, p. 88.

9. "But above all, I am an English gentleman."

10. *Seward at Washington*, vol. ii, p. 502.

11. Rhodes, *United States*, vol. iii, p. 349.

12. *Works* (London, 1863) vol. iv, pp. 154-156.

13. "If the shattered world collapsed, him, fearless, the debris would strike." Horace, *Ode* 3.

13

"War is Hell"

This speech was delivered at the Waldorf-Astoria in New York City on the occasion of Lee's birthday. The date was January 26, 1903.

MR . COMMANDER , Officers , and Members of the Confederate Veterans ' Camp of New York : -

A New Englander; by birth, descent, tradition , name and environment closely associated with Massachusetts; I was a Union soldier from 1861 to 1865 , and the one boast I make in life was and is , and will ever be, that I also bore arms and confronted the Confederacy, and helped to destroy it. Formerly of the Army of the Potomac, through long years I was intent on the overthrow of the Army of Northern Virginia. So far , moreover, as that great past is concerned, having nothing to regret, to excuse, or to extenuate, I am yet here on this day to respond to a sentiment in honor of the military leader once opposed to us, a Virginian and a Confederate. Nor, all this being thus and So, if asked why I am here, would the answer be far to seek. Primarily, as a Massachusetts man I confess to a feeling of special kindliness toward two other States of the Union, two of the original thirteen above all the other present forty and five, South Carolina and Virginia. Those, with

Massachusetts, I hold to have been, essentially, pivotal States. Communities peculiarly prolific of men the exponent of ideas, from them have gone forth those migrating columns which met in fierce grapple for the maintenance and the ascendency of that in which they believed.

So, if I may be permitted first to say a word personal to myself, when the other day, scarcely a month ago, I was called on to speak in Charleston to an audience of South Carolinians, I responded at once; and I did so because my heart went out to them as those of my countrymen to whom I had once been most bitterly opposed; countrymen still, though I had come to know that, as foemen, they were men of whom it behooved us most to take heed. As exponents of ideas, right and wrong, Massachusetts and South Carolina were peers. They had not followed; they had led. And so, as I told them, fully conscious that I was walking on ashes still hot in the very crater of what had within all our memories been the most terrific volcano of a century, walking there amid sulphurous memories, I chose for my theme the constitutional ethics of secession. In a wholly dispassionate spirit , I addressed myself to it as a purely academic question; but I wanted to know whether the time had in- deed come when the old friendly feeling was restored, and the foes of a former generation could again talk together calmly and as brethren over issues once burning. The reception of what I said justified my faith in those to whom I said it . Never have I met with more cordial welcome, never did I receive a more fraternal response.

Next came the Confederate Veterans of New York; they called, and I am here. At this banquet, your annual commemoration of Robert E. Lee, I am asked to respond to a sentiment in his honor, and, without reservation, I do so; for, as a Massachusetts man, I see in him exemplified those lofty elements of personal character which, typifying Virginia at her highest, made Washington possible. The possession of such qualities by an opponent cannot but cause a thrill of satisfaction from the sense that we also, as foes no less than as countrymen, were worthy of him , and of those whom he typified. It was a great company , that old, original thirteen; and in the front rank of that company Virginia, Massachusetts, and South Carolina stood conspicuous. So I recognize a peculiar fellowship between them, the fellowship of those who have both contended shoulder to shoulder, and fought face to face. This, however, is of the past. Its issues are settled, never to be raised again. But, no matter how much we may discuss the rights and the wrongs of a day that is dead, its victories and defeats, one thing is clear beyond dispute: victor and vanquished, Confederate and Unionist, the descendants of those who, between 1861 and 1865, wore the gray and of those who wore the blue, enter as essential and as equal factors into the national life which now is, and in future is to be. Not more so Puritan and Cavalier in England, the offspring of Cromwell and the children's children of Strafford. With us, as with them, the individual exponents of either side became in time common property, and equally the glory of all.

So I am here this evening, as I have said, a Massachusetts man as well as a member of the Loyal Legion, to do honor to the memory of him who was chief among those once set in array against us. Of him, what shall I say? Essentially a soldier, as a soldier Robert E. Lee was a many-sided man. I might speak of him as a strategist; but of this aspect of the man, enough has perhaps been said. I might refer to the respect, the confidence and love with which he inspired those under his command. I might dilate on his restraint in victory; his resource and patient endurance in the face of adverse fortune; the serene dignity with which he , in the end, triumphed over defeat. But, passing over all these well - worn themes, I shall confine myself to that one attribute of his which, recognized in a soldier by an opponent, I cannot but regard as his surest and loftiest title to enduring fame. I refer to his humanity in arms, and his scrupulous regard for the most advanced rules of civilized warfare.

On this point, two views, I am well aware, have been taken from the beginning, and still are advocated. On the one side, it is contended that warfare should be strictly confined to combatants, and its horrors and devastations brought within the narrowest limits; that private property should be respected, and devastation and violence limited to that necessary to overcome armed opposition at the vital points of conflict. This, by some. But, on the other hand, it is insisted that such a method of procedure is mere cruelty in disguise; that war at best is Hell, and that true humanity lies in exaggerating that Hell to such an extent as to make it unendurable. By so doing, it is forced to a speedy end. On this issue, I stand with Lee. Moreover, looking back over the awful past, replete with man's inhumanity to man, I insist that the verdict of history is distinct. That war is Hell at best, then make it Hell indeed, — that cry is not original with us: far from it; it echoes down the ages. Take Europe, for example. Let me cite two instances, separated by half a century, and two names which have come down to us loaded with execration and sunken deep in infamy: the instances, the repeated and complete devastation of what was known as the Palatinate, once during the war of Thirty Years and again under the orders of Louis Fourteenth; - the names, Tilly and Mélac.

You have heard of Tilly, and of the sack of Magdeburg. Tilly fully believed in making war Hell, — fast, furious and bloody. His orders were to kill and burn, burn and kill; and burn and kill again. He wanted no prisoners, and none were made. The more his subordinates killed and the more they burned, the better he was pleased. Before Tilly bathed in blood and rapine at Magdeburg, he tried his comparatively ' prentice hand elsewhere. He wished the Palatinate to be made a howling wilderness. It is a familiar story, a lamentation and an ancient tale of wrong; and you remember its outcome. Even today, as we read the story of those horrors centuries gone, we thrill with vindictive pleasure when the humane Gustavus Adolphus sprang into the arena, and bore down Hell's advocate in hopeless defeat and irrevocable death.

Again, fifty years later, the same gospel of Hell is proclaimed and enforced. Once more the Palatinate is devastated by sword and fire. War is Hell, then make it Hell indeed; and have it over! They did make it Hell; but was it over? Was it shortened even? A French general, Mélac by name, acting under the inspiration of Louis the Fourteenth, repeated Tilly's work; he could not improve upon it. He, also, believed that to carry on war, disguise it as we may, is to be cruel. It is to kill and burn, burn and kill; and again kill and burn. The Great Monarch desired him, also, so to bear himself as to leave on the inhabitants of the Palatinate an impression that future generations would know he had been there. He did so bear himself.

What was the result? Hell was indeed let loose; but so was Hate. Was the war made shorter? No! Not by an hour! It was simply made needlessly bitter, brutal and barbarous. To this day the ruins of Heidelberg remain Mélac's monument. Remembered to be cursed, pilloried with Tilly, his name in what was once the Palatinate is still a household word. Six generations of men have since passed, and, today, with those of the seventh, Mélac is a name there given to dogs. Many of you have doubtless stood, as have I, on the still shattered and crumbling battlements of Heidelberg, looking out over the peaceful valley of the Necker, and listening to its murmuring flow. Thirty years ago I was there, and I vividly recall a little incident strikingly illustrative of the exact opposite of what I am here today to say of Lee. A portrait of Mélac hung in the gallery of the castle. It hangs there still. I saw it again a year or two ago; but when I saw it first, in 1872, it bore an inscription, — an inscription eloquent of hate. Mélac had, in March, 1689, blown up the castle, burned the town, and devastated the surrounding country, given future generations to know he had been there. A Frenchman, he made war Hell to the German. Nearly two centuries later the turn of Germany came. Then, in 1870, devastating France, they inflicted on the French the misery and shame of Sedan, they besieged and captured Paris. Two years afterwards, in 1872, I read this inscription in letters large and black beneath the portrait of Mélac at Heidelberg- "1689. VERGOLTEN.[2] 1871." They had indeed been given cause to remember; nor had they forgotten. The debt, two centuries old, had been computed with interest; and payment exacted in blood and flame.

As an American, as an ex-soldier of the Union, as one who did his best in honest, even fight, to destroy that fragment of the army of the Confederacy to which he found himself opposed, I rejoice that no such hatred attaches to the name of Lee. Reckless of life to attain the legitimate ends of war, he sought to mitigate its horrors. Opposed to him at Gettysburg, I here, forty years later, do him justice. No more creditable order ever issued from a commanding general than that formulated and signed at Chambersburg by Robert E. Lee as, towards the close of June, 1863, he advanced on a war of invasion. "No greater disgrace," he then declared, can "befall the army and through it our whole people, than the perpetration of barbarous outrages upon the innocent and defenceless. Such proceedings not only disgrace the perpetrators and all connected with them, but are subversive of the discipline and efficiency of the army, and destructive of the ends of our movement. must be remembered that we make war only on- armed men." Lee did not, like Tilly and Mélac, exhort his followers to kill and burn, and burn and kill; and again kill and burn: to make war Hell. He did not proclaim that he wanted no prisoners. He did not enjoin it upon his soldiers as a duty to cause the people of Pennsylvania to remember they had been there. I thank Heaven he did not . He at least, though a Confederate in arms, was still an American, and not a Tilly nor a Mélac.

And here, as a soldier of the Army of the Potomac, let me bear my testimony to such of the Army of Northern Virginia as may now be present. While war at best is bad, yet its necessary and unavoidable bad-ness was not in that campaign enhanced. In scope and spirit Lee's order was observed, and I doubt if a hostile force ever advanced into an enemy's country, or fell back from it in retreat, leaving behind less cause of hate and bitterness than did the Army of Northern Virginia in that memorable campaign which culminated at Gettysburg. Because he was a soldier, Lee did not feel it incumbent upon him to proclaim himself a brute, or to exhort his followers to brutality.

I have paid my tribute. One word more and I have done. Some six months ago, in a certain academic address at Chicago, I called to mind the fact that a statue of Oliver Cromwell now stood in the yard of Parliament House in London, close to that historic hall of Westminster from the roof of which his severed head had once looked down. Calling to mind the strange changes of feeling evinced by the memory of that grinning skull and the presence of that image of bronze, remembering that Cromwell, once traitor and regicide, stood now conspicuous among England's worthiest and most honored, I asked why should it not also in time be so with Lee? Why should not his effigy, erect on his charger, and wearing the insignia of his Confederate rank, gaze from his pedestal across the Potomac at the Virginia shore, and his once dearly loved home at Arlington? He, too, is one of the precious possessions of what is an essential factor in the nation that now is, and is to be.

My suggestion was met with an answer to which I would now make reply. It was objected that such a memorial was to be provided for from the national treasury, and that Lee, educated at West Point, holding for years the commission of the United States, had borne arms against the nation. The rest I will not here repeat. The thing was pronounced impossible. Now let me here explain myself. I never supposed that Robert E. Lee's statue in Washington would be provided for by an appropriation from the national treasury. I did not wish it. I do not think it fitting. Indeed, I do not rate high statues erected by act of Congress, and paid for by public money. They have small significance. Least of all would I suggest such a one in the case of Lee. Nor was it so with Cromwell. His effigy is a private gift, placed where it is by Parliament. So , when the time is ripe, should it be with Lee, and the time will come. When it does come, the effigy, assigned to its place merely by an act of the Congress of a reunited people, should bear some such inscription as this : —

ROBERT EDWARD LEE.

Erected by the contributions

Of those who, wearing the Blue, or wearing the Gray,

recognize Brilliant Military Achievements,

and honor Lofty Character

evinced by Humanity in War

and by

Devotion and Dignity in Defeat

Notes:

1. Speech delivered at the thirteenth annual dinner of the Confederate Veterans ' Camp of New York , in response to a sentiment in honor

of General Robert E. Lee . The birthday of General Lee was January 19. In 1903 it was observed in New York on the 26th of the month , in the large banqueting - hall of the Waldorf - Astoria Hotel. Some six hundred persons were present at the tables or in the boxes.

2. [Editor's note] German, verb, *to relaliate, to recompense*

14

The Confederacy and the Transvaal: A People's Obligation to Robert E. Lee

This paper was read to the American Antiquarian Society in Worcester, Massachusetts on October 30, 1901.

The present seems a sufficiently proper occasion, and this a not inappropriate place, to call attention to a matter sufficiently germane to the purpose of this Society, though hardly as yet antiquarian. Historical in its character, it conveys a lesson of grave present import.

One of the most unhappy, and, to those concerned in it, disastrous wars since the fall of Napoleon, is, in South Africa, now working itself to a close apparently still remote, and in every way unsatisfactory. There is reason to think that the conflict was unnecessary in its inception; that by timely and judicious action it might long since have been brought to a close; and that it now continues simply because the parties to it cannot be brought together to discuss and arrive at a sensible basis of adjustment, — a basis upon which both in reality would be not unwilling to agree. Nevertheless, as the cable dispatches daily show, the contest drags wearily along, to the probable destruction of one of the combatants, to the great loss of the other, and, so far as can be seen, in utter disregard of the best interests of both.

My immediate purpose, however, is to draw attention to the hair-breadth escape we ourselves had from a similar experience, now thirty-six years ago, and to assign to whom it belongs the credit for that escape. In one word, in the strong light of passing events, I think it now opportune to set forth the debt of gratitude this reunited country of ours — Union and Confederate, North and South — owes to Robert E. Lee, of Virginia.

Most of those here — for this is not a body of young men — remember the state of affairs which existed in the United States, especially in what was then known as the Confederate States, or the rebellious portion of the United States, in April, 1865. Such as are not yet as mature as that memory implies, have read and heard thereof. It was in every respect almost the identical state of affairs which existed in South Africa at the time of the capture of Pretoria by General Roberts, in June a year ago.

On the 2d of April, 1865, the Confederate army found itself compelled to abandon the lines in front of Petersburg; and the same day — a very famous Sabbath — Jefferson Davis, hastily called from the church services he was attending, left Richmond to find, if he might, a new seat of government, at Danville. The following morning our forces at last entered the rebel capital. This was on a Monday; and, two days later, the Confederate President issued from Danville his manifesto, declaring to the people of the South that "We have now entered upon a new phase of the struggle. Relieved from the necessity of guarding particular points, our army will be free to move from point to point, to strike the enemy in detail far from his base. If, by the stress of numbers, we should be compelled to a temporary withdrawal from her limits [Virginia], or those of any other border State, we will return until the baffled and exhausted enemy shall abandon in despair his endless and impossible task of making slaves of a people resolved to be free." The policy and line of military action herein indicated were precisely those laid down and pm-sued by the Boer leaders during the last sixteen months.

It is unnecessary for me even to refer to the series of events which followed our occupation of Richmond, and preceded the surrender of Appomattox. It is sufficient to say that on the Friday which followed the momentous Sunday, the capitulation of the Army of Northern Virginia had become inevitable. Not the less for that, the course thereafter to be pursued as concerned further resistance on the part of the Confederacy was still to be decided. As his Danville proclamation showed, Jefferson Davis, though face to face with grave disaster, had not for an instant given up the thought of continuing the struggle. To do so was certainly practicable, — far more practicable than now in South Africa, both as respects forces in the field and the area of country to be covered by the invader. Foreign opinion, for instance, was on this point settled; it was in Europe assumed as a certainty of the future that the conquest of the Confederacy was "impossible." The English journals had always maintained, and still did maintain, that the defeat of Lee in the field, or even the surrender of all the Confederate armies, would be but the close of one phase of the war and the opening of another, — the final phase being a long, fruitless effort to subdue a people, at once united and resolved, occupying a region so vast that it would be impossible to penetrate every portion of it, much less to hold it in peaceful subjection. As an historical fact, on this point the scales, on the 9th of April, 1865, hung wavering in the balance ; a mere turn of the hand would decide which way they were to incline. Thus, on the morning of that momentous day, it was an absolutely open question, an even chance, whether the course which subsequently was pursued should be pursued, or whether the leaders of the Confederacy would adopt the policy which President Kruger and Generals Botha and De Wet have in South Africa more recently adopted, and are now pursuing.

The decision rested in the hands of one man, the commander of the Army of Northern Virginia. Fairly reliable and very graphic accounts of what took place at General Lee's headquarters in the early morning hours of April 9th have either appeared in print or been told in conversation, and to two of these accounts I propose to call attention. Apparently the second of the interviews described followed close on the first, not more than a couple of hours intervening between them. Of the first, I find this account in a book recently published by John Sargent Wise, entitled "The End of an Era." John Sargent Wise is the son of Henry A. Wise, once prominent in our national politics. Governor of Virginia in the later "fifties," the father was subsequently a brigadier-general in the Confederate service. Though in 1865 but a youth of nineteen, John S. Wise was a hot Confederate, and had already been wounded in battle. At the time now in question he chanced to have been sent by Jefferson Davis, then on his way to Danville, with dispatches to Lee ; and while seeking Lee's headquarters he came, in the early morning of April 9th, across his father. Governor and General Wise, in bivouac with his brigade. The father was then nearly sixty years of age, but the son found him wrapped in a blanket, stretched on the ground like a common soldier, and asleep among his men. A typical Southern " fire-eater " of the extreme type, Henry A. Wise was an out-and-out Secessionist and Confederate. Aroused from an uneasy slumber, almost the first wish he expressed was to see General Lee, and he asked impetuously of his whereabouts. The son knew where the headquarters of the Confederate commander were, and the two started together to go to them. John S. Wise has described vividly the aspect of affairs as they passed along: " The roads and fields were filled with stragglers. They moved looking behind them, as if they expected to be attacked and harried by a pursuing foe. Demoralization, panic, abandonment of all hope, appeared on every hand. Wagons were rolling along without any order or system. Caissons and limber-chests, without commanding officers, seemed to be floating aimlessly upon a tide of disorganization. Rising to his full height, casting a glance around him like that of an eagle, and sweeping the horizon with his long arm and bony forefinger, my father exclaimed: 'This is the end!' It is impossible to convey an idea of the agony and the bitterness of his words and gestures." Then follows this description of the interview which ensued: —

"We found General Lee on the rear portico of the house that I have mentioned. He had washed his face in a tin basin, and stood drying his beard with a coarse towel as we approached. 'General Lee,' exclaimed my father, ' my poor, brave men are lying on yonder hill more dead than alive. For more than a week they have been fighting day and night, without food, and, by God, sir, they shall not move another step until somebody gives them something to eat! '

"Come in, general,' said General Lee soothingly. 'They deserve something to eat, and shall have it; and meanwhile you shall share my breakfast.' He disarmed everything like defiance by his kindness.

" It was but a few moments, however, before my father launched forth in a fresh denunciation of the conduct of General Bushrod John-son[1] in the engagement of the sixth. I am satisfied that General Lee felt as he did; but, assuming an air of mock severity, he said, 'General, are you aware that you are liable to court-martial and execution for insubordination and disrespect toward your commanding officer?'

"My father looked at him with lifted eyebrows and flashing eyes, and exclaimed: 'Shot! You can't afford to shoot the men who fight for cursing those who ran away. Shot! I wish you would shoot me. If you don't, some Yankee probably will within the next twenty-four hours.'

"Growing more serious. General Lee inquired what he thought of the situation.

" 'Situation?' said the bold old man. 'There is no situation! Nothing remains, General Lee, but to put your poor men on your poor mules and send them home in time for spring ploughing. This army is hope-lessly whipped, and is fast becoming demoralized. These men have already endured more than I believed flesh and blood could stand, and I say to you, sir, emphatically, that to prolong the struggle is murder, and the blood of every man who is killed from this time forth is on your head. General Lee.'

"This last expression seemed to cause General Lee great pain. With a gesture of remonstrance, and even of impatience, he protested: 'Oh, general, do not talk so wildly. My burdens are heavy enough. What would the country think of me, if I did what you suggest?'

" ' Country be d ----d ! ' was the quick reply. 'There is no country. There has been no country, general, for a year or more. You are the country to these men. They have fought for you. They have shivered through a long winter for you. Without pay or clothes, or care of any sort, their devotion to you and faith in you have been the only things which have held this army together. If you demand the sacrifice, there are still left thousands of us who will die for you. You know the game is desperate beyond redemption, and that, if you so announce, no man or government or people will gainsay your decision. That is why I repeat that the blood of any man killed hereafter is upon your head.'

"General Lee stood for some time at an open window, looking out at the throng now surging upon the roads and in the fields, and made no response."[2]

It will be remembered that John Sargent Wise was individually present at this conversation, a youth of nineteen. I have as little respect as any one well can have for the recollection of thirty years since as a basis of history. Nevertheless, it would seem quite out of the question that a youth of only nineteen could have been present at such a scene as is here described, and that the words which then passed, and the incidents which occurred, should not have been indelibly imprinted upon his memory. I am disposed, therefore, to consider this reliable historical material. Meanwhile, it so chances that I am able to supplement it by similar testimony from another quarter.

Some years ago I was, for a considerable period, closely associated with General E. P. Alexander, who, in its time, had been Chief of Artillery in Longstreet's famous corps; and it was General Alexander who, on the morning of July 3, 1863, opened on the Union line at Gettysburg what Hancock described as "a most terrific and appalling cannonade," intended to prepare the way for the advance of Pickett's division. In April, 1865, General Alexander was, if my recollection serves me right, in command of the artillery of the Army of Northern Virginia. General Alexander's memory I found always singularly tenacious as well as accurate, and he delighted in reminiscence of the great war; so he many times repeated to me, or to others in my hearing, the details of an interview he had with Lee on the morning of the 9th of April, not long, it would seem, after Wise had left him. Of what he said, I have since retained a vivid recollection.

On the morning in question, General Alexander had occasion to report to Lee. He realized that the Army of Northern Virginia was then in a desperate situation. Moreover, as he well knew, the limber-chests were running low; his arm of the service was in no condition to go into another engagement. Yet the idea of an abandonment of the cause had never occurred to him as among the probabilities. All night he had lain awake, thinking as to what was next to be done. Finally he had come to the conclusion that there was but one course to pursue. The Confederate army, while nominally capitulating, must in reality disperse, and those composing it should be instructed, whether individually or as part of detachments, to get each man to his own State in the most direct way and shortest possible time, and report to the governor thereof, with a view to a further and continuous resistance. Thus, exactly what is now taking place in South Africa was to take place in the Confederacy. General Alexander told me that, as he passed his batteries on his way to headquarters, the men called out to him, in cheery tones, that there were still some rounds remaining in the caissons, and that they were ready to renew the fight. He found Lee seated on the trunk of a fallen tree before a dying campfire. He was dressed in uniform, and invited Alexander to take a seat beside him. He then asked his opinion of the situation, and of the course proper to be pursued. Full of the idea which dominated his mind, Alexander proceeded at once to propound his plan, for it seemed to him the only plan worthy of consideration. As he went on, General Lee, looking steadily into the fire with an abstracted air, listened patiently. Alexander said his full say. A brief pause ensued, which Lee finally broke in somewhat these words: "No! General Alexander, that will not do. You must remember we are a Christian people. We have fought this fight as long as, and as well as, we knew how. We have been defeated. For us, as a Christian people, there is now but one course to pursue. We must accept the situation; these men must go home and plant a crop, and we must proceed to build up our country on a new basis. We cannot have recourse to the methods you suggest." I remember being deeply impressed with Alexander's comment, as he repeated these words of Lee. They had evidently burned themselves into his memory. He said: "I had nothing more to say. I felt that the man had soared way up above me, — he dominated me completely. I rose from beside him; silently mounted my horse; rode back to my command; and waited for the order to surrender."

Then and there, Lee decided its course for the Confederacy. And I take it there is not one solitary man in the United States to-day, North or South, who does not feel that he decided right.

The Army of Northern Virginia, it will be remembered, laid down its arms on the 9th of April. But General Joseph Johnston was in command of another Confederate army then confronting Sherman, in North Carolina, and it was still an open question what course he would pursue. His force numbered over 40,000 combatants; more than the entire muster of the Boers in their best estate. Lee's course decided Johnston's. S. R. Mallory, who was present on the occasion, has left a striking account of a species of council held at Greensboro, North Carolina, on the evening of the 10th of April, by Jefferson Davis and the members of his cabinet, with General Johnston. Davis, stubborn in temper and bent on a policy of continuous irregular resistance, expressed the belief that the disasters recently sustained, though "terrible," should not be regarded as "fatal." "I think," he added, "we can whip the enemy yet, if our people will turn out." When he ceased speaking, a pause ensued. Davis at last said, " We should like to hear your views. General Johnston." Whereupon Johnston, without preface or introduction, and with a tone and manner almost spiteful, remarked in his terse, concise, demonstrative way, as if seeking to condense thoughts that were crowding for utterance: "My views are, sir, that our people are tired of the war, feel themselves whipped, and will not fight."[3]

We all know what followed. Lee's great military prestige and moral ascendancy made it easy for some of the remaining Confederate commanders — like Johnston — to follow the precedent he set; while others of them —like Kirby Smith — found it imposed upon them. A firm direction had been given to the course of events; an intelligible policy was indicated. I have in my possession a copy of the "Index," the weekly journal published in London during our Civil War. The official organ of the Confederate agents in Europe, it was intended for the better enlightenment of foreign opinion, more especially the English press. The surrender of Lee was commented upon editorially in the issue of that paper for April 27th. "The war is far from concluded," it declared. "A strenuous resistance and not surrender was the unalterable determination of the Confederate authorities . . . and if the worst comes to the worst there is the trans-Mississippi department, where the remnant of [Johnston's] army can find a shelter, and a new and safe starting-point." On the 11th of May following, the surrender of Johnston's army was announced on the same terms as that of Lee; but, in summing up the situation, the "Index" still found " the elements of a successful or at least a protracted resistance." On the 25th of May, it had an article entitled "Southern Resistance in Texas," in which it announced that, "Such a war will be fierce, ferocious, and of long duration," — in a word, such an expiring struggle as we are to-day witnessing in South Africa. In its issue of June 1st the "Index" commented on "The capture of President Davis;" and then, and not until then, forestalling the trans-Mississippi surrender of Kirby Smith, brought to it by the following mail, it raised the wailing cry, " *Fuit Ilium.* . . . The South has fallen."

Comparing the situation which then existed in the Confederacy with that now in South Africa, it must also be remembered that General Lee assumed the responsibility he did assume, and decided the policy to be pursued in the way it was decided, under no ameliorating conditions. Politically, unconditional surrender was insisted upon; and Lee's surrender was, politically, unconditional. Even more so was Johnston's; for, in Johnston's case, the modifying terms of capitulation agreed on in the first place between him and Sherman were roughly disallowed at Washington, and the truce, by an order coming thence, abruptly terminated. Then Johnston did what Lee had already done; ignoring Davis, he surrendered his army.

In the case of the Confederacy, also, an absolutely unconditional political surrender implied much. The Emancipation Proclamation of January, 1863, which confiscated the most valuable chattel property of the Confederacy, remained the irreversible law of the land. The inhabitants of the South were, moreover, as one man disfranchised. When they laid down their arms they had before them, first, a military government, and, after that, the supremacy of their former slaves. A harder fate for a proud people to accept could not well be imagined. The bitterness of feeling, the hatred, was, too, extreme. It may possibly be argued that the conditions in this country then were different from those now in South Africa, inasmuch as here it was a civil war, a conflict between communities of the same race and speech, involving the vital question of the supremacy of law. This argument, however, seems to imply that, in case of strife of this description, a general severity may fairly be resorted to in excess of that permissible between nations, — in other words, that we are justified in treating our brethren with greater harshness than we would treat aliens in blood and speech. Obviously, this is a questionable contention.

It might possibly also be claimed that the bitterness of civil war is not so insurmountable as that of one involving a question of race dominance. Yet it is difficult to conceive bitterness of greater intensity than existed between the sections at the close of our Civil War. There is striking evidence of this in the book of Mr. Wise, from which I have already quoted. Toward its close he speaks of the death of Lincoln. He then adds the following:—

"Perhaps I ought to chronicle that the announcement was received with demonstrations of sorrow. If I did, I should be lying for sentiment's sake. Among the higher officers and the most intelligent and conservative men, the assassination caused a shudder of horror at the heinousness of the act, and at the thought of its possible consequences; but among the thoughtless, the desperate, and the ignorant, it was hailed as a sort of retributive justice. In maturer years I have been ashamed of what I felt and said when I heard of that awful calamity. However, men ought to be judged for their feelings and their speech by the circumstances of their surroundings. For four years we had been fighting. In that struggle, all we loved had been lost. Lincoln incarnated to us the idea of oppression and conquest. We had seen his face over the coffins of our brothers and relatives and friends, in the flames of Richmond, in the disaster at Appomattox. In blood and flame and torture the temples of our lives were tumbling about our heads. We were desperate and vindictive, and whosoever denies it forgets or is false. We greeted his death in a spirit of reckless hate, and hailed it as bringing agony and bitterness to those who were the cause of our own agony and bitterness. To us, Lincoln was an inhuman monster, Grant a butcher, and Sherman a fiend."

Indeed, recalling the circumstances of that time, it is fairly appalling to consider what in 1865 must have occurred, had Robert E. Lee then been of the same turn of mind as was Jefferson Davis, or as implacable and unyielding in disposition as Kruger or Botha have more recently proved. The national government had in arms a million men, inured to the hardships and accustomed to the brutalities of war; Lincoln had been freshly assassinated; the temper of the North was thoroughly aroused, while its patience was exhausted. An irregular warfare would inevitably have resulted, a warfare without quarter. The Confederacy would have been reduced to a smouldering wilderness, — to what South Africa to-day is. In such a death grapple, the North, both in morale and in means, would have suffered only less than the South. From both sections that fate was averted.

It is not my purpose to enter into any criticism of the course of events in South Africa, or of the policy there on either side pursued. It will be for the future to decide whether the prolonged, irregular resistance we are witnessing is justifiable, or, if justifiable, whether it is wise. Neither of these questions do I propose to discuss. My purpose simply is to call attention, in view of what is now taking place elsewhere, to the narrow escape we ourselves, thirty-six years ago, had from a similar awful catastrophe. And I again say that, as we look to-day upon Kruger and Botha and De Wet, and the situation existing in the Transvaal and the Orange Free State, I doubt if one single man in the United States, North or South, — whether he participated in the Civil War or was born since that war ended, — would fail to acknowledge an infinite debt of gratitude to the Confederate leader, who on the 9th of April, 1865, decided, as he did decide, that the United States, whether Confederate or Union, was a Christian community, and that his duty was to accept the responsibility which the fate of war had imposed upon him, — to decide in favor of a new national life, even if slowly and painfully to be built up by his own people under conditions arbitrarily and by force imposed on them.

In one of the Confederate accounts of the great war[4] is to be found the following description of Lee's return to his Richmond home immediately after he had at Appomattox sealed the fate of the Confederacy. With it I will conclude this paper. On the afternoon of the previous day, the first of those paroled from the surrendered Army of Northern Virginia had straggled back to Richmond. The writer thus goes on: "Next morning a small group of horsemen appeared on the further side of the pontoons. By some strange intuition it was known that General Lee was among them, and a crowd collected all along the route he would take, silent and bareheaded. There was no excitement, no hurrahing; but as the great chief passed, a deep, loving murmur, greater than these, rose from the very hearts of the crowd. Taking off his hat and simply bowing his head, the man great in adversity passed silently to his own door; it closed upon him, and his people had seen him for the last time in his battle harness."

After preparing the foregoing paper, I wrote to General Alexander asking him to verify my recollection of the account of what passed at his meeting with General Lee, at Appomattox. His reply did not reach me in time for the meeting of the American Antiquarian Society, at which the paper was read. In his answer to my letter he wrote in part as follows: "I am greatly interested in what you wish, having often thought and spoken of the contrast between Lee's views of the duty of the leaders of a people, and those held at the time by President Davis, and now held by Kruger and the Boer leaders; and I have written of it, too, in my own war recollections, which I am writing out for my children.

"*Essentially,* your recollections are entirely correct: though some of the details are not exact. Two days before I had talked with General Lee over his map, and noted Appomattox Court-house as the 'danger point.' When I came up on the 9th to where he had halted on the road, he called me to him, and began by referring to previous talk, and then he asked me, 'What shall we do to-day?' For an account of our conversation I will cut out of a scrap-book two pages which contain a clipping from the 'Philadelphia Press ' of a letter I wrote twenty years ago."

The clipping referred to was from an issue of the "Press" of July, 188 L The narrative contained in it is, of course, now not easily accessible; but it is of such interest and obvious historical value, as throwing light on what was passing in Lee's mind at one of the most critical moments in the national history, that I here reproduce it in full: —

"The morning of the 9th of April, 1865, found the Confederate army in a position in which its inevitable fate was apparent to every man in it. The skirmishing which had begun in its front as its advance guard reached Appomattox Court-house the night before had developed into a sharp fight, in which the continuous firing of the artillery and the steady increase of the musketry told to all that a heavy force had been thrown across our line of march, and that reinforcements to it were steadily arriving. The long trains of wagons and artillery were at first halted in the road and then parked in the adjoining fields, allowing the rear of the column to close up and additional troops to pass to the front to reinforce the advanced guard and to form a reserve fine of battle in their rear, under cover of which they might retire when necessary. While these dispositions were taking place, General Lee, who had dismounted and was standing near a fire on a hill about two miles from the Court-house, called the writer to him, and, inviting him to a seat on a log near by, referred to the situation and asked: 'What shall we do this morning?' Although this opportunity of expressing my views was unexpected, the situation itself was not, for two days before, while near Farmville, in a consultation with General Lee over his map, the fact of the enemy's having the shortest road to the Appomattox Court-house had been noted and the probability of serious difficulty there anticipated, and in the mean time there had been ample opportunity for reflection on all of the emergencies that might arise. Without replying directly to the question, however, I answered first that it was due to my command (of artillery) that I should tell him that they were in as good spirits, though short of ammunition and with poor teams, as they had ever been, and had begged, if it came to a surrender, to be allowed to expend first every round of ammunition on the enemy and surrender only the empty ammunition chests. To this General Lee replied that there were remaining only two divisions of infantry sufficiently well organized and strong to be fully relied upon (Field's and Mahone's), and that they did not number eight thousand muskets together; and that that force was not sufficient to warrant him in undertaking a pitched battle. 'Then I answered, general, there are but two alternatives, to surrender or to order the army to abandon its trains and disperse in the woods and bushes, every man for himself, and each to make his best way, with his arms, either to the army of General Johnston, in North Carolina, or home to the governor of his State. We have all foreseen the probability of such an alternative for two days, and I am sure I speak the sentiments of many others besides my own in urging that rather than surrender the army you should allow us to disperse in the woods and go, every man for himself.'

"'What would you hope to accomplish by this?'

"I answered: 'If there is any hope at all for the Confederacy or for the separate States to make terms with the United States or for any foreign assistance, this course stands the chances, whatever they may be; while if this army surrenders this morning, the Confederacy is dead from that moment. Grant will turn 150,000 fresh men against Johnston, and with the moral effect of our surrender he will go, and Dick Taylor and Kirby Smith will have to follow like a row of bricks, while if we all take to dispersing in the woods, we inaugurate a new phase of the war, which may be indefinitely prolonged, and it will at least have great moral effect in showing that in our pledges to fight it out to the last we meant what we said. And even, general, if there is no hope at all in this course or in any other, and if the fate of the Confederacy is sealed whatever we do, there is one other consideration which your soldiers have a right to urge on you, and that is your own military reputation, in which every man in this army, officer or private, feels the utmost personal pride and has a personal property that his children will prize after him. The Yankees brought Grant here from the West, after the failure of all their other generals, as one who had whipped everybody he had ever fought against, and they call him " Unconditional Surrender " Grant, and have been bragging in advance that you would have to surrender too. Now, general, I think you ought to spare us all the mortification of having you to ask Grant for terms, and have him answer that he had no terms to offer you.'

"I still remember most vividly the emotion with which I made this appeal, increasing as I went on, until my whole heart was in it; and it seemed to me at the moment one which no soldier could resist and against which no consideration whatever could be urged ; and when I closed, after urging my suggestions at greater length than it is necessary to repeat, looking him in the face and speaking with more boldness than I usually found in his presence, I had not a doubt that he must adopt some such course as I had urged.

"He heard me entirely through, however, very calmly, and then asked: 'How many men do you estimate would escape if I were to order the army to disperse?'

"I replied: 'I suppose two thirds of us could get away, for the enemy could not disperse to follow us through the woods.'

"He said: We have here only about sixteen thousand men with arms, and not all of those who could get away would join General Johnston, but most of them would try and make their way to their homes and families, and their numbers would be too small to be of any material service either to General Johnston or to the governors of the States. I recognize fully that the surrender of this army is the end of the Confederacy, but no course we can take can prevent or even delay that result. I have never believed that we would receive foreign assistance or get our liberty otherwise than by our own arms. The end is now upon us, and it only remains to decide how we shall close the struggle. But in deciding this question we are to approach it not only as soldiers but as Christian men, deciding on matters which involve a great deal else besides their own feelings. If I should order this army to disperse, the men with their arms, but without organization or control, and without provisions or money, would soon be wandering through every State in the Confederacy, some seeking to get to their homes and some with no homes to go to. Many would be compelled to rob and plunder as they went to save themselves from starvation, and the enemy's cavalry would pursue in small detachments, particularly in efforts to catch the general officers, and raid and burn over large districts which they will otherwise never reach, and the result would be the inauguration of lawlessness and terror and of organized bands of robbers all over the South. Now, as Christian men, we have not the right to bring this state of affairs upon the country, whatever the sacrifice of personal pride in-volved. And as for myself, you young men might go to bushwhacking, but I am too old; and even if it were right for me to disperse the army, I should surrender myself to General Grant as the only proper course for one of my years and position. But I am glad to be able to tell you one thing for your comfort: General Grant will not demand an uncondi-tional surrender, but offers us most liberal terms — the paroling of the whole army not to fight until exchanged.' He then went on to speak of the probable details of the terms of surrender, and to say that about 10 a. m. he was to meet General Grant in the rear of the army and would then accept the terms offered.

"Sanguine as I had been when he commenced that 'he *must* acqui-esce in my views,' I had not one word to reply when he had finished. He spoke slowly and deliberately and with some feeling; and the completeness of the considerations he advanced, and which he dwelt upon with more detail than I can now fully recall, speaking particularly of the women and children, as the greatest sufferers in the state of anarchy which a dispersion of the army would bring about, and his reference to what would be his personal course if he did order such dispersion, all indicated that the question was not then presented to his mind for the first time.

"A short time after this conversation General Lee rode to the rear of the army to meet General Grant and arrange the details of the surrender. He had started about a half hour when General Fitz Lee sent word to General Longstreet that he had broken through a portion of the enemy's line, and that the whole army might make its way through. General Longstreet, on learning this, directed Colonel Haskell of the artillery,[5] who was very finely mounted, to ride after General Lee at utmost speed, killing his horse, if necessary, and recall him before he could reach General Grant. Colonel Haskell rode as directed, and a short distance in rear of the army found General Lee and some of his staff dismounted by the roadside. As he with difficulty checked his horse. General Lee came up quickly, asking what was the matter, but, without waiting for a reply, said: 'Oh! I'm afraid you have killed your beautiful mare. What did you ride her so hard for?' On hearing General Longstreet's message, he asked some questions about the situation, and sent word to General Longstreet to use his own discretion in making any movements; but he did not himself return, and in a short while another message was received that the success of the cavalry under General Fitz Lee was but temporary, and that there was no such gap in the enemy's line as had been supposed. Soon afterward a message was brought from the enemy's picket that General Grant had passed around to the front and would meet General Lee at Appomattox Courthouse, and General Lee accordingly returned.

"Meanwhile, as the Confederate line under General Gordon was slowly falling back from Appomattox Courthouse after as gallant a fight against overwhelming odds as it had ever made, capturing and bringing safely off with it an entire battery of the enemy's. General

Custer, commanding a division of Federal cavalry, rode forward with a flag of truce, and, the firing having ceased on both sides, was conducted to General Longstreet as commanding temporarily in General Lee's absence. Custer demanded the surrender of the army to himself and General Sheridan, to which General Longstreet replied that General Lee was in communication with General Grant upon that subject, and that the issue would be determined between them. Custer replied that he and Sheridan were independent of Grant, and unless the surrender was made to them they would 'pitch in' at once. Longstreet's answer was a peremptory order [to Custer] at once [to return] to his own lines, and 'try it if he liked.' Custer was accordingly escorted back, but fire was not reopened, and both fines remained halted, the Confederate about a half mile east of the Court-house.

"General Lee, returning from the rear shortly afterward, halted in a small field adjoining Sweeney's house, a little in rear of his skirmish line, and, seated on some rails under an apple-tree, awaited a message from General Grant. This apple-tree was not only entirely cut up for mementos within two days afterward, but its very roots were dug up and carried away under the false impression that the surrender took place under it.[6]

"About noon a Federal staff officer rode up and announced that General Grant was at the Court-house, and General Lee with one of his staff accompanied him back. As he left the apple-tree General Longstreet's last words were: 'Unless he offers you liberal terms, general, let us fight it out.'

"It would be a difficult task to convey to one who was not present an idea of the feeling of the Confederate army during the few hours which so suddenly, and so unexpectedly to it, terminated its existence, and with it all hopes of the Confederacy. Having been sharply engaged that very morning, and its movements arrested by the flag of truce, while one portion of it was actually fighting and nearly all the rest, infantry and artillery, had just been formed in line of battle in sight and range of the enemy, and with guns unlimbered, it was impossible to realize fully that the war, with all its hopes, its ambitions, and its hardships, was thus ended. There was comparatively very little conversation, and men stood in groups looking over the scene ; but the groups were unusually silent. It was not at first generally known that a surrender was inevitable, but there was a remarkable pre-acquiescence in whatever General Lee should determine, and the warmest expressions of confidence in his judgment. Ranks and discipline were maintained as usual, and there is little doubt that, had General Lee decided to fight that afternoon, the troops would not have disappointed him. About 4 p. m. he returned from the Court-house, and, after informing the principal officers of the terms of the surrender, started to ride back to his camp.

"The universal desire to express to him the unabated love and confidence of the army had led to the formation of the gunners of a few battalions of artillery along the roadside, with orders to take off their hats in silence as he rode by. When he approached, however, the men could not be restrained, but burst into the wildest cheering, which the adjacent infantry lines took up; and, breaking ranks, they all crowded around him, cheering at the tops of their voices. General Lee stopped his horse and, after gaining silence, made the only speech to his men that he ever made. He was very brief, and gave no excuses or apologies for his surrender, but said he had done all in his power for his men, and urged them to go as quickly and quietly to their homes as possible, to resume peaceful avocations, and to be as good citizens as they had been soldiers; and this advice marked the course which he himself pursued so faithfully to the end."

Notes:
1. Elsewhere in his book (pp. 358, 359), and in another connection, J. S. Wise is equally severe in his characterization of Bushrod Johnson.
2. *The End of an Era*, pp. 433-435.
3. Alfriend's *Life of Jefferson Davis*, pp. 622-626.
4. De Leon, *Four Years in Rebel Capitals*, p. 367.

5. Colonel J. B. Haskell, of South Carolina; "a born and a resourceful artilleryman, [who] knew no such thing as fear." General Longstreet evidently used General Alexander's paper in the Philadelphia Press in preparing the account, contained in his *Manassas to Appomattox,* of what occurred on the day of Lee's surrender. A further reference to Colonel Haskell may be found in Wise's *The End of an Era* (p. 360). Longstreet says that, at Appomattox, "there were 'surrendered or paroled' 28,356 officers and men." A week previous to the capitulation, Lee's and Johnston's combined forces numbered considerably over 100,000 combatants.

6. The surrender took place in the house of a Mr. McLean, a gentleman who, by a strange coincidence, owned a farm on Bull Run at the beginning of the war. General Beauregard's headquarters were at McLean's house, just in the rear of Blackburn's fort, during the first battle fought by the army, July 18, 1861. McLean moved from Bull Run to get himself out of the theatre of war. The last battle took place on his new farm and the surrender in his new residence.

15

A Plea for Military History

This speech was given to the American Historical Association on December 28, 1899.

I AM to contribute to this occasion a paper under the title of "A Plea for Military History." To this subject I have already — more than six months ago — elsewhere alluded, — in the course of an address to the Massachusetts Historical Society, on taking for the fifth time the chair as its president.

"It is scarcely an exaggeration to say that there are not many considerable branches of human know ledge concerning which the historian of the future must not in some degree inform himself. Somewhere and somehow his researches will touch upon them, remotely, perhaps, but still as factors in his problem. . . . Formerly all necessary information, it was supposed, could be acquired from books; manuscripts were better yet, for those were, without any question, what are termed 'original sources.' But the old-fashioned historian, rarely, if ever, hesitating, flies boldly at every kind of game — all are fish that come to his net. For instance, history is largely made up of accounts of operations and battles on land and on sea. Weary of threading his way

398

through a long period of most impicturesque peace, trying to make that interesting which was at best commonplace, the historian draws a breath of relief when at length he comes to a tumult of war. Here are pride, pomp, and circumstance, — a chance for descriptive power.

"The historian of the future seems now likely to pursue a different method. Recognizing the fact that he probably is not at once a litterateur, a soldier, a statesman, a lawyer, a theologian, a physician, and a biologist; that he certainly will not live forever; that he has not the cosmogony at his fingers' ends, and that to ransack every repository of information on all possible subjects transcends the powers of even the most industrious; recognizing in this degree the limits of possibility, he will be content to avail himself of the labors of others, better advised on many subjects than himself, and, becoming the student of monographs, derive the great body of his information, not, as the expression now goes, from 'original sources,' or even from personal observation, but, as we all in the end must, at secondhand. His insight will be largely into the knowledge and judgment of others, and the degree of reliance to be placed in them.

"I know of but one writer who has described military operations and battles, — those intricate movements of human pawns on a chessboard of much topo graphical uncertainty, and those scientific melees in which skill, luck, preparation, superiority of weapons, human endurance, and racial characteristics decide the question of mastery as between two marshalled mobs, — I know, I was saying, of but one writer who has described battles and military operations in that realistic way which impresses me with a sense of both personal experience and literary skill. That one is Tolstoi, the Russian philosopher and novelist. His Austerlitz and Russian campaigns of Napoleon and his Sebastopol are masterpieces. A man of imagination and consummate literary capacity, he had him self served ; and, curiously enough, in the same way, his compatriot, Verestchagin, has put upon canvas the sickening realism of war with a degree of force which could come only from familiarity with the cumbered field, and could by no possibility be worked up in the studio through the study of photographs, no matter how numerous, or the perusal of the accounts ' from our special correspondent,' no matter how graphic and detailed.

"I once, in a very subordinate capacity, though for a considerable period of time, was brought into close contact with warfare and saw much of military operations from within, or, as I may say, on the seamy side. Since then I have read in books of history, and other works more avowedly of fiction, many accounts of campaigns and battles ; and in so doing I have been most deeply impressed with the audacity, not of soldiers, but of authors. Usually, bookish men who had passed their lives in libraries, often clergymen — knowing absolutely nothing of the principles of strategy or of the details of camp life and military organization, never having seen a column on the march, or a regiment in line, or heard a hostile shot, — not taking the trouble even to visit the scene of operations or to study its topography, wholly unacquainted with the national characteristics of the combatants, — these 'bookish theoricks' substitute their imaginings for realities, and in the result display much the same real acquaintance with the subject which would be expected from a physician or an artist who undertook to treat of difficult problems in astronomy or mechanics. They are strongly suggestive of the good Dr. Goldsmith and his 'Animated Nature.' Once or twice I have had occasion to follow these authorities, — authors of standard historical works, — and in so doing have familiarized myself with the topography of the scenes they described, and worked down, as best I could, into the characters of those in command, and what are known as the 'original sources' of information as to their plans and the course of operations. The result has uniformly been a distinct accession of historical scepticism."[1]

I come now to the true occasion of my being here to-day. Having a year ago passed this general censure upon "bookish theoricks," I happily bethought me of a friend of a lifetime to whom it was possible what I had said might be assumed to apply. I refer to the late John Codman Ropes. I therefore added this qualifying sentence, and I now greatly rejoice that it occurred to me so to do ; for Mr. Ropes was present when I spoke the words I have quoted, having done me the compliment that day to leave his office that he might listen to me. The qualifying sentence was as follows: —

"That among men of the closet and the historical laboratory are to be found military students of profound, detailed knowledge and great critical acumen, no one would dispute; least of all we, with at least one brilliant and recognized exemplar in our own ranks, — a man who never saw an army in movement or a stricken field, and yet whom I once heard referred to by one who had borne a part in fifty fights, the general then commanding our army, as the first among living military critics."

The hearty applause with which the audience received these words showed that the allusion was under stood, and Mr. Kopes did not fail, later on, to express the gratification the incident afforded him. Not yet a month ago, at midnight on the 29th-30th of November last, he died. As I have already said, the friendship which existed between us was almost life long. Nearly fifty years ago we were students together at Harvard, though not classmates, and my intimacy with him and my feeling of high regard for him had increased with each passing year. In my existence his death has left a void not to be filled. That is a small matter and personal only ; but, so far as the study of military history is concerned, especially in connection with our Civil War, the loss occasioned by his death is scarcely less great. The work Mr. Ropes was engaged on must remain un finished; for the second of his four volumes was published less than a year ago, and of the third volume the beginning only had been prepared. He had brought down his narrative to the battle of Fredericksburg on one side and that of Murfreesboro on the other, following, as he did, the large strategic lines of the conflict only, and paying little attention to those minor operations, almost innumerable, which did not greatly affect the grand result. It was General Schofield, then commanding the armies of the United States, who, in a conversation I had with him more than ten years ago, referred to Mr. Kopes in the language I have quoted, as the first of living military critics. And now, standing here among historical writers, scholars and investigators, speaking over the scarcely closed grave of the man, the student and the friend, I bear such witness as I may to the fact that in my judgment General Schofield in this remark was not guilty of exaggeration. And further let me add that, in my judgment also, so far as the history of the great struggle hereafter to be known as the American Confederate Rebellion is concerned, the death of Mr. Ropes, leaving his work unfinished, is to the highest class of historical research an irreparable loss. As a student of military historical problems he was, so far as my knowledge of such goes, almost unique. Combined with a sufficient literary skill, he had a grasp of the great principles of strategy which could hardly be bettered. His knowledge of tactics, and of the details of the march and of the battlefield, was of course defective. He, too, had never seen a column on the road or a battery in action. Accordingly, when it came to this portion of his subject he could not speak as a man can speak who has himself shared in the prolonged weariness of the march or the sharp stress of conflict. He knew as little of campaign variety as he did of camp tedium. As respects all these elements of warfare — and they have much to do with the evolution of military results; far more than most writers are apt to realize — he was obliged to have recourse to his imagination; and, while imagination is in good historical writing a most important factor, yet when imagination deals with topics of which the writer has had no practical experience, it is a dangerous guide. Nevertheless, allowing for these limitations under which Mr. Ropes necessarily labored, I am free to say that, in my estimation, he has contributed more than any other one writer has done, or any other one writer is likely to do, to a correct historical under standing of the great military operations and strategic results of the first two years of the Rebellion. I felt, therefore, that it would not have been well had this meeting of the American Historical Association gone by, the first held since his death, without bearing in its record something indicative of the high appreciation in which he and his work are by us held. But for that feeling I should not trespass on your patience to day. I am well aware that our president has already fittingly forestalled me in this grateful task, and that mine is but a con-current testimony on a subject concerning which little new remains to be said. That little, however, is very appropriate to my theme, for it would not be possible on this occasion to enter "A Plea for Military History," and not to feel that in doing so the name and thought of our best exponent of " military history " — he who, in fact, had with us identified himself with it — at once suggested them selves. In all that our president has said of Mr. Ropes I concur, and to it I have sought to add what I might.

Having thus rendered my tribute, I recur to my allotted theme, and I propose to illustrate the criticism I last spring ventured upon by references to a few of the great military operations which have left distinct marks upon American history ; and, in so doing, I shall en-deavor to point out how inadequately they have been treated, having, as a rule, been treated by investigators who failed to combine technical know ledge and a professional experience with literary skill. Indeed, among writers who have undertaken to deal with problems of this class we number in the whole record of the United States, so far as I know, but one striking instance to whom this criticism plainly fails to apply, and that exceptional instance is outside the field of military operations. Captain Mahan has recently shown us what naval history becomes when handled by one who had himself sailed the ocean and had thoroughly familiarized himself with maritime conditions. In this I think all will agree. His work constitutes, indeed, a veritable addition to naval historical lore. It marks a new departure ; and it does so for the simple reason that he did combine the two qualities I have referred to, — literary skill with professional knowledge. I think it hardly less safe to say that, so far as strictly military operations are concerned, no similar American writer has yet come for ward. These operations, past and present, recent and remote, have been very copiously described and almost lovingly, as altogether too patriotically, dwelt upon ; they have been analyzed on paper, and fought over in print more than enough, but it has been either by military men who failed to possess Captain Mahan's literary gift, or by literary men who had not shared in his professional work. The result, except in the case of Mr. Kopes, has been an inadequate and more or less unsatisfactory treatment, and even his conclusions are to a degree affected by his lack of that personal observation and familiarity bred of contact which was an essential element in the success of Captain Mahan. As Gibbon, referring to his own experience, observed in a well-remembered passage of his autobiography, "The captain of the Hampshire Grenadiers has not been useless to the historian of the Roman Empire."

Coming to my first illustration, I propose to submit a few words concerning what was the most memorable incident in American military annals prior to the struggle we know as the Revolution, more properly called the War of American Independence. I refer, of course, to Wolfe's capture of Quebec. It is not too much to say that the fall of Quebec led to results which have affected the whole subsequent history of the American continent and of civilization. Though not included in his selection by Professor Creasey, the short struggle on the Plains of Abraham must, therefore, unquestionably be classed among the decisive battles of the world.

In common with every boy who was taught in an American school during the first half of the century, the story of Wolfe's victory and death had been familiar to me from childhood. None the less, though I believe I have been in every other considerable city on the North American continent, with the exception, possibly, of Vera Cruz, Quebec had until last summer unaccountably escaped me. Putting a copy of Parkman's *Montcalm and Wolfe* in my bag, I went there in September last ; and, while there, of course examined with no little interest the scene of the great exploit in that work described. The defects in Parkman's narrative, when studied on the spot, became at once apparent. Written by a scholar who spared no pains in preparation, the result yet showed on its face that it was the work of one who had never him self participated in military operations. It was deficient in precision; inferences were not drawn; technical expressions were incorrectly used; it lacked firmness of touch.

I was, in the first place, much surprised on examining the ground over which Wolfe's force reached the Plains of Abraham. All my preconceptions, derived from tradition and confirmed by Parkman's narrative, were at variance with the actual topography. From the descriptions, I had assumed that the path by which Wolfe's forces made their ascent was narrow and very steep, winding along the face of the cliff, and one by which men could go up only in single file, or at most by twos; or, as I have seen it described within a few days in the report of a discourse delivered here in Boston, it was an " ascent up precipitous cliffs, by means of overhanging boughs and projecting crags."[2] On examination, I found it quite another thing. In 1759 the legendary "narrow path" must have been, as it now is, up an acclivity, steep, it is true, but not difficult, and nowhere narrow. A somewhat precipitous gorge, it then was, as it still is, wide and well wooded, — a bit of rough hillside breaking a palisade, up which any group of athletic young men could in ten minutes easily clamber. Especially would this be true of Scotch Highlanders, of whom Wolfe's command was largely made up.

It is here, and in connection with this legendary scaling of the heights, that the technical deficiencies of Parkman's narrative become apparent. Though he had himself, unquestionably, time and again gone over the ground, yet his account fails, as that of no trained military historian would have failed, to give the exact time of the ascent. His narrative is indeed on this important point exasperatingly vague. He says: "Towards two o'clock the boats cast off and fell down with the current." He then adds that "for full two hours the procession of boats steered silently down the St. Lawrence." It must, therefore, have been four o'clock in the morning when the landing was effected, and a small scaling party climbed the heights, "closely followed by a much larger party." Meeting with no resistance, those in the advance, the escaladers, surprised, and captured or routed, a small French out post at the head of the ravine. Its commanding officer was in bed, and, wounded while trying to escape, was taken prisoner. The shots and shouts of those composing the scaling party notified their comrades below of their success, and the advance of the main body was at once ordered. Apparently this could not have really begun until 4.30 at least; and yet before 6 o'clock 5000 men were in line of battle on the Plains of

Abraham. Before 9 o'clock, more over, they had also hauled up by hand at least two pieces of artillery, besides more or less camp equipage. These facts speak for themselves. Any one who has ever participated in military movements knows that for 5000 men, carrying their arms, ammunition, knap sacks and rations, to scale a steep ascent of at least half a mile in the short space of ninety minutes, they must have been able to swarm up, not in file, nor by twos and threes, but in a tolerably solid mass. No one, viewing the locality, would seek to detract from Wolfe's achievement, — daring in conception, it was firmly executed. Throughout, it showed the hand of a true soldier.[3] But that is not in question. The point is that it was a boldly desperate, rather than a physically difficult, undertaking. Like the night as sault of any place rendered by nature or art hard of access, the success of the attempt was purely a matter of surprise and defence; and at Quebec, the surprise of the defenders being perfect, the ascent presented no great obstacle. It was neither narrow nor precipitous, as was proved by the fact that within two hours artillery and munitions were dragged up, following 5000 men. Provided, therefore, the much discussed gorge was undefended, as was the case, Wolfe's famous escalade was a by no means unprecedented military operation. Even had the gorge been defended, and by a fairly adequate force, the very steepness of the ascent, as any experienced military authority would appreciate, and as we repeatedly found in our Civil War, would have enabled those composing the attacking party to scale the cliff with no great degree of personal danger. The enemy from far above would almost inevitably have fired over the heads of their assailants. In such case, the resistance to be effective must be determined and by an adequate force; a force, moreover, which does not await attack at the summit, but stubbornly contests every foot of ground from bottom to top.

Having now got Wolfe, with 5000 men in battle array, upon the Plains of Abraham, only ninety minutes after leaving their boats, the thing which next bewildered me was why Montcalm played into his opponent's hands as he did, by hastily attacking him the next morning, — risking the fate of Quebec and of Canada, not upon the result of protracted military operations, but on the cast of sudden battle. What in Montcalm's mind led to this decision ? Here again the judgment of the skilful military historian would be of great value. On the face of things, I was unable, as I stood on the Plains of Abraham, to see how Wolfe had greatly bettered his situation by getting there instead of remaining in his camp on the other side of the river, provided always his opponent availed himself to the uttermost of his advantages. The escalade was effected on the morning of September 13. Three days before, on the 10th, the uneasy British naval commanders had held a council, and decided that the lateness of the season required the fleet to leave the St. Lawrence without delay. Among the experienced French authorities some would hardly allow their opponents a week longer of campaigning weather, while Montcalm conceded them only a month. It was merely a question of a few days more or a few days less, and the French could count on the Cana dian winter as a grim and irresistible ally, just as surely as did the Russians half a century later. As a matter of fact, the British fleet, delaying to the last moment in view of the success of Wolfe's operations, did not leave Quebec until " it was past the middle of October," as Parkman again expresses it, about five weeks after the escalade. It was, therefore, a question of prolonging the defence that amount of time only.

When the breaking of an equinoctial day revealed Wolfe securely planted on the heights west of Quebec, the outlook for him was, con-sequently, far from clear. It is true he had with him a force of 5000 very reliable troops, drawn up within striking distance of the land-side de-fences of Quebec; but, on the other hand, provided he was not attacked by the covering army, the lateness of the season left one course, and one only, open to him. He must endeavor to storm those defences. And not only must he endeavor to storm fortifications in his front, but, in so doing, he must prepare to be attacked both on his flank and rear by an enemy who, when his detachments were all concentrated, num bered nearly double his own force, though greatly in ferior to it in fighting qualities on an open field. Thus, without any sufficient artillery, Wolfe was confronted with the difficult problem of immediately capturing a stronghold, while subject to attack by a numerous covering force, much better supplied than he with artillery. So far as I can yet see, the only thing his opponent had to do was to wait until Wolfe began his necessary assault. It would have involved for him great risk.

Under these circumstances, why did Montcalm decide to take the immediate initiative? Without artillery, without even waiting until his entire force had been concentrated, he made a noisy, futile rush at the British, as if for him there was no other course open. Yet his so doing was exactly what Wolfe must most have hoped for. The result we all know. On this most interesting point, however, Parkman is curiously vague. He is even contradictory ; thus betraying the lack of professional insight. At first he says of Montcalm, when the French commander saw the English army in line of battle behind Quebec, — "He could not choose. Fight he must, for Wolfe was now in position to cut off all his supplies" (p. 293). Leaving the imminence of winter out of consideration, this is, in a way, plausible ; but a little farther on Parkman says of Montcalm's immediate successor in command of the beaten Canadian army: — "There was no need to fight at once. . . . By a march of a few miles he could have [concentrated the covering force], and by then intrenching himself he would have placed a greatly superior force in the English rear, where his position might have been made impregnable. Here he might be easily furnished with provisions, and from hence he could readily throw men and supplies into Quebec, which the English were too few to invest" (p. 306). If this was the situation the day after Montcalm suffered defeat, why was it that officer had "no choice" but to fight at once, thirty-six hours before?

Parkman fails to tell us.

To supply the tantalizing omission, even were I competent so to do, is no part of my present plan. The omission amounts, none the less, in itself, to a "Plea for Military History;" for I submit that a trained military historian, after a careful examination of the locality and every record of the battle, could form a presumably correct estimate of the considerations which acted on Montcalm, and thus caused France the loss of the key to a continent.

Coming now to a later period and events nearer home, I propose to illustrate my thesis by a brief reference to four battles in our own history, two from the War of Independence and two from that of 1812-15, - the engagements at Bunker Hill and Long Island in the one case, and those of Bladensburg and New Orleans in the other. None of these incidents in our history have, so far as I know, been treated by any writer competent to handle them from a distinctively military point of view, as, for instance, Captain Mahan has handled the naval operations of Nelson.

Recurring to Bunker Hill, the mistakes and controversies which have arisen among historians and critics in regard to that engagement have well-nigh partaken of the ludicrous. There has, in the first place, been an almost endless discussion as to who was in command, — a discussion which would have caused no man of military training a moment's pause. It has been elaborately contended that General Putnam must have been in command, because he was the officer of the highest grade upon the ground, obviously outranking Colonel Prescott. The proposition is simply absurd, as being contrary to the first and elementary principles of military subordination. General Putnam was, it is true, on the ground ; but he was on the ground as an officer having a Connecticut commission only, and in command of a detachment from that province. He held no commission from Massachusetts, much less any Continental commission. Colonel Prescott, commanding a Massachusetts regiment, had received his orders from his military superior, Major-General Ward, an officer also in the Massachusetts service. Ward thus was Prescott's superior officer ; Putnam was not. During the operations which ensued, it was open for Putnam to make to Prescott any suggestion he saw fit ; and Prescott, acting always on his own responsibility, might give to such suggestions the degree of weight he deemed proper; but he could report only to his superior in the same service as himself, — his military commander. Prescott, therefore, showed perfectly well that he knew what he was about when he offered the command to Warren, who had been com missioned by the Massachusetts authorities as a major general, when Warren appeared upon the field. Warren, very properly, declined the command, remaining purely as a volunteer. But, so far as Putnam was concerned, he was in command merely of such Connecticut troops as were cooperating with the Massachusetts detachment; and for a Massachusetts officer to have received an order as such from him would have subjected that officer to a court-martial. All this is elementary, — the very alphabet of the military organization, — and yet the lay historians who have written upon that battle have contended over the question for years.

The extraordinarily bad tactics of both sides in the affair of Bunker Hill I have dealt with elsewhere,[4] — the opportunity which the British lost, the accidental advantage which the Americans gained. Luck, combined with good marksmanship, on the one side, and blundering, bull-headed persistence on the other, were the predominating elements of the occasion; and to those features of it the historians have given scant consideration. The cause of American independence owed much that day to Yankee pluck and straight shooting; but more yet to genuine British bulldog stupidity. The race learns slowly. Its representatives then did just what they have recently attempted in South Africa.

Nevertheless, the effect of the battle of Bunker Hill upon that on Long Island fourteen months later is, from a military point of view, interesting and very worthy of study. It is not too much to say that the experience of the earlier absolutely changed the fate of the subsequent day; and, on the 17th of June, 1775, Colonel Prescott not only saved from destruction General Washington and the American army on the 27th of August, 1776, but he saved the cause of American independence itself. Sir William Howe commanded at Bunker Hill; he also commanded at Long Island. Upon the latter field of operations his movements, though slow, were skilfully planned and well carried out. For a wonder, he had recourse to a flanking movement, which was successfully executed by Clinton; and, as the result of it, Howe found himself in the early hours of that August day in an admirable position to deliver an assault, with the chances at least four out of five in his favor. But the bloody experience at Bunker Hill was fresh in his mind ; and so, having his enemy completely in his grasp, he hesitated. He allowed his opponent to elude him; and that opponent chanced to be Washington.

When, some years ago, I had occasion to make a study of operations about New York in August, 1776, I was amazed at the mistakes, from a military point of view, of which Washington was then guilty. Even more amazing, however, was the partisanship of the American historians. In their unwillingness to see any blemish in the career of Washington, their narratives amounted to little less than a falsification of history, — a literary misdemeanor, not to say crime, for which the only plea in justification possible for them to enter would be lack of technical knowledge. Suppressing incontrovertible facts, they gave credence to absurd stories. So much was I at the time surprised at the conclusions to which I found myself compelled that I took my narrative in the manuscript to Mr. Ropes, told him of my perplexity, and asked him to read my paper and give me the benefit of an outspoken criticism. I found him singularly well informed on the subject in a general way, and he readily assumed the task. A few days later he returned me my manuscript with an emphatic written indorsement of the conclusions I had reached. Subsequently the paper was printed in the *American Historical Review*[5] and may there be consulted.

Time and space do not permit of my now entering again upon this subject, nor would it be worth your or my while were I so to do. Suffice it to say that during the latter part of August, 1776, Washington appears to have disregarded almost every known principle of strategy or rule of tactics, some of them in a way almost grotesque. For instance, while lying on Long and Manhattan islands awaiting the sluggish movements of Howe, a body of Connecticut cavalry appeared, volunteering their services. Substantial, well-mounted men, they were some 400 in number. Washington declined to accept their services as mounted men, on the extraordinary ground that operations being then conducted on islands, there could be no occasion for cavalry. Men, however, were greatly needed, and he suggested that members of the troop should send back their horses, and agree to serve as infantry. When they declined so to do, he roughly dismissed them. In reaching this decision it is not too much to say that Washington betrayed a truly singular ignorance of what cannot be regarded otherwise than as the elementary principles of military movements. It was true the operations then in hand were necessarily conducted on islands; but, as it subsequently appeared, the American army did not have the necessary mounted men to do orderly and courier duty. More than that, the disaster of the 27th of August on Long Island, involving, as it did, the needless destruction of the very flower of the American army, was wholly due to the lack of a small mounted force. There were on that occasion three roads which led from Gravesend, whence the British began their movement, to Brooklyn, where Washington was in trenched. We will call these the eastern, the middle, and the western roads. Of these three roads, two, the western and the middle, the Americans had occupied in force. The eastern road they wholly neglected. It was assumed, apparently, that the enemy would never go so far out of the direct way. There is unquestionably a well-developed propensity in British commanders to butt their own heads and those of their soldiers directly against any obstacle their enemies may see fit to put in their front. They can generally be counted on so to do. Unfortunately for the American army, it so chanced, as I have already said, that for once a flanking movement suggested itself to some one in the British army at Gravesend, probably not Sir William Howe. Accordingly, having reconnoitred their front, a British division, under the command of Clinton, made a night move on Brooklyn by the easternmost of the three roads. That road, under any known rules of warfare, even the most elementary, should have been picketed, and watched by a mounted patrol. Twenty-five men would have sufficed ; fifty would have been ample. Four hundred men could have picketed the whole of Washington's front, and, holding the enemy in check, have given ample notice of his approach. To neglect such an obvious precaution was so unpardonable as not to admit of explanation. As a matter of fact, the road in question was left not only uncovered, but it was not even observed. The American army had no cavalry, its commander having sent the mounted men offered him home on the curiously suggestive ground that they could be of no possible service, as on islands "horses cannot be brought into action." By this unconsciously innocent remark the trained military expert learns that, at the time it was made, Washing ton had no conception of the duties and functions of a mounted force in connection with any extended military operations; and, accordingly, the fact, not otherwise comprehensible, is explained that during the short summer night of August 26-27, 1776, Clinton moved forward not only unopposed but actually un observed, until, in the early morning, he had got him self between the defences at Brooklyn and the right wing of Washington's army under Stirling and Sullivan, thrown forward to cover the western and the middle roads. As a result, that whole wing of the army, its flower, was crushed between Howe, advancing directly from Gravesend, and Clinton, who, by a slightly circuitous night march to the eastward, had got in its rear. The disaster was, as I have said, wholly due to the lack of cavalry on Long Island, and a consequent defective outpost service. Yet these facts, so pregnant with both inferences and consequences, are not even alluded to by any general historian of the operations. The writers of so-called history did not in their turn realize the functions of cavalry in warfare, or observe that the American army in and before New York had no mounted service, or why it had none. The disaster of August 27 on Long Island just failed to bring irretrievable ruin on the cause of American independence. Even as it was, gravely compromising Washington, its influence was perceptible on the whole course of military operations during the succeeding three years. To Washington it was a lesson from which he learned much. Thence forth he adopted Fabian tactics.

Turning now to the war of 1812-15, the influence of the battle of Bladensburg, and the consequent capture of the city of Washington, is not less apparent in the operations which resulted in the defeat of Pakenham before New Orleans and the failure of the British expedition against Louisiana than was the sharp lesson of Bunker Hill in Howe's cautious movement against the American lines at Brooklyn. The affair at Bla densburg occurred on the 24th of August ; the assault on Jackson's lines before New Orleans was delivered on the 8th of January following. Those engagements, and the tactics pursued in them, are, moreover, of peculiar interest just at this time in connection with what is taking place in South Africa. A recurrence to the events of eighty-five years ago will show how very tenacious are military traditions, with the British at least, and how racial characteristics assert them selves, no matter how much conditions change, and in spite of experience. It also, if taken in connection with the other and earlier operations I have referred to, illustrates very curiously the slight degree of reli ance which can be placed on the fundamental rules of strategy when it comes to their practical application. They are, in fact, about as dangerous to apply as they are to disregard ; for, when all is done and written, in warfare almost everything depends on the character of the man at the head — on his insight into the real facts of the situation, including the topography of the country, and the quality of the material at his command and of that opposed to him. The really great military commander, as in the case of Napoleon in his earlier days, effects his results quite as much by ignoring all recognized rules and principles as by acting in obedience to them. New Orleans was a case in point. At New Orleans, Jackson had no right to succeed ; Pakenham had no excuse for failure. The last brought defeat on his army, and lost his own life, while proceeding in the way of tradition and in obedience to accepted principles of strategy; the former achieved a brilliant success by taking risks from which any reasonably cautious commander would have recoiled.

In the first place, however, to understand the why and the wherefore of what took place at New Orleans eighty-five years ago in January, it is necessary to recall to mind what occurred at Bladensburg and in Washington eighty-five years ago last August. The general in command of the British army had been changed, for Ross was killed before Baltimore, and Pakenham, fresh from the battlefields of the Peninsula, had succeeded him; but the regiments which had simply, with a volley, a shout and a rush, walked over the American line at Bladensburg, all took part in the attempt to walk over a similar line before New Orleans. The tactics, if such they deserve to be called, were the same in each case — those of the football field. In other words, at Bladensburg the British officers, proceeding in conformity with their simple traditions and good old rules, endeavored to do, and succeeded in doing, exactly what they intended to do and failed in doing at Bunker Hill; that is, they marched directly up in front of the defending force, carried the position with little loss, routed their opponents, and then, as a matter of course in the case of Washington, captured the city those opponents were there to cover. The proceeding was perfectly simple, - very much, in fact, what we have seen recently in the Philippines, — a body of superior troops carrying by front assault weakly defended defensive points, and this with insignificant loss to themselves. At both Bladensburg and New Orleans the attempt indicated an overweening self-confidence in the attacking party, due to a dangerous contempt for their opponents. The veterans of Wellington's Peninsular campaigns had to do with raw American levies. They regarded them very much as our own volunteers have recently regarded the Filipinos.

Thus New Orleans was the sequel of Bladensburg; it goes far also to explain the recent battle on the Tugela. Thirty-four years after New Orleans, Charles James Napier, brother of the historian of the Peninsular war, writing in a reminiscent mood of the Spanish battle of Busaco, said of Pakenham, — and he and Pakenham had both been wounded at Busaco,— "Poor fellow! He was a heroic man, that Edward Pakenham, and it was a thousand pities he died in defeat; it was not his fault, that defeat." This may possibly be, and Napier was unquestionably a high authority on such a point. None the less there is a large class of military commanders commonly known in camp parlance as "butt-heads," and it is not at once apparent why Major-General Sir Edward Pakenham should not be included therein.[6] James Parton was, by birth, English, and in his life of Jack son — one of the most picturesque and vivid biographies, be it said, in the language — Parton speaks thus of Pakenham, using forty years ago language curiously applicable to operations in South Africa eighty-five years after those I am criticising:" The British service seems to develop every high and noble quality of man and soldier except generalship. Up to the hour when the British soldier holds an independent command, he is the most assured and competent of men. Give him a plain, unconditional order,— 'Go and do that! ' — and he will go and do it with a cool, self-forgetting pertinacity of daring that can scarcely be too much admired. All of the man below the eyebrows is perfect. The stout heart, the high purpose, the dextrous hand, the enduring frame, are his. But the work of a general in command demands head — a cool, calculating head, fertile in expedients ; a head that is the controlling power of the man. And this article of head, which is the rarest production of nature everywhere, is one which the brave British soldier is apt to be signally wanting in ; and never so much so as when responsibility rests upon him." For the intelligent student of military operations it is not any easier now than it was for Parton half a century ago to advance any sufficient reasons for the tactics pursued by the British commander when, on the 8th of January, 1815, he went to his own death while thrusting his storming columns against breastworks bristling with artillery and swarming with riflemen. It was simply the wanton throwing away of life to accomplish a result which could have been accomplished in another and more scientific way absolutely without loss; for New Orleans was then within the easy grasp of the British.

Had Pakenham, as he perfectly well could have done, passed a division of his army over to the western bank of the Mississippi, and then threatened New Orleans from that side of the river, operating upon Jackson's flank and rear, Jackson would have had no choice but to vacate his lines and allow New Orleans to fall. This, when too late, Jackson himself perfectly appreciated; but the British commander preferred the desperate chance of an assault. The recollection of Bladensburg lured him to destruction.

In reading the literature of that campaign, it is curious to come across the footprints of this fact. Pakenham joined the army before New Orleans on the morning of Christmas-day, 1814, only two weeks before the battle. The English had then already met with much stiffer resistance than they had anticipated, and those whom Pakenham relieved of command recognized the difficulty of the problem before them to solve. Nevertheless, as the reinforcements the new commander-in-chief brought with him stepped on shore, not a few of them expressed their fears lest they should be too late to take part in the advance, as they thought New Orleans would be captured before they could get into line. On the 7th of January, the day before the fight, as one of the Bladensburg regiments was somewhat sulkily moving to the rear for the less valued service across the river, several of its officers grumbled in passing, a new arrival wrote, that " it would be now our turn to get into New Orleans, as they had done at Washington." Among those who had been at Washington, not one had been more conspicuous than Admiral Cochrane, as, a naval officer, mounted on a brood mare, white, uneurried, with a black foal trotting by her side, he rode around personally superintending the work of destruction. And now, when the brave and unfortunate Pakenham hesitated in face of the obstacles in front of him, Cochrane, so the story goes, egged him on with a taunt, telling him, with Bladensburg fresh in mind, that " if the army could not take those mud-banks, defended by ragged militia, he would do it with 2000 sailors, armed only with cutlasses and pistols."

On the other hand, Jackson on this occasion evinced one of the highest and rarest attributes of a great commander; he read correctly the mind of his opponent — divined his course of action. The British com mander, not wholly impervious to reason, had planned a diversion to the west bank of the river, with a view to enfilading Jackson's lines, and so aiding the pro posed assault in front. As this movement assumed' shape, it naturally caused Jackson much anxiety. All depended on its magnitude. If it was the operation in chief of the British army, New Orleans could hardly be saved. Enfiladed, and threatened in his rear, Jack son must fall back. If, however, it was only a diversion in favor of a main assault planned on his front, the movement across the river might be checked, or prove immaterial. As the thing developed during the night preceding the battle, Commodore Patterson, who commanded the American naval contingent on the river, became alarmed, and hurried a despatch across to Jackson, advising him of what was taking place, and begging immediate reinforcement. At one o'clock in the morning the messenger roused Jackson from sleep, stating his errand. Jackson listened to the despatch, and at once said : — "Hurry back and tell Commodore Patterson that he is mistaken. The main attack will be on this side, and I have no men to spare. General Morgan must maintain his position at all hazards." To use a vernacular but expressive term, Jackson had "sized" Pakenham correctly, — the British commander could be depended on not to do what a true insight would have dictated, and the occasion called for. He would not throw the main body of his army across the river and move on his objective point by a practically undefended road, merely holding his enemy in check on the east bank. Had he done so, he would have acted in disregard of that first princi ple both of tactics and strategy which forbids the division of a force in presence of an enemy in such a way that the two parts are not in position to support each other ; but, not the less for that, he would have taken New Orleans. An attack in front was, on the contrary, in accordance with British military tradi tions, and the recent experience of Bladensburg. He acted, accordingly, as Jackson was satisfied he would act. In his main assault he sacrificed his army and lost his own life, sustaining an almost unexampled defeat ; while his partial movement across the river was completely successful, so far as it was pressed, opening wide the road to New Orleans. A mere diversion, or auxiliary operation, it was not persisted in, the principal attack having failed.

Possibly it might by some now be argued that, had Pakenham thus weakened his force on the east side of the river by operating, in the way suggested, on New Orleans and Jackson's flank and rear on its west side, a vigorous, fighting opponent, such as Jackson unquestionably was, might have turned the tables on him for thus violating an elementary rule of warfare — the very rule, by the way, so dangerously ignored by Washington at Brooklyn. Leaving his lines and boldly taking the aggressive, Jackson, it will then be argued, might have overwhelmed the British force in his front, thus cutting the column operating west of the river from the fleet and its base of supplies — in fact, destroying the expedition. Not improbably Pakenham argued in this way ; if he did, however, he simply demonstrated his incompetence for high command. Failing to grasp the situation, he put a wrong estimate on its conditions. It is the part of a skilful commander to know when to secure results by making exceptions to even the most general and the soundest rules. Pakenham at New Orleans had under his command a force much larger, in fact nearly double that confronting him. While, moreover, his soldiers were veterans, the Americans were hardly more than raw recruits ; but, like the Boers of to-day, they had in them good material, and were individually accustomed to handling rifles. As one of the best of Jackson's brigadiers, General Adair, afterwards expressed it, — "Our men were militia without discipline, and if once beaten, they could not be relied on again." They were, in fact, of exactly the same temper and stuff as those who were stampeded by a volley and a shout at Bladensburg; and the principle of military morale thus stated by General Adair was that learned by Washington on Long Island. Troops of a certain class, when once beaten, cannot be relied on again. They are not seasoned soldiers. The force Pakenham had under his command before New Orleans was, on the other hand, composed of seasoned soldiers of the best class. In the open field, and on anything approaching equality of position, he had absolutely nothing to fear. He might safely provoke attack ; in deed, all he ought to have asked was to tempt Jackson out from behind his breastworks on almost any terms. So fully, moreover, did he realize all this that it in spired him to his assault. It is useless, therefore, to suggest that he hesitated to divide his command, over estimating Jackson's numbers and aggressive capacity. Had he done so, he would hardly have ventured to assail Jackson in front. On the contrary, Pakenham's trouble lay not in overestimating, but in underestimating his adversary. He failed to operate on what were correct principles for the conditions which con fronted him, not because he was afraid so to do, but because he did not grasp the situation.

In case, then, dividing his command, Pakenham had thrown one half of it across the river to assail New Orleans in force, so turning Jackson's rear, and then with the other half held his position on the east bank, keeping open his communications with the British fleet, the only possible way in which Jackson could have taken advantage of the situation would have been by leaving his lines, and attacking.

Now, it so happens that resisting attack under just such circumstances is the position in which the British soldier has always developed his best staying qualities. Quebec was a case directly in point. Again, the men under Pakenham before New Orleans were even more reliable than those who only five months later at Waterloo, after the auxiliary troops had been swept from the field by the fury of the French attack, held their position from noon to a June sunset against an assaulting force of nearly twice their number commanded by the Emperor himself. Indeed, the tenacity of the English infantry under such circumstances is well known, — it is even now receiving new illustration. But concerning it there is a statement of the French marshal Bugeaud which is so curious, and which bears upon its face such evidence that it was written by a military man of practical experience, that I cannot refrain from quoting it. It is not the utterance of a " bookish theorick," but of one who knew of that whereof he spoke. Marshal Bugeaud, in making this statement, referred not to Waterloo, but to the operations in the Peninsular war, — that school in which the soldiers under Pakenham had learned their business. What he says reveals, moreover, a curious insight into the characteristics of the French and English infantry: —

"The English generally occupied well-chosen defensive positions, having a certain command, and they showed only a portion of their force. The usual artillery action first took place. Soon, in great haste, without studying the position, without taking time to examine if there were means to make a flank attack, we marched straight on, taking the bull by the horns. About one thousand yards from the English line the men became excited, spoke to one another, and hurried their march ; the column began to be a little confused.

"The English remained quite silent, with ordered arms, and from their steadiness appeared to be a long red wall. This steadiness invariably produced an effect on the young soldiers.

"Very soon we got nearer, shouting, 'Vive l'Empereur, en avant! a la bayonette!' Shakos were raised on the muzzles of the muskets; the column began to double, the ranks got into confusion, the agitation produced a tumult; shots were fired as we advanced.

"The English line remained still, silent and immovable, with ordered arms, even when we were only three hundred paces distant, and it appeared to ignore the storm about to break.

"The contrast was striking; in our inmost thoughts each felt that the enemy was a long time in firing, and that this fire, reserved for so long, would be very unpleasant when it did come. Our ardor cooled. The moral power of steadiness, which nothing shakes (even if it be only in appearance) over disorder which stupefies itself with noise, overcame our minds. At this moment of intense excitement the English wall shouldered arms, an indescribable feeling rooted many of our men to the ground — they began to fire. The enemy's steady concentrated volleys swept our ranks; decimated, we turned round, seeking to recover our equilibrium; then three deafening cheers broke the silence of our opponents ; at the third they were on us, pushing our disorganized flight. But, to our great surprise, they did not push their advantage beyond a hundred yards, retiring calmly to their lines to await a second attack."

Those thus vividly described by an hereditary race opponent, who had himself confronted them, were the identical men Jackson would have had to attack on their own ground had he found himself compelled on the 8th of January to leave his lines and assume the aggressive, as the only possible alternative to a precipitate retreat and the abandonment of New Orleans. Certainly, that day Andrew Jackson was under great obligations to Edward Pakenham.

I have referred to Washington's operations on Long Island and the short Bladensburg campaign as interesting military studies in connection with New Orleans, or as directly influencing the course of events there. But there is another and far more memorable and momentous American campaign which is deserv ing of mention in the same connection. I refer to our own army movements on the Mississippi nearly half a century later. I have in this paper contended that at New Orleans one half of the British force there assembled would have been fully equal to hold ing its own against an assault in front from any force Jackson could have brought against it. Pakenham's flank operations in front of New Orleans could, there fore, in 1815 have been conducted with quite as much safety as were those of Grant before Yicksburg in May and June, 1863. In fact, the positions in the two cases were much the same. Like Pakenham at New Orleans, Sherman, it will be remembered, before Grant's flanking operations began, assailed the works at Vicksburg in front, meeting with a disastrous repulse. Subsequently, Grant devised his brilliant, scientific movement by Grand Gulf and the Big Black, crossing the Mississippi twice and taking his opponents in the rear, exactly as Pakenham could have done from below New Orleans, though on a much larger scale and incurring far greater risks. He thus forced Pemberton to come out from behind his works, to take the chance of even tattle, in order to preserve his line of communication. He then whipped him.

And this brings us face to face with what is, after all, the fundamental condition behind all principles and theories of warfare, the individuality and tactical or strategic aptitudes — for they are very different things — of commanders. It was the Confederate general Forrest, I believe, one of the born fighters developed in our Civil War, who defined strategy as the art in warfare of "getting there first with most men." The definition is rather general; but in it there is much native shrewdness, and, moreover, it smacks strongly of practical experience. Grant illustrated its truth in one way in 1863, just as poor Pakenham illustrated its obverse in 1815. The trouble, however, with most books of so-called history is that the industrious, but, as a rule, quite inexperienced, writers thereof, fail conspicuously to get at what may be called, for want of a better term, the true inward ness of any given situation. They tell of what occurred, after a fashion; they fail to show why it occurred. The sequence is not revealed. So, where such are not written with a distinct bias of patriotism or hero worship, they are apt to repeat in a stereotyped sort of way accepted traditions or conventional theories; and when, with this, is combined a lack of familiarity and practical experience, the result is apt to be what we are very familiar with when a clergyman sets out to explain difficult problems of constitutional law, or some excellent man of affairs feels impelled to impart in some public way his views upon art.

As I have sought to show, Wolfe at Quebec, Washington on Long Island, Jackson at New Orleans, are all still interesting studies, studies than which few are more interesting. But as chance and occasion have led me to look into them, the result has been, in the first place, as I stated when I began, a distinct access of historical scepticism, followed by grave doubts as to the real value of what are known as gen eral histories, written on the plan heretofore in vogue. They fail to bear the test of rigid special analysis. Accordingly, I cannot help fancying that in some future, not now very remote, a new historical method must be developed, a method the general character of which I have this evening illustrated from a special point of view. Pursuing in other fields of knowledge the line of thought I have tried to develop in connec tion with a few familiar military episodes, the general historian on a large scale will seek to draw his narra tive not from his inner consciousness, or his assumed personal knowledge of military operations as of every thing else, or from any supposed natural aptitudes which he may infer exist in himself. On the contrary, he will turn to others, and, like some good occupant of the judicial chair, he will bring his judgment to bear, not upon the problems themselves, but upon the degree of reliability to be placed on the conclusions reached by those specially qualified for the task, who have undertaken to speak on the problems, — the laborious writers of scientific monographs. In military affairs as in others, the day of the historian of the Oliver Goldsmith type, — the facile writer who knows it all, who is at once a statesman, a diplomat, a parliamen-tarian, a lawyer, a theologian, a physician, a biologist, a mechanician, an architect, a linguist, and, though neither last nor least, a military and naval strategist, — the day of the historian of this class is practically a thing of the past; for even historical writers begin to realize that no man can be a specialist in everything; neither is it any longer given to one of finite powers to take all knowledge for his province, and to be a generalizer besides.

Notes:

1. "Historians and Historical Societies," *Proceedings of the Massachusetts Historical Society* (April, 1899), Second Series, vol. XIII. pp. 81-119.

2. "He [Wolfe] was the first to leap on shore and to scale the narrow path where no two men could go abreast. His men followed, pulling themselves to the top by the help of bushes and the crags." (Green : *A Short History of the English People*, vol. III. p. 1655.) There has been no more careful and contained British historian than J. R. Green. His name can never be mentioned otherwise than with respect. But Green had no military experience, and this quotation from his work illustrates the difficulties under which merely bookish men write. There is no reason to suppose that Wolfe " was the first to leap ashore." In practical warfare, the General in command does not act as a boatman holding a painter, or fending off with an oar. He was not the first "to scale the narrow path." There was no "narrow path," and he, very properly and in accordance with the necessities of actual field service, immediately sent a reconnoitring party up the gorge to secure the outlet at its summit. He followed, in his proper place, with the main command. The men of the main command did not " pull themselves to the top by the help of bushes and the crags," but tramped up in tolerably solid column, and deployed in the regular way when they debouched at the summit. The accounts given by Lord Mahon and in Knight's *Popular History of England* are open to similar criticisms.

3. The last word in the Quebec campaign of 1759 is to be found in the recently published volume of Colonel Townshend, *The Military Life of Field-Marshal George, First Marquess Townshend, 1724-1807* (pp. 142-251). From this it appears that the famous operation, which resulted in the fall of Quebec, was not designed by Wolfe, but was adopted by him, contrary to his own judgment, on the formal recommendation of his subordinates in command. From a purely military point of view, this should not detract from Wolfe's fame. He was then

a very sick man, probably dying; a physical wreck, in consequence of the fatigues and anxieties he had undergone. None the less, so to speak, game to the last, he, by adoption, made the plan his own, and carried it out with spirit and determination. He then had the great good fortune to be killed in the hour of victory. The problem of the Quebec campaign was, on a very small scale, the same as that which confronted Grant in his Vicksburg campaign, more than a century later. It was solved by precisely the same strategic movement. Grant's campaign was, however, of a far higher and more difficult strategic order than Wolfe's venturesome escalade.

4. *American Historical Review*, vol. I. pp. 401-413; April, 1896.

5. Vol. I. pp. 050-670; July, 1896.

6. See, also, *Proceedings of the Massachusetts Historical Society*, Second Series, vol. XIII. pp. 412-423.

4

Empire

16

The Monroe Doctrine and Mommsen's Law

Read before the American Society of International Law,
Washington, April 22, 1914.

SIXTY-EIGHT years ago the 6th of December last, J. Q. Adams, at the time serving in Congress, had occasion to meet George Bancroft, the historian, then Secretary of the Navy in the Cabinet of James K. Polk. Of what passed, Mr. Adams, after his wont, next day made a detailed diary record. In so doing he incidentally observed that the manner of the Secretary was conciliatory and apparently cordial; and then added, Mr. Bancroft "seemed anxious to know my opinion'" on the parts of the annual message of Mr. Polk, transmitted to Congress a few days previous, relating to the controversy with Great Britain over the Oregon boundary, — that known in history as the " Fifty-four Forty or Fight" message. Mr. Adams then went on as follows : — " I said that I approved entirely of Mr. Polk's repeated assertion of the principle first announced by President James Monroe in a message to Congress, that the continents of North and South America were no longer to be considered as scenes for their future European colonization. [Mr. Bancroft] said he had heard that this part of the message of

Mr. Monroe had been inserted by him at my suggestion. I told [Mr. Bancroft] that was true; that I had been authorized by [Mr. Monroe] to assert the principle in a letter of instruction to Mr. Rush, then Minister in England, and had written the paragraph in the very words inserted by Mr. Monroe in his message. It was Mr. Monroe's custom, and has been, I believe, that of all the Presidents of the United States, to prepare their annual messages, and to receive from each of the heads of Departments paragraphs ready written relating to their respective Departments, and adopt them as written, or with such modifications as the writer of the message deemed advisable. That this principle thus inserted was disagreeable to all the principle European sovereigns I well knew."

The very memorable passage in Monroe's message here referred to is familiar. It reads as follows: —

"The American continents, by the free and independent condition which they have assumed and maintain, are henceforth not to be considered as subjects for future colonization by European powers, . . . We should consider any attempt on their part to extend their system to any portion of this hemisphere as dangerous to our peace and safety. With the existing colonies or dependencies of any European power, we have not interfered and shall not interfere. But with the governments who have declared their independence, and maintained it, and whose independence we have, on great consideration, and on just principles, acknowledged, we could not view any interposition for the purpose of oppressing them, or controlling, in any other manner, their destiny, by any European power, in any other light than as the manifestation of an unfriendly disposition towards the United States"

I am here this evening scheduled to speak on the "Origin of the Monroe Doctrine" so called, and it is in that connection I quote the above passages from the "Memoirs" of J, Q. Adams, and from the 1823 message of President Monroe. Historically speaking, my understanding is that in his remarks to Secretary Bancroft, Mr. Adams only referred to the first of two distinct and widely separated passages in the message — that relating to colonization — as originating with him. The second passage bore on the aims at that time of those party to the Holy Alliance; and for this the paternity of George Canning is asserted though, as it stands in the message, it was presumably submitted, "ready written," to the President by the Secretary of State, A distinction between the two passages must, under existing conditions, be observed. As I shall presently have occasion to point out, the portion of the message of 1823 which related to colonization is now, under existing conditions, practically obsolete. It is, however, to a degree different as respects the portion relating to the independence of American nations in the sense of the popular phrase "America for the Americans." In this respect it may with a certain plausibility be claimed that the Monroe Doctrine is still alive, a sentiment the strength and vitality of which the lapse of years has not impaired.

Disposing thus of the Monroe Doctrine in both its parts, I will proceed further to premise that, as we all realize, nothing, whether in philosophy, history or law, is ever definitely settled, and every conclusion supposed to be finally arrived at is sure soon or late to be challenged. Accordingly, I want it at the outset distinctly understood that I am not now claiming for an ancestor of mine the origin of the "Doctrine" referred to. It may, I admit, as has been contended, have been developed twenty years before; nor am I prepared either to advocate or dispute cither of two later contentions, — one that his Secretary of State imposed it on a timid President, the other that a Bismarckian chief dictated it to an amazed and pallid scribe. My sole present purpose is to call attention to the fact that, as it appears in the Message of 1823, the "Doctrine" assumed shape from the pen of Mr. J. Q. Adams, then Secretary of State. Such being the case, we have a basis on which to discuss not only its origin but also its significance and intent. Knowing when it was formulated and by whom, we have to consider the environment and experiences of him who held the pen, and the objects he had in view under international conditions then prevailing.

The "Doctrine" was enunciated in the closing months of 1823. The Secretary of State, who put it in form, was then in his fifty-seventh year. Born in 1767, his earliest and strongest impressions related to personal experiences in the eventful period between 1774, when his memories began, and 1782, when, a youth, the companion of his father and the other commissioners representing the American Congress in Europe, he practically participated in the negotiation which transformed the United States from the condition of British provinces to an independent nationality. Later, he had himself come into public life during the wars of Napoleon, representing his country at various European courts, — The Hague, Berlin, St. Petersburg, and London — and, from positions of close proximity, studied anxiously the European situation as it then existed, — always with a view to American interests.

Bearing these facts in mind, it is not difficult, perhaps, to understand what J. Q. Adams was driving at when he set forth the "Doctrine." His thought naturally reverted to the conditions existing in his own country prior to and during the Revolutionary War, — that is, the "Colonial Period" and the "Provincial Status," — his mind being 'influenced and his expression colored by what he presumably had observed and gone through during a long and intimate subsequent European diplomatic experience. He was one of the very few who at that juncture understood both American conditions and European modes of thought an d procedure. Under these conditions, what must he have been aiming at when he drafted the passages submitted by him, and incorporated in President Monroe's Message of 1823? To reach a conclusion on that point, it is necessary in the first place to separate ourselves from the present' and have a clear conception of conditions then existing. It is to be remembered that in 1823 the world, just emerged from the Napoleonic wars, was still, as compared with what it now is, largely mediaeval. Napoleon, "the armed soldier of Democracy," as he has been sometimes termed in that stilted phraseology in which men so delight, had been effectually suppressed. He was extinguished; and the turn of the despots had come. The "Holy Alliance," so called, signifying the absolute suppression of popular government, was in full swing. The United States had emerged from the War of 1812 a recognized sea power; and the Spanish dependencies in America were carrying on their long struggle with the so-called "mother country" So Monroe's Secretary of

State, recalling the experiences of his early youth and the lessons he had later learned in Europe, framed the "Doctrine" as a manifesto of somewhat defiant character. Issued in the face of Europe, it was aimed at further American colonization by European powers, combined with the proposed suppression by them of the struggling Latin American nationalities. It was, so to speak, a formal notification on the part of the American Republic, designed primarily to administer a check to any colonizing intentions on the part of European powers, as colonization was understood in the period preceding the "Sphere of Influence" dispensation. Colonization, meanwhile, was in 1823 an entirely different thing from what it is now. The colony was in the European conception what it had been in the days of Athens, — a dependency and adjunct of the mother state. Going further, the Holy Alliance, *quoad* America, was a reactionary movement looking to the perpetuation of that colonial status which Mr. Adams so distinctly recalled among the memories of his childhood. Out of that status the United States had painfully struggled, and the idea of Mr. Adams was to encourage other American colonies to move along the same lines to a similar result. On the other hand, knowing little or nothing of the antecedents of those colonies and dependencies, he gravely misconceived the situation. He had his countrymen and the English-speaking communities always in mind.

Meanwhile, every single condition referred to has since ceased to exist. The character of the problem has wholly changed. In the first place, both the American continents are now occupied, and occupied by responsible and independent powers — this with the exception of certain English speaking dominions and dependencies, practically self-governing.

On the other hand, new industrial, financial, and racial movements have asserted themselves. In 1823 in this respect wholly undeveloped, the Americas, North and South, are now a favorite field for European investment. Their railroad lines, their banks, their improvements of every character, are largely held, and, in many cases, controlled and managed, in European financial circles. A tide of emigration of the most pronounced character, composed of many different currents, has developed, from every country in Europe. This, as a voluntary migration and in its present form, dates from the Irish movement which set in a score of years after the Monroe Doctrine was promulgated. The more recent movements do not need to be referred to.

It is, however, a noticeable feature in our American development that so far from bringing with them their own government, laws, and political institutions, there is no portion of the American population which would regard with so little favor the introduction of European methods or mother-country practices as emigrants to America taken as a whole. This is true of the English, the French, the German, the Italian and the Slav no less than] of the Irish. One and all, they would object even more than the stock known as "native American" to that form of colonization at which the Monroe Doctrine was aimed. The "Doctrine" as enunciated, therefore, is now obsolete. It has no apparent application to existing conditions and theories.

Moreover, it is to be remembered that it is a "Doctrine," and in no respect a natural law; and if, I next submit, there is one thing politically more dangerous than another, it is a "Doctrine" so called, misapplied, or one which, having lost its original significance, is now applied in an unintelligent way, or a "Jingo" spirit. Such a "Doctrine," degenerated into a cult or fetish, is apt to come in impact with some real underlying law of Nature and, when it does, the result is — the unexpected!

Numerous examples at once suggest themselves of these "Doctrines," hardened into accepted cults. Let one suffice. The "Balance of Power Doctrine," now a by-word, a century ago was a terrible reality. Of it John Bright — always a name to conjure with in America — has said : —

"I think I am not much mistaken in pronouncing the theory of the balance of power to be pretty nearly dead and buried. You cannot comprehend at a thought what is meant by that balance of power. If the record could be brought before you — but it is not possible to the eye of humanity to scan the scroll upon which are recorded the sufferings which the theory of the balance of power has entailed upon this country. It rises up before me when I think of it as a ghastly phantom which during one hundred and seventy years, whilst it has been worshipped in this country, has loaded the nation with debt and with taxes, has sacrificed the lives of hundreds of thousands of Englishmen, has desolated the homes of millions of families. ... I am very glad to be able to say that we may rejoice that this foul idol — fouler than any heathen tribe ever worshipped — has at last been thrown down, and that there is one superstition less which has its hold upon the minds of English statesmen and of the English people.'" Is it not barely possible that, as things are now tending, a century hence some future statesman or publicist may comment in not dissimilar terms on our Monroe Doctrine, the scope and significance of which is today, I submit, as little understood as was* the scope and significance of the "Balance of Power Doctrine" in Europe a century ago?

Returning, however, to my proper theme, the origin of the Monroe Doctrine, while to-day's existing conditions never in the remotest degree entered into the conception of the framer of that "Doctrine," and the conditions which then confronted him have since wholly disappeared — it is interesting to; consider what results he contemplated as likely to ensue at a not remote day from the position assumed. Two of those results are, I think, apparent and indisputable. I refer, of course, to results existing in his conception of the probable outcome of the future as forecast from the 1823 standpoint.

Of "Hegemony" we now hear much. As a political term it had in 1823 not come into existence. Greek in origin, even as late as 1860 it was explained in the London "Times" as leadership among states, or, as that "land of professors " phrased it, "the hegemony of the Germanic Confederation." The origin of the term must, of course, be looked for in the history of ancient Greece, where it signified the leadership of Athens on the one hand, and Sparta on the other. There can be no question that when enunciating the famous "Doctrine," Monroe's Secretary, a student of history as well as a scholarly man, had in mind a family of American States under the hegemony, or, as he would have expressed it, the leadership, of the United States; this country alone having then achieved a standing among nations, as well as independence. Using a familiar form of speech, the United States was, in Mr. Adams's mind, to be the "Big Brother" in that family circle. This fact is evidenced in the struggle over the Panama Congress, subsequently such a distinctive feature in the J. Q. Adams Administration. The scheme, as we all know, proved abortive, and subsequent experience shows clearly that neither Mr. Adams nor Mr. Clay had any realizing sense of the limitations under which, humanly speaking, hegemony was practicable. Indeed, at that time those limitations had not forced themselves on the minds of public men. Napoleon, for instance, planned that Eastern Europe, wholly irrespective of racial considerations, was to constitute a family, or circle, of kingdoms under the hegemony of France. He had not the faintest conception of a limiting law. We, a century later, after abundant lessons almost as severe as those incident to the "Balance of Power" dispensation, have had occasion to realize that hegemony, practically speaking, is only possible with communities of the same racial descent. A distinctly foreign element invariably asserts a disturbing presence. This, before his downfall. Napoleon had occasion to realize; and now the law may be studied in operation in the cases of Norway and Sweden, Holland and Belgium, Austria and Italy, Austro-Hungary, Great Britain and Ireland, and most recent of all, in that of the Balkans. It is a long record of unending discords.

Results in such cases are never satisfactory. For this reason, and under conditions now existing on the two American continents, the hegemonic application of the Monroe Doctrine is, I confidently submit, out of the question. Racial limitations bar the way. So much for hegemony, and the law of its limitation. I now pass to another law.

I will call it "Mommsen's Law," because nowhere else than in Mommsen's "History" have I seen it stated with such Germanic directness, bordering on brutality. This "Law" reads as follows: —

"By virtue of the law, that a people which has grown into a state absorbs its neighbors who are in political nonage, and a civilized people absorbs its neighbors who are in intellectual nonage, — by virtue of this law, which is as universally valid and as much a law of nature as the law of gravity, — the Italian nation (the only one in antiquity which was able to combine a superior political development and a superior civilization, though it presented the latter only in an imperfect and external manner) was entitled to reduce to subjection the Greek states of the East which were ripe for destruction, and to dispossess the peoples of lower grades of culture in the West — Libyans, Iberians, Celts, Germans — by means of its settlers; just as England with equal right has in Asia reduced to subjection a civilization of rival standing but politically impotent, and in America and Australia has marked and ennobled, and still continues to mark and ennoble, extensive barbarian countries with the impress of its nationality... It is the imperishable glory of the Roman democracy or monarchy — for the two coincide — to have correctly apprehended and vigorously realized this its highest destination.'"

Not until the framer of the Monroe Doctrine had been ten years in his grave did Mommsen lay the law down in these terms; yet Mr. Adams manifestly had its essence clearly in mind when he penned the "Doctrine " incorporated in the message of 1823. In Europe he had been a careful observer of the forcible goings-on of Napoleon — Napoleonic "Benevolent Assimilation"! He had represented this country in Russia for a number of years; and, as a reminiscence of that struggle for independence which had figured so largely in the memory of his childhood, he vividly recalled the partition of Poland. It is unnatural to assume that these memories and lessons were not uppermost in his mind when he put the Monroe Doctrine in written shape. So far as Europe and Mommsen's Law were concerned, exemplified in the case of Poland and practiced by Napoleon, he wished to lay down for America a doctrine of "hands off." And this he did.

While both "Hegemony" and "Mommsen's Law" were thus distinctly present in the enunciation of the Monroe Doctrine, the last entered into consideration only so far as Europe was concerned; and, from that point of view, the "Doctrine" served its purpose. Both Mommsen's Law and the law of hegemonic limitation are, however, still operative; nor can they be left out of consideration in any discussion of the "Doctrine" in its present possible application and practical working. The question presents itself, — Has the United States, as the original "Big Brother," and now the dominant American' world-power, taken in this matter the place of Europe? In other words, conceiving a family of American States, it is well to bear in mind that, while the Monroe Doctrine proper has become inoperative, the law of limitations in the case of "Hegemony" and "Mommsen's Law" is, and will remain, in operation. This Mr. Adams had occasion to realize in the latter years of his life, though it is questionable whether he ever appreciated the operation of the law he had vetoed as respects Europe when working to the accretion of his own country. He certainly offered all the resistance in his power to it when it presented itself under the guise of a "Reannexation of Texas," and in the name of "Manifest Destiny." Natural laws in their operation have thus a way of assuming strange names; later we meet "Mommsen's Law," rechristened as the "Ostend Manifesto," and only recently it again masqueraded as "Benevolent Assimilation." All these, however, are merely aliases; "Sphere of Influence" is the very latest. Be not in this matter deceived by forms of speech. Keep in mind the French aphorism — *Cherchez la femme!*[1]

I state these propositions in connection with my theme, the "Origin of the Monroe Doctrine." It is for others, during the discussions now begun, to refer, as Mr. Root has this evening done, to the "Doctrine" historically, to the glosses attempted on it, misconceptions which prevail concerning it, and the limitations which have developed in its operation. With these propositions I have no concern. I confine my contribution to the origin of the "Doctrine" the conditions which prevailed at the time it was enunciated, and the fact that another world has since come into existence. Furthermore, it is hardly necessary for me, addressing this particular audience, to say that I speak neither as an originator nor an advocate. I merely call attention to an alleged natural Law, propounded many years ago by an eminent publicist and historian. His statement of it may be correct, and it may be a law of universal application; possibly, on the other hand, it is a figment of Mommsen's imagination, or applicable only locally. These aspects of the case are no affair of mine. I merely quote the law as enunciated, and call attention to its possible relations with the Monroe Doctrine. I draw no inferences much less advocate or urge acceptance. I refer to this law exactly as I would refer to the law of gravity, were I here discoursing on the development of aeronautics. None the less, when the Monroe Doctrine is considered in connection with the law of hegemonic limitation and "Mommsen's Law," the apparent logic of to-day's Mexican situation[2] accentuates itself. It was, I believe Secretary Olney, who, some twenty years ago, laid down the principle that the United States is practically sovereign on this continent, and that its fiat is law upon the subject to which it confines its interposition." In other words, the United States is as respects the field in question a law unto itself. It defines the limits and character of its suzerainty. Not unnaturally the sensibilities of other members of the American family of nations were more or less disturbed by this utterance, indisputably Delphic while in no way called for by the necessities of the case in hand. However, not to be outdone, and with a view perhaps to clearing away any oracular obscurity in the previous utterance. President Roosevelt a few years later [1904] thus further expanded, while expounding, the "Doctrine": —

"It is not true that the United States feels any land hunger or entertains any projects as regards other nations of the Western Hemisphere save such as are for their welfare. All that this country desires is to see the neighboring countries stable, orderly, and prosperous. Any country whose people conduct themselves well can count upon our hearty friendship. If a nation shows that it knows how to act with reasonable efficiency and decency in social and political matters, if it keeps order and pays its obligations, it need fear no interference from the United States. Chronic wrongdoing, or an impotence which results in a general loosening of the ties of civilized society, may, in America as elsewhere, ultimately require intervention by some civilized nation, and in the Western Hemisphere, the adherence of the United States to the Monroe Doctrine may force the United States, however reluctantly, in flagrant cases of such wrongdoing or impotence, to the exercise of an international police power."

Viewed in this way, and with the law of "Hegemonic Limitation" and "Mommsen's Law," "that two handed engine at the door," is it not desirable that the still so-called "Monroe Doctrine" should at this juncture receive further and thoughtful consideration? An example of this we have had this evening in the address of Mr. Root. Freed from gloss and misconstruction, the "Doctrine" has been brought back' to a basis at least intelligible. Still, National Self-Complacency is a weakness from which even We are not altogether exempt; in certain of the Pan-American family circle "Benevolent Assimilation" may after all be looked upon as only a euphemistic form of "Nutritive Deglutition." The veil drawn aside, may not "Mommsen's Law" in all its nakedness, stand revealed? For now and here, as heretofore and elsewhere, —

"We are puppets, Man in his pride, and
Beauty fair in her flower;
Do we move ourselves, or are moved by
an unseen hand at a game
That pushes us off from the board and
others ever succeed?

. . . . . .

"For the drift of the Maker is dark an
Isis hid by the veil.
Who knows the ways of the world, how
God will bring them about?
Our planet is one, the suns are many,
the world is wide. Shall I weep if a Poland fall ? shall I
shriek if a Mexico fail?"

Notes:
1. "Search for the woman."
2. This paper was read at the first session of the Eighth Annual Meeting of the American Society of International Law, at Washington, D.C., the evening of April 22, 1914, on the previous day (Tuesday,

April 21) Vera Cruz had been occupied by the United States naval forces, acting under the order of President Wilson, issued in consequence of the Tampico incident and the consequent attitude of the Huerta Government.

17

Reflex Light From Africa

Published in *The Century*, volume 72, in 1906.

In Khartoum

Shivering in the folds of an ulster overcoat, I reached Khartoum in the early morning hours of Friday, the 10th of February, 1905. Having left our Nile steamer at Wadi-Halfa thirty hours before, we had passed two chilly, almost frosty, nights in the Nubian desert; and, about sunrise of the second morning, our train drew up on the banks of the Blue Nile, the railroad terminus. Quite naturally, the average American mind is somewhat hazy as respects the geography of interior Africa, and Khartoum is chiefly associated with vague memories of that modern knight-errant, "Chinese Gordon," and his tragic end there a score of years ago. But, for present purposes, it is sufficient to say that Khartoum is at the junction of the Blue and the White Niles, some 1750 miles from Alexandria by river, and some 1500 by river and rail, the route the traveler now takes; for the lower Nile navigation stops at the foot of the Second Cataract, at the point known as the rock of Abusir, a short distance south of Wadi-Halfa. At Wadi-Halfa, Kitchener's military railroad begins; and, traversing the frightful

441

Nubian desert 550 miles to Khartoum, cuts across the great Nile bend rendered difficult by the succession of rapids known as the Third and Fourth Cataracts. Egypt proper,—the Egypt of the Ptolemies,—ends at Phylos, just above Assuan, and at the head of the First Cataract. Then comes Nubia, and the Nubian desert while, further south is the Soudan, of which Khartoum is the capital. Further south yet is that central African district known as Uganda,—a vast interior lake region some three thousand miles from the Mediterranean. Drained by the White Nile, Uganda was first explored by Grant and Speke, and Sir Samuel and Lady Baker, during the years of our Civil War (1861-1865). In a direct north and south line, the Victoria Nyanza is almost exactly equidistant from Cairo, on the north, and from Cape Town on the south,—it is in the heart of eastern Africa. Gondokoro is the southern limit of upper Nile navigation. Some 1100 miles south of Khartoum and within 150 miles of the Albert Edward Nyanza, chief source of the White Nile, Gondokoro is almost exactly on the fifth degree north latitude. On the other hand, the tropic of Cancer passes some fifty miles only south of Assuan. The entire region between Assuan and Gondokoro,—the region now to be referred to —is, therefore, equatorial.

Coming directly to my notes of travel, and the conclusions therein drawn, I arrived, as I have said, at Khartoum, early on the morning of Friday, February 10th. Remaining there five days, until Wednesday 15th, the time was naturally spent in the usual tourist excursions, two only of which proved interesting, —that down the Blue Nile to its junction with the White Nile, and then up the latter as far as Gordon's tree, so-called; and that to the African city of Omdurman, the former capital of the Mahdi and the Califa. The first of these excursions is most inspiring; for the junction of the two Niles is impressive,—it stirs the imagination. Recalling the down-pour of the Missouri into the Mississippi,—the White Nile, broad and swift, surges forward and, crowding the Blue Nile before Omdurman over against the eastern bank, then, little by little, absorbs it. About the White Nile there is, too, something at once vast and vastly suggestive—here, nearly

2000 miles from its mouth, so great in quiet volume. One cannot resist a longing to see more of it, —in short, the ordinary tourist soon distinctly feels a touch of the fever known as "The Nile Quest."

Black Africa

As to Omdurman,[1] the morning (February 11th) spent there proved most interesting and singularly suggestive. For the first time I saw Africa,—not Egypt, but black Africa;—its streets, its habitations, its marts, its people. As an American, it then came directly home to me what those people were, and how they lived. I looked on the largest native city of a stationary, barbarous continent,—the chief commercial centre of an "inferior race," —and, comparing it with London, Paris, or New York, those material outcomes of the two species indicated the difference of their capacities. For, of course, races, like individuals of the same race, must be measured and classed by their visible output; and, as Omdurman is to London, so is the African to the Anglo-Saxon. Distinctly, the difference is too great to admit of measurement. And then comes the awful corollary—: What is the duty and what the function of the superior to the inferior race under existing conditions, and in the present advanced stage of civilization? Can we, have we a right to wrap ourselves in our somewhat Pharisaic individuality, and, taking care of ourselves, leave the less developed, or wholly undeveloped, to work out thro' force and fraud a destiny which is no destiny at all?—Unless, as in the former Soudan, an unending tale of violence and wrong be termed a destiny. But, if we have not such a right, and are under an obligation, what, I asked myself, becomes of all my philosophical theories heretofore so confidently advanced? I confess to a faltering. My morning at Omdurman, and my subsequent days in equatorial Africa, were in this respect pointedly suggestive,—indisputably educational. When thus face to face with such a problem one ponders a good deal. So far as climate was concerned, we all liked Khartoum. In the middle of the day, the sun had unmistakable power; but the nights were cool, the air dry, and an atmosphere of exhilaration pervaded the place. The hotel, close to the bank of the Blue Nile, looking to the north, while nothing to enthuse over, is good enough. In February it was crowded; in March, it was nearly empty, and shortly to close. But, generally, Khartoum proper is, in 1905, a very different place from what it was a score of years-ago in Gordon's time, and altogether unlike what Baker described in 1862. Now the winter haunt of tourists, then it was "chiefly composed of huts of unburnt bricks" extending over "a flat hardly above the level of the river at high water." Numbering some 30,000 inhabitants "densely crowded" and without drains or cesspools, its thoroughfares were necessarily redolent with inconceivable nuisances. "A more miserable, filthy and unhealthy spot," Sir Samuel Baker declared, "can hardly be imagined." It was, moreover, a human hell; for, with-out the White Nile trade it would have almost ceased to exist, "and that trade," he wrote, "is kidnapping and murder." Assuredly, even Africa does improve! Since that description was penned,—just forty years,— British rule has wrought wonders; and that rule, in its present form, dates back only to 1898. Prior to that very recent time, under the rules of the Mahdi and Califa which followed the fall of Gordon in 1885, it may well be questioned whether Khartoum's last estate was not worse than its earlier. But now, Baker's African city has been swept clean away, or relegated to the suburbs of the modern town; and Khartoum proper is a remarkably clean, well-ordered, embryotic European municipality. Its wide streets are well paved and lighted; residences and public buildings line the river front; and, at the intersection of two broad thoroughfares, immediately south of the spot where he met his death on the "palace" steps, is an imposing effigy in bronze. It is "Chinese Gordon," in easy restful attitude, sitting high on his dromedary, looking out over the desert region he sought to civilize and to rule. But, just beyond all this, not a mile away, are two native African villages,—well policed and, after a fashion, scavengered —much as Baker describes the whole place in 1863. Their inhabitants would to-morrow revert to-savagedom, murder, kidnapping and the slave trade were British rule withdrawn. As it is, however, Khartoum is the germ of a really considerable and important government and trade center of the future. The natural base from which the Nyanza upland of equatorial Africa will be developed, a great possible future lies before it: but that future is altogether dependent on the continued presence of the Anglo-Saxon.

The White Nile,—Khartoum to Taufikia and Lake No, some 550 miles,—is a magnificent river,—somewhat monotonous, but distinctly interesting. Almost absolutely without affluents, its volume when it issues from Lake No and the great papyrus swamp is half as large again as at either Omdurman or at Cairo; yet, when coming down the Blue Nile, and turning sharply to the south, you enter it at Omdurman, the White Nile is unmistekeably impressive. There is about it a surge and volume which excite a special wonder. Baker, writing in December, 1862, describes the junction of the two rivers as a vast flat as far as the eye can reach, the White Nile being about two miles broad, the banks dead level. "The Tree" which he, over forty years ago, refers to as the rendezvous for all boats when leaving for the White Nile voyage is presumably that still standing, now known as Gordon's tree,—because under it Gordon was accustomed to dis mount and sit when, by marching them out from Khartoum, he exercised his troops. Further on, Baker says he had never seen a fog in that part of Africa; and, though the neighborhood of the river was swampy, the air was clear both in the morning and evening. It is so still; and, moreover, the nights in winter are cool; nor, in spite of warning to the contrary, were we annoyed by mosquitoes. Indeed, both going up and coming down, the White Nile proper,—that is as far south as Lake No,—left a not unpleasant impression. The river as a rule is wide; the current steady. One shore at least is usually swampy ; but trees are always visible in the distance. There are numerous villages; and immense herds of cattle or goats are seen throughout. The settlements, all of the same character, are shelters of mud and reeds; but, now and again, especially on our way down, we would see a village built under great spreading trees, in the shade of which the inhabitants -idly lay during the heat of the afternoon. In the river, a hippopotamus would occasionally project his snout, and, sometimes, a whole herd would be standing in the water sunning them-selves. On the sand-banks were great flocks of water fowl of many descriptions and varied plumage, with crocodiles among them, all apparently on the friendliest terms. The country, however, does not impress the passing tourist as fertile; it is always arid and coarse. Evidently a rainless region, it nowhere invites settlement. In aspect it is distinctly monotonous and repellent,—naked barbarians occupants of a God-forsaken land! One day is a mere repetition of another,—river, shore and sky,—all in marked contrast with Egypt and the lower Nile.

In his description of the dreary region known as the Sud,—the region between Lake No and Gondokoro,— Baker refers to the natives, —and he wrote in 1863 what those who follow in the track he blazed might write to-day,—"they are something superlative in the way of sav-ages; the men as naked as they came into the world; their bodies rubbed with ashes, and their hair stained red by a plaster of ashes and cow's urine." And again he adds—"the weather to-day (Jan. 21,1863) is dull, oppressive, and dead calm. As usual, endless marshes and mosquitoes. I never either saw or heard of so disgusting a country as that bordering the White Nile from Khartoum to this point." A finer mosquito-breeding locality could not be imagined; yet they did not annoy us to any noticeable extent. They were in-disputably there; and they bothered, making a mosquito netting at nights a necessity, and mosquito-boots in the evenings very desirable; but they were neither more numerous nor more venomous than, in their season, here on the banks of Boston's Charles; and the stories heard concerning them struck us good mosquito-proof Americans as greatly exaggerated. They were mere babes and sucklings compared with the genuine Jersey breed.

But to return to Baker's narrative for one last extract he winds up by saying— "it is a heart-breaking river without a single redeeming point; I do not wonder at the failure of all expeditions in this wretched country. I could not believe that so miserable a country existed as the whole of this land. There is no game to be seen, few birds, and not even crocodiles show themselves; all the water animals are hidden in the high grass; thus there is absolutely nothing living to be seen, but day after day is passed in winding slowly through the labyrinth of endless marsh." Then referring again to the natives at the now abandoned Austrian missionary station of Kanisa, he says— "twenty or thirty of these disgusting, ash-smeared, stark-naked brutes, armed with clubs of hard wood brought to a point, were lying idly about." It was just so at the same landing place on the 27th of February, forty-two years later. The successors of those Baker saw were loitering about the wooding station, one of them a man, old-looking and emaciated, over seven feet in height,—stark naked, with a long spear in his hand,—clad all in innocence! Gondokoro also makes on the modern tourist the impression conveyed to Baker. He says of it—"it is a great improvement upon the interminable marshes; the soil is fertile, and raised about twenty feet above the river level. Distant mountains relieve the eye accustomed to the dreary flats of the White Nile." Certainly, the sight of those distant, blue foot-hills rising above the horizon to the South, is at Gondokoro a great relief. One feels that the dreary Sud has been left behind. In 1863, Gondokoro was merely a station of the ivory-traders, occupied for about two months of every year. On longer acquaintance Baker referred to it as "a perfect hell," and characterized it as "a colony of cut-throats;" but there, on the 15th of February, 1863, he ran to meet Speke and Grant, just emerging from the wilderness after their discovery of the Victoria Nyanza; and he himself was the first Englishman who, going south, had ever reached the place.

Finally, as to conclusions. During nine weeks passed in Africa, the only really suggestive experience was that obtained above the junction of the two Niles. A strong reflected light was thrown on our most perplexing home problem,—the African in America. It gave much food for thought,—first, as respects Africa; second, as respects the Negro.

Africa's Time is at Hand

Plainly, no matter what is coming to the African, Africa's time is coming. The Nile problem is in process of speedy solution; that of central and interior Africa will certainly follow hard upon it. Of the country beyond the White Nile, whether Abyssinia or that about the

Nyanzas, I know nothing; of the Nile basin I know something, not much, I admit, but a little; and the country beyond is a corollary to it. South of Khartoum,—that is up the Nile,—there is a very considerable, not, as such things go, a vast region, which if drained and then irrigated, would produce largely of cotton, sugar, rice and tobacco. It is a mere question of water in a country of unevenly distributed rainfall, —where there is any rainfall at all,—lying under a tropical sun. But it is not a country suitable for the Caucasian, —it is a country to be exploited and developed, not one to be occupied and peopled. That it will now be developed, admits of little question. The construction of the Assuan barrage, following hard on the scientific occupation of the Soudan, settles the question. There is money in it—and big money! So the work will henceforth go right along; the waters of the Nile will be economized at their sources, whether in Abyssinia or at the outlet of the Nyanzas. The gradual reclaiming and systematic irrigation of a very considerable part of the Nile basin north of Lake No will follow; and even the Sud,—that wretched, heart-rending morass,—may, not impossibly, be drained by degrees, and made habitable. Now a vast papyrus wilderness, it would then prove a great rice swamp and sugar field. So far as the natives are concerned,—what will follow? Clearly, this:—the African will at last find his place in civilization, whatever that place may prove to be. In the Soudan and Nile basin, he will not be brought, as in our Southern States, into industrial conflict with the white man. If he meets with any competitor, it will be the imported Asiatic,—the Asiatic purposely imported to do what the African will not do, or cannot so well do. The native African of the Nile basin is now a savage,—he herds cattle, and cultivates the soil to a limited extent. He is distinguished from the brute creation only by the fact of articulate speech, the use of tools and weapons of the most primitive kind, and a knowledge of the properties of fire. In such matters as clothes, food or sanitation he is in no essential respects better than various kinds of animals. A savage, he admits, like nearly all known negro savages, of an imitative domestication. Thus, in Africa, the simple question is as to how far he can be developed by external influences, and under altered conditions;

for as yet he has evinced no self-elevating capacity. If Africa proper is now to be developed, and if the laboring white man will not, because he cannot, make a home in it or in large portions of it, the field is open to the native. Can he occupy that field, and fill it; or must he, free from forced, regulated labor, languish and die out like the American aboriginal, and the Australian? A large question, it is as interesting as its answer is obscure,—as yet! Fortunately, its solution is in the best of hands —those of the British. Asiatic experience thus throws light on the African problem; and again, the problem working out in Africa is full of suggestion as respects America. One thing seems clear, without being reduced to servitude, the inferior race must be recognized as such, and, in some way, so dealt with. Facts are facts; and only confusion results when things essentially not equal are dealt with on the basis of natural equality. The world has now for some time been pondering the African problem,—pondering it in America as well as in the place of its origin;— it has been laying up a store of experiences bearing upon it,— experiences stretching through at least 2000 years. The discovery of the Nile source was delayed to our time; in its turn that discovery now bids fair to involve the future of the Negro. The wild animals of Africa are to go; will the Negro go with them? The alternative is domestication. That he will not go with the wild animal our experience shows. That he is imitative has been proven. That he can ever become, or be made self elevating in the mass remains to be shown.

The African in America

Finally, as to the African in America. What gleam of supposable light does a brief visit to the White Nile throw on our home problem? A good deal,—perhaps! In the first place, looking about me among Africans in Africa,—far removed from that American environment to which I have been accustomed,— the scales fell from my eyes. I found myself most impressed by a realizing sense of the appalling amount of error and cant in which we of the United States have indulged on this topic. We have actually wallowed in a bog of self-sufficient ignorance,—especially we philanthropists and theorists of New England. We do so still. Having eyes, we will not see. Even now we not infrequently hear the successor to the abolitionist and humanitarian of the ante-civil-war period,—the "Uncle Tom" period,—announce that the difference between the White Man and the Black Man is much less considerable than is ordinarily supposed, and that the only real obstacle in the negro's way is that—"He has never been given a chance!" For myself, after visiting the black man in his own house, I come back with a decided impression that this is the sheerest of delusions, due to pure ignorance of rudimentary facts; yet we built upon it in reconstruction days as upon a foundation-stone,— a self-evident truth! Let those who indulge in such theories go to the Soudan, and pass a week at Omdurman. That place marks in commerce, in letters and in art, in science and architecture, the highest point of development yet reached by any African race. As al-ready suggested, the difference between Omdurman and London about measures the difference between the Black and White. Indisputably great, that it admits of measurement is questionable. So far as I am advised, the Soudanese are the finest race of the whole African species. Physically, they are tall, as a whole well-formed; and, in their savage way, they are indisputably courageous. Yet in them not the slightest inherent power of development has as yet come to the surface. Baker, after living amongst them for years, calls attention to the striking elementary fact that, since the beginning of time to the day that now is, they have neither domesticated the elephant nor invented pottery. As respects pottery the Chinese, for instance, were "as civilized as they are at the present day when the English were barbarians;" the Hindoos domesticated the elephant at a period now beyond the memory of man. To-day the African uses the gourd, and kills the elephant for his ivory!

Baker was a rough, typical John Bull; and, as an authority on the subject of the negro what he wrote is very open to question. A sportsman more even than an explorer, he looked with contempt and dislike on the natives; yet he got along with them, and dominated them. He was truthful and just in his dealings with them, even if he did, when the emergency came, lash out with a strong left arm. It would be well to offset his evidence and inferences with those of Livingstone. But, when all allowances are made, there is for Americans much food for thought in Baker's conclusions. His verdict on the Soudanese was at any rate explicit,— "I believe that ten years' residence in the Soudan and this country would spoil an angel, and would turn the best heart to stone." And again—"'the apathy, indolence, dishonesty combined with dirtiness, are beyond description; and their abhorrence of anything like order increases their natural dislike to Europeans." The following we also have observed in America,— "In childhood I believe the negro to be in advance, in intellectual quickness, of the white child of a similar age, but the mind does not expand,—it promises fruit, but does not ripen; and the negro has grown in body, but not advanced in intellect." In this respect, as the individual, so is the race. "In no instance has he evinced other than a retrogression, when once freed from restraint....and his natural instincts being a love of idleness and savagedom, he will assuredly relapse into an idle or savage state, unless specially governed and forced by industry." The "restraint" in this case is not necessarily physical it may be moral: but contact with the white man is necessary to keep the negro from retrogression. He has never invented anything—not letters, nor numbers, nor tools, nor harmony, nor arts, nor architecture; nor has he voluntarily adopted anything, except rum and® fire-arms. He taught himself to handle implements and weapons, both of the rudest and most elementary kind; and he can talk. There his development stops. In architecture, he has not progressed beyond the cave, the hovel and the nest. In letters he has not devised a symbol for a sound. In science, his digits rep-resent the sum total of his capacity for computation. Art, poetry, music, —it is the same old story! Religion, law, medicine—to-day the natives of Uganda are perishing by thousands from a strange epidemic known as the "sleeping sickness." The prevailing scientific

conviction is that it is caused by a poisonous insect of the mosquito species, to whose attacks the negro is peculiarly exposed from the fact that, unlike the Hindoo, for example, he has not yet got so far as to invent garments, and cover his nakedness. And the worst of it is that, being thus, he is stationary. The instinct as well as the desire for development is lacking. Such being the indisputable fact, Baker, writing in 1865, closes his long enumeration of conditions with a startling corollary—"So long as it is generally considered that the negro and the white man are to be governed by the same laws and guided by the same management, so long will the former remain a thorn in the side of every community to which he may unhappily belong."

If true, this strikes at the very root of our American polity,—the equality of man before the law. We cannot conform to it. If the fact must be conceded,—so much the worse for the fact! By all good Americans at least, the theory will none the less be maintained, the principle confidently asserted! We are thus confronted by a condition. The existence of an uneradicable and insurmountable race difference is indisputable. The white man and the black man cannot flourish together, the latter being considerable in number, under the same system of government. Drawing apart, they will assuredly become antagonistic. An opposite theory can be maintained, and will work with more or less friction where the white greatly dominates, and the black element is a negligible quantity; when, however, the black predominates, the theory breaks down, and some practical solution is reached not in conformity with it. As Hamlet was led to observe in a quite different connection,— "This was sometime a paradox, but now the time gives it proof."

What, then, is to be our American outcome? The negro squats at our hearth-stone;—we can neither assimilate nor expel him. The situation in Egypt is comparatively simple. The country will be developed by European money and brain; and the African will find his natural place in the outcome. Facts will be recognized, and a polity adopted in harmony with them. Will the results reached there react on us in America?— Who now can say? The problem is intricate. Meanwhile one thing is clear:—the work done by those who were in political control at the close of our Civil War was work done in utter ignorance of ethno-logic law and total disregard of unalterable fact. Starting the movement wrong, it will be yet productive of incalculable injury to us.

The Negro, after emancipation, should have been dealt with, not as a political equal, much less forced into a position of superiority; he should have been treated as a ward and de-pendent,—firmly, but in a spirit of kindness and absolute justice. Practically impossible as a policy then, this is not less so now. At best, it is something which can only be slowly and tentatively approximated. Nevertheless, it is not easy for one at all observant to come back from Egypt and the Soudan without a strong suspicion that we will in America make small progress to-wards a solution of our race problem until we approach it in less of a theoretic and humanitarian, and more of a scientific, spirit. [Equality results not from law, but exists because things are in essentials like; and a political system which works admirably when applied to homogeneous equals results only in chaos when generalized into a nostrum to be administered universally. It has been markedly so of late with us.

San Domingo and Egypt - A Suggestive Parallel

Getting back to Cairo at the close of March, after six weeks of exemption from letters, newspapers or telegrams, almost the first American tidings related to a fresh phase of this same race question,—the' San Domingo imbroglio resulting from the Roosevelt-Morales negotiation. This at once suggested a parallel—San Domingo and Egypt. It was curiously suggestive. In every essential aspect,—reckless financial mismanagement, foreign indebtedness leading to international commitments, internal misrule, instability of government, even importance through proximity to an inter-oceanic canal,—the two cases, to use the lawyer's phrase, "' went on all fours"; and, if the United States were England, the American in Egypt would have felt, and would still feel, no sort of doubt as to the course to be pursued: The United States should do with San Domingo exactly what Great Britain has done, and is now doing, with Egypt,— follow closely the precedent there set. But the United States is not Great Britain; nor, again, is Great Britain the United States. Each seems able to accomplish what the other in vain attempts. We, for instance, after one fierce, final struggle for supremacy, pacified the Confederacy in twenty years; in five centuries Great Britain has not succeeded in pacifying Ireland. Great Britain can rule and successfully develop dependencies beyond the sea, peopled by those of another race. That the United States can do so likewise, or in the same degree, is altogether questionable. If we make the attempt we will assuredly exploit them to our own advantage. That we should do so is an inevitable. corollary of the protective-tariff system,—a system now ingrained in the minds of our people and embodied in our national polity. Great Britain in Egypt bids fair, I fancy, to constitute a distinct advance both in theory and practice as respects the relations of the more developed with the less developed, or wholly stationary, races,—the naturally dominant with the naturally dependent. It is not the old, brutal, altogether unsympathetic and wholly contemptu-ous, foreign domination,—it is the "veiled protectorate," or guidance through influence; the guiding head and hand wisely contenting itself with those incidental benefits which assuredly, as naturally, must and will result from such relations scrupulously observed. It is the principle on which the United States pre-eminently should act;—but, practically, can it,—or, rather, will it so act? In his conversations with Americans, Lord Cromer does not fail distinctly to point out and emphasize that the success of the British-Egyptian system depends absolutely on three things—: (1) a sympathetic attitude, and corresponding speech, on the part of those representing the protectorate. This naturally implies the utter repudiation and forgetting of that "nigger" talk so marked and loud in the earlier Englishman in India, as now in the American in the Philippines; (2) a policy and a practice looking wholly to the good, moral and material, of the community acted upon, regardless of the interests of the alien government acting upon it; and, finally, (3) a con-tinuity of personal relations, carried on through agencies not subject to political change at home. For instance Egypt is now accustomed to Lord Cromer and Lord Cromer understands Egypt; through him and by him that can be quietly accomplished which would be met with fatal resistenge if attempted directly or through any other agency. Now, it is a patent fact,—one altogether undeniable,—that these fundamental postulates of success

are one and all either conspicuously absent from or diametrically opposed to the settled and accepted principles of our political system, —the policy of protection, and periodic, sweeping changes of administration. With us these must be accepted as postulates. Accepting them as such, it is. easy to imagine the quiet shrug of the shoulders with which Lord Cromer would remark—"Under those circumstances the less you have to do with dependencies the better!"

The Philippines

While in Cairo last April, pondering Lord Cromer's freshly uttered fundamentals, a copy of an American paper reached me, and, in it, I found a letter from Secretary Taft, dated from Washington, March 16th. Naturally it attracted notice. He therein laid down the law. He said that the policy of the present "administration is the indefinite retention of the Philippine Islands for the purpose of developing the prosperity and self-governing capacity of the Philippine people." Judged by Lord Cromer's "veiled protectorate" standard, here is a contradiction in terms;—no people on earth ever yet learned self-government through government by others. The way to teach a people, as a child, to walk, is to make it walk ; not everlastingly to hold it on its feet. There is a wide difference between this system, and that now practiced in Egypt;—it is not even a protectorate, much less "a veiled protectorate," it is a pronounced foreign domination of professed benevolence: and, the more actually benevolent such a domination is, the more destructive it becomes so far as the capacity of the dependency for self-government is concerned. That road leads direct, not to a rugged spirit of self-government, but to contentment in slavery. It is in no respect Burke's "wise and salutary neglect." Here was fallacy number one. But number two was worse; and there the cloven hoof obtruded. Secretary Taft in the letter alluded to, spoke of "the prosperity they (the Philippines) will find behind the national tariff wall!" There was the fatal weakness of the proposed policy,— the dependencies are to be exploited for our benefit, through a tariff designed first, last and all the time for the protection of American interests and industries! They, Asiatics, are to serve as consumers of American "surplus" products!— a new field for American enterprise! Thus, under our political system, the dependencies are to be held subject to a change of policy with every incoming administration, and at the mercy of the American protectionist! The Filipino producer and merchant are, for instance, shortly to find themselves entangled in the meshes of our protective coast-wise navigation laws. Such entanglement will unquestionably tend to encourage and develop American shipping interests: but, at whose cost? Is this sympathy? Is this altruism? To me, pondering imperialistic problems in Cairo, Secretary Taft's letter made further discussion useless. It was a case of Q. E. D. The British policy as seen in operation in Egypt may be,—I believe it is,—a great discovery,—a veritable advance in human polity:—but its successful prosecution is not consistent with the established fiscal policy and most pronounced political tendencies of the American people. It is fundamentally irreconcilable with religious or political proselyting, and it implies a complete renunciation of all self-protective or self-aggrandising industrial ends; moreover, it is utterly impracticable under an administration subject to continual changes of agency. Therefore, what in this line may now be practicable as well as beneficial in the case of Great Britain, is not unlikely to prove a dangerous deception with us.

To one fresh from Egypt, the San Domingo imbroglio also presents difficulties. The student of the Cromer dispensation finds himself somewhat at a loss. So far as self-government is concerned, he who has faith in the African certainly has the courage of his convictions. Left to himself, the tendency of the negro, whether in Uganda or in San Domingo, is distinctly to deterioration,—he will insensibly but assuredly relapse into his normal African conditions. The fundamental and ever-lasting principles enunciated in the Declaration may suffer, and even have to be subjected to revision and limitation; but, none the less, facts are facts, and, for his own good, and ultimate possible development, the African has got to be "restrained." But how? In this respect, the Soudan is to-day a most suggestive field for study. Until subject to British domination, the Soudan, and Uganda also, were internal hells and external nuisances; and as they then were, time out of mind they had been. One has but to read Baker's account of the conditions which prevailed in that region anterior to 1890 to appreciate the utter fallacy of the theoretical rights-of-man and philanthropical African-and-brother doctrines. In plain vernacular English, they are all "rot";—"rot" which I myself have indulged in to a considerable extent, and, in face of observable facts which would not down, have had to outgrow.

On the other hand, the domination of the inferior and stationary races, by the superior, for the mere material and selfish benefit of the latter,—as illustrated in the whole former experience of mankind,—Greek, Roman, Russian, British and American,—is not change for the better. It is one long, loud lamentation, and an ancient tale of wrong. British rule in Egypt marks at last not improbably the beginning of a new era; but of, possibly, in-calculable importance to the world, it is not likely at once to displace and replace the traditional abominations. Frankly accepted to its full extent, and subject to its necessary limitations, it might, the observer is now inclined to think, offer a solution of our much talked-of American inferior race, dependency, and, modernized, Monroe-doctrine problems. For, say what we theorists will, those problems do present practical difficulties. It is well to decry naval armaments, and the construction of great fleets of battle-ships and torpedo-boats;—but there is reason in everything: and, after all, practically, under present conditions, what is a powerful nation to do? Sudden complications will arise, and armaments can no longer be improved. Facts and conditions are not as they were. For instance, the days of the armed merchant marine are over; gone, with privateering and piracy, is the militia of the sea. It now takes at least three years to construct a modern battle-ship; and the unspeakably humiliating experience of Jefferson's policy of exactly a century ago should not be wholly for-gotten. Consequently, in the present stage of development a nation, situated even as the United States most fortunately is, must be, to a measurable extent at least, in position to protect it-self, and cause itself to be respected. The question is over the term "measurable extent";—what does the phrase mean? Dislike it as I may, and denounce it as I have and still do, there is, as Lord Cromer in a talk I had with him at Cairo pointed out, both logic and common sense in the interpretation and outcome of the much abused Monroe Doctrine now being formulated. When, as Secretary of State, J. Q. Adams more than eighty years ago first enunciated that doctrine, forcing it, as a pronunciamento, on the reluctant President whose name it bears, it was with an eye to world-conditions wholly different from those of the present time. As Disraeli coolly put it, when confronted with his own utterances of an earlier day,— "Since then a great many things have happened"; and, during the last eighty years, science has put in a good deal of work. Darwin, not less than Watts, Morse and Bessemer, has had his say; and the Book of Genesis has gone the way of the Holy Alliance and "England's wooden-walls." Steam, electricity and dynamite are now very considerable factors; in 1823 in no way did they enter intopolitical prescience, or naval and military calculations. Why shut eyes? The present is probably a period of great impending change. One after another the lesser powers are, on the international chess-board, becoming mere pawns,—negligible quantities. Among nations and with races the newly discovered law known as the survival of the fittest is working in a way not less suggestive than pitiless; and,— something will come of it! In the way of world-policing—what? In the way of armament—what? That the modern iron-clad battle-ship will at no remote day, and for much the same reason, follow the ancient mail-clad man-at-arms into innocuous desuetude is altogether probable. But how about the interim? That other and old-world powers should, under present conditions, obtain naval or military footholds on this side of the two great oceans is hardly compatible with our security. Hence, the logical extension of the Monroe Doctrine to cover the case of even coaling stations. Such, as in Asiatic waters we have recently seen, imply for modern armaments a full naval foothold. But, if we throw a shield over both American continents, so far as European nations and territorial integrity are concerned, what other obligation on us does so doing imply? Lord Cromer put it to me clearly. We have got logically, as President Roosevelt insists, to hold those we shield territorially up to a reasonable sense of their debt to civilization. So far as mere lucre is concerned, the rule of *caveat emptor* is all very well,—

well in the case of Egypt in 1882, and well in that of San Domingo in 1905. Tt should be observed and enforced. Private persons, or companies, accepting foreign franchises, or making investments in strange lands, whether in Africa or the West Indies, or in the States of the Union. do so at their own risk. If the profits of the enterprises tempt them, they must take the accompanying risks. Nations have not proved a success as bailiffs. On this head Palmerston's famous Don Pacifico *civis Romanus sum* was symbolic. The *civis Romanus* is curiously

apt to be a disappointed adventurer who knowingly made a gamblers throw. In behalf of such "Hands-Off" should be the Monroe Doctrine corollary. So far all is plain. But how about negro barbarism? After all, is San Domingo none of our business? The existence of an international nuisance in immediate proximity to one's front door, whether in Africa, or in the Caribbean sea,—or in South America, for that matter,—is something not easily, nor forever, to be ignored. It may have to be abated. Theories are all right; but facts will force themselves into the account. Egypt was a fact, and so is San Domingo; and, for us rights-of-man American theorists, the last is a somewhat awkward fact. In plain language, and as an upshot of what is now taking place, our Declaration of Independence generalities have developed, in presence of the African, unforeseen limitations; but, again, that does not imply a reversion to the old-time counter-balancing barbarisms of slavery and brutal domination. The world, after all, does progress. The record of Great Britain in Hindustan, for instance, covers three centuries; that in Egypt thirty years. Lord Clive and Lord Cromer are ear-marks of a very different kind,— typical of two periods and two systems. As for British rule in the Soudan and Uganda, it dates only from 1898. That thus far it has been one of unmixed beneficence, I bear witness.

The "Veiled Protectorate"

Impressions and conclusions derived from only two Nile winters are necessarily superficial and crude. None the less, a White Nile trip, and the hard facts of Egypt and equatorial Africa, are at just this juncture, for an American, indisputably stimulating. They make him reflect; and, as the journey drew to its close, the foregoing was written down merely to clear the writer's mind. The discussion is immensely complicated, as well as interesting. It involves all sorts and conditions of men and things,—modern military and naval development, international obligations under existing facts, theories of the rights-of-man, questions of race and ethnology, policies and contentions moral and material, above all, the great final query—What is, humanly speaking, practicable?

At this writing, with what has been done in Egypt, and is to-day doing in the Soudan and Uganda fresh in mind, the impulse is strong to a belief that, properly handled, Cuba, the Philippines and San Domingo might be utilized to establish for the United States a correct, up-to-date, dependent-people policy, and one practically workable under our system of government,—a policy of influence under the "veiled protectorate," at once sympathetic and altruistic, as contra-distinguished from a system of recognized dependencies, and foreign domination.

But in effecting our results on those lines, diplomacy and the law of moral and material gravitation, not the big stick either quiescent or flourished, must be relied on; our admiration for the man-who-does-things should be tempered by a little respect for him who is wise enough to know when and how to wait. Lord Cromer has been twenty-five years in Cairo; and, to-day, there is hardly a full British battalion in Egypt.

Cuba has been measurably thus dealtwith. The Philippines should, I now believe, from the beginning have been dealt with in this way. If so, the steps hitherto there taken cannot too soon be retraced. The pleasing but slightly childish fancy that a few generations of our rule will suffice to transform Filipinos into Yankees is not likely to bear the test. As the vernacular has it—*"it will not wash!" And for that matter no amount of "wash," or white-wash, will cause the Asiatic to change his skin any more than the leopard his spots. The Malay will to the end, and in the end, be a Malay!—and he will not shade off into a town-meeting Yankee. Why in our boundless self-complacency thus nurse unending delusions! The school-marm can do much; but she cannot make that white which Nature decreed brown or black. Foreign domination, for which the American is ill-adapted, should, then, give way to the largest practicable measure of de-pendency home-rule; dictation from with-out to a sympathetic, if alien,—and, because alien, diplomatically "veiled,"—protectorate.

San Domingo next looms on the horizon. Is San Domingo more fitted for self-government than the Philippines? But for San Domingo latter-day Egypt blazes a possible path; the path of self-government subject to foreign influence. On the other hand, it must also be conceded that in the world that now is, just as every citizen, even though he may be more or less irregular in face of money obligations, must still recognize the police power, no community can ignore the debt due from it to civilization. But, again, there is a world of difference between a modern "mandate of civilisation" and the old-time *vis major* warrant. Assuming, therefore, that the influence of the "veiled protectorate," may for all concerned most advantageously displace and replace foreign domination, the self-constituted international bailiff and policeman may, when he initiates proceedings to compel satisfaction of civilization's debt, not impossibly get, at just this juncture, quite a number of very useful hints from benighted Africa.

Notes:

1.This name is pronounced with the accent on the last syllable—Om-dur-mén. The town is only six miles from Khartoum.

18

"The Solid South" and the Afro-American Race Problem"

Delivered at the Academy of Music,
Richmond, Virginia,
October 24, 1908

It will now, in less than six months, be forty-four full years since Appomattox day, — that day when, through the action of the greatest of all modern Virginians, the War of Secession was brought to a dramatic close. Forty-four years covers the whole lifetime of one entire generation of men and a third part of that of a second generation. The man of twenty-one in 1865 is, then, a man of sixty-five now, — practically on the retired list; and, if he has during the intervening years been a good citizen he, next month, will have cast his ballot at eleven presidential elections — covering the candidates from the first election of Grant to that one who may be his choice on the 3d of November. During the present canvass we have heard almost no reference at all to the War of Secession, — the embers of the great strife have not been raked over, nor its passions and enmities stirred up into a fitful blaze. Both statesman and demagogue have left it severely alone. In fact, since 1876 and the inauguration of President Hayes, appeals of that character have ceased to be in vogue — vulgarly speaking, the "bloody shirt" long since passed away as a political emblem on either side, and to the eyes and ears of the vast majority of those who will vote at the election of Tuesday week the phrase has no significance. And yet, in spite of all this, it is a significant and curious, as well as an indisputable fact that the coming election will turn on the still living memories and traditions of the great strife, and the more vital issues which grew out of it. Proverbially, the ground swell following mighty tempests is slow in subsiding.

I have said that this was an indisputable as well as a significant and curious fact; to prove it so it is merely necessary to call a moment's attention to the attitude in the present canvass of the eleven States which once constituted the Confederacy — now what is known as the Solid South. To a large extent, by no means impossibly as a controlling factor, those States will influence the result. Assuredly, without their votes conceded to him in advance, one of the two leading candidates would simply drop out of the running; and yet those States have been, and now are, ignored as a factor in the contest. In the eyes and minds of the party managers they are a mere recognized appendage of one political party, — a species of bob, so to speak, on the tail of its kite. From the beginning of the canvass this has been apparent. It was notorious at Chicago as at Denver, and before both the nominating Conventions; it has been an accepted fact throughout the somewhat languid debate now drawing to its wearisome close. By both Democrats and Republicans the South has been looked upon as a fixed political quantity, to be weighed and treated as such — and, as such, ignored!

Obviously also this curious result is due to the fact that the South has thus become solidified in presence of an overshadowing problem affecting its very existence as a free and civilized industrial community. I refer, of course, to the great Afro-American Race Problem, — in its present form, a problem the direct outcome of the War of Secession. For reasons well understood also, this underlying motive of a Solid South — the great unsolved problem of our day and country — has not entered into the presidential debate. One candidate has altogether ignored it; the other has touched on it only in the most desultory and delicate way. Indeed, in whatever aspect viewed, it must be confessed it is somewhat dynamitic in character. For that very reason I am here to discuss it, — perhaps it would be more correct to say I am here to philosophize over it, — this evening. For one without either political connections or a possible political future, there is a certain fascination in political dynamite. President Roosevelt has declared that his "spear knows no brother"; and, to the political free lance, dynamite has no terror. The explosive cannot hurt him. And so I propose on this occasion to handle the dynamite referred to with a freedom bordering on recklessness.

But I have also this evening a long way to travel, and I must do it at the double quick if I propose to reach my destination at all. None the less I have got to begin very far back. I, a Massachusetts man, am talking in Virginia and to Virginians. An old anti-slavery man, by inheritance a believer in Emancipation under the War Power, I was through four long years of active operations an officer in the Union Army, and as such was more familiar by far with Virginia — your mountains, rivers and valleys — than I ever was, or now am, with any equal extent of country in my native New England. I have traversed the Old Dominion from the Shenandoah to the James. All this you will bear in mind, and I cannot forget it; though in passing, let me add that, having since had occasion to familiarize myself more or less with every portion of the common country from Maine to Texas and California, I hold Virginia still, as respects natural endowments, to be the garden spot of the continent. I so thought it four and forty years ago; I so think it now. It has but one "out" that I know of, — nor do I fear to name that "out,"—the unhappy presence of the African!

I propose to come to that presently. Before doing so, however, you must bear with me while I indulge in a short but very necessary historical retrospect. What is the matter with our present political situation? Why is it so involved, so confused, — in a word, so chaotic and abnormal? The answer is, I think, obvious, — it is so because of the presence of an abnormal irremovable factor which impedes and indeed prevents that freedom and fluidity of action essential to political health. That factor is the Solid South.

Lord Palmerston, as Premier of Great Britain, was wont to say that people talked of political landslides and overwhelming majorities and all that sort of thing; but, for his own part, what he liked best was a strong Government confronted by a strong Opposition. Here, tersely put, lies the whole secret of a successful parliamentary or representative government, — a vigorous Opposition facing a powerful Administration. But this is exactly what our country has not got now, has not had for thirty years, and, as I see it, is most unlikely to have just so long as there is a Solid South, the result of an abnormal political, social and industrial condition.

That it was not always so, you Virginians most of all must realize. During the whole ante-war period — the antediluvian or pre-deluge epoch, so to speak — the South and especially Virginia, acting as a rule in close combination with the Democratic Party of the North, greatly influenced, where it did not control and actually shape the national policy. You remember, and I need not recall, the constitutional, financial and industrial issues of that period, — State Rights, Strict Construction, the Tariff, the Bank, the Sub-Treasury, Texas. As respects them all, a strong Government was confronted, upon well-defined issues, by a strong and intelligent Opposition. The South, then a mighty political factor, greatly influenced results. The outcome of the War of Secession marked the change of leadership so far as the Democratic Party was concerned. It then lost its head, and except at rare intervals under the lead of two marked personalities — Samuel J. Tilden and Grover Cleveland — ceased in any proper sense to be Democratic at all; it became instead Socialistic. The South, a mere fixed party appendage, was no longer to be considered, — it had become a negligible quantity. So far as skill and sagacity, to say nothing of standard and intelligence, were concerned, I think it must be admitted the change was not for the better. In every parliamentary form of government, whether here or in Europe, what in Great Britain is sometimes known as His Majesty's Opposition is quite as essential to healthy political action as is His Majesty's Government. Without the former, if I may use a very old and threadbare simile, the Ship of State becomes a vessel with no cargo in its hold to serve as ballast, — it yaws and lurches confoundedly in its course. It is the plaything of winds and waves, and the passing fancies of the helmsman. I am not an admirer, political or otherwise, of Senator Benjamin R. Tillman of South Carolina. In every possible respect I think he compares otherwise than favorably with the great traditional Carolina figures of the earlier period — I need not name them. I recognize none the less a great deal of hard common sense, mixed with characteristic profanity, in Mr. Tillman's alleged remark to David B. Hill that, in the light of the history of the last fifty years, and since the Southern direction ceased to control, "the Democratic Party could always be relied on to make a damned fool of itself, at just the wrong time"! Think, in this respect, of its record since 1864; the War, from the Northern point of view, declared a failure in July of that year; a little later the issue of paper money in time of peace urged by it, — by the traditional hard money party; then followed in rapid succession the legal tender contention; the tariff fiasco of the second Cleveland administration; that political laughing-stock, the 16 to 1 silver craze, with its Cross of Gold interlude; and now, at last, the party of which Thomas Jefferson was the fountain head gravely proposes a national guarantee of all Bank Deposits, and the Congressional licensing of interstate commerce, with Governmental Railroad ownership in the perspective. Was there ever a political record so fatuous, so absurd, so illogical, so unhistoric! In it, the break with the past is complete. I say this too in all bitterness of spirit; for, since reconstruction days, I have belonged to the Opposition to the Republican Party, and in every presidential election since 1868 would have acted and voted with that Opposition to turn the Republicans out, if the Democratic Party would only have permitted me, as a self-respecting man, so to do. Thus, for the last forty years it has been my fate to dwell almost continually in the political woods, — pondering over the Tillman aphorism!

Such is the indisputable record; what is the prospect for the future? — "Watchman, tell us of the night, what its signs of promise are?" Poor, I must confess! So far as the party in control is concerned, I am one of the politically dissatisfied. I see little that attracts, nothing to admire in the recent conduct of affairs, — the administration program, so-called. I am an individualist— in that respect a disciple of Jefferson; but I everywhere see a tendency to collectivism. Constitutionally, I am a strict constructionist, especially since the Civil War: but I have seen the Constitution treated with ill-disguised contempt; and stretched by administrative and legislative construction until, like Falstaff's waist, it has got out of all reasonable compass. A free-trader, I have looked on at protection run mad. An economist in public expenditure, I have studied the records of billion-dollar congresses. A disbeliever in costly armaments, I have been confronted with the heaviest war budget in time of peace the world sees, or history records. A believer in minding one's own business, I have seen my country masquerading, as I consider it, in the absurd character of an imperialistic World Power. Somewhat of a student of economical and business developments, I have felt growth hampered and thwarted by spectacular performances known as trust-curbing and "trust-busting." Like every other man engaged, or even interested, in considerable business enterprises, I have been denounced, abused and despoiled. And, not unnaturally I think, I find myself neither an ardent Republican nor a devoted supporter of the present methods of administration. Tired of strenuosity, I, in fact, yearn for a period of rest. Where am I to look for it? Is it to the present candidate of the Democratic Party? The question answers itself. The chief fault Mr. Bryan has to find with Mr. Taft as his opponent is that he will not carry out to their last and logical results what are known as "the Roosevelt policies." Mr. Roosevelt even has, so the candidate of the present so-called Democracy charges, confined his activity to the levying of fines and money penalties; but he, Mr. Bryan, if elected, promises to make evident the need, not of battleships but of more and enlarged penitentiaries. Judging by his language I should infer that, under the regime he proposes to install, to be a director even in any large business undertaking will constitute prima facie evidence of states-prison criminality. A negative is in such cases proverbially hard to prove.

The simple fact is, and it may as well be blurted out, Mr. Bryan, though in many respects an estimable man, is, judged by any recognized and historical test, no Democrat at all. The writer of a communication printed a few days since in the New York Sun put the case very fairly: "Even Taft," he said, "shows himself a better Jefferson-Tilden Democrat than Bryan in regard to things to be left in control of the several States. Taft at least denies that State production implies interstate commerce. Bryan affirms it." Bryan is thus "imbued with strong government theories of so extravagant a character that even Hamilton would have disowned and doubtless would have condemned them." Mr. Bryan is not a strict constructionist; he is not a hard money man; he talks of local and State government, but when it comes to legislation he advocates, as respects money, trade and means of transportation, a system of concentrated government supervision and control such as the civilized world has not yet seen. In a word, he is a Socialist of the mild type. But the very essence of American Democracy lay in its faith in the individual; in its demand for freedom from governmental control. It is just the opposite with Mr. Bryan. He is in fact the antithesis rather than the follower of Jefferson, and, unconsciously perhaps, he is masquerading under a traditional Virginia name in garments peculiar to the Northwest. To the student of our political history he presents in so doing a somewhat odd, not to say grotesquely incongruous aspect.

But many of those who feel as I do, — made restless, terrified even, by the long continuance of one party in control of the government, — thoroughly alarmed over its tendencies, its lawlessness, as they deem it, its undeniable extravagance, its scarcely dis¬ guised subservience to the protected interests, its morbid tendency to indiscriminate meddling, its disregard of constitutional limitations and avowed disposition to centralize power and authority, its constant increase of the vast army of office holders and consequent political hangers-on and "heelers," — seeing, I say, all this — and not a count in the indictment is disputable — seeing all this, many of those who feel as I feel are hot for a change — a change of any sort. The existing state of affairs, they insist, must not be continued or perpetuated; and it will surely be perpetuated if it is much longer continued. This is plausible; but are those who argue thus perfectly sure that an ill-considered and premature change under existing conditions — especially in presence of a Solid South — is not the most assured way of renewing and perpetuating just that state of affairs of which they now complain, and those tendencies, the results of which they so fearfully apprehend? Have they wholly forgotten their own recent experience, now history? Let me remind them; and, before so doing, offer to them, free of charge, a solid hunk of political wisdom.

In that respect from experience wiser than we, the English know that few things are more disastrous to a political organization dependent on parliamentary support than for it to assume the responsibility of administration prematurely, or when as a party, from disorganization or lack of acknowledged leadership, it is not in position to carry on the government successfully. By so doing it provokes an inevitable reaction; and, when that reaction comes, it will find itself powerless to stem it. As respects the policies it has at heart, its future will then be infinitely worse than its past. It will have provoked and suffered a more or less prolonged setback. The precedents, therefore, are many in which, under such circumstances, His Majesty's Opposition, even when in position so to do, has declined to overthrow His Majesty's existing Government. Wisely, those composing it have bided their time.

The significance of this reference to a foreign experience lies in its immediate application to ourselves. I doubt if there is to-day a single Democratic or so-called Opposition member of Congress — Senate or

House — and especially not one from the South — who really in his heart believes that the Democratic Party as at present composed is even remotely in condition successfully to assume the responsibility of national administration. Made up of incongruous and manifestly discordant elements, it has no established and recognized policy, and, above all, no acknowledged leadership.

And this brings me immediately to the personal equation, — face to face with Mr. Bryan. With him I propose to deal frankly, and, as I think, fairly. That Mr. Bryan is a kindly, well-intentioned man I at once admit. He is also honest, I suppose, as this world goes; though I cannot but feel that for a really honest man, the "go-it-alone," 16 to 1 delusion of 1900 was a questionable as well as novel way of extinguishing uncomfortable money obligations. He certainly then strongly advocated a bare-faced debasement of the coinage which he now admits would have proved a blunder as well as a crime; and wholly uncalled for at that. That Mr. Bryan is possessed with a consuming desire to occupy the presidential chair is apparent; but other and far better and abler men than he have been life-long victims of the same ambition. Henry Clay, Daniel Webster, Lewis Cass, Salmon P. Chase and Winfield Scott at once suggest themselves as cases in point. But the trouble I find with Mr. Bryan, as the leader of an Opposition offering to assume the responsibilities of office, is not lack of honesty or stability of temper, —the objection I make to him lies deeper; it is that he is obviously and essentially — let me out with it — an Opportunist and a Charlatan. Look at his record! Mr. Bryan began in Congress as a tariff reformer. But what did we hear of tariff reform when twice he ran for the presidency? Not one word! After Mr. Cleveland's — the "bunco-steerer's' as he termed him — experience with that, it plainly was not a winning card. So the Opportunist let a reform of the tariff drop. In place of it, the Charlatan then took up 16 to 1, with its precious Cross of Gold. I fairly acknowledge that my gorge rises as I recall the course of events and his utterances. Then followed the absurd empty- dinner-pail campaign, with its prolonged lamentation over the hopeless case of the unemployed toiler, and the utter absurdity of expecting restored prosperity except on a "go-it-alone" silver basis; all ending in the eloquent New York City outburst, — "Great is Tammany, and Croker is its Prophet!" The occasion passed; for the "unemployed," a transformation scene ensued, — a period of high wages unparalleled in history. As a result, the Cross of Gold was relegated to the dust of that lumber-room which serves as a receptacle for over-worked political emblems. Mr. Bryan had no further use for 16 to 1; and it was distinctly impolite to allude to crosses, gold or otherwise, in his presence. Next he went to Europe, and traveled on an imperial railroad; and forthwith, the Opportunist gave way to the Charlatan, and, when he came home, the theory of National and State Railroads was paraded before the eyes of an astonished American public. That novelty failed to draw, especially in the South; so it too was speedily sent to the lumber-room, to keep company with the Cross of Gold. A good card some day, perhaps, it was not, just now, a drawing one! Then came the excess-of-prosperity crisis of 1907, and, fully equal to the occasion, the Charlatan again mounted the stage; and now he pulled out from the lumber-room the dust-covered, time-honored tariff reform, and, simultaneously, invented a new elixir of life labeled the Guaranty of Bank Deposits; and also — "Rest, rest, perturbed spirit" of Thomas Jefferson! — the National Licensing of Interstate Commerce! The world, instead of being governed too much, as your prophet so loudly proclaimed, cannot, it would appear, be governed enough. Congress, presumably, has little or nothing to do; so every branch of trade is to be scrutinized by it on a 50% basis, and any one engaged in it, not panoplied by a license fresh from Washington, is to be summarily jailed. And — tell it not in the Gath of Monticello; publish it not in the streets of this, the Virginia, Askalon — these bare-faced political heresies are all proclaimed as the accepted tenets of to-day's Jeffersonian Democracy! And you Virginians are not only asked to gulp the dose down, but — I am glad to say not without some grimacing and considerable retching — you actually propose to accomplish the feat.

However, I am asked, — what is the alternative? Mr. Taft: and Mr. Taft, I am assured, is only Mr. Roosevelt's "man"; he would go into the presidential chair pledged to carry out the policies of his predecessor. This, as an alternative, I deny. I am no prophet; but I most confidently assert that did I want to see Mr. Roosevelt and his policies back, four years hence, and securely entrenched in office, I would now elect Mr. Bryan president. Surely you have not forgotten the Cleveland experience of 1892! We of the Opposition then rejoiced over a premature victory. We turned the Republicans out. What ensued? Under the stress of the financial and commercial crisis of 1893 the Democratic Party simply dissolved. Its leader went one way — the right way; and the Northern section of the party went the other, the wrong way — and Mr. Bryan, you remember, the present leader of that section of the party, pronounced Grover Cleveland a "bunco-steerer"! Now, I, a Massachusetts man, tell you, Virginians — and in your hearts you know it to be so — Mr. Bryan is not the man to succeed Theodore Roosevelt in the presidential chair. As a political character Mr. Roosevelt is tolerably well understood. I am no supporter of his. I do not like his methods, and I think he has gone far to break down constitutional and traditional barriers which I regard as very essential to our national well-being. But uncertain, impulsive and, consequently, erratic as he unquestionably is, Mr. Roosevelt is neither a Charlatan nor an Opportunist. Strenuous — altogether, in my judgment, too strenuous — aggressive, hard-hitting and effusive, he is honest; and, while to the last degree theatrical, he is in his curious way instinctively tactful. He is also courageous in both thought and deed; altogether a masterful man. And the Opposition proposes to replace this Theodore Roosevelt with William Jennings Bryan! I do not care to follow out the comparison, but on this prediction I confidently venture. Just so sure as Bryan now replaces Roosevelt, just so sure will our experience in 1896 repeat itself in 1912. In 1896 the inevitable reaction ensued. Under the lead of Mr. McKinley the Republican ascendency was restored; and it came back, more securely entrenched in power than ever, for a period of twelve years. So Roosevelt will succeed Bryan.

From the day of his inauguration the latter will be conscious of the shadow of his predecessor creeping over the succession.

You remember what the demand was only the other day on the part of the extreme wing of the Republican Party? A stampede in favor of what was called a Second Elective Term was greatly apprehended at Chicago. An I-told-you-so cry would inevitably follow the defeat of Mr. Taft. It is, I know, the unexpected which is apt to occur; but, in my judgment, a vote for Mr. Bryan on November 3 of this year is a vote for Mr. Roosevelt, and a return to Republican administration four years hence. History will repeat itself.

The single alternative is the election of Mr. Taft. It is true that what we really need to clear the political atmosphere, — a realignment of parties on an intelligible basis of division, — we will not immediately get; as I have said already, this in my judgment we cannot hope for until we have a return to normal conditions through the break-up of the Solid South. In the election of Mr. Taft, however, a long step may well have been taken towards that most desirable result. Mr. Taft I personally do not know. I have never met him; nor, indeed, have I ever met Mr. Bryan. But, when they tell me that Mr. Taft is but the shadow of Mr. Roosevelt, —that, as President, he will be but his echo, I simply do not believe it. Indeed, I know better. Mr. Taft, if he tried, could not be the echo of Mr. Roosevelt any more than, physically, he could stand in Roosevelt's shadow. That, in the main, he will carry forward the policies generally known as those of Mr. Roosevelt, I do not question. In themselves, however, those policies — a high tariff, profuse expenditure, a large naval and military establishment, an active world-power diplomatic attitude, the centralization of power and governmental control, a rigid and somewhat inquisitorial corporate supervision, a sustained purpose to counteract the tendency to large accumulations of individual wealth, the purification of political life, — all these, I say, and many other issues of like nature closely identified in the public mind with the intense activities of Mr. Roosevelt present distinct and reasonable issues on which parties may fairly divide. In themselves, properly presented and calmly argued, they are not open to criticism. But when it comes to presentation of issues and the promoting of policies Mr. Taft has what Mr. Roosevelt distinctly has not, a legal mind, disciplined by judicial training. He may to a degree be strenuous; but he is by nature neither impulsive nor sensational. This conceded, I see no objection to him in other respects. I may not advocate all that he advocates; on many points I do disagree with him fundamentally: but the issue would in any case be fairly joined. A result would then be reached in a recognized way, and with due regard to form. Is not this all that can be asked, or even desired, under a representative government?

Let me illustrate in a concrete case, — the issue of Tariff Revision. For many years somewhat of a student of this subject, and in later life brought more than once in direct contact with our protective system — sometimes as a sufferer from it, but much more frequently as what is euphoniously called a " beneficiary " — I frankly confess myself an advocate of a pure Tariff for Revenue. I would, if I could, wholly eliminate from our schedules the protective features. I believe them to be at best unnecessary, and so undesirable; and, in many cases, pernicious — a mere cover for legalized robbery. In some cases as a "beneficiary," so-called, I know, to my great profit, this to be the case. Mr. Taft declares himself distinctly and emphatically in favor of a revision of the tariff. As a tariff- for-revenue man, do I anticipate any real reduction of the present tariff schedules in case of the election of Mr. Taft? Most certainly not. Even less should I hope for any in case of the election of Mr. Bryan. Yet I believe both Mr. Taft and Mr. Bryan would honestly strive, each in his way, to bring it about. But so did Mr. Cleveland. He proved powerless; in my belief, so will they. How will the game be worked? I will tell you; it is not hard to explain.

The tariff "beneficiaries" — and I have confessed I am one of them — are wise in their day and generation. Thoroughly familiar with their business, infinitely skilled in political and legislative methods and work, no thimble-rigger at a county fair is more plausible, or a greater proficient in the game in hand. That in the next Congress, whether Mr. Taft or Mr. Bryan is President, there will be a so-called revision of the present schedules is almost certain. Yet I state what is of common knowledge when I say it is perfectly feasible to make an ostensible average reduction of 25% in the present schedules, and yet in reality increase the actual protective burden by at least 5%. It is only necessary to strike off that excess of duty which was imposed through the different schedules when the Dingley Tariff was framed, with a view to trading thereon upon the passage of the Reciprocity Treaties then in negotiation. Those treaties have not been confirmed; and now the striking off of those excess duties, judiciously applied in way of ostensible reduction, would in no way lower the actual protective system. Meanwhile, on the other hand, a neatly arranged increase of certain schedules, as suggested by Mr. Taft, would fill out and complete the protected abominations. Here is "the little joker"; and yet, as a result of the whole, it might publicly, and most plausibly, be proclaimed that a net tariff reduction of 20% had been effected.

That the whole thing was a thimble-rigging fraud would be only too manifest to the well-informed. To the unthinking, however, a campaign pledge would have been faithfully redeemed.

Mr. Taft I believe to be a perfectly honest man; but he has already told us that he has "been advised by men who know" that a certain schedule, to wit, that on pottery, could be raised to advantage. The real facts in the case of that particular "little joker" have since been exposed; and the duty on the commodity referred to is already, it seems, fixed in the Dingley Bill of Abominations at from 55% to 60%, or "practically twice the total cost of production"; and yet, as a practical example of a measure of Tariff Reform, Mr. Taft unconsciously advises such further protection as shall be in reality prohibitive!

It was Macbeth, I believe, who, on a certain occasion, energetically exclaimed:

> "And be these juggling fiends no more believed,
> That palter with us in a double sense;

> That keep the word of promise to our ear,
> And break it to our hope."

It is small matter of surprise, therefore, that, with this card up the sleeve, the tariff "beneficiaries" evince no considerable anxiety, irrespective of who may be President; nor that the Steel men, the Wool men and the Sugar men all say, privately but with confidence, that they do not apprehend their several schedules will be affected adversely. You know their persuasiveness and their power!

Seeing the game about to be put up thus clearly, you will doubtless ask why do I, as a tariff-for-revenue man, still advocate the election of Mr. Taft. My answer is immediate and direct. I bear freshly in mind the Cleveland-Wilson experience of 1894. The burnt child fears the fire. This time I want the tariff to be revised by its proclaimed friends, and not by its enemies disguised as its friends. I want, as the outcome of it all, no premature and deceptive victory, — no Dead Sea apple in guise of another Wilson- Gorman measure. Is Bryan a stronger man than Cleveland? Is Taft equally in earnest? There was thimble-rigging done in 1896, — I, at least, do not say "bunco-steering"; if one or the other is to be practiced in 1909 I want it to be practiced by those who can be held directly responsible for the game. I can then see the way to a political issue. I do not want again to be held accountable for the "little joker." The time for a real and genuine tariff revision has not yet come; nor, in my judgment, is Mr. Bryan at all the man to achieve what Mr. Cleveland under infinitely more favorable auspices wholly failed to accomplish. So, as a tariff- reformer I say in the favorite phrase of old Cervantes — "Patience; and shuffle the cards!" and on that issue, I vote for Mr. Taft.

And now at last I come to the matter which brings me here, — the political fact of a Solid South, involving as it does the Afro- American Race Problem. I have bluntly told you that, as a mere fixed appendage to the so-called Democratic machine, the South, solid though it be, receives no consideration. It trails along in a species of servitude, the doubtful elements, the factors in the game whose support it is necessary to secure, — always at a price, — being alone considered. I have also pointed out to you that, so far at least as Virginia's traditional political theories are concerned, there is absolutely, as between you and the socialistic democracy of the Northwest, nothing in common. Yet you find yourself chained as it were to the tail-board of the prairie schooner. Why is this thus? And how long is it to continue?

The *raison d'etre* of a Solid South is not far to seek. We all are cognizant of it. It is founded in the hateful memory of what is known as the Reconstruction Period; and in a lurking apprehension of action in the shape of new force bills, or a reduction of political power under the possible operation of the Fourteenth Amendment to the Constitution. The Republican Party, it is believed, still feels a secret hankering for the Negro vote. It would, if it saw its way to so doing, convert what is now a political shadow — though a sometimes convenient convention reality — into a potent and reliable ally; and this too without regard to local consequences so far as the Southern community is concerned. The bitter memory of the period from 1865 to 1876 then recurs. The portentous Race Question looms up!

And now I come to delicate ground. I, a New Englander, a Yankee of the Yankees, an anti-slavery man from my birth, an ex-officer of the Union Army, a lineal descendant of a signer of the Declaration of Independence brought up in the faith, — I, being all this by tradition, experience and environment, am to talk to you of a problem largely in its present form the creation of those of whom I am one, and a problem which you have always with you. I propose to do so frankly and freely; though much of what I have to say will, I apprehend, grate somewhat harshly on ears at home, and, not impossibly, there elicit more than one indignant rebuke and positive denial.

Coming at once to the point, — so to speak taking the bull by the horns, — let me say that I fully concur in the remark of some observing Englishman — John Morley, I think, now Lord Morley — made a year or two ago as the result of what he saw and heard during a stay in this country. He pronounced the African Race Problem in America as being as nearly insoluble as a human problem could be. It is; and, so far as we in the United States are concerned, its insolubility rests in the fact that it offers a flat negative — gives the he direct — to a fundamental principle of our social and political life and material development. The American system, as we all know, was founded on the assumed basis of a common humanity. That is, absence of absolutely fundamental racial characteristics was accepted as an established truth. Those of all races were welcome to our shores. They came, aliens; they and their descendants would become denizens first, natives afterwards. It was a process first of assimilation, and then of absorption. On this all depended. There could be no permanent divisional lines. The theory has now plainly broken down. We are confronted by the obvious fact, as undeniable as it is hard, that the African will only partially assimilate, and that he cannot be absorbed. He remains a distinct alien element in the body politic; an element from smallness of quantity negligible in New England, but in no way negligible in the South. What is to be the outcome? What is to be done? A foreign substance, it can neither be assimilated nor thrown off.

In the North, and in the community to which I belong, a great change in opinion, and consequent feeling, on this grave problem has been steadily going on for many years. It can be traced to very remote sources, — for instance to the Bible, to the Declaration of Independence, and, not least, to the writings of Mrs. Beecher Stowe. There are still those among people I know, and with whom I come in almost daily contact, who on this issue plant themselves firmly on what Rufus Choate once referred to as the "glittering generalities" of the Declaration of Independence. Our theory, they say, was what I have stated — one of assimilation and subsequent absorption, resulting in the equality of men. That theory they believe in as of general application. If the facts are not in accord with it, well — so much the worse for the facts! They must be compelled to come into accord with it. The theory is sacred, in complete harmony with the everlasting fitness of things — as they see them! The argument is thus closed.

Such, however, is not now the trend of thought of the more judicious. They reason, and reason in constantly increasing numbers, to a very different conclusion, and a conclusion of the utmost political importance to you of the South — white or black. I have watched the change, — I have undergone it, and observed its process in myself. It is interesting. To understand it we must go back about two generations, or say sixty years, into the scriptural and, so to speak, "Uncle Tom" period. The African was then a brother, — descended from a common ancestor, — to wit, Noah. He was the offspring of Ham; we of Japhet or of Shem — which, exactly, I fail to recall. Consequently, the Hamitic man, or negro, was simply God's image carved in ebony, — only partially developed under unfavorable fortuitous circumstances; — in a word, he was a potential Yankee who had, as the expression went, "never had a chance"! Uncle Tom was then held up as individual proof of the proposition. This may then fairly be referred to as the "Uncle Tom" period of the Afro- American Race Problem. I think it was the late Robert Toombs of Georgia who emphatically declared that Uncle Tom was a wholly imaginary creation; but if such a being ever existed in the flesh, developed from the African savage, it was the strongest and most irrefutable argument in favor of American slavery that ever had been, or ever could be, advanced. A system which evolved Uncle Toms out of Congo negroes should be sacredly preserved. The missionary had never succeeded in doing it; and Liberia was a dead failure. That there was force in the contention cannot well be denied.

This was only fifty years ago; yet the discussions and contentions of that day seem now strangely remote, archaic even. There is no question, however, that, absurd as it sounds to us, the reconstruction system was step by step evolved from that as a basis. So Robert E. Lee was disfranchised; while the ballot was conferred on the freemen he had himself liberated. Further comment would be superfluous. I am glad to remember that I then separated from the Republican Party on that issue.

Meanwhile, the subtle change of thought was going slowly on. The scientific was gradually, imperceptibly, superseding the scriptural; the

Ham and Japhet, and Brotherhood of Man, theory of descent was receding, — was indeed no longer gravely advanced. Darwin's "Origin of Species" was published in 1859; his " Descent of Man" in 1871; and in the light of his researches, and the inferences necessarily drawn from them, the Afro-American Race Problem assumed a new shape. Hayti and Jamaica also have served as object lessons. The solution of the problem became in the eyes of some, and those a constantly increasing number, a far more complicated and difficult proposition. After all, the promiscuous conferring of the ballot had not solved it, — indeed, far from so doing, it had only served to complicate what before was at best terribly confused. As it now presents itself it is simply this, — to devise some practical system, other than one of slavery, whereby two races of widely different interests, attainments and ideals can live together in peace and harmony under a Republican form of government.

Thus stating the problem, at once let me say, I propose to make no attempt at its solution. In the invitation which brought me here, it is stated that "the race question has in Virginia been solved in a manner which insures the supremacy of intelligence; gives to people of all races a fair opportunity to work out their destiny upon their merits, and offers a just reward to good citizenship." These are words of cheer. That they are justified by the facts of the case, I sincerely and devoutly hope. Meanwhile, I do not for a moment profess to be informed on the subject myself, or, consequently, to be in position to express an opinion. I am not here to instruct you as to facts, as to your obligations, your good deeds, or your shortcomings. I will run no risk of still further darkening a difficult case by ignorant or ill-informed counsel; above all I submit no patented panacea, warranted to work a cure. Far too intricate and confused for me to pose as one in any way competent to deal with it, I stand abashed and silent in the awe-inspiring presence of this awful and mysterious Afro-American Sphinx. On certain points only am I clear. In the first place, I recognize the fact that forty-five years, — the full lifetime of one generation and the half of the lifetime of a second, — a period longer by five years than that assigned for the sojourn of God's chosen people in the Wilderness before Israel entered on the Promised Land, — close, I say, upon a full half century has now elapsed since Lincoln issued his epoch-marking Proclamation. The African has thus passed through his full period of probation. Already the third generation of freedmen is coming forward; and from this time on it is but reasonable to demand of those composing it that they work out their own destiny. It is for the Afro-American, as for the American descendant Of the Celt, the Slav, or the Let, to shape his own future, accepting the common lot of mankind. He must not ask to be held up, or protected from outside, in so doing.

Again, while, as I have already said, the essence of the race problem is the peaceful common occupancy of the same territory by people of two widely differing races, a certain responsibility rests on us of the North, and especially us of New England; for it does not admit of denial that the connection between the existing race problem phenomena which so perplex us and the reconstruction policies and incidents to which I have so pointedly referred is that of direct and historical sequence. In this case, while we of New England may go into court with a clear conscience as to goodness of our intentions, we do not, in view of actual results, stand there with clean hands. The reconstruction policy of 1866 we forced on the helpless States of the Confederacy was worse than a crime; it was a political blunder, as ungenerous as it was gross.

Looking, therefore, into the future, illumined by the strong searchlight of the past, of one thing only do I feel assured. The solution of this problem must be worked out in the South; and, while its solution will be attended with infinite difficulty, and loud and reiterated calls for sympathy and aid from without, I am satisfied that, in the future as in the past, any external intervention of a political character will tend only to confusion, suffering and harm. And upon this conclusion I am satisfied the mind of the North is rapidly crystallizing. Individually, and in concert among ourselves, it is, and will be, incumbent on us to do whatever we clearly see our way to do towards the uplift of the Afro-American. As political communities, however, or acting through the national government, the only wise attitude for us outsiders to assume must be one of sympathetic observation. The recent terrible experience in the Illinois Springfield should satisfy us that there is Christianizing work for us at home. So I fully concur in the conclusions of one of the most hopeful as well as thoughtful of your Southern students of this problem, expressed in a recently published volume which I devoutly wish all my Northern friends would prayerfully study. Writing in Mississippi, and from the heart of the Black Belt, Mr. Alfred Holt Stone, quoting Booker T. Washington, says: " 'My own belief is, although I have never before said so in so many words, that the time will come when the Negro in the South will be accorded all the political rights which his ability, character and material possessions entitle him to. I think, though, that the opportunity to freely exercise such political rights will not come in any large degree through outside or artificial forcing, but will be accorded to the Negro by the Southern white people themselves, and that they will protect him in the exercise of those rights.' "

Naturally, you will ask me if, in speaking thus, I speak for myself only, or as representing, or thinking that I represent, a mass of growing Northern opinion. And, in any case, what bearing has it all on the pending presidential election? My answer is direct and specific. I speak only for myself; but, none the less, I know that in so doing I voice a large and growing, and in the end most influential, public opinion. Its influence has already been felt in political action. How to promote the growth of opinion, and accelerate the action, is another matter; and that rests largely with you — your moderation, your self-restraint, your sense of justice and your spirit of what is known as fair play. My reply carries also an answer to your second question, — how what I have said bears on the pending election. It bears very closely upon it. You may not realize the fact, — I doubt if you even suspect it; but, as I see it from my point of view, Virginia to-day holds, — or rather Virginia will on Tuesday, the 3d of November, hold politically a position of great strategic importance, — as important as that held by her in 1787, or again in 1861. It rests on her now, if she sees fit so to do, to serve notice on both political parties and the country that the last movement resultant from the War of Secession, and incident to the Period of Reconstruction, has come to a close; and, consequently, that the Solid South stands dissolved, and demands full political recognition. The troubled waters have become calm. What would be the result of her so doing? It scarcely needs to be pointed out. Suppose for a moment that Virginia next Tuesday week should throw a majority vote for Mr. Taft, thus serving formal notice that she had broken the tie which bound her, in common with her Confederate sisters, to what I have referred to as the tail-board of the Democratic prairie schooner, — what, I ask, would be the immediate political result of her so doing? You yourselves know, for you are not unacquainted with the nature of our Northern politicians. But I will tell you all the same, — I will shout it, if you ask me to, from your house-tops. The immediate result would be such surprise and delight in the Republican camp that the colonels and captains, as well as the rank and file, would give you anything you asked for; while, on the other hand, in their utter dismay and confusion those of the Democratic camp would let you dictate your own terms, if only you would come back to the prairie-schooner tail-board. So far as your own local questions and interests are concerned, by regaining your independence of political action you make yourselves complete masters of the situation.

I have given you my message.

19

What Mr. Cleveland Stands For

Published in *The Forum*, Vol. 13, 1892

"How is it that you, an original member of the Republican party and an officer in the Union army all through the war of the Rebellion, -how is it that you, with this political and military record, are now a supporter of the presidential candidate of the Democratic party?" This question has recently been put to me; it is a fair question; it comes from a responsible source, and is put, not idly or out of mere curiosity, but because I am believed to be one of a class, more or less numerous, and it is assumed, correctly or otherwise, that the considerations which have influenced me have also influenced those who feel and act much as I feel and act. Though the voice of almost no one carries far amid the tumult of a presidential canvass, I propose to answer the question. But before doing so, and in order to make my answer in-telligible, it is necessary to cast a rapid glance backward.

It was in 1856, the year in which the Republican party came into existence--and in which also James Buchanan was elected President-that I cast my first vote. It is needless to say that I did not vote for Mr. Buchanan. My virgin vote was deposited for John C. Fremont, the

"Pathfinder," as we then called him. And I may add, by way of reminiscence, that since then, like most men who take an interest always and occasionally an active hand in political movements, I have experienced some disappointments, and at times felt that the bottom, so to speak, of things, if it had not actually already tumbled out, was in imminent danger of so doing. But, looking back over an interval of more than a third of a century, I am now free to say that never at any time do I remember to have experienced so bitter a sense of political disappointment and temporary discouragement as when a merciful Providence, through the result of the Pennsylvania State election of October, 1856, saved the young Republican party from the grave dis- aster of a premature success. Since that time I have cast my vote in eight presidential elections; six times for the successful candidate and twice for the candidate who failed of success. So, as an adult, I have seen nine such elections; and I have further a most vivid recollection of the two others which immediately preceded those nine.

Passing in review the whole eleven of these conflicts from the standpoint of the threshold of the twelfth, I find myself forced to the conclusion that in the course of them I have been through a great deal of most unnecessary anxiety, and witnessed the expenditure of a vast amount of energy and enthusiasm with very inadequate returns; because, though generally I have been on the winning side, and so at the moment seen my country saved from what appeared to be imminent peril, yet now, looking back over the lines of that country's development and the political battle-fields which marked and more or less deflected those lines, I really cannot help feeling that so far as the country as a whole is concerned, the grand result would in the long run have been about the same whether at any particular election, with one exception only, the party I sympathized with had won the day or whether the other party had won it. The single exception was the election of 1864, the second election of President Lincoln. That election all, I think, must agree was of vital importance; and for the obvious reason, which Lincoln himself either gave or would have given, that it was not politic to attempt to swap horses while crossing a river. The country was most undeniably then crossing a river, a river swift and dangerous, and the transfer of political power from one party to the other at that time would, so far as all human judgment can decide, have been disastrous. But with this single exception, I do not see how a different result in any one of the last eleven presidential elections could have affected the grand course of events further than slightly to hasten or retard it, or possibly to deflect it to an extent in no way material.

Thus in these days of profound peace and great material prosperity, some of us, the veterans now of many noisy but innocuous presidential conflicts and of one actual and awful war-some of us, I say, seeing the general prosperity of the country we fought to preserve, and not being able to shut our eyes to the eager patriotism of the people, no matter by what party lines they may divide themselves— seeing all this, we find it somewhat difficult to work up in ourselves the old enthusiasm, or to be very earnest partisans, or to feel that every fourth year is "the most important in the country's history." Moreover, so far as the Republican party is concerned, the party of our youth and devotion, the present battle-cries of that organization have to our ears a somewhat unfamiliar sound. It was William M. Evarts, I think, who many years ago, probably during the second administration of Grant, remarked that "the Republican party was like an army the term of enlistment of which had expired." The saying was as true as it was incisive. As I hold it, there have been only two political parties in the United States since the present National Government was organized which have left behind them the record of a great work of lasting historical importance accomplished. One of those two parties was the original Federal party, the party of Washington; the other was the original Republican party, the party of Lincoln. The Federal party organized and firmly established the Union of the States under a National Government; and the Republican party triumphantly carried that Union and that Government through the crucial stress of a great civil war. All the other parties and party conflicts of these hundred years of national history are, so far as I am competent to judge, mere matters of detail, and will prove hardly deserving of the future historian's notice.

It was to meet the issues of a great crisis then manifestly impending that the Republican party came into existence in 1856, and the young men of the North enlisted in its ranks. The mottoes inscribed on its banners were plain enough and understood by all. Neither was the work before it to do matter for much question. That work it did, and it did it completely-far more completely than it was originally proposed to do it. When the work the Republican party was organized to do was thus done, and fully and irreversibly done, the term of service of those who enlisted literally for that war expired by its own limitation. New issues then presented themselves, new leaders came to the front, new battle-cries were heard, and the name of Republican attached to a party organization became a mere tradition and sentiment-a trade-mark, as it were, representing what might most aptly be described as a very valuable political good-will.

Such are the general conditions of to-day as seen by some of us, original members of the Republican party, and faithful to it until the work it was formed to do was done; then, ceasing to call ourselves. Republicans, we have seen no good reason for identifying ourselves with the Democratic or with any other political faction. We have felt satisfied with being simply citizens of that common country which, as members of the original Republican party, we helped to save. Why, then, do some of us now come forward, not calling ourselves Democrats, and earnestly advocate the election to the presidency of the candidate of the Democratic party? My answer is: We do so simply because that candidate is ex-President Cleveland. What are the political issues of the impending canvass? Some of them are old, as old as the National Government, and likely long to continue; others are new and of a passing character. These issues, new and old, may be enumerated somewhat as follows: 1. The economic and commercial system, commonly known as protective, based upon the idea that it is the business of government artificially to foster, or even call into existence, various branches of industry. 2. The purification and reform of the civil service; or, as Mr. Carl Schurz once tersely expressed it, "the disestablishment of the spoils system,' the system which the Jacksonian Democracy introduced. 3. What is known as the "currency question," now taking the form of a demand for the free coinage of silver at the national mint at an artificial ratio with gold. 4. The pension system.

What is the attitude of Mr. Cleveland so far as these issues are concerned? He has been called upon officially to confront them all, and on no occasion, so far as I know, has he failed to make his position understood, or to give the party of which he was the head a distinct, recognized, and creditable lead. He has not shuffled or vacillated; his voice at least has, upon these issues, emitted no uncertain sound. In this respect the line of responsible public action he has pursued has been in most agreeable contrast with that usually pursued by politicians, not only of the present, but of all time. The crying sin of cattle of that class, especially in these days of many newspapers and much rapid communication, is their constant endeavor to catch quickly and to reflect correctly the passing phases of public sentiment, and neither to think nor to speak for themselves. Continually playing a game of political chess and small party tactics, they are very chary of enunciating any political principles by which they are prepared to stand or fall, unless such principles are time-honored political platitudes or orthodox party shibboleth. But such has not been the practice of Mr. Cleveland. In high public position he has stood forth a clean-cut political character-a man with the courage of his convictions.

Take his course on the question of civil-service reform, that one of the issues enumerated in regard to which his record may seem to be most open to attack. Under the lead of Grover Cleveland the Democratic party came back into power in 1885 after twenty-eight years of exclusion from it. It is no exaggeration to say that those calling themselves Democrats were then simply ravenous for spoils. No more severe pressure for a general turning out of officials and a new distribution of places was probably ever brought to bear upon the head of a government than was brought to bear upon President

Cleveland after his inauguration. I have not the figures before me, nor do I care to look them up, but I think it will be found that the removals during President Cleveland's administration were fewer in number and less dictated by partisan or political considerations than those of President Harrison, who succeeded him. Yet President Harrison represented a party which when Cleveland was inaugurated had been in power for over a quarter of a century, filling every office in the gift of the Government, and many of these officials had held over notwithstanding the change which took place in 1885. President Harrison also represented the party which claims to be and which should be essentially the party of civil-service reform. Yet, so far as the use of party power for political purposes is concerned, the administration of Grover Cleveland will have little to fear from a comparison of its record with that of Benjamin Harrison. It may well be that in this matter there is little to choose as between the politicians of the two great parties; but in view of the record, it cannot but be conceded that Mr. Cleveland, in the trying position in which he was placed, acquitted himself as creditably as any man could have been expected to do. Upon the issue of a reformed civil service he showed himself as much in advance of both parties as it was wise or prudent for the recognized leader of one of those parties to be. He may not have been-probably he was not-on the skirmish line; but then a general in command is not in his proper place on the skirmish line.

On the next issue, that of protection, whether the critic be a protectionist or otherwise, he must still admit that President Cleveland's course was most creditable to him. Indeed, it may well be questioned whether any President, in dealing with an important question of public policy, ever acted from higher or more disinterested motives than did Cleveland when he took the course he did in his annual message of 1887. Before that message was sent in, it was generally conceded that all the President had to do to secure a re-election was silently to bide the time. The course of events and the drift of public opinion were in his favor. The terrible results his opponents had so confidently predicted from a return of the Democratic party to power had not come about. The country was at peace and very prosperous; the South was pacified and loyal; the Treasury was overflowing. All things indicated popular confidence in the administration and unwillingness to disturb it. Nevertheless, when President Cleveland, after the most thorough and careful investigation he could make, had convinced himself that the tariff system needed modification, he did not hesitate to cast all further ulterior consider- ations aside and boldly to indicate his opinion. It is no sort of con- sequence whether his so doing was "good politics," as it is called, or "bad politics"; it is no sort of consequence whether, as a question of party strategy, it was a success or a failure; it is no sort of consequence whether by doing as he then did President Cleveland showed skill as a political leader or com- mitted a serious political blunder, his course none the less showed character and courage; and the Anglo-Saxon race has always evinced. a proclivity for men of character and courage.

It was the same with the question of silver coinage. That issue was and is unmistakably before the country and has got to be fought out. It was unnecessary for ex-President Cleveland, as he then was, to express in February last any opinion upon it. It was perfectly within his power, by preserving a discreet silence, to hold himself in position where those in favor of a free coinage of silver and those who were opposed to it could equally lend him their support. He might have dodged the issue. Nevertheless, here again the courage and character of the man asserted themselves. His letter of February 10, 1892, to the Cooper Union meeting was, as I look upon it, under all the circum- stances of the case, one of the most creditable utterances that ever came from an American public character. He did not want to have his position misunderstood. He did not propose to stand before the country in any false or uncertain attitude. So, again, his voice, when heard, emitted no uncertain sound.

Finally, the question of pensions. On this subject I speak with some degree of feeling, because, having served through nearly four years of the Civil War, I, in common with many others who did the same, feel a sense of humiliation-I may almost say of degradation- in seeing the uniform we once wore turned into a mendicant's garb, and the garb of a very impudent and persistent mendicant at that. Under the administrations which preceded that of Cleveland the pension legislation had, as we thought, been already carried to excessive length. Grant and Garfield, we knew, were of the same opinion. Under it every man who had any reasonable claim to public consideration had received recognition, or the way to recognition was open to him. My own experience, I presume-and, indeed, I know-had in a small way been, that of nearly every one else who was in immediate command of men during the Rebellion. We had seen every dead-beat and malingerer, every bummer, bounty-jumper, and suspected deserter we had ever known or heard of rush to the front as the greedy claimant of public bounty. If there was any man whose army record had been otherwise than creditable to him, we soon heard of him as the claimant of a back pension of many hundred dollars or as being in the regular receipt of his monthly stipend. On the other hand, those good and faithful soldiers who, in the day of trial, had been found in the front rank in presence of the enemy-those men had, since the flags were furled away, developed, as a rule, the same characteristics as citizens which had distinguished them as soldiers; self- respecting and self-sustaining, they were reluctant to trade on the patriotism of their younger and better days as on a beggar's claim. They had supported the brunt of battle then, and they were able to support themselves now. Thus there were of us those who felt that this wretched largess business, this trading of political hucksters on patriotic self-sacrifice, had gone quite far enough. We therefore felt a keen sense of relief when, in February, 1887, President Cleveland sent in his veto of that Dependent Pension bill, which put a premium on self-abasement and perjury.

But President Cleveland's cogent reasoning in that message failed to commend itself to the army of pension agents, the circulars from whose offices at Washington cumbered the mails and our desks. The Republican party, that party to which we had belonged until it completed its work, took the same view of the subject. Accordingly, so far as could be judged from the outside, the issue made by that party in the campaign of 1888, which resulted in the election of Harrison, was distinct and simple. It set itself in direct opposition to the public policy which President Cleveland had enunciated as respects what may be called the "protected interests" of the country and the pension agents. It turned to those two powerful and wide-spread organizations, saying to the first: "If you will elect our candidate to the presidency and return us to power, you can come to Washington and demand such an increase of your protective duties as you shall see fit; and we will see that it is given to you." It then turned to the army of claim agents in and about the Pension Office, saying to them: "If you will elect our candidate to the presidency and cause the administration of the country to return into our hands, we will allow you the free plunder of the Treasury. President Cleveland, as you see, bars your way to it."

The result was that by a narrow vote President Cleveland was defeated and General Harrison elected to succeed him. The Republican party returned to power. After it returned to power, the record shows that it was as good as its word. Its promises were carried out. The protected interests swarmed to Washington, and in due time the McKinley Tariff bill was reported and passed. In it the demands of every producer, so far as appears, who wished to fatten at the expense of the consumer, were gratified. He had but to ask and it was given. On the other hand, the horde of claim agents ran riot in the Pension Office under " Corporal Joe" Tanner until the Treasury which President Cleveland left only too full bade fair to be empty. The record in this respect is one of which the quondam soldiers of the Republic cannot well feel proud. The Treasury was looted.

Those who feel thus on the questions now before the country feel also that the issue involved in the present canvass is by no means a vital one. Whichever way it goes, the United States will prosper and go on in its course of irresistible development along the lines marked out as the result of the discussions of the century just closed and of the irreversible course of its events. Where they are not purely fiscal and economic, the issues involved in the contest of 1892 seem destined to be largely personal. They can affect nothing which is fundamental to our Government, nor will any mistake made be irremediable. Under such circumstances it has ever been found that heresies and the errors into which people fall in consequence of them can be de- pended on in due course of time to rectify themselves. The disease is self-limited and will work its own cure. Parties, too, are strangely divided. There is, for instance, a recognized element among the Re- publicans which favors a modification of the tariff, another which in- sists on the free coinage of silver, and yet another which looks with alarm and disgust upon new pension raids on the Treasury. So also with the Democrats. Indeed, there is no one distinctive question upon which the whole Republican party is divided from the whole Democratic party, or the whole Democratic party from the Republican. The ranks are mixed. Under such circumstances, the issue is necessarily more or less an issue of individual men: Who is to be the temporary head of the Govern- ment for the next four years?

Such being the case, those who feel as I feel, caring far more for country than for faction-for things than for names-see in Mr. Cleveland a man both true and tried, a political leader far in advance of his party, a public character with the courage of his convictions, a statesman whose views on every political issue are definite and well known, a possible President who if elected can have no ulterior political ends in view, for he cannot be a candidate to succeed himself. Opposed to Mr. Cleveland, we see the partisan candidate of a political party the recent record of which has not served to fill us with admira- tion. Our pride and patriotism are not stirred at the mention of the diplomatic victories achieved by it in its disgraceful Chilian fiasco; nor does its policy of taxing every human being in the country in the name of protection in order to call into existence an industry in tin plates commend itself to our business judgment, any more than the proposi- tion that a natural and economical desire to buy "a cheap coat" indi- cates "a cheap man"; while, moreover, we look with absolute and unspeakable disgust, not unmixed with alarm, upon the noisy crowd of thieves and mendicants who, under the lead of an aggressive, well- organized staff of pension agents, constitute the acknowledged camp-following of the latter-day Republican organization, and, as such, beset the doors of the Treasury. Finally, if the published utterances of ex-President Cleveland upon all the leading issues of the day constitute what is now Democracy, then I and those who feel as I do must for the time being submit, for the reasons I have given, to be accounted Democrats. So far as the nominee for the presidency is concerned, we certainly propose next November to vote as such.

20

Mr. Cleveland's Task and Opportunities

Published in *The Forum*, Vol. 15, 1893.

THE popular hallucination which seems to prevail as to some approaching millennium whenever a new administration is inaugurated or a new Congress enters upon its work is one of the curious features in American political thought. It may be said to be perennial. Administrations come and go-Congresses meet and pass out of existence; nothing of a material character, so far as the grand result is concerned, is effected by either one or the other; and yet, as regularly as each new administration begins and as regularly as each new Congress assembles, the same expectation is seen of a new and brighter epoch.

One thing only is certain. It is eminently unjust that these great expectations should exist; for while any given President can, during the period of four years, affect the administration of the country very materially for ill, it is not in his power greatly to change things for the better. It is always easy to demoralize; it is always difficult to elevate. There have been unquestionably two periods in the history of the United States when great results were worked within the period of four or eight years. One was during Washington's presidency, when a shape was given to our institutions which has been perpetuated from that time to this; the other was during the administration of President Lincoln, when our Government passed through its ordeal of fire. For the rest, large bodies move slowly; and it would, I fancy, be extremely difficult to point out action taken in any other of the various administrations which has materially and permanently affected the public policy. Take, for instance, the tariff question: the policy inaugurated by Hamilton at the close of the last century has gone on developing from that time to this, until now, at the close of the present century, it has assumed its last phase in the McKinley bill. Again, take the judiciary: the one event of supreme importance in its history was the appointment of Chief Justice Marshall. From the date of his nomination, more than ninety years ago, down to the present day, the impulse he gave to that department of the Government has gone on increasing in force until it now moves on fixed and unchangeable lines.

It is the same with questions of internal improvement and of finance. For years, no matter what party has been in power, all these questions, when studied through a period of time, have moved in some more or less well-defined course of development, from which it would now be extremely difficult, if not impracticable, for any one administration, no matter how vigorous, to divert them.

Judging by the loose writing one sees in the newspapers and the talk heard on the streets, a foreigner might suppose that a new President, when he entered on the functions of his office, was a species of arbitrary monarch; that the whole machinery of government was at his disposal to take to pieces and put together anew, as he saw fit. Yet, as everyone who takes the trouble to think a moment in relation to the matter knows well, this is the furthest possible from being the case. A President has very little real power. He is hemmed in by restrictions or tied up by controlling influences to such an extent that what he can do even in the way of the distribution of offices is comparatively little. He finds his bed made for him; and do what he will he has to lie in it. Generally, too, he finds it, when not actually thorny, confoundedly narrow and curiously hard.

Take now the case of Mr. Cleveland. He has four years before him in which to work-only four years! A brief period in which to accomplish any considerable result; a period infinitely brief when a body of the magnitude of the United States is to be taken into the account. Probably no one appreciates this fact so thoroughly as Mr. Cleveland himself. He knows that at best he cannot accomplish much, and that he will be fortunate if he accomplishes anything which will leave a permanent mark upon our institutions; especially a white mark.

Turning, therefore, to that which is feasible and putting aside visions of the impracticable, it would seem that President Cleveland is confronted by four practical problems.

1. He is pledged to a reform of the tariff system.

2. He must struggle with the silver question.

3. It is in his power either to demoralize the civil service, or to extend the reforms which have already been begun in it.

4. He may hope to reduce the expenditures of the country again within reasonable limits by purging and correcting the pension lists.

To bring any results about, except in the extension of the reform of the civil service, the President must have the active and earnest coöperation of Congress. Without that he can accomplish nothing. In regard to one only of the four problems confronting him can Mr. Cleveland, therefore, be held to occupy a position of actual responsibility, to have a mastery of the situation.

In the matter of the civil service it is plainly in his power to set an example which his successors would find it difficult to disregard. In the United States we are gradually growing to the idea that political evils of any considerable magnitude have to work their own cure; in other words, the body politic is in this respect very like the human system, and the ills which afflict it have to run a prescribed course. They do not seem to admit of effective treatment in their earlier stages. It was so with slavery. It will be so with protection; and the disease of municipal corruption, the recurrent office-seeking epidemic and the pension fever are all in the same category. The wisest of the Massachusetts physicians wrote a treatise some half a century ago on the "Self-Limitation of Diseases," developing, in so doing, what he termed the "Expectant Treatment." In the result, he modified the medical systems of the civilized world. There is an excellent opportunity now for a similar treatise by some equally competent doctor of history on the self-limitation of political distempers and crazes. They do not seem to admit of a cure until they pass into the curative stage.

Now the disease just referred to as the recurrent, office-seeking epidemic shows at last distinct symptoms of having reached the curative stage. It has existed in the acute forms known as "the spoils system" and the "rotation in office" theory for rather more than sixty years, during which it has run into all sorts of excesses and developed every conceivable phase. The great body politic, long very sick, is now manifestly recovering. This is seen in the sort of amused, contemptuous spirit in which the community looks on, and sees its newly-elected executive head struggle in the toils from which he has not the force of will necessary to extricate himself; or, perhaps, the proper moment has not come for him to exercise his will. One thing is clear. Secretaries, senators, representatives, and governors grunt and sweat under the weary load of this particular infliction just as much as the President. When, therefore, the man and the hour do come, as come at last they surely will, the President who summarily brings this disorder within recognized limits, and places the administration of government business on a recognized business basis, will find that he has merely brought to its close a disease which had run its course. The patient is quite ready to get well and will gratefully recognize a wise and firm course of treatment.

Presumably Mr. Cleveland during his second term must, as a mere object lesson, sustain for a time the dread ordeal of hand-shaking and office-begging through which, as one of his own predecessors in office, he passed before. So he knows how it is himself. Presently, he may feel that his time has come. Should it come, and should the thing, in the presence of great pending public issues, become fairly unendurable to him, by then, once for all, widely extending the civil- service rules, regardless of the pressure of politicians and the cry for a distribution of spoils, he would unquestionably bring to his own support an additional moral confidence which would be invaluable. Of all our recent Presidents he alone finds himself in position to accomplish this result. Judging by his record and utterances, the course he will pursue is hardly open to question. So much may be gained.

As respects the tariff and a reform of the revenue department, nothing whatever can be accomplished by the President alone; and it would, I fancy, be well for the country not to entertain too large expectations on this head. The existing tariff system, it is to be remembered, is not the growth of a few recent years. On the contrary, as I have said, it began one hundred years ago; and, with slight periods of reaction, it has gone on steadily developing upon one and the same line from then till now, when it has reached the McKinley culmination. What reason is there to suppose that the present reaction is anything more than the various reactions which preceded it? If not, it is only temporary. One thing is certain, the tendency of the people of the United States is distinctly toward protection of every character. Witness the numerous trades unions, the combinations of capital against labor and of labor against capital, the popular depreciation everywhere noticeable of what are known as the influences of the natural laws of trade. In this depreciation I, personally, do not share. Nevertheless, no observing man can for a moment fail to see that within the last twenty years the movement has been almost wholly one of reaction against the teachings of the economical school of which Adam Smith was the head, and those of the political school of Jefferson. As I see it, the high protective system of this country, including the silver legislation, is but one phase, and somewhat of a superficial, surface phase at that, in this great reactionary movement, a movement by no means confined to America. On the contrary, it is working quite as violently in France, Italy, and Germany as it is here. Even in Great Britain, the birth-place and citadel of the Free-Trade and Let-Alone dispensation, we see to-day the counter-current of Trade-Unionism (which is only another name for the protection of labor through a recognized monopoly of employment at wages arbitrarily fixed), we see, I say, this direct negation of the whole theory of Adam Smith receiving parliamentary sanction. And what is this but a deep, swift under- current in the great protective reaction? To fancy, then, for a moment that it is in the power of President Cleveland or any other man, or potentate, no matter of what government he may be the head, to check or even materially affect the course of a general impulse of this character, seems to verge on the preposterous. Like other sweeping natural movements, this one must work itself out in a natural way and in its own time. How and when that will be it is unnecessary now to consider. The only point at present to be discussed is the degree to which President Cleveland, through his administration of four years, can affect it. That I hold to be small indeed.

There is no position which President Cleveland has to fill more important than that of Commissioner of Pensions. He has made his selection for the office; and the man he has selected enters upon his difficult duties with words only of commendation heard of him. The result must be awaited; yet President Cleveland will be most fortunate if, in making the selection he has made, he shall prove to have found a man who can take hold of a two-hundred-millions-a-year problem firmly, yet in such a way as not to give unnecessary offence, a man who by his military record and executive and judicial qualities will be able to hold off the claimants who are now swarming around the Treasury and compel the well-nigh innumerable leeches who are now sucking from it to let go their hold. It is not easy to see exactly what inducement was held out to the successor of Tanner and Raum to induce him to accept the office and perform its duties. Certainly a most inadequate salary can be no inducement; and it is not apparent how the new Commissioner can obtain his reward in any way except from a sense of duty performed. Here, again, the disease must, through its very excesses, work its own cure; but in the future page of history President Harrison will have to confront "Corporal" Tanner. Possibly the ex-President does not believe in an Hereafter. If so, he is fortunate in this life; and probably he will not live to see the poral" and the vanished Treasury-Surplus figuring, together with himself, in a ghostly dance through the life to come. The new Commissioner of Pensions is at least happy in his predecessors. There is a depth lower than which it is not easy to fall. A contrast is now in order; but, on the other hand, there seems no reasonable ground for hoping that Congress will in any way contribute toward making that contrast effective. When it is a question of the *panem-et-circenses* appropriations the average Senator and Member of Congress is apt to 1 develop a nervousness at the time of the roll-call in no way suggestive of the class of remedies commonly referred to as heroic. He will appropriate anything to anybody-if there are votes in it! What President Cleveland accomplishes in his wrestle with this problem, he must, therefore, accomplish unaided. Like the late Senator Benton, he will, if he accomplishes anything, be able to say, "Solitary and alone I set that ball in motion."

Finally, as respects the silver question. In order to avert what can hardly be regarded otherwise than as a possible national calamity, President Cleveland has again got to have the coöperation, and the willing coöperation, of Congress. But what are known as the silver States are a fact a fact not to be ignored. How in the face of that fact he is to secure Congressional coöperation is a problem President Cleveland has got to wrestle with. The silver States were, of course, introduced into the Union for a political purpose. They had and have no business to be in the Union. Together, although they have some twelve votes in the United States Senate, holding on the silver and other questions a secure balance of power, they do not represent the population of one State of reasonable size. They are mere rotten boroughs. The time. may come when in several of them there will be a population which would justify the representation they now have; but this time certainly will not come during the four years Mr. Cleveland is to be responsible for results. How, under such circumstances, much can reasonably be expected from him in the way of a satisfactory solution of the silver question is not apparent.

In fine, therefore, the expectation of anything like a new epoch, as it is called, resulting from the administration of Mr. Cleveland appears wholly unreasonable and most unjust to him. He has neither the time, nor the power, nor the instruments in which and with which to work. More is thus expected of him than could be accomplished under the same conditions by any man who has left a name in history; as much indeed as could result from the career of any man who, like Gladstone, has been fifty years in public life, or like Prince Bismarck, was for twenty years in secure possession of power, backed by an almost arbitrary government.

Consequently, I submit, there is no reasonable ground to suppose that this country, in entering upon the second administration of President Cleveland, enters upon any new era in its existence at all.

21

"Imperialism" and "The Tracks of Our Forefathers"

This paper was delivered to the Lexington, Massachusetts historical society on December 20, 1898.

"In a word, many wise men thought it a time wherein those two miserable adjuncts, which Nerva was deified for uniting, imperium et libertas, were as well reconciled as is possible."

—Clarendon's History of the Rebellion, B. 1. § 163.

"I put my foot in the tracks of our forefathers, where I can neither wander nor stumble."

—Burke's Speech on Conciliation with America.

What the feast of the Passover was to the children of Israel, that the days between the nineteenth of December and the fourth of January—the Yuletide—are and will remain to the people of New England. The

Passover began "in the first month on the fourteenth day of the month at even," and it lasted one week, "until the one and twentieth day of the month at even." It was the period of the sacrifice of the Paschal lamb, and the feast of unleavened bread; and of it as a commemoration it is written, "When your children shall say unto you, What mean ye by this service? that ye shall say, It is the sacrifice of the Lord's passover, who passed over the houses of the children of Israel in Egypt, when he smote the Egyptians. Now the sojourning of the children of Israel, who dwelt in Egypt, was four hundred and thirty years." And thus, by their yearly Passover, were the Jewish congregations of old put in mind what farewell they took of the land of Egypt.

So our own earliest records tell us that it was on the morning of Saturday, of what is now the nineteenth of December, that the little exploring party from the *Mayflower*, then lying at her anchor in Provincetown Harbor, after a day and night of much trouble and danger, sorely buffeted by wind and wave in rough New England's December seas, found themselves on an island in Plymouth Bay. It was a mild, "faire sunshining day. And this being the last day of the weeke, they prepared ther to keepe the Sabbath. On Munday they sounded the harbor, and marched into the land, and found a place fitt for situation. So they returned to their shipp againe [at Provincetown] with this news. On the twenty-fifth of December they weyed anchor to goe to the place they had discovered, and came within two leagues of it, but were faine to bear up againe; but the twenty-sixth day, the winde came faire, and they arrived safe in this harbor. And after wards tooke better view of the place, and resolved wher to pitch their dwelling; and the fourth day [of January] begane to erecte the first house for commone use to receive them and their goods." Such, in the quaint language of Bradford, is the calendar of New England's Passover; and, beginning on the nineteenth of December, it ends on the fourth of January, covering as nearly as may be the Christmas holyday period.

Is there any better use to which the Passover anniversary can be put than to retrospection? "And when your children shall say unto you, What mean you by this service? ye shall say, It is the sacrifice of the Lord's passover, when he smote the Egyptians, and delivered our houses." So the old story is told again, being thus kept ever green in memory; and, in telling it, the experiences of the past are brought insensibly to bear on the conditions of the present. Thus, once a year, like the Israelites of old, we, as a people, may take our bearings and verify our course, as we plunge on out of the infinite past into the unknowable future. It is a useful practice; and we are here this first evening of our Passover period to observe it.

This, too, is an Historical Society,—that of Lexington, "a name," as, when arraigned before the tribunal of the French Terror, Danton said of his own, "tolerably known in the Revolution;" and I am invited to address you because I am President of the Massachusetts Historical Society, the most venerable organization of the sort in America, perhaps in the world. Thus, to-night, though we shall necessarily have to touch on topics of the day, and topics exciting the liveliest interest and most active discussion, we will in so doing look at them,—not as politicians or as partisans, nor from the commercial or religious side, but solely from the historical point of view. We shall judge of the present in its relations to the past. And, unquestionably, there is great satisfaction to be derived from so doing; the mere effort seems at once to take us into another atmosphere,—an atmosphere as foreign to unctuous cant as it is to what is vulgarly known as "electioneering taffy." This evening we pass away from the noisy and heated turmoil of partisan politics, with its appeals to prejudice, passion, and material interest, into the cool of a quiet academic discussion. It is like going out of some turbulent caucus, or exciting ward-room debate, and finding oneself suddenly confronted by the cold, clear light of the December moon, shining amid the silence of innumerable stars.

Addressing ourselves, therefore, to the subject in hand, the question at once suggests itself,—What year in recent times has been in a large way more noteworthy and impressive, when looked at from the purely historical point of view, than this year of which we are now observing the close? The first Passover of the Israelites ended a drama of more than four centuries' duration, for "the sojourning of the children of

Israel, who dwelt in Egypt, was four hundred and thirty years; and at the end of the four hundred and thirty years all the hosts of the Lord went out from the land of Egypt." So the Passover we now celebrate commemorates the closing of another world drama of almost precisely the same length, and one of deepest significance, as well as unsurpassed historic interest. These world dramas are lengthy affairs; for, while we men are always in a hurry, the Almighty never is: on the contrary, as the Psalmist observed, so now, "a thousand years in his sight are but as yesterday when it is past, and as a watch in the night." The drama I have referred to as this week brought to its close, is that known in history as Spanish Domination in America. It began, as we all know, on the twenty-first of October, 1492; it has been continuous through six years over four centuries. It now passes into history; the verdict may be made up.

So far as I personally am concerned,—a matter needless to say of very trifling consequence,—this verdict was rendered a year ago. It was somewhat Rhadamanthine; but a twelve-month of further reflection has shown no cause in any respect to revise it. In referring to what was then plainly impending, in December, 1897, before the blowing up of the battleship *Maine*, before a conflict had become inevitable, I used this language in a paper read to the Massachusetts Historical Society: "When looking at the vicissitudes of human development, we are apt to assume a certain air of optimism, and take advancement as the law of being, as a thing of course, indisputable. We are charitable, too; and to deny to any given race or people some degree of use in the economy of Nature, or the plan of Creation, is usually regarded as indicative of narrowness of view. The fatal, final word "pessimist" is apt to be whispered in connection with the name of one who ventures to suggest a doubt of this phase of the doctrine known as Universalism. And yet, at this time when, before our eyes, it is breathing its last, I want some one to point out a single good thing in law, or science, or art, or literature,— material, moral or intellectual,—which has resulted to the race of man upon earth from Spanish domination in America. I have tried to think of one in vain. It certainly has not yielded an immortality, an idea, or a discovery; it has, in fact, been one long record of reaction and retrogression, than which few pages in the record of mankind have been more discouraging or less fruitful of good. What is now taking place in Cuba is historical. It is the dying out of a dominion, the influence of which will be seen and felt for centuries in the life of two continents; just as what is taking place in Turkey is the last fierce flickering up of Asiatic rule in Europe, on the very spot where twenty-four centuries ago Asiatic rule in Europe was thought to have been averted forever. The two, Ottoman rule in Europe, and Spanish rule in America, now stand at the bar of history; and, scanning the long four-century record of each, I have been unable to see what either has contributed to the accumulated possessions of the human race, or why both should not be classed among the many instances of the arrested civilization of a race, developing by degrees an irresistible tendency to retrogression."

This, one year ago; and while the embers of the last Greco-Turkish struggle, still white, were scarcely cold on the plain of Marathon. The time since passed has yielded fresh proof in support of this harsh judgment; for, if there is one historical law better and more irreversibly established than another, it is that, in the case of nations even more than in the case of individuals, their sins will find them out,—the day of reckoning may not be escaped. Noticeably, has this proved so in the case of Spain. The year 1500 may be said to have found that country at the apex of her greatness. America had then been newly discovered; the Moor was just subdued. Nearly half a century before (1453) the Roman Empire had fallen, and, with the storming of Constantinople by the Saracens, disappeared from the earth. That event, it may be mentioned in passing, closed another world drama continuous through twenty-two centuries,—upon the whole the most wonderful of the series. And so, when Roman empire vanished, that of Spain began. It was ushered in by the landfall of Columbus; and when, just three hundred years later, in 1792, the subject was discussed in connection with its third centennial, the general verdict of European thinkers was that the discovery of America had, upon the whole, been to mankind the reverse of beneficent. This conclusion has since been commented upon with derision; yet, when made, it was right. The United States had in 1792 just struggled into existence, and its influence on the course of human events had not begun to make itself felt. Those who considered the subject had before them, therefore, only Spanish domination in America, and upon that their verdict cannot be gainsaid; for, from the year 1492 down, the history of Spain and Spanish domination has undeniably been one long series of crimes and violations of natural law, the penalty for which has not apparently even yet been exacted in full.

Of those national crimes four stand out in special prominence, constituting counts in a national indictment than which history shows few more formidable. These four were: (1) The expulsion, first, of the Jews, and then of the Moors, or Moriscoes, from Spain, late in the fifteenth and early in the sixteenth centuries; (2) the annals of "the Council of Blood" in the Netherlands, and the eighty years of internecine warfare through which Holland fought its way out from under Spanish rule; (3) the Inquisition, the most ingenious human machinery ever invented to root out and destroy whatever a people had that was intellectually most alert, inquisitive, and progressive; and, finally (4), the policy of extermination, and, where not of extermination, of cruel oppression, systematically pursued towards the aborigines of America. Into the grounds on which the different counts of this indictment rest it would be impossible now to enter. Were it desirable so to do, time would not permit. Suffice it to say, the penalty had to be paid to the uttermost farthing; and one large instalment fell due, and was mercilessly exacted, during the year now drawing to its close. Spanish domination in America ceased,—the drama ended as it was entering on its fifth century,—and it can best be dismissed with the solemn words of Abraham Lincoln, uttered more than thirty years ago, when contemplating a similar expiation we were ourselves paying in blood and grief for a not dissimilar violation of an everlasting law,—"Yet, if God wills that this mighty scourge continue until all the wealth piled by the bondsmen's two hundred and fifty years of unrequited toil shall be sunk, and until every drop of blood drawn by the lash shall be paid by another drawn by the sword, as was said three thousand years ago, so still it must be said, 'The judgments of the Lord are true and righteous altogether!'"

But not only is this year memorable as witnessing the downfall and complete extirpation of that Spanish rule in America which began with Columbus, but the result, when it at last came about, was marked by incidents more curiously fitting and dramatic than it would have been possible for a Shakspeare to have conceived. Columbus, as we all know, stumbled, as it were, on America as he sailed west in search of Asia,—Cipango he was looking for, and he found Cuba. It is equally well known that he never discovered his mistake. When fourteen years later he died, it was in the faith that, through him, Europe had by a westward movement established itself in the archipelagoes of Asia. And now, at last, four centuries afterward, the blow which did most to end the American domination he established was struck in Asiatic waters; and, through it and the descendants of another race, America seems on the threshold of realizing the mistaken belief of Columbus, and by a westward movement establishing the European in that very archipelago Columbus failed to reach. The ways of Providence are certainly not less singular than slow in movement.

But the year just ending was veritably one of surprises,—for the historical student it would, indeed, seem as if 1898 was destined to pass into the long record as almost the Year of Surprises. We now come to the consideration of some of these wholly unanticipated results from the American point of view. And in entering on this aspect of the question, it is necessary once more to remind you that we are doing it in the historical spirit, and from the historical point of view. We are stating facts not supposed to admit of denial. The argument and inferences to be drawn from those facts do not belong to this occasion. Some will reach one conclusion as to the future, and the bearing those facts have upon its probable development, and some will reach another conclusion; with these conclusions we have nothing to do. Our business is exclusively with the facts.

Speaking largely, but still with all necessary historical accuracy, America has been peopled, and its development, up to the present time, worked out through two great stocks of the European family,—the Spanish-speaking stock, and the English-speaking stock. In their development these two have pursued lines, clearly marked, but curiously divergent. Leaving the Spanish-speaking branch out of the discussion, as unnecessary to it, it may without exaggeration be said of the English-speaking branch that, from the beginning down to this year now ending, its development has been one long protest against, and divergence from, Old World methods and ideals. In the case of those descended from the Forefathers,—as we always designate the Plymouth colony,—this has been most distinctly marked, ethnically, politically, industrially.

America was the sphere where the European, as a colonist, a settler, first came on a large scale in contact with another race. Heretofore, in the Old World, when one stock had overrun another,—and history presented many examples of it,—the invading stock, after subduing, and to a great extent driving out, the stock which had preceded in the occupancy of a region, settled gradually down into a common possession, and, in the slow process of years, an amalgamation of stocks, more or less complete, took place. In America, with the Anglo-Saxon, and especially those of the New England type, this was not the case. Unlike the Frenchman at the north, or the Spaniard at the south, the Anglo-Saxon showed no disposition to ally himself with the aborigines,—he evinced no faculty of dealing with inferior races, as they are called, except through a process of extermination. Here in Massachusetts this was so from the outset. Nearly every one here has read Longfellow's poem, "The Courtship of Miles Standish," and calls to mind the short, sharp conflict between the Plymouth captain and the Indian chief, Pecksuot, and how those God-fearing Pilgrims ruthlessly put to death by stabbing and hanging a sufficient number of the already plague-stricken and dying aborigines. That episode occurred in April, 1623, only a little more than two years after the landing we to-night celebrate, and was, so far as New England is concerned, the beginning of a series of wars which did not end until the Indian ceased to be an element in our civilization. When John Robinson, the revered pastor of the Plymouth church, received tidings at Leyden of that killing near Plymouth,—for Robinson never got across the Atlantic,—he wrote: "Oh, how happy a thing had it been, if you had converted some before you had killed any! There is cause to fear that, by occasion, especially of provocation, there may be wanting that tenderness of the life of man (made after God's image) which is meet. It is also a thing more glorious in men's eyes, than pleasing in God's or convenient for Christians, to be a terror to poor, barbarous people." This all has a very familiar sound. It is the refrain of nearly three centuries; but, as an historical fact, it is undeniable that, from 1623 down to the year now ending, the American Anglo-Saxon has in his dealings with what are known as the "inferior races" lacked "that tenderness of the life of man which is meet," and he has made himself "a terror to poor, barbarous people." How we of Massachusetts carried ourselves towards the aborigines here, the fearful record of the Pequot war remains everlastingly to tell. How the country at large has carried itself in turn towards Indian, African, and Asiatic is matter of history. And yet it is equally matter of history that this carriage, term it what you will,—unchristian, brutal, exterminating,—has been the salvation of the race. It has saved the Anglo-Saxon stock from being a nation of half-breeds,—miscegenates, to coin a word expressive of an idea. The Canadian half-breed, the Mexican, the mulatto, say what men may, are not virile or enduring races; and that the Anglo-Saxon is none of these, and is essentially virile and enduring, is due to the fact that the less developed races perished before him. Nature is undeniably often brutal in its methods.

Again, and on the other hand, the Anglo-Saxon when he came to America left behind him, so far as he himself was concerned, feudalism and all things pertaining to caste, including what was then known in England, and is still known in Germany, as Divine Right. When he at last enunciated his political faith he put in the forefront of his declaration as "self-evident truths," the principles "that all men are created equal;" that they are endowed with "certain inalienable rights," among them "life, liberty, and the pursuit of happiness;" and that governments derived "their just powers from the consent of the governed." Now what was meant here by the phrase "all men are created equal?" We know they are not. They are not created equal in physical or mental endowment; nor are they created with equal opportunity. The world bristles with inequalities, natural and artificial. This is so; and yet the declaration is none the less true;—true when made; true now; true for all future time. The reference was to the inequalities which always had marked, then did, and still do, mark, the political life of the Old World, —to Caste, Divine Right, Privilege. It declared that all men were created equal before the law, as before the Lord;[1] and that, whether European, American, Asiatic, or African, they were endowed with an inalienable right to life, liberty, and the pursuit of happiness. And to this truth, as he saw it, Lincoln referred in those memorable words I have already cited bearing on our national crime in long forgetfulness of our own immutable principles. The fundamental, primal principle was indeed more clearly voiced by Lincoln than it has been voiced before, or since, in declaring again, and elsewhere that to our nation, dedicated "to the proposition that all men are created equal," has by Providence been as-signed the momentous task of "testing whether any nation so conceived and so dedicated can long endure," and "that government of the people, by the people, for the people, shall not perish from the earth."

The next cardinal principle in our policy as a race—that instinctive policy I have already referred to as divergent from Old World methods and ideals—was most dearly enunciated by Washington in his Fare-well Address, that "the great rule for us in regard to foreign nations is, in extending our commercial relations, to have with them as little political connection as possible;" that it was "unwise in us to implicate ourselves by artificial ties in the ordinary vicissitudes of [Old World] policies, or the ordinary combinations and collisions of her friendships or enmities. Our detached and distant situation invites and enables us to pursue a different course.... Taking care always to keep ourselves by suitable establishments on a respectable defensive posture, we may safely trust to temporary alliances for extraordinary emergencies."

Accepting this as firm ground from which to act, we afterwards put forth what is known as the Monroe Doctrine. Having announced that our purpose was, in homely language, to mind our own business, we warned the outer world that we did not propose to permit by that outer world any interference in what did not concern it. America was our field,—a field amply large for our development. It was therefore declared that, while we had never taken any part, nor did it comport with our policy to do so, in the wars of European politics, with the movements in this hemisphere we are, of necessity, more intimately connected. "We owe it, therefore, to candor to declare that we should consider any attempt [on the part of European powers] to extend their system to any portion of this hemisphere as dangerous to our peace and safety."

On these principles of government and of foreign policy we have as a people now acted for more than seventy years. They have been exemplified and developed in various directions, and resulted in details —commercial, economic, and ethnic—which have given rise to political issues, long and hotly contested, but which, in their result from the purely historical point of view, do not admit of dispute. Commercially, we have adopted what is known as a system protective both of our industries and our labor. Economically, we have carefully eschewed large and costly armaments, and expensive governmental methods. Ethnically, we have avowed our desire to have as little contact as possible with less developed races, lamenting the presence of the African, and severely excluding the Asiatic. These facts, whether we as individuals and citizens wholly approve—or do not approve at all—of the course pursued and the results reached, admit of no dispute. Neither can it be denied that our attitude, whether it in all respects commanded the respect of foreign nations, or failed to command it, was accepted, and has prevailed. Striking illustrations of this at once suggest themselves.

In one respect especially was our attitude peculiar, and in its peculiarity we took great pride. It was largely moral; but, though largely moral, it had behind it the consciousness of strength in ourselves, and its recognition by others. In great degree, and relatively, an unarmed people, we looked with amaze, which had in it something of amusement, at the constantly growing armaments and war budgets of the nations of Europe. We saw them, like the warriors of the middle ages, crushed under the weight of their weapons of offence, and their preparations for defence. Meanwhile, fortunate in our geographical position,—weak for offence, but, in turn, unassailable,—we went in and out much as an unarmed man, relying on his character, his recognized force, position, and peaceful calling, daily moves about in our frontier settlements and mining camps amid throngs of men armed to the teeth with revolvers and bowie knives. Yet, evidence was not lacking of the consideration yielded to us when we were called upon, or felt called upon, to assert ourselves. I will not refer to the episode of 1866, when, in accordance with the principles of the Monroe Doctrine, we intimated to France that her immediate withdrawal from Mexico was desired; for then we had not laid down the arms we had taken up in the Rebellion. But, without remonstrance even, France withdrew. In 1891, under circumstances not without grounds of aggravation against us, a mob in Valparaiso assaulted some seamen from our ships of war. Instant apology and redress were demanded; and the demand was complied with. Yet later, the course pursued by us in the Venezuela matter is too fresh in memory to call for more than a reference. These are all matters of history. When did our word fail to carry all desired weight?

Such were our standing, our traditional policy, and our record at the beginning of the year now ending. No proposition advanced admits, it is believed, of dispute historically. Into the events of the year 1898 it is not necessary to enter in any detail. They are in the minds of all. It is sufficient to say that the primary object for which we entered upon the late war with Spain was to bring to an end the long and altogether bad record of Spanish rule in America. In taking the steps deemed necessary to effect this result, Congress went out of its way, and publicly and formally put upon record its disclaimer of any intention to enter upon a war of conquest, asserting its determination, when Spanish domination was ended, to leave the government of Cuba, and presumably of any other islands similarly acquired, to the people thereof. As an incident to our naval operations on the Pacific, the island of Hawaii was then annexed to the United States as an extra-territorial possession, or coaling station, this being effected by a joint resolution of the two Houses of Congress, under the precedent of 1845 established in the case of Texas,—a method of procedure the constitutionality of which was at the time formally called in question by the State of Massachusetts, and against which Mr. Webster made vigorous protest in the Senate. In thus possessing ourselves of Hawaii, the consent of the native inhabitants was not considered necessary; we dealt wholly with an oligarchical *de facto* government, representing the foreign element, mainly American, there resident.

Shortly after the acquisition of Hawaii, we, as the result of brilliant naval operations and successes, acquired possession of the harbor of Manila, in the Philippine archipelago, and finally the city and some adjacent territory were surrendered to us. A treaty was then negotiated, the power of Spain being completely broken, under which she abandoned all claims of sovereignty, not only over the island of Cuba, the original cause of war, but over various other islands in the Philippine, as well as in the West Indian, archipelagoes. These islands, in all said to be some 1,200 to 1,500 in number, are moreover not only inhabited by both natives and foreigners to the estimated number of ten to twelve million of souls, but they contain large cities and communities speaking different tongues, living under other laws, and having customs, manners, and traditions wholly unlike our own, and which, in the case of the Philippines, do not admit of assimilation. Situated in the tropics also, they cannot gradually become colonized by Americans, with or without the disappearance of the native population. The American can only go there for temporary residence.

A wholly new problem was thus suddenly presented to the people of the United States. On the one hand, it is asserted that, by destroying Spanish government in these islands, the United States has assumed responsibility for them, both to the inhabitants and to the world. This is a moral obligation. On the other hand, trade and commercial inducements are held out which would lead us to treat these islands simply as a commencement—the first instalment—in a system of unlimited extra-territorial dependencies and imperial expansion. With these responsibilities and obligations we here this evening have nothing to do, any more than we have to do with the expediency or probable results of the policy of colonial expansion, when once fairly adopted and finally entered upon. These hereafter will be, but are not yet, historical questions; and we are merely historical inquirers. We, therefore, no matter what others may do, must try to confine ourselves to our own proper business and functions.

My purpose, therefore, is not to argue for or against what is now proposed, but simply to test historically some of the arguments I have heard most commonly advanced in favor of the proposed policy of expansion, and thus see to what they apparently lead in the sequence of human, and more especially of American, events. Do they indicate an historic continuity? Or do they result in what is geologically known as a "fault,"—a movement, as the result of force, through which a stratum, once continuous, becomes disconnected?

In the first place, then, as respects the inhabitants of the vastly greater number of the dependencies already acquired, and, under the policy of imperialistic expansion, hereafter to be acquired. It is argued that we, as a people at once dominant and Christian, are under an obligation to avail ourselves of the opportunity the Almighty, in his infinite wisdom, has thrust upon us,—some say the plain call he has uttered to us,—to go forth, and impart to the barbarian and the heathen the blessings of liberty and the Bible. A mission is imposed upon us. Viewed in the cold, pitiless light of history,—and that is the only way we here can view them,—"divine missions" and "providential calls" are questionable things; things the assumption and fulfilment of which are apt to be at variance. So far as the American is concerned, as I have already pointed out, the historic precedents are not encouraging. Whatever his theories, ethnical, political, or religious, his practice has been as pronounced as it was masterful. From the earliest days at Wessagusset and in the Pequot war, down to the very last election held in North Carolina,—from 1623 to 1898,—the knife and the shotgun have been far more potent and active instruments in his dealings with the inferior races than the code of liberty or the output of the Bible Society.

The record speaks for itself. So far as the Indian is concerned, the story has been told by Mrs. Jackson in her earnest, eloquent protest, entitled "A Century of Dishonor." It has received epigrammatic treatment in the saying tersely enunciated by one of our military commanders, and avowedly accepted by the others, that "the only good Indian is a dead Indian." So far as the African is concerned, the similar apothegm once was that "the black man has no rights the white man is bound to respect;" or, as Stephen A. Douglas defined his position before an applauding audience, "I am for the white man as against the black man, and for the black man against the alligator." Recent lynching and shotgun experiences, too fresh in memory to call for reminder, and too painful in detail to describe, give us at least reason to pause before we leave our own hearthstone to seek new and distant fields for missionary labors. It remains to consider the Asiatic. The racial antipathy of the American towards him has been more intense than towards any other species of the human race. This, as an historical fact, has been recently imbedded in our statute-book, having previously been illustrated in a series of outrages and massacres, with the sickening details of some of which it was at one time my misfortune to be officially familiar. Under these circumstances, so far as the circulation of the Bible and the extension of the blessings of liberty are concerned, history affords small encouragement to the American to assume new obligations. He has been, and now is, more than merely delinquent in the fulfilment of obligations heretofore thrust upon him, or knowingly assumed. In this respect his instinct has proved much more of a controlling factor than his ethics,—the shotgun has unfortunately been more constantly in evidence than the Bible. As a prominent "expansionist" New England member of the present Congress has recently declared in language, brutal perhaps in directness, but withal commendably free from cant: "China is succumbing to the inevitable, and the United States, if she would not retire to the background, must advance along the line with the other great nations. She must acquire new territory, providing new markets over which she must maintain control. The Anglo-Saxon advances into the new regions with a Bible in one hand and a shotgun in the other. The inhabitants of those regions that he cannot convert with the aid of the Bible and bring into his markets, he gets rid of with the shotgun. It is but another demonstration of the survival of the fittest." (Hon. C.A. Sulloway, Rochester, N.H., Nov. 22, 1898.)

Next as regards our fundamental principles of equality of human rights, and the consent of the governed as the only just basis of all government. The presence of the inferior races on our own soil, and our new problems connected with them in our dependencies, have led to much questioning of the correctness of those principles, which, for its outspoken frankness, at least, is greatly to be commended. It is argued that these, as principles, in the light of modern knowledge and conditions, are of doubtful general truth and limited application. True, when confined and carefully applied to citizens of the same blood and nationality; questionable, when applied to human beings of different race in one nationality; manifestly false, in the case of races less developed, and in other, especially tropical, countries.[2] As fundamental principles, it is admitted, they were excellent for a young people struggling into recognition and limiting its attention narrowly to what only concerned itself; but have we not manifestly outgrown them, now that we ourselves have developed into a great World Power? For such there was and necessarily always will be, as between the superior and the inferior races, a manifest common sense foundation in caste, and in the rule of might when it presents itself in the form of what we are pleased to call Manifest Destiny. As to government being conditioned on the consent of the governed, it is obviously the bounden duty of the superior race to hold the inferior race in peaceful tutelage, and protect it against itself; and, furthermore, when it comes to deciding the momentous question of what races are superior and what inferior, what dominant and what subject, that is of necessity a question to be settled between the superior race and its own conscience; and one in regard to the correct settlement of which it indicates a tendency at once unpatriotic and "pessimistic," to assume that America could by any chance decide otherwise than correctly. Upon that score we must put implicit confidence in the sound instincts and Christian spirit of the dominant, that is, the stronger race.

It is the same with that other fundamental principle with which the name of Lexington is, from the historical point of view, so closely associated,—I refer, of course, to the revolutionary contention that representation is a necessary adjunct to taxation. This principle also, it is frankly argued, we have outgrown, in presence of our new responsibilities; and, as between the superior and inferior races, it is subject to obvious limitations. Here again, as between the policy of the "Open Door" and the Closed-Colonial-Market policy, the superior race is amenable to its own conscience only. It will doubtless on all suitable and convenient occasions bear in mind that it is a "Trustee for Civilization."

Finally, as respects entangling foreign alliances, and their necessary consequents, costly and burdensome armaments and large standing armies, we are again advised that, having ceased to be children, we should put away childish things. Having become a great World Power we must become a corresponding War Power. We are assured by high authority that, were Washington now alive, it cannot be questioned he would in all these respects modify materially the views expressed in the Farewell Address, as being obviously inapplicable to existing conditions. Under these circumstances, and in view of the obligations we have assumed, the President, and Secretaries of War and the Navy, recommend an establishment the annual cost of which ($200,000,000), exclusive of military pensions, is in excess of the largest of those European War Budgets, over the crushing influence of which we have expressed a traditional wonder, not unmixed with pity for the unfortunate tax-payer.

Historically speaking, I believe these are all facts, susceptible of verification. I do not mean to say that the arguments developing obvious limitations in the application of the principles of the Declaration and the Constitution have been avowedly accepted by our representatives, or officially incorporated into our domestic and foreign policy. I do assert as an historical fact that these arguments have been advanced, and are meeting, both in Congress and with the press, a large degree of acceptance. And hence comes a singular and most significant conclusion from which, historically, there seems to be no escape. It may or it may not be fortunate and right; it may or it may not lead to beneficent future results; it may or it may not contribute to the good of mankind. Those questions belong elsewhere than in the rooms of an historical society. Upon them we are not called to pass,—they belong to the politician, the publicist, the philosopher, not to us. But, as historical investigators, and so observing the sequence of events, it cannot escape our notice that on every one of the fundamental principles discussed,— whether ethnic, economical, or political,—we abandon the traditional and distinctively American grounds and accept those of Europe, and especially of Great Britain, which heretofore we have made it the basis of our faith to deny and repudiate.

With this startling proposition in mind, consider again the several propositions advanced; and first, as regards the so-called inferior races. Our policy towards them, instinctive and formulated, has been either to exclude or destroy, or to leave them in the fullness of time to work out their own destiny, undisturbed by us; fully believing that, in this way, we in the long run best subserved the interests of mankind. Europe, and Great Britain especially, adopted the opposite policy. They held that it was incumbent on the superior to go forth and establish dominion over the inferior race, and to hold and develop vast imperial possessions and colonial dependencies. They saw their interest and duty in developing systems of docile tutelage; we sought our inspirations in the rough school of self-government. Under this head the result then is distinct, clean cut, indisputable. To this conclusion have we come at last. The Old World, Europe and Great Britain, were, after all, right, and we of the New World have been wrong. From every point of view,—religious, ethnic, commercial, political,—we cannot, it is now claimed, too soon abandon our traditional position and assume theirs. Again, Europe and Great Britain have never admitted that men were created equal, or that the consent of the governed was a condition of government. They have, on the contrary, emphatically denied both propositions. We now concede that, after all, there was great basis for their denial; that, certainly, it must be admitted, our forefathers were hasty at least in reaching their conclusions,—they generalized too broadly. We do not frankly avow error, and we still think the assent of the governed to a government a thing desirable to be secured, under suitable circumstances and with proper limitations; but, if it cannot conveniently be secured, we are advised on New England senatorial authority that "the consent of some of the governed" will be sufficient, we ourselves selecting those proper to be consulted. Thus in such cases as certain islands of the Antilles, Hawaii, and the communities of Asia, we admit that, so far as the principles at the basis of the Declaration are concerned, Great Britain was right, and our ancestors were, not perhaps wrong, but too general, and of the eighteenth century, in their statements. To that extent, we have outgrown the Declaration of 1776, and have become as wise now as Great Britain was then. At any rate we are not above learning. As was long ago said,—"Only dead men and idiots never change;" and the people of the United States are nothing unless open-minded.

So, also, as respects the famous Boston "tea-party," and taxation without representation. Great Britain then affirmed this right in the case of colonies and dependencies. Taught by the lesson of our War of Independence, she has since abandoned it. We now take it up, and are to-day, as one of the new obligations towards the heathen imposed upon us by Providence, formulating systems of imposts and tariffs for our new dependencies, wholly distinct from our own, and directly inhibited by our constitution, in regard to which systems those dependencies have no representative voice. They are not to be consulted as to the kind of door, "open" or "closed," behind which they are to exist. In taking this position it is difficult to see why we must not also incidentally admit that, in the great contention preceding our War of Independence, the first armed clash of which resounded here in Lexington, Great Britain was more nearly right than the exponents of the principles for which those "embattled farmers" contended.

Again, consider the Monroe Doctrine, entangling foreign alliances, and the consequent and costly military and naval establishments. The Monroe Doctrine had two sides, the abstention of the Old World from interference in American affairs, based on our abstention from interference in the affairs of the Old World. But it is now argued we have outgrown the Monroe Doctrine, or at least the latter branch of it. It is certainly so considered in Europe; for, only a few days ago, so eminent an authority as Lord Farrar exultingly exclaimed in addressing the Cobden Club,—"America has burned the swaddling clothes of the Monroe Doctrine." Indeed we have, in discussion at least, gone far in advance of the mere burning of cast-off infantile clothing, and alliances with Great Britain and Japan, as against France and Russia, are freely mooted, with a view to the forcible partition of China, to which we are to be a party, and of it a beneficiary. For it is already avowed that the Philippines are but a "stopping-place" on the way to the continent of Asia; and China, unlike Poland, is inhabited by an "inferior race," in regard to whom, as large possible consumers of surplus products, Providence has imposed on us obvious obligations, material as well as benevolent and religious, which it would be unlike ourselves to disregard. It is the mandate of duty, we are told,—the nations of Europe obey it, and can we do less than they? "Isolation" it is then argued is but another name for an attention to one's own business which may well become excessive, and result in selfishness. It is true that the nations of the Old World have not heretofore erred conspicuously in this respect; and as the "Balance of Power" was the word-juggle with which to conjure up wars and armaments in the eighteenth century, so the "Division of Trade" may not impossibly prove the similar conjuring word-juggle of the twentieth century. Nevertheless, "isolation" is not compatible with the policy of a Great Nation under a call to assert itself as a World Power. Then follows the familiar argument in favor of costly military and naval establishments. But, upon this head it is needless to restate our traditional policy,—our jealousy as a people of militarism and large standing armies, to be used, if occasion calls, as a reserve police. Our record thereon is so plain that repetition grows tedious. The record of Europe, and especially of Great Britain as distinguished from other European powers, has been equally plain, and is no less indisputable. In this respect, also, always under compulsion, we now admit our error. Costly armies are necessary to the maintenance of order, Heaven's first law; and World Powers cannot maintain peace, and themselves, without powerful navies and frequent coaling stations.

Finally, even on such matters as the Protective System and the encouragement of American Labor, as against the "Pauper Labor" of Europe and of the inferior races, Great Britain has for half a century now advocated the principle of unrestricted industry and free trade,— that is the "Open Door" policy logically carried to its final results. We have denied it, establishing what we in time grew to call the distinctive American system. It is, however, now asserted that "Trade follows the Flag," and that, as respects dependencies at least, the "Open Door" policy is the best policy. If "Trade follows the Flag" in dependencies, and, by so doing, affords the American producer all needful protection and every fair advantage in those dependencies, it is not at once apparent why it fails so to do at home. Is it less docile to the flag, less in harmony with and subservient to it, in the United States, within our own limits, than in remote lands under that flag beyond the seas? And, if so, how is such an apparent anomaly accounted for? But with this question we are not concerned. That problem is for the economist to solve, for in character it is commercial, not historical. The point with us is that again, as regards the "Open Door,"—free trade and no favor, so far as all outside competition is concerned, American labor and "pauper" labor being equally outside,—on this long and hotly contested point, also, England appears on the face of things to have had after all much the best of the argument.

As regards "Pauper Labor," indeed, the reversal contemplated of established policy in favor of European methods is specially noteworthy. The labor of Asia is undeniably less well paid even than that of Europe; but it is now proposed, by a single act, to introduce into our industrial system ten millions of Asiatics, either directly, or through their products sold in open competition with our own; or, if we do not do that, to hold them, ascribed to the soil in a sort of old Saxon serfdom, with the function assigned them of consuming our surplus products, but without in return sending us theirs. The great counterbalancing consideration will not, of course, be forgotten that, like the English in India, we also bestow on them the Blessings of Liberty and the Bible; provided, always, that liberty does not include freedom to go to the United States, and the Bible does include the excellent Old Time and Old World precept (Coloss. 3: 22), "Servants, obey in all things your masters."

It is the same in other respects. It seems to be admitted by the President, and by the leading authorities on the imperialistic policy, that it can only be carried to successful results through the agency of a distinct governing class. Accordingly administration through the agency of military or naval officers is strongly urged both by the President and by Captain Mahan. Other advocates of the policy urge its adoption on the ground, very distinctly avowed, that it will necessitate an established, recognized Civil Service, modelled, they add, on that of Great Britain. If, they then argue, Great Britain can extend—as, indeed, she unquestionably has extended—her system of dependencies all over the globe, developing them into the most magnificent empire the world ever saw, it is absurd, unpatriotic, and pessimistic to doubt that we can do the same. Are we not of the same blood, and the same speech? This is all historically true. Historically it is equally true that, to do it, we must employ means similar to those Great Britain has employed. In other words, modelling ourselves on Great Britain, we must slowly and methodically develop and build up a recognized and permanent governing and official class. The heathen and barbarian need to be studied, and dealt with intelligently and on a system; they cannot be successfully managed on any principle of rotation in office, much less one which ascribes the spoils of office to the victors at the polls. What these advocates of Imperialism say is unquestionably true: The political methods now in vogue in American cities are not adapted to the government of dependencies.

The very word "Imperial" is, indeed, borrowed from the Old World. As applied to a great system of colonial dominion and foreign dependencies it is English, and very modern English, also, for it was first brought into vogue by the late Earl of Beaconsfield in 1879, when, by Act of Parliament introduced by him, the Queen of England was made Empress of India. It was then he enunciated that doctrine of *imperium et libertas*, the adoption of which we are now considering. While it may be wise and sound, it indisputably is British.

Thus, curiously enough, whichever way we turn and however we regard it, at the close of more than a century of independent existence we find ourselves, historically speaking, involved in a mesh of contradictions with our past. Under a sense of obligation, impelled by circumstances, perhaps to a degree influenced by ambition and commercial greed, we have one by one abandoned our distinctive national tenets, and accepted in their place, though in some modified forms, the old-time European tenets and policies, which we supposed the world, actuated largely by our example, was about forever to discard. Our whole record as a people is, of course, then ransacked and subjected to microscopic investigation, and every petty disregard of principle, any wrong heretofore silently, perhaps sadly, ignored, each unobserved or disregarded innovation of the past, is magnified into a precedent justifying anything and everything in the future. If we formerly on some occasion swallowed a gnat, why now, is it asked, strain at a camel? Truths once accepted as "self-evident," since become awkward of acceptance, were ever thus pettifogged out of the path, and fundamental principles have in this way prescriptively been tampered with. It is now nearly a century and a quarter ago, when Great Britain was contemplating the subjection of her American dependencies, that Edmund Burke denounced "tampering" with the "ingenuous and noble roughness of truly constitutional materials," as "the odious vice of restless and unstable minds." Historically speaking it is not unfair to ask if this is less so in the United States in 1898 than it was in Great Britain in 1775.

What is now proposed, therefore, examined in connection with our principles and traditional policy as a nation, does apparently indicate a break in continuity,—historically, it will probably constitute what is known in geology as a "fault." Indeed, it is almost safe to say that history hardly records any change of base and system on the part of a great people at once so sudden, so radical, and so pregnant with consequences. To the optimist,—he who has no dislike to "Old Jewry," as the proper receptacle for worn-out garments, personal or political,—the outlook is inspiring. He insensibly recalls and repeats those fine lines of Tennyson:

> "To-day I saw the dragon-fly Come from the wells where he did lie.
> "An inner impulse rent the veil Of his old husk: from head to tail Came out clear plates of sapphire mail.
> "He dried his wings: like gauze they grew: Thro' crofts and pastures wet with dew A living flash of light he flew."

To others, older perhaps, but at any rate more deeply impressed with the difference apt to develop between dreams and actualities, the situation calls to mind a comparison, more historical it is true, but less inspiriting so far as a commitment to the new policy is concerned. At the risk, possibly, of offending some of those present, I will venture to institute it. In the fourth chapter of the Gospel according to St. Matthew, I find this incident recorded: "The devil taketh him [the Saviour] up into an exceeding high mountain, and showeth him all the kingdoms of the world, and the glory of them; and saith unto him, All these things will I give thee, if thou wilt fall down and worship me. Then saith Jesus unto him, Get thee hence, Satan. Then the devil leaveth him, and, behold, angels came and ministered unto him." Now, historically speaking, and as a matter of scriptural exegesis, that this passage should be accepted literally is not supposable. Satan, on the occasion referred to, must not be taken to have presented himself to the Saviour *in propriâ personâ* with his attributes of horns, tail, and cloven hoof, and made an outright proposition of extra-territorial sovereignty. It was a parable. He who had assumed a lofty moral attitude was tempted by worldly inducements to adopt a lower attitude,—that, in a word, common among men. It was a whispering to Christ of what among nations, is known as "Manifest Destiny;" in that case, however, as possibly in others, it so chanced that the whispering was not from the Almighty, but from Satan. Now if, instead of recognizing the source whence the temptation came, and sternly saying, "Get thee hence, Satan," Christ had seen the proposition as a new Mission,—thought, in fact, that he heard a distinct call to Duty,—and so, accepting a Responsibility thrust upon him, had hurried down from the "exceeding high mountain," and proceeded at once to lay in a supply of weapons and to don defensive armor, renouncing his peaceful mission, he would have done exactly—what Mohammed did six centuries later!

I do not for a moment mean to suggest that, as respects the voice of "Manifest Destiny," there is any similarity between the case of the Saviour and that which we, as a people, are now considering. I am not a prophet, nor do I claim prophetic insight. We are merely historical investigators, and, as such, not admitted into the councils of the Almighty. Others doubtless are, or certainly claim to be. They know every time, and at once, whether it is the inspiration of God or the devil; and forthwith proclaim it from the house-tops. We must admit—at any rate no evidence in our possession enables us to deny—the confidential relations such claim to have with either or both of the agencies in question,—the Divine or the Infernal. All I now have in mind is to call attention to the obvious similarity of the positions. As compared with the ideals and tenets then in vogue,—principles of manhood, equality before the law, freedom, peace on earth, and good-will to men,—the United States, heretofore and seen in a large way, has, among nations, assumed a peculiar, and, from the moral point of view, unquestionably a lofty attitude. Speaking historically it might, and with no charge of levity, be compared with a similar moral attitude assumed among men eighteen centuries before by the Saviour. It discountenanced armaments and warfare; it advocated arbitrations, and bowed to their awards; spreading its arms and protection over the New World, it refused to embroil itself in the complications of the Old; above all, it set a not unprofitable example to the nations of benefits incident to minding one's own business, and did not arrogate to itself the character of a favorite and inspired instrument in the hands of God. It even went so far as to assume that, in working out the inscrutable ways of Providence, character, self-restraint, and moral grandeur were in the long run as potent in effecting results as iron-clads and gatling-guns.

Those who now advocate a continuance of this policy are, as neatly as wittily, referred to in discussion, "for want of a better name," as "Little Americans," just as in history the believers in the long-run efficacy of the doctrines of Christ might be termed "Little Gospellers," to distinguish them from the admirers of the later, but more brilliant and imperial, dispensation of Mohammed. That the earlier, and less immediately ambitious, doctrine was, in the case of the United States, only temporary, and is now outgrown, and must, therefore, be abandoned in favor of Old World methods, especially those pursued with such striking success by Great Britain, is possible. As historical investigators we have long since learned that it is the unexpected which in the development of human affairs is most apt to occur. Who, for instance, in our own recent history could ever have foreseen that, in the inscrutable ways of the Almighty, the great triumph of Slavery in the annexation of Texas, and the spoliation of that inferior race which inhabited Mexico, was, within fifteen years only, to result in what Lincoln called that "terrible war" in which every drop of blood ever drawn by the lash was paid by another drawn by the sword? Again, in May, 1856, a Representative of South Carolina struck down a Senator from Massachusetts in the Senate-chamber at Washington; in January, 1865, Massachusetts battalions bivouacked beside the smoking ruins of South Carolina's capital. Verily, as none know better than we, the ways of Providence are mysterious, and past finding out. None the less, though it cannot be positively asserted that the world would not have been wiser, more advanced, and better ordered had Christ, when on that "exceeding high mountain," heard in the words then whispered in his ear a manifest call of Duty, and felt a Responsibility thrust upon him to secure the kingdoms of the earth for the Blessings of Liberty and the Bible by so small a sacrifice as making an apparently meaningless obeisance to Satan, yet we can certainly say that the world would now have been very different from what it is had He so done. And so in the case of the United States, though we cannot for a moment assert that its fate and the future of the world will not be richer, better, and brighter from its abandonment of New World traditions and policies in favor of the traditions and policies of the Old World, we can say without any hesitation that the course of history will be greatly changed by the so doing.

In any event the experiment will be one of surpassing interest to the historical observer. Some years ago James Russell Lowell was asked by the French historian, Guizot, how long the Republic of the United States might reasonably be expected to endure. Mr. Lowell's reply has always been considered peculiarly happy. "So long," said he, "as the ideas of its founders continue dominant." In due course of time we, or those who follow us, will know whether Mr. Lowell diagnosed the situation correctly, or otherwise. Meanwhile, I do not know how I can better bring to an end this somewhat lengthy contribution to the occasion, than by repeating, as singularly applicable to the conditions in which we find ourselves, these verses from a recent poem, than which I have heard none in the days that now are which strike a deeper or a truer chord, or one more appropriate to this New England Paschal eve:

> "The tumult and the shouting dies,
> The captains and the kings depart;
> Still stands thine ancient sacrifice,
> An humble and a contrite heart.
> Lord God of Hosts, be with us yet,
> Lest we forget—lest we forget!
> "Far-called our navies melt away,
> On dune and headline sinks the fire—
> Lo, all our pomp of yesterday
> Is one with Nineveh and Tyre!
> Judge of the nations, spare us yet,
> Lest we forget—lest we forget!
> "If, drunk with sight of power, we loose
> Wild tongues that have not Thee in awe,
> Such boasting as the Gentiles use
> Or lesser breeds without the law—
> Lord God of hosts, be with us yet,

Lest we forget—lest we forget!
"For heathen heart that puts her trust
In reeking tube and iron shard—
All valiant dust that builds on dust,
And guarding calls not Thee to guard—
For frantic boast and foolish word,
Thy mercy on thy people, Lord!
Amen."

Taken in connection with the foregoing paper, the following-letter, addressed to the Hon. Carl Schurz, is self-explanatory:

Boston, December 21, 1898.

My Dear Mr. Schurz:

In a recent letter you kindly suggest that I submit to you a sketch of what, I think, should be said in an address such as it is proposed should now be put forth by the Anti-Imperialist League to the people of the United States.

I last evening read a paper before the Lexington Historical Society, in which I discussed the question of extra-territorial expansion from the historical point of view. A copy of this paper I hope soon to forward you. Meanwhile, there is one aspect, and, to my mind, the all-important aspect of the question, which, in addressing an historical society, was not germane. I refer to the question of a practical policy to be pursued by us, as a nation, under existing conditions. That Spain has abandoned all claim of sovereignty over the Philippine islands admits of no question. Whether the United States has accepted the sovereignty thus abandoned is still an open question; but this I do not regard as material. Nevertheless, we are confronted by a fact; and, whenever we criticise the policy up to this time pursued; we are met with an inquiry as to what we have to propose in place of it. We are invited to stop finding fault with others, and to suggest some feasible alternative policy ourselves.

To this we must, therefore, in fairness, address ourselves. It is, in my judgment, useless to attempt to carry on the discussion merely in the negative form. As opponents of an inchoate policy we must, in place of what we object to, propose something positive, or we must abandon the field. Accepting the alternative, I now want to suggest a positive policy for the consideration of those who feel as we feel. I wish your judgment upon it.

There has, it seems to me, been a great deal of idle "Duty," "Mission," and "Call" talk on the subject of our recent acquisition of "Islands beyond the Sea," and the necessity of adopting some policy, commonly described as "Imperial," in dealing with them. This policy is, in the minds of most people who favor it, to be indirectly modelled on the policy heretofore so successfully pursued under somewhat similar conditions by Great Britain. It involves, as I tried to point out in the Lexington paper I have referred to, the abandonment or reversal of all the fundamental principles of our government since its origin, and of the foreign policy we have heretofore pursued. This, I submit, is absolutely unnecessary. Another and substitute policy, purely American, as contradistinguished from the European or British, known as "Imperial," policy, can readily be formulated.

This essentially American policy would be based both upon our cardinal political principles, and our recent foreign experiences. It is commonly argued that, having destroyed the existing government in Cuba, Porto Rico, and the Philippines, we have assumed a political responsibility, and are under a moral obligation to provide another government in place of that which by our action has ceased to exist. What has been our course heretofore under similar circumstances? Precedents, I submit, at once suggest themselves. Precedents, too, directly in point, and within your and my easy recollection.

I refer to the course pursued by us towards Mexico in the year 1848, and again in 1866; towards Hayti for seventy years back; and towards Venezuela as recently as three years ago. It is said that the inhabitants of the islands of the Antilles, and much more those of the Philippine archipelago, are as yet unfitted to maintain a government; and that they should be kept in a condition of "tutelage" until they are fitted so to do. It is further argued that a stable government is necessary, and that it is out of the question for us to permit a condition of chronic disturbance and scandalous unrest to exist so near our own borders as Cuba and Porto Rico. Yet how long, I would ask, did that condition exist in Mexico? And with what results? How long has it existed in Hayti? Has the government of Venezuela ever been "stable"? Have we found it necessary or thought it best to establish a governmental protectorate in any of those immediately adjacent regions?

What has been, historically, our policy—the American, as distinguished from the European and British policy—towards those communities,—two of them Spanish, one African? So far as foreign powers are concerned, we have laid down the principle of "Hands-off." So far as their own government was concerned, we insisted that the only way to learn to walk was to try to walk, and that the history of mankind did not show that nations placed under systems of "tutelage,"—taught to lean for support on a superior power,—ever acquired the faculty of independent action.

Of this, with us, fundamental truth, the British race itself furnishes a very notable example. In the forty-fourth year of the Christian era the island of Great Britain was occupied by what the "Imperial" Romans adjudged to be an inferior race. To the Romans the Britons unquestionably were inferior. Every child's history contains an account of the course then pursued by the superior towards that inferior race, and its results. The Romans occupied Great Britain, and they occupied it hard upon four centuries, holding the people in "tutelage," and protecting them against themselves, as well as against their enemies. With what result? So emasculated and incapable of self-government did the people of England become during their "tutelage" that, when Rome at last withdrew, they found themselves totally unfitted for self-government, much more for facing a foreign enemy. As the last, and best, historian of the English people tells us, the purely despotic system of the imperial government "by crushing all local independence, crushed all local vigor. Men forgot how to fight for their country when they forgot how to govern it."[3] The end was that, through six centuries more, England was overrun, first by those of one race, and then by those of another, until the Normans established themselves in it as conquerors; and then, and not until then, the deteriorating effect of a system of long continued "tutelage" ceased to be felt, and the islanders became by degrees the most energetic, virile, and self-sustaining of races. As nearly, therefore, as can be historically stated, it took eight centuries for the people of England to overcome the injurious influence of four centuries of just such a system as it is now proposed by us to inflict on the Philippines.[4] Hindostan would furnish another highly suggestive example of the educational effects of "tutelage" on a race. After a century and a half of that British "tutelage," what progress has India made towards fitness for self-government? Is the end in sight?

From the historical point of view, it is instructive to note the exactly different results reached through the truly American policy we have pursued in the not dissimilar cases of Hayti and Mexico. While Hayti, it is true, has failed to make great progress in one century, it has made quite as much progress as England made during any equal period immediately after Rome withdrew from it. And that degree of slowness in growth, which with equanimity has been endured by us in Hayti, could certainly be endured by us in islands on the coast of Asia. It cannot be gainsaid that, through our insisting on the policy of non-interference ourselves, and of non-interference by European nations, Hayti has been brought into a position where it is on the high road to better things in future. That has been the result of the prescriptive American policy. With Mexico, the case is far stronger. We all know that in 1848, after our war of spoliation, we had to bolster up a semblance of a government for Mexico, with which to negotiate a treaty of peace. Mexico at that time was reduced by us to a condition of utter anarchy. Under the theory now gaining in vogue, it would then have been our plain duty to make of Mexico an extra-territorial dependency, and protect it against itself. We wisely took a different course. Like other Spanish communities in America, Mexico than passed through a succession of revolutions, from which it became apparent the people were not in a fit condition for self-government. Nevertheless, sternly insisting on non-interference by outside powers, we ourselves wisely left that country to work out its own salvation in its own way.

In 1862, when the United States was involved in the War of the Rebellion, the Europeans took advantage of the situation to invade Mexico, and to establish there a "stable government." They undertook to protect that people against themselves, and to erect for them a species of protectorate, such as we now propose for the Philippines. As soon as our war was over, we insisted upon the withdrawal of Europe from Mexico. What followed is matter of recent history. It is unnecessary to recall it. We did not reduce Mexico into a condition of "tutelage," or establish over it a "protectorate" of our own. We, on the contrary, insisted that it should stand on its own legs; and, by so doing, learn to stand firmly on them, just as a child learns to walk, by being compelled to try to walk, not by being kept everlastingly in "leading strings." This was the American, as contradistinguished from the European policy; and Mexico to-day walks firmly.

Finally take the case of Venezuela in 1895. I believe I am not mistaken when I say that, during the twenty-five preceding years, Venezuela had undergone almost as many revolutions. It certainly had not enjoyed a stable government. Through disputes over questions of boundary, Great Britain proposed to confer that indisputable blessing upon a considerable region. We interfered under a most questionable extension of the Monroe Doctrine, and asserted the principle of "Hands-off." Having done this,—having in so far perpetuated what we now call the scandal of anarchy,—we did not establish "tutelage," or a protectorate, ourselves. We wisely left Venezuela to work out its destiny in its own way, and in the fullness of time. That policy was far-seeing, beneficent, and strictly American in 1895. Why, then, make almost indecent haste to abandon it in 1898?

Instead, therefore, of finding our precedents in the experience of England, or that of any other European power, I would suggest that the true course for this country now to pursue is exactly the course we have heretofore pursued under similar conditions. Let us be true to our own traditions, and follow our own precedents. Having relieved the Spanish islands from the dominion of Spain, we should declare concerning them a policy of "Hands-off," both on our own part and on the part of other powers. We should say that the independence of those islands is morally guaranteed by us as a consequence of the treaty of Paris, and then leave them just as we have left Hayti, and just as we left Mexico and Venezuela, to adopt for themselves such form of government as the people thereof are ripe for. In the cases of Mexico and Venezuela, and in the case of Hayti, we have not found it necessary to interfere ever or at all. It is not yet apparent why we should find it necessary to interfere with islands so much more remote from us than Hayti, and than Mexico and Venezuela, as are the Philippines.

In this matter we can thus well afford to be consistent, as well as logical. Our fundamental principles, those of the Declaration, the Constitution, and the Monroe Doctrine, have not yet been shown to be unsound—why should we be in such a hurry to abandon them? Our precedents are close at hand, and satisfactory—why look away from them to follow those of Great Britain? Why need we, all of a sudden, be so very English and so altogether French, even borrowing their nomenclature of "imperialism?" Why can not we, too, in the language of Burke, be content to set our feet "in the tracks of our forefathers, where we can neither wander nor stumble?" The only difficulty in the way of our so doing seems to be that we are in such a desperate hurry; while natural influences and methods, though in the great end indisputably the wisest and best, always require time in which to work themselves out to their results. Wiser than the Almighty in our own conceit, we think to get there at once; the "there" in this case being everlasting "tutelage," as in India, instead of ultimate self-government, as in Mexico.

The policy heretofore pursued by us in such cases,—the policy of "Hands-off," and "Walk alone," is distinctly American; it is not European, not even British. It recognizes the principles of our Declaration of Independence. It recognizes the truth that all just government exists by the consent of the governed. It recognizes the existence of the Monroe Doctrine. In a word, it recognizes every principle and precedent, whether natural or historical, which has from the beginning lain at the foundation of our American polity. It does not attempt the hypocritical contradiction in terms, of pretending to elevate a people into a self-sustaining condition through the leading-string process of "tutelage." It appeals to our historical experience, applying to present conditions the lessons of Hayti, Mexico, and Venezuela. In dealing with those cases, we did not find a great standing army or an enormous navy necessary; and, if not then, why now? Why such a difference between the Philippines and Hayti? Is Cuba larger or nearer to us than Mexico? When, therefore, in future they ask us what course and policy we Anti-Imperialists propose, our answer should be that we propose to pursue towards the islands of Antilles and the Philippines the same common-sense course and truly American policy which were by us heretofore pursued with such signal success in the cases of Hayti, Mexico, and Venezuela, all inhabited by people equally unfit for self-government, and geographically much closer to ourselves. We propose to guarantee them against outside meddling, and, above all, from "tutelage," and make them, by walking, learn to walk alone.

This, I submit, is not only an answer to the question so frequently put to us, but a positive policy following established precedents, and, what is more, purely American, as distinguished from a European or British, policy and precedents.

I remain, etc.,

Charles Francis Adams.

Hon. Carl Schurz,

16 E. 64th Street, New York City.

Notes:

1. "Obviously, men are not born equal in physical strength or in mental capacity, in beauty of form or health of body. Diversity or inequality in these respects is the law of creation. But this inequality is in no particular inconsistent with complete civil or political equality.

"The equality declared by our fathers in 1776 and made the fundamental law of Massachusetts in 1780, was *Equality before the Law.* Its object was to efface all political or civil distinctions, and to abolish all institutions founded upon *birth*. 'All men are *created* equal,' says the Declaration of Independence. 'All men are *born* free and equal,' says the Massachusetts Bill of Rights. These are not vain words. Within the sphere of their influence, no person can be *created*, no person can be *born*, with civil or political privileges not enjoyed equally by all his fellow-citizens; nor can any institutions be established, recognizing distinctions of birth. Here is the Great Charter of every human being drawing vital breath upon this soil, whatever may be his conditions, and whoever may be his parents. He may be poor, weak, humble, or black,—he may be of Caucasian, Jewish, Indian, or Ethiopian race,—he may be born of French, German, English, or Irish extraction; but before the Constitution of Massachusetts all these distinctions disappear. He is not poor, weak, humble, or black; nor is he Caucasian, Jew, Indian, or Ethiopian; nor is he French, German, English, or Irish; he is a MAN, the equal of all his fellow-men. He is one of the children of the State, which, like an impartial parent, regards all its offspring with an equal care. To some it may justly allot higher duties, according to higher capacities; but it welcomes all to its equal hospitable board. The State, imitating the divine Justice, is no respecter of persons."—*Works of Charles Sumner, Vol. II., pp. 341-2.*

2. Historically speaking, the assertion in the Declaration of Independence has been fruitful of dispute. The very evening the present paper was read at Lexington the Mayor of Boston, in a public address elsewhere, alluded to the "imprudent generalizations of our forefathers," referring, doubtless, to what Rufus Choate, forty-two years before, described as "the glittering and sounding generalities of natural right" to be found in the Declaration, "that passionate and eloquent manifesto." Mr. Calhoun declared (1848) that the claim of human equality set forth in the Declaration was "the most false and dangerous of all political errors," which, after resting a long time "dormant," had, in the process of time, begun "to germinate and produce its poisonous fruits." Mr. Pettit, a Senator from Indiana, pronounced it in 1854, "a self-evident

lie." In the famous Lincoln-Douglas debate in Illinois (1860) the question reappeared, Mr. Douglas contending that the Declaration applied only to "the white people of the United States;" while Mr. Lincoln, in reply, asserted that "the entire records of the world, from the date of the Declaration of Independence up to within three years ago, may be searched in vain for one single affirmation, from one single man, that the negro was not included in the Declaration." The contention of Mr. Douglas had recently again made its appearance in the press as something too indisputable to admit of discussion. It is asserted that, in penning the Declaration, Mr. Jefferson could not possibly have intended to include those then actually held as slaves. On this point Mr. Jefferson himself should, it would seem, be accepted as a competent witness. Referring to the denial of his "inalienable rights" to the African, he declared at a later day, "I tremble for my country, when I reflect that God is just." What he meant will, however, probably continue matter for confident newspaper assertions just so long as anybody in this country wants to make out, as did Stephen A. Douglas in 1860, a plausible pretext for subjugating somebody else,—Indian, African, or Asiatic. As Mr. Lincoln expressed it, "The assertion that all men are created equal was of no practical use in effecting our separation from Great Britain, and it was placed in the Declaration, not for that but for future use. Its author meant it to be, as, thank God, it is now proving itself, a stumbling block to all those who, in after times, might seek to turn a free people back into the paths of despotism. They knew the proneness of prosperity to breed tyrants, and they meant, when such should reappear in this fair land, and commence their vocation, they should find left for them at least one hard nut to crack."—*Works*, Vol. I., p. 233.

3. Green's *Short History* (Ill. Ed.). Vol. I. p. 9.

4. The Roman legions were withdrawn from Great Britain in 410; Magna Charta was signed in June, 1215, and the reign of French kings over England came to a close in 1217. It is a striking illustration of the deliberation with which natural processes work themselves out, that the period which elapsed between the withdrawal of Rome from England, and the recovery of England by the English, should have exceeded

by more than a century the time which has as yet elapsed since England was thus recovered.

22

The Panama Canal Zone: An Epochal Event in Sanitation

Published in the
Proceedings of the Massachusetts Historical Society,
for May 1911.

Leaving New York for Colon, Monday, March 6th, we landed in New York on our return Thursday, March 30th, having passed ten days (13th to 23d) on the Isthmus and in the so-called Canal Zone. A winter voyage to Caribbean waters and a brief stay on the Darien Isthmus are not now so unusual as, under ordinary circumstances, to justify record, much less to call for one. Scarcely more exceptional than going to the Mediterranean by way of the Azores and Gibraltar, I should not, under ordinary circumstances, any more care to put detailed mention of it in the *Proceedings* of this Society than I would make record there of one of the numerous trips I have, first and last, made across the Atlantic. There are, however, even in these days, trips- and trips; and five years ago a winter trip carried me into a region- that of the White Nile- not yet become wholly familiar to the tourist. What I there heard and saw also proved, if not altogether novel, so suggestive that I made it the subject of a communication which, finding a place in our *Proceedings*,[1] also at the time attracted a certain amount of general attention. Though less unusual, the Panama experience proved not less interesting and quite as suggestive as that of five years ago in East Africa. In Central America I found myself face to face with what I cannot but feel is going at no remote day to be recognized from the strictly historical point of view as an epochal development; and, thus feeling, I propose here to put on file some account of what I saw, and of what I feel assured will in time result therefrom.

Before doing this, however, I wish to forestall an obvious, though natural criticism. Ten days, it must be admitted, are a very insufficient space of time in which to make a study of so considerable and complicated an enterprise as this Panama Canal,- an enterprise with so many different aspects; much less would any observation possible to be made in that time, by one both a layman in engineering and a novice in tropical conditions, suffice for the drawing of inferences of value, or such as would be entitled to consideration. This is altogether undeniable; and yet, for reasons which will presently appear, I propose not only to tell what I saw and repeat what I was told, but to draw inferences therefrom; always, of course, subject to correction by those better informed. And I feel moved so to do by a conviction that what I have to say is at least not matter of general knowledge; and, further, that what was altogether novel to me cannot be wholly familiar to others.

Premising this, I come to my subject. From the moment I reached the Isthmus to the day I left it, what most impressed me was not the magnitude of the undertaking, the engineering and material difficulties encountered in carrying it to a successful issue, nor yet the administrative ability displayed in overcoming those difficulties;- of all these I shall later on have something to say; but it was not these which from start to finish interested me most. What did most interest as well as surprise me was the morale apparent in those I encountered, the high standard of their physical condition, and the energy, alertness and zeal with which amid tropical surroundings all, from highest to lowest, went at their work. This was unmistakable, and apparent from the day I left New York. On the steamer were various employes, or members of the families of employes,- both sexes and all ages,- people who had been in the Zone for years and were now returning from a visit to their homes, whether for purposes of business or recreation. Not one but was ready and even glad to go back; all looked forward to remaining there for the end-till, as the expression went, they "saw the thing through." For them existence and labor in the tropics, on the Chagres River or in the Culebra Cut, had neither terrors nor deprivations, nor inconveniences even. They actually professed to like the climate and life, and to be more than satisfied with their jobs. And this expression was uniform; nor, evidently, was it in any way forced or simulated. Those I met also were unmistakably healthy in aspect; in them and in their bodily movements no indication was to be seen of that lassitude and those anremic conditions which we are accustomed to associate with any prolonged residence in the tropics, a region in the present case ten degrees only removed from the Equator. Young and old, they were a ruddy-faced, well-conditioned set, both in aspect and in action physically in good case.

So impressed from the start, as I went on these things more and more forced themselves on my notice, incessantly calling for explanation. I had heard vaguely of measures of sanitation enforced in the Canal Zone, and of a consequent decrease in the rate of mortality; but not the less the vicinage of the treacherous, death-dealing Chagres still in association remained the worst reputed region, "the foremost pest-hole," of the earth, infamous for its fevers, and interesting only because of the variety of its malarial disorders and pestilences. Its sanitary conditions might be less wholly bad; but that they should be positively, and in comparison with other places, good, surpassed reasonable belief.

If now, however, I were asked what single thing seen impressed me most of all I saw during my stay in the Canal Zone, I should reply, not the Gatun Dam nor yet the Culebra Cut, but the afternoon and evening of March 15 spent at Camp Elliott, as it is called, an elevation about equidistant from both Atlantic and Pacific, and supposed to be not far from the spot where Francis Drake, three hundred and thirty-eight years ago, caught from the branches of a lofty tree his first momentous glimpse of what men then called the South Sea. Camp Elliott, located on high ground in the midst of a tropical jungle, half a mile only from the banks of the Chagres, has for two consecutive years been the home of a detachment of U. S. marines under command of Major Smedley D. Butler. A large party of visitors had been invited there on this occasion to witness a drill, and be guests at an evening's entertainment. We went from Panama by train in the early afternoon, returning in the late evening. The force of marines at the camp numbered five hundred men, composing two battalions. As I have said, they had been stationed there two years; yet a finer, healthier-looking, more active and better conditioned body of men — "huskier " is the word — I do not remember to have seen; and, of the whole number (487) then there, I was assured by the post physician not one was that day sick in hospital. Such a record would be remarkable any-where; but half a mile away from the Chagres, it was, I submit, well calculated to excite a special wonder.

My occasions for surprise were, however, not confined to the visit at Camp Elliott; the next almost equally striking incident was of a nature peculiarly pleasing. The following evening another social engagement carried me out, this time to Culebra, the site of the much advertised "cut," or excavation. The local travel, especially the evening local travel, on the Panama railroad is heavy; surprisingly so, indeed. Trains of six coaches are crowded; and while many nationalities and all shades of color, from pure white to ebony, are represented, women and young children make up a larger proportion of the whole than is usual with us. Later in the evening we were to take the return train to Panama, a distance of perhaps a dozen miles. Coming on our way back to the Culebra station, at about nine o'clock, we found the platforms thronged much as is apt to be the case after sundown at all southern way stations,- people were there, some to take the train, others accompanying visitors about to take it, while a good many seemed to be idlers brought together by mere curiosity or to enjoy the evening's coolness. Moving along towards the point where the head of the train I was to take would probably stop, I there came across a group of American girls, eight or ten in number, and varying in age from perhaps ten to fifteen. Very nicely and neatly dressed in their thin white frocks, with heads uncovered, some of them, like ourselves, had come to take the train home, others to see their companions off. A more healthy, well-to-do and companionable group of children could not under similar conditions have been met at any station within twenty 'miles of Boston. Perfectly at home, and at ease sitting " and standing, without a thought of malaria or any other danger, they were chatting and laughing under the glare of the station lights, about which not an insect was flitting; while the hum of the mosquito was noticeable from its absence. Not one was to be heard. The material, social and meteorological conditions would in every respect have compared favorably with those to which we here are accustomed during the midsummer season; the single noticeable difference was the more complete absence of insect life, whether merely annoying or aggressively noxious. And this on the slope of the death-dealing Chagres!

I freely confess I could not understand it; nor, after a fairly intelligent effort at enlightenment from the most authoritative and best informed sources, do I really understand it yet. I questioned Colonel Gorgas, the head of the Sanitary Department, of whom and whose evidence I shall presently have more to say. I met and talked with Mr. and Mrs. C. C. Mallet; he a man of over fifty, English born, from youth a resident on the Isthmus, and, since 1908, British Minister Resident at Panama; she, of Spanish descent, born in Panama.[2] So far as the yellow fever was concerned, Madam Mallet, an Obarrio and so to the manner born, was, it may be inferred, immune, having presumably gone through the dread ordeal vicariously, as it were, in the persons of forbears more or less remote. Indeed, a belief, I was assured, exists that no child born within Panama town limits need later fear the *vomito*. Mr. Mallet, less fortunate in this respect, had, by the narrowest of possible margins, survived an attack. They both had lived in Panama before the French attempt at canal construction, all through the times of that attempt, and since during the American regime. Their reminiscences were vivid; at times, ghastly and pathetic. Very curious on the subject, I asked Madam Mallet as to the normal conditions at that period of the year; for though I remembered well both the stifling heat and the insect life I had encountered five years previous on the White Nile at the same period of the year (March) and in exactly the same latitude (10° North), between the two environments there seemed nothing in common. The White Nile was a stagnant pest-hole swarming with insect life; the Chagres was to all appearance an agreeable winter health-resort. Even Pharaoh's old plague, the common house-fly, was noticeable only from his absence. Thus puzzled, I asked Madam Mallet as to the facts, and her explanation thereof. Was it a question of season?- and was this the off season? The: reply I got was to the point, and given with Latin animation. Madam Mallet assured me that, had I found myself ten years before where I then was at the same season of the year, I would have been devoured by mosquitoes, while the flies would have been as ubiquitous as they were unbearable. To my further question of how she- born in Panama, and all her life a resident of the inmost quarter of the town of Panama itself- still in fact there domiciled- how she accounted for it, the response was quick and to the point, a reply conveyed quite as much through the movements of the hands as by the mouth,- "I explain it in one word - Colonel Goethals!"

Though indisputably gratifying and to the last degree suggestive, this answer, besides being manifestly unjust to others, especially Colonel Gorgas, was, even to a layman like myself, not in all respects satisfactory. I was quite conscious that my informant was speaking somewhat metaphorically, and had no idea that what she said would

be taken in a literal way; much less be repeated, and in print. Moreover, even when accompanied by these limitations, the explanation
left much to be accounted for. For instance, we were then sitting at
table, but behind the wire screens always prescribed by the officials in
charge of sanitation for every place of abode; the following day, however, I chanced to meet at the hotel Dr. Morton Prince of Boston,
there in company with some ladies from New York, all members of a
large excursion party come into Colon the day before. They had been
"doing" the Canal, and were to pass the night at Panama. Dining together, at about nine o'clock we all went out on the broad verandah of
the hotel, overlooking the Pacific. Not fancying the sense of enclosure
within the screened part of the gallery, Dr. Prince suggested that we
go outside, sitting and chatting in the open. We did so, a party of eight
or ten, all new-comers and clad in the light thin garments customarily
worn in the tropics. We sat there in the coolness of the early night for
perhaps an hour, no screen or protection of any kind between us and
the trees and shrubs before the hotel; a powerful electric light was
flaring directly over our heads, and yet not an insect of any kind- fly,
moth or gnat- was either visible or audible; the shard-borne beetle
with his noisy hum was as noticeably absent as was the mosquito's
sharp acrid note. All the same, when the next day I mentioned this
performance to Colonel Gorgas, he shook his head with a disapproving look; he did not like that sort of thing- it was a reckless braving of
danger; and, moreover, contrary to regulation. Indeed, I had myself to
admit on better reflection that it was a somewhat ill-considered
proceeding.

Again, and a more unaccountable experience than any I have yet
described:-While at Ancon, the suburb of Panama in which are the
United States government buildings, including the Tivoli Hotel, I
drove out, as is the custom with all tourists, to visit the site and few
remains of Old Panama, as it is called, the original Spanish settlement
on the South Sea side of Darien, the point from which Pizarro sailed
forth, which Drake half a century later reconnoitred from both its land
and water sides, and the stronghold which the buccaneer Morgan

captured, sacked and practically destroyed in 1671. Once a busy and, for those days, populous and wealthy place, of Panama Viejo- in its way, I fancy, somewhat of an historical myth- I shall perhaps presently have something to say; meanwhile in this immediate connection I will only remark that the site, fronting an exposed tidal roadstead, is a wholly uninhabited jungle, rising in the midst of which, a landmark from sea or shore, is one lofty and well-preserved cathedral tower of solid masonry compact. A mile or so away on the landward side the remains of an old cobblestone road, or causeway, lead across a stone bridge, disappearing in the tropical jungle on either side of the muddy stream spanned by a single arch of solid masonry. Facing the sea, or back from it, but hidden in the well-nigh impenetrable tropical growth, are yet other ruined foundations, walls and buttresses, and vaults in what once were cellars, These mark the sites of religious edifices or public buildings; while the ground adjacent is covered with shards or fragments of what once was rather solid masonry. As a seat of traffic, the locality was abandoned more than two centuries ago in favor of the site of present Panama. The reason for its abandonment is obvious. As a port, it was not only unprotected from gales, but its depth of water in no way met the requirements of even seventeenth century maritime construction. So, its fate already sealed, the buccaneer Morgan, in 1671, dealt its death blow to the first Panama. From that blow it never rallied.

Having, after tourist fashion and quite uninformed, made a hasty preliminary visit to the spot, a day or two later at the quarters of Admiral H. H. Rousseau and Lieut. Col. D. DuBose Gaillard- both more or less archreologically inclined- my companion, Mr. Frank D. Millet, and myself were shown an ancient and contemporary ground-plan of the vanished town, and descriptions of it from Hakluyt's *Voyages* and Esquemelin's *Narrative* were brought to our notice. So, better advised and with greatly increased interest, we determined on a second and more carefully considered visit. Leaving the hotel at half past six on the morning of Tuesday, March 21, we did not get back until eleven, having passed some three hours in going over every accessible portion of the site. In other respects most interesting, the point to which I now want to call attention was, and is, to me most interesting of all. Moreover, it is still inexplicable. Here was a tropical sea-shore locality, six hundred miles only from the Equator, undrained and densely overgrown; the day, slightly overcast at times, was yet reasonably clear; the time was between 7 and 10 o'clock, A. M.; no noticeable wind was blowing; apparently it was an ordinary day for the locality, towards the close of the dry season; yet, during those three hours of constant physical activity, the heat, though considerable, was in no degree oppressive, nor can I recall having been annoyed by fly or gnat. I heard, though I did not see them, just two mosquitoes. Limits had to be allowed to the achievements of Colonel Goethals even ; and it was not reasonable to maintain that he had extinguished the fly, the gnat and the mosquito not only in the Canal Zone, but throughout Panamanian limits. Quite unable satisfactorily to account for them, I merely state facts and report conditions as they came under my actual observation.[3]

Meanwhile, though American sanitation has not accomplished impossibilities, it has indisputably wrought wonders. Into its details I do not propose to enter. If not familiar now, they will soon become so; for the war on household disease disseminators- the fly, the mosquito, the flea, the bug and the rat- now systematically inaugurated in the Canal Zone, will at no remote day be taken up and vigorously carried on in all countries properly to be classed as civilized. In time, it will even extend to the New England tavern, boarding-house and railroad refreshment-room. The rules and directions for it s conduct will then have been simplified, and be in the hands of everyone; so I will not dwell upon them here and now in a paper designed for record only. Suffice it to say that, so far as the sanitation of the Canal Zone is con- cerned- my present thesis- it is a matter purely of drainage, screening, the free and systematic use of oils and disinfectants, and cutting and firing; the whole enforced by rigid and unremitting inspection and policing. In the case of disease also, everlasting vigilance is the price of liberty. The very considerable results already reached are due to no great engineering feat- the making of a lake where once was a morass, or the laying out and construction of a modern *cloaca maxima*[4] they have, on the contrary, been brought about as the result of patient, long continued observation, supplemented by a system of rigidly policed sanitary regulation. Very matter-of-fact, commonplace even in detail, about those results there is nothing dramatic; little that strikes the eye. The appeal, based largely on the noticeable absence of filth and a study of the bills of mortality, is to the senses rather than to the imagination.

This element of the commonplace and obvious is, however, one we are slow to recognize as always affecting the problem. In facing it we have, also, continually to guard ourselves against preconceptions. Take, for example, the dreaded Chagres fever, so-called. I endeavored to obtain from Colonel Gorgas something in the nature of a diagnosis of it as a classified disease. Naturally, the result was not satisfactory; indeed, it was quite the reverse of satisfactory. He spoke of it as an acute malarial disorder, wholly distinct from yellow fever, but in more malignant cases frequently reported as such. A moment's reflection sufficed to show me how ill-considered my query was. It is still called a fever and classified as such; but while it unquestionably is accompanied with febrile action, it is nothing more nor less than a poisoning —a poisoning exactly like that from the bite of a moccasin or rattle-snake. As such only can it properly be classified. Its cause, dramatic in a way and terribly insidious, is not far to seek.

As a river the Chagres is unique; it constitutes a class by itself. A mountain stream, a hundred and twenty miles perhaps in length, when I saw it,- towards the close of the dry season,- it was flowing sluggishly along, a yellow rivulet, meandering through a tropical morass. But the rainfall, when it comes, is in that country something of which we in New England have no conception. For instance, I was assured by no less an authority than Mr. J. B. Bishop, the Secretary of the Isthmian Canal Commission, that there was a well-established record of close upon nine solid feet of rain at a point in the Chagres water-shed, all within two successive calendar months,- or, to be more specific, a fall of one hundred and three measured inches in sixty-one days of the months of November and December, 1909. That under such conditions the Chagres has been known to rise twenty-five feet in a single day is no occasion for surprise. The conductor is simply choked. The natural result follows. The neighboring country becomes a morass; and, as the torrent rapidly recedes, the region which emerges from under it remains saturated and stagnant subject to tropical conditions, an ideal breeding-place for every noxious reptile or poisonous: insect. Hence the so-called fever; for the bite of the Hindostan cobra was infinitely less to be dreaded than was the sting of the Chagres mosquito. Formerly supposed to be of atmospheric origin, the disorder was classified as a miasmatic fever peculiar to a locality; now, under control, it is practically extinct. But, as the question I put to Colonel Gorgas showed, the name and recollection abide.

It is the same with the yellow fever; though that, as every one at last knows, has been traced down to a single one of the very numerous species of the genus mosquito- the comparatively noiseless but deadly stegomyia. Men fear the cobra and avoid the rattlesnake,- the moccasin is looked upon as very deadly, and the copper-head has become a simile; but, so far as those of the human race were concerned, cobra and rattler, moccasin and copper-head, taken separately or massed together, were mere negligible dangers as compared with the stegomyia mosquito. The cobra only bites, and in biting kills his single victim, and that is the end; the stegomyia, on the contrary, not only kills that victim but injects into countless fresh victims the deadly virus drawn 'as food from former victims. The next thing inferred is obvious; and a theory is now confidently maintained that all other forms of tropical malaria, so called, are due to approximately identical causes. In no way contagious, and in only much less if in any degree of miasmatic origin, they are absolutely preventable; and this great result, if it in ripeness of time actually materializes, while elsewhere foreshadowed, has been brought to its demonstration in the Canal Zone of to-day. Its most dramatic and monumental achievement, the prevention, and the consequent practical extinction of the yellow fever, belongs exclusively to the Medical Department of the United States

Army. It was the outcome of our Spanish War (1901), thereby made memorable. Thus the Canal Zone is an object lesson, and the Canal itself a monument; for the last was, humanly speaking, made possible by a medical triumph, the like of which in importance to mankind has not been equalled since the discoveries of anæsthetics and antiseptics.

And this it is which caused me at the outset to say that the great and most startling impression left on me by what I saw on my visit to the Zone was not the magnified ditch itself, nor the engineering feats accomplished i nor yet the construction work in progress: These are remarkable; but solely, so far as I am competent to judge, because of their magnitude and concentratedness. I have frequently seen steam shovels at work; though never so many, nor quite so busily, as now in the Culebra Cut. So I have watched pneumatic drills as they bored into the rock, and heard the detonation of the dynamite; though at Panama more drills would be working at once and in closer proximity than I ever saw before, and the blasts when the day's work was done sounded like a discharge of artillery in battle. For centuries all civilized nations have been building canals and dams, though the Gatun Dam breaks the record for bigness; the locks. too, at Panama are larger and longer, and more elaborate and imposing than any yet designed. All this is true; and yet it failed deeply to impress me. After all, it was a mere question of bigness-the something more or something less; and, as a result of organized energy and systematic co-operation of forces for rapid daily accomplishment, I still think the construction of the Pacific railroads fifty years ago at the rate of half a dozen miles a day, every material, even water, having to be hauled to the moving camp which constituted the advancing front,- this was by far a more dramatic display than anything now to be seen on the Isthmus. Again, the Gatun Dam is a great conception; but as such the recent tunnelling of the Hudson and the subterranean honeycombing of Manhattan Island, combined with the bridging of the East River, impress me more. Finally, the locks at the entrance and outlet of the proposed Chagres Lake are imposing structures; but to my mind the terminal stations built, or now in process of building, in the heart of New York city, are more imposing. As I have said, all this is a mere question of degree, and time out of mind the world has been building roads and water-ways; moreover, behind this particular water-way is the Treasury of the United States. But when it comes to the sanitation which made all that is now going on at Panama humanly and humanely possible,- vanquishing pestilence and, while harnessing the Chagres, also making it innocuous to those both working and dwelling on its banks,- this is new; and the like of it the world had not before seen. Face to face with it, reading of it in the movements of the men and the faces of the children, I frankly admit what I saw smote the imagination. Seeing the American at his very best, one felt- at least, I felt, as never before- a pardonable pride of race.

Moreover, in the Panama Canal Zone of to-day you do see the American at his best- individually and collectively. The region, and those living and laboring there, impress one coming freshly from without as singularly sober, orderly, well conducted, and policed. There is a noticeable absence of that roughness, drunkenness and immorality,- that carelessness of life and defiance of its decencies traditionally associated with our American improvised communities pushing to rapid completion some great enterprise involving lavish expenditure, both inevitable and incessant. In the building of the Union Pacific, the town of Julesburg boasted of its wickedness, Hell was at Julesburg always equalled, and not unusually or infrequently outdone. Panama once, and that not so very long ago, bade fair to perpetuate the Julesburg tradition in this particular.[5] There is to-day no Julesburg in the Canal Zone. The impression in this respect made on the newly arriving stranger is curious; hut, though instinctive, quite unmistakable. It is in the air; you are at once conscious of its presence. It was silently evidenced by the issuance during the month I was there (March) of over 20,000 postal money orders, representing a little short of half a million dollars of savings, $370,000 of which was payable in the United States. Along the banks of the Chagres the workman to-day lives cheaper, enjoys apparently better health, and saves more than he can in Massachusetts, And for all this- order, thrift, temperance, health credit is due to someone.

Until I landed at Colon, I had never met either Colonel Goethals or. Colonel Gorgas; nor, indeed, with a single exception, anyone of the small-but very able body of officers and civil officials in charge of the Canal work. Mr. Bishop I had known long, and his connection with the *Canal Record* afforded easy access to a vast store of information not otherwise accessible, and at once interesting and reliable.' His was a veritable *vox clamantis in tropico.* But, subsequently, I found reason to regard all these gentlemen with ever-increasing respect; and on what I have come to consider the best of grounds. In the course of a fairly long and somewhat varied life it has been my fortune to be brought in contact with many men- men prominent politically, and in administrative and professional work; generals in command of great armies in active warfare; executives in the direction of large enterprises; financiers; notables of the market-place. The one thing in these contacts which has always insensibly but most impressed me has been the presence or absence in individuals of that clement known.as Character. Whether there or not there, the sense of its being there, or not being there, is instinctive. If there, in the man at the head, the thing permeates. You are conscious of it in every part; and I think Madam Mallet was right. Her female instinct guided her straight to the central fact. It is so in Panama. The individuality and character of Colonel Goethals to-day permeate, and permeate visibly, the entire Zone;- unconsciously on his part, unconsciously on the part of others, his influence is pervasive.[6] Nor, in expressing this opinion of Colonel Goethals, do I for a moment wish to depreciate, much less to ignore, the zeal and fidelity shown by the heads of department in the present Canal organization. Gorgas, Hodges, Gaillard, Devol, Rousseau, Bishop, one and all, so far as my brief stay afforded me opportunities of reaching an opinion, were stamped by the same die. Of some, of course, I saw but little; others I did not meet at all: but indications of the influence of Goethals were, I thought, perceptible everywhere. Quiet, reserved, unassuming, known to everyone engaged on the work but noticed, as he quietly moved around, by no one, he gave the impression of conscious because innate but unobtrusive force. He was a natural diplomat as well as an educated engineer; and, whether dealing with labor conditions or Latin-American officials and races, the Panama situation of to-day stands in quite as much need of a skilful diplomat as of a trained engineer.

Especially was I impressed, moreover, and most favorably so, by a certain modesty of attitude and expression observed by all I talked with towards those who had preceded them in the enterprise, especially the French. Far from any tendency to a depreciatory tone, open or covert, or to an attitude of self-glorification, all I saw and heard seemed almost to seek occasion to express their sense of the advantage they had derived from the work done and the experience gained by those who had initiated the enterprise, but failed to carry it to completion. Indeed, their testimony went at times further than was justified by the facts, as I saw them. Not only did they warmly commend the French engineering, but they admitted that much of the French material, and some of the French machinery, was more durable and, considering its date, better than what now came to them from the United States. The French mechanical appliances were also pronounced most valuable. Of De Lesseps they spoke with uniform respect; even going so far as to say that the French hospital organization and efforts at sanitation had contributed very materially to the remarkable results since attained.

Listening sympathetically, and appreciating to the fullest extent the fineness of feeling which inspired these utterances, I yet found myself unable in some respects to accept them at face value. There was, on the contrary, as it seemed to me, evidence everywhere that the French had involved themselves in the enterprise, and, when in it, gone about their work in a way most ill-considered and wasteful. With preconceived ideas altogether wrong, they provoked set-backs and invited ultimate failure. The 'material they bought and used may have been of the best quality; their engineering was probably, as our engineers admit, of the most approved sort ; some of their machinery and more or fewer of their appliances may still be in use; none the less the fact stands forth plain even to the layman that, taken altogether, De Lesseps was peculiarly ill-fitted to carry to a successful close what he so confidently undertook. From the beginning to the end he was obsessed. He had, so to speak, Suez Canal on the brain. Yet it may broadly be asserted that there was not a single lesson derived from the Suez experience applicable to Panama conditions. This sweeping generalization, moreover, held true at every point,- from the sea-level structure to rainfall, from the sandy soil on the Red Sea to the rocky, mountainous range above the Chagres River. In their essential features- political, geological, racial, industrial or sanitary- the two problems were unlike; and every lesson of experience drawn from the one was well calculated to lead to disaster if applied to the other. Yet De Lesseps invariably applied them all. As respects labor and sanitation, for instance, he apparently looked at the problem from a French point of view,- a military standpoint, and one quite the reverse of humanitarian. The work would cost lives as well as money; unquestionably it would: but, as Marshal Pelissier observed in the Crimea, " One cannot make omelettes without breaking eggs." The Suez Canal had been carried to completion by Egyptian forced labor, regardless of human sacrifice; just as it is still asserted, though with most absurd exaggeration, that every tie on the Panama railroad represented the life of a man employed in its construction. It would probably approach more closely to historic truth to say that every hundred ties was in this case the unit of representation; even that, however, would mount up to a very respectable holocaust. But, after all, the greatest possible death rate involved in the digging of a sea-level canal would be small in comparison with that always and necessarily incurred in the conduct of a war of even the second or third class. In view of the result to be secured, the loss of life was from the De Lesseps and Suez point of view a somewhat sentimental consideration, and one altogether negligible.

Passing over other factors in the situation,- financial, material, industrial, in regard to all of which the methods of the French seem to have been open to obvious criticism, passing over all these, it was their sanitary and hospital arrangements which interested me most. Colonel Gorgas spoke of them with apparent respect; the French work had, he said, been carried on before the mosquito theory and observations had led to their results, and we had profited largely by the French experience. This was doubtless true; but, none the less, the stories still told of that experience, while extremely pathetic, were undeniably grewsome,- in fact, I may say, ghastly. It appears to have been nothing less than a travesty on nursing leading to a dance of death. At Ancon, just outside of Panama, they still point out a building in the American hospital grounds in which it is asserted five thousand patients died. French clinical attendance, as it is called, has never been good; it is not good to-day even in Paris, and much less so in the Provinces. In no respect is it up to our American standards. It is suggestive of the Sairey Gamp and Betsey Prigg period and methods. In the hands of so-called Sisters of Charity, the rules by them observed at Ancon were, to say the least, peculiar; and over the gates of that Ancon hospital, I was assured by those whose testimony might not be disputed, could properly have been inscribed Dante's familiar *Lasciate ogni speranza voi eli' entrate.*[7] Friends or acquaintances of those taken ill dreaded to obtain a hospital permit; it was looked upon as a graveyard billet.

As then conducted, a dollar a day was paid the Sisters by the French Company for each patient admitted to the hospital. The practice with the Sisterhood was to attend the sick during certain prescribed hours, leaving the wards at night. In the morning duty was resumed; the corpses of those who had died during ' the night were removed, and the places thus made vacant were filled by others newly admitted. During the night absences of the Sisters, the only care the patients received was from convalescents, not yet discharged. At that time it was the usual practice for those journeying to and fro across the Isthmus to carry with them more or less gold; and, in the case of such as died, this gold was a perquisite of the convalescent attendants. They divided it among themselves. It was the dead man's parting " tip."

Nor was this all; ignorance then came with its contribution, disguised in most deadly fashion under the mask of neatness and beauty. The following is from a chapter in a recently published book on the Canal:

> In the state of ignorance that prevailed as to the sources of yellow and malaria fever, the hospitals soon became known as foci of the former disease, as we can easily understand now, when we know that their verandahs and wards were filled with large plants in pots that stood in earthen basins filled with water. The French cultivated flowers extensively about their dwellings and buildings, and each flower pot afforded an ideal breeding-place for mosquitoes, that conveyed the yellowfever and malaria germs.[8]

In other words, acting in perfect good faith and according to their lights, the French medical staff unwittingly established a well-designed and arranged breeding-school of the deadly stegomyia, they being systematically propagated, and regularly supplied with non-immune subjects on which to feed. The only cause for present surprise is that under such conditions the yellow fever in that climate and locality did not become epidemic as well as endemic, and that any even temporary sojourner on the Isthmus should have escaped it. Tome, a confessed layman, it seems as if the natural laws regulating both the propagation and dissemination of the mosquito are not yet fully understood; but, in the still recent days of the De Lesseps dispensation, the death-dealing insect was looked upon as a torment but a harmless one, and the phantom of miasma was at all times invoked as a final, if not sufficient, explanation of the injuries he inflicted.

Almost a century before, the French under the lead of a greater than DeLesseps had ventured on another great West Indian enterprise. In 1801 Napoleon, he also fresh from Egypt and Suez, had sent to Hayti an army some twenty-five thousand strong, commanded

by his brother-in-law, General Leclerc, the husband of his sister
Pauline. Of that large force it is said not one man in three ever saw
France again. For, more to be feared than the liberated African resisting a return to bondage, the then wholly unsuspected stegomyia put in
his deadly work.[9] Leclerc himself fell a victim, and of the twenty five
thousand sent out to Santo Domingo under his command in 1801,
only four thousand were fit for duty in 1802. Napoleon never liked to
waste time or thought upon his failures. They were, in so far as
possible, by him treated strictly as alms for oblivion. The investigator
now, consequently, searches in vain for statistical reports of the
experiences of the French in Santo Domingo, and the number of
deaths to be there attributed to yellow fever. In Metral's *Histoire de
L'Expedition des Français, à Saint Domingue*, the whole of the third book
(pp. 105-164) is, for instance, devoted to a somewhat lurid account of
the ravages of the disease, the narrative concluding with the death of
Leclerc. The terror inspired by the fever, and the havoc it worked, are
there dwelt upon with the habitual French excesses of rhetoric; but
from it no exact figures are forthcoming. It is, however, not unsafe to
draw the conclusion that, taking into proportional account the size of
the two expeditions- 40,000 in the first case, including the naval
contingent, and 500,000 in the last- the mosquitoes of Hayti were
more destructive to the Napoleonic venture of 1801 in 'Vest Indian
waters than the frosts of Russia were to the memorable and colossal
tragedy of 18 12. There is no apparent reason why the experience in
Hayti in 1801 should not have been repeated at Darien in 1901. No less
subject to the infection, the French under the guidance of De Lesseps
were as much in the dark as to either the origin or the prevention of
the scourge as were those a century before under the command of
Leclerc.

But I propose in this connection to confine myself strictly to a
statement of what I saw, and to inferences naturally to be drawn from
it by any observing layman not wholly devoid of experience gained
elsewhere. Such an experience, as I have already said, had been mine in
Africa five years ago. I was there also at the same time of year, in

March, and at the same latitude, 10° North. The English had then been for twenty years in control in Egypt, and for several years in control in Uganda. They had established their hospitals; the work of sanitation, as they understood it, was steadily going on. Yet the house-fly was accepted as an unescapable nuisance. He swarmed, ubiquitous. No apparent prevention was thought of. A strong north wind only brought relief from him. With those I accompanied, I was recently at the Hotel Tivoli, Panama, for ten consecutive days. During that time we took our meals in a public dining-room capable of accommodating three hundred guests at a sitting. The attendants were all African; just such as we are accustomed to find in Washington, or at the hotels of every southern winter resort. I kept a careful reckoning, and during those ten days I saw on the dining-room table around which our party sat, exactly three house-flies; and yet, at the same time, I found them abundantly in evidence, though not at all to the Egyptian degree, in the fruit stalls in the public market-place not a mile away. It was certainly not the offseason for flies there.

In one of the extremely interesting occasional papers of Colonel Gorgas on the canal, he refers to the "heroism" exhibited by the French employes in coming to Panama. Every Frenchman, he says, who came to Panama knew that he was going to have yellow fever, and he also knew that every second man would die with it. "To face such chances took no little courage." Elsewhere he gives some ex-amples- cases in point. "The family of one of the chief engineers consisted of five; four died of yellow fever. . .. The family of the super-intendent of the railroad consisted of five; three of these died of yellow fever. A party of seventeen engineers came on one steamer; sixteen of these died of yellow fever. Twenty five Sisters of Charity came to Ancon Hospital at one time; twenty of these died of yellow fever. ... I think it quite reasonable to say that one-third of the Frenchmen who came to the Isthmus during the French construction died of this disease." The testimony of both Mr. and Mrs. Mallet, fortified by piteous cases of bereavement within their personal experiences, was to precisely the same effect. Colonel Gorgas says that for these people, under such conditions, to come to the Isthmus "took no little courage." To one at all acquainted with French industrial conditions the going to Panama of these victims in advance would probably be attributed to another motive,- the *res angusta domi*, In France the avenues to bread-earning occupations or employment are choked. To earn a living, especially with the slightly superannuated, almost any risk will be incurred. The Canal afforded at least a chance; the rest followed. Thus the Ancon graveyard is suggestive of many domestic tragedies, not the less pathetic because not otherwise of record.

Very different conditions in this respect now prevail in the Zone. Of those there in steady employment, though in subordinate capacities, more than the ordinary proportion are somewhat superannuated, and others have manifestly sought refuge from a too rigorous climatic condition- bronchial exiles, or those threatened by tuberculosis. For such, the region of the Chagres is now a health resort; but, computed on the basis of the French mortality, Colonel Gorgas estimates that the American loss by fever during the first five years of our work in the Zone should have been over eight thousand; it actually was just nineteen. And to-day the American skilled workman goes to the Isthmus with wife and children for the first time, or having been there returns to his work and his family, giving no more thought to the fever, whether yellow or Chagres, than we here in Massachusetts give to the small-pox,- not nearly so much as we give to bronchial affections or our annual epidemic of measles. Assuredly the world has seen nothing like it before; and, standing face to face with it, is not the American justified in a certain access of race-pride?

This is not the place nor am I the person to enter into the story of the gradual development of the mosquito theory, and its full demonstration. First advanced as a plausible suggestion, as I understand it, in 1881, not until 1901 was it at last accepted as proven. The question now is as to its further development, and the new fields into which it will lead the investigator and sanitarian.

And yet there was one aspect of the subject which in my talk with Colonel Gorgas moved my sense of humor, though in a way slightly cynical, It moved it also to such an extent that I had difficulty in preserving a proper degree of acquiescent respect for his presentation of the matter. Colonel Gorgas was obviously greatly concerned over the cost of a more perfect sanitation and the necessity of unremitting vigilance with endless precautions, all of which involved an outlay at best never less, and probably always tending to increase. To this I simply listened; for I did not care to enter into a discussion of that other aspect of the case which at once suggested itself. During my stay on the Isthmus I had heard more or less discussion of the armament proposition. Should the Canal be fortified by us, and the Zone properly garrisoned? With the Great Lakes and Suez precedents in mind, observing also the obvious world tendency to neutralization, such a policy on our part seemed to me personally a distinctly backward step. By taking it, America would be throwing away a great opportunity to stimulate by example a movement of world-advance at once obvious and impending. The drift of feeling, and consequently of opinion, was, however, even on the Isthmus, plainly the other way. Patriotism is invoked, and the sense of proprietorship makes itself felt. We built it; it will be ours; and we will not deserve to own it, or to continue to enjoy it, if we are not prepared to hold and defend it, if need be against a world in arms! Are we not the greatest and richest nation on earth?- and so forth and so on, *ad infinitum* and *ad nauseam.*

A most familiar line of appeal and argument, it is also one against which it is useless to contend, save by a silent recourse to time.[10] That Colonel Goethals strongly sympathized in it I was sure; for not only is he a professional soldier, but the evening before I listened to the plaint of Colonel Gorgas I heard Colonel Goethals, at the Hotel Tivoli, address the assembled representatives of the Society of American Engineers, and the one passage which had called forth the warmest and the most immediate expression of approval was that in which he lent his great authority to the armament proposal. So far as I could judge, sanitation and engineering were, in the thoughts of those present, considerations of quite secondary importance. I was also under the impression that Colonel Gorgas was similarly minded; I have uniformly found that all army circles instinctively so incline. I, therefore, did not care to provoke a useless discussion. None the less a comparison did not fail to suggest itself. Colonel Gorgas was gravely considering the unavoidable necessity of a continuing sanitation with the consequent expense thereby entailed. The price came high. Could those who had to provide the amount be counted on always to respond? The problem is serious; the outcome questionable. Fortification was a necessity; sanitation, a luxury. So be it! Yet even when looked at in this way, and conceding each proposition, there was, it seemed to me, something to be said in a comparative way in behalf of sanitation. In the first place it was an incident, but still a necessary one, to any really successful system of armament. That I had seen emphasized at Camp Elliott. The health of the garrison, and consequently the efficiency of the armaments, were involved. Sanitation was not therefore a matter of pure luxury. But even allowing that it was; as a luxury, is it not, comparatively speaking, one which may justifiably be indulged in? It is admitted- or, if not admitted, probable in the light of all experience- that a reasonable armament for the Zone, with a force sufficient properly to garrison the same, will entail an average annual expenditure of $15,000,000; on the other hand, the most perfect sanitation could be provided for $750,000, or five per cent of that amount. Was an expenditure of five dollars for luxury unreasonable on the part of a man, or a nation, which is spending one hundred dollars for necessities? The comparison is suggestive ; but, as it presented itself to me in my interview with Colonel Gorgas, I could not but recall Prince Hal's wondering exclamation on a familiar occasion,- " Oh, monstrous! but one half-pennyworth of bread, to this intolerable deal of sack!"

One thing, and that the essential thing, is clear; the cost of sanitation is not prohibitive. On the contrary, as compared with that of armament, it is trivial. In these days, here and abroad, both men and journals liken, as continually as wearisomely, the war-budget to an insurance premium paid to avert actual war,- the way to avoid war, it is claimed, is to be prepared for it. Without wishing to appear learned, the insurance argument may, I believe, be traced back to classic times, and the *Qui desiderat pacem, preparet bellum.*[11] More recently even Napoleon insisted, and perhaps himself believed, that his everlasting preparation and consequent perpetual wars were but preliminary to a solid and enduring peace. But, conceding the force of the argument, does not the insurance-premium figure of speech apply quite as forcibly to pestilence as to war? For instance, while preparing this paper I notice that in a recent official report Dr. L. O. Howard, the head of our Bureau of Entomology, estimates that malaria alone costs the United States one hundred millions annually, and the insect diseases generally twice that sum. It will probably be conceded that, except in connection with the warbudget, such amounts are worth saving. In the present case, moreover, the insurance premium against pestilence, besides immunity under existing conditions, further implies the opening of vast regions to development by healthy generations of human beings. Looked at from this point of view, it is at least suggestive that to-day the entire cost of a complete sanitation of our Canal Zone,- heretofore the most pestilential region on earth, and, in that respect, incomparably worse than the proverbial Roman Campagna,- to completely sanitize this region and convert it into a practical winter health-resort may involve a yearly expenditure equal to one half only of the cost of maintenance of a single battle-ship, and, possibly, a sixth part of one per cent of the regular annual war-budget of the United States alone, if we include in that budget the cost entailed on us by wars the last and least of which occurred ten years ago.

Moreover, sanitation is, it must be remembered, as yet but in its infancy. In its present stage of development it is little more than a crude, somewhat clumsy demonstration; though as such, complete. Every method and every appliance are yet to be perfected. To illustrate by example:- sanitation is at this time where steam, as a source of power, was eighty years ago,- where electricity and anæsthetics were in the early memory of those not yet old. Looked at in this way, when some measurement of the possibilities of the future is attempted, the imagination, as I have already said, staggers; at least, when at Panama, mine did.

But, a layman at best, I feel I am now venturing on somewhat dangerous ground,- the domain of prophecy. For, on the other side, tradition holds; nor, it must at once be conceded, is the case yet fully proved, and time alone- sixty years at shortest- can effect a complete demonstration. It is argued, and plausibly argued, that, so far as human life in the tropics is concerned, and continuance of energy there through successive generations as well as its extension to both sexes and all ages, the problem is to-day much where it was heretofore. It is merely proven that the adult male can, by following a prescribed mode of life and observing strict precautionary rules, live, and do a man's work, where he could not ive safely or work effectively before. Existence in a high, steady and monotonous temperature, without impairment of vitality, is still, to say the least, questionable as a possibility. Men may perhaps stand the test; can women and children, much more successive generations of women and children? In other words, was insect poison from time immemorial the root of all tropical evils so far as the human race was concerned, and to what extent do miasmas, temperature and climatic conditions generally still remain to be reckoned with? Moreover, does the presence of the mosquito, that cobra of the air- and here the thought suggested becomes even more startling explain such enigmas as Greek deterioration and the decline and fall of Rome's empire? Was it an imported, and then domesticated insect, which after all avenged a conquered world? But, then again, why not? The tsetse-fly is to-day depopulating eastern Africa.

Suggesting the problem, I withdraw from its discussion. Confessedly a layman, I make no pretence at the prophet's role. So, stating the next and most startling proposition of all on the authority of Colonel Gorgas, I shall there leave it. In the reports put by him in my hands while at Ancon I find him on record to the following effect:

But I do not believe that posterity will consider the commercial and physical success of the Canal the greatest good it has conferred upon mankind. I hope that as time passes our descendants will see that the greatest good the construction of the Canal has brought was the opportunity it gave for demonstrating that the white man could live and work in the tropics, and maintain his health at as high a point as he can, doing the same work, in the temperate zone. That this has been demonstrated none can justly gainsay. . . .

I therefore expect in the course of years to see a very large and wealthy population grow up at the Isthmus in the neighborhood of the Canal. In other words, I expect this Panama Canal to turn out to be one of the greatest commercial successes that man ever brought about. . . .

The figures (here submitted) prove that in the case of the unacclimated foreigner, women and children, as well as men, health conditions have been so changed at Panama that one can live about as well here as in the healthy parts of the United States. That in the case of the native and negro, who make up the bulk of the total population, his sanitary surroundings have been so changed that he now enjoys at Panama about the same degree of health as the ordinary inhabitant of the United States. If this can be accomplished at Panama, the same may be accomplished anywhere else in the tropics. . . .

We therefore believe sanitary work on the Isthmus will demonstrate to the world that the white man can live and work in any part of the tropics and maintain good health, and that the settling of the tropics by the Caucasian will date from the completion of the Panama Canal.

It will be noticed that in these extracts Colonel Gorgas is speaking not of acute and malignant diseases, such as the yellow or the Chagres fevers, but of the incapacity caused by malaria, so-called, generally; a manifestation not at all confined to the tropics, but, in this country, familiar to those dwelling in the neighborhood of Boston, as well as of Rome, of Philadelphia or of New York. This "incapacity" Colonel Gorgas asserts is an indication of an underlying evil to which must be attributed more fatalities than are due " to all other diseases combined." "Yellow fever," he says, " has a great effect on the death rate of a non-immune population, but it is not a noticeable cause of debility. On the other hand, malaria is a disease which may affect the individual for years; and, in a locality like Panama, is responsible for a widespread condition of debility throughout the population."

The yellow fever Colonel Gorgas dismisses almost with words of contempt, relegating it to an historic past:

> It seems to me that yellow fever will entirely disappear within this generation, and that the next generation will look on yellow fever as an extinct disease having only an historic interest. They will look on the yellow fever parasites as we do on the three-toed horse- as an animal that existed in the past, without any possibility of reappearing on the earth at any future time.

Finally Colonel Gorgas closes with this inspiriting trumpetnote, at once a challenge and a prophecy; in it he fairly throws down the gauntlet:

> I dare to predict that after the lapse of a period, let us say, equal to that which now separates the year 1909 from the Norman conquest of England, localities in the tropics will be the centers of as powerful and as cultured a white civilization as any that will then exist in temperate zones.

This paper has already extended far beyond the limits originally proposed for it ; and, purposely, I have in it said nothing of many of the subjects most discussed in connection with the Canal,- for example, the much mooted question of a sealevel or a lock construction. On this point, one of opinion purely, I see no reason why I should commit myself, or waste time and spoil paper over it. I have my own opinion on it, and a decided one; visiting the work, it could not well be otherwise. But, not being an expert on canal construction and at best a mere casual visitor of the Zone, that opinion could, if expressed, carry no weight, and would be undeserving of consideration. But there is another aspect of the subject more appropriate to this place, and to me of greater interest; and I cannot close this paper without reverting to the purely historical side of my experience, already more than alluded to. I refer, of course, to Old Panama, so called to distinguish it from the present city of that name,- the Panama of Pizarro, of Drake, and of Morgan. I have said that, greatly interested in it, its location and remains, in company with my 'artist friend, F. D. Millet, I visited the site of the original Panama twice, and made of it as complete an examination as was practicable under tropical conditions and in so brief a time. I have also said that, as a result of an examination, the place, while vastly interesting and historically suggestive, impressed both my companion and myself as being somewhat of a myth. There hangs about it an atmosphere of exaggeration curiously suggestive of Herodotus and early Greece. For myself, I freely confess that, having visited both localities, I no more believe in the tradition of Old Panama, its size, its population, its commerce and its wealth, than I believe in the accepted traditions of the battle of Marathon. In each case I am persuaded it is in large part an historical fake. As respects Marathon I am, in the *Proceedings* of this Society,[12] already on record; as respects Old Panama, I propose now to put myself on record. Turning back to the fountain head, Hakluyt was, I find, to Old Panama much what Herodotus was to Marathon. What he records, the modern investigator implicitly accepts and then proceeds to elaborate. For instance, in the recent work of Mr. Forbes-Lindsay, from which I have already quoted, is the following somewhat highly wrought description:

The ruins of Panama Viejo are overgrown with dense vegetation and a considerable portion of them has not been seen by the eye of man in two hundred years.. Enough is, however, accessible to make the place unusually interesting, and to attest to the substantial manner in which the Spaniards of old erected their buildings. The tower of the Cathedral of St. Anastasius rises above the tangle of tropical jungle and affords a prominent landmark. In the days of Panama's prosperity and pride, this was the focal point of the city, for the Church was more powerful than the temporal authority. A fine old stone bridge, in a good state of preservation, is a picturesque reminder of the period when the " Gate to the Universe" stood on this spot. There are remains of fortifications and dungeons; and the famous "paved way," which was, in reality, no more than a road of cobble-stones, may be seen where the forest is not too dense to penetrate.

So far all is not unfairly set down and in reasonable accord with ascertainable facts; but the imagination next assumes control:

In its palmy days Old Panama was the seat of wealth and splendor such as could be found nowhere else in the world than the capitals of the Orient. At the court of the Governor gathered noblemen and ladies of gentle birth. There were upwards of seven thousand houses in the place, many of them being spacious and splendidly furni shed mansions: The monasteries, convents and other ecclesiastical edifices were numerous, and contained vast amounts of treasure in their vaults. There were fine public buildings devoted to various purposes, among them pretentious stables in which were housed the " King's horses."

But, as matter of fact, a remark might here not improperly be interjected to the effect that the horses in question were in reality mules, and the stables- Latin-American shacks!

To much the same effect Mr. Hubert Howe Bancroft, or his *pro hac vice* ready writer, grows poetical as he lovingly dilates on the seventeenth century metropolis and trade-centre:

> Two or three piers of a shattered bridge, a fragment of wall, a single tower, and a few remnants of public buildings, half buried under a dense growth of creepers, still mark the spot where, in 1671, stood a city with fine streets and beautiful edifices, among which were stately churches richly adorned with altar-pieces and rare paintings, with golden censers and goblets, and tall candelabra of native silver. There were the abodes of the merchant princes of the New World, some of them the descendants of men who had fought under Cortes when he added the empire of the Montezumas to the realm of the Spanish crown. There were vast storehouses stored with flour, wine, oil, spices, and the merchandize of Spain; there were villas of cedar surrounded with beautiful gardens, where fair women enjoyed the cool evening breeze as they gazed seaward on the untroubled waters of the Pacific.' . . .[13]
>
> There the raw adventurer who at the opening of his career pressed forward with eager expectation into a dark uncertain future met the returned fortune-seeker elated with success or broken-spirited through failure. Into the lap of this great central city poured untold wealth. Her merchants were princes; her warerooms were filled with rich merchandize of every kind and from every quarter of the globe. There were to be seen stacks of yellow and white ingots from the mines of Peru, the cochineal and dye-woods of Mexico, the richest wines of Spain and Portugal, the silks, velvets and laces of France and Italy.[14]

G. W. Thornbury[15] is equally imaginative, but a trifle more specific:

> The buildings were all stately, and the streets broad and well arranged. There were within the walls eight monasteries, a cathedral, and an hospital, attended by the religious. The churches and monasteries were richly adorned with paintings, and in the subsequent fire may have perished some of the masterpieces of Titian, Murillo, or Velasquez. The gold plate and fittings of these buildings the priests had concealed. The number of rich houses was computed at 2000, and the smaller shops, etc., at 5000 additional. The grandest buildings in the town were the Genoese warehouses connected with the slave trade; there were also long rows of stables, where the horses and mules were kept that were used to convey the royal plate from the South to the North Pacific Ocean. Before the city, like offerings spread before a throne, lay rich plantations and pleasant gardens.

Of course, the writer meant from the South Pacific to the North Atlantic; but that is a mere detail. And of such stuff is what passes for history made up! Padding, pure and simple!

Now for the facts, as inferred from observations made in person and on the spot.

The report of Baptista Antonio, made in 1587, to Philip II, King of Spain, is the base on which these historical figments rest. Antonio's report is in Hakluyt's principal narrative; and, in connection with this paper, I reprint such portions thereof as relate immediately to Panama. Matter of fact and to the point, they are also quaint and refreshing. Antonio describes the geographical situation exactly as it exists to-day; and the ruins of the structures he refers to can even now be seen, or traced, in the jungle. In view of the exceptional interest which at just this juncture attaches to the place, the extracts have a distinct historical interest as well as value. Well worth reproduction, therefore, it is nevertheless difficult to make them in all respects conform to facts and appearances.

In the first place, the topography of the site and surroundings is as Antonio described it four centuries ago; but the foundations and ruins still remaining of the structures- fortifications, ways, bridges and edifices- are at variance with the statement that the town, as such, was ever of considerable size. Limited to an area of at most two hundred and fifty to three hundred acres, the ruins now remaining and the scattered fragments of tile show conclusively that Panama Viejo never could have contained within its limits either the buildings and dwellings, or the avenues, streets and ways described. Both the public edifices and the private houses were limited in size of modest dimensions, as we would phrase it- and, apparently, packed closely together. In place of the fifty thousand sometimes credited to them, they never, on any reasonable estimate, could have sufficed to accommodate a population in excess of seven thousand. Ten thousand would be a maximum. The foundations of "the royal houses builded upon a rock" are still there; so also those of the " audience or chancerie," as likewise the prison; all "adjoining together one by another along upon the rocks." But those foundations afford proof positive of the dimensions of the superstructures. By their proximity to each other, also, they show that there never could have been any "broad streets" or wide thoroughfares in the town or approaching it; and the bridge, of which we are informed that " two or three piers" only remain, never had but a single span, both short and narrow, thrown across a contemptible mud-creek, almost devoid of water in the dry season or at low tide; and that single span- a very picturesque one, by the way- is still there. That a great store of wealth for those days annually passed through Old Panama, there can be no question. The place was, however, merely a channel; and, after a fairly close inspection, I do not hesitate to repeat that the stories of its art, its population and its treasures- generally of its size and splendor- constitute about as baseless an historic fabric as the legions that fought at Marathon or the myriads that followed Xerxes. Old Panama, as seen through the imagination of modern investigators, bears, I believe, just about as much resemblance to the sixteenth century reality as Francis Drake's *Golden Hind* would bear to a present-day Atlantic liner, say the *Lusitania.*

PANAMA[16]

Panama is the principall citie of this Dioces: it lieth 18. leagues from Nombre de Dios on the South sea, and standeth in 9. degrees. There are 3. Monasteries in this said city of fryers, the one is of Dominicks, the other is of Augustines, and the third is of S. Francis fryers: also there is a College of Jesuits, and the royall audience or chancery is kept in this citie.

This citie is situated hard by the sea side on a sandy bay: the one side of this citie is environed with the sea, and on the other side it is enclosed with an arme of the sea which runneth up into the land 1000. yards.

This citie hath three hundred and fiftie houses, all built of timber, and there are sixe hundred dwellers and eight hundred souldiers with the townesmen, and foure hundred Negros of Guyney, and some of them are freemen: and there is another towne which is called Santa Cruz la Real of Negros Simerons, and most of them are imployed in your majesties service, and they are 100. in number, and this towne is a league from this citie upon a great rivers side, which is a league from the sea right over against the harbour of Pericos. But there is no trust nor confidence in any of these Ncgros, and therefore we must take heede and beware of them, for they are our mortall enemies.

There are three sundry wayes to come to this citie, besides the sea, where the enemy may assault us. The one is at the bridge which is builded upon the river : and on the one side of this, there lieth a creeke: so on this side the citie is very strong, because it is all soft muddie ground, for in no way they cannot goe upon it. And right over against it there lyeth a river which is in maner like unto a ditch or moate; and on the other side of the River there lyeth a great Lake or Pond which is full of water all the Winter, and part of the Sommer, so that on this side the city is very strong, for with very small store of souldiers this place might bee kept verie well.

The greatest danger for the surprising of this citie is the way that doth come from Nombre de Dios: for all this way is playne ground and no woods: and 2000 yardes from this citie there lyeth a river called Lavanderas, where the women doe use to wash their linnen: and this river doth goe into the creeke, according as I have certified your majestie: and being once past this river, there is a causey which goeth directly unto them. The other way which doth go towards the citie is lower downe towards the sea at a stone bridge lying upon the way which goeth to the harbour of Perico. These two wayes cannot be kept nor resisted, because it is all plaine ground and medowes.

Upon the East side of this citie there are your majesties royall houses builded upon a rocke joyning hard to the Sea side, and they doe aswell leane towards the sea as the land. The royall audience or chancerie is kept here in these houses, and likewise the prison. And in this place all your majesties treasure is kept. There dwelleth in these houses your majesties Treasurer, the Lord President, and 3. Judges, and master Atturney. All these doe dwell in these houses, and the rest of your majesties officers: which are six houses besides those of the Lord President, the which are all dwelling houses, and all adjoyning together one by another along upon the rockes. And they are builded all of timber and bourdes, as the other houses are. So where the prison standeth and the great hall, these two places may bee very well fortified, because they serve so fitly for the purpose, by reason they are builded towardes the sea, and that there lye certaine small rocks, which at a lowe water are all discovered and drie, and some of them are seene at a high water. Right over these houses to the Eastwardes there lyeth an Island about five hundred yardes from these houses, and the Island is in forme of a halfe moone; and in this order it runneth all alongst very neere the maine land: so over against these houses there lyeth the harbour where all the shippes doe use to rideat an anker, after that theyhave discharged and unladen their marchandize. For when they have their lading aboord, there can come in none but small

Barkes, and at a lowe water the shippes are all aground and drie, and so is all the space some thirtie yardes from those houses. Right over against them standeth the citie,

When newes were brought to this citie of those Pirates which were come upon this coast, the Lord President and Judges commanded that there should a sconce bee made, and trenched round about, made all of timber for the defence of this citie against the enemie, and to keep your majesties treasure. So your officers caused Venta de Cruzes to be fortified, and likewise Chagre, and Quebrada, and fortified the garrison of Ballano: for all these are places where th e enemy may land, and by this meanes spoyle all this countrey.

There are three sundry places where this citie may without diffi-culty be taken, and spoyled by the Pirates. The first is on the North seas in a certaine place which lyeth foureteene leagues from Nombre de Dios, the place is called Aele to the Eastwards, where once before certaine men of warre have entred into those seas. The other place is Nombre de Dios, although this is a bad place and naughtie wayes, and full of waters and a very dirtie way: for three partes of the yeere the countrey people doe travell upon those waters, and an other very badde way, which is the going up of certaine rockes and mountaines which they must climbe, called the mountaines of Capira, which are of height three quarters of a league, so in this place with very small store of souldiers wee can defend our selves from the fury of the enemie, so these dwellers doe say that in Sommer the wayes are very good with-out either dirt or water.

The other entrance is up the river of Chagre, which rivers mouth lyeth eighteene leagues from Nombre de Dios to the Westwards falling into the North sea, and this is the place which the citizens of Panama doe most feare, for they may come up this river to Venta de Cruzes, and so from thence march to this citie, which is but five leagues off. So up this river there goe boates and barkes which doe carry 320. Quintals waight. These are they which carry the most part of the marchandize which doe come from Spaine to be transported to Peru, and from Venta de Cruzes it is carried to Limaret which is three leagues off that place, and the dwellers doe report that it is a very good way: and if any men of warre will attempt to come into these seas, they may very easily come up this river as Iarre as Venta de Cruzes, and from thence march unto this citie, and if the enemy will, they may bring their pinnesses ready made in foure quarters, and so taken in sunder, may afterwards set them together againe: as it is reported that Francis Drake hath used it once before when he came that voyage; and so he may attempt us both by sea and land. And forasmuch as the most part of these people are marchants, they will not fight, but onely keepe their owne persons in safetie, and save their goods; as it hath bene sene heretofore in other places of these Indies.

So if it will please your majesty to cause these houses to bee strongly fortified, considering it standeth in a very good place if any sudden alarms shoulde happen, then the citizens with their goods may get themselves to this place, and so escape the terrour of the enemy: and so this will be a good securitie for all the treasure which doth come from Peru. So all the Pirats and rebels, which have robbed in these parts, have gone about what they can to stoppe this passage, and so by this meanes to stoppe the trade of Spaine, and to set souldiers in this place, for to intercept and take your majesties treasure, whereby none might be caried into Spaine. Therefore it behooveth your majestie to fortifie these places very strongly.

These places being fortified in this maner, your majesty shal have al your gold and silver brought home in safetie which commeth from Peru. And all those commodities which are laden in Spaine may come safe to this place. And if perchance any rebels should rise in these parts, which would rebel against your majesty, which God forbid, & if they should chance to joyn with any of these pirats, having this place so wel fortified, & Puerto Bello in ye North parts, & so to send some garrison your majestie needs not to feare: for here in this harbor are alwayes 10 or 12 barks of 60 or 50 tunnes apiece, which do belong to this harbor. So if any of these places shalbe intercepted, then your majestic hath no other place fitter then this to land your majesties souldiers, for then they have but 18. leagues to march by land, &

presently they may be shipped to supply these places which shal stand in most need of them. In al the coast of Peru there is no harbour that hath any shipping but onely this place, and the citie of Lima, where there are some ships and barks. The harbour being thus open without any defence, a man of war may very easily come to this place, as I have certified your majestie, thorow the streits of Magellane, & arrive at that instant, when those barks, do come from Peru with your majesties gold & silver, for sometimes they bring 5 or 6 millions in those barks; so the enemy may come and take al their treasure, & not leese one man, because here is not one man to resist him, therefore this place being thus fortified, the treasure may be kept in the fort. There is a trench made round about your majesties houses which are builded of timber: the President and Judges did cause it to be made, for that here was newes brought that there were certaine men of warre, & pirats comming for these parts. So this trench is thus maintained until such time as your majesties pleasure is to the contrary, & in such wise that your souldiers may fight lying behind the trench; so there is order given to build a platforme upon the plaine ground, and so to plant such ordinance in those places, as shall be thought most convenient.

If it wil please your majestic, here we may make a sconce or fort toward the land side, & so trench it round about and build it with stone, because here is a place and al things readie for the same purpose; and by this meanes the citie would be securely kept: as for the sea there is no danger at al, by reason that the water doth ebbe & flow twise a day, and then when it is ebbing water it wil be all ozy & muddy ground and rocks, so that in no wise at a low water the enemy can wade over the mud to come to this city, and it reacheth from the Island til you come to the bridge called Paita. Two leagues from this city there lieth a harbor called Perico downe to the Westward: this is a very sure harbour by reason of 3. Islands which do joyne in manner of a halfe moone, they lie halfe a league from the maine, the Islands do enclose the harbor round about, the harbour is a very high land, and the Ilands arc but reasonable high, there is good store of fresh water: also there hath never any ship bene cast away in this harbour, for there is 7. Iathome water at ful sea, and 3 or 4 fathome at lower water, and very good ground for their ankering, and when they will trimrne their ships, they may hale them ashore. All those ships and barks which come from Peru with gold, silver or any other kind of commodities, do first come to an anker in this harbour, and if they have a contrary weather they cannot come into the harbour of Panama; and for so much as the harbour hath no defence for the safegard of the ships, if a man of warre should chance to come into the harbour, all the barks with the treasure may be very easily taken. And likewise these barks & ships which do navigate in the South seas carrie not so much as one piece of ordinance or a rapier to defend them withal!. From this place to Venta de Cruzes is not passing 5 leagues; so that if any pinnesse should happen to arrive there, no doubt but they might robbe and take al your treasure which is in .those barks, by reason that from the shore they cannot be rescued nor holpen, because it is an Island and refuge for all ships and barks. If it would please your majestic here might some fort or defence bee made in the middlemost Island, and some ordinance planted, and this might bee made with little charges, because in the said Island there are all kinde of necessaries fi t for that purpose, so by this meanes your majestic may have both the harbour and the citie very well kept. .

And likewise there is another entering into the South sea which is called the river of Francisca, which licth on this side of the Cabeca de Cativa, and this river doth come into another river which is called Caracol, and is five leagues from this citic; and once before these Simerons brought into this place certainc Frenchmen.

THE RIVER OF CHAGRE

The river of Chagre lieth in 9. degrees and one tierce. The mouth of this river is in the North seas 18. leagues from Nombre de Dios, and 13. leagues from Puerto Bello: there is caryed up this river certaine quantitie of those merchandize which are unladen at Nombre de Dios which come from Spaine. From the mouth of this river to Venta de Cruzes are eighteene leagues. From this place where the barkes unlade their commodities, they are carried upon mules to Panama, which is but five leagues off from this place.

This river hath great store of water in the Winter. And the barkes which belong to this river are commonly of 320. Quintals that is of 16. tunnes in burthen: but in the Summer there is but small store of water: so then the barkes have much to doe to get up this river: and in many places these barks are constrained to unlade their commodities; and are drawen by mens strength and force a good way up the river, and therefore if it would please your majestie to command that all those goods may bee first unladen in Puerto Bello, and there to build a litle castle in the mouth of the said river, and at the foote of the castle to build a storehouse to unlade and keepe all the sayd goods, and there to build other barks of lesse burthen; then these would serve for Sommer, and the great barks for the Winter.

If it would please your majestic, there might a verygood high way be made on theone side of the river, and so they might bee towed, for it may bee made and not with much cost becauseit isall plaineground, and there is growing upon the sayd river great store of timber and trees which doe lie over-thwart the said River; so that they are very cumbersome and great annoiance unto the said boates, as well those that go up the said River, as also that doe come downe the said River.

And therefore if it might please your majestie to command, that Puerto Bello might be inhabited, and the towne made neerer the Rivers side, every thing would be a great deale better cheape, if the commodities were caryed up the River; for it is a great danger to cary them up by land, for it is daily seene that the mules do many times fall and breake their neckes with their lading upon their backs, as well the treasure as other kinde of commodities, because it is such a bad way. And your majestie might be at this charges and spend your revenewes of Nombre de Dios and Panama, which do yerely yield 12 or 14 thousand pezos, & this being once done it would be a great ayd and benefit to those, which doe trade and trafficke, and to those merchantes which doe send their goods over-land, and ease them much of paine and purse. because the other is a most filthy way, as any is in the world.

Notes:

1. 2 *Proceedings*, XVII. 248.

2. I had written Creole, but am given to understand that among the English-speaking people of Central America the designation Creole is, by general acceptance, now supposed to imply an infusion of African blood; that, vulgarly, it is taken to be somewhat synonymous with Mulatto. A grosser and more absurd misapprehension could hardly be imagined. It is next and elsewhere assumed that any person of European blood born in the West Indies is a Creole. This is little less incorrect than the African assumption. No one ever heard of a Scotch, or Dutch, or Irish Creole. On the contrary, as the Century Dictionary defines it, the word Creole signified originally one of West Indian or Central American birth descended from Spanish ancestors, " as distinguished from immigrants of European blood and from the aboriginal negroes and natives of mixed blood." Subsequently the significance was broadened to cover all West Indians of Latin descent. The Empress Josephine, for instance, was a French Creole. The freedom of the Creole's blood from any native or African admixture was a matter of pride. The mere suggestion of such an admixture would in old Creole days have been resented as an unpardonable insult. Under a correct acceptance of terms Mrs. Mallet would, therefore, be Creole par excellence; Madame Beauharnais was French Creole.

3. While correcting the final proof sheets of this paper, I am informed by Mr. J. B. Bishop, in a letter dated Ancon, May 24. that, during the previous ten days, " we have had a mosquito pest covering the whole zone... . During my four years of residence here I have seen nothing comparable to it. I have seen more mosquitoes in the last week than I have seen during the previous four years." He adds, " they are not poison-bearing; though in other ways as annoying as any specimens of the species I have ever seen."

4. [Editor's note] The *cloaca maxima* is the great sewer of ancient Rome and is still functional. Its mouth can still be seen on the bank of the Tiber.

5. " In 1882, actual construction was commenced [under the French], and several thousand laborers were put to work along the line, Then graft, extravagance, immorality and disease began to pervade the scene, Froude, describing conditions after a visit to the scat of French operations, declared: ' In all the world there is not, perhaps, now concentrated in any single spot so much swindling and villainy, so much foul disease, such a hideous dungheap of moral and physical abomination, as in the scene of this far-famed undertaking of the nineteenth century." Forbs Lindsay, *Panama and the Canal To-day,* 69.

6. On this point, see the paper entitled" The Panama Canal," in the report of the *Am. Inst, of Mining Engineers,* for November, 1910 , pp. 83. 84.

7. [Editor's note] "Abandon all hope, ye who enter here." This was inscribed on the gate of Hell.

8. Forbes-Lindsay, *Panama and the Canal To-day, 69-70.*

9. The Panama Canal, *Inst. of Mining Engineers,* November, 1910, 50.

10. " With her great navy and immense standing army Japan could attack our Pacific coast to-day and we should be helpless to resist her. . . . It may be hard for the average American to appreciate the military weakness of his country at the present time, especially on the Pacific coast, and to understand in what an appalling situation the United States would be should the Panama Canal, being unfortified, suddenly be seized by Japan, a nation which has twice within the last fifteen years begun war without a declaration of war and by treacherous attacks. ... . It is difficult to speak calmly of the thick-headed, thin-blooded theory that would, in the face of these facts, persuade us to leave our coasts unprotected by using our navy to guard an unfortified canal. ... With the great armed powers approaching a struggle for

supremacy in Asia, and with a part of Asia already in arms and thirsting for conquest, it would seem as though none but a fool or a traitor could fail to see that to refuse to fortify the Panama Canal is to invite war and to make our destruction easy." The foregoing extracts from a paper entitled " The Madness of an Unfortified Canal," by Mr. James Creelman, in the issue of a popular periodical (*The Cosmopolitan*) for the current month (May, 1911), may be not without historical interest. In a period of future development, probably not now remote, they will at least serve to illustrate the temper and discretion with which the discussion referred to in the text is now approached.

11. [Editor's note] "Let him who wants peace prepare for war." A Roman proverb.

12. 2 *Proceedings,* XVII. 252.

13. *History of Central America,* II. 50 2

14. *The Monarchs of the Main,* II. 158.

15. Ib. 249.

16. From a "Relation of the ports, harbors, forts, and cities in the West Indies which have been surveicd, edified, finished, made and mended, with those which have bene builded, in a certaine survey by the king of Spaine his direction and commandement: Written by Baptista Antonio, surveyour in those parts for the said King. Anno 1587. It was printed in Hakluyt's *Principall Navigations,* III. 554, and in the edition of 1904, in x. 148.

23

A National Change of Heart

This paper was read for the Massachusetts Historical Society on October 10, 1901.

A terrible and tragic episode in our national life has burned itself into history since the last meeting of the Society, — the assassination of President McKinley. Twice before have we, in common with the whole land, been shocked by like occurrences.[1] At the time of both, Mr. Winthrop occupied this chair;[2] and, on each occasion, fitting resolutions, sub mitted by him and unanimously adopted, were spread upon our records. From the precedents thus established I propose to deviate; not that I have failed to sympathize in the outburst of feeling this truly terrible event has excited, or the expressions elicited by it; but, on now reading the resolutions heretofore passed on similar occasions, they seem to me, though drawn with all Mr. Winthrop's accustomed felicity, unequal to the occasion, — in one word, almost of necessity, formal, conventional, perfunctory. I also feel that I could not express myself more adequately. Of President McKinley all has in this way been said that can be said : —

"Duncan is in his grave;

> After life's fitful fever he sleeps well;
> Treason has done his worst; nor steel, nor poison,
> Malice domestic, foreign levy, nothing,
> Can touch him further."

He cannot hear; and, as to her for whom the latter years of the dead President's life were one long record of affectionate, self-sacrificing care, no formally set down words of mine could add one iota to the expression of sympathy — deep and prolonged as sincere — which has already gone forth. This being so, silence seems best.

Still, to one aspect of this awe-impelling tragedy I wish to call attention, for that aspect has to my mind an historic interest. Perhaps, already discussed, it is an old story; if such is the case I can only excuse myself on the ground that, having been absent from the country, and only just returned to it, I am less informed as to what has been said than I otherwise might have been. But, when some event like this last murder of a high official startles and shocks the whole civilized world, the first impulse always is to attribute its occurrence to present conditions, — moral or material, — to some circumstance or teaching or appliance peculiar to the day, — and to ask in awe-struck tones, — To what are we coming? Whither do tendencies lead? In what will they result? So, as of genuine historical interest, in this connection, I want to call attention to the very noticeable fact that this murder of President McKinley by the wretched, half-witted Czolgosz[3] has no significance whatever, as respects either cause or method, in connection with the times in which we live, its destructive appliances, or its moral instruction. This, somewhat curiously, is true not only of President McKinley's assassination, but of all the assassinations of a like nature, with two exceptions, which have occurred within the last half century. Of such, I easily recall eight: (1) The Orsini attempt on Napoleon III. in 1858, which resulted in numerous deaths, though the person aimed at escaped unharmed; (2) the slaying of President Lincoln in 1865; (3) that of the Czar Alexander II. in 1881; (4) that of President Garfield three months later in the same year; (5) that of President Carnot in 1894; (6)

that of the Empress Elizabeth of Austria in 1898; and (7, 8) those of King Humbert in 1900, and, more recently, of President McKinley.

This is truly enough the age of advance, — scientific and intellectual. Strange doctrines are promulgated, and widely preached. There is a freedom given to utterances, at once wild and subversive, the like of which the world has not known before; we do not believe in the suppression of talk; the press disseminates incendiary doctrines broadcast among the partially educated, and the half, where not wholly, crazed. Then, in its turn, science has put the most deadly and destructive of appliances within easy reach of the irrational or reckless. Yet, of all the attempts I have enumerated, two only have borne an earmark of this age. The Orsini conspiracy of 1858 and the death of the Czar Alexander in 1881 brought into play implements of destruction unknown to former generations; the other six cases out of the eight had no features in any respect different from similar crimes of the long past. The impulses, the methods, and the weapons of Booth and Guiteau, in 1865 and 1881, were identical in every way with those of Gerard and Ravaillac in 1584 and 1610, three centuries before. They had in them nothing epochal, — nothing peculiar to the dynamitic age. Consider, in the first place, the aim of the assassin, the object of his animosity, — McKinley and Garfield were neither tyrants nor despots; nor were William the Silent and Henry of Navarre. On the contrary, all those named were men of a merciful, not to say singularly genial disposition. Beneficent as rulers and magistrates, they were in the popular mind connected with no severities towards individuals. In not one of these cases had the assassin, directly or indirectly, immediately or remotely, suffered injury at the hands of his victim. It was the same with Lincoln and Carnot, Humbert and Elizabeth. In ah1 these in stances, moreover, the weapons used in killing, if not identical, were common to the earlier and the later period. Henry of Navarre in 1610, President Carnot in 1894, and Elizabeth of Austria in 1898, were murdered by thrusts of a poniard ; William of Orange in 1584, King Humbert in 1900, and Presidents Lincoln, Garfield and McKinley, all within forty years, met their deaths from pistol-shots. In no one of these tragedies did the modern high explosive play any part. They were all ordinary shootings or stabbings of the old style.

Nor was it otherwise as respects motive. The more recent instances developed nothing peculiar to any age or doctrines, except that in the earlier cases the crime originated in a morbid fanaticism born of religious zeal; whereas, in the later, social and anarchistic teachings had taken the place of theological. In the process of human development, or evolution as we call it, the same character of mind was set in action to a like end by a common diseased impulse, only under another name. There is no new factor at work ; merely the teaching of social rights now operates, in a certain order of brooding minds, as the teachings of theology once did on minds of the same temper. So far as these recent murders are concerned, the world and human nature have, therefore, undergone no change. The Czolgosz of 1901 is the Gerard of 1584 reembodied, but actuated by the same impulse, and armed with his old weapon! Luccheni is Ravaillac. The three centuries between introduced no element of novelty. Indeed, the thought this recent murder has most forced on me has been one of surprise, on the whole, that such things so rarely happen. Here in America are now seventy millions of people, — gentle and simple, rich and poor, sane and insane, healthy and morbid; of those seventy millions not a few are men who, like Macbeth' s hired assassin, might truthfully enough declare themselves of those

"Whom the vile blows and buffets of the world

Have so incensed that I am reckless what

I do to spite the world;"

and, when thus thought of, it seems cause for genuine surprise that among those seventy millions there do not more frequently develop single individuals — some one person in the half million — who, seized in his brooding moments with the homicidal mania, asserts his equality and his hate by striking at the most shining mark. To my mind, contemplating mankind as an infinitely varied and well-nigh count less mass, it is the rarity of these attempts in our day, not their occasional occurrence, which should excite our special wonder.

At the time of the assassination of the President, I chanced to be in England, having left home on the 10th of August. It was a vacation trip; and, in the course of it, I thus had some opportunity to witness that singular, and very suggestive, outburst of sympathy and fellow-feeling on the part of our kin beyond the sea, which was so marked a feature of that unhappy episode. On Thursday, September 19, I was in London, and present at the memorial ser vices in Westminster Abbey. Certainly, they were most impressive. Seated in the choir, I was not in position to see the nave of the Abbey, except in part and by glimpses; but, throughout the solemn observances of that day and place, an atmosphere of genuine sympathy and deep feeling pervaded the great assembly. Every nook and corner was occupied; a sense of awe was apparent. The day had been dull and obscure, — a September noon in London, — but, towards the close of the ceremonial, as the solemn tones of the great organ, intermingled with the responses of the choir, rolled up through the arches of the vaulted roof, the clouds broke away without, and the sun shone down through the windows of stained glass on the vast congregation below. It was Milton's "dim religious light;" and the dusky atmosphere seemed laden with the smoke of incense, as the chant of the choir died slowly away.

To me personally, however, this outburst of English sentiment to-wards the United States and all things American — the demonstration of an undemonstrative people — contained within itself much food for thought. I freely acknowledge I have seen nothing like it. And, as my eyes witnessed the Present, memory called the Past to mind. What, I could not but ask myself, did it signify? In what did it originate? Was it merely external? Was it matter of policy ? Or did it indicate a true change of heart ? And if a change of heart, to what was that change due?

My thoughts then reverted to remote days and other experiences, now, in Great Britain, quite for gotten, — memories still fresh with me, though a generation has since passed on. I recalled my first experi-ences in England far back in the "sixties," in the dark and trying days of our Civil War; and again, more recently, during the commercial depression, and contest over the free coinage of silver, in 1896. Then, especially in the earlier period, nothing was too opprobrious — nothing too bitter and stinging — for English lips to utter of America, and men and things American.[4] We were, as the *Times,* echoing the utterances of the governing class, never wearied of telling us, a "dishonest" and a "degenerate" race, — our only worship was of the Almighty Dollar. A hearty dislike was openly expressed, in terms of contempt which a pretence of civility hardly feigned to veil. They openly exulted in our reverses; our civilization was, they declared, a thin veneer; democracy, a bursted bubble. In true Pharisaic spirit they made broad their phylacteries, thanking God that they were not as we, nor we as they. All this I distinctly recalled; it was the atmosphere — frigid, contemptuous, condescending — in which I had first lived and moved in London. And now what a change! and so very sudden! Nothing was too good or too complimentary to say of America. Our representatives were cheered to the echo. In the language of Lord Rosebery, at the King Alfred millenary celebration at Winchester, on the day following the McKinley observances, the branches of the great Anglo-Saxon stock were clasping hands across the centuries and across the sea; and the audience applauded him loudly as he spoke.[5]

The heartiness was all there. That at least admitted of no question. But what did it mean? Why had this people so suddenly awakened to a kinship, in which formerly they had felt something in no way akin to pride? It was over this I pondered. At last I evolved an explanation, mistaken, perhaps, — I may say probably mistaken, — but still plausible, and to me satisfactory. At the risk, perchance, of seeming un gracious, — of appearing to respond somewhat unfeelingly to an outburst of genuine sympathy on the part of a kindred people, calling on us to forgive and for get the ill-considered utterances and unwise policy of another time, I purpose here to put my much pondered explanation coldly on record.

In the first place let me premise, and, in so doing, emphasize, my sense of the little worth of the judgment of an individual, and that individual an alien, on what may be the feeling of any community, taken in the aggregate, on a question which does not at once absorb and concentrate attention. Even in our own country, except when deeply stirred by some outburst of patriotism or sympathy, — a common impulse sweeping over the land, and bending minds as a strong gust inclines one way a field of ripening grain, — except on occasions such as this, we know how little real insight the average man has into what is passing in the minds of those among whom he has from his birth lived and moved. We all are conscious of that sense of weariness which almost daily comes over us when we read, in editorial parlance, what the American People have made up their minds to do or not to do, — to have or not to have. On this point the average journalist is always fully advised. His insight is in fallible. To his conclusions, knowing by long expe rience their utter worthlessness, we pay no attention. Yet not an American goes to Europe for a vacation trip, but he comes home fully convinced that he knows more or less of the tendencies of foreign thought. Yet all the insight he has, has been picked up from newspapers and conversations in the railway carriage or the smoking-room. It is true that, in the case of Great Britain, descended from one parent stock, we speak the same language. None the less, an American in Great Britain must almost of necessity draw his inferences as to Great Britain as a community from casual sources and a narrow range of observation. He may read the *Times* and the *Saturday Review,* or the *News* and the *Spectator*; he may have an introduction into English domestic and social life, passing as a guest from one great house to an other; he may mix in business or financial circles, and be familiar with "the city;" he may belong to the church, and breathe the atmosphere of the close or the university; he may be a non-conformist, and so frequent the conventicle: — and yet, when all is said and done, he is still a stranger in a strange land. In spite of himself, except it be as the result of a long and varied sojourn, he necessarily draws his conclu sions largely from matters of accident, — chance con versations overheard or participated in at hotels and in clubs, in waiting-rooms and in railway carriages, — unsigned communications in copies of papers he may pick up, — or even from talking with bagmen, waiters, cab-drivers, and ca-sual travelling companions. In this way what may be called the general drift of public opinion, so far as it reaches him, finds its expression. Much undoubtedly in such cases depends, also, on the individual ; for, though every one is apt to generalize from his individual experience, not all men are either sympathetic or approachable. Yet, allowing for all these peculiarities of the individual, — these kaleidoscopic chances of travel, — certain large features stand forth and impress themselves ; some general inferences may at times not unsafely be drawn.

I think I know the Englishman fairly well; at any rate, I have known him through personal contact for over thirty years. I may add that I like him; and, individually, I think he does not dislike me. We certainly get on fairly well together. About him and her there is a downrightness, sometimes, it is true, bordering on brutality, which commands my respect. He does not conceal his feelings. He is not good at playing policy. But, high or low, gentle or simple, rich or poor, the Englishman and the Englishwoman respect and admire the wealthy, the successful, the masterful. This is natural, for the English themselves are essentially masterful. They are also a commercial people. Of late years the struggle for life in Great Britain, as elsewhere, has become more intense, — the cost of living higher, — the social scales more exacting. There, as in America, wealth, and the possession of wealth, has become a larger and larger factor in the common existence ; and the newspaper, with its elaborate daily accounts of what is taking place among the rich and the fashionable, has distorted ideals. Now, of recent years, — since, we will say, the close of our Civil War, or 1870, — no people on earth have been comparably so successful as the Americans in the rapid accumulation of wealth, none have shown them selves more masterful ; and, as he has more and more so shown himself, the Englishman has undergone a change of feeling towards him, — and this change is, I believe, real. Whether real or not, it certainly is sudden. The outward expression is of recent date; but the influences which have gradually brought it about have been a good while at work. The change, as now witnessed, may, I think, be traced to one re mote and several immediate causes. I will enumerate some of the more prominent.

The first was the outcome of our gigantic, prolonged Civil War. At one stage of that struggle, America - loyal America, I mean — touched its lowest estate in the estimation of those called, and in Great Britain considered, the ruling class, — the aristocracy, the men of business and finance, the army and navy, the members of the learned professions.[6] None the less, they then saw us accomplish what they had in every conceivable form of speech pronounced "impossible." We put down the Rebellion with a strong hand; and then, peacefully disbanding our victorious army, made good our every promise to pay. We accomplished our results in a way they could not understand, — a way for which experience yielded no precedent. None the less, the dislike, not unalloyed by contempt, was too deep-rooted to disappear at once, much more to be immediately transmuted into admiration and cor diality. They waited. Then several striking events occurred in rapid succession, — all within ten years.

I am no admirer of President Cleveland's Venezuela diplomacy. I do not like brutality in public any more than in private dealings. Good manners and courtesy can always be observed, even when firmness of bearing is desirable. None the less, bad for us as the precedent then established was, and yet will prove, there can be no question that, so far as Great Britain was concerned, the tone and attitude on that occasion adopted were productive of results at once profound and, in some ways, beneficial. The average English man from the very bottom of his heart respects a mail who asserts himself, — provided always he has the will, as well as the power, to make the self-assertion good. This, as a result of our Civil War, they felt we had. We had done what they had most confidently pro claimed we could not do, and what they, in their hearts, feel they have failed to do. Throughout our Rebellion they had insisted that, even if the conquest of the Confederacy was possible, — which they declared it manifestly was not, — the pacification of the Confederates was out of the question. They thought, also, they knew what they were talking about. Had they not for centuries had Ireland on their hands? Was it not there now ? Were they not perpetually floundering in a bottomless bog of Hibernian discontent? Would not our experience be the same, except on a larger scale and in more aggravated form ? The result worked out by us wholly belied their predictions. Not only was the rebellion suppressed, but the Confederates were quickly conciliated. The British could not understand it; in the case of the Transvaal they do not understand it now. They merely see that we actually did what they had been unable to do, and are still trying to do. The Spanish war showed that our work of domestic conciliation was as complete as had been that of conquest.

Then came the commercial depression of 1893, and the silver issue. Again they predicted all possible disaster. I was in London in the summers of 1896 and 1897, in close touch with financial circles. The tone and atmosphere at that time prevalent reminded me forcibly of the dark days of the Rebellion. Even as recently as four years back, nothing was too bad for the Englishman "on 'Change" to say or to predict of America, or " Americans," as our securities were called. Suddenly, and in our own way, we emerged from under the cloud, and, again erect and defiant, challenged British commercial supremacy. That they understood ; while they feared, in their hearts they admired. Then came our Spanish war; and at Manila and Santiago they saw us crush a European navy, such as it was, much as the lion they have taken for their emblem might crush some captive jackal of the desert. This they understood best, and most admired. The rest naturally followed. We were unquestionably rich, unmistakably powerful; that we too were a masterful race was evident; we fearlessly challenged supremacy; we had a way of somehow accomplishing results which they had been at much pains vociferously to pronounce altogether out of the question. So they respected and feared us; then they began, in a way, to feel proud of us. Were we, after all, not flesh of their flesh, — bone of their bone?

Finally came their own war in the Transvaal. Among the nations of Europe, Great Britain found itself in a state of extreme isolation. We ourselves know from recent experience to what this is due. Under some law of development as yet only partially understood, the leading nations of the earth have, especially within the last quarter of a century, been reaching out for dominion in every direction. In this process Great Britain, for reasons plain to every observer, took the lead. In so doing, she had a century's start; but, none the less, she came in necessary but sharp contact with others, all bent on the same work. The result was logical. A few years ago we suddenly entered on the same path, — Imperialism, it is called. We all know what followed. We came in conflict with a nation belonging to Latin Europe. Immediately, all the Latin communities were in sympathy with Spain, and looked loweringly upon us. The English, at about the same time, came in conflict with an offshoot of the Germanic stock ; and instantly all those of German blood scowled upon her. France, she had offended in Africa; Russia was traditionally a rival, and an enemy in Asia. It so chanced that a fellow feeling then brought the United States and Great Britain together. We were in a not dissimilar situation. As Mr. Richard Cobden observed long ago of his countrymen, — "We generally sympathize with everybody's rebels but our own."[7] This is not a peculiarly British characteristic. We, in America, were inclined to sympathize strongly with the rebels of South Africa; but we now have rebels of our own. Rebels, therefore, are with us not in such high favor as they were, — temporarily, of course. Thus, instinctively and insensibly, Great Britain and the United States, each being to a degree isolated, drew together in face of the Germanic and the Latin races. Especially was this so with Great Britain; for her isolation and consequent unpopularity were much the more pronounced of the two. It thus became, to a certain extent, those of the English-speaking race against the world. Blood, speech, descent, told; and it told more plainly with them than with us.

Thus, as I more and more reflected upon it, I began to realize that the change in the English heart was not only real, but altogether human, as well as eminently characteristic. I saw, also, or thought I saw, just how it came about. The mass of the English people — the great wage-earning class, the toiling millions — never had shared in the fear and dislike, so long and loudly proclaimed, of America and Democracy. They, on the contrary, throughout the slave holders' rebellion, and during our time of greatest stress, as a whole, sympathized with the national spirit and the Union cause. They instinctively felt that we somehow were fighting their battle with privilege and aristocracy. Their hearts, therefore, were true ; in them no change had to take place. The governing or influential classes, on the other hand, though prejudiced, were quick, in their way, to learn. They now felt British isolation; they feared for their trade; they found themselves in trouble in Ireland and in Africa. So their hearts turned towards their kin beyond the sea; and they turned in good earnest. The new-born sympathy was real; its expression genuine. They themselves did not analyze the motive. Perhaps it was as well they did not, for that adulation which goes forth to those whom success has crowned savors of the Philistine, rather than of the disciples of sweetness and light. None the less it is human ; and, moreover, there is much to urge in extenuation of it. But, in this case, the worship of success was but one of the factors which entered into the situation. We ourselves, it must not be forgotten, had, in the years that had passed and the bitter experiences through which we had gone, been largely transmuted. More assured of our position, we had that increased confidence in ourselves which relieved us in a degree of self-consciousness. We had a record, and a future. The national crudeness, so conspicuous in the past, was largely of the past. It was no longer necessary to assert our equality, for our equality was no longer challenged. Thus the change was as much in our selves as in the estimate held of us by others.

All this we only partially appreciate. In my own case, remembering the situation of a generation back, while I saw how differently they regarded us, I could but be to some extent conscious of a failure to realize how different we had ourselves become. In reality it was much as if, from under the parental roof, a father had watched some rebellious, self-assertive youth, who had gone forth into the world to work out his destiny in his own way and on his own account, not over and above respectful, and setting all precept and experience at defiance. At first, and for a good while, he would be looked at askance; failure would be pronounced his predestined fate. Then, by degrees, as, always asserting his equality, he overcame difficulties, — as he acquired wealth, power, fame, — the father would begin to look with pride on the stalwart, broadshouldered, big-boned youth, moving on from success to success, achieving victory after victory, ever accomplishing results before pronounced impossible, by processes peculiarly his own working out a great destiny in defiance of rule, but ever changing, developing, ripening as he did so. And gradually that father, however set in his ideas, would undergo a change of heart, not the less real because unconfessed, saying to himself:" This is my offspring, — bone of my bone, flesh of my flesh! And what an extraordinary fellow he is, — and enormously rich withal!"

And this, unless I greatly err, is the process through which Great Britain has gone, — is going; we have gone, and are going. In any event, I now submit it as a tentative explanation of an extremely noticeable recent something, — a manifestation no less unmistakable than suggestive. As a change of demeanor, too, it was not otherwise than agreeable to some of us, as, last month, we sat in quiet reminiscent mood during the ringing plaudits. The "Old Home" had not always welcomed us back in just that way; we probably were other than we had been; they certainly looked upon us with more kindly eyes.

Notes:
1. 2 April 20, 1865, following- the death of President Lincoln ; and October 13, 1881, following- that of President Garfield.

2. Robert C. Winthrop was President of the Massachusetts Historical Society from 1855 to 1885.

3. [Editor's note] Leon Czolgosz was a Polish-American born in Detroit who shot President McKinley at the World's Fair in Buffalo, New York on September 6th, 1901: less than a month before Adams delivered this speech. McKinley succumbed to an infection of his two gunshot wounds eight days after the shooting, making Theodore Roosevelt President. After a truly speedy trial which hinged on his sanity, Czolgosz was executed by the state of New York with the

electric chair only forty-five days after the shooting, and only weeks after Adams gave this speech.

4. See *supra*, pp. 74-79; also *Life of C. F. Adams*, American Statesmen Series, pp. 291-305; for a collection of parliamentary utterances from the pages of Hansard, see Blaine: *Twenty Years of Congress*, vol. II. pp. 478-481.

5. Mr. E. L. Godkin, formerly editor of the *Nation*, called attention to this great change of tone in the very last published communication from his pen, dated Lyndhurst, England, July 31, 1901, printed in the New York Evening Post of the 10th of the following month. Mr. Godkin is peculiarly qualified to speak on this point. A Briton by birth, he has, after long residence in this country, been a frequent visitor in England during recent years, returning there recently in failing health. " The American," he wrote in the letter referred to, " who in any profession enjoys ever so slight a distinction at home, has little idea what a great man he is until he comes to England. It is, how ever, just as well for him in this respect that he comes now instead of ten years earlier. ... At the present time American fortunes, and freedom in distributing them, and wide financial operations generally, have so captured the English imagination that they now hasten to embrace indiscriminately the cousins whom they snubbed for a century, and to pronounce them and their works good, one and all."

6. *Supra*, pp. 62, 63.

7. *Speeches*, vol. II. p. 88.

24

To the Honorable Theodore Roosevelt, President of the United States, Regarding the Philippines

This open letter was signed by Adams, Carl Schurz, Edwin Burritt Smith, and Herbert Welsh. It was published in a supplement to *City and State*, Vol. XIII, No. 5, July 31, 1902.

Sir: On the 16th of April last the Secretary of War, under your personal order, issued a "memorandum" of instructions sent to General Chaffee, relating to outrages and acts of torture alleged to have been perpetrated in the Philippines. Shortly after, a meeting of persons interested therein was held in New York. At this meeting we were appointed a committee "to take all necessary steps to effect the full disclosure of the facts connected with processes and executions in the course of military operations in the Philippine Islands." The duty thus imposed has since engaged our attention; and, in the performance thereof, we have investigated many cases of alleged outrage, besides otherwise seeking to inform ourselves in relation thereto.

In this connection we now desire to express the gratification afforded us by your "review" of the 14th inst., as Commander-in-Chief, of the findings of the court-martial in the case of General J. H. Smith. Taken in connection with the previous memorandum of April 15th, that review will, provided it be followed by corresponding general action, in our opinion, do much towards the re-establishment of the national prestige and the restoration of the morale of the army. At this time, therefore, it is of more than a national, it is distinctly of international service; for, brought into new relations with remote, and, possibly, less developed races, it is manifestly above all desirable that the United States should aim to elevate others to a higher standard, rather than itself sink to a lower. Especially opportune, in our judgment, is your very commendable reminder to officers in high and responsible positions that, in a warfare with national dependents, such as that recently waged by us in the East, it behooves all such officers to be "peculiarly careful in their bearing and conduct so as to keep a moral check over any acts of an improper character by their subordinates." The level here reached is lofty, and in healthy contrast with that spirit, far too prevalent, which seeks excuse, if not justification, for the excesses of the present, in every instance of inhumanity which can possibly be exhumed either from colonial history, otherwise happily forgotten, or from the regrettable records of our Indian warfare.

While thus, however, expressing our sense of obligation, we wish most respectfully to call your attention to certain conclusions which we have in the course of our own inquiries found ourselves compelled to reach. These conclusions, we are not unaware, may be somewhat at variance with those reached by you; none the less, in stating them our desire is to contribute, if in our power so to do, toward the more complete realization of the ends set forth in the memorandum to General Chaffee of April 15th.

Coming directly to the point, and speaking historically, our investigations have led us to conclude that the demoralization of the officers and soldiers of our army in the Philippines, including all branches of the service and all grades of rank, was far more general, as well as pronounced, than might be inferred from your review of the court-martial findings in the case of General Smith. The essential facts charged in this case, we believe we have reason to say, were rather notorious than exceptional. Demoralizing influences, very prejudicial to any high standard of military morale, were, under the circumstances, inevitable. This led to lamentable results, calling for the firm hand and stern correction found, and most fortunately applied, in your orders of April 15th and July 14th. For that application, while the country is under great obligation to you, the army is, in our estimate, under obligation still greater.

In the Chaffee memorandum of April 15th is this language: "The fact that any such acts of cruelty and barbarity appear to have been done indicates the necessity of a most thorough, searching, and exhaustive investigation, and you will spare no effort to uncover every case which may have occurred, and bring the offenders to justice." These words, and the inquiries and courts-martial instituted in obedience thereto, unquestionably had a most clarifying effect. Their influence was immediate, great, and beneficent. Meanwhile, we would respectfully submit that the good of the army, and the future of our Eastern dependencies, demand that investigation should not stop at this point, or with results already reached. The inquiries we, as a committee, have made, necessarily imperfect, have yet been sufficient to satisfy us that General Smith and Mayor Waller were not the sole culprits; nor should they suffice in the character of scapegoats.

In your "review" of July 14th, you say that these cases were exceptional. Your means of information on this point should unquestionably be infinitely better than ours, for you have access to the files of the War Department; we have not. Meanwhile, it is always to be borne in mind that one side only of this painful story has been heard, and that side only in part. The testimony of representative Filipinos has been jealously and systematically suppressed. Judicial and impartial examination on the spot has been denied, or pronounced impracticable. From the very nature of things armies and army organizations are much the same everywhere, and a recent foreign experience, still very fresh in public memory, forcibly suggests what may be expected from military tribunals and investigations when the esprit de corps is enlisted, or "the honor of the army" is thought to be involved. In the present case, occasionally, and by accident merely, have fragments of information come to general knowledge; broken glimpses only have been permitted to reach the public eye. Certain facts have been elicited in the proceedings before the Senate Philippine Committee, or through the imperfect reports of evidence given in the more notorious of the courts-martial proceedings; but these, though

very suggestive, are far from complete, much less exhaustive. To our minds, they indicate unmistakably a condition of great and general demoralization. Of this, the findings of the courts-martial referred to afford conclusive evidence; as also do the published orders of commanding officers, and the reports of provincial governors. A general, for instance, high in command, permits himself to say, "I will burn everything that stands, and kill everything that lives in Batangas to have peace." If nothing else, this is suggestive of another memorable utterance of the same nature—an utterance with which the name of Warsaw is mournfully associated. As eighteen centuries ago, so now—" Solitudinem faciunt, pacem appellant. " Another general, a degree only less high in grade, is on record as declaring in language, not classic certainly, but, though less terse, equally forcible with that just quoted, "By the Great Horn Spoon I will make them want peace, and want it badly!" As the not unnatural result of military operations so inspired, an official report indicates that, out of a total population in a single district of 300,000, not less than 100,000 perished. Is this "assimilation," we would ask, "benevolent" in character? In the case of Samar, and the now familiar order there to burn everything, and kill "all over ten," the Secretary of War asserts that, owing "to the good sense and self-restraint of General Smith's subordinates and their regard for the laws of war, . . . his intemperate and unjustifiable instructions were not followed." We are not aware that any reliable statistics on this head are generally accessible; but the evidence is that Samar, with its population of 200,000 Christian beings, was not exempt from the results usual in cases where war, pestilence, and famine combine in the work of destruction. Fire and the sword there had full sway.

Language such as that just quoted, openly used by commanding officers, can have but one effect. To all inferiors and subordinates, it is an incentive at once direct and powerful to the systematic commission of acts of the character revealed in the printed evidence of the Senate Philippine Committee. To pretend otherwise is in our judgment merely to add cant and hypocrisy to cruelty. In the case under consideration, the courts-martial subsequently convened habitually, as well as naturally, recorded findings of which those in the Smith and Waller cases were typical. A reprimand has been the not unusual punishment deemed adequate for the killing in cold blood of natives by officers, whether those killed were at the time prisoners or only suspects, if, indeed, even that.

At first, also, the charges of the infliction of torture, by the so-called "water cure" met with an indignant denial. One general, recently promoted for the capture or killing of those whose bread and salt he, starving, had just begged and eaten, even went to the length of recording his belief that in no case had the "water cure" ever been administered by an American. When the actual notoriety of the practice thus denied was proved, evidence of utter demoralization is found in the testimony given before sympathetic courts-martial by officers, apparently inclined to be humorous, to the effect that, before administering to others a torture not unknown to those familiar with the processes of the medieval Inquisition, they had first had it tried on themselves. As so applied, they had found it productive of no injurious effects; in certain cases even, they alleged, it had proved most beneficial to the health. With a state of demoralization such as evidence of this character implies in both witness and tribunal, it is not easy to deal either seriously or with patience. The impudence of the mockery is manifest.

Where, in other cases, inquiry revealed the systematic use of torture by subordinates, the officer in responsible command is pronounced free from blame on the ground that his praiseworthy absorption in other duties of his position was so complete that such trivial incidents failed to attract his notice. Such a finding is certainly suggestive; it is also reminiscent of Dreyfus incidents; but, in France, as here, "the honor of the army" was alleged to be assailed. Much, indeed, has in these connections been heard of the "honor of the army," French and American. May we be permitted to suggest that the good name of the United States now, as of France then, is also entitled to some degree of consideration? Of the national conscience, in either case, we do not speak.

Finally, every severity known to a state of war,—practices which have excited the special reprobation of the American people when reported as features of the hostilities in Cuba, under the Spanish regime, or in South Africa, during the Boer War,—has been of undisputed and frequent occurrence in the Philippines. From the early beginning of operations there, it has been the general practice, if not actually the order, to kill those wounded in conflict; and, in this matter, the depth of the general demoralization reached can perhaps best be studied in the statement of an officer high in command, when confronted with statistics undeniably showing that the killed of the enemy in all engagements with us largely outnumbered the wounded and the prisoners combined, that this unprecedented result—admitting of but one explanation—was due to the fact that our soldiers were so trained as marksmen that they almost invariably struck vital points; and, moreover, that the Filipinos, even in panic flight, made a practice of carrying off their wounded with them! Such evidence gravely given is not only proof conclusive of utter military demoralization, but, we submit, it is with difficulty distinguished from what is usually known as audacious mendacity.

In like manner as respects concentration camps. These, as a feature in recent Spanish and South African operations, excited in us as a people the deepest indignation, combined with the most profound sympathy for those thus unmercifully dealt with. When resorted to by our officials in the Philippines, these camps are represented as a species of recreation grounds, into which the inhabitants of large districts rejoiced to be drawn, and from which they departed with sorrow. Reports to which we can, on the other hand, refer in a responsible army journal give of them accounts not essentially different from the accounts received of similar camps established elsewhere. By one army officer they have been likened to "suburbs of Hell." Meanwhile, the most persistent effort on our part has failed to obtain from the War Department or any official source any statistics of disease or mortality in those camps. The published statistics relating to the British camps in South Africa of a similar nature were, on the contrary, precise and periodical. Such being the case, the reports of our medical inspectors on the concentration camps in the Philippines are contrary to reason, and opposed to all human experience. As such, we hold them to be little less than an insult to the intelligence of those to whom they were addressed.

In the course of a communication addressed to the Chairman of the Senate Committee on the Philippines, on the 14th of February, the Secretary of War, the Hon. Elihu Root, took occasion to express himself as follows: "The war in the Philippines has been conducted by the American army with scrupulous regard for the rules of civilized warfare, with careful and genuine consideration

for the prisoner and the non-combatant, with self-restraint, and with humanity never surpassed, if ever equaled, in any conflict, worthy only of praise, and reflecting credit upon the American people." These words of sweeping commendation and unqualified indorsement were written by the Honorable Secretary when all the essential facts since brought to light were within his official cognizance. You have given public assurance that the Secretary is more desirous than yourself even, if that be possible, to probe to the bottom every responsible allegation of outrage and torture, to the end that nothing be concealed, and no man be for any reason favored or shielded. The draft on our credulity thus presented is large, but we accept your assurance. Meanwhile, permit us to point out that such very sweeping and somewhat uncalled-for commendation and approval, so far as we are advised altogether unprecedented in character, coming directly, and in the midst of active operations, from the fountain head of military authority, are scarcely calculated "to keep a moral check over acts of an improper character by subordinates." It is charitable to assume that the pressure of official business, at the time of the communication referred to, was such that the Secretary failed to recall what correspondents had brought to his notice, or fully to advise himself as to what the files of his department might have to disclose.

Such are certain of the conclusions reached by us from as careful a study as it has been in our power to make of facts thus far procurable. We have endeavored to supplement and perfect the evidence; but our efforts to that end have encountered obstructive embarrassments. We presented a formal memorial to Congress, asking for a complete and impartial investigation to be made on the spot; no action was taken thereon. We sought to have witnesses called by the Senate Philippine Committee, and a more complete inquiry instituted, in which both sides should be heard; our efforts were unavailing. Finally, when evidence led up to the threshold of revelation, officers of the proper department of the army appointed to make inquiry reported "that considerations of public policy, sufficiently grave to silence every other demand, require that no further action be taken." It was apprehended that "facts would develop implicating many others." Again was there danger that "the honor of the army" would be assailed. So further investigation was summarily stopped.

The allegations we make are grave; the condition of affairs we describe, serious. As a national record it is discreditable. The good name of the country is implicated, as also is the professional character of officers of the army, some of them retired, many still in high command. That we ourselves are responsible persons, and that we represent responsible persons, needs scarcely be alleged, much less proved. We stand ready to cooperate directly, and in utmost good faith, in the line of Secretary Root's order of April 15th, to the end that all offenders may be brought to justice, and the guilty punished. A careful examination of the law has satisfied us that no process possible for us to initiate would elicit further facts, or suffice to bring culprits to account. In this communication we have made references the personal application of which is obvious, and of record. To those thus referred to, courts of military inquiry are open; and, if demanded, would doubtless be by you at once accorded. Before such courts, if once convened, we will hold ourselves prepared to substantiate any or all charges here advanced.

Finally, acknowledging the great service rendered in the orders herein referred to, as the result of the investigations we have made and the study we have given to the documentary evidence already adduced, we find ourselves, though with deep regret, compelled to take issue with you on one important point. In your "review" of July 14th you say: "Almost universally the higher officers have so borne themselves as to supply the necessary checks over acts of an improper character by their subordinates." We, on the contrary, have found ourselves compelled to the belief that the acts referred to were far more general, the demoralization more all pervasive. This, we submit and are prepared to show, is established by the evidence before the Senate Philippine Committee; by the findings of the courts-martial published, or on the files of the War Department; and by documentary proof already accessible. There is indeed no tribunal before which further proof could be adduced. None the less, from the material thus by mere chance made accessible to us here, many thousand miles from the scene and long after the time of these occurrences, we hold ourselves ready to direct your attention to concrete cases the investigation of which would demonstrate the following criminal acts, contrary to all recognized rules and usages of war, on the part of officers and soldiers of the United States:

1. Kidnapping and murder, under circumstances of aggravated brutality.

2. Robbery.

3. Torture, both of men and of women, and rape of the latter.

4. The infliction of death on other parties, on the strength of evidence elicited through torture.

The facts in one of these cases, the most aggravated, were early brought to the attention of the Chairman of the Senate Philippine

Committee (the Hon. Henry Cabot Lodge) and an investigation urged. It was by him promised; but, for reasons of the nature of which we are unadvised, though presumably from a tender regard for "the honor of the army," no action was taken. The murder of a priest of the Roman Catholic Church, a man educated, refined, and, so far as appears, guilty only of the possession of money, was in this case in question. According to witnesses, still believed to be accessible, he was foully done away with by a commissioned officer of the United States, now in New England. In yet another case, we are prepared to produce evidence of outrage and torture perpetrated on a Philippine female by those wearing our uniform, and of summary death inflicted on others upon the strength of evidence wrung from her by torture.

There is no tribunal before which these cases can be brought for judicial inquiry. Nevertheless, until such a tribunal exists and is in operation, your order of April 15th, that all offenders shall summarily be brought to justice and the guilty punished, is not effective; for much, we have reason to assert, and stand ready to prove, has been, and still remains, "concealed," while many wrong-doers, for various "reasons," have been, and still are, "favored or shielded."

Mr. Andrew Carnegie is also a member of our Committee. He is in Europe, and it has been impossible to consult him in preparing this communication, or to obtain his signature to it. A copy has been forwarded to his address, with a request that he will, after due consideration, communicate with you directly concerning it.

Again thanking you in our own names and in the names of those we represent for the strong words you have so opportunely spoken, and the good work already done, we submit the foregoing to your consideration.

(Signed)

We remain, etc.,

Charles Francis Adams, Chairman

Carl Schurz,

Edwin Burritt Smith,

Herbert Welsh.

25

The Doctrine of Equality and the Race Problem

This essay was the introduction for volume 14 of Marion Miller's series, *Great Debates of American History: Slavery from 1790 to 1857*. This was published in 1913.

So far far as the institution of slavery is concerned-in its relations to ownership and property in those of the human species-I have seen no reason whatever to revise or in any way to alter the theories and principles which I entertained when I entered Harvard in 1853, and in the maintenance of which I subsequently bore arms between 1861 and 1865. Economically, socially, and from the point of view of abstract political justice, I hold that the institution of slavery, as it existed in this country prior to the year 1865, was in no respect either desirable or justifiable. That it had its good and even its elevating side, so far at least as the African is concerned, I shall not deny. On the contrary, I see and recognize those features of the institution far more clearly now than I should have said would have been possible in 1853. That the institution in itself, under conditions then existing, tended to the elevation of the less advanced race I frankly admit I did not then think. On the other hand, that it exercised a most pernicious influence upon

606

those of the more advanced race, and especially upon that large majority of the more advanced race who were not themselves owners of slaves -of that I have become with time even more and more satisfied. The noticeable feature, however, so far as I individually am concerned, has been the entire change of view as respects certain of the fundamental propositions at the base of our whole American political and social edifice brought about by a more careful and intelligent ethnological study. I refer to the political equality of man, and to that race absorption to which I have alluded-that belief that any foreign element introduced into the American social system and body politic would speedily be absorbed therein, and in a brief space thoroughly assimilated. In this all- important respect I do not hesitate to say we theorists and abstractionists of the North, throughout that long anti-slavery discussion which ended with the 1861 clash of arms, were thoroughly wrong. In utter disregard of fundamental scientific facts , we theoretically believed that all men-no matter what might be the color of their skin or the texture of their hair-were, if placed under exactly similar conditions, in essentials the same. In other words, we indulged in the curious and, as is now admitted, utterly erroneous theory that the African was, so to speak, an Anglo-Saxon, or, if you will, a Yankee, "who had never had a chance," a fellowman who was guilty, as we chose to express it, of a skin not colored like our own. In other words, though carved in ebony, he also was in the image of God.

Following out this theory, under the lead of men to whom scientific analysis and observation were anathema if opposed to accepted cardinal political theories as enunciated in the Declaration of Independence as read by them, the African was not only emancipated, but, so far as the letter of the law, as expressed in an amended Constitution, would establish the fact, the quondam slave was in all respects placed on an equality, political, legal, and moral, with those of the more advanced race. As one who largely entertained the theoretical views I have expressed, I do not hesitate here to say, as the result of sixty years of more careful study and scientific observation, that the theories then entertained by us were not only fundamentally wrong, but further involved a problem in the presence of which I confess to-day I stand appalled.

It is said, whether truthfully or not, that, when some years ago John Morley, the English writer and thinker, returned to England after a visit to this country, he remarked that the African race question, as now existing in the United States, presented a problem as nearly, to his mind, insoluble as any human problem well could be. I do not care whether Lord Morley made this statement or did not make it. I am prepared, however, to say that, individually, so far as my present judgment goes, it is a correct presentation. To us in the North, the African is a comparatively negligible factor. So far as Massachusetts, for instance, or the city of Boston more especially, is concerned, as a problem it is solving itself. Proportionately the African infusion is there becoming less-never large, it is incomparably less now than it was in the days of my own youth. Thus manifestly a negligible factor, it is also one tending to extinction. Indeed, it would be fairly open to question whether a single Afro-American of unmixed Ethiopian descent could now be found in Boston. That the problem presents itself with a wholly different aspect in Carolina is manifest. The difference too is radical; it goes to the heart of the mystery.

As I have already said, the universal "melting- pot" theory in vogue in my youth was that but seven or, at the most, fourteen years were required to convert the alien immigrant-no matter from what region or of what descent-into an American citizen. The educational influences and social environment were assumed to be not only subtle but all-pervasive and powerful. That this theory was to a large and even dangerous extent erroneous the observation of the last fifty years has proved, and our Massachusetts experience is sadly demonstrating it to-day. It was Oliver Wendell Holmes who, years ago, when asked by an anxious mother at what age the education of a child ought to begin, remarked in reply that it should begin about one hundred and fifty years before the child is born. It has so proved with us; and the fact is to-day in evidence that this statement of Dr. Holmes should be accepted as an undeniable political aphorism. So far from seven or fourteen years making an American citizen, fully and thoroughly impregnated with American ideals to the exclusion of all others, our experience is that it requires at least three generations to eliminate what may be termed the "hyphen" in citizenship. Not in the first, nor in the second, and hardly in the third, generation, does the immigrant cease to be an Irish- American, or a French- American, or a German-American, or a Slavonic-American, or yet a Dago. Nevertheless, in process of time, those of the Caucasian race do and will become Americans. Ultimately their descendants will be free from the traditions and ideals, so to speak, ground in through centuries passed under other conditions. Not so the Ethiopian. In his case we find ourselves confronted with a situation never contemplated in that era of political dreams and Scriptural science in which our institutions received shape. Stated tersely and in plain language, so far as the African is concerned the cause and, so to speak, the motive of the great struggle of 1861 to 1865-we recognize the presence in the body politic of a vast alien mass which does not assimilate and which cannot be absorbed. In other words, the melting- pot theory came in sharp contact with an ethnological fact, and the unexpected occurred. The problem of African servitude was solved after a fashion; but in place of it a race issue of most uncompromising character evolved itself.

I am by no means prepared to go the length of an English authority in recently saying that "emancipation on two continents sacrificed the real welfare of the slave and his intrinsic worth as a person to the impatient vanity of an immediate and theatrical triumph." This length, I say, I cannot go; but so far as the present occasion is concerned, with such means of observation as are within my reach, I find the conclusion difficult to resist that the success of the abolitionists in effecting the emancipation of the Afro- American, as unexpected and sweeping as it was sudden, has led to phases of the race problem quite unanticipated at least. For instance, as respects segregation. Instead of assimilating, with a tendency to ultimate absorption, the movement in the opposite direction since 1865 is pronounced. It has, moreover, received the final stamp of scientific approval. This implies much; for in the old days of the "peculiar institution" the relations between the two races were far more intimate, kindly, and even absorptive than they now are.

That African slavery, as it existed in the United States anterior to the year 1862, presented a mild form of servitude, as servitude then existed and immemorially had almost everywhere existed, was, moreover, incontrovertibly proven in the course of the Civil War. Before 1862 it was confidently believed that any severe social agitation within, or disturbance from without, would inevitably lead to a Southern servile insurrection. In Europe this result was assumed as of course; and, immediately after it was issued, the Emancipation Proclamation of President Lincoln was denounced in unmeasured terms by the entire London press. Not a voice was raised in its defence. It was regarded as a measure unwarranted in civilized warfare, and a sure and intentional incitement to the horrors which had attended the servile insurrections of Haiti and San Domingo; and, more recently, the unspeakable Sepoy incidents of the Indian mutiny. What actually occurred is now historic. The confident anticipations of our English brethren were, not for the first time, negatived; nor is there any page in our American record more creditable to those concerned than the attitude held by the African during the fierce internecine struggle which prevailed between April, 1861, and April, 1865. In it there is scarcely a trace, if indeed there is any trace at all, of such a condition of affairs as had developed in the Antilles and in Hindustan. The attitude of the
African toward his Confederate owner was submissive and kindly. Although the armed and masterful domestic protector was at the front and engaged in deadly, all-absorbing conflict, yet the women and children of the Southern plantation slept with unbarred doors-free from apprehension, much more from molestation.

Moreover, during the old days of slavery there was hardly a child born, of either sex, who grew up in a Southern household of substantial wealth without holding immediate and most affectionate relations with those of the other race. Every typical Southern man had what he called his "daddy" and his "mammy," his "uncle, " and his "aunty," by him familiarly addressed as such, and who were to him even closer than are blood relations to most. They had cared for him in his cradle; he followed them to their graves. Is it needful for me to ask to what extent such relations still exist ? Of those born thirty years after emancipation, and therefore belonging distinctly to a later generation, how many thus have their kindly, if humble, kin of the African blood? I fancy I would be safe in saying not one in twenty.

Here, then, as the outcome of the first great issue occupying the thought and exciting the passions of the period before the Civil War, is a problem wholly unanticipated—a problem which, merely stating, I dismiss.

5

Historiography

26

The Sifted Grain and the Grain Sifters

An address at the dedication of the building of the State historical society of Wisconsin at Madison, October 19, 1900.

"But whoever shall represent to his fancy, as in a picture, that great image of our mother Nature, in her full majesty and lustre, whoever in her face shall read so general and so constant a variety, whoever shall observe himself in that figure, and not himself but a whole kingdom, no bigger than the least touch or prick of a pencil in comparison of the whole, that man alone is able to value things according to their true estimate and grandeur." — Hazlitt edition (1892) of Cotton's Montaigne, vol. i. p. 161.

On occasions such as this, a text upon which to discourse is not usual; I propose to venture an exception to the rule. I shall, moreover, offer not one text only, but two; taken, the first, from a discourse prepared in the full theological faith of the seventeenth century, the other from the most far-reaching scientific publication of the century now drawing to its close.

"God sifted a whole Nation that He might send choice Grain over into this Wilderness," said William Stoughton in the election sermon preached according to custom before the Great and General Court of Massachusetts in April, 1668. To the same effect Charles Darwin wrote in 1871: "There is apparently much truth in the belief that the wonderful progress of the United States, as well as the character of the people, are the results of natural selection; for the more energetic, restless and courageous men from all parts of Europe have emigrated during the last ten or twelve generations to that great country and have there succeeded best;" and the quiet, epoch-marking, creed-shaking naturalist then goes on to express this startling judgment, which, uttered by an American, would have been deemed the very superlative of national vanity:-"Looking to the distant future, I do not think [it] an exaggerated view [to say that] all other series of events as that which resulted in the culture of mind in Greece, and that which resulted in the Empire of Rome only appear to have purpose and value when viewed in connection with, or rather as subsidiary to, the great stream of Anglo-Saxon emigration to the West."[1]

Such are my texts; but, while I propose to preach from them largely and to them in a degree, I am not here to try to instruct you to-day in the history of your own State of Wisconsin, or in the magic record relating to the development of what we see fit to call the North- west. Indeed I am not here as an individual at all; nor as one in any way specially qualified to do justice to the occasion. I am here simply as the head for the time being of the oldest historical society of this continent, and, for that matter, so far as I can ascertain, the oldest society in the world, if reference is made to societies organized exclusively for the preservation of historical material and the furtherance of historical research. As the head of the Massachusetts Historical Society, I have been summoned to contribute what I may in honor of the completion of this edifice, the future home of a similar society, already no longer young; — a society grown up in a country which, when the Massachusetts institution was formed, was yet the home of aboriginal tribes, -a forest-clad region known only to the frontiersman and explorer. Under such circumstances, I did not feel that I had a right not to answer the call. It was as if in our older Massachusetts time the pastor of the Plymouth, or of the Salem or Boston Church had been invited to the gathering of some new brotherhood in the Connecticut Valley, or the lighting of another candle of the Lord on the Concord or the Nashua, there to preach the sermon of ordination and extend the right hand of fellowship.

And in this connection let me pause for an instant to mention one historical fact in connection with your State which I fancy is new to all of you. Is there a human being here, with the exception of him addressing you, who is aware of the fact that this portion of Wisconsin, -Madison itself and all the adjoining counties, — was once, territorially, a part of the colony of Massachusetts Bay?[2] I gravely doubt it; and yet such is indisputably the fact. The fact, also, lends a certain poetic, though remote, propriety to my taking this part, here to-day assigned me.

Accepting that part, I none the less, as I have said, propose to break away from what is the usage in such cases. That usage, if I may have recourse to an old theological formula, is to improve the occasion historically. An address, erudite and bristling with statistics, would now be in order. An address in which the gradual growth of the community or the institution should be developed, and its present condition set forth; with suitable reference to the days of small things, and a tribute of gratitude to the founders, and those who patiently built their lives into the edifice, and made of it their monument. The names of all such should, I agree, be cut deep over its portico; but this task, eminently proper on such occasions, I, a stranger, shall not undertake here and now to perform. For it others are far better qualified. I do not, therefore, to-day propose to say a single word of St. Francis Xavier or Nicollet; of Jean Cartier, Père Marquette or Radisson, any more than of those faithful and devoted benefactors and secretaries of this institution from Lyman C. Draper to Reuben Gold Thwaites; but, leaving them and their deeds and services to be commemorated by those to the manner born, and, consequently, in every respect better qualified than I for the work, I propose to turn to more general subjects and devote the time allotted me to generalities, and to the future rather than to the past.

In an address delivered about eighteen months ago before the Massachusetts Historical Society, I discussed in some detail the modern conception of history as compared with that which formerly prevailed. I do not now propose to repeat what I then said. It is sufficient for my present purpose to call attention to what we of the new school regard as the dividing line between us and the historians of the old school, the first day of October, 1859, — the date of the publication of Darwin's "Origin of Species;" the book of his immediately preceding the "Descent of Man," from which my text for to-day was taken. On the first day of October, 1859, the Mosaic cosmogony finally gave place to the Darwinian theory of evolution. Under the new dispensation, based not on chance or an assumed supernatural revelation, but on a patient study of biology, that record of mankind known as history, no longer a mere succession of traditions and annals, has become a unified whole, -a vast scheme systematically developing to some result as yet not understood. Closely allied to astronomy, geology and physics, the study of modern history seeks a scientific basis from which the rise and fall of races and dynasties will be seen merely as phases of a consecutive process of evolution, - the evolution of man from his initial to his ultimate state. When this conception was once reached, history, ceasing to be a mere narrative, made up of dis- connected episodes having little or no bearing on each other, became a connected whole. To each development, each epoch, race and dynasty its proper place was to be assigned; and to assign that place was the function of the historian. Formerly each episode was looked upon as complete in itself; and, being so, it had features more or less dramatic or instructive, and, for that reason, tempting to the historian, whether investigator or literary artist, -a Freeman or a Froude. Now, the first question the historian must put to himself relates to the proper adjustment of his particular theme to the entire plan, - he is shaping the fragment of a vast mosaic. The incomparably greater portion of history has, it is needless to say, little value, - not much more than the biography of the average individual;

it is a record of small accomplishment, -in many instances a record of no accomplishment at all, perhaps of retrogression; — for we cannot all be successful, nor even everlastingly and effectively strenuous. Among nations in history, as among men we know, the commonplace is the rule; but, whether ordinary or exceptional, conspicuous or obscure, - each has its proper place, and to it that place should be assigned.

Having laid down this principle, I, eighteen months ago, proceeded to apply it to the society I was then addressing, and to the history of the Commonwealth whose name that society bears; and I gave my answer to it, such as that answer was. The same question I now put as concerns Wisconsin; and to that also I propose to venture an answer. As my text has indicated, that answer, also, will not in a sense be lacking in ambition. In the history of Wisconsin I shall seek to find verification of what Darwin suggested, evidence of the truth of the great law of natural selection as applied also to man.

Thus stated, the theme is a large one, and may be approached in many ways; and, in the first place, I propose to approach it in the way usual with modern historical writers. I shall attempt to assign to Wisconsin its place in the sequence of recent development; for it is only during the last fifty years that Wisconsin has exercised any, even the most imperceptible, influence on what is conventionally agreed upon as history. That this region before the year 1848 had an existence, we know; as we also know that, since the last glacial period when the earth's surface hereabouts assumed its present geographical form, -some five thousand, or, perhaps, ten, or even twenty thousand years ago, it has been occupied by human beings, — fire-making, implement-using, garment-wearing, habitation-dwelling. With these we have now nothing to do. We, the historians, are concerned only with what may be called the mere fringe of Time's raiment, the last half century of the fifty or one hundred centuries; the rest belong to the ethnologist and the geologist, not to us. But the last fifty years, again, so far as the evolution of man from a lower to a higher stage of development is concerned, though a very quickening period, has, after all, been but one stage, and not the final stage, of a distinct phase of development.

That phase has now required four centuries in which to work itself out to the point as yet reached; for it harks back to the discovery of America, and the movement to- wards religious freedom which followed close upon that discovery, though having no direct connection with it. Martin Luther and Christopher Columbus had little in common except that their lives overlapped; but those two dates, 1492 and 1517,- the landfall at San Salvador, and the theses nailed on the church door at Wittenberg, - those two dates began a new chapter in human history, the chapter in which is recounted the fierce struggle over the establishment of the principles of civil and religious liberty, and the recognition of the equality of men before the law. For, speaking generally but with approximate correctness, it may be asserted that, prior to the year 1500, the domestic political action and the foreign complications of even the most advanced nations turned on other issues, dynastic, predatory, social; but, since that date, from the wars of Charles V., of Francis I., and of Elizabeth, down to our own Confederate rebellion, almost every great struggle or debate has either directly arisen out of some religious dispute or some demand for increased civil rights, or, if it had not there its origin, it has invariably gravitated in that direction. Even Frederick of Prussia, the so-called Great-that skeptical, irreligious, cut-purse of the Empire, -the disciple and protector of Voltaire and the apotheosized of Thomas Carlyle, - even Frederick figured as "the Protestant Hero"; while Francis I. was "the Eldest Son of the Church," and Henry VIII. received from Rome the title of "Defender of the Faith."

Since the year 1500, on the other hand, what is known as modern history has been little more than a narrative of the episodes in the struggle not yet closed against arbitrary rule, whether by a priesthood or through divine right, or by the members of a caste or of a privileged class, whether ennobled, plutocratic or industrial. The right of the individual man, no matter how ignorant or how poor, to think, worship and do as seems to him best, provided always in so doing he does not infringe upon the rights of others, has through these four centuries been, as it still is, the underlying issue in every conflict. It seems likely, also, to continue to be the issue for a long time to come, for it never was more firmly asserted or sternly denied than now; though to-day the opposition comes, not, as heretofore, from above, but from below, and finds its widest and most formidable expression in the teachings of those socialists who preach a doctrine of collectivism, or the complete suppression of the individual.

That proposition, however, does not concern us here and now. Our business is with the middle period of the nineteenth century, and not with the first half of the twentieth; and, no matter how closely we confine our- selves to the subject in hand, space and time will scarcely be found in which properly to develop the theme. Two and fifty years ago, when, in the summer of 1848, Wisconsin first took shape as a recognized political organization, -a new factor in man's development, human evolution was laboring over two problems,-nationality and slavery. Slavery that is, the ownership of one man or one class of men by another man or class of men- had existed, and been accepted as a matter of course, from the beginning. Historically the proposition did not admit of doubt. In Great Britain, bondage had only recently disappeared, and in Russia it was still the rule; while, among the less advanced nations its rightfulness was nowhere challenged, with us here in America it was a question of race. The equality of whites before the law was an article of political faith; not so that of the blacks. The Africans were distinctly an inferior order of being, and, as such, not only in the Southern or slave States, but throughout the North also, not entitled to the unrestricted pursuit on equal terms of life, liberty and happiness. Hence a fierce contention, the phase as it presented itself on the land discovered by Columbus in 1492, of the struggle inaugurated by Luther in 1517. Its work was thus, so to speak, cut out for Wisconsin in advance of its being, its place in the design of the great historical scheme prenatally assigned to it. How then did it address itself to its task? how perform the work thus given it to do? Did it, standing in the front rank of progress, help the great scheme along? Or, identifying it-self with that reactionist movement ever on foot, did it strive with the stars in their courses?

Here, in the United States, the form in which the issue of the future took shape between 1830, when it first presented itself, and 1848, when Wisconsin entered the sisterhood of States, is even yet only partially understood, in such occult ways did the forces of development interact and exercise influence on each other. For reasons not easy to explain, also, certain States came forward as the more active exponents of antagonistic ideas,— on the one side Massachusetts; on the other, first, Virginia, and, later, South Carolina. The great and long sustained debate which closed in an appeal to force in the spring of 1861 must now be conceded as something well-nigh inevitable from fundamental conditions which dated from the beginning. It was not a question of slavery; it was one of nationality. The issue had presented itself over and over again, in various forms and in different parts of the country ever since the Constitution had been adopted, - now in Pennsylvania; now in Tennessee; now in New England; even here in Wisconsin; but, in its most concrete form, in South Carolina. It was a struggle for mastery between centripetal and centrifugal forces. At the close, slavery was, it is true, the immediate cause of quarrel, but the seat of disturbance lay deeper. In another country, and under other conditions, it was the identical struggle which, in feudal times, went on in Great Britain, in France and in Spain, and which, more recently, and in our own day only, we have seen brought to a close in Germany and in Italy, — the struggle of a rising spirit of nationality to overcome the clannish instinct, the desire for local independence. In the beginning Virginia stood forward as the exponent of State Sovereignty. Jefferson was its mouthpiece. It was he who drew up the famous Tennessee resolutions of 1798–99, and his election to the presidency in 1800 was the recognized victory of the school of States' Rights over Federalism. Later the parties changed sides, —as political parties are wont to do. Possession of the government led to a marked modification of views; new issues were presented; and, in 1807, the policy which took shape in Jefferson's Embargo converted the Federalist into a disunion organization, which disappeared from existence in the famous Hartford Convention of 1814-15. New England was then the centre of the party of the centrifugal force, and the issues were commercial. Fortunately, up to 1815 the issue between the spirit of local sovereignty and the ever-growing sense of nationality had not taken shape over any matter of difference sufficiently great and far-reaching to provoke an appeal to force. Not the less for that was the danger of conflict there, -a sufficient cause and suitable occasion only were wanting, and those under ordinary conditions might be counted upon to present themselves in due course of time. They did present themselves in 1832, still under the economical guise. But now the moral issue lurked behind, though the South did not yet stand directly opposed to the advancing spirit of the age. But Nullification—the logical outcome of the theory of absolute State Sovereignty was enunciated by Calhoun, and South Carolina took from Virginia the lead in the reactionary movement from nationality. The danger once more passed away; but it is obvious to us now, and, it would seem, should have been plain to any cool-headed observer then, that, when the issue next presented itself, a trial of strength would be well-nigh inevitable. The doctrine of State Sovereignty, having assumed the shape of Nullification, would next develop that of Secession, and the direct issue over Nationality would be presented.

Almost before the last indications of danger over the economical question had disappeared, Slavery loomed ominously up. They did not realize it at the time, but it was now an angry wrangle over a step in the progressive evolution of the human race. The equality of man before the law and his Maker was insisted upon, and was denied. It was a portentous issue, for in it human destiny was challenged. The desperate risk the Southern States then took is plain enough now. They entered upon a distinctly reactionary movement against two of the foremost growing forces of human development, the tendency to nationality and the humanitarian spirit. Though they knew it not, they were arraying themselves against the very stars in their courses

Under these circumstances the secession-slavery movement between 1835 and 1860 was a predestined failure. Because of fortuitous events the chances of the battlefield, the impulse of individual genius, the exigencies of trade or the blunders of diplomats it might easily have had an apparent and momentary triumph; but the ultimate result the Slave Power, as such, had in view, the creation about the Gulf of Mexico of a great tropical nationality, based on cotton culture and African servitude, — this result was directly in the teeth of the irresistible tendencies of mankind in its present stage of development. It was in every respect radically reactionary, and could at most only have amounted to a passing anomaly.

While the Southern, or Jamestown, column of Darwin's great Anglo-Saxon migration was thus following to their legitimate conclusions the teachings of Jefferson and Calhoun, the Virginia and South Carolina schools of State Sovereignty, Slavery and Secession, -the distinctively Northern column, - that entering through the Plymouth and Boston portals, instinctively adhering to those principles of Church and State in the contention over which it originated, -found its way along the southern shores of the Great Lakes, through northern Ohio, southern Michigan, and northern Illinois, and then, turning north and west, spread itself over the vast region beyond the great lakes, and towards the upper waters of the Mississippi. But it is very noteworthy how the lead and inspiration in this movement still came from the original source. While in the South it passed from Virginia to Carolina; in the North it remained in Massachusetts. Three men then came forward there, voicing more clearly than any or all others what was in the mind of the community in the way of aspiration, whether moral or political. These three were: William Lloyd Garrison, Daniel Webster and John Quincy Adams; they were the prophetic voices of that phase of American political evolution then in process. Their messages, too, were curiously divergent; and yet, apparently contradictory, they were, in reality, supplementary to each other. Garrison developed the purely moral side of the coming issue. Webster preached nationality, under the guise of love of the Union. Adams, combining the two, pointed out a way to the establishment of the rights of man under the Constitution and within the Union. While, in a general way, much historical interest attaches to the utterances and educational influence of those three men during the period under discussion, the future political attitude of

Wisconsin, then nascent, was deeply affected by them. To this subject, therefore, I propose to devote some space; for, deserving attention, I am not aware that it has heretofore received it. In doing so I cannot ignore the fact of my own descent from one of the three I have named but I may say in my own extenuation that John Quincy Adams was indisputably a considerable public character in his time, and when I, a descendant of his, undertake to speak of that time historically, I must, when he comes into the field of discussion, deal with him as best I may, assigning to him, as to his contemporaries, the place which, as I see it, is properly his or theirs. Moreover, I will freely acknowledge that an hereditary affiliation, if I may so express it, was not absent from the feeling which impelled me to accept your call. However much others had forgotten it, I well remembered that more than half a century ago, in the days of small things, it was in this region, as in central New York and the Western Reserve, that the seed cast by one from whom I claim descent fell in the good ground where it bore fruit an hundred fold.

Recurring, then, to the three men I have named as voicing systematically a message of special significance in connection with the phase of political evolution, or of development if that word is preferred, then going on, — Garrison's message was distinctly moral and humanitarian. In a sense, it was reactionary, and violently so. In it there was no appeal to patriotism, no recognition even of nationality. On the contrary, in the lofty atmosphere of humanitarianism in which he had his being, I doubt if Garrison ever inhaled a distinctively patriotic breath; while he certainly denounced the Constitution and assailed the Union. He saw only the moral wrong of slavery, its absolute denial of the fundamental principle of the equality of men before the law and before God, and the world became his, - where freedom was, there was his country. To arouse the dormant conscience of the community by the fierce and unceasing denunciation of a great wrong was his mission; and he fulfilled it: but, curiously enough, the end he labored for came in the way he least foresaw, and through the very instrumentality he had most vehemently denounced, it came within that Union which he had described as a compact with death, and under that Constitution which he had arraigned as a covenant with Hell. Yet Garrison was undeniably a prophet, voicing the gospel as he saw it fearlessly and without pause. As such he contributed potently to the final result.

Next, Webster. It was the mission of Daniel Webster to preach nationality. In doing so he spoke in words of massive eloquence in direct harmony with the most pronounced aspiration of his time, — that aspiration which has asserted itself and worked the most manifest results of the nineteenth century in both hemispheres, in Spain and Prussia during the Napoleonic war, in Russia during the long Slavonic upheaval, again more recently in Germany and in Italy, and finally in the United States. The names of Stein, of Cavour and of Bismarck are scarcely more associated with this great instinctive movement of the century than is that of Daniel Webster. His mission it was to preach to this people Union, one and indivisible; and he delivered his message.

The mission of J. Q. Adams during his best and latest years, while a combination of that of the two others, was different from either. His message, carefully thought out, long retained, and at last distinctly enunciated, was his answer to the Jeffersonian theory of State Sovereignty, and Calhoun's doctrine of Nullification and its logical outcome, Secession. Secession. With both theory and doctrine, and their results, he had during his long political career been confronted; on both he had reflected much. It was during the administration of Jefferson and on the question of Union that he had, in 1807, broken with his party and resigned from the Senate; and with Calhoun he had been closely associated in the cabinet of Monroe. Calhoun also had occupied the vice-presidential chair during his own administration. He now met Calhoun face to face on the slavery issue, prophetically proclaiming a remedy for the moral wrong and the vindication of the rights of within the Union and under the Constitution, through the exercise of inherent war powers, whenever an issue between the sections should assume the insurrectionary shape. In other words, Garrison's moral result was to be secured, not through the agencies Garrison advocated, but by force of that nationality which Webster proclaimed. This solution of the issue, J. Q. Adams never wearied of enunciating, early and late, by act, speech and letter; and his view prevailed in the end. Lincoln's proclamation of January, 1863, was but the formal declaration of the policy enunciated by J. Q. Adams on the floor of Congress in 1836, and again in 1841, and yet again in greater detail in 1842.[3] It was he who thus brought the abstract moral doctrines of Garrison into unison of movement with the nationality of Webster.

The time now drew near when Wisconsin was to take her place in the Union, and exert her share of influence on the national polity, and through that polity on a phase of political evolution. South Carolina, by the voice of Calhoun, was preaching reaction, through slavery and in defiance of nationality: Massachusetts, through Garrison and Webster, was proclaiming the moral idea and nationality as abstractions; while J. Q. Adams confronted Calhoun with the ominous contention that, the instant he or his had recourse to force, that instant the moral wrong could be made good by the sword wielded in defence of Nationality and in the name of the Constitution.

As 1848 waxed old, the debate grew angry. J. Q. Adams died in the early months of that memorable year; but his death in no way affected the course of events. The leadership in the anti-slavery struggle on the floor of Congress and within the limits of the Constitution had passed from him four years before. He was too old longer to bear the weight of armor, or to wield weapons once familiar; but the effect of his teachings remained, and were living realities wherever the New England column had penetrated, throughout central New York, in "the Western Reserve," and especially in the region which bordered on Lake Michigan. Garrison still declaimed against the Union as an unholy alliance with sin; while, in the mind of Webster, his sense of the wrong of slavery was fast being overweighted by apprehension for nationality. In the mean time, a war of criminal aggression against Mexico in behalf of Calhoun's reactionary movement had been brought to a close, and the question was as to the partition of plunder. On that great issues hinged, and over it was fought, the presidential election of 1848. A little more than fifty years ago, that was the first election in which Wisconsin participated. The number of those who now retain a distinct recollection of the canvass of 1848 and the questions then so earnestly debated are not many; I chance to be one of those few. I recall one trifling incident connected, not with the canvass but with the events of that year, which, for some reason, made an impression upon me, and now illustrates curiously the remoteness of the time. I have said that J. Q. Adams died in February, 1848. Carried back with much funereal state from the Capitol at Washington to Massachusetts, he was in March buried at Quincy. An eloquent discourse was there delivered over his grave by the minister of the church of which the ex-President had been a member. He who delivered it was a scholar, as well as a natural orator of high order; and, in the course -of what he said he had occasion to refer to this remote region, then not yet admitted to statehood, and he did so under the name of "the Ouisconsin." That discourse was delivered on the 11th of March, 1848; and, on the 29th of the following May, Wisconsin became a State.

Returning now to the presidential election of 1848, it will be found that Wisconsin, the youngest community in the Union, came at once to the front as the banner State of the West in support of the principles on which the Union was established, and the maintenance and vindication of those fundamental principles within the Union and through the Constitution. In that canvass the great issues of the future were distinctly brought to the front. The old party organizations then still con- fronted each other, the Henry Clay Whigs were over against the Jacksonian Democracy; but in that election Lewis Cass, the legitimate candidate of the Democracy, a Northern man with Southern principles, so far as African slavery was concerned a distinct reactionist from the principles of the great Declaration of 1776, -Lewis Cass, of Michigan, was opposed to General Zachary Taylor, of Louisiana, himself a slaveholder, and nominated by a party which in presenting his name carefully abstained from any enunciation of political principles. He was an unknown political quantity; and no less a public character than Daniel Webster characterized his nomination as one not fit to be made. It yet remained to be seen that, practically, the plain, blunt, honest, well- meaning old soldier made an excellent President, whose premature loss was deeply and with reason deplored. His nomination, however, immediately after that of Cass, proved the signal for revolt. For the disciples of J. Q. Adams in both political camps it was as if the cry had again gone forth, "To your tents, O Israel!"—and a first fierce blast of the coming storm then swept across the land. In August the dissentients met in conference at Buffalo, and there first enunciated the principles of the American political party of the future, - that party which, permeated by the sentiment of Nationality, was destined to do away with slavery through the war power, and to incorporate into the Constitution the principle of the equality of man before the law, irrespective of color or of race. Now, more than half a century after the event, it may fairly be said of those concerned in the Buffalo movement of 1848 that they were destined to earn in the fulness of time the rare distinction of carrying mankind forward one distinct stage in the long process of evolution. In support of that movement Wisconsin was, as I have already said, the banner western State. In its action it simply responded to its early impulse received from New England and western New York. Thus the seed fell in fertile places and produced fruit an hundred fold. The law of natural selection, though not yet formulated, was at work.

The election returns of 1848 tell the story. They are still eloquent. The heart of the movement of that year lay in Massachusetts and Vermont. In those two States, taken together, the party of the future polled, in 1848, a little over 28 per cent. of the aggregate vote cast. In Wisconsin it polled close upon 27 per cent.; and this 27 per cent. in Wisconsin is to be compared with 15 per cent. in Michigan, 12 per cent. in Illinois, less than 11 per cent. in Ohio, and not 4 per cent. in the adjoining State of Iowa. In the three neighboring States of Michigan, Illinois and Iowa, taken together, the new movement gathered into itself 12 per cent. of the total voting constituency, while in Wisconsin it counted, as I have said, over 26 per cent. Thus, in 1848, Wisconsin was the Vermont of the West; sending to Congress as one of its three representatives Charles Durkee, a son of Vermont, the first distinctively anti-slavery man from the Northwest. Wisconsin remained the

Vermont of the West. From its very origin not the smallest doubt attached to its attitude. It emphasized it in words when in 1849 it instructed one of its Senators at Washington "to immediately resign his seat" because he had "outraged the feelings of the people" by dalliance with the demands of the Slave Power; it emphasized it by action when five years later its highest judicial tribunal did not hesitate to declare the Fugitive Slave Law of 1850 "unconstitutional and void." At the momentous election of 1860, Wisconsin threw 56 per cent. of its vote in favor of the ticket bearing the name of Abraham Lincoln; nor did the convictions of the State weaken under the test of war. In 1864, when Wisconsin had sent into the field over 90,000 enlisted men to maintain the Union, and to make effective the most extreme doctrine of war powers under the Constitution, even then, in the fourth year of severest stress, Wisconsin again threw 55 per cent. of its popular vote for the reëlection of Lincoln. A year later the struggle ended. Throughout the ordeal Wisconsin never faltered.

Of the record made by Wisconsin in the Civil War, I am not here to speak. That field has been sufficiently covered, and covered by those far better qualified than I to work in it. I will only say, in often quoted words, that, none then died more freely or in greater glory than those Wisconsin sent into the field, though then many died, and there was much glory. When figures so speak, comment weakens. Look at the record: Fifty-seven regiments and thirteen batteries in the field; a death roll exceeding 12,000; a Wisconsin regiment (2d) first in that roll of honor which tells off the regiments of the Union which suffered most, and two other Wisconsin regiments (7th and 26th), together, fifth; while a brigade made up three quarters of Wisconsin battalions shows the heaviest aggregate loss sustained during the war by any similar command, and is hence known in the history of the struggle as the "Iron Brigade." Thirteen Wisconsin regiments participated in Grant's brilliant movement on Vicksburg; five were with Thomas at Chickamauga; seven with Sherman at Mission Ridge; and, finally, eleven marched with him to the sea, while four remained behind to strike with Thomas at Nashville. Thus it may truly be said that wherever, between the 13th of April, 1861, and the 26th of April, 1865, death was reaping its heaviest harvest, -whether in Pennsylvania, in Virginia, in Tennessee, in Mississippi, in Georgia, — at Shiloh, at Corinth, at Antietam, at Gettysburg, in the salient at Spottsylvania, in the death-trap at Petersburg, or in the Peninsula slaughter-pen, wherever during those awful years the dead lay thickest, there the men from Wisconsin were freely laying down their lives.

It is, however, no part of my present purpose to set forth here your sacrifices in the contest of 1861-65. What I have undertaken to do is to assign to Wisconsin its proper and relative place as a factor in one of the great evolutionary movements of man. As the twig was bent, the tree inclined. The sacrifices of Wisconsin life and treasure between 1861 and 1865 were but the fulfilment of the promise given by Wisconsin in 1848. The State, it is true, at no time during that momentous struggle rose to a position of unchallenged leadership either in the field or the council chamber. Among its representatives it did not number a Lincoln or a Sherman; but it did supply in marked degree that greatest and most necessary of all essentials in every evolutionary crisis, a well-developed and thoroughly distributed popular backbone.

This racial characteristic, also, I take to be the one great essential to the success of our American experiment. In every emergency which arises there is always the cry raised for a strong hand at the helm, - the ship of state is invariably declared to be hopelessly drifting. But it is in just those times of crisis that a widely diffused individuality proves the greatest possible safeguard, the only reliable public safeguard. It is then with the State as it is with a strong, seaworthy ship manned by a hardy and experienced crew, in no way dependent on the one pilot who may chance to be at the wheel. In any stress of storm, the ship's company will prove equal to the occasion, and somehow provide for its own salvation. Under similar political conditions, a community asserts, in the long run, its superiority to the accidents of fortune, - the aberrations due to the influence of individual genius, those winning numbers in the lottery of fate, and evinces that staying power, which, no less now and here than in Rome and Great Britain, is the only safe rock of empire. The race thus educated and endowed is the masterful race, the master of its own destiny, it is master of the destiny of others; and of that crowning republican quality, Wisconsin, during our period of national trial, showed herself markedly possessed. While individuals were not exceptional, the average was unmistakably high.

And this I hold to be the highest tribute which can be paid to a political community. It implies all else. Unless I greatly err, this characteristic has, in the case of Wisconsin, a profound and scientific significance of the most far-reaching character; and so I find myself brought back to my text. As I have already more than once said, others are in every way better qualified than I to speak intelligently of the Wisconsin stock, — of the elements which enter into the brain and bone and sinew of the race now holding as its abiding-place and breeding-ground the region lying between Lake Michigan and the waters of the upper Mississippi, - between the State of Illinois on the south and Lake Superior on the north. I speak chiefly from impression, and always subject to correction; but my understanding is that this region was in the main peopled by men and women representing in their persons what there was of the more enterprising, adventurous and energetic of three of the most thoroughly virile and, withal, moral and intellectual branches of the human family,—I refer to the Anglo-Saxon of New England descent, and to the Teutonic and the Scandinavian families. Tough of fibre and tenacious of principle, the mixed descendants from those races were well calculated to illustrate the operation of a natural law; and I have quite failed in my purpose if I have not improved this occasion to point out how in the outset of their political life as a community they illustrated the force of Stoughton's utterance and the truth of Darwin's remarkable generalization. By their attitude and action, at once intelligent and decided, they left their imprint on that particular phase of human evolution which then presented itself. They, in so doing, assigned to Wisconsin its special place and work in the great scheme of development, and forecast its mission in the future.

I have propounded an historical theory; it is for others, better advised, having passed upon it, to confirm or reject.

There are many other topics which might here and now be discussed, perhaps advantageously, - topics closely connected with this edifice and with the occasion, topics relating to libraries, the accumulation of historical material, and methods of work in connection with it; but space and time alike forbid. A selection must be made; and, in making my selection, I go back to the fact that, representing one historical society, I am here at the behest of another historical society; and matters relating to what we call "history" are, therefore, those most germane to the day. Coming, then, here from the East to a point which, in the great future of our American development, - a century, or, perchance, two or three centuries hence, - may not unreasonably look forward to being the seat of other methods and a higher learning, I propose to pass over the more obvious and, possibly, the more useful, even if more modest, subjects of discussion, and to try my hand at one which, even if it challenges controversy, is indisputably suggestive. I refer to certain of the more marked of those tendencies which characterize the historical work of the day. Having dealt with the sifted grain, I naturally come to speak of those who have told the tale of the sifting. Looking back, from the standpoint of 1900, over the harvested sheaves which stud the fields we have traversed, the retrospect is not to me altogether satisfactory. In fact, taken as a whole, our histories — I speak of those written by the dead only -have not, I submit, so far as we are concerned, fully met the requirements of time and place. Literary masterpieces, scientific treatises, philosophical disquisitions, sometimes one element predominates, sometimes another; but in them all something is wanting. That something I take to be an adequately developed literary sense.

In dealing with this subject, I am well aware my criticism might take a wider range. I need not confine myself to history, inasmuch as, in the matter of literary sense, the shortcomings, or the excesses rather, of the American writer, are manifest. In the Greek, and in the Greek alone, this sense seems to have been instinctive. He revealed it, and he revealed it at once, in poetry, in architecture and in art, as he revealed it in the composition of history. Of Homer we cannot speak; but Herodotus and Phidias died within six years of each other, each a father in his calling. With us Americans that intuitive literary sense, resulting in the perfection of literary form, seems not less conspicuous for its absence than it was conspicuous for its presence among the Greeks. In literature the American seems to exist in a medium of stenographers and typewriters, and with a public printer at his beck and call. To such a degree is this the case that the expression I have just used- literary form — has, to many, and those not the least cultured, ceased to carry a meaning. Literary form they take to mean what they know as style; while style is, with them, but another term for word-painting. Accordingly, with altogether too many of our American writers, to be voluminous and verbose is to be great. They would conquer by force of numbers the number of words they use. I, the other day, chanced across a curious illustration of this in the diary of my father. Returning from his long residence in England at the time of the Civil War, he attended some ceremonies held in Boston in honor of a public character who had died shortly before. "The eulogy," he wrote, "was good, but altogether too long. There is in all the American style of composition a tendency to diffuseness, and the repetition of the same ideas, which materially impairs the force of what is said. I see it the more clearly from having been so long out of the atmosphere."

The failing is national; nor in this respect does the American seem to profit by experience. Take, for instance, the most important of our public documents, the inaugurals of our Presidents. We are a busy people; yet our newly elected Presidents regularly inflict on us small volumes of information, and this, too, notwithstanding the fact that in the long line of inaugural commonplaces but one utterance stands out in memory, and that one the shortest of all, -the immortal second of Lincoln. Our present chief magistrate found himself unable to do justice to the occasion, in his last annual message, in less than eighteen thousand words; and in the Congress to which this message was addressed, two Senators, in discussing the "paramount" issue of the day, did so, the one in a speech of sixty-five thousand words; the other in a speech of fifty-five thousand. Webster replied to Hayne in thirty-five thousand; and Webster then did not err on the side of brevity. So in the presidential canvass now in progress. Mr. Bryan accepted his nomination in a comparatively brief speech of nine thousand words; and this speech was followed by a letter of five thousand, covering omissions because of previous brevity. President McKinley, in his turn, then accepted a renomination in a letter of twelve thousand words, - a letter actually terse when compared with his last annual message; but which Mr. Carl Schurz subsequently proceeded to comment on in a vigorous address of fourteen thousand words. Leviathans in language, we Americans need to be Methuselahs in years. It was not always so. The contrast is, indeed, noticeable. Washington's first inaugural numbered twenty-three hundred words. Including that now in progress, my memory covers fourteen presidential canvasses; and by far the most generally applauded and effective letter of acceptance put forth by any candidate during all those canvasses was that of General Grant in 1868. Including address and signature, it was comprised in exactly two hundred and thirty words. With a brevity truly commendable, even if military, he used one word where his civilian successor found occasion for fifty- two. As to the opponent of that civilian successor, he sets computation at defiance. Indeed, speaking of Mr. Bryan purely from the historical standpoint, I seriously doubt whether, in all human experience, any man ever before gave utterance to an equal number of words in the same space of time.

Leaving illustration, however, and returning to my theme, I will now say that in the whole long and memorable list of distinctively American literary men,-authors, orators, poets and story-tellers, I recall but three who seem to me to have been endowed with a sense of form, at once innate and Greek; those three were Daniel Webster, Edgar Allan Poe and Nathaniel Hawthorne. Yet, unless moulded by that instinctive sense of form, nothing can be permanent in literature any more than in sculpture, in painting or in architecture. Not size, nor solidity, nor fidelity of work, nor knowledge of detail, will preserve the printed volume any more than they will preserve the canvas or the edifice; and this I hold to be just as true of history as of the oration, the poem or the drama.

Surely, then, our histories need not all, of necessity, be designed for students and scholars exclusively; and yet it is a noteworthy fact that even to-day, after scholars and story-tellers have been steadily at work upon it for nearly a century and a half, -ever since David Hume and Oliver Goldsmith brought forth their classic renderings, — the chief popular knowledge of over three centuries of English history between John Plantagenet (1200) and Elizabeth Tudor (1536) is derived from the pages of Shakespeare. There is also a curious theory now apparently in vogue in our University circles, that, in some inscrutable way, accuracy as to fact and a judicial temperament are inconsistent with a highly developed literary sense. Erudition and fairness are the qualities in vogue, while form and brilliancy are viewed askance. Addressing now an assembly made up, to an unusual extent, of those engaged in the work of instruction in history, I wish to suggest that this marked tendency of the day is in itself a passing fashion, and merely a reactionary movement against the influence of two great literary masters of the last generation,- Macaulay and Carlyle. That the reaction had reason, I would by no means deny ; but, like most decided reactions, has it not gone too far? Because men weary of brilliant colors, and mere imitators try to wield the master's brush, it by no means follows that art does not find its highest expression in Titian and Tintoretto, Rembrandt, Claude and Turner. It is the same with history. Profound scholars, patient investigators, men of a judicial turn of mind, subtile philosophers and accurate annalists empty forth upon a patient, because somewhat indifferent, reading public volume after volume; but the great masters of literary form, in history as in poetry, alone retain their hold. Thucydides, Tacitus and Gibbon are always there, on a level with the eye; while those of their would-be successors who find themselves unable to tell us what they know, in a way in which we care to hear it, or within limits consistent with human life, are quietly relegated to the oblivion of the topmost shelf.

I fear that I am myself in danger of sinning somewhat flagrantly against the canons I have laid down. Exceeding my allotted space, I am conscious of disregarding any correct rule of form by my attempt at dealing with more subjects than it is possible on one occasion adequately to discuss. None the less I cannot resist the temptation, - I am proving myself an American; and having gone thus far, I will now go on to the end, even though alone. There are, I hold, three elements which enter into the make-up of the ideal historian, whether him of the past or him of the future; these three are learning, judgment and the literary sense. A perfect history, like a perfect poem, must have a beginning, a middle and an end; and the well proportioned parts should be kept in strict subservience to the whole. The dress, also, should be in keeping with the substance; and both subordinated to the conception. Attempting no display of erudition, pass the great historical literatures and names in rapid review, and see in how few instances all these canons were observed. And first, the Hebrew. While the Jew certainly was not endowed with the Greek's sense of form in sculpture, in painting or in architecture, in poetry and music he was, and has since been, preeminent. His philosophy and his history found their natural expression through his aptitudes. The result illustrates the supreme intellectual power exercised by art. Of learning and judgment there is only pretence; but imagination and power are there and, even to this day, the Hebrew historical writings are a distinct literature, we call them "The Sacred Books." We have passed from under that superstition; and yet it still holds a traditional sway. The books of Moses are merely a first tentative effort on the road subsequently trodden by Herodotus, Livy and Voltaire; but their author was so instinct with imagination and such a master of form that to this day his narrative is read and accepted as history by more human beings than are all the other historical works in existence combined in one mass. No scholar or man of reflection now believes that Moses was any more inspired than Homer, Julius Cæsar or Thomas Carlyle; but the imagination and intellectual force of the man, combined with his instinct for literary form, sufficed to secure for what he wrote a unique mastery only in our day shaken.[4]

The Greek follows hard upon the Jew; and of the Greek I have already said enough. He had a natural sense of art in all its shapes; and, when it came to writing history, Herodotus, Thucydides and Xenophon seemed mere evolutions. Of the three, Thucydides alone combined in perfection the qualities of erudition, judgment and form; but to the last-named element, their literary form, it is that all three owe their immortality.

It is the same with the Romans, Livy, Sallust, Tacitus. The Roman had not that artistic instinct so noticeable in the Greek. He was, on the contrary, essentially a soldier, a ruler and organizer; and a literary imitator. Yet now and again even in art he attained a proficiency which challenged his models. Cicero has held his own with Demosthenes; and Virgil, Horace and Juvenal survive, each through a mastery of form. Tacitus, it is needless to say, is the Latin Thucydides. In him again, five centuries after Thucydides, the three essentials are combined in the highest degree. The orbs of the great historical constellation are wide apart, -the interval that divided Tacitus from Thucydides is the same as that which divided Matthew Paris from Edward Gibbon; — twice that which divides Shakespeare from Tennyson.

Coming rapidly down to modern times, of the three great languages fruitful in historical work, the French, English and German, those writing in the first have alone approached the aptitude for form natural to the Greeks; but in Gibbon only of those who have, in the three tongues, devoted themselves to historical work, were all the cardinal elements of historical greatness found united in such a degree as to command general assent to his pre- eminence. The Germans are remarkable for erudition, and have won respect for their judgment; but their disregard of form has been innate, — indicative either of a lack of perception or of contempt.[5] Their work accordingly will hardly prove enduring. The French, from Voltaire down, have evinced a keener perception of form, nor have they been lacking in erudition. Critical and quick to perceive, they have still failed in any one instance to combine the three great attributes each in its highest degree. Accordingly, in the historical firmament they count no star of the first magnitude.

Their lights have been meteoric rather than permanent. In the case of Great Britain it is interesting to follow the familiar names, noting the shortcoming of each. The roll scarcely extends beyond the century, -- Hume, Robertson and Gibbon constituting the solitary remembered exceptions. Of Gibbon, I have already spoken. He combined in highest degree all the elements of the historian, — in as great a degree as Thucydides or Tacitus. He was an orb of the first order; and it was his misfortune that he was born and wrote before Darwin gave to history unity and a scheme. Hume was a subtle philosopher, and his instinctive mastery of form has alone caused his history to survive. He was not an investigator in the modern sense of the term, nor was he gifted with an intuitive historical instinct. Robertson had fair judgment and a well-developed though in no way remarkable sense of form; but he lacked erudition, and, as compared with Gibbon, for example, was content to accept his knowledge at second hand. Telling his story well, he was never master of his subject. -

Coming down to our own century, and speaking only of the dead, a series of familiar names at once suggest themselves, Mitford, Grote and Thirlwall; Arnold and Merivale; Milman, Lingard, Hallam, Macaulay, Carlyle, Buckle, Froude, Freeman and Green, — naming only the more conspicuous. Mitford was no historian at all; merely an historical pamphleteer. His judgment was inferior to his erudition even, and he had no sense of form. Grote was erudite, but he wrote in accordance with his political affinities, and what is called the spirit of the time and place; and that time and place were not Greece, nor the third and fourth centuries before Christ. He had, moreover, no sense of literary form, for he put what he knew into twelve volumes, when human patience did not suffice for six. Thirlwall was erudite in Thirlwall was erudite in a way, and a thinker and writer of unquestionable force; but his work on Greece was written to order, and is what is known as a "standard history." Correct, but devoid of inspiration, it is slightly suggestive of a second-class epic. Arnold is typical of scholarship and insight; his judgment is excellent: but of literary art, so conspicuous in his son, there is no trace. Merivale is scholarly and academic. Milman was hampered by his church training, which fettered his judgment; learned, as learning went in those days, there is in his writings nothing that would attract readers or students of a period later than his own. Lingard was another church historian. A correct writer, he tells England's story from the point of view of Rome. Hallam is deeply read, and judicial; but the literary sense is conspicuously absent. His volumes are well-nigh unreadable. Freeman is the typical modern historian of the original-material-and-monograph school. He writes irrespective of readers. Learned beyond compare, he cumbers the shelves of our libraries with an accumulation of volumes which are not literature.

Of Henry Thomas Buckle and of John Richard Green I will speak together, and with respectful admiration. Both were prematurely cut off, almost in what with historical writers is the period of promise; for, while Green at the time of his death was forty-seven, Buckle was not yet forty-one. What they did, therefore, and they both did much, — was indicative only of what they might have done. Judged by that, *-ex pede Herculem*, I hold that they come nearer to the ideal of what a twentieth century historian should be than any other writers in our modern English tongue. That Buckle was crude, impulsive, hasty in generalization and paradoxical in judgment is not to be gainsaid; -but he wrote before Darwin; and, when he published his history, he was but thirty-six. What might he not have become had he been favored with health, and lived to sixty. Very different in organization, he and Green alike possessed in high degree the spirit of investigation and the historical insight, combined with a well-developed literary sense. Men of untiring research, they had the faculty of expression. Artists as well as scholars, they inspired. Their early death was in my judgment an irreparable loss to English historical lore and the best historical treatment.

I come now to Macaulay, Carlyle and Froude, the three literary masters of the century who have dealt with history in the English tongue; and I shall treat of them briefly, and in the inverse order. Froude is redeemed by a sense of literary form; as an historian he was learned, but inaccurate, and his judgment was fatally defective. He was essentially an artist. Carlyle was a poet rather than an historian.

A student, with the insight of a seer and a prophet's voice, his judgment was fatally biased. A wonderful master of form, his writings will endure; but rather as epics in prose than as historical monuments. Macaulay came, in my judgment, nearer than any other English writer of the century to the great historical stature; but he failed to attain it. The cause of his failure is an instructive as well as an interesting study.

Thomas Babington Macaulay is unquestionably the most popular historian that ever wrote. His history, when it appeared, was the literary sensation of the day, and its circulation increased with each succeeding volume. Among historical works, it alone has in its vogue thrown into the shade the most successful novels of the century, those of Scott, Thackeray and Dickens, Jane Eyre, Robert Elsmere, and even Richard Carvel, the last ephemeral sensation; but, of the three great attributes of the historian, Macaulay was endowed with only one. He was a man of vast erudition; and, moreover, he was gifted with a phenomenal memory, which seemed to put at his immediate disposal the entire accumulation of his omnivorous reading. His judgment was, however, defective; for he was, from the very ardor of his nature,[6] more or less of a partisan, while the wealth of his imagination and the exuberance of his rhetoric were fatal to his sense of form. He was incomparably the greatest of historical raconteurs, but the fascination of the story overcame his sense of proportion, and he was buried under his own riches. For it is a great mistake to suppose, as so many do, that what is called style, no matter how brilliant, or how correct and clear, constitutes in itself literary form; it is a large and indispensable element in literary form, but neither the whole, nor indeed the greatest part of it. The entire scheme, the proportion of the several parts to the whole and to each other, the grouping and the presentation, the background and the accessories constitute literary form; the style of the author is merely the drapery of presentation. Here was where Macaulay failed; and he failed on a point which the average historical writer, and the average historical instructor still more, does not as a rule even take into consideration. Macaulay's general conception of his scheme was so imperfect as to be practically impossible; and this he himself, when too late, sadly recognized. His interest in his subject and the warmth of his imagination swept him away, they were too strong for his sense of proportion. Take, for instance, two such wonderful bits as his account of the trial of the seven bishops, and his narrative of the siege of Londonderry. They are masterpieces; but they should be monographs. They are in their imagery and detail out of all proportion to any general historical plan. They imply a whole which would be in itself an historical library rather than a history. On the matter of judgment it is not necessary to dwell. Macaulay's work is unquestionably history, and history on a panoramic scale; but the pigments he used are indisputably Whig. Yet his method was instinctively correct. He had his models and his scheme, he made his preliminary studies, he saw his subject as a whole, and in its several parts; but he labored under two disadvantages:- In the first place, like Gibbon, he was born. and wrote before the discoveries of Darwin had given its whole great unity to history; and, in the second place, he had not thought his plan fully out, subordinating severely to it both his imagination and his rhetoric. Accordingly, so far as literary form was concerned, his history, which in that respect above all should, with his classic training, have been an entire and perfect chrysolite, was in fact a monumental failure. It was not even a whole; it was only a fragment.

Coming now to our own American experience, and still speaking exclusively of the writings of the dead, it is not unsafe to say that there is as yet no American historical work which can call even for mention among those of the first class. The list can speedily be passed in review, Marshall, Irving, Prescott, Hildreth, Bancroft, Motley, Palfrey and Parkman. Except those yet living, I do not recall any others who would challenge consideration. That Marshall was endowed with a calm, clear judgment, no reader of his judicial opinions would deny; but he had no other attribute of an historian. He certainly was not historically learned, and there is no evidence that he was gifted with any sense of literary proportion. Irving was a born man of letters. With a charming style and a keen sense of humor, he was as an historical writer defective in judgment. Not a profound or accurate investigator, as became apparent in his Columbus and his Washington, his excellent natural literary sense was but partially developed. Perhaps he was born before his time; perhaps his education did not lead him to the study of the best models; but, however it came about, he failed, and failed indisputably, in form. Prescott was a species of historical pioneer,- - an adventurer in a new field of research and of letters. Not only was he, like Macaulay and the rest, born before Darwin and the other great scientific lights of the century had assigned to human history its unity, limits and significance, but Prescott was not a profound scholar, nor yet a thorough investigator; his judgment was by no means either incisive or robust, and his style was elegant, as the phrase goes, rather than tersely vigorous. He wrote, moreover, of that which he never saw, or made himself thoroughly part of even in imagination. Laboring under great disadvantages, his course was infinitely creditable; but his portrait in the gallery of historians is not on the eye line. Of Hildreth, it is hardly necessary to speak. Laborious and persevering, his investigation was not thorough; indeed he had not taken in the fundamental conditions of modern historical research. With a fatally defective judgment, he did not know what form was.

George Bancroft was in certain ways unique, and, among writers and students, his name cannot be mentioned without respect. He was by nature an investigator. His learning and philosophy cannot be called sound, and his earlier manner was something to be forever avoided; but he was indefatigable as a collector, and his patience knew no bounds. He devoted his life to his subject; and his life came to a close while he was still dwelling on the preliminaries to his theme. A partisan, and writing in support of a preconceived theory, his judgment was necessarily biased; while, as respects literary form, though he always tended to what was better, he never even approximately reached what is best. He, too, like Macaulay, failed to grasp the wide and fundamental distinction between a proportioned and complete history and a thorough historical monograph. His monumental work, therefore, is neither the one nor the other. As a collection of monographs, it is too condensed and imperfect; as a history, it is cumbersome, and enters into unnecessary detail. From a literary point of view Motley is unquestionably the most brilliant of American historical writers. He reminds the reader of Froude. Not naturally a patient or profound investigator, he yet forced himself to make a thorough study of his great subject, and he was gifted with a remarkable descriptive power. A man of intense personality, he was, however, defective in judgment, if not devoid of the faculty. He lacked calmness and method. He could describe a siege or a battle with a vividness which, while it revealed the master, revealed also the historian's limitations. With a distinct sense of literary form, he was unable to resist the temptations of imagination and sympathy. His taste was not severe; his temper the reverse of serene. His defects as an historian are consequently as apparent as are his merits as a writer.

Of Palfrey, the historian, I would speak with the deep personal respect I entertained for the man. A typical New Englander, a victim almost of that "terrible New England conscience," he wrote the history of New England. A scholar in his way, and the most patient of investigators, he had, as an historian, been brought up in a radically wrong school, that of New England theology. There was in him not a trace of the skeptic, nor a suggestion of the humorist or easy-going philosopher. He wrote of New England from the inside, and in close sympathy with it. Thus, as respects learning, care and accuracy, he was in no way deficient, while he was painstaking and conscientious in extreme. His training and mental characteristics, however, impaired his judgment, and he was quite devoid of any sense of form. The investigator will always have recourse to his work; but, as a guide, its value will pass away with the traditions of the New England theological period. From the literary point of view the absence of all idea of proportion renders the bulk of what he wrote impossible for the reader.

Of those I have mentioned, Parkman alone remains; perhaps the most individual of all our American historians, the one tasting most racily of the soil. Parkman did what Prescott failed to do, what it was not in Prescott ever to do. He wrote from the basis of a personal knowledge of the localities in which what he had to narrate occurred, and the characteristics of those with whom he undertook to deal. To his theme he devoted his entire life, working under difficulties even greater than those which so cruelly hampered Prescott. His patience under suffering was infinite; his research was indefatigable. In this respect, he left nothing to be desired. While his historical judgment was better than his literary taste, his appreciation of form was radically defective. Indeed he seemed almost devoid of any true sense of proportion. The result is that he has left behind him a succession of monographs of more or less historical value or literary interest, but no complete, thoroughly designed and carefully proportioned historical unit. Like all the others, his work lacks form and finish.

The historical writers of more than an hundred years have thus been passed in hasty review, nor has any nineteenth century compeer of Thucydides, Tacitus and Gibbon been found among those who have expressed them- selves in the English tongue. Nor do I think that any such could be found in other tongues; unless, perchance, among the Germans, Theodor Mommsen might challenge consideration. Of Mommsen's learning there can be no question. I do not think there can be much of his insight and judgment. The sole question would be as to his literary form; nor, in that respect, judging by the recollection of thirty years, do I think that, so far as his history of Rome is concerned, judgment can be lightly passed against him. But, on this point, the verdict of time only is final. Before that verdict is in his case rendered, another half century of probation must elapse.[7]

There is still something to be taken into consideration. I have as yet dealt only with the writers; the readers remain. During the century now ending, what changes have here come about? For one, I frankly confess myself a strong advocate of what is sometimes rather contemptuously referred to as the popularization of history. I have but a limited sympathy with those who, from the etherealized atmosphere of the cloister, whether monkish or collegiate, seek truth's essence and pure learning only, regardless of utility, of sympathy or of applause. The great historical writer, fully to accomplish his mission, must, I hold, be in very close touch with the generation he addresses. In other words, to do its most useful work, historical thought must be made to permeate what we are pleased to call the mass; it must be infiltrated through that great body of the community which, moving slowly and subject to all sorts of influences, in the end shapes national destinies. The true historian, - he who most sympathetically, as well as correctly, reads to the present the lessons to be derived from the experience of the past, -I hold to be the only latter-day prophet. That man has a message to deliver; but, to deliver it effectively, he must, like every successful preacher, understand his audience; and, to understand it, he must either be instinctively in sympathy with it, or he must have made a study of it. Of those instinctively in sympathy, I do not speak. That constitutes genius, and genius is a law unto itself; but I do maintain that instructors in history and historical writers who ignore the prevailing literary and educational conditions, therein make a great mistake. He fails fatally who fails to conform to his environment; and this is no less true of the historian than of the novelist or politician.

In other words, what have we to say of those who read? What do we know of them? Not much, I fancy. In spite of our public libraries, and in spite of the immensely increased diffusion of printed matter through the agency of those libraries and of the press, what those who com- pose the great mass of the community are reading, what enters into their intellectual nutriment, and thence passes into the secretions of the body politic,-this, I imagine, is a subject chiefly of surmise. The field is one upon which I do not now propose to enter. Too large, it is also a pathless wilderness. I would, however, earnestly commend it to some more competent treatment at an early convention of librarians or publishers. To-day we must confine ourselves to history. For what, in the way of history, is the demand? Who are at present the popular historical writers? How can the lessons of the past be most readily and most effectually brought home to the mind and thoughts of the great reading public, vastly greater and more intelligent now than ever before?

This is something upon which the census throws no light. There is a widespread impression among those more or less qualified to form an opinion that the general capacity for sustained reading and thinking has not increased or been strengthened with the passage of the years. On the contrary, the indications, it is currently supposed, are rather of emasculation. Everything must now be made easy and short. There is a constant demand felt, especially by our periodical press, for information on all sorts of subjects, historical, philosophical, scientific, -but it must be set forth in what is known as a popular style, that is introduced into the reader in a species of sugared capsule, and without leaving any annoying taste on the intellectual palate. The average reader, it is said, wants to know something concerning all the topics of the day; but, while it is highly desirable he should be gratified in this laudable, though languid, craving, he must not be fatigued in the effort of acquisition, and he will not submit to be bored. It is then further argued that this was not the case formerly; that in what are commonly alluded to as "the good old times," - always the times of the grandparents, people had fewer books, and fewer people read; but those who did read, deterred neither by number of pages nor by dryness of treatment, were equal to the feat of reading. To-day, on the contrary, almost no one rises to more than a magazine article; a volume appalls.

This is an extremely interesting subject of inquiry, were the real facts only attainable. Unfortunately they are not. We are forced to deal with impressions; and impressions, always vague, are usually deceptive. At the same time, when glimpses of a more or less remote past do now and again reach us, they seem to indicate mental conditions calculated to excite our special wonder. We do know, for instance, that in the olden days,- before public libraries and periodicals, and the modern cheap press and the Sunday newspaper were devised, -when books were rarities, and reading a somewhat rare accomplishment, -the Bible, Shakespeare, Paradise Lost, the Pilgrim's Progress and Robinson Crusoe, the Spectator and Tatler, Barrows' Sermons and Hume's

History of England were the standard household and family literature; and the Bible was read and reread until its slightest allusions passed into familiar speech. Indeed, the Bible, in King James's version, may be said to have been for the great mass of the community, those who now have recourse to the Sunday paper, -the sum and substance of English literature. In this respect it is fairly open to question whether the course of evolution has tended altogether toward improvement. Now and again, however, we get one of these retrospective glimpses which is simply bewildering; and, while indulging in it, one cannot help pondering over the mental conditions which once apparently prevailed. The question suggests itself, were there giants in those days?-or did the reader ask for bread, and did they give him a stone? We know, for instance, what the public library and circulating library of to-day are. We know, to a certain extent, what the reading demand is, and who the popular authors We know that, while history must content itself with a poor one in twenty, the call for works of fiction is more than a third of the whole, while nearly eighty per cent. of the ordinary circulation is made up of novels, story books for children, and periodicals. It is the lightest form of pabulum. This, in 1900. Now, let us get a glimpse of "the good old times." In the year 1790, a humorous rascal named Burroughs -once widely known as "the notorious Stephen Burroughs" — found himself stranded in a town on Long Island, New York, a refugee from a Massachusetts gaol and whipping-post, the penalties incurred in or at both of which he had richly merited. In the place of his refuge, Burroughs served as the village schoolmaster; and, being of an observant turn of mind, he did not fail presently to note that the people of the place were "very illiterate," and almost entirely destitute of books of any kind, "except schoolbooks and bibles." Finding among the younger people of the community many "possessing bright abilities and a strong thirst for information," Burroughs asserts that he bestirred himself to secure the funds necessary to found the nucleus of a public library. Having in a measure succeeded, a meeting of "the proprietors" was called "for the purpose of selecting a catalogue of books;" and presently the different members presented lists "peculiar to their own tastes." Prior to this meeting it had been alleged that the people generally anticipated that the books would be selected by the clergyman of the church, and would "consist of books of divinity, and dry metaphysical writings; whereas, should they be assured that histories and books of information would be procured," they would have felt very differently. And now, when the lists were submitted, "Deacon Hodges brought forward 'Essays on the Divine Authority for Infant Baptism,' 'Terms of Church Communion,' 'The Careful Watchman,' 'Age of Grace,' etc.; Deacon Cook's collection was 'History of Martyrs,' 'Rights of Conscience,' 'Modern Pharisees,' 'Defence of Separates;' Mr. Woolworth exhibited Edwards against Chauncy,' 'History of Redemption,' 'Jennings's Views,' etc.; Judge Hurlbut concurred in the same; Dr. Rose exhibited 'Gay's Fables,' 'Pleasing Companion,' 'Turkish Spy,' while I," wrote Burroughs, "for the third time recommended 'Hume's History,' 'Voltaire's Histories,' 'Rollin's Ancient History,' 'Plutarch's Lives,' etc."

It would be difficult to mark more strikingly the development of a century, than by thus presenting Hume's History and Rollin as typical of what was deemed light and popular reading at one end of it, and the Sunday newspaper at the other. As I have already intimated, they were either giants in those days, or husks supplied milk for babes. Recurring, however, to present conditions, the popular demand for historical literature is undoubtedly vastly larger than it was a century ago; nor is it by any means so clear as is usually assumed that the solid reading and thinking power of the community has at all deteriorated. That yet remains to be proved. A century ago, it is to be borne in mind, there were no public libraries at all, and the private collections of books were comparatively few and small. It is safe, probably, to assume that there are a hundred, or even a thousand, readers now to one then. On this head nothing even approximating to what would be deemed conclusive evidence is attainable; but the fair assumption is that, while the light and ephemeral, knowledge-made-easy reading is a development of these latter years, it has in no way displaced the more sustained reading and severe thought of the earlier time. On the contrary, that also has had its share of increase. Take Gibbon, for instance. A few years ago, an acute and popular English critic, in speaking of the newly published "Memoirs" of Gibbon, used this language:-"All readers of the 'Decline and Fall,' - that to say, all men and women of a sound education," etc. If Mr. Frederic Harrison was correct in his generalization in 1896, certainly more could not have been said in 1796; and, during the intervening hundred years, the class of those who have received "a sound education" has undergone a prodigious increase. Take Harvard College, for instance; in 1796 it graduated thirty-three students, and in 1896 it graduated four hundred and eight, an increase of more than twelvefold. In 1796, also, there were not a tenth part of the institutions of advanced education in the country which now exist. The statistics of the publishing houses and the shelves of the bookselling establishments all point to the same conclusion. Of course, it does not follow that because a book is bought it is also read; but it is not unsafe to say that twenty copies of Gibbon's "Decline and Fall" are called for in the bookstores of to-day to one that was called for in 1800.

On this subject, however, very instructive light may be derived from another quarter. I refer to the Public Library. While discussing the question eighteen months ago, I ventured to state that, "in the case of one Public Library in a considerable Massachusetts city I had been led to conclude, as the result of examination and somewhat careful inquiry, that the copy of the 'Decline and Fall' on its shelves, had, in over thirty years, not once been consecutively read through by a single individual." I have since made further and more careful inquiry on this point from other, and larger, though similar institutions, and the inference I then drew has been confirmed and generalized. I have also sought information as to the demand for historical literature, and the tendency and character of the reading so far as it could be ascertained, or approximately inferred. I have submitted my list of historical writers, and inquired as to the call for them. Suggestive in all respects, the results have, in some, been little less than startling. Take for instance popularity, and let me recur to Macaulay and Carlyle. I have spoken of the two as great masters in historical composition, — comparing them in their field to Turner and Millet in the field of art. Like Turner and Millet, they influenced to a marked extent a whole generation of workers that ensued. To such an extent did they influence it that a scholastic reaction against them set in, — a reaction as distinct as it was strong. Nevertheless, in spite of that reaction, to what extent did the master retain his popular hold? I admit that my astonishment was great when I learned that between 1880, more than twenty years after his death, and 1900, besides innumerable editions issued on both sides of the Atlantic, the authorized London publishers of Macaulay had sold in two shapes only, — and they appear in many other shapes, — 80,000 copies of his History and 90,000 of his Miscellanies. Of Carlyle and the call for his writings I could gather no such specific particulars; but, in reply to my inquiries, I was generally advised that, while the English demand had been large, there was no considerable American publishing house which had not brought out partial or complete editions of his works. They also were referred to as "innumerable." In other words, when a generation that knew them not had passed away, the works of the two great masters of historical literary form in our day sold beyond all compare with the productions of any of the living writers most in vogue ; and this while the professorial dry-as-dust reaction against those masters was in fullest swing.

With a vast amount of material unused,[8] and much still unsaid, I propose, in concluding, to trespass still further on your patience while I draw a lesson to which the first portion of my discourse will contribute not less than the second. A great, as well as a very voluminous, recent historical writer has coined the apothegm, -"History is past politics, and politics are present History." The proposition is one I do not now propose to discuss, except to suggest that, however it may have been heretofore, what is known as politics will be but a part, and by no means the most important part, of the history of the future. The historian will look deeper. It was President Lincoln who said in one of the few immortal utterances of the century, an utterance, be it also observed, limited to two hundred and fifty words, that this, our, nation was "conceived in liberty, and dedicated to the proposition that all men are created equal;" and that it was for us highly to resolve "that government of the people, by the people, for the people, should not perish from the earth." It was James Russell Lowell, who, when asked in Paris by the historian Guizot many years since, how long the Republic of the United States might reasonably be expected to endure, happily replied, -"So long as the ideas of its founders continue dominant." In the first place, I hold it not unsafe to say that, looking forward into a future not now remote, the mission of the Republic and the ideas of the founders will more especially rest in the hands of those agricultural communities of the Northwest, where great aggregations of a civic populace are few, and the principles of natural selection have had the fullest and the freest play in the formation of the race. Such is Wisconsin; such Iowa; such Minnesota. In their hands, and in the hands of communities like them, will rest the ark of our covenant. In the next place, for the use and future behoof of those communities I hold that the careful and intelligent reading of the historical lessons of the past is all important. Without that reading, and a constant emphasis laid upon its lessons, the nature of that mission and those ideas to which Lincoln and Lowell alluded cannot be kept fresh in mind. This institution I accordingly regard as the most precious of all Wisconsin's endowments of education. It should be the sheet anchor by which, amid the storms and turbulence of a tempestuous future, the ship of State will be anchored to the firm holding- ground of tradition. It is to further this result that I to-day make appeal to the historian of the future. His, in this community, is a great and important mission; a mission which he will not fulfil unless he to a large extent frees himself from the trammels of the past, and rises to an equality with the occasion. He must be a prophet and a poet, as well as an investigator and an annalist. He must cut loose from many of the models and most of the precedents of the immediate past, and the educational precepts now so commonly in vogue. He must perplex the modern college professor by asserting that soundness is not always and of necessity dull, and that even intellectual sobriety may be carried to an excess. Not only is it possible for a writer to combine learning and accuracy with vivacity, but to be read and to be popular should not in the eyes of the judicious be a species of stigma. Historical research may, on the other hand, result in a mere lumber of learning; and, even in the portrayal of the sequence of events, it is to a man's credit that he should strive to see things from the point of view of an artist, rather than, looking with the dull eye of a mechanic, seek to measure them with the mechanic's twelve-inch rule. I confess myself weary of those reactionary influences amid which of late we have lived. I distinctly look back with regret to that more spiritual and more confident time when we of the generation now passing from the stage drew our inspiration from prophets, and not from laboratories. So to-day I make bold to maintain that the greatest benefactor America could have far more immediately influential than any possible President or Senator or peripatetic political practitioner, as well as infinitely more so in a remote future would be some historical writer, occupying perhaps a chair here at Madison, who would in speech and book explain and expound, as they could be explained and expounded, the lessons of American history and the fundamental principles of American historical faith.

It was Macaulay who made his boast that, disregarding the traditions which constituted what he contemptuously termed "the dignity of history," he would set forth England's story in so attractive a form that his volumes should displace the last novel from the work-table of the London society girl. And he did it. It is but the other day that an American naval officer suddenly appeared in the field of historical literature, and, by two volumes, sensibly modified the policy of nations. Here are precept and example. To accomplish similar results should, I hold, be the ambition of the American historian. Popularity he should court as a necessary means to an end; and that he should attain popularity, he must study the art of presentation as much and as thoughtfully as he delves amid the original material of history. Becoming more of an artist, rhetorician and philosopher than he now is, he must be less of a pedant and colorless investigator. In a word, going back to Moses, Thucydides and Herodotus; Tacitus, Gibbon and Voltaire; Niebuhr, Macaulay, Carlyle, Buckle, Green, Mommsen and Froude, he must study their systems, and, avoiding the mistakes into which they fell, thoughtfully accommodating himself to the conditions of the present, he must prepare to fulfil the mission before him. He will then in time devise what is so greatly needed for our political life, the distinctively American historical method of the future. Of this we have as yet had hardly the promise, and that only recently through the pages of Fiske and Mahan; and I cannot help surmising that it is to some Eastern seed planted here in the freer environment of the more fruitful West that we must look for its ultimate realization.

Appendix A

THE fact that the southern portion of the State of Wisconsin was formerly, in a certain sense at least, a portion of Massachusetts, is, even historically, more curious than interesting or valuable. In regard to it the following extracts are from a Report of its Council made to the American Antiquarian Society at Worcester, October 21, 1890,[10] by Samuel A. Green, than whom, on a matter of this sort connected with Massachusetts history, there is no higher living authority. "The Colonial Charter of Massachusetts Bay, granted by Charles I., under date of March 4, 1628-9, gave to the Governor and other representatives of the Massachusetts Company, on certain conditions, all the territory lying between an easterly and westerly line running three miles north of any part of the Merrimack River, and extending from the Atlantic Ocean to the Pacific, and a similar parallel line run- ning south of any part of the Charles River." The exact words of the original instrument, bearing on the matter under discussion, were: "All that parte of Newe England in America which lyes and extendes betweene a great river there comonlie called Monomack river, alias Merrimack river, and a certen other river there called Charles river, being in the bottome of a certen bay there comonlie called Massachusetts, alias Mattachusetts, alias Massatusetts bay: And also all those lands and hereditaments whatsoever which lye and be within the space of three English myles to the northward of the saide river called Monomack, alias Merrymack, or to the norward of any and every parte thereof, and all landes and hereditaments whatsoever, lyeing within the lymitts aforesaide, north and south, in latitude and bredth, and in length and longitude, of and within all the bredth aforesaide, throughout the mayne landes there from the Atlantick and westerne sea and ocean on the east parte, to the south sea on the west parte: "

"Without attempting to trace in detail, from the time of the Cabots to the days of the Charter, the continuity of the English title to this transcontinental strip of territory, it is enough to know that the precedents and usages of that period gave to Great Britain, in theory at least, undisputed sway over the region, and forged every link in the chain of authority and sovereignty."

"At that time it was supposed that America was a narrow strip of land, — perhaps an arm of the continent of Asia, and that the distance across from ocean to ocean was comparatively short. It was then known that the Isthmus of Darien was narrow, and it was there- fore incorrectly presumed that the whole continent also was narrow."

"By later explorations this strip of territory has been lengthened out into a belt three thousand miles long. It crosses a continent, and includes within its limits various large towns of the United States. The cities of Albany, Syracuse, Rochester, Buffalo, Detroit, and Milwaukee all lie within the zone. There have been many social and commercial ties between the capital of New England and these several municipali- ties, but in comparison with another bond they are of recent date, as the ground on which they stand was granted to the Massachusetts Company by the Charter of Charles I., more than two hundred and sixty years ago."

"After the lapse of some years the settlers took steps to find out the territorial boundaries of the Colony on the north in order to establish the limits of their jurisdictional authority. To this end at an early day a Commission was appointed by the General Court, composed of Captain Simon Willard and Captain Edward Johnson, two of the foremost men in the Colony at that time."

"It will be seen that the Commissioners were empowered, under the order, to engage 'such Artists & other Assistants,' as were needed for the purpose. In early days a surveyor was called an artist, and in old records the word is often found with that meaning. Under the authority thus given, the Commissioners employed Sergeant John Sherman, of Watertown, and Jonathan Ince, of Cambridge, to join the party and do the scientific work of the expedition."

"In October, 1652, the Commissioners made a return to the General Court, giving the result of their labors, and including the affidavits of the two surveyors. According to this report they fixed upon a place then called by the Indians Aquedahtan as the head of the Merrimack river. By due observation they found the latitude of this spot to be 43° 40' 12"; and the northern limit of the patent was three miles north of this point."

An extension of the northern limit thus indicated would, crossing Lake Michigan, run west, from a point about three miles south of Sheboygan, through Fond du Lac, Green Lake and Marquette counties, some six miles north of their southern boundaries, thus bisecting Wisconsin.

Appendix B.

The full record of J. Q. Adams's utterances on this most important subject has never been made up. (See Works of Charles Sumner, vol. vi. pp. 19-23; vol. vii. p. 142.) Historically speaking, it is of exceptional importance; and, accordingly, for convenience of reference, a partial record is here presented. In 1836, Mr. Adams represented in Congress what was then the Massachusetts "Plymouth" district. In April of that year the issue, which, just twenty-five years later, was to result in overt civil war, was fast assuming shape; for, on the 21st of the month, the battle of San Jacinto was fought, resulting immediately in the independence of Texas, and more remotely in its annexation to the United States and the consequent war of spoliation (1846-48) with Mexico. At the same time petitions in great number were pouring into Congress from the Northern States asking for the abolition of slavery, and the prohibition of the domestic slave trade, in the District of Columbia; the admission into the Union of Arkansas, with a constitution recognizing slavery, was also under consideration. In the course of a long personal letter dated April 4th, 1836, written to the Hon. Solomon Lincoln, of Hingham, a prominent constituent of his, Mr. Adams made the following incidental reference to the whole subject, indicative of the degree to which the question of martial law as a possible factor in the solution of the problem then occupied his mind: - "The new pretensions of the Slave representation in Congress, of a right to refuse to receive Petitions, and that Congress have no Constitutional power to abolish slavery or the slave trade in the District of Columbia forced upon me so much of the discussion as I did take upon me, but in which you are well aware I did not and could not speak a tenth part of my mind. I did not, for example, start the question whether by the Law of God and of Nature man can hold property, hereditary property in man I did not start the question whether in the event of a servile insurrection and War, Congress would not have complete, unlimited control over the whole subject of slavery even to the emancipation of all the slaves in the State where such insurrection should break out, and for the suppression of which the freemen of

Plymouth and Norfolk Counties, Massachusetts, should be called by Acts of Congress to pour out their treasures and to shed their blood. Had I spoken my mind on those two points the sturdiest of the abolitionists would have disavowed the sentiments of their champion."

A little more than seven weeks after this writing, Mr. Adams made the following entries in his diary: -

May 25th." At the House, the motion of Robertson, to recommit Pinckney's slavery report, with instructions to report a resolution declaring that Congress has no constitutional authority to abolish slavery in the District of Columbia, as an amendment to the motion for printing an extra number of the report, was first considered. Robertson finished his speech, which was vehement.

"Immediately after the conclusion of Robertson's speech I addressed the Speaker, but he gave the floor to Owens, of Georgia, one of the signing members of the committee, who moved the previous question, and refused to withdraw it. It was seconded and carried, by yeas and nays.

"The hour of one came, and the order of the day was called joint resolution from the Senate, authorizing the President to cause rations to be furnished to suffering fugitives from Indian hostilities in Alabama and Georgia. Committee of the whole on the Union, and a debate of five hours, in which I made a speech of about an hour, wherein I opened the whole subject of the Mexican, Indian, negro, and English war."

It was in the course of this speech that Mr. Adams first enunciated the principle of emancipation through martial law, exercised under the Constitution in time of war. He did so in the following passage : —

"Mr. Chairman, are you ready for all these wars? A Mexican war. A war with Great Britain if not with France? A general Indian war? A servile war? And, as an inevitable consequence of them all, a civil war? For it must ultimately terminate in a war of colors as well as of races. And do you imagine that, while with your eyes open you are wilfully kindling, and then closing your eyes and blindly rushing into them; do you imagine that while in the very na- ture of things, your own Southern and Southwestern States must be the Flanders of these complicated wars, the battlefield on which the last great battle must be fought between slavery and emancipation; do you imagine that your Congress will have no constitutional authority to in- terfere with the institution of slavery in any way in the States of this Confederacy? Sir, they must and will interfere with it- perhaps to sustain it by war; perhaps to abolish it by treaties of peace; and they will not only possess the constitutional power so to interfere, but they will be bound in duty to do it by the express provisions of the Constitution itself. From the instant that your slaveholding States become the theatre of war, civil, servile or foreign, from that instant the war powers of Congress extend to interference with the institution of slavery in every way in which it can be interfered with, from a claim of indemnity for slaves taken or destroyed, to the cession of the State burdened with slavery to a foreign power."

The following references to this speech are then found in the diary: -

May 29th.- "I was occupied all the leisure of the day and evening in writing out for publication my speech made last Wednesday in the House of Representatives one of the most hazardous that I ever made, and the reception of which, even by the people of my own district and State, is altogether uncertain."

June 2d. "My speech on the distribution of rations to the fugitives from Indian hostilities in Alabama and Georgia was published in the National Intelligencer of this morning, and a subscription paper was circulated in the House for printing it in a pamphlet, for which Gales told me there were twenty-five hundred copies ordered. Several mem- bers of the House of both parties spoke of it to me, some with strong dissent."

June 19th. "My speech on the rations comes back with echoes of thundering vituperation from the South and West, and with one uni- versal shout of applause from the North and East. This is a cause upon which I am entering at the last stage of life, and with the certainty that I cannot advance in it far; my career must close, leaving the cause at the threshold. To open the way for others is all that I can do. The cause is good and great."

So far as the record goes, the doctrine was not again propounded by Mr. Adams until 1841. On the 7th of June of that year he made a speech in the House of Representatives in support of a motion for the repeal of the Twenty-first Rule of the House, commonly known as "the Atherton Gag." Of this speech, no report exists; but in the course of it he again enunciated the Martial Law theory of Emancipation. The next day he was followed in debate by C. J. Ingersoll, of Pennsylvania, Chairman of the Committee on Foreign Affairs, who took occasion to declare that what he had heard the day previous had made his "blood curdle with horror: " -

"Mr. Adams here rose in explanation, and said he did not say that in the event of a servile war of insurrection of slaves, the Constitution of the United States would be at an end. What he did say was this, that in the event of a servile war or insurrection of slaves, if the people of the free States were called upon to suppress the insurrection, and to spend their blood and treasure in putting an end to the war -a war in which the distinguished Virginian, the author of the Declaration of In- dependence, had said that God has no attribute in favor of the master' - then he would not say that Congress might not interfere with the institution of slavery in the States, and that, through *the treaty-making power*, universal emancipation might not be the result."

The following year the contention was again discussed in the course of the memorable debate on the "Haverhill Petition." Mr. Adams was then bitterly assailed by Henry A. Wise, of Virginia, and Thomas F. Marshall, of Kentucky. Mr. Adams at the time did not reply to them on this head; but, on the 14th of the following April, occasion offered, and he then once more laid down the law on the subject, as he understood it, and as it was subsequently put in force :—

"I would leave that institution to the exclusive consideration and management of the States more peculiarly interested in it, just as long as they can keep within their own bounds. So far I admit that Congress has no power to meddle with it. As long as they do not step out of their own bounds, and do not put the question to the people of the United States, whose peace, welfare and happiness are all at stake, so long I will agree to leave them to themselves. But when a member from a free State brings forward certain resolutions, for which, instead of reasoning to disprove his positions, you vote a censure upon him, and that without hearing, it is quite another affair. At the time this was done I said that, as far as I could understand the resolutions proposed by the gentleman from Ohio (Mr. Giddings), there were some of them for which I was ready to vote, and some which I must vote against; and I will now tell this House, my constituents, and the world of mankind, that the resolution against which I should have voted was that in which he declares that what are called the slave States have the exclusive right of consultation on the subject of slavery. For that resolution I never would vote, because I believe that it is not just, and does not contain constitutional doctrine. I believe that so long as the slave States are able to sustain their institutions without going abroad or calling upon other parts of the Union to aid them or act on the subject, so long I will consent never to interfere.

"I have said this, and I repeat it; but if they come to the free States and say to them you must help us to keep down our slaves, you must aid us in an insurrection and a civil war, then I say that with that call comes a full and plenary power to this House and to the Senate over the whole subject. It is a war power. I say it is a war power, and when your country is actually in war, whether it be a war of invasion or a war of insurrection, Congress has power to carry on the war, and must carry it on according to the laws of war; and by the laws of war an invaded country has all its laws and municipal institutions swept by the board, and martial law takes the place of them. This power in Congress has, perhaps, never been called into exercise under the present Constitution of the United States. But when the laws of war are in force, what, I ask, is one of those laws? It is this: that when a country is invaded, and two hostile armies are set in martial array, the commanders of both armies have power to emancipate all the slaves in the invaded territory. Nor is this a mere theoretic statement. The history of South America shows that the doctrine has been carried into practical execution within the last thirty years. Slavery was abolished in Colombia, first, by the Spanish General, Morillo, and, secondly, by the American General, Bolivar. It was abolished by virtue of a military command given at the head of the army, and its abolition continues to be law to this day. It was abolished by the laws of war, and not by municipal enactments; the power was exercised by military commanders, under instructions, of course, from their respective Governments. And here I recur again to the example of General Jackson. What are you now about in Congress? You are passing a grant to refund to General Jackson the amount of a certain fine imposed upon him by a Judge under the laws of the State of Louisiana. You are going to refund him the money, with interest; and this you are going to do because the imposition of the fine was unjust. And why was it unjust? Because General Jackson was acting under the laws of war, and because the moment you place a military commander in a district which is the theatre of war, the laws of war apply to that district...

"I might furnish a thousand proofs to show that the pretensions of gentlemen to the sanctity of their municipal institutions under a state of actual invasion and of actual war, whether servile, civil, or foreign, is wholly unfounded, and that the laws of war do, in all such cases, take the precedence. I lay this down as the law of nations. I say that the military authority takes for the time the place of all municipal institutions, and slavery among the rest; and that, under that state of things, so far from its being true that the States where slavery exists have the exclusive management of the subject, not only the President of the United States but the commander of the army has power to order the universal emancipation of the slaves. I have given here more in detail a principle which I have asserted on this floor before now, and of which I have no more doubt, than that you, Sir, occupy that Chair. I give it in its development, in order that any gentleman from any part of the Union may, if he thinks proper, deny the truth of the position, and may maintain his denial; not by indignation, not by passion and fury, but by sound and sober reasoning from the laws of nations and the laws of war. And if my position can be answered and refuted, I shall receive the refutation with pleasure; I shall be glad to listen to reason, aside, as I say, from indignation and passion. And if, by the force of reasoning, my understanding can be convinced, I here pledge myself to recant what I have asserted.

"Let my position be answered; let me be told, let my constituents be told, the people of my State be told, a State whose soil tolerates not the foot of a slave, that they are bound by the Constitution to a long and toilsome march under burning summer suns and a deadly Southern clime for the suppression of a servile war; that they are bound to leave their bodies to rot upon the sands of Carolina, to leave their wives and their children orphans; that those who cannot march are bound to pour out their treasures while their sons or brothers are pouring out their blood to suppress a servile, combined with a civil or a foreign war, and yet that there exists no power beyond the limits of the slave State where such war is raging to emancipate the slaves. I say, let this be proved I am open to conviction; but till that conviction comes I put it forth not as a dictate of feeling, but as a settled maxim of the laws of nations, that in such a case the military supersedes the civil power."

The only comment on this utterance made by Mr. Adams in his diary was the following:-"My speech of this day stung the slaveocracy to madness."

Here the proposition rested until 1861, when the course of events brought into forcible application the principles abstractly enunciated twenty years before by Mr. Adams.

Appendix C

Owing to the hold which the Hebrew theology has obtained on all modern thought, the standards of judgment usually applied to histori-cal characters have not been applied to Moses. He has been treated as exceptional. Meanwhile, judged by those standards, it may not unfairly be questioned whether Moses was not the most many-sided human being of whom any record exists, and the one whose influence on the history of the race has been most far-reaching. He constitutes almost a class by himself, in that he seems to have been equally great as a philosopher, a law-giver, a theologist, a poet, a soldier, an executive magistrate and an historian. Compare him, for instance, with Julius Cæsar, also a many-sided man, whose influence over human events is perceptible even to the present time. A consummate military commander and political organizer, Cæsar wrote his Commentaries. As a strategist he may have been superior to Moses; and yet it is very questionable whether he ever executed a more brilliant or successful movement than the march out of Egypt or the passage of the Red Sea. The campaigns of the Israelites seem to have been uniformly both planned and carried out in a very masterly way. On the other hand, as a literary product the De Bello Gallico is in no way comparable to Exodus. As a philosopher, the authority of him who wrote the book of Genesis was undisputed until well into the present century, and is even now implicitly accepted by the great mass of those calling themselves Christians. The binding character of the decalogue is still recognized, and it lies at the basis of modern legislation. As apoet, Homer distinctly pales before the Israelite; while both Dante and Milton drew from him their inspiration. There is no epic which in sublimity of movement as well as human interest compares with the books of Moses. As a chief magistrate, the Hebrew moulded, or at least left his imprint, on a race which has proved the most marked and persistent in type the earth has yet produced. Jesus Christ was of it. Finally, as an historian, while the learning and judgment of Moses would not stand the test of modern criticism, his narrative was accepted as incontrovertible until within the memory of those now living, and has passed into common speech.

What other man in all recorded history presents such a singular and varied record?

Appendix D

In the address delivered at the opening of the Fenway Building of the Massachusetts Historical Society, in April, 1899, occurred the following: -

"It would be very interesting to know how many young persons now read Gibbon through as he was read by our fathers, or even by ourselves who grew up in 'the fifties.' Accurate information on such a point is not attainable; but in the case of one public library in a considerable Massachusetts city I have been led to conclude as the result of examination and somewhat careful inquiry, that the copy of the 'Decline and Fall' on its shelves has, in over thirty years, not once been consecutively read through by a single individual. That it is bought as one of those 'books no gentleman's library should be without,' I know, not only from personal acquaintance with many such, but because new editions from time to time appear, and the booksellers always have it in stock;' that it is dipped into here and there, and more or less, I do not doubt; but that it is now largely or systematically read by young people of the coming generation, I greatly question."

This passage was at the time remarked upon, and subsequently led to a considerable correspondence. In the course of that correspondence, as occasion offered, I endeavored further to inform myself, through publishers, booksellers, librarians, instructors and students. To reach any really valuable results such an inquiry would, of course, have to cover a broad field and be systematically conducted. This was out of my power. None the less the questions involved are of moment, and a thorough investigation by a competent and unprejudiced person, with abundance of time at his disposal, could hardly fail to be suggestive, and, not improbably, might reveal some quite unexpected conditions, educational as well as popular. While the correspondence carried on by me was desultory, as well as limited, some of the points developed by it are more or less noteworthy and may incite others to a better arranged inquiry. I, therefore, give space to them.

From publishing firms and booksellers not much of value could be obtained. The former are, not unnaturally, more or less reticent on matters connected with their business; while the booksellers not only run into special lines, but their trade is subject to local conditions. With both, also, the question of copyright has to be taken into consideration. So far as conclusions could be drawn from information derived from these sources, they would seem generally to be that the demand for books of an historical character has increased largely and is still increasing, and that for both the more expensive and the cheaper editions; but there is nothing indicative of a special or disproportionate increase in the case of history as compared with other branches of literature. Among what may be called the standard English and American writers, the demand is for the writings of Gibbon, Macaulay, Carlyle and Green; and for those of Prescott, Motley and Fiske. In Boston it seems of late to be somewhat in the following proportions: Green 150, Macaulay 100, Carlyle and Gibbon 75, Prescott 50, Motley 30. Text-books and what may be called the ephemeral historical writings are not taken into consideration. Taking the English-speaking public in all parts of the world as a whole, Macaulay and Carlyle would seem to be the two standard historical writers incomparably most in vogue. Even in America there have been numerous editions of the works of both of these writers to single editions of American works of a similar character. For Gibbon alone of the older writers does there seem to be any active demand. One feature in the demand is noticeable. The readers of history seem largely to buy and own the copies they use. The public libraries will alone absorb full editions of any new work; but, of the standard writers, they as a rule buy the better and more expensive impressions, while the great mass of cheap reprints and second-hand copies is absorbed by a vast reading public, which formerly did not exist at all and of which little is now known. Its demand is, however, on the lines indicated.

The fact just referred to, that what may be termed the sustained readers of history, or those equal to continuous historical reading, prefer to own their own copies of the books they read, and to a large extent contrive to do so either through the bargain-stand or the cheap reprint, has a very close bearing on the inferences to be drawn from the statistics and experience of the public libraries. These agencies are all modern, and their influence has not yet had time in which fully to assert itself. A development of the last half century, they are yet in the formative, or plastic, state. As regards them and their influence on the reading of historical works, further inquiry and correspondence have led to a revisal of first impressions. As respects historical reading and study now going on, I gravely doubt whether any safe inferences can be drawn from this source. As a rule about five (5) per cent, of the books called for at the desks of our public libraries are classified as historical; but, on the other hand, further investigation leads me to infer that those who resort to the public libraries for books of this sort do so as a rule either educationally, that is, in connection with school studies, or they are ephemeral readers. This appears clearly on examination in a public library of almost any historical work in several volumes. The first will almost invariably bear marks of heavy handling, and will probably have been sent to the binder; the succeeding volumes will show fewer and fewer signs of use; while the closing volumes, except the index volume, will be quite fresh. People who read such works through with profit or pleasure probably own them. Observation from the Public Library point of view is, therefore, on this subject, apt to be deceptive.

For instance, an official of one of the largest and most extensively used public libraries in the country writes me, speaking of Gibbon, "It is my opinion that a fair percentage of those who undertake Gibbon put the job through. You can draw about any inference you please on the relative place Gibbon now holds." Another, almost equally well placed from the same point of observation, has written to me, "There is no doubt that the fact [you observe] as to the condition of the several volumes of Gibbon on the shelves of the Public Library of Quincy could be verified by observation in this library, and, in all probability, in most other public libraries in this country." My own inference now is that the people who read "The Decline and Fall," — and they are many, — own it. The copies in the public libraries are used for experimental purposes, or for topical reference.

On the general subject, I find many suggestive paragraphs in my Public Librarian correspondence. The following for instance : —

"The fact of the matter is that very few people nowadays have the time and patience to read a prolix history through by course, or even to wade through the novels which were constructed with so great elaboration of exciting incident for the edification of our grandfathers. It is our experience that Gibbon and Hallam and Lingard and Hume and Bancroft are never read entire. It may be said that the attempt is seldom if ever made to do so. There is sometimes an effort to master Macaulay, or Carlyle, or Motley, or Prescott; but it is evident that this is too often with flagging interest. The historical writings of Francis Parkman and John Fiske are in great popular demand. These are so broken up into separate topics that the task set before the reader does not appear formidable, and when he has read up on one topic he is quite likely to be lured by the interesting narrative and the fascinating style into a continuance through other works of the same author. Captain Mahan's books are much read, as are also Green's shorter history and McCarthy's 'History of our own Times,' and the recent histories of Schouler and Rhodes.

"Though there is less reading by course of voluminous histories than formerly, the study of history was never more popular. The tendency of the times is toward condensation. We want our facts in a nutshell; we cannot spend time over unimportant details; the historian is expected to separate the chaff from the grain. So we have numerous condensed histories and biographies, some of which are excellent, though some show too clearly the characteristic of having been made-to-order at the expense of the publisher. But the fact that the publishers find them profitable is good evidence that such books are the kind which many persons are buying.

"Much of the historical reading with which we come into contact in this library is by topic, under the guidance of clubs and instructors, and therefore systematic."

"I don't see how you can hope to induce the average person of moderate intelligence to do more than read the newspapers and a few monthly magazines in these days. History does not come to him any longer through the volume; it comes to him through the morning paper, as it never did before. Historians are still a little too much inclined to write histories in the old style; even John Fiske does, it would seem. Whereas entirely new conditions of life and knowledge would seem to call for a new kind of history, what kind I cannot tell you."

"I doubt if ten undergraduates at Yale have read Gibbon during the past five years; many, however, have read Carlyle's 'Frederick,' and more his "French Revolution.""

"I find myself more and more astonished at the narrowing range of reading. It may be that I don't see the whole thing or that I form wrong estimates, but I am in accord with the more observing of my associates when I tell you that the reading habits of the 'average' reader are not desultory — I wish they were — but sharply defined and within most contracted limits. Let me specify in the matter of United States History. When I was a youngster we used to have large plans for reading Bancroft, or Hildreth, or the biographies of famous Americans. To-day it is noticeable that the generation recently graduated from the Public Schools seems to have imbibed no general taste for reading — and does not seek to expand its small acquirements beyond a given point. For several years, off and on, I have been the civil service examiner for this Library, and I can assert that the only knowledge of American History, or worse, of American historical writings, is confined to the work of one Montgomery, of whom, I dare say, you never heard. Very rarely a young reader knows of Fiske, more rarely of Higginson — once in a while of Barnes, a new name to you, I fancy. But of the important names, simply nothing. What is true in these examination papers, is true also of the people who come to read. They largely confine themselves to this sort of historical reading.

"In the past few years there has also been a gradual restriction of the limits of literary tastes. Children, in our schools, and I suppose the tendency comes from the West, are fed on very limited pap. Longfellow, Whittier, and a few others are the only names known to them — and there seems to be no encouragement of a general taste. So far as we then are able to discern, everything is 'patriotic' — patriotic speeches, poems, history, one might hazard the statement that in the 'nature studies' so popular now, — what we used to call 'natural history' — the bugs, beetles, butterflies and flowers must be patriotic too. This all may seem exaggerated and fanciful, but I assure you that it is not to us. We trace it to a sort of spurious conception of specialization among teachers and especially among school committees. Whatever the cause, I submit to you that it is a depressing fact that children should grow up with a particular knowledge of Longfellow and Mr. Montgomery's history, and not the least acquaintance with the general works of literature and history, at least of America and England. This is one reason why Gibbon is not read more — nobody hears about him to-day — or of Grote, or Mommsen, — though Macaulay still has his readers."

The truth seems to be that, so far as the general public is concerned, — that largest portion of the body politic which is finally influenced by its secretions, — no conclusions are reliable the inductions to which do not include the Sunday newspaper and the periodical. These circulate by the million, and are most carefully shaped to meet the demand of the day. They all give much space to historical topics, dealing with them in popular form. Formerly, neither the medium nor the method existed. Their function and influence have never been adequately investigated. As a literature, besides creating a new field of enormous size, the periodical and the Sunday paper have, as leisure reading, largely superseded the Bible, Pilgrim's Progress, Robinson Crusoe and all literature of that class.

Turning now to the educational institutions, — especially those of the more advanced grade, — and the student class, it would, I think, be found that a great change has taken place in recent years. Not only have new methods been introduced, but a branch of education has been called into being. Formerly, — that is prior to thirty years ago, — history was taught in our colleges merely as a subject concerning the authors and leading facts of which a so-called educated man should have some knowledge; it is now taught as, at once, a science and a philosophy. Approached in this way by a newly created race of instructors, it naturally and almost necessarily runs into vagaries, — what may best be described as educational "fads." The original research, topical, period and realistic methods seem to be those now most in vogue. As intimated in the text, the artistic side is in disrepute, while little or no attention is paid to history as literature. It has the aspect of a revival on a more scientific basis of Carlyle's Dr. Dryasdust dispensation, and can hardly be considered inspiring. The following extracts from letters I have received throw light on this subject: —

"I have nowadays under my instruction only such seniors and graduates of and as elect my courses, perhaps sixty or seventy individuals each year. Among these I should suspect that perhaps one in ten might have read Carlyle's 'Revolution.' I should be astonished to find that one in twenty had read even half of Macaulay or Gibbon, or one in fifty Bancroft. As for 'Frederick the Great,' that would be as rarely perused as Augustine's 'City of God.' One in five might know something of Parkman, Fiske and Mahan, on account of their general popularity, however, rather than any stimulus due to college work. Green's book enjoys a greater popularity, I should presume, than any of the others.

"I will venture to add the following reflections in extenuation of what you appear to deem an indication of a reluctance on the part of the present generation to apply themselves patiently to prolonged and serious tasks. It is undoubtedly true that the methods of instruction in our more conspicuous institutions of learning militate against 1 the habit of steady, or "course" historical reading,' but I should be very loath to add, as you do, 'and sustained thought,' among our students. There is indeed little encouragement to read long works through, and certainly there is little tendency to extol any writer as a prophet. But it is not impossible that the causes of the discredit into which the older method has fallen may indicate after all increasing insight and discrimination. These causes appear to me to be, first, a growing tendency to a broader and more sympathetic method of dealing with the past. We are no longer chiefly interested in political events, nor are the best writers of to-day guilty of the *tendenz* so apparent in the partisan treatments of Gibbon, Hume, Prescott, Macaulay and Motley.

"The broader conception of history leads, secondly, to a topical treatment of the subject; students turn to special rather than general works of reference. An advanced student is taught to turn often to a monograph or the most recent edition of a technical encyclopaedia rather than to so-called 'standard' general treatments."

" Personally, I feel that we shall be able sometime to combine the advantages both of form and readableness with the requirements of scientific truth and relevancy."

"I should say that the studious habit of the men runs rather to topical than to course reading; and that, outside the range of their fixed studies, they take their pleasure from poetry and fiction rather than from the historians. I should say that such general historical reading as I remember to have been the delight of my own undergraduate (1875-9) days is now less common than it used to be.

"The tendency is decidedly towards 'other and more recent methods.' Macaulay and Carlyle are too much decried in the classroom. Even Green is looked upon askance as a bit too 'literary,' I suspect; and the men who would be scholars are sternly bidden to the methods of colorless investigators. Let us pray that we shall some day come to a sane balance in these matters, and not start young historians copying false standards of either extreme."

"I am nearly certain that the average undergraduate who has anything to do with historical electives in the more important colleges now reads in a year more history than did the average undergraduate of a generation ago. But the methods of instruction now employed make it likely that he reads chapters or portions of books, reads with a view to getting various lights upon particular transactions or episodes of history, rather than to read consecutively through works comprising several volumes each.

"I am sure that the average undergraduate has not less patience or grit than the average undergraduate of my time. I think he works more ; but he works in a different manner. I have taken counsel chiefly, in respect to your questions, of our assistant librarian, who remembers pretty well what books are taken out from the library. He knows no recent instance of a student having read through Gibbon's 'Decline and Fall.' Carlyle's 'Frederick the Great' has recently been attempted by one or two, but not completed. Carlyle's 'French Revolution' has been a good deal read. Of a consecutive reading of Bancroft he remembers no instance. Some have read through Motley's 'Dutch Republic' Probably no one has also gone through his ' History of the United Netherlands.' John Fiske's writings are much in demand.

"I believe you would find very few college libraries in which the last volume of Gibbon showed signs of having been much used at any period, though Vol. I. is often worn out.

"It is not the first time that the question has arisen in my mind whether our students ought not to-day to be given the opportunity to do more reading that is not positively required. But I presume that I shall answer the question, as I have always answered it before, by concluding that it is a better plan to make sure that all the students do enough work and, toward that end, to fill up the time of all, even of those who, without constraint, would read enough."

"The habit of reading practised by university students in history to-day is that of topical comparison — or at least (if the student or the references be at fault) topical cumulation. Thus in the last decade a considerable number of pamphlets of references on American history have been published, doing on a small scale what the 'Guide' of Professors Channing and Hart does on a larger one. Judging from these guides, and my own experience and observation, I should say that this method of topical analysis and references is the method used at present not only in universities but in colleges and larger high schools. A generation ago, doubtless, a student was thrown upon the text-book, recitation system; but if he were ambitious, then he would obtain his comparative view of history by reading — independent or required — in the classic works. To-day the comparative study is made easy, and is more or less required; but it is applied peacemeal, not broadly: to individual topics, narrow points. The student reads his authors 'in little' on each phase of a movement. In this way he rounds out each whole while details are fresh in mind — however he may lose in other respects. Now the fact is, that the topical reading is so exacting that a student has little time for the more generous reading of his authors. In other words, so far as his university courses are concerned, the chapter and page system is very largely forced upon a student. In view of such tendencies — which I have reason to believe are general and dominant — it would seem unlikely that the consecutive reading through of classics will again become more common. It could scarcely become less common."

"The modern method of setting men to work to answer problems or draw conclusions from various writers in a report or essay leads men to use a book for a purpose, and such part of it, therefore, as they want, rather than to sit down and read consecutively a single author until they have finished him. In addition, doubtless, the hurry, the scattered interests in things athletic and public, in college contests and exhibitions, in social 'functions,' the general lack of repose and of steady application also contribute to explain the situation. These latter excesses are lamentable; but the modern method of historical study is in my opinion the right one, even were it not the only feasible one under modern conditions."

"My experience and observation goes to show that steady or course historical reading among the undergraduates of the present day is avoided as far as possible. No more reading is done than is absolutely essential to satisfy the requirements of the instructor in the written weekly papers, and in the mid-year and final examinations. Furthermore, the amount of required reading which the students actually do is regulated by their ambitions to obtain high, medium, or low grades in their history courses. Of course there are exceptions in the students who do far more than the required reading simply because they are greatly interested in the subject-matter itself, but, in my opinion, the average student of to-day does no more than he really has to."

"I should say students of to-day read widely in history, but not with very great steadiness: the greatest bursts are nearest the examination periods."

Finally a recently graduated Harvard student, and an undergraduate, to whom in my curiosity on the' subject I was led to apply for information as to the reading tendencies among the younger generation so far as history from a literary point of view was concerned, kindly replied to my queries as follows : —

"In general my answer to your questions is decidedly that there is very little reading done by undergraduates in the older and more solid authors. The general tendency seems to be towards newer and abridged works like M. Duruy's 'Middle Ages and

Modern Times.' What little reading is done in books like Gibbon, Carlyle, Hallam, etc., is done in little 'dabs': there is no thought of a consecutive study of them. Especially is this true in the case of Gibbon. I had almost said that the 'Decline and Fall' is as little known here now, as in the days when its use was forbidden as ' unorthodox.' It was one of the books out of which the freshmen in History were advised to read a hundred pages, and though I told all my boys that they ought at least to look into it and know who Gibbon was, the general tendency was to fight shy of so weighty a work, and rather to read in books like' Professor Emerton's 'Introduction to the Middle Ages.' The ordinary undergraduate is too much scared by Macaulay's allusiveness to get very far with him. I think I am correct in stating that I attended a course in which ten or fifteen lectures were devoted to the French Revolution, and Carlyle was not mentioned. Sorel and Von Siebel and Rose seem to have displaced him. Green is read a little more, I think.

"Of course it is the exception rather than the rule for the ordinary undergraduate to read solid books which are not recommended in his courses. I don't think there is any great difference between the present undergraduate methods and those of the undergraduates of my day."

"I think that most undergraduates do very little steady reading in history, the general tendency being to keep very near the minimum amount of prescribed reading in courses. Many men make sincere resolves to read more, and begin to read long works, but those who read from beginning to end are few indeed. A great deal of historical information is gained indirectly through indiscriminate magazine reading, especially in regard to current events. I have found that most of my acquaintances are usually familiar with So-and-So's article in this or that magazine, from month to month.

"I have myself read the whole of Gibbon several times from beginning to end, but I have never known of another undergraduate who had ever read so much as one volume through. Of eleven men to whom I addressed the question this morning none had read Gibbon through, three had never read a page of his writings, and eight had read 'a few chapters,' these chapters having been required in a freshman course (History 1). None had ever read him voluntarily.

"I like the style of Macaulay best, but it is more because of his English than because of his historical methods. Nine of the eleven men questioned also favored Macaulay, and for the same reason, I fancy. Most undergraduates learn to admire him in English A, and in answering your question the men did not seem to discriminate between his English style and his historical methods. None seemed to have any opinion as to the merits of the methods of the different writers, not ever having given any thought to the question.

"I have myself read Hume, Gibbon, Macaulay, Ridpath, Fiske, Bancroft, Prescott, Irving, much biography and many Memoirs, especially of American statesmen and of the Napoleonic era, because I like them ; but I think very few men do this. Of the men questioned, eight had read Bryce's 'American Commonwealth,' which is required in one of Professor Mac Vane's Government courses here. Two had read a part of McMaster's 'United States,' in connection with Professor Hart's History 13, and one man, inspired by work done in Professor MacVane's History 12, had read May's 'Constitutional History of England ' from beginning to end. Most men here have read Bryce.

"In the sense implied in your question, no, or very few, undergraduates read the long works nowadays. Most of the men I questioned looked at me rather quizzically when I asked them this question, as much as to say, 'What do you take us for?'"

The inference from all of which is obvious. In our institutions of advanced education, literary form as an element in good historical work, when not actually discountenanced, is now wholly ignored. The method in vogue is suggestive of that pursued by the critic of the

Eatanswill Gazette, in his admired review of the work on Chinese metaphysics. The student is expected to improve himself in literature in the English Department, and in history and the historical methods in the Historical Department; and, subsequently, combine his information.

Notes:

1. *The Descent of Man* (ed. 1874), vol. ii. pp. 218, 219.

2. See Appendix A, p. 51.

3. See Appendix B, p. 53.

4. See Appendix C, p. 58.

5. "Not only does a German writer possess, as a rule, a full measure of the patient industry which is required for thinking everything that may be thought about his theme, and knowing what others have thought; he alone, it seems, when he comes to write a book about it, is imbued with the belief that that book ought necessarily to be a complete compendium of every- thing that has been so thought, whether by himself or others."- *The Athenæum*, September 8, 1900, p. 303.

6. "It is well to realize that this greatest history of modern times was writ- ten by one in whom a distrust in enthusiasm was deeply rooted. This cynicism was not inconsistent with partiality, with definite prepossessions, with a certain spite. The conviction that enthusiasm is inconsistent with intellectual balance was engrained in his mental constitution, and confirmed by study and experience. It might be reasonably maintained that zeal for men or causes is an historian's undoing, and that 'reserve sympathy' — the principle of Thucydides is the first lesson he has to learn." J. B. Bury, Introduction to his edition (1896) of Gibbon, vol. i. pp. lxvii.-lxviii.

7. "C'est sous ces deux aspects qui sont en réalité les deux faces de l'esprit de Mommsen, le savant et le politique-qu'il convient d'étudier cet ouvrage.

"Dans l'exposé scientifique de l'Historie romaine on ne sait ce qu'on doit le plus admirer, ou de la science colossale de l'auteur ou de l'art avec la- quelle elle est mise en œuvre. "C'était une entreprise colossale que celle de résumer tous les travaux sur la matière depuis Niebuhr. Mommsen lui-même avait contribué à ce travail par la quantité fabuleuse de mémoires qu'il avait écrits sur les points les plus spéciaux du droit romain, de l'archéologie ou de l'histoire. Or tout cela est assimilé d'une manière merveilleuse dans une narration his- torique qui est un des chefs-d'œuvre de l'historiographie. L'histoire romaine est une œuvre extraordinaire dans sa condensation, comme il n'en existe nulle autre au monde, enfermant dans des dimensions si restreintes (3 volumes in 80) tant de choses et de si bonnes choses. Mommsen raconte d'une manière si attrayante que dès les premières lignes vous êtes entraîné. Ses grands tableaux sur les premières migrations des peuples en Italie, sur les débuts de Rome, sur les Etrusques, sur la domination des Hellènes en Italie; ses chapitres sur les institutions romaines, le droit, la religion, l'armée et l'art; sur la vie économique, l'agriculture, l'industrie et le commerce; sur le développement intérieur de la politique romaine; sur les Celtes et sur Carthage; sur les péripéties de la Révolution romaine depuis les Gracques à Jules César; sur l'Orient grec, la Macédoine; sur la sou- mission de la Gaule: tout cela forme un ensemble admirable. —

"Comme peintre de grands tableaux historiques, je ne vois parmi les historiens contemporains qu'un homme qui puisse être comparé à Mommsen, c'est Ernest Renan : c'est la même touche large, le même sens des propor- tions, le même art de faire voir et de faire comprendre, de rendre vivantes les choses par les détails typiques qui se gravent pour toujours dans la mé- moire." Guilland, L'Allemagne Nouvelle et ses Historiens (1900), pp. 121- 22.

[Editor's note] "The work should be studied for these two reasons, which are the two sides of Mommsen's mind: the scholar and the politician. In the scientific presentation of Roman History we do not know what we should admire most, or the colossal science of the author or the art with which it is implemented. "It was a colossal undertaking to summarize all the work on the subject since Niebuhr. Mommsen himself had contributed to this work with the fabulous quantity of memoirs he had written on the most special points of Roman law, archeology and history. Now all this is assimilated in a marvelous way in a historical narration which is one of the masterpieces of historiography. Roman history is an extraordinary work in its condensation, like no other in the world, enclosing in such limited dimensions (3 volumes in 80) so many things and such good things. Mommsen narrates in such an engaging way that from the first lines you are drawn in. His large paintings on the first migrations of peoples in Italy, on the beginnings of Rome, on the Etruscans, on the domination of the Hellenes in Italy; its chapters on Roman institutions, law, religion, the army and art; on economic life, agriculture, industry and commerce; on the domestic development of Roman politics; on the Celts and on Carthage; on the adventures of the Roman Revolution from the Gracchi to Julius Caesar; on the Greek East, Macedonia; on the submission of Gaul: all this forms an admirable whole. — As a painter of large historical paintings, I see among contemporary historians only one man who can be compared to Mommsen, it is Ernest Renan: it is the same broad touch, the same sense of proportions, the same art of making people see and understand, of making things come alive through typical details which are engraved forever in the memory." Guilland, *New Germany and its Historians.*

8. At least twenty (20) American publishing houses have brought out complete editions of Macaulay, both his Miscellanies and the History of England. Many of these editions have been expensive, and they seem uniformly to have met with a ready demand. Almost every American publishing house of any note has brought out editions of some of the Essays. The same is, to a less extent, true of Carlyle. Seven (7) houses have brought out complete editions of his works; while three (3) others have put on the market imported editions, bearing an American imprint. Separate editions of the more popular of his writings—some cheap, others de luxe-have been brought out by nearly every American publishing concern.

9.See Appendix D, p. 59.

10. *Proceedings* (New Series), vol. vii. pp. 11-32.

27

An Undeveloped Function

This paper was delivered at the annual meeting of the Ameri-can Historical Association in Washington, D.C. in 1901. Adams was then president of the AHA.

"History is past Politics, and Politics are present History."
-Edward A. Freeman

"Politics are vulgar when they are not liberalized by history, and history fades into mere literature when it loses sight of its relation to practical politics."
-Sir John Seeley

Here are aphorisms from two writers, both justly distinguished in the field of modern historical research. Sententious utterances, they would probably, like most sententious utterances, go to pieces to a greater or less extent under the test of severe analysis. They will, how-ever, now serve me sufficiently well as texts.

That politics should find no place at its meetings is, I believe, the unwritten law of this Association; and by politics I refer to the discus-sion of those questions of public conduct and policy for the time being uppermost in the mind of the community. Taking into consideration the character and purpose of our body, and the broad basis on which its somewhat loose membership rests, the rule may be salutary. But there are not many general propositions not open to debate; and so I propose on this occasion to call this unwritten law of ours in question. While so doing, moreover, I shall distinctly impinge upon it.

Let us come at once to the point. May it not be possible that the un-written law, perhaps it would be better to speak of it as the tacit under-standing, I have referred to, admits of limitations and exceptions both useful and desirable? Is it, after all, necessary, or from a point of large view even well-considered, thus to exclude from the list of topics to be discussed at meetings of historical associations, and especially of this Association, the problems at the time uppermost in men's thoughts? Do we not, indeed, by so doing abdicate a useful public function, surrender an educational office? Do we not practically admit that we cannot trust ourselves to discuss political issues in a scholarly and historical spirit? In one word, are not those composing a body of this sort under a species of obligation, in a community like ours, to contribute their share, from the point of view they occupy, to the better understanding of the questions in active political debate? This proposition, as I have said, I now propose to discuss; and, in so doing, I shall, for purposes of illustration, draw freely on present practical politics, using as object lessons the issues now, or very recently, agitating the minds of not a few of those composing this audience,—indeed, I hope, of all.

I start from a fundamental proposition. The American Historical Association, like all other associations, whether similar in character or not, either exists for a purpose, or it had better cease to be. That purpose is, presumably, to do the best and most effective work in its power in the historical field. I then next, and with much confidence, submit that the standard of American political discussion is not now so high that its further elevation is either undesirable or impracticable. On the contrary, while, comparatively speaking, it ranks well both in tone and conduct, yet its deficiencies are many and obvious. That, taken as a whole, it is of a lower grade now than formerly, I do not assert;

though I do assert, and propose presently to show, that in recent years it has been markedly lower than it was in some periods of the past, and periods within my own recollection. That, however, it is not so high as it should be, that it is by no manner of means ideal, all will, I think, admit. If so, that admission will suffice for present purposes.

My next contention is perhaps more open to dispute. It is a favorite theory now with a certain class of philosophers, somewhat inclined to the happy-go-lucky school, that in all things every community gets about what it asks for and is qualified to appreciate. In political discussion—as in railroad or hotel service, and in literature or religion—the supply as respects both quality and quantity responds with sufficient closeness to the demand. There is, however, good reason for thinking that, with the American community or at least with some sections and elements thereof, this at best specious theory does not at the present time hold true. Our recent political debates have, I submit, been conducted on a level distinctly below the intelligence of the constituency; the participants in the debate have not been equal to the occasion offered them. Evidence of this is found in the absence of response. I think I am justified in the assertion that no recent political utterance has produced a real echo, much less a reverberation; and it would not probably be rash to challenge an immediate reference to a single speech, or pointed expression even, which during the last presidential campaign,[1] for instance, impressed itself on the public memory. That campaign, seen through the vista of a twelve-month, was, on the contrary, from beginning to end, with a single exception, creditable neither to the parties conducting it, nor to the audience to whose level it was presumably gauged.

Perhaps, however, I can best illustrate what I have to say—enforce the lesson I would fain this evening teach—by approaching it through retrospect. So doing, also, if there is any skill in my treatment, I cannot well be otherwise than interesting; for I shall largely deal with events within the easy recollection of those yet in middle life. But, while those events are sufficiently removed from us to admit of the necessary perspective, having assumed their true proportions to what preceded and has followed, they have an advantage over the occurrences of a year ago; for the controversial embers of 1900 may still be glowing in 1901, —though, I must say, to me the ashes seem white and cold and dead enough. Still, I do not propose to go back to any very remote period, and I shall confine myself to my own recollection, speaking of that only of which I know, and in which I took part. My review will begin with the year 1856,—the year of my graduation, and that in which I cast my first vote; also one in which a President was chosen, James Buchanan being the successful candidate.

But it must be premised that each election does not represent a debate; not infrequently it is merely a stage in a debate. It was so in 1856; it has been so several times since. Indeed, since 1840,—the famous "Log Cabin and Hard Cider" campaign of "Coon-Skin Caps," and "Tippecanoe and Tyler too," probably the most humorous, not to say grotesque, episode in our whole national history, that in which the plane of discussion reached its lowest recorded level,—since 1840 there have been only six real debates, the average period of a debate being, therefore, ten years. These debates were, (1) that over Slavery, from 1844 to 1864; (2) that over Reconstruction, from 1868 to 1872; (3) Legal Tenders, or "Fiat Money," and Resumption of Specie Payments were the issues in 1876 and 1880; (4) the issue of 1888 and 1892 was over Protection and Free Trade; (5) the debate over Bimetallism and the Demonetization of Silver occurred in 1896; and, finally, (6) Imperialism, as it is called, came to the front in 1900. Since 1856, therefore, the field of discussion has been wide and diversified, presenting several issues of great moment. Of necessity also the debates have assumed many and diverse aspects, ethical, ethnological, legal, military, economical, financial, historical. The last is that which interests us.

The first of the debates I have enumerated, that involving the slavery issue, is now far removed. We can pass upon it historically; for the young man who threw his maiden vote in 1860, when it came to its close, is now nearing his grand climacteric. Of all the debates in our national history that was the longest, the most elevated, the most momentous, and the best sustained. It looms up in memory; it projects itself from history. As a whole, it was immensely creditable to the people, the community at large, for whose instruction it was conducted. It has left a literature of its own, economical, legal, moral, political, imaginative. In fiction, it produced *Uncle Tom's Cabin*, still, if one can judge by the test of demand at the desks of our public libraries, one of the most popular books in the English tongue. In the law, it rose to the height of the Dred Scott decision; and, while the rulings in that case laid down have since been reversed, it will not be denied that the discussion of constitutional principles involved, whether at the bar, in the halls of legislatures, in the columns of the press or on the rostrum, was intelligent, of an order extraordinarily high, and of a very sustained interest. It was to the utmost degree educational.

So far as the historical aspect of that great debate is concerned, two things are to be specially noted. In the first place the moral and economical aspects predominated; and, in the second place, what may be called the historical element as an influencing factor was then in its infancy. Neither in this country nor in Europe had that factor been organized, as it now is. The slavery debate was so long and intense that all the forces then existing were drawn into it. The pulpit, for instance, participated actively. The physiologist was much concerned over ethnological problems, trying to decide whether the African was a human being or an animal; and, if the former, was he of the family of Cain. Thus all contributed to the discussion; and yet I am unable to point out any distinctly historical contribution of a high order; though, on both sides, the issue was discussed historically with intelligence and research. Especially was this the case in the arguments made before the courts and in the scriptural dissertations; while on the political side, the speeches of Seward and Sumner, of Jefferson Davis and A. H. Stevens, leave little to be desired. The climax was, perhaps, reached in the memorable joint debate between Lincoln and Douglas, of which it is not too much to say the country was the auditory. The whole constituted a fit prologue to the great struggle which ensued.

Beginning in its closing stage, in December, 1853, when the measure repealing the Missouri Compromise of 1820 was introduced into the Senate of the United States, and closing in December, 1860, with the passage of its Ordinance of Secession by South Carolina, this debate was continuous for seven years, covering two presidential elections, those of 1856 and 1860. So far as I know, it was *sui generis*; for it would, I fancy, be useless to look for anything with which to institute a comparison except in the history of Great Britain. Even there the discussion which preceded the passage of the Reform Bill of 1832, or that which led up to the repeal of the Corn Laws in 1846, or, finally, the Irish Home Rule agitation between 1871 and 1892, one and all sink into insignificance beside it. Of the great slavery debate it may then in fine be said that, while the study of history and the lessons to be deduced from history contributed not much to it, it made history, and on history has left a permanent mark.

Of the canvass of 1864, from our point of view little need be said. There was in it no great field for the historical investigator, the issue then presented to the people being of a character altogether exceptional. The result depended less on argument than on the outcome of operations in the field. There was, I presume, during August and September of that year, a wordy debate, but the people were too intent on Sherman as he circumvented Atlanta, and on Sheridan as he sent Early whirling up the valley of the Shenandoah, to give much ear to it. Had this Association then been in existence, and devoted all its energies to elucidating the questions at issue, I cannot pretend to think it would perceptibly have affected the result.

Nor was it greatly otherwise in the canvass of 1868. The country was then stirred to its very depths over the questions growing out of the war. The shattered Union was to be reconstructed; the slave system was to be eradicated. These were great political problems; problems as pressing as they were momentous. For their proper solution it was above all else necessary that they should be approached in a calm, scholarly spirit, observant of the teachings of history. Never was there a greater occasion; rarely has one been so completely lost. The assassination of Lincoln silenced reason; and to reason, and to reason only, does history make its appeal. The unfortunate personality of Andrew

Johnson now intruded itself; and, almost at once, what should have been a calm debate degenerated into a furious wrangle. Looking back over the canvass of 1868, and excepting Gen. Grant's singularly felicitous closing of his brief letter of acceptance—"Let us have peace!"—I think it would be difficult for any one to recall a single utterance which produced any lasting impression. The name even of the candidate nominated in opposition to Grant is not readily recalled. In that canvass, as in the preceding one, I should say there was no room for the economist, the philosopher, or the historian. The country had, for the time being, cut loose from both principle and precedent.

The debate over Reconstruction, begun in 1865, did not wear itself out until 1876. In no respect will it bear comparison with the debate over slavery which preceded it. Sufficiently momentous, it was less sustained, less thorough, far less judicial. Towards its close, moreover, as the country wearied, it was gravely complicated by a new issue; for, in 1867, began that currency discussion destined to last in its various phases through the life-time of a generation. It thereafter entered, in greater or less degree, into no less than nine consecutive presidential elections, two of which, those of 1876 and 1896, actually turned upon it.

The currency debate presented three distinct phases: first, the proposition, broached in 1867, known as the greenback theory, under which the interest-bearing bonds of the United States, issued during the Rebellion, were to be paid at maturity in United States legal tender notes, bearing no interest at all. This somewhat amazing proposition was speedily disposed of; for, early in 1869, an act was passed declaring the bonds payable "in coin." But, as was sure to be the case, the so-called "Fiat Money" delusion had obtained a firm lodgment in the minds of a large part of the community, and to drive it out was the work of time. It assumed, too, all sorts of aspects. Dispelled in one form, it appeared in another. When, for instance, the act of 1860 settled the question as respects the redemption of the bonds, the financial crisis of 1873 re-opened it by creating an almost irresistible popular demand for a government paper currency as a permanent substitute for specie.

Finally, when seven years later this issue was put to rest by a return to specie payments, the over-production of silver, as compared with gold, already foreshadowed the rise of one of the most serious and far-reaching questions which have perplexed modern times. Thus as the ethical and legal issues which were the staples of public discussion from 1844 to 1872 were disposed of, or by degrees settled themselves, a series of material questions arose, destined, even if at times in a some-what languid way, to occupy public attention through thirty years.

It is difficult to say what the dividing issue of 1876 really was. The country was then slowly recovering from the business prostration which followed the collapse of 1873. The issues involved in Recon-struction, if not disposed of, were clearly worn out, and to them the country would not respond, turning impatiently from their further discussion. Those issues might now settle themselves, or go unsettled; and, though that conclusion was reached thirty years ago, they are not settled yet. The living debate was over material questions, the cause of the prolonged business depression, and the remedy for it. The favor-ite specific was at first a recourse to paper money. The government printing-press was to be set in motion in place of the mint; and even hard-money Democrats of the Jacksonian school united with radical Republicans of the Reconstruction period in guaranteeing a resultant prosperity. Again the teachings of history were ignored. What, it was contemptuously exclaimed in the Senate, do we care for "abroad"! From this calamity the country had been saved by the veto of President Grant in 1874; and, the following year, an act was passed looking to the resumption of specie payments on the 1st of January, 1879. Seven-teen years of suspension were then to close. Over this measure the parties nominally joined issue in 1876. The Republicans, nominating Governor Hayes, of Ohio, demanded the fulfilment of the promise; the Democrats, nominating Governor Tilden, of New York, insisted on the repeal of the law. Yet it was well understood that the candidate of the Democracy favored the policy of which the law in debate was the concrete expression. The contest was thus in reality one between the "ins" and the "outs." We all remember how it resulted, and the terrible strain to which our machinery of government was in consequence subjected. In the wrangle which ensued the material and business interests of the country recuperated in a natural way, just as had repeatedly been the case before, and more than once since; and the United States then entered on a new era of increased prosperity. This brought the paper money debate to a close. The issues presented had, in the course of events, settled themselves.

But not the less for that, in the canvass of 1876 a field of great political usefulness was opened up to the historical investigator; a field which, I submit, he failed adequately to develop. A public duty was left unperformed. It was in connection with what John Stuart Mill has in one of his *Essays and Dissertations* happily denominated "The Currency Juggle." From time immemorial to tamper with the established measures of value has been the constant practice of men of restless and unstable mind, honest or dishonest, whether rulers or aspirants to rule. History is replete with instances. To cite them was the function of the historical investigator; to marshal them, and bring them to bear on the sophistries of the day was the business of the politician. A professorial discussion in a meeting of such an organization as this would then have been much to the point; and yet, curiously enough, a new historical precedent was about to be worked out. That was then to be done which had never been done before; a country which had gone to the length the United States had gone in the direction of "Fiat Money"—two-thirds of the way to repudiation—was actually to retrace its steps, and resume payments in specie at the former standards of value. History would have been searched in vain for a parallel experience.

The administration of President Hayes was curiously epochal. During it the so-called "carpet-bag governments" disappeared from the southern states; the country resumed payments in specie; and, on the 28th of February, 1878, Congress passed, over the veto of the President, an act renewing the coinage of silver dollars, the stoppage of which, five years before, constituted what was destined thereafter to be referred to as "the crime of 1873." This issue, however, matured slowly. Public men, having recourse to palliatives, temporized with it; and, through four presidential elections it lay dormant, except in so far as parties pledged themselves to action calculated, in the well-nigh idiotic formula of politicians, to "do something for silver." The canvasses of 1880 and 1884 are, therefore, devoid of historical interest. The first turned largely on the tariff; and yet, curiously enough, the single utterance in that debate which has left a mark on the public memory was the wonderful dictum of Gen. Hancock, the candidate of the defeated opposition, that the tariff was a local issue, which, a number of years before, had excited a good deal of interest in his native state of Pennsylvania. The gallant and picturesque soldier, metamorphosed into a political leader *pro hac vice*, simply harked back to the "Log Cabin" and "Coon-skin" campaign of 1840, when, a youth of sixteen, he was on his way to West Point.

Nor is the recollection of the debate of 1884 much more inspiring. It was a lively contest enough, under Grover Cleveland and James G. Blaine as opposing candidates, a struggle between the "outs" to get in and the "ins" not to go out. But a single formula connected with it comes echoing down the corridors of time, the alliterative "Rum, Romanism and Rebellion" of the unfortunate Burchard. An interlude in the succession of great national debates, the canvass of 1884 called for no application of the lessons of history.

That of 1888, presenting at last an issue, rose to the dignity of debate. In his annual message of the previous December, the President, in disregard of all precedent, had confined his attention not only to the tariff, but to a single feature in the tariff, the duty on wool. In so doing he had, as the well-understood candidate of his party for re-election, flung down the gauntlet; for, only three years before, the Republicans, in the presidential platform, had laid particular emphasis on "the importance of sheep industry" and "the danger threatening its future prosperity." They had thus pledged themselves to "do something" for wool, as well as for silver, and the President now struck at wool as "the tariff-arch keystone." But, while in this debate the economist came to the front, there was no pronounced call and, indeed, small opportunity for the historian. The silver issue was in abeyance; the pension list and civil service were not calculated to incite to investigation; nor had history much to say on either topic. As to the sheep, now so much in evidence, the British wool-sack might afford a text suggestive of curious learning in connection with England's once greatest staple—how, for instance, as a protective measure it was by one Parliament solemnly ordained that the dead should be buried in woolens. But it will readily be admitted that the historic spirit does not kindle over tariff schedules. The lessons of experience to be drawn from revenue tables appeal rather to the school of Adam Smith than to the disciples of Gibbon.

Returning to the review of our national debates, we find that in 1892 the shadow of coming events was plainly perceptible. The tariff issue had now lost its old significance; for the infant industries had developed into trade and legislation-compelling trusts. These were suggestive of new and, as yet, inchoate problems; but to them the constituency was not prepared intelligently to address itself. Populism was rife, with its crude and restless theories; a crisis in the history of the precious metals was clearly impending, with the outcome in doubt; indiscriminate and unprecedented pension giving had reduced an overflowing exchequer to the verge of bankruptcy. The debate of 1892 accordingly dropped back to the politician's level, that of 1876, 1880 and 1884. In it there was nothing of any educational value; nothing that history will dwell upon. The "ins" pointed with pride; the "outs" sternly arraigned the "ins"; while the student, whether of economics or history, there found small place and a listless audience. The memory of the canvass which resulted in the second administration of Cleveland is quite obliterated by the issues, altogether unforeseen, which the ensuing years precipitated.

Of quite another character were the two canvasses of 1896 and 1900. Still fresh in memory, the echoes of these have indeed not yet ceased to reverberate; and I assert without hesitation that, not since 1856 and 1860 has this people passed through two such wholesome and educational experiences. In 1896 and in 1900, as in the debates of forty years previous, there was a place, and a large place, for the student, whether investigator or philosopher. Great problems, problems of law, of economics and ethics, problems involving peace and war, and the course of development in the oldest as in the newest civilizations, had to be discussed, on the way to a solution. That the prolonged debate running through those eight years was at all equal to the occasion, I do not think can be claimed. Even his most ardent admirers will hardly suggest that Mr. Bryan in 1896 and 1900 rose to the level reached by Lincoln forty years before, nor do the utterances of either Mr. Roosevelt, Mr. Depew or Mr. Hanna bear well a comparison with those of Seward, Trumbull and Sumner. And that this momentous, many-sided debate failed to rise to the proper height was due, I now unhesitatingly submit, to the predominance in it of the political "boss," and the absence from it of the scholar. In it, those belonging to this Association, and to other associations similar in character to this, did not play their proper part; they proved themselves unequal to the occasion. Indeed, in the whole wordy canvass of 1896 I now recall but two instances of the professor or philosopher distinctively taking the floor; but both of those were memorable. They imparted an elevation of tone to discussion, immediately and distinctly perceptible, in the press and on the platform. I refer to the single utterance of Carl Schurz, before a small audience at Chicago, on the 5th of September, 1896, and to the subsequent publications of President Andrew D. White, in which, from his library at Ithaca, he drew freely on the stores of historical experience in crushing refutation of demagogical campaign sophistry. Amid the petulant chattering of the political magpies it was refreshing to hear those clear-cut, incisive utterances,—calm, thoughtful, well-reasoned. I have been told that in its various forms of republication, no less than five millions, and some authorities say ten millions, of copies of that Chicago speech of Mr. Schurz were then put in circulation. It was indeed a masterly production, a production in which a high key-note was struck and sustained. But the suggestive and extremely encouraging fact in connection with it was the response it elicited. Delivering himself at the highest level to which he could attain, Mr. Schurz was only on a level with his audience. To the political optimist that fact spoke volumes; it revealed infinite possibilities.

Twelve presidential canvasses, and six great national debates have thus been passed in rapid review. It is as if, in the earlier history of the country we had run the gamut from Washington to Van Buren. Taken as a whole, viewed in gross and perspective, the retrospect leaves much to be desired. That the debates held in Ireland and France during the same time have been on a distinctly lower level, I at once concede. Those held in Great Britain and Germany have not been on a higher. Yet ours have at best been only relatively educational; as a rule extremely partizan, they have been personal, often scurrilous, and intentionally deceptive. One fact is, however, salient. With the exception of the first, that of 1856–1860, not one of the debates reviewed has left an utterance which, were it to die from human memory, would by posterity be accounted a loss. This, I am aware, is a sweeping allegation; in itself almost an indictment. Yet with some confidence I challenge a denial. Those here are not as a rule in their first youth, and they have all of them been more or less students of history. Let each pass in rapid mental review the presidential canvasses in which he has in any degree participated, and endeavor to recall a single utterance which has stood the test of time as marking a distinct addition to mankind's intellectual belongings, the classics of the race. It has been at best a babel of the commonplace. I do not believe one utterance can be named, for which a life of ten years will be predicted. Such a record undeniably admits of improvement. Two questions then naturally suggest themselves: To what has this shortcoming been due? Wherein lies the remedy for it?

The shortcoming, I submit, is in greatest part due to the fact that the work of discussion has been left almost wholly to the journalist and the politician, the professional journalist and the professional politician; and, in the case of both there has in this country during the last forty years, been, so far as grasp of principle is concerned, a marked tendency to deterioration. Nor, I fancy, is the cause of this far to seek. It is found in the growth, increased complexity and irresistible power of organization as opposed to individuality, in the parlance of the day it is the all-potency of the machine over the man, equally noticeable whether by that word "machine" we refer to the political organization or to the newspaper.

The source of trouble being located in the tendency to excessive organization, it would seem natural that the counteracting agency should be looked for in an exactly opposite direction—that is, in the increased efficacy of individualism. Of this, I submit, it is not necessary to go far in search of indications. Take, for instance, the examples already referred to, of Mr. Schurz and President White, in the canvass of 1896, and suppose for a moment efforts such as theirs then were made more effective as resulting from the organized action of an association like this. Our platform at once becomes a rostrum, and a rostrum from which a speaker of reputation and character is insured a wide hearing. His audience too is there to listen, and repeat. From such a rostrum, the observer, the professor, the student, be it of economy, of history, or of philosophy, might readily be brought into immediate contact with the issues of the day. So bringing him is but a step. He would appear, also, in his proper character and place, the scholar having his say in politics; but always as a scholar, not as an office-holder or an aspirant for office. His appeal would be to intelligence and judgment, not to passion or self-interest, or even to patriotism. Congress has all along been but a clumsy recording machine of conclusions worked out in the laboratory and machine-shop; and yet the idea is still deeply seated in the minds of men otherwise intelligent that, to effect political results, it is necessary to hold office, or at least to be a politician and to be heard from the hustings. Is not the exact reverse more truly the case? The situation may not be, indeed it certainly is not, as it should be; it may be, I hold that it is, unfortunate that the scholar and investigator are finding themselves more and more excluded from public life by the professional with an aptitude for the machine, but the result is none the less patent. On all the issues of real moment,—issues affecting anything more than a division of the spoils or the concession of some privilege of exaction from the community, it is the student, the man of affairs and the scientist who to-day, in last resort, closes debate and shapes public policy. His is the last word. How to organize and develop his means of influence is the question.

"Here's what should strike, could one handle it cunningly:
Help the axe, give it a helve!"

So far as the historian is concerned, this Association is, I submit, the helve to the axe.

Of this the presidential election which closed just a year ago affords an apt illustration, ready-at-hand. No better could be asked. What might then well have been? The American Historical Association, as I have already said, is composed of those who have felt a call for the investigation and treatment of historical problems. Its members, largely instructors in our advanced education, feel that keen interest in the issues of the day natural and proper in all good citizens, irrespective of calling. They want to contribute their share to discussion; and, in that way, to influence results, so far as in them lies. From every conceivable point of view it is most desirable that they should have facilities for so doing. I hold, therefore, that in the last presidential canvass, a special meeting of this Association, called to discuss the issues then pending, might well have tended to the better general and popular comprehension of those issues, and to the elevation of that debate. Conducted on academic principles and looking to no formal expression of results in any enunciated platform of principles, such a gathering would have exercised an influence, as perceptible as beneficial, in lifting the discussion up into the domain of philosophy and research. It would have brought the lessons of the past to bear on the questions of the day. In any event, it would certainly not have descended to that contemptible *post ergo propter* formula, which, on the one side or the other, has in every presidential canvass been the main staple of argument.

What were the issues of the last presidential canvass? On what questions did its debate turn? Three in number, they were I think singularly inviting to those historically minded. To the reflecting man the matter first in importance was what is known as "imperialism," the problem forced upon our consideration by the outcome of the war with Spain. Next I should place the questions of public policy involved in the rapid agglomerations of capital, popularly denominated trusts. Finally the silver issue still lingered at the front, a legacy from the canvass of four years previous. The debate of 1900 is a thing of the past. Each of those issues can now be discussed, as it might well then have been discussed, in the pure historical spirit. Let us take them up in their inverse order.

Historically speaking, I hold there were two distinct sides to the silver question; and, moreover, on the face of the record, the advocates of bimetallism, as it was called, had in 1896 the weight of the argument wholly in their favor. In his very suggestive work entitled *Democracy and Liberty*, Mr. Lecky refers to the discovery of America as producing, among other far-reaching effects, one which he considers most momentous of all. To quote his words: "The produce of the American mines created, in the most extreme form ever known in Europe, the change which beyond all others affects most deeply and universally the material well-being of man: it revolutionized the value of the precious metals, and, in consequence, the price of all articles, the effects of all contracts, the burden of all debts." This was during the sixteenth century, the years following the great event of 1492. Again, the world went through a similar experience within our own memories, in consequence of the California and Australia gold-finds, between 1848 and 1852. These revolutions were due to natural causes, and came about gradually. They were also of a stimulating character. From the beginning of modern commercial times, however, to the close of the last century, the exchanges of all civilized communities had been based on the precious metals; and silver had been quite as much as gold a precious metal for monetary purposes. Shortly after 1870 the policy of demonetizing silver was entered upon; and, in 1873, the United States gave in its adhesion to that policy. Thereafter, in the great system of international exchanges, silver ceased to be counted a part of that specie reserve on which drafts were made. Thenceforth, the drain, as among the financial centers, was to be on gold alone. In the whole history of man no precedent for such a step was to be found. So far as the United States was concerned the basis, on which its complex and delicate financial fabric rested, was weakened by one-half; and the cheaper and more accessible metal, that to which the debtor would naturally have recourse in discharge of his obligations, was made unavailable. It could further be demonstrated that, without a complete readjustment of our currencies and values, the world's accumulated stock and annual production of gold could not, as a monetary basis, be made to suffice for its needs. A continually recurring contest for gold among the great financial centers was inevitable. "A change which," in the language of Lecky, "beyond all others affects most deeply and universally the material well-being of man" had been unwittingly challenged. The only question was: would the unexpected occur? Then, if it did occur, what might be anticipated? Such was the silver issue, as it presented itself in 1896. On the facts, the weight of argument was clearly with the advocates of silver.

Four years later, in 1900, the unexpected had occurred. As then resumed, the debate was replete with interest. The lessons of 1492 and 1848 had a direct bearing on the present, and, in the light by them shed, the outcome could be forecast almost with certainty; but it was a world-question. Japan, China, Hindostan entered into the problem, in which also both Americas were factors. It was a theme to inspire Burke, stretching back, as it did, to the Middle Ages, and involving the whole circling globe. Rarely has any subject called for more intelligent and comprehensive investigation; rarely has one been more confused and befogged by a denser misinformation. The discoverer and scientist, moving hand in hand, had, during the remission of the debate, been getting in their work, and under the touch of their silent influence, the world's gold production rose by leaps and bounds. Less than ten millions of ounces in 1896, in 1899 it had nearly touched fifteen millions; and in money value, it alone then exceeded the combined value of the gold and silver production of the earlier period. What did this signify? History was only repeating itself. The experiences of the first half of the sixteenth century and the middle decennaries of the nineteenth century were to be emphasized during the opening years of the twentieth.

So much for the silver question and its possible treatment. In the discussion of 1900, the last word in the debate of 1896 remained to be uttered. A page in history, both memorable and instructive, was to be turned. Next trusts—those vast aggregations of capital in the hands of private combinations, constituting practical monopolies of whole branches of industry, and of commodities necessary to man. Was the world to be subject to taxation at the will of a moneyed syndicate? The debate of a year ago over this issue, if debate it may be called, is still very recent. In it the lessons of history were effectually ignored; and yet, if applied, they would have been sufficiently suggestive. The historian was as conspicuous for his absence as the demagogue was in evidence.

The cry was against monopoly and the monopolist, a cry which, as it has been ringing through all recorded times, suggests for the historical investigator a wide and fruitful field. Curiously enough the first lesson to be derived from labor in that field is a paradox. Practically, so far as extortion is concerned there is almost nothing in common between the old time monopoly and the modern trust. Of examples of the first, the record is monotonously full. Mere agents of the government, sometimes the favorites of the Crown, the whole machinery of the state has time out of mind been put at the service of monopolists to enable them to exact tribute from all. To the student of English history the names and misdeeds of Sir Richard Empson and Sir Giles Mompesson at once suggest themselves; while others more familiar with the drama recall Sir Giles Overreach, or that powerful scene in Ruy Blas in which the Spanish courtiers wrangle together, coming almost to blows, over a division among themselves of the right to extort. The old system still survives. For example, in France to-day the manufacture and sale of salt is a government monopoly. A prime necessity of life, no person not specially authorized may engage in the production of salt, or import it. If a peasant woman, living on the sea-coast of Brittany or Normandy, endeavors to procure salt for her family by the slow process of evaporating a pailful of sea water in the sun, she is engaged in an illicit trade, and becomes amenable to law. Her salt will certainly, if found, be confiscated. So of improved pocket matches. In France, their manufacture is a government revenue monopoly. They are notoriously bad. Those made and sold in Great Britain are on the contrary noted for excellence. If, however, a box of English matches is found in the pocket of a traveller passing from England to France, it is taken from him and the contents are destroyed at once; indeed he is fortunate if he escapes the payment of a fine. This is monopoly; the whole strength of a government being put forth to exact an artificial profit on the sale of a commodity in general use. There is an historical literature pertaining to the subject, a lamentation, and an ancient tale of wrong.

The curious feature in the present discussion, that which in the mind of the student of things as opposed to words imparts a special interest to it, is that, while the trust or vast aggregation of capital and machinery of production in the hands of individuals intended to control competition is in fact the modern form of monopoly, it is in its methods and results the direct opposite of the old time monopoly; for, whereas, the purpose and practice of that was to extort from all purchasers an artificial price for an inferior article through the suppression of competitors, the first law of its existence for the modern trust is, through economics and magnitude of production, to supply to all buyers a better article at a price so low that other producers are driven from the market. The ground of popular complaint against them is not that they exact an inordinate profit on what they sell, but that they sell so low that the small manufacturer or merchant is deprived of his trade. This distinction with a difference explains at once the wholly futile character of the politician's outcry against trusts. It is easy, for instance, to denounce from the platform the magnates of the Sugar Trust to a sympathizing audience; and yet not one human being in that audience, his sympathies to the contrary notwithstanding, will the next morning pay a fraction of a cent more per pound for his sugar, that by so doing he may help to keep alive some struggling manufacturer who advertises that his product does not bear the trust stamp.

As to the outcome of conflicts of this character history tells but one story. They can have but one result, a readjustment of industries. A single familiar illustration will suffice. Any one who chooses to turn back to it, can read the story of the long conflict between the loom and the spindle. Formerly, and not so very far back, the distaff and spinning-wheel were to be seen in every house; homespun was the common wear. To-day the average man or woman has never seen a distaff, or heard the hum of a spinning-wheel. Ceasing long since to be a commodity, homespun would be sought for in vain. Yet the struggle between the loom of the manufacturing trust and the old dame's spinning-wheel was, literally, for the latter, a fight to the death; for, in that case, the livelihood of the operator was at stake. Her time was worth absolutely nothing, except at the wheel; she must needs work for any wage; on it depended her bread. A vast domestic, industrial readjustment was involved; one implying untold human suffering. The result was, however, never for an instant in doubt. The trust of that day was left in undisputed control of the field; and it always must, and always will be, just so long as it supplies purchasers with a better article, at a lower price than they had to pay before. The process does not vary; the only difference is that each succeeding readjustment is on a larger scale and more far-reaching in its effects.

Such, stripped of its verbiage and appeals to sympathy, is the trust proposition. But the popular apprehension always has been, as it now is, that this supply of the better article at a lower price will continue only until the producer, the monopolist has secured a complete mastery of the situation. Capital, it is argued, is selfish and greedy, corporations are proverbially soulless and insatiable; and, as soon as competition is eliminated, nature will assert itself. Prices will then be raised so as to assure inordinate gains; and when, in consequence of such profits, fresh competitors enter the field, they will either be crushed out of existence by a temporary reduction in price, or absorbed in the trust.

All this has a plausible sound; and of it as a theory of practical outcome the politician can be relied on to make the most. But on this head what has the historical investigator to say? His will be the last word in that debate also; his verdict will be final. The lessons bearing on this contention to be drawn from record cover a wide field of both time and space; they also silence discussion. They tend indisputably to show that the dangers depicted are imaginary. The subject must, of course, be approached in an unprejudiced spirit and studied in a large, comprehensive way. Permanent tendencies are to be dealt with; and exceptional cases must be instanced, classified and allowed for. Attempts, more or less successful, at extortion in a confidence of mastery, can unquestionably be pointed out; but, in the history of economical development, it is no less unquestionable that, on the large scale and in the long run, every new concentration has been followed by a permanent reduction of price in the commodity affected thereby. The world's needs are continually supplied at a lower cost to the world. Again, the larger the concentration, the cheaper the product; until now a new truth of the market place has become established and obtained general acceptance, a truth of the most far-reaching consequence, the truth that the largest returns are found in quick sales at small profits. To manage successfully one of those great and complex industrial combinations calls for exceptional administrative capacity in individuals, for men of quick perception and masterful tempers. These men must be able correctly to read the lessons of experience, and, accepting the facts of the situation, they must find out how most exactly to adapt themselves to those facts. No theorist, be he politician or philosopher, appreciates so clearly as does the successful trust executive the fundamental laws of being of the interests they have in charge. They have good cause to know that under conditions now prevailing, competition is the sure corollary of the attempted abuse of control; and, moreover, that the largest ultimate returns on capital, as well as the only real security from competition, are found not in the disposal of a small product at large profits, but in a large output at prices which encourage consumption. Throwing exceptional cases and temporary conditions out of consideration, as not affecting final results, the historical investigator will probably on this subject find himself much at variance with the political canvasser. That the last will get worsted in the argument hardly needs be said.

Does history furnish any instance of a financial, an industrial or a commercial enterprise,—a bank, a factory, or an importing company,—ever having been powerful enough long to regulate the price of any commodity regardless of competition, except when acting in harmony with and supported by governmental power? Is not the monopolist practically impotent, unless he has the constable at his call? To answer this question absolutely would be to deduce a law of the first importance from the general experience of mankind. So doing would call for a far more careful examination than is now in my power to make, were it even within the scope of my ability; but if my supposition prove correct, the corollary to be drawn therefrom is to us as a body politic and at just this juncture, one of the first and most far-reaching import. In such case, the modern American trust, also, so far as it enjoys any power as a monopoly, or admits of abuse as such, must depend for that power and the opportunity of abuse solely on governmental support and cooperation. Its citadel is then the custom house. The moment the United States revenue officer withdrew his support, the American monopolist would cease to monopolize, except in so far as he could defy competition by always supplying a better article at a price lower than any other producer in the whole world. And here, having deduced and formulated this law, the purely historical investigator would find himself trenching on the province of the economist. The so-called protective system would now be in question. Thus again, as so often before, the tariff would become the paramount issue. But the tariff would no longer stand in the popular mind as the beneficent protector of domestic enterprise; it would, on the contrary, be closely associated with the idea of monopoly, it would be assailed as the Bastille of the monopolist. From the historical and economical points of view, however, the debate would not, because of that, undergo any diminution of interest. Whatever the politician might in discussion assert, or the opportunist incorporate into legislation, we may rest assured that this issue will ultimately settle itself in accordance with those irresistible underlying influences which result in what we know as natural evolution. History is but the record of the adjustment of mankind in the past to the outcome of those influences, moral, geological, industrial and climatic; and, in this respect, when all is said and done, it is tolerably safe to predict that the future will present no features of novelty. If, then, we can measure correctly the nature of the influences at work, experience furnishes the data from which the character, as well as the extent, of the impending readjustment may be surmised. For such a diagnosis the historian and economist are requisite.

It remains to pass on to the third and last of the matters in debate during 1900, that known as imperialism. This was the really great issue before the American people then; and it is the really great issue before them now. That issue, moreover, I with confidence submit, can be intelligently considered only from the historical standpoint. Indeed, unless approached through the avenues of human experience, it is not even at once apparent how the question, as it now confronts us, arose and injected itself into our political action; and accordingly, it is in some quarters even currently assumed that it is there only fortuitously, a feature in the great chapter of accidents, a passing incident, which may well disappear as mysteriously and as suddenly as it came. Studied historically, I do not think this view of the situation will bear examination. On the contrary, I fancy even the most superficial investigator, if actuated in his inquiry by the true historical spirit, would soon reach the conclusion that the issue so recently forced upon us had been long in preparation, was logical and inevitable, and for our good or our evil must be decided, rightly or wrongly, on a large view of great and complex conditions. In other words, there may be reason to conclude that an inscrutable law of nature, at last involving us, has long been and now is evolving results. It is one more phase of natural evolution, working itself out, as in the case of Rome twenty-five centuries ago, through the survival and supremacy of the fittest.

I need hardly say, I feel myself now venturing on some dangerous generalizations; and yet I do not see how the American investigator, who endeavors to draw his conclusions from history, can recoil from the venture. His deductions will probably be erroneous—indeed, they are sure to be so to some extent; and, in making them, he is more than likely to betray a very considerable capacity in the line of superficiality. None the less, even if it be of small value, he is bound to offer what he has. If the seed he throws bears no fruit, it can do small harm.

Mr. Leslie Stephen, in one of his essays, truly enough says: "The Catholic and the Protestant, the Conservative and the Radical, the Individualist and the Socialist, have equal facility in proving their own doctrines with arguments, which habitually begin, 'All history shows.' Printers should be instructed always to strike out that phrase as an erratum, and to substitute 'I choose to take for granted.'" And elsewhere the same writer lays it down as a general proposition that: "Arguments beginning 'all history shows' are always sophistical." What is by some known as the doctrine of manifest destiny is, I take it, identical with what others, more piously minded, refer to as the will, or call, of God. The Mohammedan and the modern Christian gospel-monger say "God clearly calls us" to this or that work; and with a conscience perfectly clear, they then proceed to rob, slay and oppress. In like manner, the political buccaneer and land-pirate proclaims that the possession of his neighbor's territory is rightfully his by manifest destiny. The philosophical politician next drugs the conscience of his fellowmen by declaring solemny that "all history shows" that might is right; and with time, the court of last appeal, it must be admitted possession is nine points in the law's ten. It cannot be denied, also, that quite as many crimes have been perpetrated in the name of God and of manifest destiny as in that of liberty. That, at least, "all history shows." But, all the same, just as liberty is notwithstanding a good and desirable thing, so God does live and will, and there is something in manifest destiny. As applied to the development of the races inhabiting the earth it is, I take it, merely an unscientific forth of speech; the word now in vogue is evolution, the phrase "survival of the fittest." When all is said and done, that unreasoning instinct of a people which carries it forward in spite of and over theories to its manifest destiny, amid the despairing outcries and long-drawn protestations of theorists and ethical philosophers, is a very considerable factor in making history; and, consequently one to be reckoned with.

In plain words then, and Mr. Stephen to the contrary notwithstanding, "all history shows" that every great, aggressive and masterful race tends at times irresistibly towards the practical assertion of its supremacy, usually at the cost of those not so well adapted to existing conditions. In his great work Mommsen formulates the law with a brutal directness distinctly Germanic:

"By virtue of the law, that a people which has grown into a state absorbs its neighbours who are in political nonage, and a civilized people absorbs its neighbours who are in intellectual nonage—by virtue of this law, which is as universally valid and as much a law of nature as the law of gravity—the Italian nation (the only one in antiquity which was able to combine a superior political development and a superior civilization, though it presented the latter only in an imperfect and external manner) was entitled to reduce to subjection the Greek states of the East which were ripe for destruction, and to dispossess the peoples of lower grades of culture in the West—Libyans, Iberians, Celts, Germans —by means of its settlers; just as England with equal right has in Asia reduced to subjection a civilization of rival standing, but politically impotent, and in America and Australia has marked and ennobled and still continues to mark and ennoble, extensive barbarian countries with the impress of its nationality."

Professor Von Holst again states a corollary from the law thus laid down in terms scarcely less explicit, in connection with a well-known and much discussed act of foreign spoliation in our own comparatively recent history: "It is as easy to bid a ball that has flown from the mouth of the gun to stop in its flight, and return on its path, as to terminate a successful war of conquest by a voluntary surrender of all conquests, because it has been found out that the spoil will be a source of dissension at home." And then Von Holst quotes a very significant as well as philosophical utterance of William H. Seward's, which a portion of our earnest protestants of to-day would do well to ponder: "I abhor war, as I detest slavery. I would not give one human life for all the continents that remain to be annexed; but I cannot exclude the conviction that the popular passion for territorial aggrandizement is irresistible. Prudence, justice, cowardice, may check it for a season, but it will gain strength by its subjugation. ... It behooves us then to qualify ourselves for our mission. We must dare our destiny." One more, and I have done with quotations. The last I just now commended to the thoughtful consideration of those classified in the political nomenclature of the day as Anti-Imperialists. A most conscientious and high-minded class, possessed with the full courage of their convictions, the efforts of the Anti-Imperialists will not fail, we and they may rest assured, to make themselves felt. They enter into the grand result. Nevertheless, for them also there is food for thought, perhaps for consolation, in this other general law, laid down in 1862 by Richard Cobden, than whose, in my judgment, the utterances of no English speaking man in the nineteenth century were more replete with shrewd sense expressed in plain, terse English:

"From the moment the first shot is fired, or the first blow is struck, in a dispute, then farewell to all reason and argument; you might as well attempt to reason with mad dogs as with men when they have begun to spill each other's blood in mortal combat. I was so convinced of the fact during the Crimean war, which, you know, I opposed, I was so convinced of the utter uselessness of raising one's voice in opposition to war when it has once begun, that I made up my mind that as long as I was in political life, should a war again break out between England and a great Power, I would never open my mouth upon the subject from the time the first gun was fired until the peace was made, because, when a war is once commenced, it will only be by the exhaustion of one party that a termination will be arrived at. If you look back at our history, what did eloquence, in the persons of Chatham or Burke, do to prevent a war with our first American colonies? What did eloquence, in the persons of Fox and his friends, do to prevent the French revolution, or bring it to a close? And there was a man who at the commencement of the Crimean war, in terms of eloquence, in power, and pathos, and argument equal—in terms, I believe, fit to compare with anything that fell from the lips of Chatham and Burke—I mean your distinguished townsman, my friend Mr. Bright—and what was his success? Why, they burnt him in effigy for his pains."

Turning from the authorities, and the lessons by them deduced from the record called History, let us now consider the problem precipitated on the American people by the Spanish war of 1898. That question,—the burning political issue of the hour,—I propose here and now to discuss. I propose to discuss it, however, from the purely historical standpoint, and not at all in its moral or economical aspects. So far then as this question is concerned, the last presidential vote, that of 1900, settled nothing, except that the policy which had assumed a certain degree of form in the treaty of Paris should not be reversed. All else was left for debate, and ulterior settlement. Certain lessons, calculated greatly to influence the character of that settlement, can, I submit, now be most advantageously drawn from history. At formulating those lessons I propose here to try my hand.

The first and most important lesson is one which, in theory at least, is undisputed; though to live up to it practically calls for a courage of conviction not yet in evidence. That a dependency is not merely a possession, but a trust, a trust for the future, for itself and for humanity, is accepted by us in this debate as a postulate; accordingly, our dependencies are in no wise to be exploited for the general benefit of the alien owner, or that of individual components of that owner, but they are to be dealt with in a large and altruistic spirit with an unselfish view to their own utmost development, materially, morally and politically. And, through a process of negatives, "all history shows" that only when this course is hereafter wisely and consecutively pursued, should that blessed consummation ever be attained, will the dominating power itself derive the largest and truest benefit from its possessions.

As yet no American of any character, much less of authority, has come forward to controvert this proposition. That it will be controverted, and attempts made by interested parties to sophisticate it away through the cunningly arranged display of exceptional circumstances, can with safety be predicted. In this respect, to use a cant phrase, "we know how it is ourselves." We all remember, for instance, the unspeakable code of factitious morals and deceptive philosophy manufactured to order in these United States as a "Gospel of Niggerdom" less than half a century ago. Coming down to more recent times, we can none of us yet have forgotten the wretched sophistry ignorantly resurrected from the French Revolution and assignat days in glorification of "Fiat Money," and a business world emancipated at last from any heretofore accepted measures of value. The leopard, rest assured, has not changed its spots since either 1860 or 1876. The "New Gospel" phase of the debate now on is, however, yet to develop itself. But, assuming the correctness of the proposition I have just formulated, a corollary follows from it. A formidable proposition, I state it without limitations, meaning to challenge contradiction, I submit that there is not an instance in all recorded history, from the earliest precedent to that now making, where a so-called inferior race or community has been elevated in its character, or made self-sustaining and self-governing, or even put on the way to that result, through a condition of dependency or tutelage. I say "inferior race"; but, I fancy, I might state the proposition even more broadly. I might, without much danger, assert that the condition of dependency, even for communities of the same race and blood, always exercises an emasculating and deteriorating influence. I would undertake, if called upon, to show also that this rule is invariable,—that, from the inherent and fundamental conditions of human nature it has known and can know no exceptions. This truth, also, I would demonstrate from well-nigh innumerable examples, that of our own colonial period among the number. In our case, it required a century to do away in our minds and hearts with our dependential traditions. The Civil War, and not what we call the Revolution, was our real war of Independence. And yet in our time of dependency you will remember we were not emasculated into a resigned and even cheerful self-incapacity as the natural result of a kindly, paternal and protective policy; but, as Burke with profound insight expressed it, with us the spirit of independence and self-support was fostered "through a wise and salutary neglect." But, for present purposes, all this is unnecessary, and could lead but to a poor display of commonplace learning. The problem to-day engaging the attention of the American people is more limited. It relates solely to what are called "inferior races"; those of the same race, or of cognate races, we as yet do not propose to hold in a condition of permanent dependency; those we absorb, or assimilate. Only those of "inferior race," the less developed or decadent, do we propose to hold in subjection, dealing with them, in theory at least, as a guardian deals with a family of wards.

My proposition then broadens. If history teaches anything in this regard it is that race elevation, the capacity in a word for political self-support, cannot be imparted through tutelage. Moreover, the milder, the more paternal, kindly and protective the guardianship, the more emasculating it will prove. A "wise and salutary neglect" is the more beneficent policy; for, with races as with individuals, a state of dependency breeds the spirit of dependency. Take Great Britain for instance. That people, working at it now consecutively through three whole centuries, after well-nigh innumerable experiences and as many costly blunders, Great Britain has, I say, developed a genius for dealing with dependencies, for the government of "inferior races"; a genius far in advance of anything the world has seen before. Yet my contention is that, to-day, after three rounded centuries of British rule, the Hindus, the natives of India, in spite of all material, industrial and educational improvements—roads, schools, justice and peace—are in 1900 less capable of independent and ordered self-government, than they were in the year 1600, the year when the East India Company was incorporated under a patent of Elizabeth. The native Indian dynasties, those natural to the Hindus, have disappeared; accustomed to foreign rule the people have no rulers of their own, nor could they rule themselves. The rule of aliens has with Hindostan thus become a domestic necessity. Remove it—and the highest and most recent authorities declare it surely will some day be removed—chaos would inevitably ensue. What is true of India is true of Egypt. That, under British rule, Egypt is to-day in better material and political case than ever before in its history, modern, biblical, hieroglyphic or legendary, scarcely admits of dispute. Schools, roads, irrigation, law and order, and protection from attack, she has them all;

> "But what avail the plough or sail,
> Or land or life, if freedom fail?"

The capacity for self-government is not acquired in that school.

But of this England itself furnishes an example in its own history, an example well-nigh forgotten. In fundamentals human nature is much the same now as twenty centuries back. During the first century of the present era, the Romans, acting in obedience to the law laid down by Mommsen—the law quoted by me in full, and the law of which Thomas Carlyle is the latest and most eloquent exponent, the law known as the Divine Right of the most Masterful—acting in obedience to that law, the Romans in the year of Grace 43 crossed the British channel, overthrew the Celts and Gauls gathered in defence of what they mistakenly deemed their own, and, after reducing them to subjection, permanently occupied the land. They remained there four centuries, a hundred years longer than the English have been in Calcutta. During that period they introduced civilization, established Christianity, constructed roads, dwellings and fortifications. Materially, the condition of the country vastly improved. The Romans protected the inhabitants against their enemies; also against themselves. During hundreds of years they benevolently assimilated them. Doubtless on the banks of the Tiber the inhabitants of what is now England were deemed incapable of self-government. Probably they were; unquestionably they became so. When the legions were at last withdrawn, the results of a kindly paternalism, secure protection and intelligent tutelage became apparent. The race was wholly emasculate. It cursed its independence; it deplored its lost dependency. As the English historian now records the result—"They forgot how to fight for their country when they forgot how to govern it."

Man is always in a hurry; God never!—is a familiar saying. Certainly, nature works with a discouraging indifference to generations. Each passing race of reformers and regenerators does indisputably love to witness some results of its efforts; but, in the case of England, in consequence of the emasculation incident to tutelage, and dependency on a powerful, a benevolent and beneficent foreign rule, after that rule ended—as soon or late such rule always must end—throughout the lives of eighteen successive generations emasculated England was over-run. At last, with some half dozen intermediate rulers, the Normans succeeded the Romans. They were conquering masters; but they domesticated themselves in the British Islands, and in time assimilated the inhabitants thereof, Saxons, Picts and Celts, benevolently or otherwise. But, as nearly as the historian can fix it, it required eight hundred years of direst tribulation to educate the people of England out of that spirit of self-distrust and dependency into which they had been reduced by four centuries of paternalism, at once Roman and temporarily beneficent. Twelve centuries is certainly a discouraging term to which to look forward. But steam and electricity have since then been developed to a manifest quickening of results. Even the pace of nature was in the nineteenth century vastly accelerated.

Briefly stated then, the historical deduction would seem to be somewhat as follows: where a race has in itself, whether implanted there by nature or as the result of education, the elevating instinct and energy, the capacity of mastership, a state of dependency will tend to educate that capacity out of existence; and the more beneficent, paternal and protecting the guardian power is, the more pernicious its influence becomes. In such cases, the course most beneficial in the end to the dependency, now as a century ago, would be that characterized by "a wise and salutary neglect." Where, however, a race is for any cause not possessed of the innate saving capacity, being stationary or decadent, a state of dependency, while it may improve material conditions, tends yet further to deteriorate the spirit and to diminish the capacity of self-government; if severe, it brutalizes; if kindly, it enervates. History records no instance in which it develops and strengthens.

Following yet further the teachings of experience, we are thus brought to a parting of the ways, a parting distinct, unmistakable. Heretofore the policy of the United States, as a nationality, has, so far as the so-called inferior races are concerned, been confined in its operation to the North American continent; but, as a whole and in it's large aspects, it has been well defined and consistent. We have proceeded on the theory that all government should in the end rest on the consent of the governed; that any given people is competent to govern itself in some fashion, and that, in the long run, any fashion of self-imposed government works better results than will probably be worked by a government imposed from without. In other words, the American theory has been that, in the process of nature and looking to ultimate, perhaps remote, conditions, any given people, not admitting of assimilation, will best work out its destiny when left free to work it out in its own way. Moreover, so far as outside influence is concerned, it can, in the grand result, be more effectively exercised through example than by means of active intervention. Where we have not therefore forcibly absorbed into our system foreign and inferior races or elements, and more or less completely assimilated them, we have, up to very recently, adopted and applied what may perhaps in homely speech best be described as a "Hands-off and Walk-alone" doctrine, relying in our policy towards others on the theory practiced at our private firesides, the theory that self-government results from example, and is self-taught. I have already quoted Richard Cobden in this connection; I will quote him again. Referring, in 1864, to the British foreign policy, then by him as by us denounced, though by us now imitated, Cobden said: "I maintain that a man is best doing his duty at home in striving to extend the sphere of liberty, commercial, literary, political, religious, and in all directions; for if he is working for liberty at home, he is working for the advancement of the principles of liberty all over the world."

Mexico and Hayti afford striking illustrations of a long and rigid adherence to this policy on our part, and of the results of that adherence. Conquering and dismembering Mexico in 1847, we, in 1848, left it to its own devices. So completely had the work of subjugation been done, that our representatives had actually to call into being a Mexican government with which to arrange terms of peace. With that simulacrum of a national authority we made a solemn treaty; and, after so doing, left Mexico to work out its destiny, if it could, as it could. In spite of numerous domestic convulsions and much internal anarchy, from that day to this we have neither ourselves intervened in the internal affairs of our southern continental neighbor, nor long permitted such interference by others. To Mexico, we have said "Walk-alone"; to France, "Hands-off." The result we all know. It has gone far to justify our theory of the true path of human advancement. Forty years is, in matters of race development, a short time. A period much too short to admit of drawing positive, or final, inferences. Dr. Holmes was once asked by an anxious mother when the education of a child should begin; his prompt, if perhaps unexpected, reply was: "Not less than 250 years before it is born." To-day, and under existing conditions, Mexico, though republican in name and form only, is self-governing in reality. It is manifestly working its problem out in its own way. The statement carries with it implications hardly consistent with the might-is-right latter-day dispensation voiced by Mommsen and Carlyle.

Hayti presents another case in point, with results far more trying to our theory. We have towards Hayti pursued exactly the policy pursued by us with Mexico. Not interfering ourselves in the internal affairs of the island, we have not permitted interference by others. For the condition of affairs prevailing in Hayti, occupied by an inferior race, apparently lapsing steadily toward barbarism, the United States is morally responsible. Acting on the law laid down in the extract I have given from the pages of Mommsen, we might at any time during the last quarter of a century have intervened in the name of humanity, and to the great temporary advantage of the inhabitants of the one region "where Black rules White." The United States, in pursuance of its theories, has abstained from so doing. It has abstained in the belief that, in the long run and grand result, the inhabitants of Hayti will best work out their problem, if left to work it out themselves. In any event, however, exceptional cases are the rocks on which sound principles come to wreck; and, so far as the race of man on earth is concerned, it is better that Hayti should suffer self-caused misfortune for centuries, as did England before, than that a precedent should be created for the frequent violation of a great principle of natural development. Yet the case of Hayti is crucial. Persistently to apply our policy there evinces, it must be admitted, a robust faith in the wisdom of its universal application. The logical inference, so far as the Philippine Islands is concerned, is obvious.

Historically speaking, those now referred to are the only two theories of a national policy to be pursued in dealing with the practical dependencies, which challenge consideration, the American and the British. The others, whether ancient and abandoned, or modern and in use,—Phoenician, Roman, Spanish, French, Dutch, German or Russian,—may be dismissed from the discussion. They none of them ever did, nor do any of them now, look to an altruistic result. In all, the dependency is confessedly exploited on business principles, with an eye to the trade development of the alien proprietor. Setting these aside, there remain only the American, or "Walk-alone and Hands-off" theory; and the British, or "Ward in Chancery" theory. The first is exemplified in Mexico and Hayti; the last in Hindostan and Egypt. The question now in debate for the United States may, therefore, be concisely stated thus: taking the Philippine Islands as a subject for treatment, and the ultimate elevation of the inhabitants of those islands to self-government as the end in view, which is the policy best calculated to lead to the result desired,—the traditional and distinctively American system, as exemplified in the cases of Mexico and Hayti, or the modern and improved British system, to be studied in Hindostan and Egypt?

Subject to limitations of time and space I have now passed in review the great political debates which have occupied the attention of the American public during the last half century. I have endeavored to call attention to the plane on which those debates have been conducted, and to the noticeable absence from them of a scholarly spirit. The judicial temper and the patience necessary to any thorough investigation have in them, I submit, been conspicuously lacking. Then, starting from the point of view peculiar to this Association, I have examined the issues presented to the country in the last presidential canvass, and, for purposes of illustration, I have discussed them, always in a purely historical temper.

While the result of my experiment is for others to pass upon, my own judgment is clear and decided. I hold that the time has now come when organizations such as this of ours, instead of, as heretofore, scrupulously standing aloof from the political debate, are under obligation to participate in it. As citizens, we most assuredly should, in so far as we may properly so do, contribute to results, whether immediate, or more or less remote. As scholars and students, the conclusions we have to present should be deserving of thoughtful consideration. The historical point of view moreover, is, politically, an important point of view; for only when approached historically, by one looking before as well as after, can any issue be understood in its manifold relations with a complex civilization. Indeed, the moral point of view can in its importance alone compare with the historical. The economical, vital as it unquestionably often is, comes much lower in the scale; for, while an approach through both these avenues is not infrequently necessary to the intelligent comprehension of questions of a certain class, such, for instance, as the tariff or currency, it is very noticeable that, though many issues present themselves, slavery or imperialism for example, into which economical considerations do not enter as controlling factors, there is scarcely any matter of political debate which does not to some extent at least have to be discussed historically. Still, though our retrospect has proved this to be the case, the scarcely less significant fact also appears that not more than one presidential canvass in two involves any real issue at all, moral or economical. Of the last twelve elections, covering the half century, six were mere struggles for political control; and so far as can now be seen, the course of subsequent events would have been in no material respect other than it was whichever party prevailed. Judging by experience, therefore, in only one future canvass out of two will any occasion arise for a careful historical presentation of facts. The investigator will not be called upon; and, if he rises to take part in the discussion, he will do no harm for the excellent reason that no one will listen to him. In the other of each two canvasses it is not so. There is then apt to be a real debate over a paramount issue; and, in all such, the strong search-light of experience should be thrown, clearly and fully, over the road we are called upon to traverse. In every such case, the presentation, provided always it be made in the true historical spirit, should by no means be of one side only. On the contrary, every phase of the record should have its advocate; every plausible lesson should be drawn. The facts are many, complicated and open to a varied construction; and it is only through the clash of opposing views that they can be reduced to comparative system, and compelled to yield their lessons for guidance.

As I have also, more than once already, observed, this Association is largely made up of those occupying the chairs of instruction in our seminaries of the higher education. From their lecture rooms the discussion of current political issues is of necessity excluded. There it is manifestly out of place. Others here are scholars for whom no place exists on the political platform. Still others are historical investigators and writers, interested only incidentally in political discussion. Finally some are merely public-spirited citizens, on whom the oratory of the stump palls. They crave discussion of another order. They are the men whose faces are seen only at those gatherings which some one eminent for thought or in character is invited to address. To all such, the suggestion I now make cannot but be grateful. It is that, in future, this Association, as such, shall so arrange its meetings that one at least shall be held in the month of July preceding each presidential election. The issues of that election will then have been presented, and the opposing candidates named. It should be understood that the meeting is held for the purpose of discussing those issues from the historical point of view, and in their historical connection. Absolute freedom of debate should be insisted on, and the participation of those best qualified to deal with the particular class of problems under discussion, should be solicited. Such authorities, speaking from so lofty a rostrum to a select audience of appreciative men and women could, I confidently submit, hardly fail to elevate the standard of discussion, bringing the calm lessons of history to bear on the angry wrangles and distorted presentations of those whose chief, if not only, aim is a mere party supremacy.

Note:

1. [Editor's note] The 1900 race was between the Republican incumbent William McKinley and the Democrat William Jennings Bryan. McKinley rode a wave of popularity after the victory in the Spanish-American War, which included the annexation of the Polynesian kingdom of Hawaii.